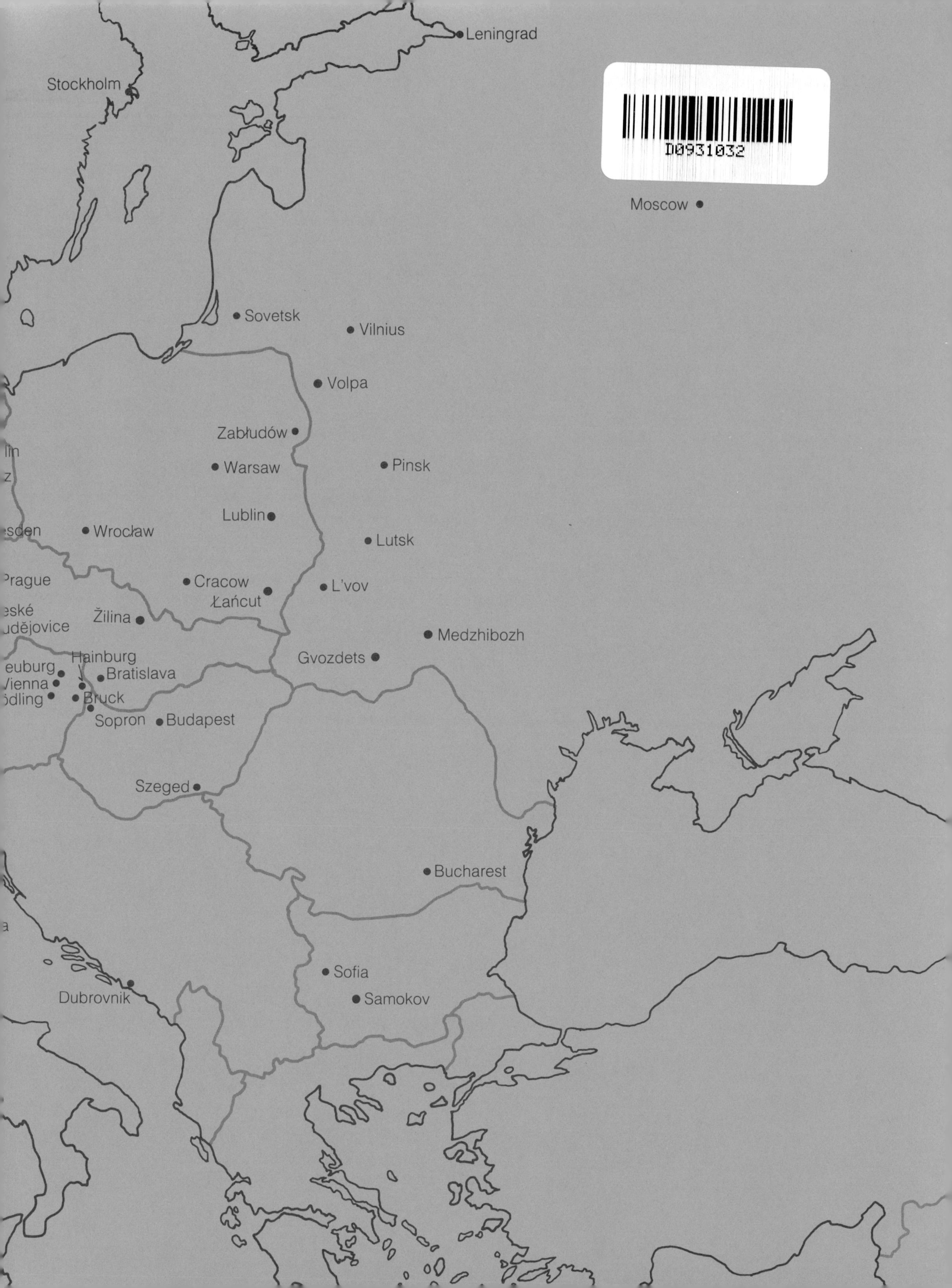
Leningrad
Stockholm
Moscow
Sovetsk
Vilnius
Volpa
Zabłudów
Warsaw
Pinsk
Lublin
Wrocław
Lutsk
Cracow
Łańcut
L'vov
Žilina
Medzhibozh
Hainburg
Gvozdets
Bratislava
Bruck
Sopron
Budapest
Szeged
Bucharest
Sofia
Samokov
Dubrovnik

SYNAGOGUES OF EUROPE

Synagogues of Europe

Architecture, History, Meaning

Carol Herselle Krinsky

The Architectural History Foundation,
New York, New York

The MIT Press,
Cambridge, Massachusetts,
and London, England

ARCHITECTURAL HISTORY FOUNDATION BOOKS

I *On Domestic Architecture,* Sebastiano Serlio's Sixth Book. Introductions by James S. Ackerman, Adolf K. Placzek, and Myra Nan Rosenfeld. 1978.
II *Space Into Light, The Churches of Balthasar Neumann,* Christian F. Otto. 1979.
III *Borromini and the Roman Oratory, Style and Society,* Joseph Connors. 1980.
IV *Le Corbusier Sketchbooks,* Volumes 1 and 2, 1981; Volumes 3 and 4, 1982.
V *Frank Lloyd Wright's Hanna House, The Clients' Report,* Paul R. and Jean S. Hanna. 1981. *The Hanna House Documents,* 1982.
VI *In Search of Modern Architecture: A Tribute to Henry-Russell Hitchcock,* edited by Helen Searing. 1982.
VII *Campus, An American Planning Tradition,* Paul Venable Turner. 1984.
VIII *The Law Courts, The Architecture of George Edmund Street,* David B. Brownlee. 1984.
IX *Synagogues of Europe: Architecture, History, Meaning,* Carol Herselle Krinsky. 1985.

AMERICAN MONOGRAPH SERIES

Bertram Grosvenor Goodhue, Richard Oliver. 1983.
The Almighty Wall, The Architecture of Henry Vaughan, William Morgan. 1983.
On the Edge of the World, Four Architects in San Francisco at the Turn of the Century, Richard Longstreth. 1983.
Mizner's Florida, American Resort Architecture, Donald W. Curl. 1984.
Charles A. Platt, The Artist as Architect, Keith Morgan. 1985.

Second printing with revisions, 1985

Carol Herselle Krinsky is Professor of Fine Arts at New York University. She is author of *Rockefeller Center* and is currently president of the Society of Architectural Historians.

Library of Congress Cataloging in Publication Data
Krinsky, Carol Herselle.
Synagogues of Europe.

Bibliography: p. 436
Includes index.
1. Synagogue architecture—Europe. 2. Synagogues—Europe. I. Title. II. Series.
NA5450.K75 1985 726'.3'094 84-26171
ISBN 0-262-11097-0

Designed by Lauren Tresnon Klein.

Publication of this book has been aided by a grant from The Millard Meiss Publication Fund of the College Art Association of America. MM

The foundation gratefully acknowledges the support of Mrs. Barnett Newman, Baron Guy de Rothschild, and Mr. and Mrs. Michael S. Klein.

Table of Contents

Selected Examples

Acknowledgments

It is always a pleasure to acknowledge publicly my debt to the many people who have offered information, located photographs, and corrected mistakes. Some thanks are offered at the end of the discussions of individual synagogues in the second part of the book. If I have omitted names, I have done so inadvertently, and I hope that people who have been kind in the past will be forgiving now.

Several scholars must have special acknowledgment here because of their exceptional and wide-ranging efforts on my behalf: Sybil Milton (Leo Baeck Institute), Moshe Barasch (Hebrew University), Joseph Gutmann (Wayne State University), and Adolf K. Placzek (Avery Librarian Emeritus). The library and staff at the Leo Baeck Institute, YIVO, Avery Library, Hebrew Union College, the Jewish Theological Seminary, and the New York Public Library Jewish Division have been kind, helpful, and resourceful. At these institutions, I must single out Fred Bogin, Marek Web, Fruma Mohrer, Lucjan Dobroszycki, and the late Zosa Szajkowski. Other scholars who have been generous with their time and knowledge include Steve Zipperstein and Abraham D. Glicksberg. Space will not permit me to name everyone in European institutions who has helped me, but J. J. F. W. van Agt, Sándor Scheiber, Nikolaus Vielmetti, and Evžen Lukeš spent exceptional amounts of time assisting a visiting scholar on a tight schedule. The organizations that have been generous with their facilities and collections include the Royal Institute of British Architects; United Synagogue; Federation of Synagogues; Liberal Synagogue; Consistoire Israélite; Archives Nationales; Caisse Nationale des Monuments Historiques; Rijksdienst voor de Monumentenzorg; Institut für die Geschichte der deutschen Juden-Hamburg; the Germania Judaica Library-Cologne; Zentralrat der Juden in Deutschland-Düsseldorf; *Allgemeine unabhängige jüdische Wochenzeitung*; municipal photograph libraries and archives in several German cities; Oesterreichische Nationalbibliothek; Bundesdenkmalamt; Jewish Community-Vienna; Jewish community office and the Jewish Historical Institute in Warsaw; Państwowy Instytut Sztuki; the Polish Historic Monuments Service; Art History Department, Jagiellonian University-Cracow; Jewish Historical Museum-Budapest; State Jewish Museum; National Technical Museum-Prague; and the institutions named in my picture credits.

Apart from those named already, I have enjoyed and benefited from meetings and correspondence with other scholars in this field, especially Rachel Wischnitzer, Harold Hammer-Schenk, and Hannelore Künzl. Early in this project, Richard Krautheimer suggested references; throughout my work I have had in mind the standard he set over fifty-five years ago with his own classic work on central European synagogues.

Friends, colleagues, and family members do much to help any author. My husband, Robert D. Krinsky, has offered every kind of support to this project, and he and our children have been patient, forgiving, and excellent traveling companions. My mother, Jane Gartman Herselle, our aunt, Charlotte Krinsky, and friends and New York University colleagues including Jane Costello, Edward Sullivan, Pearl Ehrenreich, Henry Berman, and Ethel Hirsch have taken photographs for me and collected notes during their travels. James Duncan Berry and Pamela Lawrence undertook some routine tasks with far from routine intelligence and good cheer. Jim Morgan's and Nora Beeson's astute criticisms and stimulating opinions led to substantial improvements, and Moira Duggan provided exemplary copy-editing. I am also glad to thank Madelaine Fava for redrawing several plans. It has been a pleasure to work with Karen Banks, Lauren T. Klein, Pamela Stinson, and Julianne Griffin of the Architectural History Foundation.

I gratefully acknowledge sabbatical leaves from New York University and a grant-in-aid for travel in eastern Europe from the American Council of Learned Societies.

Abbreviations

The following abbreviations are used in the notes and bibliographies.

AJYb	*American Jewish Year Book* (sometimes *Yearbook*).
Aronius, *Regesten*	J. Aronius, *Regesten zur Geschichte der Juden im fränkischen und deutschen Reiche bis zum Jahre 1273,* Berlin, 1902.
AZJ	*Allgemeine Zeitung des Judenthums.*
Bachi, "Appunti"	A. Bachi, "Appunti sulla architectura della sinagoga," *Israel. La rassegna mensile,* ser. 2, VIII (1933).
Bendt & Bothe	V. Bendt and R. Bothe, eds., *Synagogen in Berlin. Zur Geschichte einer zerstörten Architektur,* Berlin, 1983 (Stadtgeschichtliche Publikationen herausgegeben von Rolf Bothe, 1).
Gans, *Memorbook*	M. H. Gans, *Memorbook: History of Dutch Jewry from the Renaissance to 1940,* Baarn, 1977.
Grotte, *Deutsche*	A. Grotte, *Deutsche, böhmische und polnische Synagogentypen vom XI bis Anfang des XIX Jahrhunderts,* Berlin, 1915 (Mittheilungen der Gesellschaft zur Erforschung jüdischer Kunstdenkmäler, Frankfurt am Main, vols. 7 and 8).
Gutmann, *Synagogue*	J. Gutmann, ed., *The Synagogue. Studies in Origins, Archaeology, and Architecture,* New York, 1975.
Hammer-Schenk, "Opplers"	H. Hammer-Schenk, "Edwin Opplers Theorie des Synagogenbaus," *Hannoversche Geschichtsblätter* XXXII, #1/3 (1979).
Hammer-Schenk, *Synagogen*	H. Hammer-Schenk, *Synagogen in Deutschland: Geschichte einer Baugattung im 19 und 20 Jahrhundert,* Hamburg, 1981.
Hammer-Schenk, "Untersuchungen"	H. Hammer-Schenk, "Untersuchungen zum Synagogenbau in Deutschland von der ersten Emanzipation bis zur gesetzlichen Gleichberechtigung der Juden (1800–1871)," diss., Tübingen, 1974.
Krautheimer, *Mitt. Syn.*	R. Krautheimer, *Mittelalterliche Synagogen,* Berlin, 1927.

Nahon, *Arks*	U. Nahon, *Holy Arks and Ritual Appurtenances from Italy in Israel,* Tel Aviv, 1970.
Piechotka	K. and M. Piechotka, *Wooden Synagogues,* Warsaw, 1959.
Pinkerfeld	J. Pinkerfeld, *Bate ha-knesset be-Italyah,* Jerusalem, 1954.
Wischnitzer, *Architecture*	R. Wischnitzer, *The Architecture of the European Synagogue,* Philadelphia, 1964.

SYNAGOGUES OF EUROPE

Preface

Architecture, like politics, is an art of the possible. Kings or parliaments or great corporations can order spectacular structures and will see to it that their dreams come true. Less powerful people build as best they can.

The usual books on architectural history are filled with examples of sophisticated and often immense buildings that were erected for those who could express themselves in architecture or who could sum up the dominant cultural tendencies in the majority society. This book is different because its subject is different. It discusses synagogues in Europe, the religious buildings of a minority which did not receive normal civil rights in any European country until the French granted them in 1791. The Jews therefore had to temper their architectural ambitions to suit political and social circumstances. This history deals with some distinguished extant buildings, with some modest ones, and with others known only from fragmentary historic records. If Jews were invited into a town—usually to perform financial or commercial services that local people could not manage—their synagogues might be attractive and comfortable. When they were merely tolerated in the places where they lived, the Jews might have built simple synagogues concealed from public view. When Christians disobeyed the doctrines of their own church and actively persecuted Jews, they often destroyed synagogues, or expelled the Jews and converted the synagogues to other uses. Synagogues therefore reveal especially clearly the connections between architecture and society, including the effect of the larger society on the minority's self-image.

A study of synagogue architecture is timely. We are increasingly willing to admit separate ethnic studies into our schools. We are ready to appreciate diversity rather than to segregate and dismiss alternatives to the majority culture.

Similarly, we now admit into the canon of architectural history more than the cathedrals and palaces that form much of the traditional writing on this subject. While great buildings created by the most refined architects and clients will always dominate, increasing numbers of recent studies have dealt with vernacular architecture, colonial buildings, tenements, middle-class houses, hospitals, even prisons and asylums. We want to know what happened to the ordinary person, the unsung hero, the unfortunate, the members of minority groups. Study of the cultural context also helps us to understand the special qualities of the masterful creation.

Evidence for the architectural and daily environment of the ordinary person is usually less complete than the evidence we have for traditionally appreciated masterpieces. Enough survives, however, even for the buildings of an often persecuted minority, to give an adequate image of synagogues and of the Jewish ideas and rules embodied in their design.

This study is divided into two parts. The first gives a general picture of the conditions under which European synagogues were designed. It describes the synagogue's nature, the main furnishings that affect its appearance or spatial arrangement, the changes in its architecture through the centuries, and the messages that these buildings convey. Given the Jews' special status in Christian society, their buildings would ordinarily not have included the latest ideas in church design; indeed, various synagogue forms existed simultaneously, and their styles could overlap and endure far longer than those of churches. Synagogues were often small and furnished only as funds became available. It is therefore appropriate to speak about groups of buildings or tendencies in synagogue design, rather than about a sequence of great individual structures like those built for Christian worship, civic, or commercial use.

Nevertheless, even the modest buildings claim our attention because they changed slowly, providing visual documentation of the Jews' historical and cultural position. There were impressive structures in Spain, Poland, Italy, England, and the Netherlands before the nineteenth century, and many others were built there and elsewhere after ca. 1830. The destruction of many monuments and documents prevents a detailed discussion of the contributions and influence of each generation of synagogues; despite this, we will be dealing with significant architectural achievements. In addition, as evidence of majority-minority relations, synagogues may be especially interesting today when few countries of the western world have one established religion, an ethnically pure population, or a single cultural direction.

Toledo, Figs. 181, 184
Pinsk, Fig. 77
Vilnius, Fig. 93
Venice, Figs. 218, 221
London, Figs. 242, 243
Amsterdam, Figs. 225–228

The second part of the book offers short and specific accounts of individual synagogues in many European countries. They were chosen to exemplify all architectural types and styles; all sizes of synagogues; unique survivors; many of the geographic regions where Jews settled in significant numbers (though not all modern nations); and a range in congregational ritual from strict orthodoxy to liberalism. The examples come from all centuries from which we have synagogue remains. The examples are not meant to constitute a *catalogue raisonné* or a complete history of synagogues in each region; I have picked examples to illustrate tendencies described in the first part and, for the sake of convenience, have grouped them geographically.

Some buildings are found in one part of this study but not in the other. This is either because an understanding of synagogue architecture does not require a corresponding entry, or because, in many cases, useful and accurate detailed information about Jewish communities and their buildings in eastern Europe and the U.S.S.R. has vanished or become inaccessible. We can use a synagogue known only from pictures to illustrate a point even if we cannot provide a complete and accurate account of the building's history.

The present work concentrates on central and western European monuments, as most surviving buildings, documents, photographs, and scholarly studies pertain to those areas. Moreover, most synagogues in eastern Europe were simple rooms with modest furnishings, though often loved by their congregations as if they were their own homes. Adherents of the ultraorthodox, mystically-oriented Hasidic sect, which was prominent especially in eastern Europe from the late eighteenth century onward, profess indifference to their surroundings during prayer and devote more attention to rooms where they study.[1] Karaites, a small minority of Jews who do not follow the Talmud, the record of orally transmitted Jewish law, also had modest synagogues.[2] These were especially simple rooms because they dispensed with the furnishings associated with Talmudic study and requirements. Deeply pious traditional Jews often echoed Talmudic authorities who asked why the money used for handsome synagogues had not been used instead to support studies of the Torah, which is Jewish law in its widest sense.[3] Consequently, ideas about synagogue architecture were more fully formulated in central and western Europe, whence the ideas traveled eastward in all but the seventeenth and eighteenth centuries during the flowering of Jewish community life in Poland and in the present western Soviet republics. Destruction of synagogues and documents precludes discussion of some impressive buildings in certain eastern European and Balkan localities, such as Salonica, where Jews concentrated and were essential to urban development before 1939, Białystok, Kaunas, and Odessa. The eastern monuments included here will, however, indicate the general circumstances under which comparable buildings were erected elsewhere.

A few notes on terms are in order. I have used the current official United States Government names for cities, as national borders have shifted, bringing about name changes. For example, the Austrian town known as Rimalev to its Yiddish-speaking inhabitants, and recorded as Grzymałów on maps when the area of Galicia returned to Poland in 1918, is now transliterated as Grimailov, as it is in the Ukrainian S.S.R.; Pressburg and Pozsony are the German and Hungarian names for Bratislava. Readers will find some well-known old names beside the modern ones in the Index. I have used common English names of famous cities, but I have used Livorno rather than the once-famous name of Leghorn.

The term *Ashkenazic* is used here to mean the German and Polish (and Hasidic) rites unless I make a clear distinction. These rites are used in all European countries in synagogues attended by Jews who trace their origin to German- and Polish-speaking regions. The term *Sephardic* refers to Spanish and Portuguese rather than to Levantine, Italian, or other Mediterranean-area rites. I mean by *ark* the cabinet or other container for the scrolls of the Pentateuch (*Torah* in Hebrew). The ark is known as the *aron ha-kodesh* to Ashkenazic Jews and as the *hekhal* to Sephardic Jews. I have used the Ashkenazic term *bimah* rather than the Sephardic *tevah* to denote the desk used during the reading from the Torah and any platform, railing, canopy, or decoration associated with it. I use an English plural form, *bimahs*, instead of the transliterated Hebrew *bimot*. By prayer hall, I mean the principal room of a synagogue, containing the ark and the bimah. At Professor Joseph Gutmann's suggestion, I have used the Hebrew transliterations found in the *Encyclopedia Judaica*, 1971.

Synagogues of Europe is dedicated to the memory of my late maternal grandfather, Solomon Gartman. His family history incorporated many places included here. Originally Spanish, the family sought refuge in Italy after 1492, gradually moved north to Germany, and later migrated to the vicinity of Ternopol, Ukrainian S.S.R., which then belonged to Austria. When uprooted from his birthplace there he worked in a factory in New York. His solace lay in religious studies, and he spent almost every day of his retirement in the Jewish Division of the New York Public Library. He would not have had other than a grandfatherly interest in my subject, as he typified pious Jews who care deeply for the word and little for the place in which it is read, but as I have spent many hours in "his" part of the same library, it is fitting to offer this book as a memorial to him.

1 The Synagogue: An Introduction

Origin and Definition

A synagogue is a building with a threefold purpose: to house Jewish congregational worship, study, and community meetings. The community is so central to the idea of a synagogue that any location in which ten Jewish men gather for prayer may serve as a synagogue, while certain prayers can be offered only if ten men are present. The quorum of ten, rather than the building itself, constitutes the synagogue in its most fundamental sense.[1] The very word *synagogue* comes from the Greek *synagein,* to bring together.[2]

A Greek rather than Hebrew word became the basis for our modern term, because the Hebrew Bible, or Old Testament, lacks a word for it. When the Bible was written between the ninth and second centuries B.C.,* Jews worshipped in sacrificial temples. Being farmers and herdsmen, they offered up what they had raised so that the Lord would continue to make the land abundant. The temples were also places where Jews, as isolated monotheists, could reinforce their faith.

The greatest of all temples was the one King Solomon built in Jerusalem in ca. 955 B.C. In ca. 620 B.C., it became the central sanctuary of Judaism, when the strong King Josiah suppressed other temples during a period of religious and political consolidation. In 586 B.C., the Babylonians invaded Jerusalem, destroyed Solomon's Temple, and carried away many of the city's inhabitants to the Euphrates Valley. When the captives mourned their loss of the Temple, the prophet Ezekiel consoled them with the words that the Lord had spoken to him:

> Thus says the Lord God: Although I removed them far off among the nations, and although I have scattered them among the countries, yet have I been as a little sanctuary in the countries where they are come. [Ezek. 11:16]

In addition to this spiritual sanctuary, Jews in exile may have established sacrificial shrines to imitate the lost one in Jerusalem. They might have held community meetings. But they may not yet have had synagogues—community assembly places where sacrificial prayers, or close substitutes, were offered at the beginning and end of meetings.

---

*Jews who do not accept the use of B.C. and A.D. substitute B.C.E. (Before the Common Era) and C.E., respectively.

When the Jews were allowed to return to their homeland in the late sixth century B.C., they built a more modest Temple in Jerusalem. The former exiles and their descendants might have continued to hold community meetings outside the Temple, but the centuries between the exile and the Hasmonean revolt against Syrian rule (167 B.C.) marked a time of priestly ascendancy when there was little room for religious institutions to develop in competition with the Temple. Some documents of the third century B.C. and later refer to *proseuchai,* places of prayer both pagan and Jewish, but the only one that was clearly a synagogue postdates the Hasmonean revolt.[3] Earlier *proseuchai,* such as the one mentioned in III Maccabees 7:17–23, may have been loyalty shrines where Jews could pray for and honor the ruler, since they could not do so in pagan temples.[4]

A controversial modern hypothesis places the origin of the synagogue as a building for religious assembly in the period after the Hasmonean revolt. At this time, the Pharisees—scholars outside the traditional priestly power center at the Temple—became rivals to the formerly preeminent Temple priests and their associates.

> The goal of the priestly religion was fertility of the land, which was achieved by sacrificial offerings through intermediary priests at a centralized cultic shrine—the Temple at Jerusalem. The Pharisaic goal, on the other hand, was to assure the individual of the salvation of his soul after death and bodily resurrection in the messianic age. All this could be achieved through *halakhoth* (a system of laws) decreed by the new scholar class—the Pharisees. The basic law code that underwrote the priestly religion was the Pentateuch; the salvationary religion of the Pharisees rested on a divinely revealed two-fold Law—the Written and the Oral.[5]

Explanation of the Law, including readings from the Pentateuch and Prophets, required meeting places which may well have evolved into synagogues—buildings for both community meeting and prayer.

The link between secular and religious activities is the Law, or Torah, considered in its widest sense as the Lord's will and deed recorded first in the Pentateuch but also elsewhere in the Hebrew Bible and in authoritative orally transmitted laws reputedly issued from the time of Moses onward. The Oral Law is considered valid because the Lord would not have commanded people to keep the Sabbath holy,[6] for instance, without telling them how to do so. The Written Law, the Five Books of Moses, divided into periodic readings and supplemented by appropriate passages from other Biblical books, is preserved on Torah scrolls which each synagogue must have and which are holier than the building itself. Every synagogue has a repository for the scrolls, called an ark, and has a reader's platform and table, called a bimah. Together, they preserve the Law and allow it to be communicated.

Whatever the date of its origin, the synagogue developed markedly after A.D. 70. In that year, the Romans destroyed the Temple of Jerusalem which had been reconstructed under Herod the Great beginning in 20 B.C. With the center of sacrificial worship gone, Jews had to strengthen other institutions to shelter worshippers and students of the Torah. Ever since that time, Judaism has been congregational rather than hierarchical and centralized. Each local group of Jews looked to its synagogue to preserve the interrelated faith, laws, and traditions of a people who believed that the Lord had set them apart and who were often obliged to live a segregated existence with their own institutions to sustain them. The religious-educational and communal activities are both implicit in the Latin term *scola* (= school; *scuola, escolo, Judenschul, shul*), used since the twelfth century, at least, which could later denote a synagogue as well as a religious school.[7]

Jewish congregations built synagogues in the Holy Land and around the Mediterranean basin until the Islamic conquest in the seventh century. Examples of synagogues outside the Holy Land include those of the busy Roman port of Ostia, the important city of Sardis in Turkey, and the small provincial town of Stobi in Yugoslavia. Archaeologists have found other synagogues deep in the Middle Eastern hinterlands, as at Dura-Europos in Syria, and there may have been some in northern Europe, as at Cologne. Some were independent buildings, others—like some of the earliest churches—rooms in structures housing other activities. Some were inside the city walls; some lay outside them. Sites might be chosen near rivers, because flowing water is important to several purification rituals. Several synagogues stood in courtyards. Examples are known with porticoed entrances and carved ornament, while others were modest in appearance. They shared a purpose but had varied forms. Similarly, special Bible lessons and prayers and legal decisions might vary from place to place and from one congregation to another, even in the same locality.

Ostia, Fig. 202

Temple and Synagogue

Synagogues and religious schools became identified as material rather than as spiritual "little sanctuaries" (Ezekiel 11:16) in the Talmud, the fundamental Jewish legal work. The Talmud has come down to us in two versions compiled after A.D. 200, known as Jerusalem (j.) and Babylonian (b.) because they were written in the Holy Land and Babylonia respectively.[8] The Babylonian sages wrote of the synagogues and houses of study there as representing Ezekiel's "lesser sanctuary" and they applied the words, "Lord, thou hast been our dwelling place" (Ps. 90:1) to their synagogues and religious schools.[9] Jews everywhere later gave the status of "lesser sanctuary" to their own establishments. A fourteenth-century Spanish synagogue at Córdoba contains an inscription recording that the building is a "miniature sanctuary and a house of testimony built by Isaac Moheb . . . in the year 75 [=1315] as a temporary structure. Arise, O God, hasten to rebuild Jerusalem!" A fifteenth-century Italian rabbi wrote about "the synagogue, the house of our Lord, the small sanctuary."[10] Jews who joined the nineteenth-century Reform movement even called their synagogues temples because the modern buildings replaced the Temple for the indefinite future.

Even if synagogues, being "lesser sanctuaries," are unequal to the Temple, they are the places where Jews keep alive the memory of Temple services. Regulations governing sacrifices at the Temple are read and explained in synagogues, with the recitation serving as a lesser form of the deed. Hosea's words, "We will render for bullocks the offering of our lips" (14:3), was applied to the recitation of sacrificial procedures and to prayers in general. Prayers are recited at hours corresponding to those of Temple offerings. The separation of men from women in the synagogue is based on the existence of a women's court at the Temple and of a women's gallery during a festival held there. These practices explain why Jewish authorities can say that "he who prays in the synagogue, it is as if he prayed in the ancient Temple."[11]

The relationship between the Temple and synagogues was expressed in words more than in architecture, because Temple and synagogue remained fundamentally different. The former served all the people of Israel. The latter serves only a congregation, usually a local community; it may even be private property. The Temple was holier, having been instituted by the Lord. It was therefore unique, while any individual aspect of a synagogue will be due to earthly factors, such as region and date of origin, materials used, design decisions, and the orthodoxy of its congregation. The Temple's sanctity was permanent, so that the building could never have been sold or used for another purpose. Because a synagogue's sanctity comes from the activity pursued within it, the congregation may sell the building and move elsewhere. The sanctuary in Jerusalem was an imposing architectural complex, where a formal arrangement of platforms and open courts led to a supremely holy building with an inner sanctum that could be entered only by designated individuals. A synagogue may be anything from a small room to a grand church-like edifice.

The Temple ritual emphasized sacrificial services, usually performed out of doors by a priestly caste. The synagogue, however, must enclose a congregation. Synagogue worship, being essentially internal, does not require the assistance of a priest who is ordained or consecrated. Any ten male Jews over the age of thirteen constitute the *minyan,* a quorum needed for the establishment of a congregation and the conduct of complete services. Prayers in a synagogue usually have been led by a distinguished member and later by a cantor, while the rabbi (teacher) took responsibility for education and for textual or legal exegesis. Rabbinical ordination shows only that the person has graduated from a theological seminary, which is different from priestly consecration. Almost any Jew with the requisite learning could hope to become a rabbi or cantor, but the Jewish Temple priests were selected partly on the basis of hereditary membership in a caste.

It is therefore not surprising that relatively few synagogues were related visually to the Temple. Even the Reform temples did not imitate the architecture of the ancient Temple. Synagogues that imitated the Temple at all did so

Warsaw, Fig. 99
Hamburg, Fig. 154

Worms, Fig. 170

by including a few evocative details. For practical as well as associative reasons, synagogues usually had a courtyard and a hand-washing basin, as the Temple did. A synagogue with a vestibule followed by the prayer hall and the final recess for the ark recalls the arrangement of Herod's Temple, although considerations of efficient planning rather than imitation seem to have caused the similarities. The easternmost of the two columns inside the twelfth-century Worms synagogue had Biblical inscriptions on its abacus referring to Solomon's Temple: Perhaps the Worms columns were meant to be latter-day versions of Jakhin and Boaz, the two columns at Solomon's Temple. The Spanish-Portuguese synagogue of 1674 at Amsterdam has unusual sloping and curving buttresses derived from an illustrated reconstruction of Solomon's Temple made in 1642.[12] In some synagogues, a piece of wall was left unplastered or unpainted to remind worshippers of the Temple's destruction.[13] The designers could hardly do more than this, because the ancient descriptions of the Temple were unclear and scholarly illustrators offered an almost bewildering variety of dissimilar reconstructions.

Copenhagen, Fig. 235
Stockholm, Fig. 237
Budapest, Fig. 38

Symbolic and suggestive resemblances were most frequent in the nineteenth century, when some clients and architects expected that synagogues, like other buildings of the time, would convey specific messages. A three-part synagogue facade with the center part rising highest and all three sections flat-topped reflects not only a basilican interior but also the facade of Solomon's Temple as it was shown in many reconstructions. A pair of columns or turrets flanking the facade or doorway may refer to Jakhin and Boaz. The cupola flanked by turrets on the synagogue at Nijmegen may be derived from fanciful structures meant to indicate the Temple in fifteenth-century Netherlandish paintings.[14]

The Talmudic sages had other ideas about the resemblance between the "lesser" and greater sanctuaries. They did not specify forms and styles, but established more general correspondences. A worshipper should face Jerusalem during the recitation of eighteen prescribed benedictions because Daniel "went to his house where he had windows in his upper chamber open towards Jerusalem; and he got down on his knees three times a day and prayed and gave thanks before his God" (Daniel 6:11). The congregation should turn toward the Holy City.[15] Because Daniel's room had windows, the synagogue must have them, too.[16] The Talmud interprets allusions to height in Ezra 9:1 and Proverbs 1:21 to mean that the synagogue should be taller than other houses in a town, and located on the highest site.[17] Of course, the sages realized that outside authorities might not allow synagogues to be higher than towers and turrets or, by extension, the palaces that had these towers,[18] but people did not normally live in towers higher than a synagogue. In order further to exalt the religious over the mundane, the Talmud refers to men "going down" before the ark[19] which contains the Torah; in a literal interpretation, this can mean that the ark must be raised over the congregation below it. The first record of an ark in a wall niche or an enclosure approached by steps dates from the third century A.D.

Talmudic writers said that a "little sanctuary" could accommodate certain activities that would be unacceptable at the Temple of Jerusalem or in a house of study. This is so because in a synagogue one prays principally for one's own benefit, but one learns to understand the Law and seeks moral guidance in a house of study, although people may pray there as well.[20] The Talmudic sage Raba in Babylonia said, "Just as wearing a shoe is forbidden on the Temple mount but permitted in the synagogue, so spitting is forbidden on the Temple mount but permitted in the synagogue." The synagogue is "on the same footing as a man's house" as compared to the Temple, but "just as a man objects to his house being made into a short cut but does not object to the wearing of shoes or spitting there, so in the case of a synagogue the using of it as a short cut is forbidden but wearing the shoe in it and spitting in it is not forbidden."[21] People engaged in a discussion of the Law may enter a synagogue during a storm to continue this pious pursuit, but otherwise a synagogue should not serve as a mere shelter from heat and rain. A sage and his disciples may dress in synagogues—and even eat and sleep there according to later interpretations of this passage—because they virtually live in the synagogue,[22] but other people may not eat or drink there or use a synagogue as a place of social resort.

A synagogue may be turned into a house of study, but the latter may not be turned into a synagogue, for religious objects and buildings must only increase in holiness.[23] A synagogue may be sold if the money is used to buy a bimah or an ark, the holiest furnishings in a synagogue. If a bimah is sold, the money may be used to purchase cloth covers for the Torah scrolls. If a scroll cover is sold, the proceeds may be applied to scrolls, the holiest objects of all.[24]

Conversely, authorities who approve the sale of a community synagogue to private parties should specify the possibility of repurchase, because the sanctity of the building is reduced when a quorum is not present to perform certain acts of sanctification. A synagogue may, however, be sold for some secular purpose if the money received for it will be applied to a new synagogue or other sacred use. A synagogue may never be sold if it is to be used for anything involving uncleanness, such as a bath, a tannery, a laundry, or even a ritual bath.[25] A synagogue may not be pledged or lent once it has been used as a synagogue. A synagogue in ruins may be used only for certain secular purposes, because some sanctity remains associated with it. Ideally, the ruin would be left untouched, with wild grass and weeds growing to arouse compassion in the viewer. "And I will bring your sanctuaries into desolation" (Lev. 26:31) suggested to Talmudic sages that the "little sanctuaries" should be left as the Lord foretold.[26] One may not use even a ruined synagogue as a shortcut, unless a road passed through that location before the synagogue was built, or unless the passerby entered to pray rather than merely to avail himself of a convenient path.[27]

We see from these rules that synagogues must have had at least two doors or they could not have been used as shortcuts. Moreover, Proverbs 8:34 says, "Happy is the man who obeys Me and waits each day at my gates."[28] While

Babylonian sages spoke of a synagogue with one door, they also mentioned examples with two, the second apparently arranged inside the first, thus implying a vestibule (Fig. 1).[29] This passage has been interpreted in later times to require a vestibule, although a literal reading of the Talmud seems to allow some latitude.

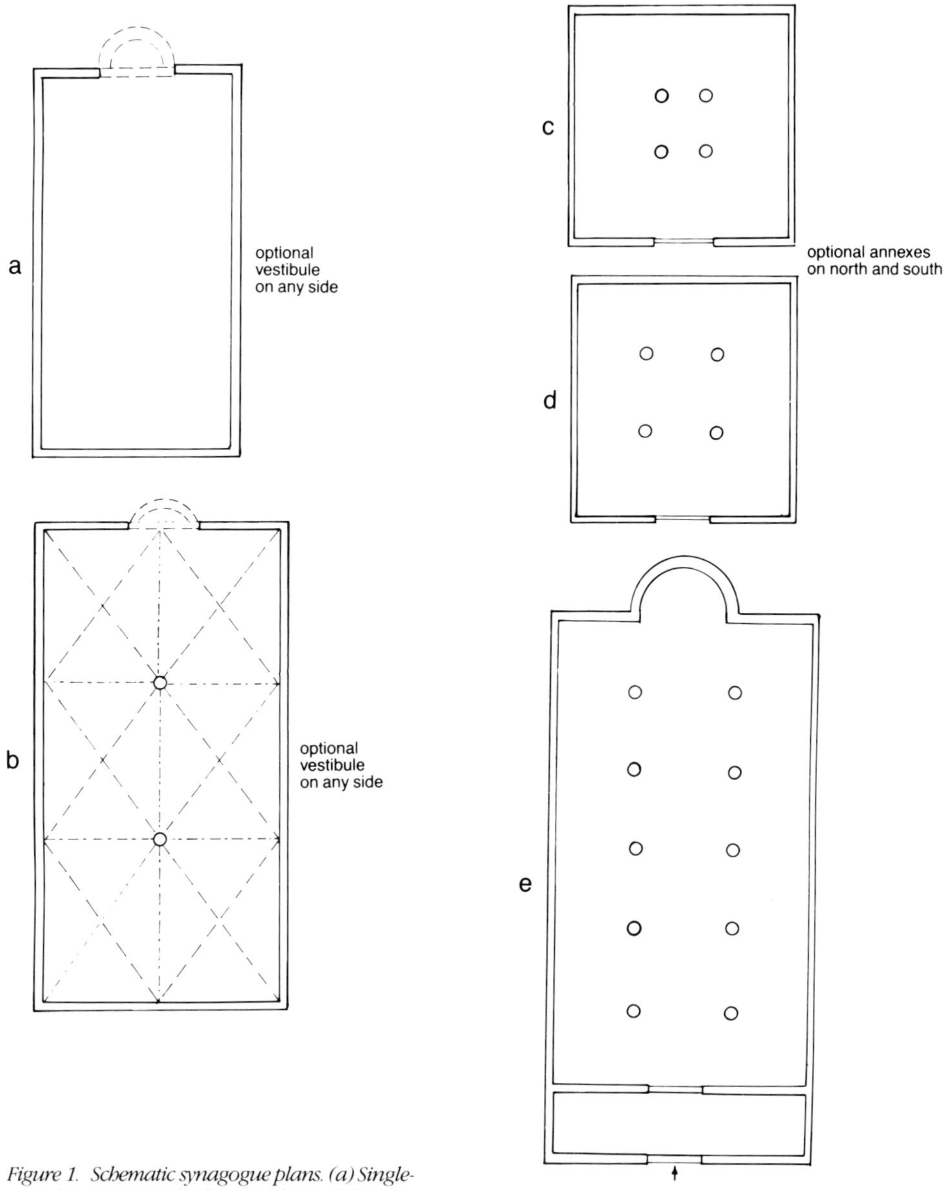

Figure 1. Schematic synagogue plans. (a) Single-naved, with optional ark recess. (b) Double-naved, with optional ark recess. (c) Four-pillar tabernacle (eastern Europe). (d) Four-pillar (Sephardic). (e) Galleried, triple-naved, with optional apse.

Secular Buildings and Synagogues

The synagogue can, however, be used for certain secular purposes as well as for prayer because the Torah fuses sacred and secular elements. The divine will is expressed in everyday activity, and daily affairs have sacred implications. The link between heaven and earth forged by the Law is what Talmudic sages had in mind when they permitted devout men to "go to synagogues and houses of study to watch over public affairs on the Sabbath."[30] The outer courts at the Temple had sheltered some commercial activities, but the public activities of a synagogue outnumber them and are more strongly emphasized. The synagogue or its courtyard[31] is the center for proclamations, for legal decisions, and for the taking of oaths.[32] Some commercial announcements and notices of lost or stolen property could be made there.[33] Government authorities could order that notices be read there for several weeks in succession to make sure that all Jews had the chance to hear them.[34] Other proclamations had to do with the conduct of worshippers, with applications for charity or for money to ransom prisoners, with fines or excommunications levied on the wayward, with food laws, or with such matters as community refusal to patronize Jewish butchers who violated the Sabbath by selling meat. Festivals and weddings were celebrated in synagogues or their courtyards, depending upon the century and country. Synagogues in the Roman Empire offered the right of asylum, and slaves could be manumitted there.[35] The community's archive, law court, pillory, and treasury might also be established in the synagogue, with some of these facilities benefiting from the right of religious buildings to offer sanctuary.

Within the main prayer room, the liturgy requires the ceremonial removal of the Torah scrolls from their repository and their transference to the reader's desk, their solemn replacement, and the bearing of the scrolls around the synagogue in processions held on holy days a few times during the year. Jewish worship, involving the congregation's united activity, can dispense with the multiple altars and chapels found in certain churches, and needs no ambulatories, crypts, shrines, or architectural settings for those who pray apart, such as monks or hermits. Simple solutions based on local custom were devised for accommodating these simple Jewish religious activities. A congregation needed only a covered enclosure and enough space for the people, the ark, and the bimah (see Fig. 1a); the Talmudic requirements had few architectural consequences.

Worshippers who used movable chairs and reading desks, as most Jews did before the mid-nineteenth century, could easily push the furniture aside during processions. Thus both liturgy and the Talmud had limited impact on synagogue architecture. Adherents of the different local rites could worship in similar buildings in which at most the position of the bimah and the arrangement of chairs might be altered.

Endingen, Fig. 131
Lengnau, Fig. 132

Any unified space suits the needs of a synagogue. A synagogue can be established in an inn, as at Plauen in Germany (1867–93), and in a private house, even one owned by Christians when Jews could not own real property, as at Haguenau in Alsace (twelfth to fourteenth century).[36] A Parisian congregation had a synagogue in 1910 in the Hôtel de Sens, which was built in the fifteenth century as the residence of the Archbishop of Sens.[37] At Regensburg, the Jews bought a particularly useful house because it had a domestic chapel which they easily transformed into a synagogue (1841–1913). Other congregations conducted community activities in separate buildings and only rented quarters for prayer, as in Zurich in 1383 and Bad Nauheim before 1929. Large domestic spaces may so closely resemble synagogue rooms that the recess in a wall of a large room at "Jews' Court," a house in Lincoln, has been identified both as an ark niche and as a fireplace, and the house called Moyses Hall in Bury St. Edmunds was long believed to have been a synagogue.[38]

The first Berlin Reform congregation prayed in a diorama, a sort of exhibition building, and Jews in Łaszczów converted the former knights' hall of a sixteenth-century castle into a synagogue. Synagogues have also been made from or converted into gymnasiums. At Poznań in 1940–41, a synagogue became a swimming pool. A convent in Strasbourg which was nationalized under the French Revolution was turned into a "Hospice of Brutus" and then a riding academy before Jews adapted it to a synagogue in 1833. Dutch synagogues at Den Briel (1804) and Dordrecht (1856) were converted meat-market halls. These changes were made, of course, by later owners who were not Jewish. In turn, synagogues have been turned into exhibition halls, art galleries and museums, art schools, a broadcasting facility, concert halls, a hotel, and a restaurant. A plain small-town synagogue stripped of liturgical furniture is like any other meeting room, making it possible for the former synagogue at Schlüchtern to become the tourist office, and another, erected in 1715, to serve as the town hall of Monsheim. The Kalte Shul (or Great Synagogue) in Slutsk became a bakery in the 1920s, and a synagogue at Gorlice has been one since the 1940s. In the Soviet Union, lumber is stored in the former synagogue of Voronezh, and the Great Synagogue of Kiev now houses a puppet theater.[39]

At the Liberal synagogue built in 1930 in Berlin-Prinzregentenstrasse, the rabbi and congregation considered that a screen drawn across the Torah scroll recess separated the sacred and profane parts of the prayer hall, allowing the latter to be used for concerts, lectures, and other culturally edifying purposes. The postwar Berlin community center in Fasanenstrasse also has a multiuse auditorium, and the purpose of all Jewish community centers is to combine sacred and suitable secular activities.

Even purpose-built synagogues resemble other buildings on the outside. That is appropriate in two important ways. First, Jewish worship has traditionally been an activity directed inside—inside the heart and intellect of the worshipper, within his close-knit community. It is a religion of intense fellowship rather than one of hierarchy, external fixed authority, and international eminence. Second, unlike Christians and Moslems, Jews have avoided converting others. Beautiful churches, exquisite symbolic or narrative carvings, and glass paintings can increase a potential convert's desire to attach himself to the source of such wonders. Moreover, the miraculous events of the eucharistic ceremonies can be enhanced by the sense of the marvelous which is given by great ecclesiastical architecture, particularly that of the Roman Catholic church. These things were extraneous to Judaism, except in certain eastern European mystical circles at various times between the seventeenth and nineteenth centuries.

Synagogues have been hard to identify also because for hundreds of years they tended to be small and modest (Figs. 2, 3). A little building with a pointed Gothic window, nestling against the town wall at Buren beside other humble houses, was actually the local synagogue in the nineteenth century. Just how modest others were can be estimated from nineteenth-century petitions for new ones. In the Bas-Rhin department of France, where Jews were especially numerous, petitioners reported on the dirty, crowded, and structurally unstable condition of existing synagogues in at least thirteen towns. Health authorities feared an epidemic among the seventy Jews of Ringendorf who packed themselves into a synagogue 5.25 meters square. Even allowing for exaggeration by those pleading for a new building, the old synagogue must have been wretched and uncomfortable. These conditions were found in comparatively benevolent France; in places where Jews were openly persecuted, the synagogues can only rarely have been better than these French ones. The Liège synagogue in 1859 was situated over a stable![40]

Dubrovnik, Figs. 46, 47
Lengnau, Figs. 132, 133

Figure 2. Medzhibozh, Baal Shem Tov Synagogue and House of Study, mid-18th century and later, exterior.

Figure 3. Medzhibozh, Baal Shem Tov Synagogue and House of Study, interior.

Of course, before the nineteenth century, there were seldom enough Jews in any town to warrant a large synagogue. Lavish investment in building would have been foolhardy even in the wealthier Jewish centers, given the appeal of synagogues as targets for expropriation. After Hasidism became a leading factor in eastern European Judaism in the eighteenth century, several large synagogues were built where nineteenth-century Hasidic leaders had their seats, but most Hasidic Jews are more deeply attached to houses of study than to synagogues.[41]

Synagogues, Churches, and Mosques

Synagogues are comparable in several respects to buildings of other faiths as well as to secular buildings. Christian worship also is conducted indoors, and Christian denominations also meet for both civic and religious activity. In the first centuries of Christianity, the new religion adapted ideas found in synagogues, such as orientation toward Jerusalem and the location of ritual furnishings facing the Holy City. Christian worshippers, too, assembled on the top floors of their buildings. Early churches were also community centers with courtyards and meeting rooms. Later, parish schools were established in church porches, just as synagogues were used for education. Christopher Wren even made one project for St. Paul's Cathedral in London with porticoes to accommodate the many secular activities conducted inside and adjacent to it.[42] Churches' forms have responded to changes of locale, liturgy, and period, as synagogue forms have done. Just as Wren could design his city churches in a great variety of forms and plans, synagogues can be varied in their appearance. The plans of many synagogues are close or even identical to those of aisleless chapels. Synagogues, like chapels, have been established in old-age and youth homes, hospitals, and schools.[43] Some early churches of the Franciscan and Dominican orders, needing plans suited to preaching, shared with synagogues the one- or two-aisled plans of chapter houses, hospital wards, and other broad spaces (Fig. 4; see Fig. 1b).[44] These friars needed something other than traditional religious architecture, just as the Jews did. A Protestant church in which preaching or bearing witness takes precedence over most ceremony may also resemble a meeting room or auditorium, as a synagogue may. Galleried churches inspired the design of galleried synagogues in the Netherlands after the seventeenth century, for "similar social and religious conditions [led] to corresponding results."[45] Protestant churches were remodeled into synagogues in the British Isles from the late eighteenth century onward[46] and small churches sometimes became synagogues on the Continent.[47] Some Jews will not establish a permanent synagogue in a building with images or pray in the direction of images; nevertheless, a synagogue is allowed to have a statue in it if the statue is not meant to be worshipped.[48] Quakers and Jews emphasize a meeting in a unified space and are otherwise traditionally indifferent to the setting for prayer. The Quakers were also a minority group, sometimes victims

Wrocław, Fig. 179

Amsterdam, Figs. 224, 226, 228

London, Figs. 246, 247

Figure 4. Regensburg, double-naved synagogue, interior, early 13th century, with Renaissance bimah, engraving by Albrecht Altdorfer, 1519.

of discrimination, yet successful in education and business.[49] Like synagogues, Christian Science churches, out of the mainstream of Christian tradition, may sometimes use styles noticeably different from those of local traditional churches. This is true of Christian Science churches in London, which tend to be unusually dull, as if to avoid the aesthetic preoccupations of other groups. In general, non-Anglican churches in Great Britain use variations of styles that are uncommon in the Anglican church, as synagogues do in other ways.

Synagogues can, then, easily be transformed into churches by simply removing the bimah, setting up an altar, and segregating an area for the clergy if that is required. After the Jews were expelled from or relocated in a town, as was frequently the case, their community property often passed to the dominant church in the area. Synagogues thus became Catholic churches in Paris in the 1180s, in thirteenth-century England, in Spain in 1391 and at many dates thereafter until the final expulsion of Jews in 1492, in Silesia in 1494, in Vienna in 1670—and these are just a few examples. A special liturgy exists for the dedication of a converted synagogue to Roman Catholic use.[50] Unified synagogue spaces and galleried synagogues suit Protestant needs especially well. The Methodists of Głogów worshipped in a former synagogue. In Great Yarmouth, a synagogue became a mission. Former synagogues at Eschwege, Groningen, Höchberg, Liberec, Plau, and Rexingen are now churches, their congregations having been dispersed or killed during the Nazi period. In 1952, the Jews of Aix-en-Provence sold their 112-year-old synagogue to Protestants.[51] The new uses do not violate Jewish law, because Christians are not idolaters. Moreover, because Christians can obtain any available building for a church, it is not the sale of the synagogue alone that makes a church possible.[52]

Toledo, Figs. 181, 184

Many synagogues even looked like Christian buildings. In the nineteenth century, small Dutch synagogues at Veghel and Gennep resembled chapels, and the German synagogue at Buchau am Federsee, complete with belfry, looked like a Protestant church.[53] The competition entries submitted to the École des Beaux-Arts in 1918 and 1919 as synagogue and Protestant church designs looked remarkably alike.[54] Synagogues, however, avoid Latin-cross plans because the form seems unsuitably Christian, and because there is no liturgical or functional need for it in a synagogue.

České Budějovice, Figs. 43, 45

Buchau, Figs. 125, 126

Of course, despite certain physical and practical similarities, churches differ fundamentally from synagogues. Most Christian worship emphasizes the sacrifice of Jesus which, as represented or reenacted in eucharistic rites, replaces the Temple sacrifice. That is why the liturgy for the dedication of Roman Catholic churches evokes the Temple of Solomon and not the synagogue, even though the church may consider itself the institution that succeeds the synagogue. The architectural consequence of having a fundamental rite enacted by a consecrated person at the east is that the church plan focuses on one point primarily; as we shall see, this was not the case in most synagogues.

Unlike most Christian denominations where there has been a central authority and supervision of church districts, Judaism depends only upon ten men in a quorum. A group of craftsmen acting on their own may set up a synagogue that opens at hours convenient for them. A rich man may set up a private synagogue for his friends. Men who want to pray with people from their home towns sometimes establish synagogues. There are, in fact, so many synagogues in any center of Jewish settlement that it is a standard subject of Jewish humor. The splitting of the local Jewish population into many congregations tends to keep synagogue buildings smaller and more modestly decorated than churches which are built with the funds of an entire parish or diocese.

Mosques, too, share features with synagogues and churches. All are places for public worship and assembly where important announcements may be made. All can be centers for the religious instruction of youth. All can be improvised from existing buildings, including those of other faiths as well as secular buildings. In all, conversion to new uses may be made mainly by changing the focal point, if that needs changing, to direct the worshipper's mind toward a holy city. The holy city for Jews and Christians is Jerusalem, but Mohammed himself originally prayed toward Jerusalem before Mecca was made the focal point, and Caliph Abd-el-Malik (ruled 685–705) substituted a rock on the Temple Mount in Jerusalem for the traditional Arab Ka'ba shrine at Mecca. Moreover, Mohammed and his earliest followers—like Jews at many periods in history—were uninterested in architecture. They used whatever buildings were at hand, simply establishing the direction in which prayer should be said, even if that meant praying across the aisles of a captured church. Existing local styles affected both mosque and synagogue architecture. The five-aisled Mudéjar-style synagogue of Toledo, known as Santa María la Blanca, could be mistaken for a mosque, and has been used as both a synagogue and a church. *Toledo, Figs. 180, 181* Human images in early synagogues, such as those of Dura-Europos (ca. 245), had their counterparts in images of Abraham, Mary, Jesus, and prophets which Mohammed knew were in the Ka'ba and which apparently remained for at least a century.[55] Most synagogues and all mosques since about the late eighth century have prohibited human imagery, although many synagogues and mosques display decorations including animals, plants, and buildings.

Mosques and synagogues share enough features to make conversion of these buildings possible. On one occasion, the Spanish Catholics who captured mosques from the Moors gave the mosques of the Jewish quarter to the Jews for use as synagogues.[56] Russian authorities in the nineteenth century turned over a captured Turkish mosque to Jewish Russian soldiers for their religious services.[57] Rabbinical authorities do not prohibit temporary use of a mosque for Jewish worship, but some rabbis hesitate to establish a permanent synagogue in one.[58]

Recently, some British synagogues have been sold for conversion to mosques, as Jews have moved away from areas now inhabited by Islamic immigrants. Current Arab-Israeli conflicts, however, led to complications: Jews were reluctant to see the change made at the Spitalfields Great Synagogue in London which is now the Jamme Masjid, and Manchester's Great and New Synagogue congregation sold its building for use as a warehouse, forgoing a higher price offered by Moslems who hoped to convert it into a mosque.[59] *London, Figs. 246, 247*

There are, to be sure, significant differences between synagogues and mosques. A synagogue is a building for a group apart, but early Moslems occasionally shared a building with members of other faiths. Although individual sects in Islam may each have their own small mosques in a large town, just as groups of Jews may establish independent synagogues, the Moslem services held on Fridays may be attended by all Islamic groups worshipping together in one or more "cathedral" or "Friday" mosques which have no precise counterpart in Judaism.[60] If followers of different Jewish rites worship under one roof, they generally occupy separate rooms or apartments, whereas members of various Islamic sects may each have their own areas or niches in a single mosque.

Unlike most synagogues, mosques—especially large ones—are closely tied to the local Moslem ruler's residence, as Solomon's palace stood near the Temple. This is different from the synagogue standing near the seat of a Christian nobleman whose will determined the fate of local Jews. And while a synagogue was part of a Hasidic leader's complex of buildings, the Hasidic leader was not the official secular ruler of his town.

A large forecourt surrounded by porticoes stands in front of many mosques, perhaps reflecting the arrangement of Mohammed's house. Although many synagogues have courtyards, they can be rear or side courts, they tend to be irregular in shape, and they are seldom porticoed. Inside a mosque, there is a raised pulpit platform, the *minbar,* which was originally occupied by the local chief; while some medieval Spanish bimahs seem to have been similar constructions (Fig. 5), most bimahs are raised only slightly and are occupied by scholars and esteemed members of the community rather than by secular leaders. Some mosques even contain enclosures in which the ruler could pray

Figure 5. Medieval Spanish synagogue, London, British Library MS Or. 2884, fol. 17b, Haggadah, 14th century.

without fear of assassination. Nothing of the sort is known in synagogue architecture or furnishing.

It is customary for Moslems to spread prayer rugs in parallel lines on the floor of a mosque. Maimonides described North African or Spanish synagogues in which worshippers sat on the floor, but they did not kneel or face in one direction only, as Moslems face Mecca. Since the climate north of the Mediterranean coast makes sitting on the floor unhealthy,[61] European Jews installed movable furniture as well as benches around the walls and around the bimah. Karaites do prostrate themselves on the floor, but only briefly, and the members of this Jewish movement generally sit on benches, as other Jews do. The furniture arrangement naturally affects the interior appearance and the circulation patterns in synagogues, adding to their differences from mosques.

Prague, Fig. 49
Endingen, Fig. 131
Lengnau, Fig. 132

The poverty of most Jews throughout history, the legal regulations applied to them, and the uncertain skills of builders were all important reasons why the Jews were likely to adapt any building that they were permitted to use for a synagogue. In such variable and often humble settings, they must have been unaccustomed to thinking about architecture. Moreover, the Talmud recommends that one be oblivious to one's surroundings during prayer.[62] These factors hindered the development of a Jewish architectural tradition.

Amsterdam, Figs. 223, 224
London, Figs. 246, 247

A Jew's faith is expressed in every aspect of his life rather than culminating in communion rites. Thus he may practice his religion fully even if he cannot attend a synagogue. The synagogue is a neutral setting for private devotions carried on, if possible, with nine other men in order to perform all the acts of sanctification set down in rabbinic law. A Jew must establish a synagogue if there is a quorum in his town,[63] but the traveler, the lone Jew in an area, the invalid, and others cut off from synagogue life can worship through prescribed behavior and private prayer, independent of priests, altars, or consecrated surroundings.

A building set apart is consequently something of only limited importance. In his novel, *Warsaw,* Sholom Asch described a congregation as having "come from their work without making any preparation, without any show of reverence, as if their God were one of themselves. With Him there was no need of ceremony." The congregation prayed in the courtyard, in "a little edifice of new planks with a shingled roof. There lived the poor occupants' God. His dwelling was just as wretched as theirs."[64]

Of course, this relative indifference to architectural surroundings varied among groups and individuals. A synagogue built as a pious foundation might have a different character from one built by someone who hoped to make a profit from selling seats. In the nineteenth century, when architecture often expressed nationalistic self-proclamation, Jews had to consider the image of their newly emancipated minority group in the larger society where the Christian church and the nation often were intertwined. Throughout European history, the shifting balance between constraint and freedom for the Jews determined the architecture of the synagogue.

2 Ritual Arrangements

Pious Jews at prayer may be indifferent to beauty in the synagogue, but they are sensitive to the correct arrangement of synagogue furnishings. The ritual furniture is connected to liturgy, and to ancestral traditions that help to maintain the cohesion of the minority group. The interior arrangements were subject to some changes, which varied with time, local custom, and the degree of the congregation's orthodoxy.

A synagogue will always need an ark, the repository for the Torah scrolls, and a bimah, the table and platform from which the scrolls are read. The congregation will need seats, because men spend long hours in the building and are supposed to follow the Talmudic requirement to pray several times a day with a quorum in the synagogue. There must be enough room for reading desks, and for storing prayer books and the prayer shawls and phylacteries that the orthodox wear. There should be a hand-washing basin for the traditional purification before prayer. The synagogue may also have a resting room for the sick and aged, and toilets as well, because services last all day long during the New Year and Day of Atonement High Holy Days in the autumn.

Bimah

Amsterdam, Figs. 224, 226, 228

Bratislava, Fig. 27
Prague, Fig. 49
Cracow, Fig. 71
Worms, Fig. 172
Volpa, Fig. 97
Fürth, Fig. 147
Endingen, Fig. 131

Vilnius, Fig. 92

The bimah is the principal influence on the synagogue's plan. The officiant reads there from the Torah scrolls and leads the congregation in turning toward Jerusalem during prayer. The bimah is the primary focus of attention, emphasized by its design and location, and by light, which is often most intense around it. The bimah table alone will suffice to hold the scrolls, but the table usually is raised on a platform with a railing enclosing it. The table is supposed to be made of wood, to imitate the wooden pulpit from which Ezra read the Law, as recorded in Nehemiah 8:4. The railing may be made in any shape and material, or a high, screen-like enclosure may substitute for a railing (see Figs. 4, 5). The enclosure may be covered, either with a small vault or an openwork roof. The platform and its cover may be square, rectangular, or polygonal. If polygonal, it is usually octagonal, but at Mulhouse before 1865, and at Endingen a century earlier, the bimah was hexagonal, while the mid-nineteenth-century example at Hirsingue was decagonal.[1] Following a post-Talmudic tradition, a synagogue's floor may be lowered under the bimah platform so that prayers can rise "out of the depths" (Ps. 130:1). This has been done from Vilnius

(Great) to London (Bevis Marks), from Altona (Ashkenazic) in northern Germany to Kórnik in Poland.

London, Fig. 243

The bimah usually stands on the main axis of the building[2] and is often emphasized by an architectural feature, such as a skylight or lantern above it or pillars beside it. The bimah's screen, cover, and lighting emphasize the officiant and the Torah that he reads, providing a common focus of attention and promoting group cohesion. Modifications in the bimah's position admit a number of spatial and architectural possibilities in synagogue design.[3] In Ashkenazic synagogues, the bimah has generally been placed near the center of the prayer hall, following the precepts of the sixteenth-century legal authority, Rabbi Moses Isserles.[4] In synagogues of the Italian rite, the bimah traditionally was set up across the room from the ark, either across the long axis or, exceptionally, across the short one, as at Padua;[5] sometimes, it stood on a balcony behind a railing. The two eighteenth-century synagogues at Carpentras and Cavaillon in the southern French Comtat Venaissin also had bimahs raised on balconies across the room from the ark. Sephardic-rite bimahs generally stand near the opposite end of the long axis from the ark, although in the twelfth century the great Sephardic legal codifier, Maimonides, had pointed out that a central bimah allowed everyone to hear easily.

Budapest, Fig. 37
Vilnius, Fig. 93
Prague, Fig. 49
L'vov, Figs. 82, 85
Vienna, Fig. 66
Ancona, Figs. 188, 189
Carpentras, Figs. 104, 105
Cavaillon, Fig. 107
Amsterdam, Figs. 223, 228
London, Fig. 243

The bimah, as locus of instruction, competes with the ark which terminates the axis facing Jerusalem, the direction in which prayers are addressed. In Italian, Sephardic, and Comtadin synagogues, worshippers divide their attention between two poles along the east-west axis—the ark at the east and the bimah at or near the west. In orthodox Ashkenazic synagogues, the congregation experiences a tension between the centralizing tendencies of a room designed around a central bimah and the axial tendencies given by the ark location. Reform Ashkenazic synagogues place both ark and bimah at the east; the ark, at the terminal point, tends to dominate the bimah.

Ansbach, Fig. 120
Hamburg, Fig. 150
Plauen, Fig. 157

Where the bimah is far from the ark, seats may run parallel to the axis of the building, allowing the congregation to look either to the right or to the left, avoiding 180-degree turns. The worshippers face each other, thereby establishing personal contact. The exchange of glances and gestures across a room, the division of attention between the left and the right, can establish a certain equivalency or unity in the room because importance is given to all parts of it, all people inside, and all activities. There may be two objects of attention, but the movement of hands, eyes, and bodies establishes currents of motion which link the parts of the synagogue and the people within it. The collegial sense given by this seating arrangement explains its use also in church choirs and university chapels.

Venice, Fig. 220
Amsterdam, Fig. 224

Interaction between the building and its users may also be found in synagogues with a central bimah (see Fig. 1c), especially if the synagogue accommodates a three-quarter circle, or three sides of a square of worshippers who are linked by their common focus on the bimah. The rabbi and cantor, and sometimes the synagogue elders, may sit beside the ark, completing the "circle" by facing the congregation. A nearly circular grouping will emphasize the

Bruck, Figs. 31–33
Frankfurt, Fig. 145
Livorno, Fig. 199
Milan, Fig. 201
London, Fig. 245

primacy of the bimah over the ark because the people will turn toward the readers, and the central bimah will be the resting place for all eyes. This has been easy to arrange in synagogues with movable seating. When the service called for the congregation to stand—such as when Torah scrolls were taken from the ark or replaced—movable reading stands in front of each set could be turned to allow prayers to be read in the proper direction. A path could be cleared for those who wanted to embrace and kiss the Torah while it was being carried between the ark and the bimah.[6]

Vienna, Fig. 66
Endingen, Fig. 131
Lengnau, Fig. 132

In many Ashkenazic synagogues, fixed seats were backed up against the bimah railing or enclosure, even if the other seats were movable. The bimah seats may have been devised to accommodate more people while making sure that one worshipper would not always have to see the back of the person in front of him, or to give readers the benefit of light from candles on the bimah. Seats around the bimah, considered places of honor, were allocated to men of distinction or to those who contributed generously to synagogue building and furnishing. The occupants of those seats faced the perimeter of the building, not the bimah.[7] This arrangement emphasized the individual, inward direction of prayer, rather than a group's united concentration on the same focal point, while retaining a sense of community because each worshipper faced another member of the congregation.

Prague, Fig. 49
Volpa, Fig. 97

In the nineteenth century, Reformers preferred fixed seating. They wanted to tidy up visual irregularities, just as they wanted to replace individual cantillation with uniform prayers. Fixed seats made it necessary to provide aisles, whereas in older synagogues worshippers could thread their way around movable chairs and lecterns. Most importantly, fixed seating meant that the bimah had to be moved to a place from which all the people in the fixed seats could see it conveniently—of course, to the east.

Israel Jacobson, an early Reformer, was the first to move the bimah eastward; he did so in the synagogue of his boys' school at Seesen, in Lower Saxony, in 1810. Such an innovation was more acceptable in a school than in a community synagogue. That it was still a questionable thing to do is shown by the fact that Jacobson left the bimah in the center of a synagogue that he later established in his house in Berlin. Gradually, however, the bimah in Reform synagogues moved farther toward the ark,[8] eventually becoming part of a grand composition of ark, ark platform, bimah, and sometimes a lectern or pulpit.

Seesen, Fig. 167

The unity and orderliness of Reform services, which included vernacular rather than only Hebrew elements, provided a conceptual parallel for the united and churchly composition of a bimah near an ark. Polite and sophisticated congregations of German-speaking "Israelites"[9] who admired the neat simplicity of church arrangements, and people who wanted to become integrated "citizens of the Mosaic persuasion" rather than being considered Jewish in mentality as well as religion, did not want to keep traditional arrangements which gave synagogues a foreign cast. At the same time, as the Jewish population increased because of immigration or better control of disease, existing synagogues became crowded before new ones could be built. By moving the

Szeged, Fig. 57
Leningrad, Fig. 89
Berlin, Fig. 124
Florence, Fig. 194

bimah to the east, the congregation gained seating room where there had previously been simply an open space between the bimah and the ark.

As an independent, freestanding entity, the Ashkenazic bimah had preserved the centrality of reading and learning in the heart of the congregation. When it moved eastward under the elevated ark, it became visually subordinate to the ark. Likewise, in less traditional orthodox and in Reform synagogues, the old orthodox practice of individual prayer at individual paces was suppressed in favor of a single leader or unified choir. When there was music, the congregation followed the pace set by an organist.[10] The congregation no longer had to participate continuously, and the congregational space was no longer a forum for the dynamic interplay between the axial tension and the centrifugal force emanating from the bimah. With a single, static culmination point at the east, the interior became a theatrical or ceremonial and rather church-like space for a mass of people. Seated quietly and in fixed seats, members of the congregation could turn their attention from the remote officiant, just as they might ignore the action of a play. An Italian Jewish observer, Augusto Bachi, remarked that the huge number of nineteenth-century synagogues had been built in the age of least faith; he compared the situation to that of the Roman Catholic church during the Italian Renaissance.[11]

Budapest, Fig. 39
Paris, Fig. 111
Berlin, Fig. 124
Lengnau, Fig. 135

At the same time, especially in western and central Europe, the role of both orthodox and Reform rabbis changed. This came about because new legal and social conditions offered increasing civil rights (under continued government regulation of religion). The rabbi became an official representative of his congregation, responsible to the state and often paid by state funds; he might now have to be a certified graduate of a theological seminary, not simply an authority approved by his fellow Jews alone. His former work as judge was reduced by the law courts, which now dealt with affairs that older privileges and charters had reserved for Jewish religious courts. His former importance as a teacher was diminished when state-sponsored schools admitted Jewish youth. As adult Jews grew more interested in secular culture in which they could now share, they had less time for Hebrew and traditional religious studies. Thereafter, congregation members continued to read the Torah along with the traditional cantor who led prayers from the bimah, but many laymen left the advanced study of Judaism to the rabbis. Changes in the role of the rabbi implied a change in the interior arrangements of the synagogue in which he officiated. The east end became more formal, and it became more remote, just as did many rabbis.

Ark

The ark and its contents are the holiest features in the synagogue. The Torah scrolls, bound in strips of fabric, are encased in a cloth cover adorned with a silver Torah shield; the scroll handles are sometimes terminated by silver finials. The ark in early times was a portable chest, sometimes stored outside the prayer hall. In that case, there might be no special architectural arrangement for it in the synagogue. This remained true in later synagogues if the ark was a large chest whether portable or not, or if the synagogue occupied a building that could not be altered. Medieval synagogues sometimes had niches in the eastern wall, in which the ark container was inserted (see Fig. 1a). Framed by decorations around the niche, the medieval ark seems to have remained a modest object, with the bimah remaining visually dominant. From the sixteenth century onward, the size and decoration of the ark frames and cabinets increased, and in this way competed visually with the bimah; this is still the case today.

Toledo, Fig. 184

The predominance of neoclassical architectural styles and the general sobriety of design around 1800 contributed to a change in the ark's appearance. It was still large and conspicuous, but it stood in an apse rather than in a niche (see Fig. 1e). An apse evoked Roman apses, which had been associated with Roman law and divine authority; some early synagogues that were erected under Roman rule also had apses to shelter Torah scrolls—repositories of divine Law. Apses were most familiar, however, from Christian churches, where they were associated with miraculous and sacramental activities that had no connection to Judaism. Reform-temple apses, where the bimah, pulpit, and elevated ark were close together at the east, looked particularly church-like. This distressed the orthodox who avoided imitating practices of other religions. Ironically, the Reformers' commanding apse compositions, glorifying the Torah repository, contrasted with the Reform movement's comparatively earthbound and rational approach to worship and Torah study.[12] Their synagogue arrangements revealed their aspirations to social and intellectual assimilation, not their most serious feelings about modern worship. The apsed synagogue therefore does not appropriately embody aspects of belief or tradition for either orthodox or Reform Jews.

Paris, Fig. 109

Hamburg, Fig. 150

The ark has taken on symbolic associations, which are post-Talmudic. The Mishnah section of the Talmud uses the word *tevah* for ark, *tevah* being the word for Noah's ark; Sephardic Jews still use this word. In the Middle Ages, the word *aron ha-kodesh,* or holy ark, used for the Ark of the Covenant (2 Chron. 35:3), was applied to synagogue arks by Ashkenazic Jews. This ark is supposed to have been installed in the Holy of Holies at Solomon's Temple. When Jews examined all the conclusions to be drawn from the nature of the synagogue as a "little sanctuary," they apparently compared the holiest part of the synagogue to the holiest part of the Temple. Accordingly, the ark in a synagogue is covered by a curtain which is likened to the veil that divided the Holy of Holies from the preceding room at the Temple. The ark is made strong—for security, of course, but perhaps to suggest a latter-day version of the Holy of Holies, which was also an impenetrable place containing the evidence of the Lord's relationship to the congregation. The ark container occasionally imitated aspects of buildings in the Holy Land, so that it could come as close as possible to the Temple ark. (In fact, no one knew what the Temple ark looked like, and

Solomon's Temple may not even have had one.)[13] The synagogue ark at Kiel had the form of Rachel's tomb, and the synagogue ark at Trieste symbolized Mount Sinai.[14] At least the latter idea had some relationship to the Torah.

Trieste, Fig. 213

Lighting

Jews must read and recite prayers, and they are honored by being called to the bimah to read from the Torah scrolls. Synagogue worship invites active participation. It is characteristic of Judaism that until the Reform movement became influential in the nineteenth century, Ashkenazic Jews took it for granted that each Jew would say his prayers aloud, but not necessarily at the same speed as his neighbor; this tradition continues in many orthodox congregations.

Individual reading makes the distribution of good lighting important. Large windows were especially desirable in places where the Christian authorities taxed each candle used for synagogue illumination. Synagogues often had only small windows, however, or windows placed high on the walls, out of the reach of stone-throwing vandals. High windows also allowed for the later addition of side annexes high enough to hold standing adults without blocking the main prayer hall windows. A local official could have ordered small openings to prevent the sound of Jewish prayer from reaching other ears, or the Jews may have found it prudent to limit the spread of the sounds they made, because Christians could close a synagogue from which prayers could be heard at an "offensive" level. Other windows might be small if a builder hesitated to open too much of a wall that supported a vaulted ceiling. Sometimes a darkened interior satisfied emotional or psychological needs.

Mödling, Fig. 20
Sopron, Fig. 21
Prague, Fig. 49
Prague, Fig. 48
Cracow, Fig. 70

Vilnius, Fig. 93

Where adjacent buildings prevented adequate light from entering through the synagogue's perimeter windows, or where the synagogue was too wide to be lit by windows alone, skylights opened in the ceiling, sometimes directly above the bimah. They became more prevalent during the nineteenth century, when glass became cheap to manufacture and widely available.[15]

Ancona, Fig. 190
Venice, Fig. 217
Paris, Fig. 113
Berlin, Fig. 124
Stockholm, Fig. 238

To be sure, people also pray at night and in gray weather, and at these times artificial light is more important than window light. Candelabra stood on the bimah railing or hung from the bimah framework and from ceilings and the parapets of galleries. They added light to the center of the prayer hall and illuminated the bimah's all-important reading desk. Metal reflectors often enhanced the light. On the walls there might be sconces or a shelf for candles, placed above the heads of congregation members to prevent the candles from being easily knocked over and causing fires. The candle shelf can still be seen in the Altneuschul of Prague. Lights above the heads of those who are praying accentuate the humble position of the worshippers whose prayers emerge from below. If the upper parts of a building are obscured, the worshipper may feel that he is praying from a spot divorced from the understandable limits of an ordinary room. This increases mystical feelings, and lends an aura of the supernatural which was fostered in certain eastern European Jewish circles

Prague, Fig. 49
Lengnau, Fig. 132
Prague, Fig. 49

during the late Renaissance. Midnight and other nocturnal services were introduced during this period. The constant flickering of candlelight complemented the rhythmic cantillation of worshippers who prayed at individual paces, as it did their traditional back-and-forth motion during prayer. The synagogues must have had an active humming effect which is different from the hieratic stateliness of Roman Catholic ritual or the more static and rationalistic atmosphere of some Protestant denominations.

Vilnius, Fig. 93

The Eternal Light hangs in front of the ark in most modern synagogues. It is a lamp first lit at the synagogue's dedication when the Torah scrolls are placed in the ark.[16] It is a reminder of the perpetual lamp of the Temple, and it is one of the links between the synagogue as a "lesser sanctuary" and the ancient great sanctuary in Jerusalem. The light also has been interpreted as a symbol of the Lord's presence among the people,[17] or as representing the spiritual light which went forth from the sanctuary at Jerusalem,[18] or as a symbol of the Law which Jews must keep alive.[19] The light has no specific form. It is usually a hanging lamp suspended in front of the ark, where it reinforces the axiality of synagogue space and lends additional richness to the ark area. In late-Renaissance Polish synagogues, the lamp stood in a niche in the entrance wall, perhaps to reduce the danger of fire inside the prayer hall.[20]

Pulpit

A pulpit[21] has been included in synagogue interiors since the fifth or sixth century, although some may have existed earlier. It has not been included in every synagogue and only in the eighteenth century did it become commonplace. It is used for reading texts which are less holy than those read at the bimah table, and for offering prayers. A Jewish pulpit is likely to be a modest piece of furniture, distinguished from a Christian pulpit or a secular speaker's desk only by the occasional application of ornaments showing the six-pointed star or the lion of Judah or some other traditional image.

Sofia, Fig. 59
Florence, Fig. 194

The pulpit did not have a fixed location. At a period now unknown, Sephardic Jews began to conduct the service from the bimah alone and therefore dispensed with a pulpit. Where one is included, it can affect the spatial arrangement of a synagogue by drawing attention to the ark area if it is near the ark, or to a cross axis or other focal point. In Ashkenazic synagogues of the traditional orthodox type, the pulpit is often placed near the bimah. In Reform temples it is part of the east-end ark-and-bimah composition and the pulpit reinforces the unitary spatial direction.[22]

London, Fig. 152

Choir and Organ

The choir and the organ[23] required suitable space, once they were introduced in Reform temples. Usually, the western gallery was given over to them, but sometimes they were placed in a broad recess above or around the Torah container. This further emphasized the single direction for synagogue activity that Reformers created when they moved the bimah eastward near the ark.

Szeged, Fig. 57
London, Fig. 152

Arrangements for Women

The connection between the Temple of Jerusalem and the "lesser sanctuaries" suggested that arrangements found in the Temple be carried over to synagogues. At least on some occasions,[24] women were separated from men at the Temple, and Talmudic interpreters took this to mean that the sexes should remain apart in synagogues.[25] Orthodox Jews support this interpretation with appeals to the respect for one's elders that can be achieved by following their tradition of segregated worship.[26] In addition, "Synagogues can purify a Jew from evil thoughts and lift him up to the level of a virtuous man." If, however, a pious man sees a woman while he recites the fundamental "Shema" prayer, the orthodox believe that the sight may arouse lustful or frivolous thoughts which defile him and his prayer.[27] A barrier of some sort between men and women prevents the possibility of this temptation. Then, too, if mixed seating is allowed, a seat formerly occupied by a deceased father might be occupied by someone other than his son; this endangers property rights established in Jewish law, and it means the abandonment of family practice and tradition.[28]

Our discussion so far has concentrated on synagogue arrangements as they were designed for men. For a long time, a women's section was only an afterthought, as comparatively few women attended synagogue services. Jewish law exempts women from required attendance because of their domestic obligations. Women were not counted in the quorum and did not read from the Torah at the bimah, or become rabbis or cantors.[29] The women's section is considered less sacred than the men's, and the barriers between the two are only means to a holy end, not intrinsic elements of a "little sanctuary."[30] Synagogues generally have had fewer seats for women, and women have been more numerous than men in synagogues only under exceptional circumstances, such as the absence or death of men in wartime.[31] As late as the eighteenth century, it was unusual for an unmarried woman to attend Ashkenazic services except on the joyous holy days of Purim and Simhat Torah.[32] Separate women's services led by women or men in the vernacular included sentimental accounts of religious subjects. The women's sections lacked both ark and bimah because only men had the duty to learn Hebrew and read the Torah.

Cracow, Fig. 72
L'vov, Fig. 83

The women's area was often cramped, dark, and ill-ventilated, unless it was a curtained or screened part of the men's space. Women had to strain forward to hear or see what was happening beyond the partitions separating them from the men. The furnishings might be minimal, or even inadequate.[33] Sometimes, steps to the women's area were provided in adjacent buildings from which a portion of the wall beside the synagogue would be removed to permit access.

A women's section could be a ground floor room, as at Worms, or an extra aisle, as in the Pinkas Synagogue in Prague. Being separated by screens or walls from the men's areas, the women's sections did not enlarge or complicate the space of the main hall.

Worms, Figs. 169, 171

Least agreeable were the women's areas situated under the men's synagogue.[34] Here the women held a literally "lower" position. Moreover, if a synagogue is to be the highest apartment in a building, a room below it cannot enjoy the same sanctity. A grille in the floor of the men's area allowed women to hear the services and to see the Torah scrolls when they were held close to the grille.

Cracow, Fig. 72
L'vov, Fig. 82

Ancona, Figs. 189, 190

Fürth, Fig. 147

A women's annex elevated above the men's floor level, at the side and scarcely visible from the men's area, is known in many synagogues from the fourteenth century on. The annex could be along any or all sides, but it was not normally beyond the ark.[35] If the annex rose along one side of the men's hall, it could darken the main room by blocking existing windows or by preventing other windows from being cut into that wall. If the openings of the annex were small and/or many-tiered, they established a rhythm competing with the rhythm of windows in the opposite side of the room.[36] This opposition might add interest to the design of a plain rectilinear interior or other simple space, but usually it was visually awkward.

L'vov, Fig. 84
Ansbach, Fig. 121

The raised annex demands the construction of more than one storey, and while that may be expensive it provides some ground floor space under the women's section which can be used for additional men's seating or for a schoolroom, meeting room, office, library, weekday synagogue, or vestibule. A single exterior wall could thus economically shelter more than one activity. The raised women's annex itself could later become part of the main space if the grilles were removed or if the openings were enlarged; the annex would then look like a gallery, although the original architect would not have designed his synagogue with a gallery in mind.

The separate annex persisted at least through the late nineteenth century. Israel Zangwill, in his novel, *Children of the Ghetto,* described one in London. It was a room that

> had no connection with the men's; it was simply the room above part of theirs, and the declamations of the unseen cantor came but faintly through the flooring, though the clamor of the general masculine chorus kept the pious *au courant* with their husbands.[37]

From the late sixteenth century onward, a gallery for women was installed in the main room of many synagogues, eventually becoming expected in all but the humblest ones of the type Zangwill described or in those with small congregations. It was characteristic of Renaissance architecture to seek harmonious ordering of all parts of a building, and the earlier ad hoc additions of oddly-sized, oddly-shaped annexes were certainly not harmonious. A synagogue on an open site may be given almost any shape, and designing a wider building than was customary presented few problems. Architects may even have welcomed the challenge of incorporating galleries into their designs. Outside stairs to the galleries could add variety to the form of a box-like building, as at the old synagogue of Cracow/Kazimierz, Olesno, and Myslkovice, or they could form part of the exterior design, as they did in a competition project by Felix Ascher for the Hamburg-Oberstrasse synagogue. The stairs could also look awkward, as the exterior staircase did at the Sephardic synagogue of Amsterdam (1675) in its original form.

Cracow, Fig. 70
Łańcut, Fig. 80

Inside the building, gallery supports that extend to the ceiling allow the synagogue interior to be wider than it could be without the extra supports. At Livorno, after a remodeling in 1789, the handsome synagogue had a graceful rhythmic design in which tiers of arches formed the boundaries of superimposed galleries. Even in the startling synagogue of 1958–62 that replaced it, the sweeping curved gallery adds élan to the interior and emphasizes the centrality of the plan. On a narrow site, however, a gallery can be a liability to the architect. Squeezing in adequate seating for women may make the entire interior seem cramped when the galleries take up too much of the space above the men's heads. The architect could, of course, raise the ceiling high enough to separate the gallery clearly from the men's level, and this was done in the Spanish and German synagogues of Venice. In these, oval galleries provided counterpoint to the oblong spaces and to the major axis. They also united all parts of the rooms, reducing the bilateral division that can occur where seats parallel the main axis, as they do in these synagogues. The long oval preserved the polarity of ark and bimah, while it offered a unifying sweep of line which linked the people, the furnishings, and the space as if to express their harmony of purpose. A curving gallery may emphasize centrality and unity in a synagogue even if it only extends around part of the interior.[38] Alternatively, if a gallery is aligned with the long walls of an oblong synagogue, it can emphasize the east-west axis. If a western gallery is used as an organ or choir loft, there will be side galleries for women unless the congregation is small enough to be seated on the main floor.

Livorno, Fig. 196
Livorno, Figs. 198, 199
Paris, Fig. 113
Venice, Figs. 217–222
Essen, Fig. 140

Gallery supports may be massive and somber, light and springing, regular and tranquil, or dramatic in their bulk or elongation. An unusual arrangement of supports is found in the large Sephardic synagogue of Amsterdam (1675) in which the women's galleries rest on independent supports and occupy just half the width of the aisles, never approaching the main piers which rise to the ceiling. Standing apart, not visually integrated, they look like the appendages that women's galleries still were in the seventeenth century. When architects step the women's seats up toward the outer walls, women can see the events in the men's area below without crowding into the space immediately beside the grilles.[39]

Amsterdam, Fig. 228

Reformers in the nineteenth century lowered or abolished the grilles. Existing walls that separated women's from men's areas were pierced with wide openings, as at Worms, or were eliminated. Eager to promote Jewish family activity, Reformers permitted women to see and hear the services easily, and allowed men to see the women at prayer, although they kept the sexes apart.

Worms, Figs. 169, 170
Hamburg, Fig. 150
London, Fig. 152

Only Liberal Jews, who extended Reform ideas in the present century, permitted mixed seating, but even in the Liberal Prinzregentenstrasse synagogue of 1930 in Berlin, women who had no families with whom to share mixed pews still sat with other women.[40]

Because much of the Reform service was conducted in the vernacular, women were expected to read and follow it. The women's section then needed good lighting. If large numbers of women were expected to stay at the long High Holy Day services, they needed more resting rooms and toilets. All members of the family, comfortably seated in synagogues planned in a modern and professional manner, were to demonstrate the (twentieth-century American) slogan that "the family that prays together stays together"—especially in the face of the social forces that tempted Jewish youth to convert to Christianity.

Auxiliary Spaces

A synagogue may be surrounded by other annexes and buildings, and it may even be part of a multisynagogue complex, as was the case at the Great Synagogue courtyard in Vilnius. The synagogue may have only a vestibule, or it may have under one roof a vestibule, women's section, children's schoolroom, house of study, rabbinical courtroom, small winter or weekday synagogue, apartments for the synagogue officiants and caretaker, guild or fraternity rooms, and community offices (Fig. 6). Adjacent to it may be a matzah bakery, social hall, ritual bath, kasher slaughterhouse, and temporary mortuary. A synagogue courtyard should be large enough for open-air services at the time of the new moon and for a tabernacle used at the Sukkot holiday. Several houses of study stood near the main synagogue at Pinsk, and the once-famous Strashun Library was a few steps from the Great Synagogue at Vilnius. In suburban London, an architect today may be asked to provide room for child care while women attend services. Synagogue kitchens may now be large enough to allow preparations for wedding and bar mitzvah receptions. A prayer hall obscured from view by these facilities may seem all the more impressive when worshippers finally enter it.

Amsterdam, Fig. 227

Some of these auxiliary spaces can also be found in churches. Before the secular state took over education, a parish school was sometimes housed in the porch of a church, and there were parish halls for festivities. Monasteries included libraries, bakeries, and other outbuildings.

Prague, Fig. 51

The principal annex is the vestibule, for a synagogue is seldom entered directly from a street or courtyard. The Talmudic passage in b. Berakoth 8a, telling worshippers to enter the synagogue by two doors, may have a metaphorical meaning, but it has generally been taken literally. Thus it requires a door from the outside into a vestibule, followed by a second door into the prayer hall. There may also be an entrance porch. Rabbi Judah Loeb of Prague said that in the vestibule one dismisses the influence of the mundane world

Bratislava, Figs. 29, 30
Budapest, Fig. 40
Warsaw, Fig. 99
Berlin, Fig. 123

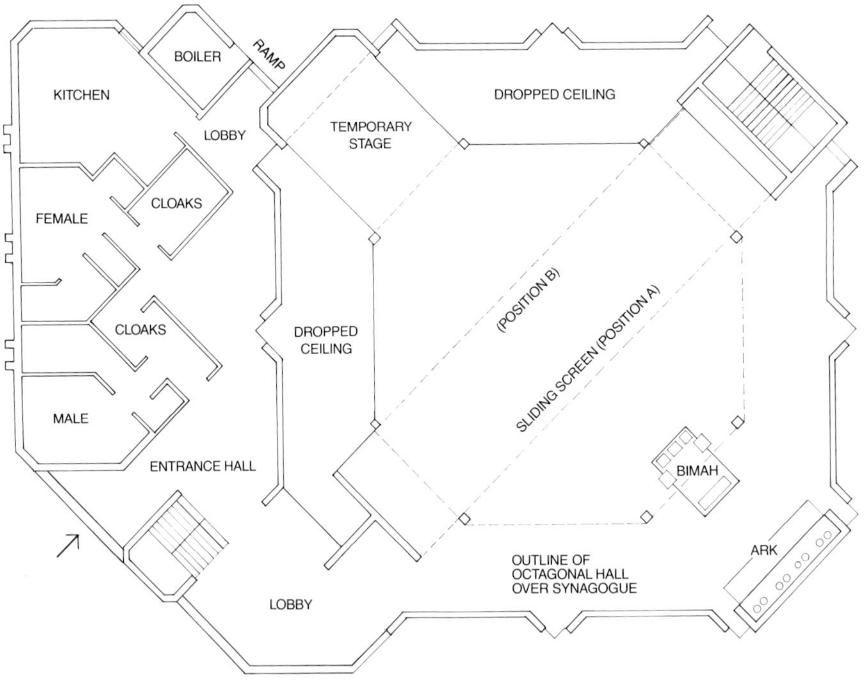

Figure 6. Pinner, plan, 1979.

before passing into a holy environment.[41] The synagogue vestibule was used also for community activities, especially from the late sixteenth to the eighteenth century when Jews were more or less self-governing in eastern Europe. A court proceeding could be held there, and in the seventeenth-century synagogues at Przysucha, Lutsk, Vilnius, and L'vov-Suburban there were pillories in a corner for punishing prisoners; the Prague-Altneuschul also contained a jail at one time.[42] As in Christian or secular buildings, the vestibule also provides a convenient place where one may remove outer clothing and greet friends. Synagogue vestibules usually have a hand-washing fountain, and the stairs up to the galleries are reached from the vestibule in nineteenth- and twentieth-century buildings. *L'vov, Fig. 85*

Some synagogues had no vestibules, such as those of Miltenberg, Rouffach, Bamberg, Speyer, Cracow/Kazimierz-Old, and Szydłów. The Old Synagogue at Cracow/Kazimierz and the Gniezno synagogues added vestibules only in the sixteenth century. The vestibule at Pińczów was added ca. 1600, and that of Worms was built in the seventeenth century. After the late sixteenth century, the vestibule was more often built along with the prayer hall itself.

The vestibule's floor often rose a few steps above that of the prayer hall. This was done either to allow prayers to rise "out of the depths" or to increase the apparent loftiness of the prayer hall in towns where outside authorities restricted the prayer hall's height above street level.

In a large synagogue with community facilities, there is often a second synagogue, one with a southern exposure. Like a chapel, it is a small room. This is the winter or weekday synagogue, used at the times suggested by the names. If only a few people come to services, it is easier and cheaper to heat a small room for them. In Reform temples, where services are held only on the Sabbath and holy days, a weekday synagogue is superfluous, but there may be a small auxiliary synagogue for winter use or for weddings.

The weekday synagogue is almost always rectangular, with a group of seats set apart for women. There is usually no gallery. The arrangements are like those in any very small synagogue in which no one has attempted architectural elaboration. The chief difference is that the interior of a small full-time synagogue will be endowed with as many lamps, as beautiful a Torah curtain, and as handsome an ark as local resources permit; the weekday synagogue tends to be a plain room, since the main synagogue receives the finest objects. The weekday synagogue may be light and pleasant in design, as is one recently added to the Hendon United Synagogue in London, or it may be a converted large room intended originally for other purposes, as at the rue des Tournelles synagogue in Paris. It may also be situated beside the main room so that both spaces can be united on High Holy Days for the crowds who come only on those days.

Another synagogue annex may be a house of study, of which the best-known example is the seventeenth-century "Rashi Chapel" appended to the synagogue at Worms. A house of study may have its own ark and bimah. An annexed room for this purpose is common in places where Jews were restricted in their ability to rent or own land. In centers of large Jewish population in eastern Europe, however, Jews had more latitude, and the house of study more easily could be a separate building.

Worms, Figs. 169, 173

Community offices, dwellings for the synagogue staff, guild meeting rooms, and children's schoolrooms are known in many examples after about 1500, from the wooden synagogues of Poland to the St. John's Wood United Synagogue in London, the seat of the Ashkenazic Chief Rabbi of England. The ritual bath and the matzah bakery can be in the synagogue building itself, as they are at Carpentras, but the danger of fire led most communities to build a separate baking oven. Even a kasher slaughterhouse could be under the synagogue, as it was at Horb, although this was unusual.

There are several reasons why synagogues were located in the midst of other buildings and annexes. A synagogue that was separated from the street by other buildings would be less likely to be damaged by accident or design (Fig. 7). The sound of prayer would be less audible to municipal officials who could close a noisy synagogue. If the synagogue was not visible from the street, it could sometimes follow the injunction to rise higher than other buildings in the town—or at least in the Jewish part of town. The open space around the synagogue was useful for gatherings before and after services, for a market, for a court where Jewish-Christian disputes could be adjudicated, and for outdoor

Figure 7. Celle, synagogue in rear courtyard, 1792, exterior in 1981.

ceremonies such as the prayer service offered at the new moon. The best extant example of a courtyard with annexes around the synagogue is that of the Sephardic synagogue in Amsterdam. *Amsterdam, Fig. 227*

If the courtyard lay between the synagogue and a building used as the office and school or rabbi's house, the courtyard could be embellished with applied arches (as at Worms) or a portico (as at Düsseldorf). The idea of setting a synagogue in a formal, isolated position in a court seems to have taken hold in the seventeenth century, and it persisted, where the Jews could afford this design, until they could build synagogue facades along the street.

In the last two centuries, the Reform movement, general cultural assimilation, and new rights to own property and attend state schools led many Jews to abandon such traditions as daylong attendance at Jewish schools, the use of a ritual bath, or the eating of kasher meat. Jewish children at state schools assimilated culturally to the majority population. Many women visited the ritual bath only under unusual circumstances—for instance, if a rabbi refused to perform a wedding for a woman who had not done so. In many towns, the premises formerly used for traditional rituals were abandoned, converted, or reduced in size. After hundreds of these facilities were destroyed between 1933 and 1945, they were rarely rebuilt, as there were few Jews left to use them. Those that were built after the Second World War were primarily in Jewish hospitals, community centers, and old-age homes. In community centers, a room used for a children's school at one time can be used for a wedding reception at another. The residents of old-age homes are the Jews who are most likely to want the traditional facilities. These are the people who may best remember the solemn and joyous ways in which the Jewish community used its special facilities in former times.

3 The European Synagogue from Antiquity to Modern Times

Over the centuries, modifications in ritual arrangements and degrees of orthodoxy brought about changes in the synagogue's form. Most synagogues were simple rectangular boxes, but in places where Jews enjoyed special protection or the benefits of enlightened laws, they could erect synagogues showing ingenuity, good workmanship, and careful design.

Under Roman Law

Within the Roman Empire, Judaism was a licit though unofficial religion. Jews reached widely dispersed locations outside the Holy Land, and may have built synagogues in more localities than we can now identify. Only two late-antique buildings in Europe are universally accepted as synagogues—those of Ostia and Stobi, the latter still being excavated. Synagogues in the Holy Land, Turkey, and Syria provide further information about early synagogue architecture, but conditions varied from one region to another and only two synagogues in the Holy Land are dated securely.

Ostia, Fig. 202

Synagogues could be oriented toward Jerusalem, although some were not, even in the Holy Land. Sometimes, neighboring buildings or town walls or other urban features made correct orientation impossible, as at Stobi. In any case, orientation to Jerusalem is a Talmudic requirement, and the Talmud may not have been universally available or accepted everywhere in earliest times.

All the buildings known were rectilinear with plain exteriors. Entrances could open either on a short side or a long side, the latter constituting the "broadhouse" type. Some dispensed with interior columns or piers, while others had rows of columns forming a nave and side aisles. Plans are known in which columns ran parallel to three or even four sides of the interior.

Some synagogues may have had galleries. A large one at Alexandria is believed to have been a galleried basilica, but this plan is unknown in Europe before the seventeenth century. Archaeological evidence offers no support for the theory that ancient synagogue galleries were meant for women. Richard Krautheimer has observed that the practical and rational character of early Judaism makes it unlikely that there were rules or ritual reasons for separating the sexes.[1]

The ark in early synagogues[2] was simply a portable container for the scrolls. It could be stored in secure quarters outside the prayer hall, and it became an object of attention only when it was brought into the prayer hall. It therefore needed no architectural accommodation, although it could be placed in the apse, as at Ostia. (At Aegina the 5.5-meter width of the apse suggests that it had some function other than sheltering a portable ark; indeed, some scholars have doubted that the building *was* a synagogue.) The ark normally faced Jerusalem. However grand the portable ark may have been, it probably could not compete visually with the dominance of the stationary bimah, unless the bimah was a simple table.

Archaeologists have discovered a great deal of art in these early buildings,[3] ranging from large murals with Biblical figures to small objects for ritual use. Some decoration guided archaeologists who had to determine the ancient use of a newly found building fragment. A floor mosaic or special stone paving, for example, may mark the location of a bimah, enabling scholars to identify the remains as those of a synagogue.

The finds put to rest the old idea that Jews did not commission works of art for their synagogues, especially if the art included images of living beings. The murals of Dura-Europos in Syria, ca. 245, show that Jews sometimes admitted extensive programs of figural decoration. Elsewhere, images ranged from a seven-branched candlestick to an eagle, and even a lion carved in the round at the synagogue of Sardis. While many Jews interpret the Second Commandment's proscription of graven images to prohibit anything that might be worshipped as an idol, others believe that the Commandment forbids only images intended for veneration, or three-dimensional objects that might easily become idols to the credulous.[4] Apparently, the Jews of the late Roman Empire were able to differentiate their own images from the idols that surrounded them in pagan society.

The artistic decoration was Roman in style, as was the overall appearance of each known synagogue. By its silence on synagogue form and style, the Talmud implies that no one expected synagogues to look distinctive. This allowed wide latitude in later ages.[5] It was natural for a minority in society to adopt cultural features from the majority, and the Jews continued to erect synagogues designed in local styles until nationalist and other currents of thought after ca. 1800 stimulated new ideas about a special Jewish style.

In the first few decades after Emperor Constantine the Great recognized Christianity as a tolerated religion within the Roman Empire (313), synagogues kept their special status as religious buildings, enjoying protection from illegal occupation, theft, and some taxation. Perhaps as early as 380, however, restrictions were placed on the construction of new synagogues. Jewish difficulties increased after 385, when Christianity became the official state religion.[6] When the Bishop of Callinicum in Mesopotamia had the local synagogue burnt, the emperor ordered the bishop to make restitution. Nevertheless, St. Ambrose, who was then Bishop of Milan, wrote a letter in 388 lamenting the penalty and regretting that he had not ordered the same action against synagogues. As Ambrose saw the matter, those who protected the synagogue became allies of Jews and therefore enemies of Christ. Between 393 and 418, the emperor and officials of the law had to reiterate that Judaism was a tolerated religion, and that Jews could practice their faith without having their synagogues destroyed or despoiled. The protective decrees decreased in strength while they increased in number—which suggests that they were increasingly disobeyed.

Roman imperial laws also added restrictive clauses. In 397, a law prevented accused people from seeking asylum in synagogues. In 415, new synagogue building was expressly prohibited for the first time, and only old ones enjoyed such protections as remained in the law. If synagogues were built illegally after the effective date of a law of February 15, 423, a proportional decrease in synagogues was to be made in places where the law would otherwise allow them. Some synagogues were destroyed to stop Jews from practicing their religion, but three laws issued during the first half of 423 took away the incentive for arson by stating that owners of a burnt building still owned the land (where a new synagogue might be erected under more lenient laws someday). If, however, Christians merely desecrated a synagogue, Jews would vacate it, leaving the Christians to consecrate the intact structure as a church! The confiscation of synagogues for use as churches coincided with the growth of the Christian population and the consequent need for more churches. The Jews had to be given a new plot of land in compensation, but a malevolent adminstrator could choose an undesirable site. Moreover, the law did not require impartial arbitration of claims for confiscated ritual objects and furniture.[7] In issuing these laws, then, the emperor preserved some protective elements, thereby emphasizing the stability of imperial law itself, but he added new clauses recognizing *faits accomplis* and the general course of anti-Jewish activity being followed by clerics and laymen.

Although there were exceptions to the trend—Theodoric, the Arian Ostrogoth who was King of Italy from 493 to 526, forced Christians to pay for the rebuilding of synagogues in Ravenna which they had set afire in 519[8]—synagogues on the whole were increasingly vulnerable. Both the Visigothic code of Roman law applicable to southern Gaul and Spain (the Breviary of Alaric, 506) and Justinian's Code (529, 534), repeating some provisions of the earlier Theodosian legal code (438), protected synagogues from destruction, expropriation, or temporary use by other groups but at the same time prohibited new ones and fined those who built them. Justinian (ruled 527–65) even broke his own protective laws, for he alone among emperors until that time despoiled and converted some synagogues over which he gained military control. He also legitimized illegally converted synagogues once they had been consecrated as churches.[9] With this in mind, Christians destroyed the Clermont-Ferrand synagogues in 576, and any Jew who did not convert emigrated to

Marseille, thus removing everyone from the city who might petition to rebuild the synagogue. There was no one to protect the synagogue at Orléans when it was attacked in 585 or that of Syracuse in the seventh century.[10]

Fortunately for the Jews, Pope Gregory the Great (pontificate 590–604) was a man of integrity. He chastised church officials whose religious zeal led them to approve of illegal or excessive actions against Jews. Gregory protected synagogues because he believed that forced conversions were undesirable, and that the destruction of a Jew's traditional place of prayer was an unsound inducement to conversion.[11] Gregory did, however, appease Christians by permitting the removal and relocation of a synagogue if it was so near a church that the sounds within disturbed Christians in the church.[12]

Middle Ages to the Late Eighteenth Century

After the death of Justinian in 565, the Roman Empire separated permanently into eastern and western parts, and large-scale secular government broke down in the West. Jews then became subject to many local laws—some of them based on Roman law—and to more widely applicable church laws.[13]

LEGAL POSITION OF SYNAGOGUES

The synagogues' legal position became more precarious. The oldest extant manuscripts of the Gelasian sacramentary (seventh and eighth centuries)[14] include a prayer to be offered on the dedication of a church that had been a synagogue. One may imagine that many of these prayers were said after forced baptism became acceptable in seventh-century Spain.[15] We may assume that in synagogues still in Jewish hands, the congregations eliminated any human imagery that remained, for controversies about iconoclasm in the seventh and eighth centuries in both Christian and Moslem countries must have made the Jewish minority wary of causing offense to the majority population.

In the ninth century, some secular authorities in the Carolingian territories granted dispensations to build new synagogues. We know this because a bishop complained about the practice. There is no specific explanation for these exceptions, but from later history we know that the authorities gained commercial and financial advantage from Jewish settlement. At a time when hardly anyone could read, Jews continued to be literate in Hebrew in order to learn the Torah, and they could use their literacy in trade and in the practice of moneylending, which was forbidden to Christians. Accordingly, individuals who could use the services of Jews granted dispensations, including the right to have a synagogue. If legal dispensations were written down as part of a local Jewry law (a law governing the Jews) the document was called a privilege. Jews built most of their synagogues through such personal—and retractable—favors until modern civil emancipation statutes let them build synagogues under terms comparable to those under which Christians built churches.

The practice of granting local privileges continued even when stronger central governments developed in the twelfth century, as in Anjou, England, and the Papal States. During the legal renascence at this time, Christians made convenient legal compilations, drawing on Roman and church law which applied over much of Europe. The newly codified statutes repeated old measures that prohibited forcible conversion of Jews, allowed synagogue buildings and services to remain undisturbed, and permitted the repair of synagogues if the buildings were not enlarged or made more beautiful and conspicuous. The general tone of the laws was severe, however, reflecting new currents in European society.[16] This was the time of the definitive development of the feudal system, but the Jews who practiced moneylending and trade did not fit within the rural-and-military-based system, although the Jews were essential to the economy. Moreover, this was the period of the Crusades, when Jews were included among the "enemies of Christ," many of whom were massacred and their places of worship burned.

Sustained by the need for their services, by the funds of their richest coreligionists, and no doubt by some acts of Christian good will, Jews survived riots and occasional expulsions as well as they could. From the twelfth century onward, we have better information about their settlements and about the circumstances under which synagogues were built.

Local Jewry laws governed Jewish activities, including the building of synagogues.[17] Many towns excluded Jews completely.[18] Some towns governed by bishops were especially strict with the Jews they admitted, allowing them to work inside the walls during the day but forcing them to go to out-of-town inns or suburban settlements at night.[19] If Jews were expelled from a town and later readmitted, they might have to pay for readmission and buy back their old synagogues.[20] The government could dictate exactly where they were to live—usually in a single small area.[21] Even without coercion, the Jews preferred to live close to the synagogue they attended at least once a day and to be near other Jews for security and for the maintenance of customs and friendship. A town might therefore have a Jews' street or compound, just as it had a drapers' or ironmongers' street. Sometimes, as at Speyer and Verona, Jews even welcomed the establishment of an enclosed ghetto because they felt safer from harm and better able to live according to Jewish law when locked behind gates.[22]

LOCATION

Jewish quarters and their synagogues tended to have specific locations. Sometimes, as in Berlin, Łańcut, Rheda, and Tata, they were near the town or suburban residence of the ruler who protected the Jews in exchange for their

Berlin, Figs. 117, 118
Łańcut, Figs. 80, 81

Figure 8. Wörlitz, synagogue in ducal park, 1789–90, facade.
Figure 9. Wörlitz, interior.

commercial services. A drawing by Jean-Jacques Lequeu of ca. 1790 shows a synagogue under a rocky escarpment, where—had it ever existed—it would have been a garden ornament like the synagogue (alias Venus Temple) in the ducal park at Wörlitz (Figs. 8, 9).[23] In the Middle Ages, when the Jews came to a town in which they were meant to stimulate commerce, the Jewish quarter and synagogue were often near the central commercial area. As Christians developed their own business expertise, they sometimes expelled the Jews from the city centers and expropriated the synagogues, especially from the late fourteenth century onward, as at Dresden, Świdnica, Cologne, and Nuremberg.[24] After one of their frequent expulsions, those Jews who returned might have to live near an overflowing, insect-infested river, as in Rome or Prague. They occupied a site of that sort in Libeň between two arms of the Vltava River, in a district that also happened to be near the local nobleman's castle but on the undesirable side of it.[25] The Jews might be placed near the city walls or limits,[26] as in their first settlements at Brussels and Carpentras, and in Frankfurt am Main, Kalisz, Szydłów, L'vov, Warsaw, Padua, Nuremberg, and Worms. This was where poor people lived, becoming the first victims of invaders. In Venice, Vienna after 1670, and Amsterdam, the Jews occupied terrain separated by water from the rest of the city. The most memorable out-of-town synagogues were erected in eastern Poland in the seventeenth and early eighteenth centuries when the threat of Cossack raids terrified both Jews and Christians. The

Jews of Lutsk were told in 1626 that if they wanted a masonry synagogue it would have to be located outside the city walls and be fortified for use in civil defense.[27] Elsewhere, Jews lived in suburbs under more peaceful circumstances, as in Kazimierz near Cracow and Kappel near Buchau am Federsee.

Illegal synagogues existed at various times, hidden in courtyards, or in upstairs rooms. In times of religious strife, churches, too, have sometimes been concealed, but they have generally been permitted and were easily visible. To this day, Jews must gather in private rooms in Soviet cities where synagogues are illegal, and only scraps of information about them reach the West. Even legal synagogues were often located upstairs in buildings that seemed to be ordinary dwellings, with only a few large windows to reveal their special use.

Dubrovnik, Fig. 46
Trieste, Fig. 208
Amsterdam, Fig. 223

There was one case of extreme caution that was made necessary by the Spanish zeal for uncovering heresy and religious dissent after Jews were expelled from the Iberian peninsula in the 1490s. A small congregation met in an underground synagogue, described in 1848 by a correspondent of the *Jewish Chronicle,* a London weekly newspaper. The writer repeated a story narrated in the first person by a middle-aged Polish Jew who had seen a synagogue in the cellar of a house in a Spanish city which he kept anonymous for the sake of security; from the context, the city appears to have been in southern Spain. This

> walled-in cavern, about twelve yards long and nine yards wide, received its light from two holes in the ceiling, which looked into the garden . . . and through which you could see the thick shrubs encompassing them. From the center of the ceiling was suspended the [continual light] which was faithfully kept burning. . . . I noticed a wooden box, hung with black velvet and containing . . . [three scrolls of the Law] and one . . . [scroll containing the lessons from the Prophets]. On the top was a wooden tablet, on which the Ten Commandments were engraved. The carving on both relics appeared to be from a masterly hand. From the one side of the Ark was suspended a Jewish calendar . . . containing the names of Jews who, not known as Jews, play no insignificant part in the annals of the history of Spain. On the other side of the box hung a tablet in black borders containing the names of all the deceased members of the small congregation which altogether did not amount to above seventy. . . . In the centre of the Synagogue stood a black marble table covered with Philacteries . . . scarfs . . . and Hebrew Prayer books. . . . Several chairs round the table and a few brass candlesticks were all the utensils I could discover in this poor synagogue.[28]

The account sounds somewhat fantastic, to be sure, but it may be accurate. A clandestine synagogue is exactly what one would expect in a place where Judaism had to be practiced in secret.

BUILDING CHARACTERISTICS

Many governments prevented the Jews from owning the land on which their synagogues stood[29] and could fix the rent to be paid the Christian landowner.

Under these rules, Jews usually built modest synagogues because a lease could be terminated and the building taken away with the land, especially if the owner had some influence over the local judiciary.

Cologne, Fig. 127
Lengnau, Fig. 133

Christian authorities also could dictate the size and seating capacity of a synagogue.[30] Limited seating restricted the number of Jews who could live in a town or visit it. When more seats were required than were needed by the resident population, they were meant to accommodate traveling Jewish merchants (who promoted the town's economy and paid taxes).

If the Jews were confined to a single street or area, the synagogues were sometimes in multistorey buildings, which made economical use of the scarce land. There were seven- to ten-storey "skyscrapers" in the Jewish streets or quarters at Frankfurt am Main, Venice, and Mikulov, in which a synagogue was supposed to be located on the top floor. A synagogue in an apartment house was difficult to identify from the street.

When a freestanding synagogue building did have an interesting facade, it was often not that of a prayer hall. Before civil emancipation, many prayer halls, such as those at Riga, Düsseldorf, Cleve, and Celle (see Fig. 7), lay at the rear of a building lot, with community offices, schoolrooms, or the rabbi's house facing the street. The front building protected the prayer hall from vandals and from noise, and kept the sound of Jewish prayer from reaching the ears of Christians.

BUILDERS

Powerful individuals, and later the guilds, controlled the training and practice of many crafts. Because Jews often were restricted to financial work or the selling of second-hand merchandise, they could not normally practice building or erect their own synagogues. Until the present century, most synagogues were therefore designed and built by Christian architects and craftsmen. The result depended upon the sensitivity of both the congregation's leaders and the architect, balanced more precariously than might have been the case with a church commission. In any case, from the Middle Ages until the nineteenth century, there were few major synagogues for which sophisticated architects were needed.

In a large Jewish community, one or more of the men might have done construction work. This would explain the designation of a certain Mar Simson (whose name sounds Jewish) as the builder of a medieval synagogue in Nuremberg.[31] "Builder" may refer either to the person who paid for the synagogue or to the craftsman, but Mar Simson seems to have been the latter because the documents also mentioned the donor of money. At Oporto, Don Joseph ibn Aryeh was "the officer who supervised the work."[32] Building is not among the trades known to have been practiced by Spanish Jews, but Francisco Cantera y Burgos has proposed that a late-fifteenth-century artisan named Juce Gali was a Jew and that he worked in the Mudéjar style on buildings used by

Christians.[33] Although we lack evidence that they designed and built synagogues, Jews in Prague, Palermo, and Cracow were carpenters in the fifteenth century.[34] Apparently, there were Jewish masons in Nuremberg in the fourteenth century, as a certain Joseph is recorded there in 1338,[35] but in the next century, a decree in that city prohibited Jews from doing any building for Christians. With work opportunities thus restricted, the younger generation of Jews was unlikely to follow Joseph in his career. A few Jews are documented as synagogue builders elsewhere, however. In the important Jewish community of Prague, an architect named Herz built the High Synagogue around 1600. Judah Goldschmied, also known as Judah Coref or Zoref de Herz (d. 1625), built much of the Pinkas Synagogue, and part of the Meisel Synagogue.[36] A mason named David signed a contract for the synagogue at Gniezno in 1582; Isaac Moses Frenkel, a craftsman, built the wooden synagogue of Marosszentkirály in Hungary; and Jacob ben Meir Halevi built a synagogue porch in Velké Meziříčí.[37]

After the late seventeenth century, Jewish names appeared more often as builders of wooden synagogues in Poland, although some identifications of Jewish architects are not persuasive.[38] The Jewish population of Poland rose from 3,000 in ca. 1400 to at least 300,000 by ca. 1750, and substantial Jewish communities, especially in the south and east, enjoyed considerable autonomy within the limits set by the government. In these areas, Jews could more easily become builders and decorators, and they had the potentially large clientele that they lacked in the smaller Jewish centers of western Europe. Perhaps Jews also worked in some capacity on masonry buildings. Szymon Zajczyk, who was a leading student of Polish synagogues, thought that the local four-pillar, nine-bay masonry synagogue type was conceived by a gifted architect—no doubt a Christian—but that less sophisticated builders, perhaps including Jews, constructed the buildings (see Fig. 16).[39]

Lublin, Fig. 76
Pinsk, Figs. 78, 79
Łańcut, Fig. 81
L'vov, Fig. 85
Vilnius, Figs. 92, 93

In other cases, the person named as builder was the donor of building funds. Inscriptions tell us that the builders at Córdoba (1315), Toledo (1350–60), and Seville (thirteenth century) were the rich patrons or owners of the synagogues. Samuel Melli, who built the Ferrara synagogue in 1485, bought the building housing it in 1481, and he was surely the proprietor rather than the mason.[40] So, it seems, were David ben Israel who acquired the stones of the doors to the Rouffach synagogue in ca. 1290–1300[41] and Isaac Koblenz who built the synagogue in Friedberg in Hessen in 1240.[42] The Hebrew inscription naming the Jewish builder at Worms certainly refers to the donor, since the vaulted structure required professional training unavailable to Jews in the twelfth century. Moreover, the ornament is close in form to that of Worms and Fritzlar cathedrals, where Jews are unlikely to have worked. Even in the nineteenth century, people spoke of donors as having "built" the synagogues of Paris-rue Buffault (Daniel Osiris Iffla), Milan (Salomone Ottolenghi), Trieste (Moses Uzeglio), Belfast (the Jaffe family, who paid for two successive synagogues), and Versailles (the Rothschild family). We know the names of many

Toledo, Fig. 184
Worms, Fig. 170
Milan, Fig. 200
Trieste, Figs. 212, 213

Christian architects who designed large and sometimes handsome synagogues in western and eastern Europe before the Jews received civil rights,[43] and in some small Bohemian towns, for instance, the modest synagogues were built by the same men who erected the local Roman Catholic churches.[44]

OTHER REGULATIONS

The Jews and their synagogues were subject to many regulations in addition to those concerning location and builders. We have already touched on the government's ability to close private synagogues and confiscate buildings. When Pope Paul IV instituted the ghetto in Rome,[45] he ordered the destruction of several earlier synagogues, contrary to the church's own laws which protected existing synagogues.

Useful Jewish doctors, merchants, and financiers received privileges that were denied to other Jews. Governments sometimes favored the Sephardic Jews because they were thought to be rich in comparison to the great mass of Ashkenazic Jews, who lived in poverty.[46] The exceptions and modifications made to laws explain how the Jews managed to survive and build synagogues between the Middle Ages and modern times.[47] Even papal power had limits, for late-sixteenth-century bulls protecting and oppressing Jews[48] seem to have been binding only during the pontificates of their writers, and some towns in papal territory allowed Jews to live outside the ghettoes for years after the pope had told the town leaders to confine their Jewish populations.[49] After the Jews were expelled from Spain (1492) and Portugal (1496), some were welcomed elsewhere as suppliers of capital and commercial expertise. During the late sixteenth and seventeenth centuries, avowed Sephardic Jews and Marranos—Jewish converts to Christianity—found shelter and the chance to practice or revert to Judaism in the Netherlands, England, and Livorno. When Ashkenazic Jews came later, restriction to a single synagogue in a town could be overcome by treating Sephardic and Ashkenazic Jews as separate "nations" with each one entitled to its own house of worship,[50] a right generally accorded to resident foreign merchants. Christians might regulate a minor urban synagogue differently from the official community synagogue or one owned by a privileged individual.

Livorno, Figs. 195, 196
London, Figs. 242, 245

Venice, Figs. 217–222
Amsterdam, Figs. 225–228

Eleventh and Twelfth Centuries

A number of eleventh- and twelfth-century synagogues of which we have documents or remains were large rooms in houses, as was the first synagogue at Speyer. Synagogues of this type were located on upper floors in the homes of men who found it honorable or prestigious—and possibly profitable—to have a synagogue. The rooms were simple spaces furnished with a bimah and a niche or chest for the ark. If the resident of the house owned the synagogue, he might rent out the seats and receptacles for prayer shawls and books.

Cologne, Fig. 127

Other synagogues, such as those of Frankfurt am Main (ca. 1150–1241), or Speyer in its late-eleventh-century form, were separate buildings, the latter an apsed building made of red sandstone (see Fig. 1a). The separate building about which we know the most is the men's prayer hall at Worms, built in 1174–75. Unlike the single-naved buildings just mentioned,[51] this one was double-naved. Inside a rectilinear stone building, two piers along the main axis divided the interior into six vaulted bays. The entrance arch and the pier capitals were finely carved with plant ornament, and they have much in common with the style and craftsmanship of parts of the Worms and Fritzlar cathedrals. From this we may assume that the Worms synagogue was unusually large and elaborate. The Jewish community there was learned and relatively rich, and the synagogue building benefited from the donations of several members whose generosity was recorded in inscriptions.

Worms, Figs. 170, 172

The bimahs at Worms and Mainz at this period had rectilinear cage-like enclosures, wooden at Mainz and made of wood or stone at Worms. A niche for the Torah scrolls is known in the eastern wall of central European synagogues from the late twelfth century onward, at about the time that Ashkenazic liturgical forms became more firmly established.[52] Inside the prayer hall, the niche looked like a small opening in the wall. A bolted door or a grille secured the Torah scrolls. The door might be covered by a curtain and valance to recall the veil of the Holy of Holies in the Temple of Jerusalem.[53] If women who were not obliged to attend synagogue came to worship before their own quarters were erected, they may have sat behind curtains or screens, or even in an adjacent room within a house. A document notes that a partition was put up on the Sabbath between men and women "during the time of preaching."[54] Before that time, the women—who lacked knowledge of Hebrew and could not follow the men's prayers—would have been in an annex or perhaps not yet in any part of the synagogue.[55]

Images appeared in synagogues at this time, when figurative art was widely used by the church. Most of what we know about synagogue art is gleaned from legal texts which preserve the few surviving notices of it.[56] They record varied opinions about the admissibility of images, their contents, and their location. Jewish scholars in northern France, known as Tosafists, permitted the three-dimensional representation of the human form if it were incomplete, and the twelfth-century Rabbi Ephraim ben Isaac of Regensburg allowed people to pray in a synagogue where there were cloths decorated with birds and fish. Profiat Duran in the fourteenth century wrote that looking at beautiful shapes and at pleasing sculpture and paintings in a synagogue enlarged and enlivened the heart and increased the power of the mind.[57] Pictures of David, Goliath, and strange beasts were familiar to Rabbi Solomon ben Isaac of Troyes, a preeminent Ashkenazic legal commentator (alias RaSHI, 1040–1109). Even if those images were not in a synagogue, the Cologne synagogue had stained glass windows depicting serpents and lions. Maimonides (1135–1204) permitted animals but not humans to be portrayed in the round. That these images were available to people at prayer—perhaps in private houses—is clear from his cautions against praying in front of an image, lest it distract the mind.

Other scholars disapproved of imagery. The mid-twelfth-century Rabbi Eliakim ben Joseph of Mainz, a sort of Jewish Bernard of Clairvaux, ordered the glass images at Cologne to be removed. He disapproved of images of the sun, moon, and dragons as well. In the next century, Rabbi Meir ben Baruch of Rothenburg preferred not to have images of figures on synagogue walls, and did not want to see birds and beasts decorating prayer books. He disapproved of paintings of any sort on the synagogue's focal wall, where they provided distraction from prayer. Plant decorations are the only ornaments at Worms and Prague-Altneuschul in central Europe. In Spanish synagogues in Toledo, Córdoba, and Seville, Moslem artists or those working in the Islamic Mudéjar style used nonfigurative ornament exclusively. The documentary references to synagogue art may be rare precisely because there was little of it.[58]

Worms, Fig. 170
Toledo, Figs. 181, 182

Thirteenth through the Early Sixteenth Century

We know more about synagogue architecture in the thirteenth through the early sixteenth century, sometimes from prints (Regensburg), old descriptions (Eger), excavations, fragments, and photographs. Those known to modern scholars were rectangular masonry buildings, as they had been earlier. They were small, indicating the limited Jewish population in any town. Building proportions were relatively high, reflecting contemporary church design, although the synagogues were far smaller, and some synagogues were longer in proportion than the 3:2 ratio found in twelfth-century synagogues at Frankfurt am Main, Speyer, and Worms.

The Gothic Ashkenazic synagogues continued to use the older single- or double-naved plans[59] with aisles separated by one,[60] two,[61] or three[62] cylindrical or polygonal piers (see Figs. 1a, 1b, 4). The capitals were carved by craftsmen whose work can be found on Christian and secular buildings in the area. Some synagogues had wooden ceilings or wooden vaults.[63] Others had masonry vaults, most of them quadripartite, although the Prague-Altneuschul and Miltenberg synagogue vaults had five ribs[64] and Sopron-Uj Street #22-24 had six-ribbed bays. Vaulted ceilings required thick supporting walls and sometimes thick buttresses as well, but no flying buttresses were needed on these modest buildings. Small windows opened high up in the walls. Ornamental details differed with local traditions, dates, and artisans, and if the few surviving examples are typical, plant and nonfigurative ornament was used exclusively.

Prague, Fig. 50
Prague, Fig. 49
Toledo, Figs. 184, 185

Ark niches were common at this time,[65] and the Prague-Altneuschul ark had a carved frame. New features appeared in this period, while others were revived or clarified. Some masonry vaulting had extra ribs, distinguishing the perimeter vault webs from those of the center, as in the three synagogues just mentioned. The bimah table stood on a platform surrounded by a traceried cage of wood or metal from which lamps could be hung,[66] elaborating earlier

Sopron, Figs. 23, 24
Sopron, Fig. 23
Prague, Fig. 49

Worms, Fig. 171

bimah frames. Women's participation may have increased, because a women's area was built in synagogues in several regions, although not in all synagogues.[67] The women's annexes were invisible from the men's prayer hall. The women's floor level was higher than the men's, perhaps because women's prayers need not come from the "depths" and because women need not "go down before the ark." The synagogue vestibule became a distinct feature at this time, and its floor sometimes lay a few steps above that of the men's prayer hall, so that men's prayers could come from below.[68] The vestibule and entrance might be along the north or south side, as they could be in churches.

Toledo, Figs. 180, 183
Tomar, Fig. 186
Amsterdam, Fig. 223

In Spain and Portugal, synagogue plans ranged from a single room with an adjacent vestibule and women's area above it,[69] to five-aisled[70] or three-aisled basilicas,[71] to Tomar's squarish room with nine vaulting bays held on four pillars. Five-aisled synagogues later disappeared from synagogue architecture, while the three-aisled type was used by Sephardic Jews in the seventeenth century, but probably under the influence of church architecture rather than because of centuries-old Iberian memories. The box survived because it suited a synagogue's needs and because of its economy; later examples need not have owed a debt to Toledo or Córdoba. The four-pillar type may be as old as the fourteenth century, if the architectural abbreviation in a Spanish manuscript of the Haggadah (Passover service) stands for that plan (see Fig. 5). It was echoed in later Sephardic communities, at Samokov and Sofia-Cahal de Francos, in Gibraltar, on Rhodes in 1731, in the Danish colonial town of Charlotte Amalie in the Virgin Islands, and as far away as Istanbul.

Samokov, Fig. 53

Toledo, Fig. 184

The Iberian synagogues known today were plain on the exterior, with lavishly decorated interiors using Mudéjar plaster ornament, like that found in buildings made for Christians and Moslems in the same centuries. The ark composition at the "Tránsito" synagogue in Toledo was a triad of niches cut into a sumptuously decorated eastern wall,[72] a wall so thick that the Torah repository did not have to project beyond it. The Haggadah manuscript shows a bimah of the time—a platform raised high above the congregation, in the center of the synagogue.

Italian medieval synagogues, occasionally mentioned, await scholarly investigation.[73]

Sixteenth through the Eighteenth Century

Endingen, Fig. 131
Lengnau, Figs. 132, 133

During the sixteenth through the eighteenth century, most synagogues were still single-naved with a women's annex, and they continued to have flat ceilings under gabled roofs, or barrel and groin vaults. Two-aisled synagogues were apparently only repaired, not newly built. Where the Jewish population was substantial, with a flourishing culture and adequate finances, architectural innovation leavened the tradition of simple synagogue architecture and decoration.

In some towns of central and eastern Europe, the synagogues commanded pleasant views,[74] rose well above the nearby houses,[75] stood at the bend of the main street,[76] or on a square or marketplace,[77] and were situated near water where the New Year purification ceremony was held.[78] From the sixteenth century onward, Jews built comparatively large synagogues in the parts of Poland where they were allowed to live. They erected other big buildings in Amsterdam, London, and Altona during the seventeenth and eighteenth centuries. A prince's court architect might design a synagogue for Jews who were useful, and the building would then be attractive even if it were small in size, as was the case at Ansbach, Łańcut, Karlsruhe, and Wörlitz (see Figs. 8, 9).[79]

Cracow, Figs. 70–75
Pinsk, Fig. 77

Amsterdam, Figs. 223–228
London, Figs. 242–245
Ansbach, Figs. 119–121
Łańcut, Figs. 80, 81

EMPHASIZING THE ARK AND BIMAH

Christian architects continued to design most synagogues, so that the architecture of the Jewish minority reflected cultural developments in the surrounding society. The Renaissance tendency to order spaces hierarchically, and to define them clearly, influenced synagogue design. At the end of the sixteenth century, synagogue architecture experienced a spurt of rationalized development. This can be seen in the arrangements for the bimah and ark and in the overall plan, especially in the women's section and the vestibule.

The more forceful definition of each part of the synagogue corresponds to the intellectual tendency of the time to clarify Jewish law. The sixteenth-century Sephardic codifier, Joseph Caro, and his younger contemporary, the Ashkenazic commentator Moses Isserles, known as ReMO, wrote legal works that still govern most aspects of orthodox Jewish life.[80] They brought all the elements in the Jewish legal system up to date, and made the laws more specific

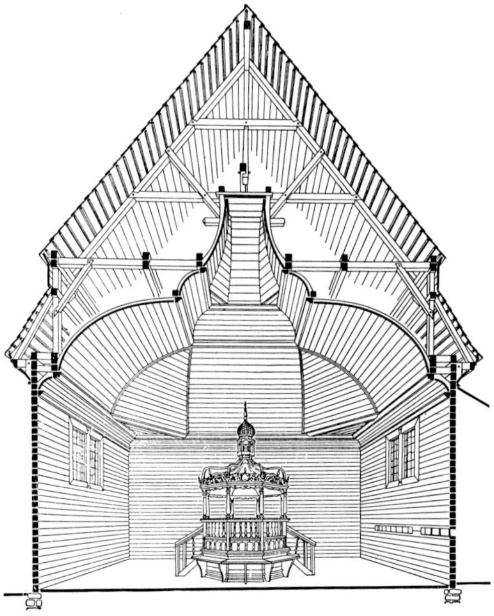

Figure 10. Gvozdets, wooden synagogue, interior ca. 1682, with cupola 18th century.

and formal; they set the laws more clearly in view, just as designers did with the components of a synagogue.

Cracow, Figs. 71, 74

Isserles insisted that the Ashkenazic synagogue have a bimah in the center (Fig. 10); if the bimah were close to the ark, it might imitate alien—in this case Christian—customs[81] such as the placement of a pulpit near an altar. The definition of "center" could be calculated from wall to wall, or from the west end of the ark steps to the western wall. Sometimes the bimah was slightly displaced. At Khodorov, the bimah and its steps almost filled the area under the west side of the recess in the central cupola. Because the space between the ark and the bimah was free of seats, a bimah could be moved slightly east of center to allow more seating west of it. A position in the exact center mattered less than the principles of separating the ark and the bimah, and keeping the bimah in the midst of the congregation.

Carpentras, Figs. 104, 105
Cavaillon, Fig. 107
Ancona, Figs. 188, 189
Livorno, Figs. 195, 196

Italian, Sephardic, and southern French bimahs were placed near the wall opposite the ark, since Caro had not required a central position. The synagogues were small, so that the officiant did not have to be in the center in order to be heard. Sephardic bimahs were usually tables inside balustraded enclosures, while those of Italian and Comtadin synagogues were tables set under canopies that may have been influenced by Roman Catholic altar baldaquins.

As new elements of mysticism became prominent in Judaism, they affected some of the rules and traditional practices in synagogue building. The concomitant of mysticism was greater emphasis on prayer (directed to Jerusalem and the ark wall) than on reading (at the bimah). The ark and its wall became magnets that pulled as hard as the bimah had done. The ark grew larger and more visually emphatic, so that the tension between the east end and the central bimah was no longer necessarily resolved in favor of the bimah. Now the ark might be introduced by an arch, projecting canopy, or sculpted frame. Steps led to the ark, so that worshippers below literally prayed "out of the depths," and "going up to the Law" became a physical reality as well as a metaphor.

L'vov, Fig. 83

Worms, Fig. 170
Venice, Fig. 221

Endingen, Fig. 131
Amsterdam, Fig. 228

Berlin, Fig. 118
Volpa, Fig. 97

The ark might have the form of a classical aedicula or temple front, with columns and a pediment or even two superimposed pediments. An ark would be especially large if it contained a collection of Torah scrolls. In the seventeenth and eighteenth centuries, eastern and central European arks with sumptuously carved borders looked like framed altarpieces. So close were some arks to Christian altarpieces that congregations could accept the church altarpieces donated by Emperor Joseph II for use as arks when he closed certain churches in Bohemia and Moravia.[82] By the eighteenth century, some synagogues had apse-like ark recesses. Ark enclosures often were adorned with densely packed carved forms that made a heavy lacework collar around the ark recess. Balusters or columns might be added to animals, plants, and other ornaments in low relief, for even the most brilliantly developed of these spectacular designs exhibit the tendency of folk art to mix motifs. The doors were made of fine wood or ornamental metalwork if the congregation could afford to commission them. Above the ark, carved rays or tablets of the Law could be silhouetted against a window[83] to give the same dramatic effect as light shining behind a crucifix or saint in baroque Roman Catholic churches.

When the Torah scrolls were removed from their resting place, they were displayed from the platform. Within the ark—a kind of spiritual treasure chest—the Law became enshrined like a precious object of both material and religious significance.

The heightened tension between the eastern wall and a focal point in the center of the room gave the synagogue a more sumptuous and energetic character than it had had earlier. This character can also be found in contemporary baroque churches. By intensifying overtly aesthetic features in the synagogue, those who commissioned the elaborate arks and more sophisticated bimahs showed their sensitivity to visual effects, even if they interpreted strictly the Second Commandment's injunction against the making of images.

MASONRY SYNAGOGUES

The vaulted room. A number of new synagogue plans evolved when the ark threatened to overwhelm the bimah. Sephardic- and Italian-rite synagogues were rectangular rooms with the bimah far from the ark. Southern French and some Italian synagogues had the bimah raised on a platform over the western side of the prayer hall, leaving the floor of the prayer hall free for seating. From the seventeenth to the nineteenth century, square synagogues were designed in eastern Europe in which the centrality of the bimah was given special architectural emphasis to balance the attraction of the ark. These synagogues were found especially in Poland, Lithuania, Belorussia, and the Ukraine, but there were examples in central Europe as well.

Carpentras, Figs. 104, 105
Cavaillon, Fig. 107
Ancona, Figs. 188–190
Livorno, Figs. 195, 196
Amsterdam, Figs. 223, 224, 227, 228
London, Figs. 242, 243

Lublin, Fig. 76
Pinsk, Figs. 78, 79
Łańcut, Figs. 80, 81
L'vov, Fig. 85
Vilnius, Figs. 92, 93

In masonry synagogues, one type of square plan called for a large room[84] covered by vaults that rose toward the center, drawing attention to the bimah there. Among these synagogues were the High Synagogue in Prague, and the synagogue at Gusyatin. Centralizing cloister vaults, along with shallow vaults, were common in northern Bohemia. When part of a vault sprang from the wall directly over the ark, the ark gained emphasis too.[85]

The bimah in these buildings was often a large platform of central plan, crowned by an openwork canopy of metal, wood, or stone. Examples are still preserved at the Old Synagogue in Cracow/Kazimierz (in a two-naved building), Zamość, and Holešov (to which the Dřevohostice bimah was moved after 1945). Substantial masonry buildings at Szydłów and Pińczów had stone-framed bimahs that seemed to fill the large, square spaces. The metal-framed bimahs did not interrupt sight lines, as the stone ones did.

Cracow, Fig. 71

Steps leading to the bimah, usually on its north and south sides, created a minor axis of movement which countered the east-west axis enough to help draw attention to the central and separate position of the bimah.

Lublin, Fig. 76
Pinsk, Figs. 78, 79
Łańcut, Fig. 81
L'vov, Figs. 85–87
Vilnius, Figs. 92, 93

The four-pillar plan. Other masonry synagogues had four interior pillars supporting a vault of equal or nearly equal bays.[86] In a more frequently used plan, four pillars formed eight equal bays surrounding a smaller ninth one.[87] An advantage of a nine-bay plan was that it had three perimeter bays in each of its four sides. A window in each bay provided the total of twelve synagogue windows recommended in Jewish mystical lore. In addition, the plan gave a unique appearance to synagogue interiors. They did not imitate buildings of other religions, for the four pillars and the concentration on the bimah made these synagogues different from Eastern Orthodox or Roman Catholic central-plan churches. The eastern European Jews would have shied away from church-like buildings with towers and domes.[88] Moreover, nine vaults or cloister vaults are easier to construct than large domes.

Pinsk, Fig. 79
Łańcut, Fig. 81
Vilnius, Figs. 92, 93

The most important feature of the eight-plus-one vault plan was its emphasis on the bimah in the distinctive central bay. A vault was often erected partway up and between the four central pillars to form a cupola with a lantern over the bimah, as at Pinsk. Lamps suspended inside the cupola created unusual effects that enhanced mystical attitudes in the congregation. Sometimes the vaulting over the central bay sank to meet the roof of a tabernacle created by the four pillars and by walls connecting them, as at Łańcut.[89] This gave extra emphasis to the bimah. When the surrounding vaults were partly sustained by the tabernacle pillars—as was generally the case—and when the vaults could be read either as bowing to focus on the central bay or as springing outward like a divine message from the central bay, the architecture further enhanced the meaning of the bimah and the activities conducted there. If the vault crowns reached equal heights in all the bays, the vault of the central, smaller bay would be emphasized, creating a special, domical form above the bimah; the Great Synagogue at Vilnius offered an example of this.

The four pillars could block some people's view of the bimah, however. If the tabernacle was too large, the congregation to the west of it had no view of the ark. This part of the synagogue might then have been left empty, wasting the space there, or it may have been allocated to paupers. On the other hand, because the internal supports allowed the synagogue to be larger, those who had formerly sat to the west of the bimah might now sit to the north or south of it. As for the reader's invisibility, worshippers looked at their own prayer books most of the time, and synagogues were small enough so that everyone could hear the reader's voice.

Cracow, Fig. 72
Berlin, Fig. 117
Ansbach, Fig. 121

Women's galleries. Just as the ark and bimah became more emphatic, other parts of a synagogue were more systematically arranged. The women's area, which had often been located on the north or south, was more regularly placed over a western vestibule, opposite the ark. Outside, two levels of windows identified the vestibule with the women's section above it; these windows were distinct from the wider and longer ones of the men's prayer hall.[90] This plan survived into the twentieth century, especially in small orthodox synagogues and in small Jewish communities.

North-south women's galleries integrated with the men's space developed at this period and became increasingly common. These buildings resembled galleried churches, especially Protestant ones, for which the type may have been invented. Churches with galleries hold many people in a compact space, so that they can hear the sermon. Since Jewish services also include readings, explanations, and sermons, architects familiar with galleried church designs built galleries along the sides of synagogues[91] to accommodate both men and women, who were separated by barriers. In the eighteenth century, if not earlier, women may have taken over all the gallery space.

The first known side galleries to be integrated with the design of the men's prayer hall were those of the Sephardic synagogue of 1639 in Amsterdam.[92] *Amsterdam, Figs. 223, 224* The synagogue was converted from a large room in the upper floors of an existing building, and no annex area was available. Women, therefore, had to be seated somewhere in the main space. Within two decades, the London-Creechurch Lane synagogue had integrated galleries[93] and the Spanish and German synagogues of Venice were equipped with oval galleries set into long *Venice, Figs. 217–222* prayer halls. As all of these synagogues stood on crowded lots or in preexisting buildings, the galleries in the main room may have been a space-saving expedient. Most of these early examples were Sephardic; reports about the innovations in one town may have reached family members or business contacts in another town.[94]

Synagogues with integrated galleries are of two main types. One is the galleried basilica, divided into nave and aisles by the gallery supports that rise to the roof. The Amsterdam synagogue of 1639 was of this type. *Amsterdam, Figs. 223, 224* The second, the galleried box, has supports only under the galleries, and therefore can be built less expensively. The Bevis Marks Synagogue in London (1699–1701) is *London, Fig. 243* one early example. Twentieth-century architects often eliminate the ground *London, Figs. 249, 251* floor supports that block sight lines.

The vestibule. The vestibule, too, received further definition. In earlier synagogues, it seems to have been added on to the west, north, or south side, wherever there was room for it. But a western vestibule suited Renaissance taste for an orderly sequence of spaces along a single axis—from an outdoor court, to a vestibule where mundane activity could be abandoned, and then to the prayer hall[95] with its eastern culmination at the ark.

Fortification. Some squarish masonry synagogues were fortified for the defense of Polish towns near the Russian-Ukrainian borders (Fig. 11). Fortified religious buildings had been known earlier—for instance, thirteenth-century churches in southwestern France. But the fortified synagogue derived its form independently, from contemporary and local sources. Like other masonry structures, the synagogues had thick, firmly buttressed walls, with windows puncturing only their upper parts. Some had battlements and others had attics, often with the arcades that decorated local secular buildings of the Renaissance. Interiors were masonry-vaulted, with either an undivided space or a four-pier, nine-bay arrangement. Decorations included arches under the windows (especially in southern areas such as Podolia and Volhynia) and a row of vertical strips or pilasters (especially in the northern Polish areas).

Figure 11. Lutsk, fortified synagogue, 1626–28, exterior.

WOODEN SYNAGOGUES

Another distinctive synagogue type was found in a broad belt of eastern Europe, concentrated in a boomerang-shaped area stretching from the Vilnius region in the northeast to the Łódż area in the southwest, and then eastward to the vicinity of Chernovtsy. These were the famous wooden synagogues, all destroyed by the end of the Second World War (Fig. 12). Those of which pictorial records remain were erected between the seventeenth century and the early nineteenth century; some were rebuilt, apparently in their old forms, during the 1800s. The oldest known was that of Khodorov near L'vov (1651), and the most spectacular examples, those of Volpa and Przedbórz, were built in the mid-eighteenth century. They had two principal plans, both apparently derived from Renaissance masonry synagogues: the simpler, axial plan favored in central and south Poland but known elsewhere also; and the centralized type that was more common in northern Poland, Belorussia, and Lithuania.

Volpa, Figs. 94, 96

Axial plans. The first plan was rectilinear, including a square or nearly square prayer hall and a western vestibule with a women's gallery above it. The

Figure 12. Zabludów, wooden synagogue, late 17th century (?), remodeled 1765, exterior.

western section was sometimes elaborated to include a house of study, rabbinic courtroom, community offices, guild chapels, and other spaces. The western part was sometimes crowned by onion-domed towers, or it could be embellished by decorative gables, columns, or a porch. About twenty examples were recorded in measured drawings and photographs, including synagogues at Gąbin, Pilica, Uzlyany, and Warka. The locations of the women's section and entrance stairs varied and helped to differentiate one of these synagogues from another. When the number of women worshippers was too great for the space available in the western gallery, annexes for women were built on the north *Volpa, Fig. 95* and/or south sides as well. The height and depth of the western vestibule and gallery structure might vary, too. That of Janów Trembowelski was plastered and looked like a house of a different height from the prayer hall behind it. At Lutomiersk, the synagogue roof hung over the ground floor and rested on six columns to form a porch behind which a divided staircase ascended to a balcony.

Central plans. The second, central, type of synagogue had a square or almost square men's prayer hall not more than 15 meters on each side, bounded on all but the east side by annexes for women, community offices, the vestibule, and other customary spaces. The annexes of the axial synagogue type seem not to have been envisioned at the start of building, but in the centralizing type, the men's prayer hall was the core around which subsidiary elements clustered. This building type was more likely to have multitiered angular or curving roofs and corner pavilions at the northwest and southwest. The pavilions were sometimes enlarged by galleries around their upper storeys as well as by shingled roofs, either pitched at two or more different slopes or curving in bell shapes. The central synagogue type more often used curvilinear or domical wooden vaulting, or cupolas (the latter beginning in the eighteenth century, especially in the Grodno-Białystok region), while most axial synagogues were barrel vaulted. Centrally emphatic vaults, ascending quickly and energetically, seemed to lift the prayers of the worshippers who swayed rhythmically as if adding impetus to the movement in the architecture. Examples of the central synagogue type were those of Grodno and nearby Volpa, and others at Sidra, Sopotskin, and Zabłudów (which was remodeled in this form) (see Figs. 10, 12). Some synagogues of this sort, such as that of Volpa, had four supports to hold a central cupola or the center of a flat ceiling. This was the wooden synagogues' equivalent of the nine-bay, four-pier masonry synagogue plan, with more widely spaced supports in the wooden buildings. Wooden buildings had no structural need for supports under a cupola, but masonry buildings were more prestigious and permanent, so that carpenters and joiners used them as models.

Volpa, Figs. 95, 96

Volpa, Fig. 96

At Śniadowo the bimah was too weak in design to fill the space satisfactorily; at Valkininkas, the eclectic-classical bimah was proportionately taller and more lavish and could therefore hold its own, but it clashed with the style and scale of the building around it. At Volpa, however, the scale was more satisfactory and the bimah incorporated the lower parts of the four piers. This united the structure and the essential furnishing in an intelligent way. At Sidra, where the ceiling was flat rather than domical, a large, square bimah stretched from the floor to the ceiling, clearly showing its connection to the building. Even if it did so imperfectly, a roofed, wooden, central-plan bimah in a wooden synagogue with a central cupola linked the covering above the sacred text to the covering over the congregation and, by implication, to the dome of heaven.

In technique and ornamental detail, the wooden synagogues were close to wooden churches and manor houses. In addition, the synagogues' curves, their brio, their surprising spatial sequences, and their ornamental elaboration parallel aspects of late baroque and rococo architecture in all materials.

When the painter and architect El Lissitzky was sent in 1916 by the Jewish Ethnographical Society in Russia to visit Jewish sites in the Dnieper River valley, he recorded his reactions to the wooden synagogue at Mogilev. He experienced different sensations from those he had felt in western European historicizing and monumental synagogues: "It is like a child enveloped by a netting, opening his eyes upon awakening and being startled by insects and butterflies glittering in the rays of the sun . . . the whole structure organized by the painter [of the abundant synagogue murals] is full of a few simple colors, giving you the impression of a world alive and blooming."[96]

DECORATION

The synagogue at Mogilev was just one of the many richly painted synagogues in eastern Europe. Complex currents of Jewish thought at the time—legal, mystical, superstitious, astrological—found aesthetic expression in these buildings. Cultural cohesion fostered the development of Jewish legend and folklore. The experience of false messiahs, persecutions, and ephemeral prosperity combined with happier moments, and the result was a plentiful background of images and ideas from daily life to mix with those derived from religious tradition and pious legend.

Earlier, in the sixteenth century, rabbis such as Joseph Caro, Moshe ben Joseph of Trani, Meir Katzenellenbogen of Padua, and David ben Zimrah agreed that there was no need for images in the synagogue. They felt that spiritual danger ensued when images were present. This conservative opinion helped worshippers to avoid any chances of idolatry or of emulating other religions' practices. At Iráklion early in that century, Jews who were wary of potential idolatry even bribed the local governor to order the removal of a sculptured lion which a rich Jew had placed on top of the synagogue ark.[97]

By the late seventeenth century, however, if not earlier, congregations in eastern Europe were decorating their synagogues with abundant images. The synagogues looked as lively and sumptuous in their way as late baroque churches did. The busy and vigorous effects were enhanced by new ornamental forms, particularly in Poland and parts of the present-day Soviet Union, including Mogilev on the Dnieper.

L'vov, Fig. 84
Volpa, Fig. 97

In the relatively self-sufficient Jewish communities of eastern Europe, Jewish craftsmen were at work executing the arks at Gvozdets (1731) and Uzlyany, and no doubt others elsewhere in eastern Europe (as well as in Livorno, 1745). Lions often flanked the ark opening, recalling the lion ornaments of Solomon's palace. The many representations of a lion joined by a deer, a leopard, and an eagle came from a saying of Rabbi Judah ben Tema in part of the Mishnah, Ethics of the Fathers, 5:20: "Be fearless as a leopard, light as the eagle, swift as a deer, and strong as a lion to do the will of your heavenly father." Foliate ornament in the dense twinings of folk art surrounded many Polish arks of the

Figure 13. Bechhofen, interior with murals by Eliezer Sussman, 1733.

seventeenth century through the early nineteenth century. Sometimes carved birds and animals inhabited the vines and leaves, as at Mukachevo and Khodorov (1652).

The ark, in a sumptuous carved frame, stood behind ornamental metal gates. Lamps, reflectors, and candles increased the visual impressiveness of the synagogue. Inscriptions were especially common decorations, whether painted on walls or made of stucco or inscribed on plaques. Some large inscriptions substituted for scarce or expensive prayer books. Photographs record the inscription-covered walls of synagogues in many countries, such as those of

Casale, Fig. 192

Ellrich am Sudharz, Casale Monferrato, and Yablonov near Chernovtsy.[98]

Some synagogues were decorated with pictorial murals,[99] which included motifs seen also in ark carvings (Fig. 13). As early as 1640, those in the Isaac synagogue of Cracow/Kazimierz included animals as well as views of the Holy Land's cities of Hebron, Jerusalem, and Machpelah. At Khodorov, mid-seventeenth-century pictures showed Jerusalem framed by Leviathan and a tree; this was the work of a Jewish artist, Israel ben Mordecai Liśnicki of Jaryczów. Jerusalem appeared also in paintings at Kamenka-Bugskaya and at several synagogues with Polish folk-style decorations. The Hasidic synagogue of Rymanów had a mural of the Wailing Wall in Jerusalem (perhaps a marker for directing prayer to that city), as well as images of animals and plants. The venerable Jewish center at Worms was honored by its depiction in the synagogue of Mogilev on the Dnieper, a work executed by Chaim ben Isaac Segal of Slutzk (ca. 1740); this artist painted synagogue decorations at the nearby towns of Kopys and Dolginovo, too.

The Temple's ritual objects also were depicted in synagogues. At Yablonov in 1674, the table of showbread appeared on the north wall, and the seven-branched lampstand on the south. The wall paintings at Bechhofen had the same objects on the same walls. It is no longer possible to say whether or for how long this was a scheme common in central and eastern Europe.

Lions, fruit, flowers, vines, leaves, urns, palmettes, birds, and curtains painted to reveal the ark were among the motifs often used in synagogue decoration. Occasionally, a more unusual subject appeared, as at Yablonov where an elephant with a tower on its back represented strength. On the west wall of the same synagogue was a picture of an open door, illustrating the Talmudic statement that all gates to heaven may now be closed except for the door of tears through which prayers are brought to the Lord's throne. At Targowica around 1800, zodiac signs were included among the birds, urns, and plant forms in the cupola. The synagogue at Przedbórz had paintings of a city and of musical instruments, perhaps those mentioned in the book of Psalms.

A group of eighteenth-century German synagogues has attracted attention because of their copious folk-art ornamentation (see Fig. 13). These wooden village synagogues were painted—sometimes from floor to ceiling—with the flowers and vines, urns, birds, beasts, and inscriptions which we know from eastern European synagogues of the seventeenth and eighteenth centuries. The synagogues were decorated by eastern European Jews who had migrated to the west during the late seventeenth and eighteenth centuries. The artists worked for congregations of fellow migrants whose customs and rite differed from those of native German Jews. Polish connections probably explain the presence of comparable paintings of the seventeenth (?) century at Holešov in Moravia. The German synagogue group includes those of Bechhofen (1733), Horb (1735), Unterlimpurg (1739), and Kirchheim (1739–40), all of which were decorated by Eliezer ben Solomon Sussman, who may have come from Brody in Galicia.[100]

Figural representations were rare, but the High Synagogue in Cracow/Kazimierz had paintings of Biblical subjects including the sacrifice of Isaac, Noah's ark, and the harps hung by the waters of Babylon. In western Europe at Sens before 1750, there were paintings representing Jewish ceremonies (but they need not have included figures).[101] In 1674, Aaron de Chaves executed a panel painting showing Moses and Aaron holding the tablets of the Law; it was displayed in the Spanish-Portuguese synagogue of London and a copy was made at an unknown date for the Ashkenazic Great Synagogue of London.

The eastern European spatial elaboration was absent from synagogues in western Europe, unless they were influenced by currents from the east, but the late Renaissance synagogue[102] everywhere was a place of heightened intensity, where impressive visual features helped to direct the congregation's attention and prayers. The distracting visual riches led, however, to increasing aestheticism. In this respect, too, one sees Renaissance secular influence in synagogue architecture and design, although the Jews initially may have reacted to the visual effects with mystical fervor rather than secular appreciation.

Late Eighteenth Century to the First World War

The eighteenth-century Enlightenment in western Europe formed the background for vast changes in the situation of Jews and synagogues from about 1800 to the start of persecution under Hitler. The questioning of traditional doctrine during the Enlightenment fostered intellectual currents which gave many Christians a better understanding of Judaism. Some Christians even met Jews socially, as in the salons of cultivated Jewish women in Berlin and Vienna around 1800.

During the course of the nineteenth century, particularly in western and central Europe, civil rights replaced the Jews' easily retractable privileges. As a result, thousands of large and small synagogues were built, located both in traditional places of Jewish settlement and in places from which the municipality had formerly excluded Jews. Warsaw offers a dramatic example, for at one time Jews could live only in its suburb of Praga; in 1864, however, there were 72,000 Jews in the city and suburb, and in 1910 there were 306,000, constituting 40 percent of the city's population.[103] By 1914, there were imposing synagogues in every European country except Norway, where the Jewish communities were very small, and Spain, where Jews were allowed to identify their buildings publicly only after 1966.

Later nineteenth-century synagogues could rise on wide streets or plazas, just as churches did, and their roofs and domes formed notable accents in the cityscapes of Berlin, Nuremberg, Turin, and Florence, among other places. Synagogues in Malacky, Sofia, and many towns in western Europe were even built near large churches. At Głubczyce, there was an ecumenical urban composition: On three sides of a rectangular plaza stood a Protestant church, a Roman Catholic church, and a large synagogue.

Sofia, Fig. 58
Berlin, Fig. 122
Florence, Fig. 193
Turin, Fig. 214

In much of eastern Europe, the majority of Jews were less fortunate. Those who became subject to Russia after the three partitions of Poland (1772, 1793, 1795) could live only in specified places in twenty-five provinces, known as the Pale of Settlement. Initiated in 1791 and lasting until the Russian Revolution of 1917, the Pale confined most of the Jews subject to the czar in 4 percent of his territory. They usually lived in squalor and had only modest synagogues. Exceptions included the buildings of a few Hasidic leaders whose followers eagerly offered funds and furnishings, and imposing synagogues donated by rich individuals. None were great works of architectural design as far as we know, but at times their abundant detail and their elaborate arks and bimahs made them memorable. The most conservatively pious Jews would not have missed beautiful architecture. Knowing that the Talmud requires Jews to pray several times a day, they may have expected their synagogues to be somewhat informal or cozy, not like the building used only once a week by less devout Jews who would have wanted more impressive structures to attract them.

Warsaw, Figs. 101, 102

Much of this part of the world was economically backward, for the nobility had avoided middle-class commerce, while the masses lacked enough education to conduct business on any but a petty scale. A few Jews adept at manufacturing, banking, and railroad building therefore began to acquire residential privileges in parts of Russia during the reign of Catherine the Great (ruled 1762–96) and were allowed to open discreet synagogues.

When Czar Alexander II (ruled 1855–81) allowed designated Jews to acquire land and live in some new areas, he meant to Russianize them, and only the culturally assimilated Jews benefited from his measures. These Jews still received privileges rather than rights through much of the nineteenth century. It was they who built large synagogues in major cities such as Odessa, Kiev, and Moscow.[104] After Alexander's death, the Jewish masses were subjected to pogroms and while a few synagogues were erected, others fell victim to vandals who seemed immune from prosecution. These hardships were among the causes of the great westward migration of Jews from the areas subject to the czars. In part because of general improvements in public health and sanitation, the remaining Jews increased in number and occasionally needed new synagogues. The migration had a profound effect on synagogue building in central and western Europe. Many Jewish communities in Great Britain, for example, owe their strength to the Russian and eastern European Jews who sought a new life in the British Isles in the decades after 1880. Occasionally, the migrants required synagogues in unusual places. Those who traveled overseas on ships of the Hamburg-America Line eventually obtained a large prayer room in one of the shipping company's emigrant halls in Hamburg.[105]

Leningrad, Figs. 88, 89
Moscow, Figs. 90, 91
Warsaw, Figs. 99, 100

Gradual Legal Improvement

In western and central Europe, the improvement in the Jews' status received special impetus from the French Declaration of the Rights of Man in 1789 and the subsequent revolution. To be sure, it took considerable debate in the French legislative assembly before these rights were applied to the Jews. The varying status of individual Jewish groups is shown by the fact that the rights were granted first, in January 1790, to the richer Sephardic Jews of the Bayonne-Bordeaux area, then to the Jews of the Comtat Venaissin, and finally, in

1791, to the Ashkenazic Jews who were particularly numerous in Alsace. Nevertheless, as early as 1789, Jews were allowed to build synagogues in places where only prayer rooms had existed earlier. By 1792, there were four synagogues in Paris. During the year-long Reign of Terror that started in July 1793, synagogues as well as churches were nationalized and desecrated; the Metz synagogues, for instance, were used as animal barns. Because the extremists tended to be more hostile to the important Roman Catholic church than to the comparatively insignificant Jews, some nationalized churches were never given back, and several were later sold for use as simple synagogues. Under the Directorate, the decree of February 1795 on religious liberty let the Jews recover some of their old synagogues.[106]

The Dutch, temporarily under French control, granted Jews substantial rights in 1796, and Napoleon spread his somewhat less generous rules governing Jews to conquered territories near France, including Westphalia. These legal provisions remained influential there, though not identical, during the succeeding three decades of monarchic restoration and conservative reaction that followed Napoleon's fall in 1814.

Emancipation and equal-status laws became increasingly common from the revolutionary year of 1848 onward. Jews generally won the right to own real estate, to collect religious taxes from their congregations, and to receive some state religious tax revenue. They usually were allowed to erect synagogues if they followed the local building codes applicable to other structures. These rights accumulated gradually and increased especially with the unification of Germany and Italy and the definition of each part of the Austro-Hungarian empire in the years around 1870.

All religious groups continued to be subject to some official constraints. If there was an established church, the ministry of religion could close unauthorized nonconforming churches, or deny them building funds. The authorities could also influence the choice of architect and style. Sometimes the state intervened indirectly, using intermediary organizations composed of Jews (or other nonconformists). These organizations were led by culturally assimilated Jews who were prepared to acquiesce to government pressure in affairs that they considered secondary, in exchange for freedom to conduct Jewish religious and community affairs in the ways they thought best. The leaders became a kind of Jewish "establishment" who seem to have represented the majority of Jews in their area, but not necessarily the most orthodox or most Reform. In French- and German-speaking countries, the organizations were known respectively as consistories (*consistoires*) and communities (*Gemeinde*).

Consistories were introduced under Napoleon in France, Belgium, northern Italy, Westphalia, and the Rhine Provinces. Jews in these places were incorporated into a body led by rabbis and laymen who were responsible to the ministry of religion. The Consistoire Israélite officially embraced all the Jews of France until a law of 1905 made religion independent of the state, and Jews in other areas had *consistoires* as long as French rule continued.[107] Regional consistories in France, with two thousand or more members, built one large consistorial synagogue in the region's largest town (Paris eventually had several) and smaller local ones, all affiliated with the central office in Paris. These synagogues received state subsidies, as churches did, so that the Jews could afford to build synagogues of impressive size in Paris, Lyon, Strasbourg, and other seats of regional consistories, if government supervisors approved. From about 1830 onward, the consistorial officials actively sponsored synagogues, and chose Jewish and Christian, municipal and private architects. *Paris, Figs. 108–111*

In Germany, Austria, and Switzerland, Jews were organized by government order into Gemeinde, legal corporate entities. They differed from consistories in being local—comprising congregations in a city and nearby villages—rather than parts of a central organization. According to laws which were originally Prussian (1847) but which were adopted in united Germany after 1870, Jews were automatically Gemeinde members and had to contribute financially to the Gemeinde's chief synagogue. If a Jew chose to worship separately because his degree of orthodoxy differed from that which the Gemeinde officials had settled on, he would still have to contribute to the treasury of the main synagogue. The rules encouraged the building of a single, large, easily supervised synagogue in each town. The government occasionally exercised its powers in malevolent ways—for instance, by offering obviously inconvenient sites for new synagogues at Munich, Berlin, and Strasbourg[108]—but the Gemeinde itself determined the degree of orthodoxy and thus the interior arrangement of the bimah and the admissibility of an organ, choir, and colored window glass.

Independent or dissident synagogues—those not administered by the consistory or Gemeinde—would have to be built either by rich or by passionately sectarian Jews. These synagogues were erected by the ultraorthodox (Israelitische Religionsgesellschaft, Hasidic groups) and by Reform Jews who simplified and revised traditional religious practice after ca. 1800. Reform Jews tended to be richer than the ultraorthodox, because the cultural assimilation that had given impetus to Reform made it easier for them to succeed in business and thc professions. Even if they were a numerical minority, they were still able to afford their own synagogues in Berlin and Hamburg when the Gemeinde there remained more traditional. If the Gemeinde followed Reform, the orthodox could apply for a contribution from wealthy orthodox Jews, the Rothschilds in particular. In 1876, ultraorthodox Jews won the right to secede from the Gemeinde; thereafter the Berlin Adath Israel and Frankfurt Adath Jeshurun congregations financed impressive synagogues of their own.[109] In Budapest, the official community agreed to erect synagogues for various levels of orthodoxy. Liberal Jews organized their ultra-Reform congregations in the present century, and built imposing synagogues before the Second World War in Berlin, Hamburg, and London. *Hamburg, Figs. 149, 150* *Frankfurt, Figs. 144, 145* *Hamburg, Figs. 153, 154*

Outside the areas with consistories and communities, Jewish organizations lacked the same powers to tax and discipline for the benefit of a chief district synagogue. The more loosely organized areas might therefore have more synagogues. Each one might be relatively small unless it was sponsored by rich people or by a government that helped useful, assimilated Jews to build a synagogue. Numerous small synagogues allowed the varied sects and degrees of orthodoxy to have their own premises, but larger synagogues, if they meant *fewer* synagogues, pleased government supervisors who wanted to keep track of Jewish activities more efficiently.[110]

Development of Large Synagogues

The large synagogues that went up in many cities from the 1850s onward were, then, sometimes built for reasons other than simply to accommodate a rising Jewish population. When synagogues were planned, advocates argued that existing buildings were overcrowded on major holy days. Opponents, who usually lost the arguments, wanted to solve the problem by hiring halls to accommodate the overflow. They hoped that building funds could be applied to charity rather than to bricks and mortar. Traditionalists among them were concerned about the spiritual danger if they imitated the practice of building large churches. They knew that assimilation in general culture and assimilation in architecture often went together, and that the plans of many nineteenth-century synagogues were virtually indistinguishable from those of contemporary Protestant churches.

Proponents of new, large buildings usually won the arguments, because Jews able to approach the majority society responded to its values. They found hired halls and small synagogues socially unsatisfactory. Indifferent Jews might have dropped their membership, or withheld contributions from a congregation that met in unattractive premises. It was feared that Jewish youths exposed to the lure of Christian social advantage might desert the old faith if they had no synagogues able to compete with imposing churches. Jews who wanted to confirm their place in modern society built large synagogues that would, as they put it, be worthy of their cities and show the congregations' gratitude for their new civil status.

Erecting infrequently filled, costly structures for such reasons as these had little to do with the prayer and Torah study that are the essential purposes of a synagogue. A building seating a thousand or more people inevitably detracts from a sense of intimate community, which is another fundamental aspect of a synagogue. Moreover, the impressive buildings aroused the hostility of anti-Semites, who accused the Jews of materialism and ostentation, even though churches in the same community were larger and more elaborate than the synagogues.

Budapest, Fig. 39
Berlin, Fig. 124

Synagogue Location

The Jews' forward march was interrupted by other pitfalls. Rights did not guarantee prosperity, and many Jews remained too poor to pay for decent synagogues. The 1806 census in the Bas-Rhin department of France showed that this Alsatian center of Jewry had 150 Jewish communities but only 120 synagogues,[111] and under the still oppressive regimes in most eastern European lands, the majority of Jews prayed in miserable places.

It was also true that some enlightened activity endangered historic synagogues, for when municipalities drained and paved and embanked the unwholesome and flood-prone areas where they had formerly confined the Jews, they removed some synagogues that lay in the path of new streets and much-needed open spaces. Prague lost several old synagogues in this way, as did Rome and Sofia, but urban renewal schemes skirted the most venerable synagogues in Prague, Livorno, L'vov, and Amsterdam. The house demolitions, canal fillings, and road widenings actually made some synagogues more visible than they had been earlier, although these buildings were severed from their historical settings. The open space around the Prague-Altneuschul and the imposing facade added to the Livorno synagogue when one side became visible from a new plaza were products of late-nineteenth-century metropolitan improvement.

Livorno, Fig. 197

Freedom to live where they chose allowed Jews, like Christians of the time, to leave villages for cities, and as village synagogues gradually emptied, many fell into ruin. Fortunately, a few were moved to local museums. Examples are that of Kirchheim, which went to the Mainfränkisches Museum at Würzburg where bombs destroyed it during the Second World War; that of Hornburg, which was installed in a disused church that became the local museum of Braunschweig; and that of Horb, which the Municipal Museum of Bamberg has lent to the Israel Museum.

Jews who were free to relocate established branch or independent synagogues in suburbs, especially in western and central Europe.[112] If they did not, those living far from the old synagogue might attend services only occasionally, for they risked criticism if they were seen riding to Sabbath services. Other Jews came to their synagogues only on the Sabbath and holy days; even so, few big synagogues were filled for ordinary Sabbath services, although weekday synagogues attracted a daily quorum. Diminished synagogue attendance had less effect on eastern European communities, because orthodoxy and traditional practice were dominant there, and Jews tended to move into cities such as Warsaw and L'vov from the suburbs in which they had formerly been confined.

When the Jews moved more easily about the world at large, they could satisfy their social, commercial, and cultural needs outside their limited community. Thus, increased opportunity might decrease group and religious cohesion. It became hard to exert social pressure on Jews who stopped praying several times a day, or who gave their sons only a perfunctory Jewish education. Even obtaining permission to have the synagogue's facade on a public street could loosen community connections, for Jews no longer had to enter the synagogue through its courtyard, where the congregation assembled near the house of study.

As community ties were relaxed, and as Jews migrated more freely, some found themselves destitute but without the customary support of close-knit families and Jewish community charities. To control beggary and unemployment, the Dutch Welfare Society set up an agricultural colony at Veenhuizen in about 1820, and the government required some poor Jews to move there. Consequently, the colony had a modest synagogue from 1839 to 1890.[113] Other Jews turned to crime, and when they became subject to general law, they lost the religious courts that formerly had governed certain kinds of lawbreaking. Prison synagogues were provided just as Christian chapels were. Although the proportion of Jewish convicts has generally been far below the Jewish percentage of population in any area, prisons close to large Jewish settlements inevitably contained Jewish inmates. In 1868, the *Jewish Chronicle* mentioned rooms set aside for synagogue use in prisons at Prague, Portsmouth, and Suben, and the same newspaper reported on others at Bayreuth and Nanterre. The synagogue in Maidstone prison was consecrated in 1939.[114]

The Reform Movement

The trends toward cultural integration also encouraged some culturally assimilated Jews around 1800 to abandon the distinctive practices of worship that had developed in times of political and cultural isolation. These Jews lived mainly in Germany, Vienna, and western Europe, where their social status improved earlier than it did in eastern Europe. They hoped to bring Judaism into harmony with modern conditions by eliminating liturgical traditions and prayers that had no application in nineteenth-century Europe. Understanding that those half-ignorant of Hebrew recited prayers only by rote, the modern-minded faithful wanted to introduce vernacular prayers and sermons to make synagogue attendance meaningful.

The result of their plans was the movement known as Reform Judaism, a term we have already mentioned. Changes in prayers accompanied aesthetic changes related to aspects of low-church Protestantism. In those Protestant churches, the emphasis was on preaching, especially about aspects of godly behavior, rather than on dogma and ritual. The congregations sat in rooms that were essentially meeting and preaching halls rather than sanctuaries of incarnate mysteries, and they listened to a minister (who, like a rabbi, might be married), rather than to a celibate priest. The designers of Protestant churches made all parts of a building visible, and made sure that the minister could be heard throughout the building. These elements were familiar in Judaism. Major differences between Protestant and traditional Jewish practice included seating the entire family together rather than segregating women, and having unified responsive reading and hymn singing, the latter regulated by an organ and a trained choir.

The serene orderliness of these Protestant procedures appealed to those assimilated German Jews who began the Reform movement. In the age of a proper Biedermeier parlor, the age of Jane Austen, a Reform-minded Jewish family shunned the shouting, vigorous movement, and uncoordinated praying known in traditional Ashkenazic synagogues, was aghast at the smoking and eating done in exceptionally lax congregations, and would probably have looked askance at the informality in some Catholic and evangelical Protestant churches.[115] Reformers evidently believed that decorum reinforced religious activity. They saw the rabbi and cantor as leaders of organized prayers, which should be recited by one voice or by the congregation in unison, rather than by each individual at his own pace. These prayers were to be offered in clean synagogues, where informal behavior was supposed to be unknown. Everyone was to sit sedately, focusing on the east where the bimah had moved from the center of the room.[116] It was easy to see beyond the bimah, because Reformers removed the old stone-framed bimah enclosures and substituted simpler tables instead, as at Worms. Scores of galleried basilican synagogues were erected for Reform worship, and there was little to distinguish the Jews' buildings from Protestant churches (see Fig. 1e). That was part of the point: Reform temples were meant to appeal especially to assimilated youths who might be tempted to follow other ambitious young Jews in converting to Christianity. The rows of neat pews revealed the status of congregation members, since those who sat closest to the east enjoyed the greatest wealth or prestige.[117]

Worms, Figs. 170, 172

In Reform temples, and even in orthodox synagogues used by assimilated Jews, changes also occurred in the auxiliary areas. In fashionable synagogues, there might be open porches to shelter those who alighted from carriages in the rain. These synagogues would also have cloakrooms and resting rooms for women. If the rabbi and cantor lived off the premises, they had office and robing rooms in the synagogue (though contrary to Jewish custom, even orthodox rabbis wore ministerial robes if the government insisted on them). There might be a dressing and waiting room for brides, and a social hall to replace the old separate "Tanzhaus," or festival building. Such changes as these suggest that the synagogue came increasingly to be viewed as a place for polite activity. It is understandable that aesthetic considerations came to the fore in the conduct of services and in decisions about architectural form and style that would please the culturally assimilated congregation, whatever rite it followed.

Warsaw, Fig. 98
Paris, Fig. 110
Brussels, Fig. 114

Architectural rapprochement with churches had its limits, of course. Synagogues avoided a church plan in which the apse—for the ark in a synagogue, for the altar in a church—lay behind a bay covered with a dome or cupola. The dome or cupola or lantern could have illuminated the easterly bimah in a Reform temple, thereby distinguishing the bimah's space from that of the ark. But because this plan separates the congregation from anyone beyond the domed bay, it suits the special status of a priest and does not suit a rabbi or cantor. In addition, as this plan had been invented specifically for Roman Catholic churches, using it would have obviously imitated the practice of another religion, something which even the Reformers must have hesitated to do without good reason.

Builders and Architects*

Before emancipation, while some Jews had entered the construction trades in eastern and central Europe,[118] the design and supervisory positions in private and governmental architecture had been reserved for Christians.[119] After the middle of the nineteenth century, it became possible for Jews to take architectural qualifying examinations. As pious boys could not have drawn, written, handled money, or ridden on the Sabbath, Jewish architects and construction engineers came from prosperous and culturally assimilated families who may not have observed all the traditional practices of Judaism. Custom and prejudice may have kept some Christians from giving jobs to Jewish architects,[120] so that the architects tended to work for their coreligionists. One exception, Richard Wolffenstein, who had many Christian clients, had a Christian partner, Wilhelm Cremer, who came first in the firm's name. Some architects of Jewish descent, such as George Basevi in England and Georg Heinrich Friedrich Hitzig in Germany, were converts to Christianity or the sons of converts.[121]

Where emancipation came early, as in France, Jews became architects earlier than in many other places. The first of these seems to have been Jacob Silveyra, one of the architects of the Paris synagogue in rue Notre Dame de Nazareth (1819–22). His name and his birthplace in Bordeaux suggest that he was of Sephardic ancestry. As Sephardic Jews were the social superiors of Ashkenazic Jews, and were often richer as well, Silveyra may have had an unusual opportunity to study architecture, no doubt privately, as was then usual. When Jewish architects were available, congregations who chose architects directly rather than by competition frequently employed their fellow Jews.[122] The Strasbourg consistory addressed a letter on July 23, 1855, to the prefect of the Bas-Rhin department, complaining of excessive stylistic variety, badly adapted to the ritual, which existed in local synagogues. Wishing to avoid luxury and superfluity, they said, they petitioned for a Jewish architect to be attached to the consistory who would supervise construction and repairs made by the official department architect.[123]

Paris, Figs. 108, 109

In tolerant England, Jewish architects designed several synagogues in London and the southern counties. Elsewhere—and even in most of southern England outside the metropolis—Christian architects worked for Jewish communities, probably for lack of Jewish architects in the provinces. The most interesting example of a Christian synagogue architect occurred in Leicester, where it was the city's mayor, Arthur Wakerley, who designed the Highfield Street synagogue (1897–98).[124] We know of one English Jew, David Mocatta, who practiced architecture during the first half of the nineteenth century. A comparatively wealthy man from a culturally assimilated Sephardic family, he obtained several commissions from other Jews of the same class or rite, including Sir Moses Montefiore, for whom Mocatta designed a private synagogue in Ramsgate (1831–33). Mocatta, who became interested in Reform, designed the

Ramsgate, Figs. 252, 253

*See Appendix I for a list of selected architects.

first Reform temple in London in Bruton Street (1842), was superintending architect for its successor in Margaret Street (1849), and was a consultant to the firm of Davis & Emanuel which designed the third temple in Upper Berkeley Street (1867–70). Mocatta may also have been a consultant at the imposing orthodox New Synagogue in Great St. Helen's (1838).[125]

London, Figs. 151, 152

More Ashkenazic Jews began to enter British architectural practice in the second half of the century.[126] They soon predominated in synagogue architecture, at least in the largest cities where congregations could afford the services of professionally trained architects rather than mere local builders. Nathan Solomon Joseph and his nephew, Delissa Joseph, working in separate firms, designed a dozen synagogues. The Josephs were related to the Chief Rabbi of the Ashkenazic Jews in Great Britain, which surely helped them to get commissions.

In the early and mid-nineteenth century, there were few Jewish architects in Germany. One whose work is known to posterity was A. Rosengarten, who designed the synagogue at Kassel in 1837–38 and three more synagogues in Hamburg between 1853 and 1857. He was born in Kassel where the rights gained by Jews under Napoleon were never fully rescinded by the restoration government, and where Jews of Rosengarten's generation could enter certain professions. He studied architecture during the 1830s at the building office in Kassel, and worked for twelve years in the Hessian state service. Trips to Paris in 1839 to study under Labrouste and to Rome in 1841 reveal his cosmopolitan culture and his aspirations.[127] P. E. Bacharach from Homm, active in 1854, advertised himself as a synagogue architect.[128] By this time, Jewish architects could take examinations and practice privately.

Kassel, Figs. 164, 165

Succeeding generations of Jewish architects received training and synagogue commissions.[129] Several made synagogues a specialty of their practice, among them Edwin Oels Oppler and Richard Wolffenstein.

Hannover, Figs. 162, 163
Wroclaw, Figs. 177, 178

In the Netherlands, we know only of Leon Winkel (1822–84), a civil engineer who designed the Delft synagogue in 1861–62, and E. M. Rood, who designed the Amsterdam-Gerard Doustraat (1892) and Monnikendam (1894) synagogues.

There were more Jewish synagogue architects in the Austro-Hungarian Empire by the late nineteenth century. Lipót Baumhorn, the most prolific synagogue architect, designed twenty-four.[130] Max Fleischer of Vienna was an important spokesman and designer for congregations that wanted to assimilate culturally. Alfred Grotte, an architectural engineer, published seminal works on synagogue architecture and history, and he designed several synagogues in towns that are now in Czechoslovakia and Poland.[131]

Szeged, Figs. 56, 57

České Budějovice, Figs. 43–45

In Italy, Marco Treves worked with two Christian architects on the main synagogue of Florence (1874–82) and designed the synagogue at Pisa (1863), which impressed Sir Moses Montefiore with its beauty. Other Italian Jewish architects and engineers of synagogues were known in Trieste and Milan.[132]

Florence, Figs. 193, 194

From the late nineteenth century to the start of Nazi persecution, Jews were freer than they had ever been to enter the architectural and engineering professions.[133] Emmanuel Pontremoli, who taught at the Ecole des Beaux-Arts in Paris, designed the synagogue of Boulogne-sur-Seine in 1909–11. Joseph DeLange, one of the few Belgian Jewish architects, designed synagogues in Antwerp (built between 1910 and 1929), one in Anderlect, and one in Ostend (ca. 1900–1910), and Jules Hofman designed one in Antwerp in 1911–13. In pre-Revolutionary Russia, Lev I. Bachman had collaborated with an older Christian architect on the main synagogue in Saint Petersburg, and I. G. Gevirts, who became dean of the Leningrad academy architecture school after the 1917 Revolution, designed two small synagogues and the large one near the Jewish cemetery (1911).

Antwerp, Fig. 115

Antwerp, Fig. 116

Leningrad, Figs. 88, 89

After 1918, Erich Mendelsohn, who was famous for having built the Einstein Tower in Potsdam and other secular buildings, designed a small synagogue (1925–26) for a Jewish community center in Tilsit, now Sovetsk (Figs. 14, 15).[134] Richard Neutra entered the Vienna-Hietzing synagogue competition (1924) early in his distinguished career, which was devoted largely to secular buildings. Artur Szalatnai designed a simple orthodox synagogue for Bratislava (1923) that mixed evocative elements with geometric forms, and Otto Eisler designed a chaste International Style synagogue at Brno (1935).[135] Dutch Jewish architects designed most of the synagogues in their country at this time, using a wide range of modern styles.[136] Jewish architects designed most of the synagogues in Hungary, including at least eight in Budapest, where the Jews, who were free to live where they chose, needed several new synagogues outside their old centers in Obuda and south-central Pest.[137]

Vienna, Fig. 68

Bratislava, Figs. 28–30

Amsterdam, Figs. 229–234

In the late nineteenth and early twentieth centuries, competitions often were held for all kinds of public buildings, and they were also part of architectural education. Jews often sponsored design competitions for synagogues,[138] just as Christians did for churches and civic structures. The clients hoped to benefit from the good ideas of many competitors, and the architects hoped for work and a boost to their reputations. Most of the synagogue competitions were open to all architects, but a few were limited to local practitioners (Offenbach, 1912; Amsterdam-Lekstraat, 1934), to invited architects (Görlitz, 1909), or to Jewish participants (Antwerp-van den Nestlei, 1923; Vienna-Hietzing, 1924). The inclusiveness of most of these competitions shows that the sponsors wanted to secure the best possible building and viewed synagogues as building types intelligible to people of all religions. Just as they were pleased to find civic officials at synagogue dedications, or to notice music-loving Christians listening to synagogue cantors, the Jews sponsored open competitions, thereby linking themselves and their institutions to the larger society.

Rome, Fig. 205
Trieste, Figs. 210, 211

Amsterdam, Figs. 233, 234

Vienna, Figs. 66–68

In recent decades congregations in Great Britain, France, and Germany have sometimes employed Christian architects, although Jewish architects are available. Perhaps a pious architect of any faith can design a synagogue with a properly "religious" character, however elusive may be the definition of "religious." Moreover, Jews come from such varied backgrounds and have such varied approaches to their religion that it seems impossible to define

Figure 14. Sovetsk, Three Patriarchs' Lodge Synagogue, 1925–26, exterior.

Figure 15. Sovetsk, Three Patriarchs' Lodge Synagogue, plan, sections.

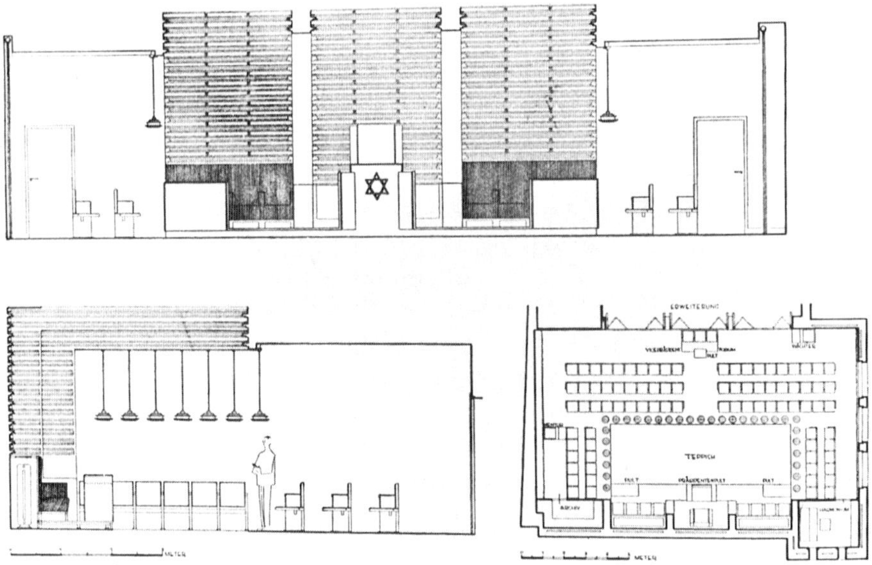

a standard "Jewish feeling" which only a Jewish architect might add to a synagogue. Nor have Jews ever agreed on a specific style. A congregation hoping for the atmosphere of a traditional eastern European "shul," for instance, will find that hard to create in modern society and in modern materials; besides, that atmosphere may even be foreign to some congregation members (see Figs. 2, 3).

To suppose that a Christian can design a synagogue well is different from saying that the architect's religion never matters.[139] A Jewish architect may be more familiar with synagogue architecture and liturgy, and may have personal experience of the architectural success or failure of other synagogues. Jewish architects were usually more sensitive to the potentially damaging social connotations of style in the nineteenth century, when style represented the self-image of nations and groups. Where Jews were segregated or despised, it must have been difficult for Christian architects to deal easily with unfamiliar people and unfamiliar requirements. In church building, the ostensible client and the real client were the same, while in synagogue architecture, the real client might be a nobleman who allowed "his" Jews to have a synagogue, or the real client to be satisfied might be society at large which looked over the shoulders of nineteenth- and twentieth-century Jews who tried to be both patriotic and true to their unique traditions. Rarely will a Christian share the Jews' sense of insecurity, relieved by episodes of stable residence and social acceptance. Rarely will a Christian feel the conflict between Jewish tradition and isolation on the one hand and the modern desire for cultural assimilation on the other hand. It was, after all, Christian synagogue architects of the nineteenth century who introduced the Egyptian, Islamic, and Byzantine styles that made Jews seem most alien from European and western Christian culture.

Canterbury, Fig. 241
Dresden, Fig. 130
Bucharest, Fig. 34
Budapest, Fig. 38
Vienna, Figs. 64, 65

In addition, there might be only limited prestige to be gained by working on a synagogue, whether one was Jewish or not. Men with good local reputations sometimes designed them, and the synagogue of rich Jews, or one ordered by a prince or tolerant government, would take on the prestige of the patron. It may, however, be significant that the well-known Christian architect Otto Wagner designed a synagogue in Budapest when he was a young man seeking commissions, and Peter Behrens designed one for Žilina when he was past his prime. Wagner omitted the Budapest synagogue from his later publication of his work. He might, of course, have abjured his earlier historicist styles, but it is surely not coincidental that anti-Semitism was rife in government and popular circles in Vienna while Wagner was working on civic buildings. Richard Neutra, who separated himself from Jewish life, published his Vienna-Hietzing synagogue project, but concealed its identity as a synagogue and Jewish community center, referring to it only as a community building.[140] Clearly, architects with mixed feelings about their clients might design beautiful monuments, but these might not be ideal embodiments of the clients' own emotions and aspirations.

Samokov, Figs. 52, 53
Warsaw, Figs. 98–100
Budapest, Figs. 40–42
Žilina, Figs. 158–160
Vienna, Fig. 68

Architectural Style

When Jews expressed a preference for a specific style, they often did so for reasons that were social and political rather than religious, since an adequate synagogue can consist of only a box with scarcely any identifiable style. Regional differences in ritual and social context, and varying degrees of orthodoxy reflecting internal religious "politics," might even lead Jews within one group, such as Reform or Hasidism, to build synagogues in several styles. The great variety and the options available testify to some confusion, as is natural for a group that had never before been able to exercise free choice. It also testifies to the institutional flexibility that is possible in a religion that has no central authority. This flexibility is also necessary for a minority that must respond to external pressure. The style of synagogues has borne silent but authoritative witness to the changing position of Jews in European society.

Before about 1830, synagogues generally used the styles found in secular and Christian buildings. Folk-art decorations embellished rustic churches and box-like village synagogues (see Fig. 13) , while urban synagogues used whatever style of ornament was then in vogue. A synagogue facade seldom called for special treatment, because synagogues were often concealed at the rear of a building lot. Masons and carvers had therefore to modify plans rather than styles to suit their Jewish clients. Even though the customs of Karaites and Hasids[141] may differ from those of other Jews, adherents of these movements usually had plain, low, vernacular buildings, or they adapted older buildings without altering their style. Israel of Medzhibozh (1700–1760), the humble founder of Hasidism, prayed in a house of study that set an example of indifference to worldly display (see Figs. 2, 3).

Budapest, Fig. 37
Vienna, Fig. 63
Wroclaw, Figs. 174–176

Several synagogue architects of the late eighteenth and early nineteenth centuries clearly had art in mind as well as Jewish needs. They built circular or oval synagogues that were anomalies in the history of synagogue design but that suited the worldly taste of the Christian rulers and Jewish elite who commissioned them from Christian architects between ca. 1790 and ca. 1840. The synagogue at Wörlitz built in 1789–90 by court architect Friedrich Wilhelm von Erdmannsdorf was a round pavilion in the gardens of the Jews' patron (see Figs. 8, 9); the synagogue was also known as the Temple of Vesta—which shows the congregation's dependent position before emancipation as the private domain of the Grand Duke of Anhalt-Dessau.[142] A suburban Jewish settlement at Floss in the Upper Palatinate erected a synagogue in 1815–17 with an elongated polygonal plan that was close to an oval. The Seitenstettengasse synagogue in Vienna of 1824–26 by Josef Kornhäusel, built at the instigation of a small group of rich and assimilated men, is a dignified oval building with a central cupola on a windowed drum that rises above the central bimah. The Avignon synagogue interior of 1846–48 by J. A. Joffroy had a curve of columns in two storeys—Ionic below Corinthian.[143] The synagogue of 1851–53 at Meerssen in Limburg by Johannes Lambertus Lemmens has a semicircular

Vienna, Figs. 61–63

gallery beside a rectilinear men's area; its external elevation—with bare brick walls relieved by pilasters, low conical roof, and polygonal lantern—resembles that of Wörlitz. The Meerssen plan varied that of the Maastricht synagogue of 1839–40 by Mathieu Hermans, where the women's gallery and entrance were contained in a two-thirds-circle addition to the men's square prayer hall.[144] A hexagonal synagogue was designed as an innovation but never built; an octagonal synagogue in stripped Romanesque style was, however, erected at Weissensee in Austria,[145] but polygonal and curved centralized plans virtually disappeared by the mid-nineteenth century, when other historicist styles and Greek- or Latin-cross plans associated with them displaced neoclassical buildings. It is possible to say that the neoclassical synagogues' forms showed the congregation's unity and therefore expressed Jewish community worship. It is also possible to imagine the architects imposing these buildings on the clients, while enjoying the chance to design charming buildings that were delightful to secular connoisseurs.

Occasionally, the style of a synagogue served as an instrument of official policies that defined the Jews' place in society. At Karlsruhe, in 1798, the synagogue stood on an unusually prominent street-corner site on one of the avenues radiating from the vast open space in front of the Margrave of Baden's residence, implying that the ruler was a tolerant man. The court architect, Friedrich Weinbrenner, designed it, in another sign of lordly benevolence. The building, however, had a street facade of an exotic modified Egyptian type, so that it could not be mistaken for anything but the property of outsiders, and the synagogue was situated near a city gate, far from the center of town where proximity to the ruler meant prestige. The archduke combined a sop to the Jews who helped him financially with a charming accent in a city plan that was of aesthetic importance to him.[146]

In Munich in 1825, the Bavarian king donated white marble palm capitals to the new basilican synagogue designed by a government architect, Jean-Baptiste Métivier. Non-German, non-European details presumably suited a building for the "foreign" group. The neoclassical-Egyptian combination of styles may illustrate the opinions of Leo von Klenze, the royal architect, who thought that ancient Hebrew architecture was reminiscent of Egyptian, and that later the Temple of Herod was built in a Roman style; as he considered both Egyptian and Roman architectural styles inferior to the Greek, he avoided associating the Jews with the best aspects of ancient culture.[147]

The question of style assumed special importance in the nineteenth century.[148] The problem seemed to arise suddenly, and it led to experiment and excitement, proud achievement and ironic failure in synagogue design. There was a new awareness among Jews of having to decide how a synagogue should look—and by extension, how the Jews themselves wanted to be seen.

In the nineteenth century, both religious revival and nationalism stimulated searches for the expression of group tradition. Especially where there was an established church, religious and national identity were connected. When

Christians preempted the Gothic style as the clearest sign of national history—as they did in England, France, and elsewhere—something else had to be found for the Jews because of their religious and ethnic differences.

The matter of Jewish self-expression became all the more urgent as nineteenth-century governments granted increasing residential and civil rights to Jews, for with emancipation Jews no longer had to pray in the usual nondescript synagogues, often hidden from public streets (see Fig. 7). When this newly visible minority emerged with the ordinary rights of other citizens, and when the minority members donned modern clothing, their synagogues somehow had to be dressed appropriately, too. Nineteenth-century Jews wanted to express their new social position architecturally, by something more than mounting tablets of the Law on a synagogue facade, or inserting six-pointed stars in window tracery. These two signs of identity often were used at this time, but the Jews wanted the entire building to be expressive as well.

Some Jews wanted to proclaim their differences by means of a special style, while others wanted to assimilate in every way short of conversion to Christianity. Some Jews emphasized their Middle Eastern heritage, while others professed allegiance only to their European homelands and avoided the slightest suggestion of exoticism. At the turn of the twentieth century, while some Jews embraced Zionism, especially in the face of pan-Germanism, pan-Slavism, and other closed ethnic-political-religious systems, others continued to press for full local acceptance.

Most governments wanted the Jews to assimilate culturally, sometimes because of enlightened good will and the desire to develop all groups in a city for the common good. These motives seem to have inspired suggestions by the city officials at Gdańsk that the Jewish leaders commission a synagogue in the local neo-Renaissance style favored for all public buildings in the 1870s and 1880s.[149] Other governments promoted cultural uniformity in order to control the entire population more easily, or even to promote conversion to Christianity. The most extreme example of enforced assimilation was the absurd demand of General Tomatcheff, Governor of Odessa, that all synagogues display crosses beside the Russian crown on the outside of the buildings. He withdrew this demand a year later, but the intolerant atmosphere may be gauged from the demand made then of a religious teacher who asked to open a new synagogue: He had to aver that it was in order to pray for the czar and the fatherland.[150]

In general, the Jews of western and central Europe welcomed opportunities to join the rest of society in manners, education, and in other ways that did not compromise their fidelity to Judaism. After the mid-1870s, when most Jews west of Hungary had mastered the customs and deportment of their Christian fellow-citizens, they had to face growing anti-Semitism of a new racial type, which denigrated Jews no matter how they behaved. The question of Jewish integration with the surrounding culture was thus a constant one, affecting every suggestion offered about synagogue style. It became clear that Jews would not be any more integrated in architecture than in society itself. Their own varied responses to integration fostered a century of inventive experimentation in expressive styles.

The nineteenth century was, of course, an exceptionally challenging period in which to define a suitably Jewish style of architecture. It was a period of enormous change in building technology, impressive achievement in Holy Land archaeology, and growth of lithography, photography, and illustrated periodicals which presented a bewildering array of possible models. The rapid changes, the speed with which new aesthetic ideas could be spread, and the disjunction between technical progress and the use of old styles all confronted the stability and cultural resolution that are normally basic to the development of tradition.

The frequent equation of moral good with political and technological progress led to technological and aesthetic innovation in synagogue architecture. Congregations seem to have welcomed new materials such as cast iron, artificial stone, and papier-mâché. Jews espoused no artistic theories favoring traditional or structurally expressive materials. Just as they had always moved to new havens, innovated in finance, and worked out new ways to survive, so now they adjusted to new technology. Synagogues at Berlin, Leipzig, and Budapest were only a few of the large synagogues designed in the 1850s that were precocious examples of the use of undisguised cast iron in religious buildings.[151] Iron was economical, and it made possible the thin structural members that gave synagogues convenient sight lines, glazed domes and skylights, and unusual visual effects. Cast iron, employed in many synagogues, could suggest changes in style; it would have been absurd to copy a thick-piered Romanesque building in cast iron, which was admired precisely because so little of it could hold so much weight, but slender Islamic columns could be imitated admirably in iron. In the twentieth century, the flexibility of reinforced concrete made possible the accordion-pleated synagogue at London-Dollis Hill and the angular, ribbed synagogue at Livorno.

Bratislava, Fig. 27
Budapest, Fig. 39
Berlin, Fig. 124

London, Figs. 248, 249
Livorno, Figs. 198, 199

Technological change did not always affect style. A synagogue building committee might feel that what was most dignified and safe from criticism was the style that had been used in the town for years. In towns large enough to have both orthodox and Reform synagogues, one congregation might purposely avoid the style used by the other, as in Košice during the 1920s, and in Frankfurt am Main at the start of the present century.

Rectilinear synagogues were built in almost every historic style. Central-plan synagogues could be Byzantine or Islamic, reflecting the frequency of central plans in the original buildings in those styles, but they might also be decorated with Gothic ribs and tracery, or with Egyptian and Mesopotamian motifs.[152] The only style absent from synagogues of large towns or culturally assimilated Jews was one that recalled the fortified or folk-style synagogues of eastern Europe; having left that culture behind, modern urban Jews wanted no reminders of it.

Fürth, Fig. 148

Some synagogues were pure in style, such as the Egyptian example at Canterbury or the *art nouveau* building by Hector Guimard in Paris. Most were

Canterbury, Fig. 241
Paris, Figs. 112, 113

eclectic, in an age when the German writer and architectural teacher Wilhelm Stier wrote that pluralism was the style of his time, and suited everyone.[153]

To be sure, the choice of style must have been almost accidental if the sponsors knew little about the visual arts. N. S. Joseph, the Jewish architect of the Central Synagogue in London, submitted both Moorish and Italian designs to the building committee in 1867. The committee secretary wrote in his minutes that one design was Byzantine, then crossed out that word and substituted *Moorish* for it. The building committee favored the Islamic mode as somehow "more adapted to an ecclesiastical building" meant for Jews.[154] The result of these confused notions was a basilica with iron gallery supports, a rib-vaulted ceiling, and restrained eclectic detail, much of it Moorish. Abraham Hirsch called his Romanesque design for Lyon "Byzantine" (reflecting imprecision in the books available to him in the 1850s) and based on the best "oriental," sources which he did not identify.[155] An unknown architect in Berlin in 1841, who designed a synagogue for a competition, produced a building in the neoclassical manner of Karl Friedrich Schinkel, with the identifying motto: "Im griechischen Style aufgefasst, Ist's Frage ob's für Juden passt" (Executed in the Greek style, questionable whether it suits Jews).[156] Stylistic labels were used at this time of unstable terminology for their ability to evoke a mixture of ideas—Eastern and Western in these cases—not because they were archaeologically descriptive.

The architectural decoration either depended upon the style chosen—an Islamic-style synagogue might have wall paintings imitating Near Eastern fabrics, for instance—or it could be entirely independent of the building, as it was when the synagogue was a plain box with little stylistic identity. A lion of Judah decorated many ark compositions, as did paired tablets of the Law. The shapes of six-pointed stars and seven-branched candlesticks, old and familiar symbols, even determined the shape of window openings, as at London-Dollis Hill (1937). Colored glass windows, known by the mid-nineteenth century, became increasingly acceptable, although some rabbis forbade them on the grounds that they imitated the customs of Christians. In 1904, Rabbi Immanuel Löw published a detailed account of the many windows in the lavish Neolog (moderate Reform) synagogue at Szeged,[157] and the elaborate decorative scheme for windows, doors, and other elements at Essen was published in 1913.[158] Thanks to these explanations, other congregations found it easy to plan their own decorative programs. Among the most popular subjects in windows were the palm branch and citron, which are used during the autumn Feast of Tabernacles, and the tablets of the Law.

London, Figs. 248, 249

Szeged, Fig. 57
Essen, Fig. 140

Many synagogues kept the inscriptions surviving from older times, or added others. Painted imitation stone or marble or brick became popular, and it can be seen in metropolitan synagogues such as Budapest-Dohány Street and in country towns such as Volpa. Landscapes and views of the Holy Land were painted on synagogues' walls and vaults in the mid-nineteenth-century at Lackenbach, Rechnitz, and Mikulov. Only rarely were figures included, as in Leon

L'vov, Fig. 86
Toledo, Fig. 185
Casale, Fig. 192
Budapest, Figs. 38, 39
Volpa, Figs. 94–97

Schenker's paintings in the Popper synagogue at Cracow/Kazimierz in the 1930s,[159] at Györ where there were landscapes and scenes from the stories of Elijah, Elisha, and Jeremiah,[160] and in Fritz Landauer's and Heinrich Lömpel's competition entry for Augsburg just before the First World War.[161]

An examination of the major synagogue styles will make these general observations more specific. The connotations of each help to explain why some Jews hoped for a style of their own, why others chose one or another historic style, and why style expressed ideas about Jewish aspirations.

EGYPTIAN

We may wonder why anyone ever wanted an Egyptian synagogue. Ancient Hebrews had been slaves in Egypt. Egyptian architecture served a pagan religion, and Jews were not supposed to imitate the practices of other religions, especially polytheistic ones. Egyptian architecture had been created for another climate and for construction in materials that were not all available in Canterbury, England, or Hobart, Tasmania, whose synagogues are the most thoroughly Egyptian in design.

Canterbury, Fig. 241

Nevertheless, Jews accepted Egyptian style occasionally between the 1790s and about 1850.[162] Sometimes they had no choice, because their patron, the local ruler, made the decision (as at Karlsruhe and Munich). Sometimes they had no knowledge of alternatives, but sometimes they concentrated on the good connotations of the style. It was famous for its strength and longevity, just as Judaism had to be strong to survive for so long. It was not used for European churches, so it could be appropriated by Jews who were then starting to look for means of self-expression as they rose in social and legal status. Then, too, after Napoleon's invasion of Egypt in 1798, Egyptian forms were in fashion for a time. Egyptian style then affected the synagogues of groups sympathetic to France, where the fashion for Egyptian design was most intense; the Compostellhof Reform temple at Frankfurt am Main was built ca. 1815 by assimilated Jews who valued the rights granted to them under temporary French rule. It was commonly believed that the Temple of Solomon looked more or less Egyptian, and some Temple reconstructions published during the 1820s and 1830s reflected this belief, although none was a direct source for known synagogue designs. While it was acknowledged that Solomon's Temple was built for Jews, not pagans, and that the builder was a Phoenician, Hiram of Tyre, it seems to have been conveniently assumed that the Jews and the Phoenicians were influenced by Egyptian architecture. The protest by a Jewish architect, A. Rosengarten, that there was as much difference between the Temple and a synagogue as between a synagogue and a church[163] did not convince all Jews or all Christians, even if they read what he had to say.

As Rosengarten realized, an exotic style could have unfortunate connotations. Anyone hostile to Jews could connect it to a group that still lived apart from the rest of the population in the early nineteenth century. It might be said that as ancient Egyptians had not developed the arch, dome, or flying buttress, the Jews had not progressed to the recognition of Jesus as the Messiah.

ROMANESQUE AND *RUNDBOGENSTIL*

Supplanting Egyptian and other ancient styles after about 1840[164] were styles that offered more ornamental variety and more subtle interpretive possibilities: Romanesque, Byzantine, and Islamic—sometimes mixed. Archaeological impurity, applied with imagination, made synagogues all the more evocative of an unusual mood, presumably one that was religious and specifically Jewish. If the building has round arches, elaborate small-scale ornament, muted and warm color, and colored glass windows that admit dim light, many people still think that the style is Jewish, even if it means equating murk and mystery with Judaism.

In Germany, where dynamic Jewish communities took the lead in building innovative synagogues, a style was popular from about 1830 onward that mixed elements of Romanesque, classical, and Renaissance architecture. *Rundbogenstil*—to use the common name for this round-arched style—was more Romanesque than anything else when it was applied to synagogues. It was used especially in the German- and French-speaking countries and in Great Britain, where the Gothic style represented the national heritage of Christian natives and the height of spirituality;[165] Gothic would not normally be used for the Jews there. Since it was generally assumed that Romanesque and Byzantine architects would have built Gothic churches if only they could have, their styles were considered inferior to Gothic. Just as the Jews had not progressed to an acceptance of Christianity, Romanesque and Byzantine architecture had not progressed as far as Gothic. Romanesque (or Byzantine—the terms were often confused) could therefore be applied to synagogues.[166]

Hamburg, Figs. 149, 150
London, Figs. 151, 152
Kassel, Fig. 164
Warsaw, Figs. 101, 102

Romanesque style was also believed to be suited to experimentation, for Romanesque architects were supposed to have tried to create buildings that came ever closer to being Gothic. Experimentation was certainly appropriate in synagogues, for no one knew how to design paradigms for them. Experiments also suited Protestant churches, for Protestantism had developed many new denominations lacking ancient architectural traditions. In England and Wales, both nonconformist chapels and synagogues may be eclectic Romanesque rather than Church of England Gothic. Romanesque was also considered a good style for Protestant building because it was less susceptible to mystical interpretation than Gothic. The same interest in a style that was religious but comparatively earthbound made the style acceptable for synagogues. To be sure, there are elaborate Protestant churches; there are striped or twin-towered Romanesque revival synagogues[167] that recall such recent Roman Catholic buildings as the Cathedral of Marseille; and the largest Romanesque synagogues looked like Rhenish cathedrals and impressive Parisian churches;[168] but these buildings were exceptions.

Paris, Figs. 110, 111
Brussels, Fig. 114
Hannover, Figs. 162, 163
Wrocław, Figs. 177, 178

There were practical advantages to using Romanesque style. It was often vaulted, as Gothic was, and vaults were thought to be good acoustically for preaching. Romanesque style better suited galleried buildings, and genuine Romanesque and Byzantine buildings often had them; galleries intersected and thus disfigured long Gothic windows, while Romanesque windows, usually smaller, could be arranged in tiers, thereby revealing on the exterior the presence of two storeys inside the building. Byzantine and Romanesque were styles associated with brick construction, and many synagogues were built of brick, which cost less than stone. Romanesque style was also used for such secular brick buildings as warehouses, railway tunnel entrances, and viaducts, so that if anyone wanted to deprecate the religious quality of a Jewish building he would have other round-arched brick buildings with which to compare the synagogue. More affirmatively, Jews could relate a Romanesque brick synagogue to well-built and functional secular architecture.

Most of all, Romanesque style provided an image for synagogues that suited Jews as well as Christians who held varying opinions of Jews. Most Jews did not want to be mistaken for Christians, but they did want equal rights and opportunities. They wanted their religion recognized as something other than a mysterious practice in an old foreign tongue. The Romanesque style, neighbor to Gothic, comparable but independent, represented the status that many Jews sought for themselves. Jews and Christians agreed that the style was serious and clear and simple and restful; to Jews who were accused of being vulgar or socially maladroit, this evaluation made Romanesque especially welcome. Jews could emphasize these connotations when others spoke of Romanesque as obscure and stolid, or as representing the last traces of pagan design, which Gothic eradicated. Romanesque style was also evidence of the Jews' long residence in Europe. Far from being foreigners, Jews had lived in the Rhineland, in Rome, and in southern France from the time of the Roman imperial conquests. Romanesque was a medieval European style; it could identify its users as Europeans rather than exotic easterners.[169]

Worms, Figs. 168, 170, 171

Architects could revive regional variations of Romanesque to show the appropriateness of the style in a particular country or district. There was even a Romanesque synagogue still standing in Worms until 1938, and in Britain and Rome a number of Romanesque houses remain which used to be identified as former synagogues.[170] If the Jews used Romanesque styles in their synagogues, it would show their desire to identify themselves with the majority culture and local history—to become "Germans of the Jewish religion," Belgians of the "Mosaic persuasion"—in short, to become fellow citizens. Several Jewish architects of the mid-nineteenth century (Rosengarten, Oppler, Hirsch) recommended and built Romanesque synagogues, while others (Aldrophe, L. Levy, and Wolffenstein) built them later.[171]

BYZANTINE

To many Christian Europeans, Jews remained Middle Eastern foreigners. Eastern Mediterranean architecture, whether Byzantine or Ottoman, was famous for exotic domed forms which could characterize Jewish buildings, too, as Eastern. As there were examples of Byzantine architecture at Venice and Ravenna, and offshoots of it in Romanesque architecture in western France, it had a legitimate western European position also. It shared with native Romanesque such characteristics as thick exterior walls, round arches, and certain decorative motifs, so that Byzantine architecture could be considered a kind of Eastern (that is, Jewish) Romanesque, useful if Christians thought it proper to temper the visual patriotism of Jews.[172] Sighing in print, the Jewish artist Leo Pinkhof explained to readers of the Dutch Jewish weekly *De Vrijdagavond* why the Christian architect of the Groningen synagogue of 1906 had made it look so odd: "Jewish is eastern. Byzantine is also eastern. Thus, Byzantine style in synagogues . . . and in the crypt under the apse, instead of the tomb of one or another saint, a central heating system under the ark."[173]

One popular Byzantine plan was the shallow-armed Greek cross with a dome or cupola in the center.[174] When the eastern arm was shallow, it did not look like the space for a priest. Seats filled part of the floor under the dome—if the dome was a broad one—and there were seats in the arms of the cross both at ground level and in the galleries. The plan provided a compact space in which the congregation could be concentrated. It thereby avoided some faults of the long-naved galleried basilicas, which stressed the east-west axis and culminating ark, and which had dozens of rows of worshippers looking at the backs of the heads in front of them. The domed central plan brought people into visual contact with each other, as well as with the bimah and ark. If the bimah remained in the center, the dome above it emphasized its centrality and the reader knew that he was literally in the center of his congregation. (If the bimah moved eastward, however, there was nothing special under the great dome.) Domes and cupolas are acoustically unreliable; moreover, they are costly and require suitably broad building lots. All the same, they allowed the Jews to make a dramatic impact on a city skyline, while avoiding the towers with which Christian churches called attention to themselves. Domes also imparted grandeur and amplitude to the interior, suiting the congregations' self-image during the period of Jewish social and economic improvement.[175]

London, Fig. 152
Florence, Figs. 193, 194
Trieste, Figs. 210–213

Jews themselves sometimes chose to show both patriotism (by using Romanesque) and distinctiveness (by using Byzantine elements), especially when they saw their political, social, and economic status improving so steadily that revealing their differences in religion alone would not hurt them. Abraham Hirsch, the Jewish architect of the Lyon synagogue of 1864, wrote that he had used elements of Byzantine architecture to reconcile the Eastern origin of the religion with a modern plan and modern materials.[176] When *Der Architekt* published Ludwig Paffendorf's unexecuted design for the Düsseldorf synagogue, the text explained that the style mixing "Syrian" (that is, early Christian and Byzantine) and Romanesque had been chosen because Syrian had influenced Romanesque;[177] the writer knew that his readers would add "just as Eastern Jewry had an impact on the West." As it happens, the building was Byzantine in overall form, but its details came from no farther east than the Viennese modernist circle of Otto Wagner. This was appropriate, according to the text, because Jews kept up to date and their buildings should not be old-fashioned. These interpretations of Byzantine style show contemporary ideas about the historical and current position of Jews in society: old and Eastern, or up to date, but not comfortably rooted in the history of generations of Christian Europeans in the West.

MOORISH-ISLAMIC

Antwerp, Fig. 115

Budapest, Fig. 39

Budapest, Fig. 38

Bucharest, Fig. 34
Vienna, Fig. 64
Stockholm, Fig. 237

Islamic forms, also associated with the Middle East, were used more often than Byzantine designs in synagogue architecture. Many synagogues had horseshoe arches that could be round or pointed, cusped or smooth.[178] There were polychromed wall patterns taken from engravings of mosques or palaces.[179] Inscriptions could be integrated with the ornament, which avoided all figural representation. Slender cast-iron piers imitated the delicate supports of the Alhambra and, being slender, they did not obstruct sight lines. A bulbous dome might rise over the ark, or over turrets that resembled minarets.[180] If a crenellated horizontal cornice rose higher in the center than on the sides of a facade[181] it evoked not only reconstructions of Solomon's Temple but also mosque or Islamic palace facades and the porch and wall composition in the Patio of the Lions at the Alhambra. In some of the Islamic-style synagogues, sniffed the Jewish architect A. Rosengarten, "the crescent alone is wanting at the summit."[182]

Dresden, Fig. 130

Islamic features first appeared conspicuously in a synagogue in Germany in 1832, at the Ingenheim synagogue by Friedrich von Gärtner. It was followed immediately thereafter by two synagogues designed by August von Voit of Munich.[183] Islamic styles had already been used in country villas and places of amusement, but synagogue architects used them for their Eastern connotations, not to trivialize their clients' houses of worship. In 1838–40, Gottfried Semper designed the interior of the Dresden synagogue, using thin piers and details taken from illustrations of the Alhambra. His design became well known upon its publication in the *Allgemeine Bauzeitung* in 1847, and its Moorish interior decoration was taken up in scores of synagogues later.[184]

By the 1850s, Islamic styles had become acceptable alternatives to classical or Romanesque styles in synagogue architecture.[185] The exotic details of the Leipzig synagogue, built in 1855 by Otto Simonson, a Jewish architect, were especially well known to Jews, as Jewish merchants from many countries attended the city's famous trade fair; in addition, six lithographs of the building were published. Pictures of several other synagogues with what everyone called Moorish forms appeared in the architectural and lay press and in prints.

The prestige of Semper, Ludwig von Förster, and Ernst Zwirner,[186] all of whom designed such synagogues, made the style increasingly popular.

These Christian architects found artistic bonds between ancient Jewish architecture and Islamic architecture. Förster said that the two columns named Jakhin and Boaz that stood in front of Solomon's Temple had lived on in the form of minarets; that is why he added slim towers to the synagogues he designed.[187] A Reform temple at Odessa was built in "Arabian" style in 1859, to imitate the Temple of Solomon as closely as an unpretentious building could do.[188] It did not matter that the connections between Temple and synagogue were based on fantasy, for buildings other than synagogues have also been inspired by creative mistakes.

Other nineteenth-century writers believed that the pointed arches of Islamic buildings had influenced the development of Gothic architecture. From this perspective, Islamic architecture was an Eastern relative of Gothic, and therefore praiseworthy.[189] It could be applied to synagogue architecture because it was Eastern, as Jews were supposed to be, and it was not too inferior to Gothic. One cannot imagine Zwirner, who had directed the completion of Cologne's Gothic cathedral, designing a synagogue in the cathedral's style, but he could use the Eastern, Jewish, form of Gothic for the synagogue. The colorful surfaces of Islamic buildings also appealed to mid-nineteenth-century taste just at the time when many new, large synagogues were going up. The use of an uncommon style allowed room for the display of artistic imagination. In their search for originality and a new national style, such brilliant American architects as Louis Sullivan and Frank Lloyd Wright later used exotic ornament; something of the same desire for group expression must have been present in connection with Moorish synagogue architecture.

The use of style to define nationality can be seen in government-sponsored architecture in the colonies ruled by imperial European countries in the nineteenth century. It is instructive to compare the use of Eastern elements in synagogues with their use in British buildings in India during the second half of the nineteenth century. In the case of synagogues, Western Christians devised an Eastern style for newly visible and respectable people who had lived for centuries in Europe, whereas in India, the Western Christian conquerors eventually tried to approach a clearly impressive Eastern heritage which they had earlier ignored or contemned. In both cases, however, the dominant group, not understanding the history and cultural variety of the subject group, searched for a mix of East and West to offer people who might have wanted something else if given their own choice. The dominant group always found the Eastern elements exotic, just as the Jews and Indians seemed to be. The frequently awkward results of both domestic and foreign colonial design show the difficulty of speaking fluently an unfamiliar language still in the process of formation.[190]

Not all the connotations of Islamic style, then, were good ones. Nationalistic anti-Semites promoted a suspiciously foreign and Eastern image of Jews, which

Islamic styles reinforced in the popular mind. More sophisticated anti-Semites said that aspects of Islamic architecture reflected Jewish character; Islamic architecture was thought not to be architectonically rational—as Gothic was—but merely superficially decorative. Likewise, Jews were supposed to lack true reason and an understanding of (Christian) truth. Islamic decoration was said to show abstraction from nature and limited intellectual range. It was said to show an arbitrary mix of things that are contradictory. Those ignorant of serious Talmudic study thought of Jewish scholarship in similar terms. On a mundane level, Jews were accused of having their minds on earthly display and not on spiritual matters; similarly, Islamic architecture was considered seductive but not uplifting.[191]

Bratislava, Figs. 25, 26
Berlin, Fig. 122
Turin, Fig. 216

The Jews themselves often disagreed about the appropriateness of this style. Generally speaking, Jews who felt secure and optimistic in their European towns thought it good to develop a distinctive architectural style. As long as their position was improving—as it was everywhere before the mid-1870s—they found that looking different, even exotic, was a harmless way of appearing proud of their religious difference. A newspaper account of the consecration of the Odessa Reform temple made special note of the respectable position held by the "numerous and wealthy Jewish community of that commercial emporium" in contrast to the squalor and misery of Jews in Galicia and Volhynia.[192] In general, Jews and their buildings were increasingly acceptable in society. Had not Sir Walter Scott made the Jewish Rebecca a more impressive heroine in *Ivanhoe* than the pallid Christian Rowena?

Jews who had a comfortable self-image found suitable an Eastern style that was not used in European church architecture. The orthodox were especially anxious to avoid any suggestion of religious assimilation to Christianity, which was more likely than Islam to tempt European Jews from their ancestral faith. The use of secular Islamic buildings as prototypes suited their purposes well. Comfortably assimilated Jews, far removed from ghettoes and from dealing in old clothes, could dismiss any association of Islamic style with Levantine hagglers. Proponents of Islamic styles pointed out that Judaism had arisen in the Holy Land, where Jewish architectural forms might have influenced the later Islamic ones in that area; Förster propounded this idea, too. Orthodox prayers expressed the hope of returning to the Holy Land. Later, Zionists proposed building a Jewish state there. Sephardic Jews could use Moorish style to allude to their own history in the Mediterranean, a heritage which they considered far more distinguished than that of Ashkenazic Jews. The Viennese Turkish congregation made much of their ties to the Pasha, evidently in an effort to be seen as unrelated to the Galician Hasids and poor *shtetl* émigrés who were flocking to Vienna when the Turkish congregation built its Moorish-style synagogue.[193] The Castello di Sammezano in Tuscany, owned for three centuries by descendants of a Portuguese Jew who had been converted by a cardinal, was redecorated by later owners in the Moorish style taken from Spanish models. Perhaps alluding to the exceptional history of the former owners, the rooms look much like the interior of the synagogue at Florence of 1874–82. The style chosen seems to reinforce the exotic, Jewish, and Islamic associations.[194] The use of Moorish style here celebrates the uniqueness of the place. Similarly, Jews who wanted to show that they were culturally separate but otherwise equal to their fellow citizens built Moorish synagogues.

Florence, Fig. 194

Other Jews protested. They probably noticed that when it came to marriage, Ivanhoe chose Rowena, not the unusual Jewish girl. They pointed out that Islamic architecture had developed too late to reveal anything about the architecture of ancient Judaism. Others noted that Christianity, too, originated in the East but only Jews worshipped in buildings which seemed not to have arisen on European soil. At Bad Nauheim in 1865, when synagogue plans were submitted to the building police supervisor, he politely asked the Jews to alter the Gothic windows and consider using a style suited to their religion, such as Moorish, so that the synagogue would not look like a Christian building.[195] Siegfried Kusnitzky, a Jewish architect in Frankfurt, wrote in 1881 to his potential clients in Gdańsk, asking rhetorically, "What has the Jewish religion to do with the Moorish and Byzantine style? Why do specifically Jewish houses of worship have to present themselves as so extraordinarily fantastic?"[196] In eastern European lands that had been ruled by the Turks, identifying Judaism with Islam cannot have been entirely complimentary. In all strongly nationalistic countries, especially those with state churches, there were political and social dangers in store for Jews if they were set apart.

Another disadvantage of an Eastern style was its association with theaters and other places of amusement, from the Prince Regent's "Indian" Royal Pavilion at Brighton to the Vigadó in Budapest. When a Jewish observer wanted to criticize the redecorated synagogue in rue Notre Dame de Nazareth, in Paris, he likened it to a "café-concert Alcázar."[197] Could a style used in buildings for common entertainment be suited to a place of worship? If Christians did not think so, why should Jews have to pray in such buildings?

Perhaps because of these problems, the Moorish mode seems to have been used more often for synagogue interiors than for exteriors. Moreover, interior views and details were more frequent in architectural publications about Islamic buildings, and they could be adopted easily. Islamic buildings are often plain outside and lavish inside; this suited Jews who preferred to present a laconic impression to the Christian public and to reserve their enthusiasm for the special "Eastern" private space indoors. Islamic styling showed that some Jews felt secure enough to proclaim their difference from the Christian majority by using Moorish forms outside, but the more frequent use indoors suggests that the Jewish proclamations were sometimes made *sotto voce.*

Dresden, Figs. 129, 130
Endingen, Figs. 136, 137
Essen, Figs. 139, 140
Frankfurt, Figs. 144, 145

Remarkable as it may seem at first, Moorish-style synagogues did not imitate the four medieval synagogues that had survived in Spain. The Spanish buildings interested nineteenth-century Jews for their inscriptions alone. Jews connected these buildings with their own synagogues only late in the century, and never imitated them even then.[198] Although the Córdoba and Seville synagogues were illustrated in a publication of 1837, and the two in Toledo were published in 1842,[199] synagogue building committees lacked ready access to these books. Either the buildings were decrepit, or they had been made into churches after the expulsion of Jews from Spain in 1492. The plans were unrelated to nineteenth-century plans. The Spanish aisled basilicas lacked integral galleries, the women's sections being in annexes outside the prayer hall. The Córdoba synagogue was a tiny box. Also, the ornament in Spain was mainly of stucco relief which would have been costly and hard to imitate well; as few details of it were available, architects found it more convenient to study the well-published Alhambra. Spain itself was a country with a poor standing among Jews, for Spanish Christians had cut short the flowering of Jewish medieval scholarship by persecution, subsequent expulsion in 1492, and the later torture and burning of people thought to be secret Jews. There were no acknowledged Jews in nineteenth-century Spain. Moreover, the Spanish-Portuguese Jews in Europe were often visibly anxious to keep their distance from other Jews, whom they treated like poor, unworthy distant relatives. Ashkenazic Jews had no reason to flatter the Sephardic Jews by imitating their medieval buildings. Those Sephardic Jews who traced their ancestry to Turkey rather than to Spain would have had no reason to use the Spanish architectural forms and patterns, or to justify their choice of style by reference to Iberian examples. Even the Jewish architect of the Sephardic synagogue in Manchester said that his Moorish building was based on the Alhambra,[200] but said nothing about the glories of a Jewish golden age in medieval Spain. For Christians who wanted to keep Jews out of the mainstream of society, stressing the mysterious Middle Eastern aspects of Moorish style suited their purposes better than references to intellectual distinction in European Spain. It seems to have been a well-intentioned Christian art critic in Russia, V. V. Stassov, who first connected the Moorish style of Spanish medieval synagogues to Moorish style in modern synagogues.[201] His privileged Russian Jewish readers were in terms of their status and cultivation much like the élite court Jews of Spain who sponsored synagogues, and his idea took hold among them, although no Moorish synagogues in Russia actually resembled the Spanish examples.

Toledo, Figs. 180–185

Leningrad, Figs. 88, 89

GOTHIC

A far less common alternative was the Gothic synagogue. A Gothic cathedral plan would have made no sense for the Jews, who did not need processional aisles and chapels, and who wanted to stress the bipolar tension between bimah and ark rather than the east end alone. But a simpler Gothic building such as a chapel or a church without a transept could serve as a synagogue model. This actually occurred, although seldom. More often, a few Gothic details were added to a synagogue.

The entrance portal of the Bordeaux synagogue has pointed arches, and the side door tympana have applied Gothic tracery. The Roonstrasse synagogue at Cologne has flying buttresses and a rose window of transitional Romanesque-Gothic form. The Sheffield-North Church Street synagogue of 1871–72 was considered to be Gothic[202] and the synagogue at Łódź-Spacerowej[203] had Gothic tracery in the apse. Most of the Gothic elements in European synagogues were merely pointed window and arch frames, bits of tracery, and railings.[204] Some of the pointed openings may have been thought of as Islamic rather than Gothic, because pointed arches are known also in Islamic architecture; this may have been the reference intended at Leningrad. *Leningrad, Figs. 88, 89*

From the 1830s to the early 1850s, when ideas about the meaning of styles were still being formulated, and when the legal position of Jews was improving rapidly, synagogue interiors at Fürth, Regensburg, and Prague-Altschul were made to look Gothic.[205] The Jews of Fürth (in 1831) and Prague (in 1837), who had long lived in these towns, thus emphasized that their roots in local soil were as deep as those of their Christian neighbors. The synagogue style implied that the religious sentiments of both faiths were comparable; not surprisingly, the synagogues received the Gothic decorations under assimilated Reform administrations. At Regensburg, where everyone concerned with the synagogue must have known the two prints by Albrecht Altdorfer showing the town's medieval synagogue (see Fig. 4), it was unnecessary to point out the Jews' medieval heritage. The new synagogue could be a converted chapel in an up-to-date Gothic revival style; there was no need to imitate the medieval two-naved building seen in Altdorfer's prints. That Jewish overtures of fraternity were reciprocated at this period of optimism is apparent from news reports in 1851 that prominent Christian gentlemen at Krefeld had contributed to the building fund of the (classical-Renaissance) synagogue which was completed there in 1853.[206]

Fürth, Fig. 148

In a later generation, Gothic synagogues seem to have been designed as defensive statements by Jews who were then targets of racial and political anti-Semitism. Western European cities and seaports were flooded with wretched Jews fleeing from starvation, economic restrictions, and pogroms in the east; these refugees did nothing to enhance the social status of the Jews already living in western cities. Such populists as Georg Schoenerer and Karl Lueger in Vienna were gaining political power with the help of anti-Semitic rhetoric. At this period, Max Fleischer, the Jewish architect of three Gothic synagogues in Vienna and one in České Budějovice, addressed his fellow architects, most of whom were Christian. Understandably avoiding any reference to contemporary politics, he allowed history to explain his work: synagogues had always followed prevailing architectural styles. Jews had used Gothic designs in the Gothic era, so that modern Jews could revive this style as legitimately as Christians could. He was simply using a style associated with profound religious feeling. Moreover, he had managed to achieve a monumental effect by using this style, even with economical materials.[207] The insistent tone of this lecture was one of justification rather than easy discourse.

České Budějovice, Figs. 4[illegible] 45

At Lüneburg in 1892–94, *Stadtbaumeister* Kampf repeated Fleischer's arguments[208] and designed a brick synagogue in the north German Gothic manner. The local style and materials helped the Jews to integrate in a city where they had only recently been allowed to live. The Bismarckstrasse synagogue in Berlin, designed by E. George and built in 1897, was another north German brick Gothic building that carried the message of affiliation with German culture.[209] The Kaiser himself promoted certain styles as being desirably national—northern brick Gothic and Rhenish Romanesque among them—and Jews in Lüneburg and Berlin responded to his exhortations.

Rabbi Max Grünwald, who studied synagogue buildings and Jewish art, agreed that Gothic was part of the Jews' heritage and could convey deep religious feelings. He added that the Gothic style was associated with the growing independence of the medieval bourgeoisie from the Church, a matter presumably to be remembered by others in later ages who stood outside the Church. By noting that the pointed arch was of Eastern derivation, he adroitly associated Gothic arches more with Eastern Jews who had come west than with Christians who had merely received and not developed this arch.[210]

At Dortmund, the Jews said that the synagogue's Gothic ornament showed their desire to take into account the Gothic style of the neighboring post office. The underlying reason for the synagogue's style was expressed in the dedication sermon: The building showed that the Jews were like their fellow citizens.[211] As it happened, the synagogue and post office barely resembled each other, revealing that the Jews and Christians of Dortmund were farther apart than the sermon claimed. At Krefeld, where the Jews thought of themselves as Germans of the Jewish faith, and where Zionism and Jewish ethnic identification had little appeal, the community sponsored, from 1900 to 1902, a late-Gothic early-Renaissance replacement for the Gothic synagogue of 1851–53. Johann Reck, a Christian, concealed an oriental interior within the traceried exterior. The congregation here, as at Dresden, accepted their difference from the surrounding society when they were together indoors, but stressed their similarity to other Germans outside.[212]

It is less clear why Alfred Grotte, a Jewish architect and writer about synagogue architecture, used late-Gothic style when he remodeled the Meisel Synagogue at Prague in 1893–1905. As the genuine Gothic Altneuschul and Pinkas synagogues stood in the same neighborhood, he did not need to stress the long history of Jews in Prague, but his elaborate version of the style, recalling that of the late-Gothic churches of the city, may have been meant to reaffirm the Jews' local ties.[213] Perhaps, too, he thought that the Renaissance style of the Meisel Synagogue was insufficiently religious-looking, and agreed with Fleischer that Gothic was more spiritually elevating.

Gothic synagogues elsewhere were built apparently because congregations and architects liked their appearance and spiritual connotations, not because they wanted to make public statements about politics and integration. In Budapest, Sándor Fellner designed a Gothic interior for the Ujlak synagogue

(1888), which was concealed from the street behind a round-arched apartment house facade.[214] The Haarlem synagogue interior was remodeled in 1896 with Gothic forms; Jews in the Netherlands experienced less discrimination or personal danger than did Jews in central and eastern Europe, and the Dutch Jews seem to have felt at ease using Gothic details.[215] Anti-Semitic violence was little known in France and England, but Jews there rarely used Gothic designs. This was probably because French and English Christians thought that they had invented the style, and used it in their state churches.

LATE-NINETEENTH-CENTURY STYLES

While French, British, and Belgian synagogues continued to use Romanesque styles much of the time, several other tendencies became evident in synagogue design, especially in central and eastern Europe.

German-speaking countries. In the German-speaking lands, newly reorganized after 1867 in Austria-Hungary, and newly organized and imperialist after 1871 in Germany, the Jews were less secure, their status constantly threatened by ethnic-nationalist currents that made little place for them, and by the streams of poor Jews emigrating from Austrian Galicia, the Russian areas,[216] and small towns generally. Moreover, after the economic crisis of 1873, Jews became the target of the racial anti-Semitism which offered a simple outlet for the distress of credulous and desperate Christians. No longer able to despise urbanized Jews for speaking poor German, living apart in crowded quarters, and dealing in second-hand goods, anti-Semites had to find other grounds for excluding their well-educated and culturally assimilated fellow citizens. They found these in racial anti-Semitism which imputed to all Jews intrinsic characteristics which no amount of cultural integration could erase.[217] In such circumstances, some central European Jews shied away from oriental designs which made their difference obvious, and began to build Gothic synagogues again. German Jews also built in the Rhenish Romanesque style, which they knew the Kaiser admired for its nationalistic connotations. These massive synagogues, made of weighty blocks lying heavily on the ground, may be read as stubborn confirmations of the Jews' rights to citizenship and residence; Jews were not to be treated like Eastern wanderers without roots, for they had lived in the Rhineland since late Roman imperial times.[218] The buildings were not, of course, always accepted in the spirit in which they were built. As early as 1872, when a precursor of the late-nineteenth-century Romanesque synagogues was erected at Wroclaw by the Jewish architect Edwin Oppler, critics said that it was odd to see a Jewish building designed in a Christian style, and that local religious architecture was so seldom Romanesque that the synagogue looked exotic (meaning Jewish) anyway.[219]

České Budějovice, Figs. 43–45

Wroclaw, Figs. 177, 178

In Austria-Hungary, many synagogues erected before the 1880s took their inspiration from Förster's synagogue of 1853–58 in Vienna, the leading metropolitan synagogue, which was conveniently available for copying in the pages

Vienna, Figs. 64, 65
Bucharest, Fig. 35

of Förster's own *Allgemeine Bauzeitung.*[220] Some synagogue designers created twin-tower facades but rarely went farther toward assimilation with church architecture. With rare exceptions, they did not imitate the twin-towered Dohány Street synagogue in Budapest, which Förster had also designed, because it probably seemed too expensive to copy; it was also less completely published, the *Allgemeine Bauzeitung* having ignored it when it was not finished to Förster's design.

Budapest, Figs. 38, 39

After 1896, when Judaism was placed legally on a par with Christianity in Hungary, and when Jewish optimism and Magyarization increased as well, there was an efflorescence of lavish, wildly eclectic synagogue designs. The work of Lipót Baumhorn is central to this trend. Ten years after his rather sober striped oblong synagogue of 1890 at Esztergom, his Szeged synagogue of 1900–1903 was a surprising contrast; it had a central cupola rising high over a Greek-cross plan, mixed Gothic, Moorish, and Romanesque ornament, busy surfaces, and a pinnacled skyline. Competition drawings by other architects for this project were almost as opulent. Synagogues by Baumhorn and others at Braşov, Szolnok, Târgu Mures, Salgótarján, and Subotica were built in the same mode. Perhaps they were meant to celebrate the differences between these provinces of the empire and Vienna itself. Perhaps the designers hoped that by combining stylistic features from many countries and all ages they could produce something Jewish—international, appearing in all periods of European and Middle Eastern history, and not conventionally Christian. In their eclecticism and joyous abundance, the synagogues are related to such secular buildings as theaters and apartment houses, but not to churches; in this respect, their style may have satisfied Christians who wanted Jews kept at arm's length as well as Jews who did not want to imitate church architecture.

Szeged, Figs. 56, 57

Rome, Fig. 205
Trieste, Fig. 210

Poland and adjacent areas. In Poland and the Russian borderlands, the architecturally distinctive new synagogues of the nineteenth century were generally financed by the new class of industrial entrepreneurs who had developed industries such as textiles (Łódż), tobacco, tanning, and milling (Vilnius), lumber (Minsk), and railroads (Moscow). This class stood apart from Christians because of religious differences and consequent social standing. It stood apart from other Jews because the rich enjoyed privileges accorded to useful businessmen, and because most other Jews were extremely poor and subject to persecution. The entrepreneurs, however, were not afraid to be known as both Jewish and prosperous, and they paid for comparatively large eclectic-style synagogues that emphasized Moorish features. These buildings looked different from the humble *shuls* of the masses and from churches as well. Horseshoe arches, striped surfaces, bulbous cupolas, semi-Gothic tracery, Romanesque columns, and Lombard bands were known in Russian and provincial Byzantine architecture of eastern Europe; now they were combined in a new building type. From Rumania to Latvia, Silesia to Russia, the provincial eclectic synagogue was more the rule than the exception for synagogues

Leningrad, Figs. 88, 89

Bucharest, Figs. 34, 35

erected by the local Jewish magnates. Communities throughout eastern and east-central Europe sponsored comparable synagogues, such as that of Prague-Královské Vinohrady, while the tall towers crowned by bulbous cupolas at Mysłowice in Upper Silesia made the polychromed building look like a Moorish church![221] The classical styles on the exterior of the Moscow and Warsaw-Tłomacka Street synagogues are among the few exceptions.

Moscow, Fig. 90
Warsaw, Figs. 98, 100

Italy. After 1870, Italian unification and the emancipation of the Jews made conspicuous synagogues possible there, too. In gratitude for their emancipation,[222] the Jews of Turin and Florence determined to erect synagogues that would embellish these first two capitals of the new Italy. Perhaps they also wished to make the synagogues more inspiring in a period of declining Jewish worship[223] and of youthful temptation to convert in order to succeed in society. This had earlier been of concern in Vienna, Berlin, and elsewhere. In Turin, the Jewish leaders asked Alessandro Antonelli, a leading engineer, to design a synagogue which became the tallest building in Italy (although by the time it was finished it was no longer a synagogue). In Milan, Luca Beltrami, one of the city's most prominent architects, received the synagogue commission. In Rome, the Jews were able to erect a new building in a commanding position near the newly embanked Tiber.

Florence, Figs. 193, 194
Turin, Figs. 214, 215
Milan, Fig. 200
Rome, Fig. 206

Each of these synagogues looked different, reflecting the local patriotism of the traditional regions of Italy, although not any traditional local style. At Milan, Beltrami designed a striped medieval church, probably inspired by central European assimilative synagogue designs. In Florence, Treves, Falcini, and Micheli designed a Byzantine domed building with golden Islamic surface ornament, borrowing ideas from transalpine facades and domed central plan buildings but clarifying and monumentalizing them for the unusually open and conspicuous site. For the Roman synagogue, Armanni & Costa produced a central-plan, compact, rectilinear structure with a moderately high cupola, all in a so-called Babylonian style. Antonelli at Turin was the most original; he designed a square building framed with Renaissance columns and surmounted by a four-sided parabolic cupola and a spire. These synagogues and others express the Jews' confidence in their new condition in Italy and their attachment to distinctive cities. Their styles, unusual in Italy, show that the Jews felt able to announce their differences from the Roman Catholic majority, even when racial anti-Semitism had infected other countries.

Milan, Fig. 200
Florence, Figs. 193, 194
Rome, Figs. 206, 207
Turin, Figs. 214, 215

EARLY-TWENTIETH-CENTURY STYLES

In the early twentieth century, while many congregations remained architecturally conservative, some tried to adapt their synagogues to modern conditions. If approaching the future meant clearing away outmoded aspects of the past, architects could simplify older architectural forms and concentrate on basic elements of geometry, massing, textures, and contrasts of materials. A good many synagogues of the early twentieth century were compact and massive buildings of impressive monumentality, simplifying forms known in Byzantine and Romanesque architecture, especially domed central plans, and contrasts of curves against rectilinear blocks. They differed from early synagogues in that the surfaces were simpler and the massive blocks were compacted rather than independently articulated. The interest in interpenetrating parts connects these geometric and heavy buildings to ideas of the *art nouveau*. Examples of this stylistic tendency were German synagogues at Augsburg and Essen-Steelerstrasse, and Austro-Hungarian synagogues at Sarajevo-Sephardic, Trieste, and Trenčin. Several of them look like Westernized versions of Hagia Sophia or other Byzantine and Islamic buildings in Istanbul. Whether or not the architects meant to characterize the Jews as Eastern, the perfume of the orient still clung to these synagogues. Those at Bamberg, Görlitz, Nijmegen, and several designs for the Offenbach competition of 1912, had compactly clustered block-like parts, with prominent heavy towers. In these buildings, vertical lines, hardly interrupted by horizontal elements, led the observer's eye to the tower. Unification and smoothness seem to have been the architects' general goals.[224]

Essen, Figs. 138–140
Frankfurt, Figs. 144, 145
Trieste, Figs. 212, 213

Other synagogue architects used aspects of the classical heritage in combination with these cleaner forms and monumental simplifications, representing a return to elemental shapes and original styles (Fig. 16). Association with fundamental sources and forms also corresponded to Judaism's position as the foundation of Christianity. Cubic and classical elements placed the synagogue within a general European cultural tradition. By taking up forms sanctified by

Figure 16. Offenbach, 1913–16, exterior in 1981.

the ancients, by the architects of Napoleon (who was to some extent a liberator of the Jews), and by Karl Friedrich Schinkel—forms which contemporary architects were reviving in secular and Christian architecture—Jews projected an image of themselves as indigenous and cultivated. Because the classical heritage was part of French and English national history, and was regarded as a third "German" style along with Rhenish Romanesque and northern brick Gothic, classicism absolved Jews from charges of mere secularism and internationalism. Classical revival provided a safe umbrella under which Jews could take shelter from the storms of anti-Semitism.

Massive synagogues at Mainz, Offenbach, Bad Wildungen, Berlin-Kottbuser Ufer, and the exterior of the Frankfurt-Westend synagogue exemplify this tendency.[225] They were all built for assimilated Jews who were inclined to think about decorum and reason rather than the mysteries of the Kabbalah or spontaneous enthusiasm in religion. E. Hiller, an architect, wrote in 1906 that the synagogues needed not mysterious atmosphere but rather restful and sober lines, a sense of enclosure and heaviness, and yet adequate width—all giving a feeling of permanence possible in the enlightened countries of the modern world.[226] Nevertheless, the stripped-classical exterior of the Frankfurt-Westend Reform synagogue hid Egyptian and Assyrian details within.[227] The congregation, like others which tried to be purely German and fully Jewish, accepted this split between their public and private faces.

Synagogues in Germany at Mainz, Offenbach, and Bad Wildungen were based on a circular plan, which had been uncommon before the late nineteenth century. The round synagogue combined elemental purity of form—unfettered by history or geography—with an expression of unity that is part of Jewish communal worship. The circular form can also be interpreted as a symbol of universality and an allusion to the omnipresent Lord.

Even in synagogues that clung more closely to Romanesque and eclectic models, architects gradually eliminated "excessive" detail. We see this clearly in the synagogues at Antwerp. While Joseph Hertogs had created an elaborate eclectic main community synagogue there in 1891–93, Joseph DeLange's and Jules Hofman's synagogues of 1910–29 grew ever more simple.[228] British, German, and Dutch synagogue architects also gradually toned down their enthusiasm for inventive combinations of forms and styles. Some turned to the *art nouveau* or *Jugendstil* in search of a style that had fewer historical associations.

Antwerp, Figs. 115, 116

Cologne, Fig. 128
Paris, Figs. 112, 113

At this time, synagogue—and church—decorations often became merely ornamental, lacking conviction and expressive power. They contrasted with the unaffected, joyous abundance of older folk art decorations, with their richness of association in communities where Jewish rather than secular culture dominated. Among the exceptionally good examples of synagogue decoration were windows that Johan Thorn Prikker, a Christian artist, designed for the Krefeld synagogue of 1902.[229] His geometric abstractions of the ark and *mizrah* and the bold strength of his six-pointed stars dramatically heightened the worshipper's attention and emphasized the Torah and Holy Land. They did not, however, have anything to do with the architecture of the building, which had extremely elaborate late-Gothic detail applied to an earlier and simpler round-arched building.

1914 to 1933

During the First World War, the Jews were the object of especially vicious excesses. Between 1914 and 1918, combatants on both sides destroyed synagogues both humble and elaborate; the synagogue of the Hasidic leader at Belz is an example of the latter.[230] In 1914, Jews were attacked in the Staszów synagogue, where eleven of them were hanged. German soldiers kept horses in the synagogue at Pruszków, and in 1915 German soldiers slaughtered pigs in the synagogue of Snekshni.[231]

In the war years, synagogues as well as Christian chapels were set up in prisoner-of-war camps and military bases, as at Döberitz, or in refugee camps, such as those of Mikulov and Bruck an der Leitha. They were simple and small, to contain a limited population. The Döberitz building looked like a tiny chapel with a low turret; at Bruck and Mikulov the synagogues were made of wood covered by creosote but with such sensitivity to tradition that they must have reminded their users of the places of worship in their native Galicia.

Bruck, Figs. 31–33

Even after the Revolution, the condition of Jews and their synagogues in Russia remained difficult. In 1919 and 1920, reports reached the West that at Fastov in the Ukraine, soldiers poured naphtha on synagogues, and then set them aflame while they were full of people seeking refuge.[232] There were other grisly examples as well. What brutality did not accomplish could be achieved by harsh new laws. In 1921, the Bolsheviks inaugurated a systematic campaign to close synagogues;[233] sixty were closed in 1928, including one seized in Poltava on the eve of the High Holy Days. Although some synagogues were understandably requisitioned by the new Soviet government to serve as emergency housing, others were taken with feeble excuses.

The Jews' situation in eastern Europe was also unfavorable. Despite pressure brought by western powers on the Balkan states, only Greece granted Jews emancipation as early as 1870–72. At the Congress of Berlin in 1878, the other Balkan states agreed to alleviate the civil condition of the Jews, but Serbia and Bulgaria did so reluctantly and Rumania did virtually nothing until in 1919 the Treaty of Versailles forced the government to make some changes. The same treaty reconstituted Poland, but the new Polish government waited until 1921 and 1931 to pass enabling laws that were supposed to assure the minority rights promised in the treaty. Between 1919 and 1939, Polish Jews built only simple synagogues, and rehabilitated some existing ones, while both Christian and Jewish scholars intensified earlier research into the architectural history of synagogues in the eastern lands.

In central and western Europe, immediately after the war, synagogues of dramatic form and overwhelming mass were designed, perhaps to recover a sense of former stability. In a synagogue competition held at the École des

Beaux-Arts in Paris in 1918,[234] the young prizewinners seem to have been inspired by the synagogues of Strasbourg (returned to France), Essen (known from a detailed publication), and other central-plan structures of the previous decades. Fritz Landauer, one of the architects of a massive domed synagogue at Augsburg, used an almost unchanged 1912 drawing for the 1924 competition for a synagogue in Vienna-Hietzing.[235] At Enschede in the Netherlands, K.P.C. deBazel designed a chunky, geometric, pared-down Moorish-Byzantine synagogue which was dedicated as late as 1928. Two synagogues at Košice would have been considered progressive if they had been designed before the war. The Neolog synagogue, with its portico and domed rotunda, was a simplified Pantheon, a younger brother to the geometric, classical buildings of the prewar years. The orthodox synagogue, characteristically avoiding styles used by contemporary Christians, was a smooth version of a Middle Eastern structure, with a low, twin-towered, and battlemented porch and vestibule preceding the prayer hall.[236] The respective assimilationist and separatist styles reflect prewar attitudes, but the modernization of older styles may show the desire of Jews in new, democratic Czechoslovakia to participate in contemporary culture. The simple porticoed synagogue at Bratislava of 1923 used smooth-walled geometric forms inside and out, but hinted at tradition by incorporating a metal cage bimah with pointed arches (as at Prague's Altneuschul) and low arcades with small windows to recall the old *shuls* of the past.

Bratislava, Figs. 28–30
Vienna, Fig. 66
Prague, Fig. 49

Architects of several synagogues surely meant them to look very different from the historicist buildings used by more traditional Jews. At Hévíz, the Neolog synagogue was a small gabled structure with three entrances, each surmounted by long rectangular windows under a peaked roof; the effect was that of a picturesque cottage facade shorn of surface ornament and texture. The bright and charming Oslo synagogue of 1918–20 looks like a little country church, with bare surfaces relieved by a low turret at one side of a porch.[237] The Linnaeusstraat synagogue at Amsterdam presented a more elaborate and sophisticated image of a modified church. Its style, based on the early-twentieth-century Arts and Crafts movement, approached the bolder manner of the Amsterdam school of architecture of the late teens and twenties.[238] The Liberal synagogues of London, Paris, and Berlin[239] used varieties of classical design—the first and last of these also modifying the form of the Pantheon.

Amsterdam, Figs. 229, 23

Some synagogue architects designed modest buildings with clearer contours, more marked textural contrasts, and larger windows than they might have used before the war. Synagogues in London-Willesden Green, Liverpool-Greenbank Drive, Dieburg (projects by Rudolf Joseph, 1928–29), and Zurich are among the buildings showing contemporary tendencies toward simplicity and clarity.[240] These synagogues, like many of the pavilions at the 1925 Paris Exposition des Arts Décoratifs et Industriels Modernes, were still eclectic and retrospective in approach, simplifying older styles. The facades were often symmetrical with forms gently salient at ends and entrances, following older traditions, but at least edges were not encumbered by quoins, pinnacles, or crenellations. The interior surfaces were generally smooth and sparsely decorated in paler and clearer tones than those of the shadowy, domed, modernized-oriental synagogues of the previous generation. Lacking firm character, they are unlikely to provide emotional inspiration to worship, but they may be well lit, efficiently planned, easy to maintain, unobtrusive (suggesting that Jews fit in well to contemporary society), and not noticeably ugly.

Two synagogues composed of austere geometric elements nevertheless have domes that mediate between the Byzantine-inspired synagogues of the previous generation and the taste of the International Modern avant-garde for pure geometric form freed from specific suggestions of time and place. For the Jews

Žilina, Figs. 158–160

of Žilina, Peter Behrens, the well-known Berlin architect, designed a synagogue with a hemispheric dome encased in a rectilinear exterior. Outside, the mathematical severity is broken by a cornice line that steps up at the corners, perhaps a Middle Eastern allusion. Varied materials—rough stone relieved by smooth plaster—modify the simplicity. Behrens's synagogue is related to its contemporaries by its faint historicism and the mixture of materials. The second building, the Heroes' Memorial Synagogue in Budapest, also combines a taste for simple geometry with reminiscences of such ancient buildings as the "Tomb of Rachel" in the Holy Land, as they both use hemispheric-domed cubic forms and contrasting materials.[241]

Avant-garde architects abandoned older models. Harry Rosenthal's quiet, weighty geometric blocks created a meditative atmosphere in the synagogue which he designed for a private home ca. 1929. The Oberstrasse Liberal syn-

Hamburg, Figs. 154, 155

agogue in Hamburg (1931) had a similar massive, cubic character. Among the synagogues designed by famous architects was one in Sovetsk in 1925–26 (see Figs. 14, 15), which Erich Mendelsohn designed as an unadorned rectilinear prayer room with smooth wall planes and crisp lines. Richard Neutra's com-

Vienna, Fig. 68

petition entry of 1924 for the Hietzing district synagogue in Vienna had the horizontals, ribbon windows, flat roofs, and starkly simple surfaces that were hallmarks of International Modern architecture. In this case they were inspired by such recent sources as the long, low lines of Frank Lloyd Wright's prairie houses, and the dynamic work of Mendelsohn. The Jacob Obrechtplein syn-

Amsterdam, Figs. 231, 232

agogue in Amsterdam is close to the interpretation of Wright's style made by the prominent Dutch architect, W. M. Dudok, whose style also apparently influenced the remodeling in 1939 of the formerly Moorish-striped synagogue of 1891 in Rotterdam-Botersloot. Synagogues distantly derived from works by Wright or Ludwig Mies van der Rohe in the 1920s, which seemed to have horizontal blocks sliding beside and behind each other, were designed for Paris-rue J. Lacroix and London-Hendon United in the mid-1930s. Fritz Landauer abandoned his interest in domed and faintly exotic synagogues by the

Plauen, Figs. 156, 157

end of the 1920s and designed a synagogue for Plauen as a box set partly on stilts imitating some of Le Corbusier's Citrohan House projects of the 1920s. An unexecuted design of 1929 by Wiener & Jaretzki for the Klopstockstrasse synagogue in Berlin apparently took its inspiration from the street facade of

Le Corbusier's villa "Les Terrasses" at Garches.[242] Without copying other work, but in the International Modern Style, Otto Eisler created a chaste rectangular synagogue for the sophisticated Jewish community at Brno, and Edward Lewis designed a similar one for the Liberal congregation at Hove, near Brighton in Sussex.[243]

The theoretical interest among architects of the time in using industrial materials to produce architecture for the machine age found its expression at the London-Dollis Hill synagogue. It was begun in 1937 by the engineer E. Owen Williams, who took only details such as window shapes from other sources, which included the seven-branched lampstand and the star of David. This synagogue of reinforced concrete had dramatically new accordion-pleated sides whose stiffness obviated the need for interior supports.

London, Figs. 248, 249

The problem of synagogue decoration became especially acute in the 1930s when modernist art theory began to affect synagogue design.[244] As modernism eschewed applied ornament and found meaning in pure form, it provided little comfort for those who had been used to the evocative moods and the play of color and light in older historicist synagogues. Nevertheless, a persistent desire for visual variety and for easily understood adjuncts to worship has led to the installation, even in modern buildings, of colored windows and large ark compositions, the latter with rampant lions, six-pointed stars, and other familiar symbols. Windows were also designed with semiabstract ritual objects or allusions to the Jews' historical sufferings and their hopes for peace and brotherhood.

Between the wars the artistic and architectural range in synagogues extended from the cautiously conservative to the dramatically new. The choice depended upon the congregation's confidence in the future or on its desire to affirm itself in the face of rising anti-Semitism.

1933 to 1983

After the National Socialists came to power in Germany in 1933, synagogues there were burned, blown up, or seriously vandalized. After 1938 the destruction spread to Austria, Czechoslovakia, Rumania, and other occupied countries where the government supported anti-Semitic activity. Synagogues were spared only if fire or bombing would have damaged nearby buildings owned or occupied by Christians, or if the synagogues were too sturdy to be blown up easily. A few synagogues survived because the government found them useful for other purposes.[245] Jews under Hitler's rule were forced to sell synagogue buildings at low prices and to surrender ritual objects. Informal synagogues were established in some internment and forced labor camps, and even in some concentration camps, either quietly set up by the inmates or more ostentatiously by authorities trying to pacify their prisoners and to conceal the horrifying living conditions from outside observers. Some descriptions and drawings exist of the bare rooms, freezing or stifling attics, and dank cellars in which the prisoners prayed.[246] Valiant anti-Nazis, however, set up a secret synagogue in the Roman Catholic orphanage of La Brise Neige in Grenoble,[247] while a few hidden prayer rooms served for pious people who were still free.

During the Second World War, a synagogue in a conquered country might become a stable, warehouse, laundry, hospital, garbage dump, brothel, or prison for deportees.[248] Churches were not used for such things, lest the Christian majority be additionally aroused against their conquerors. Synagogues also suffered from arsonists, vandals, and thieves who stole building materials. Bombs dropped by both sides ruined many synagogues as well as churches, including the eighteenth-century synagogues in London, Livorno, and Rotterdam. All the remaining wooden synagogues of eastern Europe were destroyed, along with masonry ones. Just over a dozen prewar synagogues survived in all of Greece. Learning whether the destruction in each case was due to local anti-Semites, Soviet or Axis soldiers, or citizens desperate for firewood depends upon the reliability of witnesses to these events.

Livorno, Figs. 195–197
London, Figs. 244, 245

The approximately six million Jews killed during the Second World War included the entire Jewish population of many towns. The survivors generally congregated in cities, continuing to lead a small-town existence only in isolated pockets of northern Rumania and Soviet Georgia. In some cities, burned-out synagogue shells could be restored or remodeled; Cologne's Roonstrasse synagogue, for instance, was tall enough to be cut in half horizontally by a floor separating the prayer hall above from community rooms and offices below.[249] New synagogues were needed elsewhere because the surviving synagogues were too large to be restored, maintained, and heated by the few remaining Jews who were often old, poor, and sick. New synagogues had to be built at Hamburg (Fig. 17), where the prewar Oberstrasse synagogue became a broad-

Hamburg, Figs. 153, 154

Figure 17. Hamburg, 1960, exterior in 1981.

casting studio, and at Essen where the synagogue of 1913 became a crafts and industrial arts exhibition center. In other cities, synagogues without congregations were demolished if their decrepit condition constituted a public hazard or if no new use could be found for them. Late-Renaissance synagogues at Mikulov are in danger of collapse, and the handsome Renaissance revival synagogue at Krems was torn down in the late 1970s because no one could think of a way to convert it to a new function. *Essen, Figs. 139, 140*

Population movements, not only population destruction, affected postwar synagogue location. Bomb damage and its psychological impact were so severe in the East End of London, that thousands of its prewar inhabitants moved away and never returned. It seemed pointless to rebuild the Ashkenazic Great Synagogue of 1790 for an orthodox congregation that was no longer there. The suburbs of London then experienced a new wave of synagogue building, in such districts as Ilford, Edgware, and Pinner (see Fig. 6). Southern France and the Paris region accommodated thousands of North African-born Jews who fled their countries following Arab-Israeli crises or the Algerian war of independence. This meant that new Sephardic synagogues were needed in major centers of North African Jewish population. It also led to the reuse of the Carpentras synagogue by a new congregation of immigrants, and to the conversion of the Paris-rue des Tournelles synagogue from an Ashkenazic to a Sephardic house of worship. The suburbs of Paris have massive housing projects where Jews have congregated and established new synagogues. The first synagogue at Blanc-Mesnil was located near noisy airport flight paths and beside a motorcycle garage, but gradually the congregations were able to erect synagogues in more pleasant locations. Three waves of postwar Polish persecution drove many Polish Jews to western Europe. The ultraorthodox and Hasidic migrants required new synagogues, and these are in Jewish residential areas to suit worshippers who will not travel on the Sabbath. For those who go by air to distant places, Jewish prayer rooms are available at the airports in Zurich, close to the interfaith chapel at Paris-Orly, and between the Moslem and Christian oratories at Paris-Roissy. *Carpentras, Figs. 104, 105*

Many postwar synagogues are of the community-center type, because providing social services to the elderly and to émigrés is a major task. Where Jewish cultural assimilation and intermarriage are widespread, community centers try to keep younger Jews within the fold by offering religious, social, cultural, and even athletic facilities. Community-center synagogues tend, then, to be found in rebuilt German communities, in centers of immigration, in comfortable suburbs, and in university towns. With one or two exceptions, the centers are architecturally inconspicuous. Essen has a hemispheric synagogue as part of the Jewish center, but others such as those of Caen and Dortmund could be confused with small commercial buildings or schools. *Essen, Figs. 141, 142*

The establishment of the State of Israel in 1948 had an unforeseen effect on the history of the synagogue. A few abandoned synagogues were actually transported to the new nation, where they were reassembled in museums, while dozens of arks, bimahs, lamps, curtains, and other synagogue furnishings also were sent to Israel, where many are being used in synagogues. Small Italian synagogues which had been abandoned even before the Second World War provided a major source of these artifacts, and several publications have been devoted to them.[250] When the last Jews in small communities die or become unable to sustain the local synagogues, the furnishings from these places—Dubrovnik, for example—may also make their way to museums or to Israel.

Dubrovnik, Figs. 46, 47

When permanent synagogues could be built again in Europe after the late 1940s, most of their architects worked in the International Modern style, whether the architects were Jewish or Christian.[251] During the periods of economic stringency that followed both world wars, skilled craftsmen, building materials, and money were all scarce. There was a need for practical rather than traditionally impressive architecture. An aesthetic emphasizing rationality was particularly appealing to counteract the terrifying madness of the Holocaust. The public welcomed machine-produced materials, and admired the ability of technology to repair the artifacts of a culture that man had damaged. Even the morality of the machine could be favorably interpreted—serving all without prejudice, precise but adaptable. Revival styles were held in low esteem, perhaps because their ornament seemed frivolous, or perhaps because they recalled the attitudes of the discredited past. Surely people sensed, too, that the old exotic synagogues had set Jews apart in society.

Milan, Fig. 201
Belfast, Figs. 239, 240
London, Figs. 250, 251

The simplicity of modern form also accorded well with a religion that appealed to the mind and to man's ethical sense. A modern synagogue could be beautiful because of universals suited to a house of faith: its use of light, its simple tranquillity, its proportions. The survivors of years of terror would not have to be offended by expenditure on sumptuous, earthly decoration and furnishing. The Lord's own light, pure geometry, and man's refinement of simple details would dignify the synagogue. The theoretical basis for these attitudes had been embodied before the war in synagogue designs by Neutra, Mendelsohn (see Figs. 14, 15), Landauer, Eisler, and Elzas. In an age of new conditions and new hopes it was time to spread the message more widely.[252]

Vienna, Figs. 67, 68
Plauen, Figs. 156, 157
Amsterdam, Figs. 233, 234

Contemporary synagogues are generally reticent in appearance, with exceptions such as Livorno and Essen. Many of the synagogue and community center buildings are rectilinear boxes with more or less glass as considerations of security, style, or thermal control dictate. The International Modern taste for pure geometric forms, the reduction of these forms to simplistic formulae, and considerations of economy and speed in building have produced functionally adequate but not memorable synagogues at Sarcelles, Fontainebleau, Creteil, Caen, Dortmund, London-Smith Terrace, and Villeurbanne.[253] They are differentiated largely by the design of concrete screens, or the presence of angles rather than curves, or broad expanses of glass against concrete walls. Most of the British and Irish synagogues are slightly more varied in form and materials, while in France the buildings are somewhat more attractive. The Manchester-Heaton Park synagogue has a central block and projecting wings—the same form seen in the prewar Hamburg Oberstrasse synagogue—but the Manchester example is thinner and more timid, with a disproportionately large glass

Essen, Figs. 141, 142
Livorno, Figs. 198, 199

Hamburg, Fig. 153

entrance wall. The flimsy looking Dublin-Terenure synagogue has a shed porch and varied window rhythms including six-pointed stars, a fussy elaboration of the prewar Amsterdam-Lekstraat synagogue.

Amsterdam, Figs. 233, 234

Other synagogue architects were more imaginative. Two Dutch synagogues, those of Rotterdam-Bentinckiaan and Amsterdam-Liberal, combine boxes with freestanding planes, and they differentiate even outside between the prayer hall and community rooms. The Dutch architects also varied the building textures by juxtaposing concrete, glass, stone facing, metal, and other materials.

Angular forms appear in some synagogue plans and rooflines, as in Leeds-Queenshill, Manchester-Meade Hill Road, Manchester-Stenecourt, and London-Finchley United. A popular synagogue plan is the polygon, known in many examples from the 1950s through the 1970s, including those of Hamburg, Belfast, Norwich, London-Kingsbury, London-Pinner, Manchester-Whitefield-Park Lane, and Livorno (see Figs. 6, 17).[254] Hexagonal synagogues may suggest the connected points of a six-pointed star, but any polygon is an excellent shape for a place dedicated to a united congregation. Moreover, a polygon comes close to being a circle, the form that requires the least perimeter wall for the enclosure of a given volume, but with its straight walls, a polygon is easier and cheaper to build. Polygonal plans have also been widely used for Roman Catholic churches since the Second Vatican Council emphasized closer communication between its clergy and laity and among the laymen themselves. The similarity may please Jews who want their buildings simply to stand among others, not to stand out.

London, Figs. 250, 251
Belfast, Figs. 239, 240
Livorno, Figs. 198, 199

Curved forms appear occasionally. Simple spaces, free of suggestions of exotic grandeur, have curved roofs at Strasbourg, London-Grove End Road, and Oss; curving walls at Offenbach, Paderborn, and Düsseldorf; and three low domes over a large auditorium-synagogue at Berlin-Fasanenstrasse. One of the largest curved roof spans is that of the United Synagogue at London-Edgware, which owes its size and roofline to its origin as an exhibition hall at the 1951 Festival of Britain.

The dome as a Jewish as well as a universal symbol reappeared only on rare occasions, as at Hagen, Bremen, and Essen, all built around 1960. The day of the massive domed synagogue is over; so, too, are the culture of recent emancipation that fostered it and the large communities that sponsored it. At Essen, the domed prayer hall is simply a thin-shelled hemisphere set directly on the entrance pavement. Because the congregation is surrounded only by a simulated dome of heaven, this hemisphere has a different effect from that of older synagogues with domes atop rectilinear and cross-shaped spaces. Those raised domes intimated that the cosmos was remote from man's space. At Essen, one can make direct contact with a celestial form of pure simplicity.[255]

Essen, Figs. 141, 142

A few exceptional synagogues still include evocative forms. The Strasbourg Synagogue de la Paix recalls older galleried basilican synagogues. The peaked roofs at Minden[256] and Hengelo suggest the Tent in the Wilderness, the latter perhaps through the intermediary of designs made decades earlier, such as

Žilina, Fig. 161
Vienna, Fig. 66

Josef Hoffmann's for Žilina, or Hugo Gorge's and Fritz Landauer's for Vienna-Hietzing.[257] The Rotterdam-Bentincklaan synagogue has an entrance wall that is supposed to bring to mind the Wailing Wall in Jerusalem, and the stone-faced basement on the Amsterdam-Liberal synagogue may be meant to suggest the geometric stone structures of Judea. The Bremen synagogue, a domed cube, also evokes the forms of tombs in the Holy Land. The Berlin-Fasanenstrasse community center preserved fragments of the 1912 synagogue on the site, in order to keep fresh the memory of Berlin Jewry before 1933. At Livorno, the Jewish architect Angelo di Castro wanted to recall the Tent in the Wilderness, and also wanted to provide more visual excitement than is normal in the chaste International Modern Style. He created a synagogue with the angles and fins that were popular in Italian design during the late 1950s and early 1960s. This bold building was meant to be noticed. Its form and style affirmed that the Jews had not been completely destroyed, nor had their hopes for a vigorous future in their old homes.[258]

Livorno, Figs. 198, 199

Several postwar synagogues had compact shapes, sometimes with curves and a few reminiscences of the solid geometric style of the 1930s. Synagogues of this type include those of Offenbach, Minden, and Düsseldorf, all of the 1950s.[259] Later developments of the International Modern Style also used clear contrasts between solids and voids from about 1960 onward, as in synagogues at Belfast, Hamburg, and Creteil (see Fig. 17).

Belfast, Figs. 239, 240

Whether solid or fragile in appearance, most of the synagogues emphasize openness and unity inside, unless the synagogues are ultraorthodox with women screened from view. The majority of postwar synagogues therefore look like secular auditoriums, as do many churches.

Some of the most challenging synagogue designs have been those for which architects had to work with surviving parts of buildings, or build new synagogues in sympathy with a historic setting. The nature of the problem varied from one city to another. At London-Great Cumberland Place, the local government's Historic Buildings service required the preservation of the existing elevation of the late-eighteenth-century crescent of adjacent buildings and the spacing of their windows. The main prayer hall, several apartments, the weekday synagogue, reception rooms, banquet rooms, stairs, women's guild room, a committee room, and a car park all had to fit behind the old facade and yet have nothing above the prayer hall. In East Berlin, the Rykestrasse synagogue was restored substantially to its original appearance, as if to demonstrate that the new Communist government, while antagonistic to religion in general, was not to blame for the vandalism of the Hitler years. In The Hague, the Sephardic synagogue of 1725 was converted in 1976 for use by the Liberal congregation (the only branch of Judaism that has expanded in the Netherlands). At Milan, the architects built a completely new synagogue behind the ruins of the old facade. The Reform synagogue of Frankfurt had its old Egyptian-Mesopotamian decoration drastically simplified and modernized, its present light walls and geometric ornament adding to the sweep of the architecture.

Milan, Figs. 200, 201

The favorable condition of synagogues in western Europe, and their stable position in Hungary, contrasts with the situation in the Soviet Union, eastern Europe, and the Balkans outside Greece. Whereas there were formerly hundreds of synagogues in the Soviet Union, by 1966 the authorities had closed all but sixty-two. Forty-three of them, or about 65 percent, were concentrated in Soviet Georgia and the Caucasian and Central Asian Republics—areas with only about 13 percent of the Jewish population of the U.S.S.R. at that time.[260] The absence of synagogues forces the most earnest Jews to form clandestine quorums, and it discourages those who fear the authorities from praying with a quorum at all.

Jewish communities in eastern Europe and the Balkans are now very small.[261] If there is a synagogue, it is a room or a prewar synagogue. Restoration in these areas has either been archaeologically studious (Warsaw, Bucharest) rather than creatively interpretive, or it has led to the conversion of rehabilitated synagogues for use as public libraries (Przemyśl-Sheinbach, Sroda, Strzyzów, Zamość, Piotrków Trybunalski), art museums (Lesko, Rzeszów-New Town), city archives (Rzeszów-Old Town), and a concert hall (Częstochowa). Less worthy uses include warehouses (Bochnia, Łęczna, Szydłowiec, Chrzanów, Košice, Voronezh, Góra Kalwaria-Hasidic), garages (Ostrolęka, Włodawa—part of one synagogue), and a puppet theater (Kiev-Great). A few have been restored as active or potential Jewish museums (Cracow/Kazimierz-Old, Łańcut, the Prague synagogues) or as historic monuments (Warsaw-Nozyk, Włodawa, Samokov). Some contain exhibition cases (Prague, Cracow/Kazimierz-Old) or memorial inscriptions, especially the names of 77,000 martyred Czech Jews at the Prague-Pinkas Synagogue. Services are held in the Altneuschul and Jerusalémská Street synagogues of Prague. When the towns lack congregations or Torah scrolls, the surviving buildings bear mute witness to the wanton destruction of life. However beautiful or evocative they may be, the synagogues are mere shells, for the living synagogue, always the quorum of ten men, can no longer be assembled in many parts of Europe.

Bucharest, Figs. 34, 35
Warsaw, Figs. 101, 102
Prague, Figs. 48, 49, 51
Samokov, Figs. 52, 53
Cracow, Figs. 70–72
Łańcut, Figs. 80, 81

Some Thoughts on the Meaning of the Synagogue

The diverse aspects of synagogue architecture share a common ability to indicate changes in the status and interests of the buildings' sponsors. Humble, box-like synagogues blended with the local vernacular townscape in those places where the congregation played a useful role in the local economy, but was unable to build anything to rival a parish church. The prevalence of modest structures indicates the norm; exceptional synagogues prove that human and architectural history cannot be bound by rules.

Charming synagogues situated in ducal parks (see Figs. 8, 9), and designed in court-oriented styles, made it clear that Jews were chattels of the noblemen who protected them. Large synagogues in many cities revealed the extent to

Łańcut, Figs. 80, 81
Berlin, Figs. 117, 118
Ansbach, Figs. 119–121

Budapest, Figs. 36–42
Leningrad, Figs. 88, 89
Moscow, Figs. 90, 91
Warsaw, Figs. 98, 100
Berlin, Figs. 122, 124
Vilnius, Figs. 92, 93

Warsaw, Figs. 101, 102
Florence, Figs. 193, 194
Milan, Fig. 200
Toledo, Figs. 184, 185
Ramsgate, Figs. 252, 253

Florence, Figs. 193, 194
Turin, Figs. 214, 215

which governments eager for Jewish assistance in commerce and banking were willing to allow handsome buildings to be erected. Imposing synagogues in eastern Europe, at Białystok, Brody, and Vilnius, for instance, indicated the large part of the population constituted by Jews before 1939—a contingent too large to be repressed. Fine synagogues sponsored by individuals manifest the widespread tendency to seek immortality in building, especially if the patrons have no children to ensure continuity in other ways.[262] A large, well-built synagogue might also be erected where the Jewish community felt optimistic. This was the case at Marseille where in 1863 the rabbi claimed that the new synagogue represented continuous civic progress and the Jews' own faith in the future.[263] The Jews of Turin in the 1860s and of Florence in the 1870s planned lavish new buildings as expressions of gratitude for emancipation.[264] At the dedication of the massive synagogue of Mainz in 1912, the rabbi stressed that the size and location of the new building showed Jews in Germany to be free and not second-class citizens.[265] Eager to be part of the national culture, while maintaining their old religion, French Jews called their synagogues "temples," the term used for the churches of Protestants, whose legal position resembled that of Jews when Roman Catholicism was France's state religion.[266] Ludwig Geiger, editor of the German Jewish weekly *Allgemeine Zeitung des Judenthums,* said on behalf of like-minded German Jews that in the nineteenth century "the question of assimilation does not exist; we are completely assimilated. . . . By assimilation, we mean total integration into Germanness, into its nationality, language, and culture, without, however, giving up our religious beliefs."[267]

The fervent tone of his statement revealed the Jews' awareness of the uncertainty of their position. This was the situation in many places, and a writer in *Le Nouvelliste* of Marseille made that clear. When he looked at his city's new Romanesque (that is, western European) synagogue, he declared that it combined inspirations from the most beautiful Arabic and Byzantine architecture in a manner perfectly appropriate to the nature of the building.[268] Evidently, he did not look at the real building, but only at his mental image of Jews as Eastern and exotic. (This was, to be sure, an image embraced by those Jews who hoped to emphasize their distinctive traditions, now that they felt free to do so.) The emphasis of Jews' special character continued; the art historian Elena Bassi saw in the oval gallery of the Scuola Spagnola in Venice an "oriental" character, although she wrote in the same paragraph that the gallery is related to Western secular theater design.[269] Feelings of difference and of superiority led anti-Semites to regard handsome synagogues as ostentatious and aggressive.

Venice, Figs. 220–222

The synagogue can be used as a literary setting for the Jews' own conflicts over integration and separation. Among those who passed from the ghetto into the modern world, a humble, traditional synagogue might be the place in which a young person felt most acutely her emotional distance from many aspects of the past, as in Israel Zangwill's widely read novel, *Children of the*

Ghetto. In Ludwig Hatvany-Deutsch's novel, *Bondy Jr.,* which describes the urbanization and acculturation of several generations of Hungarian Jews, the Dohány Street synagogue in Budapest appeared to his upwardly mobile protagonist as a dragon, looming in the mist and improperly understood.[270] For young people in real life, such dragons represented personal and social conflicts and obstacles to be resolved and overcome.

Budapest, Fig. 38

Synagogues built since the Second World War have often been rededicated with hesitant expressions of confidence in the moral and religious revival of mankind after the Holocaust. The *Stuttgarter Zeitung* discussed the new synagogue of that city as a symbol of confidence or trust, and as a place of meeting (*Vertrauen*).[271] The Grand Rabbi of the Bas-Rhin consistory, Abraham Deutsch, said that the use of a stone from the Holy Land in the new synagogue at Strasbourg indicated that the Jews' emotional ties to Israel did not make them forget that they lived in France and wanted to live in France. In 1982 Ionel Schein, a Jewish architect, wrote about the implications of his recently opened synagogue in Paris. A small rectilinear building set at the base of a high-rise secular structure, the synagogue has no principal face, as though to suggest its modesty and indifference to man-centered hierarchies. Executed in commonplace materials including glass and tile, the synagogue projects an interest in everyday things of the present, avoiding symbolism and references to other times and countries. It is a place merely—or one might better say, importantly—for the convergence of individuals and ideas, a place of rest and of welcome.[272]

If the synagogue has expressed special meanings at certain times, it has also kept some stable meanings.[273] The synagogue does not have to be a place of sacred mystery, but one where earthbound men can meet. It is a place of community, where a Jew wants to be part of a quorum rather than a lone sinner concerned with his salvation. The synagogue does not have to be prominently situated in a town, asserting spiritual against secular claims to power. It is, instead, a home to the pious Jew, filled with those who in their devotion transform even the meanest building into a house of assembly, a house of learning, and a house of prayer.

Notes

PREFACE

1. "In some towns where the Khasidim abound, the synagogue is almost empty and kept open for the women who are not admitted into the Beth hamidrash [house of religious study for adult men] of the Khasidim, and a few old Jews attend to conduct worship in the synagogue for the sake of the women" (*Jewish Chronicle*, March 25, 1859, p. 3). See also J. R. Mintz, *Legends of the Hasidim,* Chicago and London, 1968, pp. 31, 48.
2. Karaite synagogues are mentioned at Lutsk in the 16th century and at Odessa, Dnepropetrovsk, Vilnius, and Trakai in the 19th and 20th centuries. Karaites were also numerous in the mid-19th century at Feodosia, Ferekep, and Simferopol, and must have had synagogues there. See: *Jewish Chronicle,* July 15, 1859, p. 7; A. Frostig, "Zur Genese und Geschichte der Karäer in Polen," *Anthropos* LXXV, #1–2 (1980), pp. 24–48.
3. *Talmud* (Babylonian version, herein cited as b.) tractates Shekhalim 49b, Peah 21b, ed. I. Epstein, London, 1936ff.

CHAPTER 1

1. Babylonian Talmud (= b.) Sanhedrin 2b.
2. This word was used in the Greek Septuagint Bible translation of the Hebrew *edah*, an outdoor assembly. It gradually became attached to religious assembly, and to Jewish ones in particular.
3. Philo, *Legatio ad Cajum,* ed. A. Pelletier, Paris, 1972, para. 156, pp. 179–81; ed. E. M. Smallwood, Leiden, 1961, p. 92 and notes (to paras. 153–56), pp. 232–38.
4. E. Rivkin, "Ben Sira and the Non-Existence of the Synagogue," in *In the Time of Harvest: Essays in Honor of Abba Hillel Silver,* ed. D. J. Silver, New York and London, 1963, pp. 320–54. I am grateful to Joseph Gutmann for this important reference.
5. Ibid.; see also J. Gutmann, "The Origin of the Synagogue," *Archaeologischer Anzeiger—Beiblatt zum Jahrbuch des Deutschen Archaeologischen Instituts* LXXXVII, #1 (1972), p. 39, reprinted in idem, ed., *Synagogue;* pp. 72–76; see also S. Zeitlin, "The Origin of the Synagogue," *Proceedings of the American Academy of Jewish Research* II, 1930–31, pp. 69–81, reprinted in Gutmann, *Synagogue,* pp. 14–26; see also J. Gutmann, ed., *Ancient Synagogues. The State of Research,* Chico, Calif., 1981.
6. Ex. 20:8; Deut. 5:12.
7. Krautheimer, *Mitt. Syn.,* pp. 90–91 and notes; N. Golb, "Nature et destination du monument juif découvert à Rouen," *Proceedings of the American Academy of Jewish Research* XLVIII, 1981, pp. 155–56, differentiates *synagoga* from *scuola* in medieval and later Latin texts. The distinction was not always made from the late Renaissance onward, it seems, and the Yiddish word *shul* can mean either building type.
8. b. Meg 29a. The Talmud is composed of two parts, the Mishnah and the Gemara. The Mishnah, compiled after ca. A.D. 200, records both written and oral law. It also includes a smaller amount of nonlegal material that is considered less binding, such as proverbs, parables, and homilies. The Gemara is a record of discussions and elaborations of the Mishnah offered by early scholars. Practices accepted by

the majority of scholars or by a recognized Jewish authority also receive the status of law. Of inferior legal status are the minority opinions recorded in the Gemara, or later scholars' opinions which are not accepted by the majority of authorities. For the Talmud, see H. L. Strack, *Introduction to the Talmud,* transl. from the 5th German ed., Philadelphia, 1931.

Even the authoritative portions of the Talmud require formulation into law or binding precedent, and the laws need codification. The principal legal codes and compilations which orthodox Jews consider authoritative include: 1. *The Mishneh Torah* or *Yad ha-Hazakah* (for synagogues, see Hilkhot Tefillah part, chap. 11), finished ca. 1180 by Moses ben Maimon, better known as Maimonides, or to Jews as the RaMBaM (1135–1204), who worked in Spain and Egypt. 2. The *Arba'ah Turim* by Jacob ben Asher (1269–1343), active in Spain. 3. The *Shulhan Arukh,* written in 1564–71 by Joseph Caro (1488–1575) who lived in Bulgaria and the Holy Land. Commentaries explain the laws, resolve problems that arose after the laws were put into effect, and resolve differences between Sephardic and Ashkenazic practice. The Ashkenazic rabbi, Moses Isserles, known as ReMO (1510–72), active in Kazimierz near Cracow, prepared the authoritative Ashkenazic commentary to the *Shulhan Arukh.* Responsa, authoritative legal opinions, can also be recognized as legally binding.

9. b. Berakoth 6a, 6b. Megillah 29a. Religious schools include the *cheder* (elementary school) and *yeshivah* (college). The former, often annexed to the synagogue, is not a "lesser sanctuary" comparable to a synagogue. The *yeshivah* may be in a separate building with its own synagogue, but a school for young men is not yet a "little sanctuary" either. The adult house of study, *bet ha-midrash,* is even holier than a synagogue, according to the Talmud, and may contain all necessary synagogue furnishings because the devout spend many hours there and wish to pray. See below, for its relative degree of holiness.
10. Judah ben Eliezer Minz, active in Padua, 15th century, quoted in S. B. Freehof, *A Treasury of Responsa,* Philadelphia, 1963, p. 94. See also Jerusalem Talmud (=j.) Mishnah Yoma VII, 1; Sotah VI, 7, for parallels between synagogue and Temple.
11. j. Berakoth, as translated by B. Litvin, *The Sanctity of the Synagogue,* New York, 1959, p. 48. See also M. Rosenmann, *Die Ursprung der Synagoge und ihre allmähliche Entwicklung,* Berlin, 1907, pp. 26–31 for synagogue-Temple parallels. See also *The Zohar,* trans. by H. Sperling, M. Simon, and P. P. Levertoff, London, 1934, reprint ed., 1978, tractate Beshalah 59b, p. 186; A. Hirsch, "Temple consistorial israélite de Lyon," *Revue générale de l'architecture et des travaux publics* XXIII (1865), cols. 219–20.
12. J. J. Leon Templo, *Retrato del Templo de Selomo,* Middelburg, 1642. See comparative illustrations in J. van Agt, *Synagogen in Amsterdam,* The Hague, 1974, p. 44.
13. O. Böcher, *Die alte Synagoge zu Worms,* Worms, 1960, pp. 101–3. For the unplastered wall, see A. Eisenberg, *The Synagogue Through the Ages,* New York, 1974, p. 180.
14. Two columns or turrets: see L. von Förster's discussion of his Vienna-Tempelgasse synagogue in *Allgemeine Bauzeitung* XXIV (1859), pp. 14–16. The Helsinki synagogue has two little columns in relief on the facade. The Warsaw-Tłómacka Street synagogue had two huge columns at the entrance to the ark recess. For Nijmegen, compare Jan van Eyck (?), *Crucifixion,* Berlin-Dahlem, Staatliche Gemäldegalerie. The intermediary between painting and synagogue may be the Jerusalemkerk at Bruges with its distinctive tower. The architect at Nijmegen, Oscar Leeuw (who may have been Jewish), worked for the Historic Monuments Service and surely knew the Jerusalemkerk, at least in pictures.
15. In late antiquity, the Stobi synagogue was not oriented to Jerusalem (information courtesy of Dean Moe), nor was Budapest's early-20th-century Hevrah Kaddi-

sha Hospital synagogue, which therefore some Jews declined to use; see D. S. van Zuiden in *De Vrijdagavond* V (Aug. 17, 1928), p. 311. The congregation could, however, turn toward Jerusalem during prayer. The Talmud contains minority opinions suggesting that one may pray in other directions because the Holy Presence is everywhere: b. Baba Batra 25a. On differences between archaeological remains and Jewish legal requirements, see F.-G. Hüttenmeister, "Synagogues et écoles en Palestine Ier-VIIe siècle," in B. Blumenkranz, ed., *Art et archéologie des juifs en France médiévale,* Toulouse, 1980, pp. 143–56, esp. pp. 150–56.

16. b. Berakoth 31a, 34b.
17. b. Shabbat 11a. See also *Shulhan Arukh,* Orah Hayyim 150, para. 2, and Isserles' commentary to it.
18. Jews might have had to make their houses taller than synagogues if they lived in tall tenements in crowded ghettoes. Some special circumstance caused the architect to build an apartment for the synagogue caretaker above the prayer hall at Hamburg-Hoheluftchaussee in 1909; the architect was S. Engel. See K. Goldenberg, "Die Kultus-und Profanbauten der Juden erläutert an Hand von Hamburg - Altona - Wandsbek," diss. Dresden Technische Hochschule, ca. 1922, p. 59. Christian civil authorities at Carpentras made the Jews reduce the synagogue's height; see below, Carpentras and Cavaillon. At least twice, Jews solved the problem by erecting poles on synagogue roofs that reached the necessary height while remaining innocuous (b. Shabbat 11a). Such poles are known at Fürth near Nuremberg and at Frankfurt an der Oder, 18th century; see L. Löw, "Der synagogale Ritus," *Monatsschrift für Geschichte und Wissenschaft des Judenthums* XXXIII (1884), p. 220. In 1787, Jews in Třebíč, Moravia, had to lower the synagogue roof because the building's lights were too prominently visible from the local castle: H. Gold, *Die Juden und Judengemeinde Mährens,* Brno, 1929, pp. 523–27. Modern skyscrapers obviously make it impossible to build taller synagogues. Synagogues in prisons or other extraordinary places may also be unable to follow the usual rules.
19. b. Berakoth 34a.
20. b. Megillah 26b–27a.
21. b. Berakoth 62b.
22. b. Megillah 28b; on decorum, see also *Shulhan Arukh,* Orah Hayyim, 150, 1.
23. b. Megillah 26b–27a; j. Megillah III, 1.
24. b. Megillah 26a–27a; j. Megillah III, 1–3.
25. The Talmud allows only urban synagogues to have apartments for synagogue attendants (b. Yoma 11a–12a), since they would not be contaminated by village conditions such as keeping animals in a house. Considerations of health may underlie the separation of funerary chambers from prayer halls. A synagogue of "Roman" (Syrian, in that context) Jews which opened into a room where a corpse was deposited was remarkable enough to be mentioned.
26. b. Megillah 28a–28b. The need for space in crowded ghettoes led some Jews to build on sites of ruined synagogues.
27. b. Berakoth 62b; b. Megillah 28a, 29a.
28. b. Berakoth 8a–8b; j. Berakoth V, 1.
29. b. Berakoth 8a.
30. b. Kethuboth 5a.
31. j. Megillah III, 3.
32. Examples: J. Aronius, *Regesten,* #663, #772; M. Wiener, *Regesten zur Geschichte der Juden in Deutschland während des Mittelalters,* vol. 1, Hannover, 1862, #475, pp. 172–73, #614, pp. 197–99; F. Baer, *Die Juden im christlichen Spanien,* Berlin, 1935, p. 217.
33. *Encyclopedia Judaica,* 1971, s.v. Synagogue.
34. Krautheimer, *Mitt. Syn.,* p. 91. See also bulletin boards in the Amsterdam-Sephardic synagogue, and photographs at YIVO, New York, of the Vilnius-Great Synagogue notices.
35. Slaves: S. Baron, *A Social and Religious History of the Jews,* vol. 1, New York, 1937, p. 88. Asylum: H. L. Gordon, "The Basilica and the Stoa in Early Rabbinical Literature," *Art Bulletin* XIII (1931), pp. 352–75, esp. p. 359 citing *Corpus inscriptionum latinarum,* Berlin, 1863, vol. 3,

supp. #6583. Butchers: at Zittsheim, 1839, G. Plaut, *The Rise of Reform Judaism,* New York, 1963, pp. 213–15. See also *Encyclopedia Judaica,* 1971, s.v. Synagogue.

36. E. Scheid, "Histoire de la synagogue de Haguenau," *L'univers israélite* XXXVI (Dec. 15, 1880), with article concluded in succeeding issues.

37. G. Hillairet, *Dictionnaire historique des rues de Paris,* 4th ed., Paris, 1966, p. 527. I owe this reference to Barbara Michaels.

38. I. Meyer, *Zur Geschichte der Juden in Regensburg,* Regensburg, 1913, pp. 74–75. For Zurich, Krautheimer, *Mitt. Syn.,* p. 88; for Bad Nauheim, R. Stahl, *Geschichte der Nauheimer Juden* (Bad Nauheimer Jahrbuch 8, #9/12), Bad Nauheim, 1929, p. 13; for Plauen: W. Goldberg, ed., *Blätter der Erinnerung an die Weihe der Synagoge Plauen i/V,* Plauen, 1930, p. 7; for Lincoln and Bury, see V. D. Lipman, *The Jews of Medieval Norwich,* London, 1967, pp. 22–25 and nn. 2–3, where Lipman argues against these identifications contra H. Rosenau, "Note on the Relationship of Jews' Court and the Lincoln Synagogue," *Archaeological Journal* XCIII (1936), pt. 1, pp. 51–56, and in her dissertation, "The Architectural Development of the Synagogue," London, Courtauld Institute, 1939, p. 58, agreeing with C. Roth, *Medieval Lincoln Jewry and its Synagogue,* London, 1934.

39. For conversions to and from synagogues, see *Jewish Chronicle,* May 1, 1846, p. 131; J. F. van Agt, "Synagogues in the Netherlands," *Studies on the History of Dutch Jewry* III (1981), p. 108 (I thank Drs. van Agt for the Dutch MS version of the Hebrew article); idem, "Nieuwe functies voor oude Synagogen," *Plan* VII, #10 (1976), pp. 54–56; U. Kaploun, *The Synagogue,* Philadelphia, 1973, p. 57; *Encyclopedia Judaica,* 1971 in *Yearbook* 1974, p. 288 for Burgas; L. Gostynski, *Les pierres racontent,* Paris, 1973, pp. 52–53 for Biecz; *AJYb* 1968 (1967), p. 380; N. Chinitz and S. Nachman, *Slutzk and Vicinity Memorial Book,* New York and Tel Aviv, 1962, p. xvii; I. Heller and Z. Vajda, *The Synagogues of Hungary,* New York, 1968, p. 2; A. Diamant, *Materialien zum 40 Jahrestag der Synagogenzerstörung in Hessen,* Frankfurt am Main, 1978, p. 18; H. Rutkowski, *Kazimierz Dolny: Krajobraz i Architektury,* Warsaw, 1965, fig. 105; *New York Times,* Feb. 13, 1977, X, part 2, pp. 1, 38; for Schlüchtern, Diamant, *Zerstörte Synagogen, vom November 1938,* Frankfurt am Main, 1978, p. 111; E. Krausz, *Leeds Jewry. Its History and Social Structure,* Cambridge, 1964, p. 16; B. Postal and S. Abramson, *Traveler's Guide to Jewish Landmarks in Europe,* New York, 1971, passim; photographs at YIVO, New York, and Leo Baeck Institute, New York (esp. of Franconian synagogues, taken by I. Schweirz).

40. Paris, Archives Nationales, F 19 11112-11115. Towns of Krautergersheim, Neuwiller, Niederbronn, Reichshoffen, Saare-Union (before 1828), Saverne (before 1833), Scherwiller, Schweinheim, Strasbourg (before 1812), Trimbach, Uhrwiller, Westhouse, Zellwiller. For Liège: *Jewish Chronicle,* Jan. 14, 1859, p. 7.

41. J. R. Mintz, *Legends of the Hasidim,* Chicago and London, 1968, pp. 31, 48.

42. Exhibited in July–Aug., 1982, Whitechapel Art Gallery, London.

43. For general information on the women's section and its effect on plans, see Krautheimer, *Mitt. Syn.,* pp. 132–35.

44. R. Krautheimer, *Die Kirchen der Bettelorden in Deutschland,* Cologne, 1925.

45. H. Rosenau, "The Synagogue and Protestant Church Architecture," *Journal of the Warburg and Courtauld Institutes* IV (1941), p. 83, reprinted in Gutmann, *Synagogue,* pp. 309–16.

46. London: Cannon Street Road, Commercial Road Great Synagogue, Philpot Street Great Synagogue, Rouel Road, Stepney Orthodox, Woolwich, all from C. Roth, *The Federation of Synagogues,* London, 1937, p. 34. The Spitalfields Great Synagogue met in a former Huguenot church later used by Methodists, the West London (Reform) Synagogue first met in a former chapel in Bruton Street, the Liberal congregation first met in a chapel in Hill Street from 1911–28, and the North London Progressive congregation re-

modeled a Methodist church. See also E. Jamilly, "Anglo-Jewish Architects and Architecture," *Jewish Historical Society of England. Transactions* XVIII (1958), pp. 127–41. For Dublin, where a Presbyterian church became a synagogue in 1835, and where the Hill Street synagogue was a Roman Catholic church, see C. Roth, *The Rise of Provincial Jewry, London* [1950], pp. 70–71, and *AJYb,* 1963, p. 202; the Edinburgh-Graham Street synagogue had belonged to Protestants, see D. Daiches, *Two Worlds: An Edinburgh Jewish Childhood,* New York, 1954, p. 14; Ilana Samuels, Cardiff, and Dow Marmur, London, kindly informed me that synagogues in Cardiff had also been chapels. See also H. Guttmann, "Zur Rechtslage der Synagoge im Mittelalter," *Emlékkönyv néhai Dr. Kohn Sámuel,* ed. S. Hevesi, S. Löwinger, et al., Budapest, 1941, pp. 177–91.

47. Churches became synagogues also on the continent of Europe, e.g.:
Antwerp, ex. St. Salvator: *Encyclopedia Judaica,* 1971, s.v. Antwerp;
Bussum, ex. Hersteld Apostolische Gemeente, remodeled 1931 by J. Baars;
Capriata d'Orba: S. Foà, *Gli ebrei nel Monferrato,* Alessandria, 1914, p. 124;
Coburg: *Encyclopedia Judaica,* 1971, s.v. Coburg;
Dijon, ex. Maltese Knights' church sold 1820: Z. Szajkowski, "Synagogues during the French Revolution of 1789–1800," *Jewish Social Studies* XX, #4 (1958), p. 227;
Dordrecht, ex. St. Mary's convent: J. Zwaarts, "Joodse gemeente buiten Amsterdam," in H. Brugmans and A. Frank, *Geschiedenis der Joden in Nederland,* vol. 1, Amsterdam, 1940, p. 404;
Kronshtad: *Jewish Chronicle,* July 11, 1862, p. 5;
Naaldwijk: Gans, *Memorbook,* p. 450;
Orla: L. Dobroszycki and B. Kirshenblatt-Gimblett, *Image Before my Eyes,* New York, 1977, p. 62;
Paris, ex. Chapel of the Collège de Boissy, rue Suger (Sephardic synagogue 1770–1826): E. Haymann, *Paris Judaica,* Paris, 1977, p. 46;
Rouen, ex. Ste.-Marie-la-Petite, nationalized in French Revolution, sold in 1792 to a private owner, made into synagogue 1865: Szajkowski, "French Revolution," p. 227;
St. Dié: Archives Nationales F 19 11122, s.v. St. Dié;
Strasbourg, a convent nationalized under the Revolution became a "hospice of Brutus" and then a riding academy before being made into a synagogue in 1833: H. Haug, "De la première synagogue à la Synagogue de la Paix," *La synagogue de la Paix,* Strasbourg, 1958, pp. 12–26, esp. p. 14;
The Free Christian congregation of Szczecin asked in 1850 to use the synagogue for its meetings, as civic officials refused them the use of the town auditorium: *Jewish Chronicle,* Apr. 5, 1850;
Toulouse, Jews petitioned to use a former church: Szajkowski, "French Revolution," p. 226;
Utrecht, Mennonite church bought and rebuilt as a synagogue, 1792: Gans, *Memorbook,* p. 492;
Verdun, church nationalized under the Revolution sold to Jews in 1805: Szajkowski, "French Revolution," p. 227;
Zwolle, former Dominican chapel converted in the 19th century: information courtesy J. J. van Agt.

48. S. B. Freehof, *Reform Jewish Practice and its Rabbinical Background,* New York, 1963, pp. 39–44. See b. Avodah Zarah 43b. It was possible to confuse a synagogue with a pagan temple, too (b. Sanhedrin 61b), and a synagogue at Tiberias became a pagan temple: J. Baumgarten, "Art in the Synagogue: Some Talmudic Views," in R. Gordis and M. Davidowitz, eds., *Art in Judaism,* New York, 1975, p. 37 n. 53, reprinted with corrections in Gutmann, *Synagogue,* pp. 79–89.

49. A Quaker meetinghouse does not, however, have the synagogue's focal points (ark and bimah). It avoids elaborate decoration and evocative styles, it rarely reaches the size of the largest synagogues, and it allows men and women to sit together.

50. Latin text: J. Parkes, *The Conflict of the*

Church and the Synagogue, Cleveland, 1961, p. 401. See also L. H. Stookey, "The Gothic Cathedral as the Heavenly Jerusalem. Liturgical and Theological Sources," *Gesta* VIII (1969), pp. 35–41, esp. pp. 35–38.

51. London-Threadneedle Street (1243) and Basinghall Street (by 1256): H. G. Richardson, *The English Jewry under Angevin Kings,* London, 1960, p. 197 n. 1. Spain: F. Baer, *Die Juden im christlichen Spanien,* 1 Teil: *Urkunden und Regesten,* 2 Band: *Kastilien/Inquisitionsakten,* Berlin, 1936, p. 234, #249 (Seville, Aug. 2, 1391); Strzegom, Świdnica, and Oleśnica: A. Grotte, *Synagogenspuren in schlesischen Kirchen* (Schriften der Gesellschaft zur Förderung der Wissenschaft des Judentums, 41), Wrocław, 1937, pp. 22, 26–35, and E. Hitzig, *Katalog der vom "Verein Jüdisches Museum Breslau" in den Räumen des Schlesischen Museums für Kunstgewerbe und Altertumer veranstaltete Ausstellung . . . ,* Wrocław, 1929, p. 13. Glogów: R. Krautheimer, review of A. Grotte, *Synagogenspuren,* in *Jewish Social Studies* I (1939), p. 482 including some disagreement with Grotte's ideas on the Silesian buildings mentioned above. Brno: M. Wiener, *Regesten,* vol. 1, p. 247, #223. Cologne: A. Kober, *Cologne,* Philadelphia, 1940, p. 97. Vienna: S. Krauss, "Wiener Synagogen in der Vergangenheit," *Menorah* IV, #1 (Jan. 1926), p. 16. Aix-en-Provence: R. Berg, C. Chemouny, and F. Didi, *Guide juif de France,* Paris, n.d., p. 138. Paris and elsewhere: S. Grayzel, *The Church and the Jews in the XIIIth Century,* rev. ed., New York, 1966, pp. 357–58. Naples: A. Milano, *Storia degli ebrei in Italia,* Turin, 1963, p. 443. Eger after 1350: "Die Ruinen der ehemaligen Juden-Synagoge zu Eger," *Mitteilungen der kaiserlichen königlichen Central-Commission zur Erforschung und Erhaltung der Baudenkmale* I (1856), pp. 89–90; I am grateful to Evžen Lukeš for finding this for me. A synagogue in Great Yarmouth became a mission hall in 1892, see V. D. Lipman, *A Social History of the Jews in England,* London, 1954, p. 108. It was after the Second World War that synagogues in Eschwege and Liberec were turned into churches (A. Diamant, *Zerstörte Synagogen,* alphabetical list of cities, where Liberec is listed as Reichenberg), as were synagogues in Plau (see H. Eschwege, *Die Synagoge in der deutschen Geschichte,* Dresden, 1980, p. 173), Höchberg in Franconia (photograph by I. Schweirz, Leo Baeck Institute, New York), and Groningen (Gans, *Memorbook,* p. 480).
52. Freehof, *Reform Jewish Practice,* pp. 33–35.
53. Examples in L. Ehrmann, "Synagogen," in *Die jüdischen Denkmäler in der Tschechoslowakei,* ed. S. H. Lieben, Prague, 1933, pp. 1–9, figs. 1–24; I. Schweirz's photographs of Franconian synagogues at the Leo Baeck Institute Archives in New York; P. Rieger, *Jüdische Gotteshäuser und Friedhöfe in Württemberg,* Augsburg, 1932.
54. École nationale supérieure des Beaux-Arts, *Les concours d'architecture de l'année scolaire* X, 1918–19, pls. 3–18 (synagogues). Compare XI, 1919–20, pls. 185–204 ("temples protestantes").
55. K. A. C. Creswell, *A Short Account of Early Muslim Architecture,* Harmondsworth, 1958, p. 2 for pictures in the Ka'ba, p. 7 for churches being used as mosques. The Great Mosque of Damascus was popularly believed to have been a synagogue; see M. Schreiner, "Les juifs dans al-Beruni," *Revue des études juives* XII (1886), p. 263.
56. F. Baer, *Die Juden im christlichen Spanien,* 1 Teil, 2 Band, p. 50, #67. Note that women have occupied auxiliary positions in mosques just as Jewish women occupied separate areas in synagogues.
57. *Jewish Chronicle,* July 11, 1862, p. 5.
58. Freehof, *Reform Jewish Practice,* vol. 2, p. 41.
59. That the Jews of Highgate (London) did not object to synagogue land being sold for use as a Hindu temple (*AJR Information* XXXII [Nov. 1977], p. 3) suggests that Arab-Israeli politics rather than religious scruples underlie the current distress at selling synagogue property to the Moslems.
60. Even when the Jews of an area desig-

nated one synagogue as the central "lesser sanctuary" it might not be well attended in comparison with small local prayer rooms. A synagogue may be set up in honor of a scholar (ReMO at Cracow/Kazimierz, or the little synagogue on the hill there honoring Nathan Spira who died in 1582), or it may be named for a scholar (Ba'al Ha-Turim Synagogue, Khios, named for Jacob ben Asher who was thought to have worshipped there: P. P. Argenti, *The Religious Minorities of Chios: Jews and Roman Catholics*, Cambridge, 1970, p. 198). A synagogue may be named in memory of a private person (e.g., the Magnus Memorial Synagogue at Chatham near Rochester). The act of remembering a person in Judaism does not have the same connotations or implications of divine presence as do *kubbahs* (Islamic vaults) and Christian *memoria*. A synagogue does not have to be dedicated to anyone. It can be called "the Great" (= chief synagogue of a certain group, but not necessarily the largest one in town), or "choral" (reflecting the use of a choir customary in Reform services); it can be named for the town of origin of those who founded it or for the trade followed by congregation members; or it can be given a name such as Gates of Prayer, Holy Law, or House of Israel.

61. Jews sit on the synagogue floor on the anniversary of the destruction of the Temple in Jerusalem, but this day of mourning and the actions associated with it are exceptional.
62. j. Berakoth V, 1.
63. j. Mishnah Berakoth V, 1
64. Translated by W. and E. Muir, New York, 1933, p. 487.

CHAPTER 2

1. For drawings of the 13th through 16th centuries, see T. M. Metzger, *Jewish Life in the Middle Ages*, New York, 1982, pp. 71–74. For Hirsingue and other 19th-century examples, drawings at the Leo Baeck Institute, New York, Archives.
2. Engravings of ca. 1519 by Albrecht Altdorfer show the bimah of Regensburg's medieval synagogue slightly off axis. Perhaps that was the artist's idea, so that he could show enough of the bimah to make it intelligible.
3. This tension in synagogue design was first and most authoritatively discussed by Krautheimer, *Mitt. Syn.*
4. He was preceded in this by Maimonides, *Mishneh Torah*, Tefillah XI, 3 (completed ca. 1180); see also Deut. 31:11 as a possible Biblical source for this idea.
5. The transverse arrangement is seen also at the Old Kloyz in Vilnius, but that was built as a house of study. It was seen also at Rotterdam, 1725, and Celle, 1780. The bimah is in the center of a synagogue in a 15th-century Mantuan manuscript of Jacob ben Asher's *Arba'ah Turim*, Vatican Library, Cod. Rossi 555, illustrated in C. Roth, ed., *Jewish Art*, New York, 1961, cols. 415–16.
6. A. Perlin, "The Liturgy and Liturgical Context Surrounding the Reading of the Torah: Shabbat Morning in the Ashkenazic Rite," M.A. thesis, Hebrew Union College-Jewish Institute of Religion, New York, 1982, p. 80.
7. Prague-Altneuschul; Worms–before the 19th century; Frankfurt am Main–after 1711; Łańcut; Volpa, etc. Seating plans of various dates survive for Worms, Bischheim in Alsace, Casale Monferrato, and Amsterdam.
8. Grotte, *Deutsche*, p. 13, lists pre-Reform bimahs that were located at the east. The number of prayers uttered during the moving of the scrolls between ark and bimah depended upon the distance between these ritual furnishings: Perlin, "Reading the Torah," p. 58. Perhaps these congregations said fewer prayers than did others.
9. Cecil Roth clarified the different words by quoting an anecdote in Italian, concerning an anti-Semite who says that he borrows money from an Israelite (a term of respect), owes it to a Hebrew (a neutral term), and has to pay it back to a Jew (a term used derisively).
10. Sephardic prayers are uttered in unison, but writers on the changes in Ashkenazic

worship related the changes to church practice, not to Sephardic influence.

11. Bachi, pp. 25–46. Lax attendance and poor observance of religious practice were not only 19th-century phenomena, see T. Endelman, *The Jews of Georgian England, 1714–1830,* Philadelphia, 1979, pp. 132–34.
12. Similarly, A. Z. Idelsohn, *Jewish Liturgy and its Development,* New York, 1932, p. 276.
13. The ark described in Kings "is that of the priestly and Deuteronomic writers" (J. Gutmann, "Deuteronomy: Religious Reformation or Iconoclastic Revolution?" in J. Gutmann, ed., *The Image and the Word: Confrontations in Judaism, Christianity, and Islam,* Missoula, 1977, p. 12).
14. K. Goldenberg, "Die Kultus-und Profanbauten der Juden. Erläutert an Hand von Hamburg-Altona-Wandsbek," diss., Dresden Technische Hochschule, ca. 1922, p. 41.
15. Paris-rue Notre Dame de Nazareth, Paris-rue Pavée, Budapest-Dohány Street, Stockholm. In small synagogues: Ancona-Levantina, Ramsgate, Cheltenham.
16. See Jewish encyclopedias, s.v. Eternal Light, or *ner tamid* in Hebrew.
17. b. Shabbat 22b.
18. *Midrash Rabbah* Ex. 36:1, H. Freedman and M. Simon, London, 1961, p. 438.
19. Ibid., Ex. 36:2, p. 438; Ex. 36:3, p. 439; Lev. 31:4, p. 397.
20. S. Klass, *Responsa of Modern Judaism,* New York, 1966, vol. 2, pp. 297 98; Grotte, *Deutsche;* and A. Breier, M. Eisler, and M. Grünwald, eds., *Holzsynagogen in Polen,* Baden bei Wien, 1934.
21. See Jewish encyclopedias, s.v. Pulpit.
22. Very elaborate ones are found at Casale Monferrato and Florence.
23. The installation of organs was sharply criticized by orthodox rabbis who felt that using an organ imitated Christian practice. They preferred the traditional irregular and personal way of chanting prayers. By 1886, however, at least 65 synagogues had organs, and many more had them after that date. The list of 65 synagogues is in *Magyar Zsidó Szemle* III (1886), pp. 506–7.
24. b. Sukkah 51b; b. M. Middoth II, 5; in Zechariah 12:12 we read that wives mourned separately.
25. For a general account of the women's section, see Krautheimer, *Mitt. Syn.*, pp. 132–35. The Talmud, j. Berakoth III, 3, says that women must hear the Torah reading and follow prayers; b. Megillah 23a says that women have the right to read from the Torah but "the sages said that a woman should not read the Torah out of respect for the congregation."
26. Prov. 1:8, 6:20; for the connection of these verses concerning forsaking the teachings of one's parent, see B. Litvin, *The Sanctity of the Synagogue,* New York, 1959, p. 146.
27. b. Berakoth 16a on the effect of synagogues. Litvin, *Sanctity of the Synagogue,* pp. 130–35, 164–65, 218 on defiling thoughts.
28. Litvin, *Sanctity of the Synagogue,* p. 134.
29. b. Megillah 23a. See also Perlin, "Reading the Torah," pp. 110–11. Only Liberal (U.S.A. Reform) seminaries ordain women as rabbis. The first woman graduate of the Berlin theological academy was imprisoned at Terezín where Chief Rabbi Unger would not let her conduct services. Before her death, she was allowed to comfort other inmates and to teach; see R. Feder, "Religious Life in Terezín," *Terezín,* Prague, 1965, p. 52. In Renaissance Florence, women used Hebrew letters but Italian words: U. Cassuto, *Gli ebrei a Firenze nell'età del rinascimento,* Florence, 1918, p. 217 (Pubblicazioni del R. Istituto di Studi Superiori, Practici e di Perfezionamento in Firenze. Sezione di Filosofia e Filologia).
30. Litvin, *Sanctity of the Synagogue,* pp. 258–59.
31. One exception may be the Pinkas Synagogue at Prague, where more seats seem to have been allocated to women: H. Volavková, *The Pinkas Synagogue,* Prague, 1955, p. 78. Perhaps part of the space later used for women's seats was built originally for other purposes.
32. C. Roth, *The Great Synagogue, London, 1690–1940,* London, 1950, p. 74.
33. J. J. Schudt, *Jüdische Merckwürdigkeiten,*

Frankfurt am Main, 1715, bk. 6, chap. 32, para. 6, pp. 220–21; Grotte, *Deutsche,* p. 21; on crowding to the door to see the Torah being raised, W. P. Eckert, "Aus den Akten des Trienter Judenprozesses," *Miscellanea Medievalia. Veröffentlichungen des Thomas-Instituts an der Universität Köln, IV: Judentum im Mittelalter. Beiträge zum christlich-jüdischen Gespräch,* Berlin, 1961, p. 319.

34. The women's area under the men's prayer hall is known in towns of the Comtat Venaissin and in nearby Avignon. For a description, see T. Platter, Jr., *Beschreibung der Reisen durch Frankreich, Spanien, England, und die Niederlände, 1595–1600,* Basel and Stuttgart [1968], p. 128. For women seated in the sexton's wine cellar, see Litvin, *Sanctity of the Synagogue,* p. 146. See also Wischnitzer, *Architecture,* pp. 71–72 and p. 284 n. 37.
35. If a synagogue was set up in a narrow building, the women's annex might have to be on the ark or entrance end, rather than along the sides. If the ark was moved, as it was at Casale Monferrato, the preexisting annexes might remain on the new ark wall.
36. Fürth, as remodeled in 1692; Frankfurt am Main after 1711.
37. I. Zangwill, *Children of the Ghetto,* Philadelphia, 1892, vol. 2, p. 317.
38. Perhaps the oval gallery of the Venetian synagogues was avoided elsewhere, as in Trieste, because people objected to having a gallery over the ark.
39. Hasidic and ultraorthodox synagogues have grilles or screens preferably about 1.5 m. or more in height; less strict congregations have lower barriers. See S. Rubenstein, *The Synagogue. An Illustrated Analysis of the Aspects of the Synagogue,* New York, 1972–73, p. 6.
40. A. Rosengarten, the Jewish architect who helped to design the Kassel synagogue ca. 1840, said that the congregation did not require grilles to hide the women, though that had been customary earlier; see R. Hallo, *Kasseler Synagogengeschichte (= Die Geschichte der Judengemeinde Kassel),* Kassel, 1932, p. 62. On the Prinzregentenstrasse synagogue, see S. Baron, *A Social and Religious History of the Jews,* New York, vol. 3, 1937, p. 149 n. 25. Men and women now sit together at the Neolog (moderate Reform) Dohány Street synagogue in Budapest. Perhaps the congregation does not insist on the rules, or finds it impossible to monitor a huge synagogue that has become a tourist attraction.
41. I. Levy, *The Synagogue,* London, 1963, p. 39, cites Loeb, *Kitve Maharil,* Jerusalem, 1960, p. 189.
42. Przysucha: L. Dobroszycki and B. Kirshenblatt-Gimblett, *Image before my Eyes,* New York, 1977, p. 61. L'vov: M. Bałaban, *Zydzi Lwowscy na przełomie XVI-go wieku,* L'vov, 1906, figs. 24, 54, and Grotte, *Deutsche,* p. 17. For Prague: S. Baron, *Social, Religious History,* vol. 2, 1937, p. 93.

CHAPTER 3

1. Krautheimer, *Mitt. Syn.,* p. 54; A. Seager, "Ancient Synagogue Architecture: An Overview," in J. Gutmann, ed., *Ancient Synagogues: The State of Research,* Chico, Calif., 1981, pp. 39ff.; F.-G. Hüttenmeister, "Synagogues et écoles en Palestine, Ier–VIIe siècles," in B. Blumenkranz, ed., *Art et archéologie des juifs en France médiévale,* Toulouse, 1980, pp. 143–56, esp. p. 145 with further references. The function of galleries and apses (see below) may not have been fixed until the religion itself became more clearly defined by the compilation of the Talmud; see Krautheimer, *Mitt. Syn.,* p. 55.
2. See Gutmann, ed., *Ancient Synagogues;* F.-G. Hüttenmeister and G. Reeg, "Die antiken Synagogen in Israel," *Beiheft zum Tübinger Atlas des Vorderer Orients* 12/1, Wiesbaden, 1977; G. Foerster, "A Survey of Ancient Diaspora Synagogues," in L. I. Levine, ed., *Ancient Synagogues Revealed,* Jerusalem, 1981, pp. 164–71. If the Aegina building was a synagogue, the apse may have been used to seat congregational elders. That was perhaps done at Sardis, where the ark was not kept in the apse; see A. Seager, "The Synagogue at Sardis," in Levine, *Ancient Synagogues*

Revealed, pp. 178–84. For Stobi, see also J. Wiseman, "Stobi in Yugoslavian Macedonia. Archaeological Excavations and Research 1977–78," *Journal of Field Archaeology* V, #4 (1978), pp. 391–429; J. Wiseman with D. Mano-Zissi, "Excavations at Stobi," *American Journal of Archaeology* LXXV (1971), pp. 395–411; LXXVI (1972), pp. 407–24; LXXVII (1973), pp. 391–403; D. Moe, "The Cross and the Menorah," *Archaeology* XXX (1977), pp. 148–57; A Marmorstein, "The Synagogue of Claudius Tiberius Polycharmus in Stobi," *Jewish Quarterly Review* XXVII (1937), pp. 373–84. For the existence of a synagogue in Solin, Dalmatia, near Split, see Y. Eventov, *A History of Yugoslav Jews,* vol. 1, Tel Aviv, 1971.

3. *Encyclopedia Judaica,* 1971, s.v. Art; L. A. Mayer, ed., *Bibliography of Jewish Art,* Jerusalem, 1967; C. Roth, ed., *Jewish Art,* London, 1961; R. Gordis and M. Davidowitz, eds., *Art in Judaism,* New York, 1975; J. Gutmann, "Prolegomenon," and "The Second Commandment and the Image in Judaism," in idem, ed., *No Graven Images: Studies in Art and the Hebrew Bible,* New York, 1971, pp. xi–lxiii, 1–14.
4. J. Gutmann, "Deuteronomy: Religious Reformation or Iconoclastic Revolution?" in idem, ed., *The Image and the Word: Confrontations in Judaism, Christianity, and Islam,* Missoula, 1977, pp. 5–25; I. Z. Kahana, "Synagogue Art in Halakhic Literature," *Bet ha-knesset,* ed. M. Hacohen, Jerusalem, 1955, pp. 255–308 (in Hebrew); D. Kaufmann, "Zur Geschichte der Kunst in den Synagogen," *Gesammelte Schriften,* ed. M. Brann, Frankfurt am Main, 1908, pp. 87–103; S. Klass, *Responsa of Modern Judaism,* Brooklyn (New York), 1966, vol. 2, pp. 298–300.
5. The Talmud is also silent about imagery, specifics of ark and bimah design, and women's accommodation. On post-Talmudic prescriptions, see C. Touati, "La synagogue dans la littérature rabbinique," in B. Blumenkranz, ed., *Art et archéologie,* pp. 133–35.
6. Relevant statutes are in the Theodosian Code: Lib. I, tit. 9, art. 14; Lib. IX, tit. 45, art. 2; Lib. XVI, tit. 8, art. 9, 12, 20–22, 25–27; Novella 3, para. 3 (=Justinianic code Lib. I, tit. 9, art. 18). Letters of Gregory the Great, J. P. Migne, ed., *Patrologia (Latina),* Paris, 1896, vol. 77 (Lib. I, ep. XXXV), col. 489; (Lib. I, ep. XLVII) cols. 509–11; (Lib. IX, ep. VI), cols. 944–45.
7. P. P. Argenti, *The Religious Minorities of Chios: Jews and Roman Catholics,* Cambridge, 1970, esp. pp. 43–45; J. Juster, *Les juifs dans l'empire romain. Leur condition juridique, économique, et sociale,* Paris, 1914, vol. 1, esp. pp. 456–72; J. Parkes, *The Conflict of the Church and the Synagogue,* Cleveland, 1961, esp. pp. 379–91; E. Synan, *The Popes and the Jews in the Middle Ages,* New York, 1965.
8. Juster, *Les juifs . . . ,* vol. 1, pp. 456ff.
9. Justinianic Code Lib. I, tit. 5, art. 17; Novella 37 of 535; Ecloga, App. 4, 13; see Juster, *Les juifs . . . ,* p. 473 (n. 9 to p. 472).
10. Clermont-Ferrand: Aronius, *Regesten,* p. 14, #38; Orléans, ibid., p. 18, # 48; Syracuse, ibid., p. 310 n. 68.
11. See above, n. 7. On avoiding forced baptism, see J.P. Migne, ed., *Patrologia (Latina)* vol. 77, (Lib. I, ep. XLVII), cols. 509–11.
12. Ibid. (Lib. II, ep. VI), col. 457. This was used as the precedent for removing a synagogue in London in 1272; see H. G. Richardson, *The English Jewry under Angevin Kings,* London, 1960, p. 195. For Troyes: G. Caro, *Sozial-und Wirtschaftsgeschichte der Juden im Mittelalter und der Neuzeit,* Frankfurt am Main, 1924, vol. 2, p. 107; for Sens: S. Grayzel, *The Church and the Jews in the XIIIth Century,* Philadelphia, 1933, Doc. #14, pp. 106–7; for Segovia: O. d'Araujo, "La grande synagogue de Ségovie," *Revue des études juives* XXXIX (1912), pp. 209–16; for London, 1765: C. Roth, *The Great Synagogue, 1690–1940,* London, 1950, p. 137; for Thionville, 1806: A. Kohn, "Zur Geschichte der Juden in Diedenhofen," *Festschrift zur Einweihung der neuen Synagoge in Diedenhofen, 19 September, 1913,* Thionville, 1913, p. 34. In the 20th century, noisy prayers constituted the pretext for removing synagogues at Znamenka and Lublin (*AJYb* 1913–1914 [1913], p. 328). If they really

were built too close to churches, under the law such construction should have been prevented in the first place.

13. Among the books useful here are: Aronius, *Regesten;* B. Blumenkranz, *Juifs et chrétiens dans le monde occidental 430–1096,* Paris, 1960 (École pratique des hautes-études, Sorbonne. Sixième section: Sciences économiques et sociales. Études juives), esp. pp. 294ff.; H. Guttmann, "Zur Rechtslage der Synagoge im Mittelalter," *Emlékkönyv néhai Dr. Kohn Sámuel,* eds. S. Hevesi and L. Löwinger, Budapest, 1941, pp. 177–91, esp. pp. 189–91; S. Katz, *The Jews of the Visigothic and Frankish Kingdoms of Spain and Gaul,* Cambridge, Mass., 1937; G. Kisch, *The Jews in Medieval Germany: A Study of their Legal and Social Status,* Chicago, 1949, esp. pp. 294–95.
14. H. Wilson, *The Gelasian Sacramentary,* Oxford, 1894, p. 141. A sacramentary is one of the early service books of the Roman Catholic Church, containing the celebrant's part of the Mass and prayers to be offered at baptisms, ordinations, and consecrations. The name of Pope Gelasius (pontificate 492–96) was associated wrongly with this version of the sacramentary.
15. Sixteenth council of Toledo, 633, cited by Blumenkranz, *Juifs et chrétiens,* p. 313.
16. Among the pertinent sources are: F. Baer, *Die Juden im christlichen Spanien,* Berlin, 1936; S. Baron, *A Social and Religious History of the Jews,* New York, 1952ff.; M. Bersohn, *Dyplomataryusz dotyczący Żydów w dawnej Polsce, 1388–1782,* Warsaw, 1910; P. Bloch, *Die Generalprivilegien der polnischen Judenschaft,* Poznań, 1892; G. Caro, *Sozial und Wirtschaftsgeschichte;* V. Colorni, *Gli ebrei nel sistema del diritto comune fino alla prima emancipazione,* Milan, 1956; H. Fischer, *Die Verfassungsrechtliche Stellung der Juden in den deutschen Städten während des dreizehnten Jahrhunderts,* Wrocław, 1931; S. Grayzel, *The Church and the Jews;* S. Krauss, "The Christian Legislation on the Synagogue," *Ignace Goldziher Memorial Volume,* Part II, Jerusalem, 1958, pp. 14–42; M. Stern, *Urkündliche Beiträge über die Stellung der Päpste zu den Juden,* Kiel, 1893; S. Stern, *Der preussische Staat und die Juden,* 3 Teil: *Die Zeit Friedrichs des Grossen,* New York, 1949 (Schriftenreihe wissenschaftlicher Abhandlungen des Leo Baeck Instituts, 24), Tübingen, 1971; O. Stobbe, *Die Juden in Deutschland während des Mittelalters in politischer, socialer, und rechtlicher Beziehung,* 3d ed., Braunschweig, 1923.
17. E.g., provincial synod of Gniezno archdiocese, 1267: Aronius, *Regesten,* pp. 301–3, #724, the statute of the Jewry in *Statutes of the Realm* (England), vol. 1, pp. 221, 221a; for Austria: Duke Frederick of Austria, 1244, in Stobbe, *Die Juden in Deutschland,* p. 267.
18. P. Bloch, *Die Generalprivilegien;* Grotte, *Deutsche,* pp. 66–67 for expulsions and new settlements in Bohemia.
19. J. Zwarts, "Joodse gemeente buiten Amsterdam," in H. Brugmans and A. Frank, eds., *Geschiedenis der Joden in Nederland,* vol. 1, Amsterdam, 1940, p. 450. Jews lived in Fürth near Nuremberg, Altona near Hamburg, Maarssen near Utrecht, Obuda near Buda and Pest, Praga near Warsaw, etc. Jews also slept in Przytyk and worked in Radom, slept in Rozprza and worked in Piotrków: Piechotka, p. 16.
20. Expelled from England, 1290, Spain, 1492, and Portugal, 1496. Pius V tried to banish them from most towns in the papal states with his bull, *Hebraeorum gens sola,* issued February 26, 1569. For France, see G. Caro, *Sozial-und Wirtschaftsgeschichte,* vol. 1, p. 358. The Jews' goods were confiscated in Mainz in 1096, Speyer in 1195, Frankfurt am Main in 1241: see Aronius, *Regesten,* p. 88, #186, pp. 151–52, #337, pp. 226–27, #529. Synagogues granted as gifts, e.g., Basel, 1401, see M. Wiener, *Regesten zur Geschichte der Juden in Deutschland während des Mittelalters,* Hannover, 1862, p. 55, #17; Erfurt and Halle, 1467, ibid., p. 90, #78; London-Threadneedle Street, Basinghall Street before 1256, see Richardson, *English Jewry,* p. 197; Brno, 1454 (where part of the synagogue became an

abattoir), Wiener, *Regesten,* p. 247, #223. Görlitz's Jews had to move in and out of town, see A. Levy, *Geschichte der Juden in Sachsen,* Berlin, 1900, pp. 28–29.

21. Location: Frankfurt am Main (M. Stern, *Urkündliche Beiträge,* pp. 64–65, #59), Cologne (Aronius, *Regesten,* p. 127, #296), and Trier (ibid., pp. 209–10, #475).
22. Speyer, 1084: *Encyclopedia Judaica,* 1971, s.v. Jewish Quarter; Turin, Jews regretted the passing of the ghetto: *Jewish Chronicle,* May 11, 1860, p. 2; Verona, Jews rejoiced at the creation of a ghetto that ensured their safety and hindered assimilation: N. Pavoncello, *Gli ebrei in Verona dalle origini al secolo XX,* Verona, 1960, p. 31. Sephardic Jews in Venice moved near the existing ghetto before they had to be enclosed in one.
23. For Wörlitz, see Figs. 8, 9 and H. Eschwege, *Die Synagoge,* pp. 90–91, and Wischnitzer, *Architecture,* p. 160; Rheda: W. Weinberg, *Tale of a Torah Scroll,* Cincinnati, 1976, p. 2. I am grateful to Professor Werner Weinberg for a helpful letter and for a copy of this publication. Lequeu: H. Rosenau, "Architecture and the French Revolution: Jean Jacques Lequeu," *Architectural Review* CVI (August 1949), pp. 111–16, esp. pp. 112–13; idem, "German Synagogues in the Early Period of Emancipation," *Publications of the Leo Baeck Institute. Yearbook* VIII (1963), pp. 214–25, esp. pp. 219–20; also Buda, Łańcut, Lublin, Będzin, Casale Monferrato, Cífer, Riga, Ostrog, Prague, Wrocław. For Provence in general, see D. Iancu-Agou, "Topographie des quartiers juifs en Provence médiévale," *Revue des études juives* CXXXIII, #1–2 (1974), pp. 11–156.
24. Ejected from Dresden and Meissen: A. Levy, "Notes sur l'histoire des juifs de Saxe," *Revue des études juives* XXV (1892), pp. 223–26; from Cologne: A. Kober, *Cologne,* Philadelphia, 1940, p. 97; from Świdnica: A. Grotte, *Synagogenspuren in schlesischen Kirchen,* Wrocław, 1937, pp. 29–30 (Schriften der Gesellschaft zur Förderung der Wissenschaft des Judentums, 41); from Nuremberg: see Jewish encyclopedias, ad loc. London's Jews settled in the East End beyond the city limits because the city authorities allowed only freemen to open retail shops and Jews could not be freemen: Roth, *Great Synagogue,* p. 153.
25. Libeň: B. Nosek, "Die jüdische Gemeinde in Libeň [ex Lieben] im 16 bis 19 Jahrhundert," *Judaica Bohemiae* XVI, #2 (1980), pp. 103–18, esp. pp. 104–5.
26. See Acts 16:13.
27. R. Wischnitzer, "Starinnaia synagoga ve Lutsk," *Novy Voskhod,* 1913, #1, cols. 48–52; M. Bersohn, *Dyplomataryusz,* pp. 128–29.
28. H.S.N., "The Jews of Spain in the Nineteenth Century," *Jewish Chronicle,* April 28, 1848, pp. 515–16; May 5, 1848, pp. 523–24; May 12, 1848, pp. 531–32; May 26, 1848, pp. 547–48.
29. In some parts of Germany ca. 1500 the Jews could own land but they could not own it elsewhere: G. Kisch, *Jewry Law in Medieval Germany,* New York, 1949, p. 110. Popes protected Jews' rights to own land in much of Italy north of Rome: M. Stern, *Urkündliche Beiträge,* pp. 38ff., #31, p. 54, #49. The bull *Cum nimis absurdum* governing papal lands (1555) said, "nec . . . bona immobilia possedere possint." Permission to own land varied with place and century.
30. Seating capacity and limiting Jewish population in Prussia: H. Sachar, *The Course of Modern Jewish History,* Cleveland and New York [1958], p. 36 concerning Hamburg, 1710. In Rome, under popes Julius II in 1504 and Clement VII in 1524, and in Saxony in 1711, privileged Jews were allowed to pray but only in low voices in private houses: M. Stern, *Urkündliche Beiträge,* pp. 68ff., #68, #69; A. Levy, *Geschichte,* p. 55. Italian Jews in Nijkerk could have a synagogue in 1728 if it looked like a house on the exterior; J. Zwarts, "Joodse gemeenten buiten Amsterdam," p. 435.
31. A. Müller, *Geschichte der Juden in Nürnberg, 1146–1945,* Nuremberg, 1968, p. 20 (Beiträge zur Geschichte und Kultur der Stadt Nürnberg, 12).
32. C. Roth, "Jewish Art and Artists before

Emancipation," in Roth, ed., *Jewish Art,* p. 511. M. Lowenthal, *A World Passed By,* New York, 1933, p. 185, says that Joseph was called "supervisor and master of the work." The distinction may be significant, as "officer" could refer to the head of a lay building committee rather than to a master builder.

33. F. Cantera y Burgos, "España medieval: Arqueología," *The Sephardi Heritage,* ed. R. D. Barnett, New York, 1971, pp. 29–68, esp. p. 60. It is not clear how we know that Gali was a Jew and not, say, a convert to Christianity at that time. He built the *cimborio* of the Seo de Zaragoza soon afterward, with Christian and Moslem architects, according to Cantera y Burgos.
34. M. Wischnitzer, *A History of Jewish Crafts and Guilds,* New York, 1965, p. 211. Documents refer also to Sicilian Jewish building craftsmen, and there was a Jewish carpenters' guild in Palermo in the 1480s, according to the Jewish traveler and writer, Obadiah de Bertinoro; see M. Wischnitzer, "Notes to a History of the Jewish Guilds," in J. Gutmann, ed., *Beauty in Holiness: Studies in Jewish Customs and Ceremonial Art,* New York, 1970, p. 25.
35. Krautheimer, *Mitt. Syn.,* n. 142; A. Wolf, "Etwas über jüdische Kunst und ältere jüdische Künstler," *Mitteilungen der Gesellschaft für jüdische Volkskunde* V, #1, Heft 9 (1902), pp. 45, 48–49.
36. V. Benda, *The State Jewish Museum in Prague,* Prague, n.d., p. 19. This information, from Judah's tombstone, is translated into English in Wischnitzer, *Architecture,* p. 78.
37. Gniezno: A. Warschauer, *Geschichte der Stadt Gnesen,* Poznań, 1918, pp. 131ff.; Hungary: I. Heller and Z. Vajda, *The Synagogues of Hungary. An Album,* New York, 1968, p. 18; carpenters: M. Wischnitzer, *A History . . . ,* p. 175; brick manufacturer, builder: ibid., pp. 178–79; Poland: Z. Zajczyk, "Architektura barokowych bożnic murowanych w Polsce," *Biuletyn Naukowy* (= *Biuletyn Historii Sztuki*) I, #4 (1933); Piechotka, esp. p. 34. Jewish craftsmen named Moses ben David, David Fels, and Joseph Tudesco worked on the London-Creechurch Lane synagogue (17th century) but they were not designers: see Roth, *Great Synagogue,* pp. 2–3.
38. Tradition credits Simcha ben Solomon Weiss from Lutsk as builder of the 18th-century Nasielsk synagogue (M. Bersohn, "Einiges über die alten Holzsynagogen in Polen," *Mitteilungen der Gesellschaft für jüdische Volkskunde* VII, #2, Heft 14 [1904], p. 12), though he may have been only the painter-decorator. Jewish painters embellished synagogues with folk art decoration, but there is no evidence that they designed or constructed buildings (Zajczyk, "Architektura barokowych," p. 195). Ezekiel ben Moses from Sokal need not have constructed the Lukov (ex Maciejów) masonry synagogue ("1781, year of completion of the decoration. Work of Ezekiel son of Moses from Sokal," quoted in M. Wischnitzer, *A History . . . ,* p. 231). Jewish goldsmiths made Christian liturgical objects but are less likely to have worked on a building before emancipation (Wolf, "Etwas über jüdische Kunst . . . ," *Mitteilungen,* V, #1, Heft 9 [1902], pp. 43–44) for they would have had to work beside Christians who were, moreover, members of restrictive construction guilds (M. Bersohn, "Einiges über die alten Holzsynagogen in Polen," *Mitteilungen der Gesellschaft für jüdische Volkskunde* IV, #2, Heft 8 [1901], p. 169). After emancipation, in the late 19th century, Ludwig Levy designed a Protestant church and Gioachino Levi won a competition to paint the Mondoví cathedral in 1859 (*Jewish Chronicle,* Feb. 11, 1859). See also *AZJ,* 1860, p. 168 for Jewish-Christian collaboration on churches and synagogues at Düdelsheim in Hessen in the 1850s and 1860s, and Wolf, *Mitteilungen,* neue Reihe I, Heft 1 (= VIII, Heft 15) (1905), p. 44.
39. Zajczyk, "Architektura barokowych"; in the second half of the 18th century, Hillel Benjamin of Łask near Łódź built the timber synagogue at Lutomiersk and the wooden synagogue of Zolochev; see Bersohn, in *Mitteilungen,* IV, #2, Heft 8 (1901), pp. 182–83. S. Goldberg con-

nected Hillel's name to the synagogue at Kórnik in "Die Holzsynagoge zu Kurnik," *Mitteilungen zur jüdischen Volkskunde,* n.F. III, Heft 1 (= X, Heft 21) (1907), pp. 67–69.

40. A. Balletti, *Gli ebrei e gli estensi,* Reggio Emilia, 1930, p. 95.
41. Krautheimer, *Mitt. Syn.,* p. 194, gives the German translation of the Hebrew inscription as "David, Sohn des R. Israel, die Steine der Pforten erworben hat." Can this mean that David inherited the ownership of the synagogue?
42. G. Lukomski, *Jewish Art in European Synagogues,* New York, 1947, p. 46.
43. Matteo Gucci is thought to have remodeled the Old Synagogue in Cracow/Kazimierz ca. 1570. Paolo Romano is said to have designed the Isaac Nachmanowicz Synagogue in L'vov, 1582. Francesco Olivieri was probably responsible for the Isaac Jacobowicz Synagogue in Cracow/Kazimierz, 1638–44. Peter Ronka of Poznań built that of Brest in Belorussia, mid-16th century. See Piechotka, passim. To be sure, an architect who worked for the local ruler, as Gucci and Romano did, need not have worked for the Jews whom the rulers supervised, although historians assume that they did so.
44. L. Ehrmann, "Synagogen," *Die jüdischen Denkmäler in der Tschekoslowakei,* ed. S. H. Lieben, Prague, 1933, p. 7. A. Grotte, "Historische Baudokumente jüdischer Wanderung in Böhmen and Mähren," *Jahrbuch der Gesellschaft für die Geschichte der Juden in der Čechoslovakischen Republik* VII (1935), pp. 399–409.
45. The bull that instituted the ghetto was *Cum nimis absurdum,* issued July 14, 1555.
46. The best example of this is the granting of civil rights to the Sephardic Jews in France in 1790 and to Ashkenazic Jews only in 1791. The Sephardim were not eager to have the rights granted to the lowly Ashkenazim (Z. Szajkowski, "Relations among Sephardim, Ashkenazim, and Avignonese Jews in France from the 16th to the 20th Centuries," *Jews and the French Revolutions of 1789, 1830, and 1848,* New York, 1970, pp. 235–66, esp. pp. 243–49, 261–66; also idem, "Emancipation of Jews During the French Revolution. A Bibliography of Books, Pamphlets, and Printed Documents, 1789–1800," *Studies in Bibliography and Booklore* III, #3–4 [December 1958], p. 87). In Livorno, Sephardim did not want synagogues other than their own (S. Baron, *Social, Religious History,* vol. 14, 1969, p. 92). In England, Sephardim were reluctant to admit Ashkenazim lest the former be obliged to support the more numerous poor of the latter group (Roth, *Great Synagogue,* p. 253). The Sephardim in Manchester rebuffed overtures made by Ashkenazic Jews (*History of the Manchester Congregation of Spanish and Portuguese Jews [1873–1923],* Introduction by H. Pereira Mendes, Manchester, 1923, pp. 24–33).
47. Privileges, see Aronius, *Regesten,* pp. 71–74, #170 for Speyer (1096); Baron, *Social, Religious History,* vol. 14, 1969, p. 165 for M. Meisel at Prague; M. Stern, *Urkündliche Beiträge,* p. 21, #7 for Lublin, 1567; A. Milano, "La costituzione 'Livornina' del 1593," *Israel. La rassegna mensile* XXXIV (1968), pp. 394–410, and idem, "Gli antecedenti della 'Livornina' del 1593," ibid., XXXVIII (1972), pp. 343–40. Granting privileges even in papal territories brought into existence 115 synagogues in 46 cities between 1565 and 1569; M. Stern, *Urkündliche Beiträge,* pp. 143–45, #134, #135. Colorni, *Gli ebrei,* p. 8 points out that the canon law promulgated after the closing of the *Extravagantes comunes* was not binding on localities that had no supporting measures or that did not publish the church document officially. His pp. 8–13 and 47, with notes, give a succinct account of applicable church law and principal bulls affecting synagogues.
48. Pius V's bull, *Hebraeorum gens sola,* issued on Feb. 26, 1569, restricted Jews in the Papal States to Rome and Ancona. Sixtus V's bull, *Christiana pietas* of Oct. 2, 1586, revoked it, but Clement VIII's bull, *Caeca et obdurata* of Feb. 25, 1593, revoked *Christiana pietas.* All the same, Clement VIII authorized a synagogue at

Sermide by a bull of Aug. 8, 1598.

49. S. Baron, *Social, Religious History,* vol. 14, 1969, pp. 116–17 gives the dates when the ghetto was instituted in various Italian cities.
50. Five separate congregations with separate synagogue rooms were allowed in Rome, but they had to share a single building. There were several synagogues and oratories in Venice for different ritual groups.
51. Rouffach; Bamberg; Miltenberg; České Budějovice; Poznań-Old; Frankfurt am Main, 1460; Prague-Pinkas; Cracow/Kazimierz-Old. This type persisted.
52. Krautheimer, *Mitt. Syn.,* p. 87.
53. Exodus 27:21, 36:35, 40:21.
54. Mordecai ben Hillel (d. 1290), in his Shabbat, Chap. III, para. 311, cited in S. Freehof, *Reform Jewish Practice and its Rabbinical Background,* New York, 1963, pp. 184–85; Rabbi Eliezer ben Joel Halevi, ca. 1200, cited by I. Elbogen, *Der jüdische Gottesdienst und seine geschichtliche Entwicklung,* Leipzig, 1913, n. 127; RaSHi, cited in Touati, "La synagogue dans la littérature rabbinique," p. 134.
55. Krautheimer, *Mitt. Syn.,* p. 134 and n. 30, and see above, Chap. 2, n. 34. The women's section of the later synagogue at Brest in Belorussia was a separate building, see L. Dobroszycki and B. Kirshenblatt-Gimblett, *Image before my Eyes,* New York, 1977, p. 60.
56. For the meaning and impact of the Second Commandment, and for Talmudic and medieval sources about synagogue art, see works by the following cited in the bibliography below, s.v. Art: L. A. Mayer; J. M. Baumgarten, B. Cohen, B. Jacob, and C. Roth in Gordis and Davidowitz, pp. 13–52, 64–71; J. Gutmann in *No Graven Images,* pp. xi–14, and in *The Image and the Word,* pp. 5–25; I. Z. Kahana, "Synagogue Art in Halakhic Literature." See also *Encyclopedia Judaica,* 1971, s.v. Art, and D. Kaufmann, "Zur Geschichte der Kunst in den Synagogen," *Gesammelte Schriften,* ed. M. Brann, Frankfurt am Main, 1908, pp. 87–103.
57. Wolf, in *Mitteilungen,* neue Reihe I, Heft 1 (= VIII, Heft 15) (1905), p. 39.
58. While notices about synagogue decorations are rare, those concerning illustration of manuscripts and books are comparatively frequent.
59. Double naves: Prague-Altneuschul; Regensburg; Passau; Worms-men's synagogue and the later women's annex; Erfurt (2d synagogue) ca. 1357; Chełm, probably 17th century; Świdnica; Oleśnica; Cracow/Kazimierz-Old. For Świdnica and Oleśnica, see A. Grotte, *Synagogenspuren in schlesischen Kirchen,* Wrocław, 1937 (Schriften der Gesellschaft zur Förderung der Wissenschaft des Judentums, 41).
60. Worms: Women's annex; Eger.
61. Prague-Altneuschul; Cracow/Kazimierz-Old. It is sometimes said (e.g., H. Frauberger, "Über Bau und Ausschmückung alter Synagogen," *Mitteilungen der Gesellschaft zur Erforschung jüdischer Kunstdenkmäler* II [1901]) that the two columns represent Jakhin and Boaz at the Temple of Solomon, but this interpretation is not known before the 17th century, according to Krautheimer, *Mitt. Syn.,* p. 110.
62. Regensburg (although A. Grotte thought that there were four internal supports: "Die Beeinflussung jüdischer östlicher Sakralkunst durch Prager Vorbilder," *Jahrbuch der Gesellschaft für die Geschichte der Juden in der Čechoslovakischen Republik* VI [1934], p. 457).
63. Toledo, both extant synagogues, although the present ceilings are later; Vatican MS Rossi 555, Mantua, 1435 (Roth, *Jewish Art,* opp. cols. 415–16); Catalan painting of "Christ Among the Doctors," Metropolitan Museum of Art, New York; Italian Machsor MS of 1425, G. Weill Collection (*L'Arche,* #79–80 [Aug.–Sept. 1963], p. 123).
64. For a discussion of extra ribs, see below, Prague-Altneuschul, Sopron; also Krautheimer, *Mitt. Syn.,* p. 107. It is unlikely that extra ribs were added to avoid a cross shape, as explained below.
65. Ostia, 4th century; Prague-Altneuschul, 14th century. Ark chests are shown in 14th-century and later manuscripts illustrated in T. and M. Metzger, *Jewish Life in*

the Middle Ages, New York, 1982, figs. 88–93, 96–98, on pp. 62–69.

66. Also Zamość and Dřevohostice (now transferred to Holešov); an 18th-century example is at Prague-Pinkas. See also A. Grotte, "Alte Almemorgitter," *Ost und West* XVII, #5/6 (1917), cols. 157–62.
67. Prague-Pinkas; Worms; Toledo (both extant synagogues); Strasbourg; Cologne; Speyer after 1349, probably replacing one destroyed in anti-Jewish persecutions of that year.
68. Prague-Altneuschul; Sopron (both medieval synagogues); Tomar.
69. Córdoba; Toledo-Tránsito.
70. Toledo-Blanca.
71. Segovia.
72. There is a niche also at Córdoba, 1315.
73. Wischnitzer, *Architecture,* cited the main sources to ca. 1962; see also D. Cassuto, "Costruzioni rituali ebraiche nell'alto medioevo," *Gli ebrei nell'alto medioevo,* Spoleto, 1980, pp. 1017–57 (Settimane di studio del Centro italiano sull'alto medioevo, 26, Spoleto, 1978).
74. Będzin; Druya.
75. Vilnius-Great; Ostrog; Ostrołęka; Lyuboml; Szczebrzeszyn; also Carpentras, where the Jews were not numerous or greatly privileged.
76. Łuków.
77. Gorokhov; Piotrków Trybunalski.
78. Druya, Gorodok. Most of the Polish-Ukrainian examples in nn. 74–78 come from illustrations in R. Abramovitch, *The Vanished World,* New York, 1947. For Gorodok (ex. Gródek Jagielloński), see G. Lukomski, *Jewish Art in European Synagogues,* New York, 1947.
79. See Wischnitzer, *Architecture,* for these.
80. Joseph Caro (1488–1575), *Shulhan Arukh,* written 1564–71; Caro lived in Bulgaria and the Holy Land. Moses Isserles (1510–72), alias ReMO, *Mappa.* First printed edition of *Shulhan Arukh* with *Mappa:* 1578. Isserles lived in the Kazimierz suburb, now a district of Cracow. For the bimah's central position, see *Mappa* to *Shulhan Arukh,* Orah Hayyim 150:5. A note on popular religious appellations: the name ReMO, from Rabbi Moses, identifies this specific, distinguished scholar from other rabbis named Moses. Another famous abbreviated name is RaSHI, for Rabbi Shlomo (Solomon) ben Isaac, a medieval scholar active at Worms.
81. Imitating alien religions is to be avoided: I Kings:11; see also *Mishnah Rabba,* ed. H. Freedman and M. Simon, London, 1939 on Exodus 36:1 (p. 435).
82. Grotte, *Deutsche,* p. 71.
83. Obuda by A. Landherr, 1820, perhaps with earlier ark, photo courtesy R. Wischnitzer; Kremenets, photo at Leo Baeck Institute, New York: Rogóźno, Grotte, *Deutsche,* p. 52.
84. L'vov-Isaac Nachmanowicz Synagogue, Pińczów, Szczebrzeszyn, Zamość, Prague-High.
85. Grotte, *Deutsche,* passim; for northern Bohemia, see pp. 66–86.
86. Trenčin, L'vov-Suburban. Sephardic synagogues at Tomar, Samokov, Sofia-Cahal de Francos, Gibraltar, Charlotte Amalie. Four main supports stood free in the Amsterdam Sephardic synagogue (1670s) and Altona-Ashkenazic synagogue (surely by 1832, perhaps in 1682 or 1716), but these plans emphasize the longitudinal direction and the columns form a nave and aisles rather than a central canopy as seen at Tomar. For Altona, see R. Klee-Gobert with H. Ramm, *Die Bau und Kunstdenkmäler der Freien und Hansestadt Hamburg,* II, *Altona, Elbevororte,* 2d ed., Hamburg, 1970, p. 102 (I am grateful to H. Hipp for the gift of this book), and Eschwege, *Die Synagoge in der deutschen Geschichte,* p. 86. The vault scheme and overall character of the tiny synagogue of Tomar make a connection with Polish four-support synagogues unlikely. There is no known connection between Byzantine nine-bay church plans and the Polish synagogues.
87. Late 16th century: Przemyśl; 17th century: Brody, Lublin-MaHaRSHaL, L'vov-Suburban, Ostrog, Pinsk, Rzeszów-Old Town, Slonim, Vilnius-Great, Zholkva; 18th century: Łańcut, Lukov, Mikulov, Rzeszów-New Town; 19th century: Jarosław-Great. Date unknown: Druya, Novogrudok, Przeworsk, Rymanów-Great, Tar-

nów.

88. The hemispheric domes at Priluki and Plock may have been added to older buildings in the 19th century.
89. Also Lutsk, Novogrudok, Mikulov-Altschul.
90. Prague-Klaus, Berlin-Heidereutergasse, Ansbach, etc.
91. H. Rosenau, "The Synagogue and Protestant Church Architecture," *Journal of the Warburg and Courtauld Institutes,* IV (1941), pp. 80–84; J. J. van Agt, *Synagogen in Amsterdam,* The Hague, 1974, p. 15.
92. The galleries known at the Meisel Synagogue of Prague in 1689 may have been as old as 1592; see Krautheimer, *Mitt. Syn.,* pp. 135–36, but the evidence is uncertain. For Amsterdam, see van Agt, *Synagogen in Amsterdam,* pp. 13–18.
93. W. S. Samuel, *The First London Synagogue of the Resettlement,* London, 1924 (*Jewish Historical Society of England, Transactions,* X).
94. The integrated gallery may have spread to the mixed Ashkenazic-Sephardic synagogue at Altona, dedicated 1647, burned 1713; an "Oberweiberschul mit einem Geländer" is mentioned in a document cited by K. Goldenberg in "Die Kultus und Profanbauten der Juden. Erläutert an Hand von Hamburg-Altona-Wandsbek," diss., Dresden Technische Hochschule ca. 1922, p. 50.
95. The vestibule had no fixed position. At the late-13th and early-14th-century synagogues of Prague-Altneuschul, Regensburg, and Córdoba, it ran along the south wall. At Sopron-Uj Street #22–24 and later at Pińczów ca. 1600, it was on the north.
96. E. Lissitzky, "The Synagogue of Mogilev. Reminiscences." *Rimon* III (1923), pp. 9–12 (Hebrew). My translation is close to that of A. Kampf who quotes more of the text in "In Quest of Jewish Style in the Era of the Russian Revolution," *Journal of Jewish Art* V (1978), pp. 48–75, esp. p. 52.
97. For these sources, see Kahana, *"Synagogue Art in Halakhic Literature,"* esp. pp. 260–63, and J. Caro, *Avkat Rokhel* (a collection of responsa), #66, translated in S. B. Freehof, ed., *A Treasury of Responsa,* Philadelphia, 1966, pp. 108ff.
98. Inscriptions in Toledo are given in publications by Cantera y Burgos, see below, Toledo. For Ellrich: R. Wischnitzer, "Die Synagoge in Ellrich am Südharz," offprint from *Monatsschrift für Geschichte und Wissenschaft des Judenthums,* 1939; D. Davidowicz, *Wandmalereien in alten Synagogen: Das Wirken des Malers Elieser Sussmann in Deutschland,* Hameln and Hannover, 1969; idem, *Wall Paintings of Synagogues in Poland,* Jerusalem, 1968 (Hebrew). It is likely that the practice of using mural inscriptions began in the later 16th century; see Wolf in *Mitteilungen* V, #1, Heft 9 (1902), p. 50.
99. Paintings in central and eastern Europe: see Davidowicz, *Wandmalereien,* and L. Joel, "Uber jüdische Kunst und Synagogen," *Literarische Warte,* supplement to *Der Israelit* (Frankfurt), July 2, 1914; M. Kremer, "Jewish Artists and Guilds in Former Poland, 16th–18th Centuries," in Gutmann, ed., *Beauty in Holiness,* pp. 34–65; Piechotka; Grotte, "Historische Baudokumente"; and publications by H. Frauberger, H. Strauss, E. Toeplitz, and A. Wolf, cited in the bibliography below, s.v. Art. See also M. Wischnitzer, "Notes to a History of the Jewish Guilds," in Gutmann, ed., *Beauty in Holiness,* pp. 15–33, and idem, *A History . . . ,* esp. pp. 230–31.
100. Davidowicz, *Wandmalereien,* passim.
101. H. Gross, "Étude sur Simson ben Abraham de Sens," *Revue des études juives* VI (1883), p. 169. The Monheim synagogue was adorned ca. 1715–41 with figurative Biblical scenes executed in stucco relief; see Wolf, *Mitteilungen,* neue Reihe I, Heft 1 (= VIII, Heft 15) (1905), p. 40. Documented Jewish artists who decorated wooden synagogues in Poland from the 17th to the early 19th century include: David Friedlander at Grójec and Wyszogród (1810); Samuel Goldbaum (building artisan or painter) at Kępno; Ezekiel ben Moses from Sokal at Lukov (1781); Ber ben Israel (carver of the ark at Uzlyany); Judah Leib ben Baruch at Pogrebishchenskiy; Simcha ben Solomon

Weiss from Slutzk at Nasielsk; Michael Jechiel ben Peretz and Samuel ben Solomon at Zhidachov; Israel ben Mordecai from Jaryczów at Khodorov and Gvozdets (1652); Isaac Baer ben Jehuda Loeb from Jaryczów and his son at Gvozdets (ca. 1729); Isaac Loeb ben Jehuda Hacohen is another version of the father's name.

102. R. Wischnitzer, "Mutual Influences between Eastern and Western Synagogue Architecture from the 12th to the 18th Century," *YIVO Annual of Jewish Social Science* II–III (1947), pp. 25–68, reprinted in Gutmann, *Synagogue,* pp. 265–308. I. Fishoff, "The Architecture of Italian Synagogues: Artistic and Historical Aspects," *Pe'amim. Studies in the Cultural Heritage of Oriental Jewry* VIII (1981), pp. 3–19, esp. p. 19; Pinkerfeld, passim.

103. A census taken by the Germans in Warsaw in 1939 showed 370,000 Jews there. Jewish encyclopedias give additional population statistics.

104. Some new Hasidic centers developed, and had substantial synagogues, e.g., Belz. New industrial cities such as Łódź, and regional capitals such as Warsaw, Kiev, Odessa, Moscow, Riga, and Saint Petersburg (later Leningrad) attracted many Jews and had imposing late-19th-century synagogues built by privileged and culturally assimilated Jews.

105. Architekten-und Ingenieurs-Verein, *Hamburg und seine Bauten, unter Berücksichtigung der Nachbarstädte Altona und Wandsbek,* vol. 2, Hamburg, 1900, p. 90 and fig. 161; "... nach Amerika," *Auswanderung in die Vereinigten Staaten,* exhibition July 4–Sept. 26, 1981, Museum für Hamburgische Geschichte, Catalogue, Heft 5. Introduction by J. Bracker, p. 47; J. Huret, *En Allemagne. De Hambourg aux Marches de Pologne,* Paris, 1908, p. 163; *Aus alter und neuer Zeit,* supplement to *Israelitisches Familienblatt, Beilage* to #24 (June 1925); *Jewish Chronicle,* Feb. 12, 1904; K. Himer, *Die Hamburg-Amerika Linie im sechsten Jahrzehnt ihrer Entwicklung 1897–1907,* Hamburg, 1907, p. 123; B. Kahn, "Die jüdische Auswanderung, I," *Ost und West* V, #7/8 (1905), cols. 457–92; *AJYb,* 1914–15 (1914), p. 247; H. Harbeck, *Hamburg wie es war,* Hamburg, 1966, fig. 23. The predecessor of the synagogue of ca. 1905 on the Veddel shipping island was one set up in 1892 on the Amerika Kai at Steinwerder; see *Deutsche Bauzeitung,* 1912, p. 466.

106. Z. Szajkowski, "Synagogues during the French Revolution of 1789–1800," *Jewish Social Studies* XX, #4 (1958), pp. 215–31. P. Girard, *Les juifs de France de 1789 à 1860,* Paris, 1976, passim. On the Metz synagogues: A. Cahen, "Le rabbinat de Metz pendant la période française (1567–1871)," *Revue des études juives* XIII (1886), pp. 105–26, esp. pp. 108–110.

107. See Jewish encyclopedias, s.v. Consistory, Community, and translations of those words. Belgian Jews later had their own consistory until 1892.

108. For Munich: Hammer-Schenk, "Untersuchungen," p. 49. See below, Berlin. For Strasbourg: Hammer-Schenk, *Synagogen,* p. 405 (Hamburger Beiträge zur Geschichte der deutschen Juden, 8); the reference is to the synagogue of the 1890s, erected when this Alsatian city belonged to Germany, and was called Strassburg.

109. H. Schwab, *The History of Orthodox Jewry in Germany,* London, 1950, p. 86 lists seceding groups. As of 1876, Jews in Württemberg and Bavaria still had no secession law.

110. For France, 19th century to 1905: P. C. Albert, *The Modernization of French Jewry,* Hanover, 1977, p. 220. Dresden: Hammer-Schenk, "Untersuchungen," p. 185; Bavarian law of 1813 reducing the number of house synagogues, ibid., p. 83; Livorno, 18th century: A. Toaff, "Cenni storici sulla comunità ebrea e sulla sinagoga di Livorno," *Israel. La rassegna mensile* XXI, #9/10 (Sept.–Oct. 1955), p. 415 n. 1; Zürich, 1383: B. Weinert, "Skizzen zur Geschichte der Juden in Zürich," *Jüdisches Jahrbuch für die Schweiz* IV (1919/1920), p. 193; Bratislava: S. Krauss, "Pressburger Synagogen," *Die Juden und die Judengemeinde Bratislava in Vergan-*

genheit und Gegenwart, ed. H. Gold, Brno, 1932, p. 96.

111. Szajkowski, "Synagogues during . . . ," p. 230.

112. For example, Leeds: E. Krausz, *Leeds Jewry. Its History and Social Structure,* Cambridge, 1964; Manchester: B. Williams, *The Making of Manchester Jewry, 1740–1875,* Manchester, 1876. Exhibitions of Anglo-Jewish history and the *Jewish Chronicle* have included maps showing London's Jewish population and synagogue location. See also Sachar, *Modern Jewish History,* pp. 498–99.

113. T. Brouwer, "Veenhuizen, de voormalige synagoge," *Bijdragen Rijksdienst voor Monumentenzorg. Koninklijke Nederlandse Oudheidkundige Bond, Bulletin* LXXVI, #4–5 (Dec. 1977), p. 240. I owe this reference to J. J. van Agt.

114. R. Lehmann, *Nova Bibliotheca Anglo-Judaica,* London, 1961, s.v. Maidstone. Portsmouth: *Jewish Chronicle,* Nov. 13, 1868, p. 3; London-King's Bench Debtors' Prison *minyan* before 1850: V. D. Lipman, *Social History of the Jews in England,* London, 1954, p. 16. Lipman, p. 136, cites statistics showing that only 55 Russian and Polish immigrant Jews in England and Wales were in jail in 1894, well below the proportion of other prisoners to the general population. Nanterre: *Jewish Chronicle,* July 30, 1874, p. 280. Ensisheim: Leo Baeck Institute Archives, s.v. Ensisheim for 1834 and 1854, fols. 2311–14. Bollwiller, 1833–56, ibid., s.v. Bollwiller, fols. 2167–72 for 1846 and 1856. Bayreuth: *Jewish Chronicle,* Nov. 14, 1856. Suben: *Jewish Chronicle,* March 5, 1868, p. 8. Prague: *Jewish Chronicle,* July 13, 1868, p. 3.

115. J. J. Schudt, *Jüdische Merckwürdigkeiten,* Frankfurt am Main, 1715, Bk. 6, chap. 32, esp. pp. 222–24. Description of a Volhynian orthodox synagogue written by a supporter of Reform: I. B. Levinson, in Sachar, *Modern Jewish History,* pp. 192–93. Offenbach: Hammer-Schenk, *Synagogen,* p. 126. Fighting in synagogues: L. Finkelstein, *Jewish Self-Government in the Middle Ages,* New York, 1964, pp. 48, 187. Culturally assimilated visitors found the Prague-Altneuschul services lacking in decorum: *Jewish Chronicle,* June 1, 1855, p. 137, and Oct. 16, 1868, p. 6. Noise in synagogues at Salonica: Réchad Bey, "Turquie: Salonique, 22 novembre, 1892. Les synagogues," *Archives israélites* LIII, #52 (Dec. 29, 1892), p. 412. Budapest-Kazinczy Street orthodox synagogue, games of hide-and-seek, etc.: A. Unger, "Denominations in Contemporary Jewry," *Reconstructionist* XXXII (Feb. 18, 1966), p. 23. Edinburgh: D. Daiches, *Two Worlds. An Edinburgh Jewish Childhood,* New York, 1954, p. 50. The cantor at Nijmegen in the 18th century was not supposed to take snuff during the reading from the Torah; see Zwarts, "Joodse gemeenten buiten Amsterdam," p. 433. London-Creechurch Lane: *The Diary of Samuel Pepys, M.A., F.R.S.,* New York, 1968, vol. 3, p. 303, for October 14, 1663. Intimate, informal fellowship explains some of the "misbehavior" cited by these writers, as does, perhaps, the Talmudic comparison of the synagogue and a man's own home. See also Sachar, *Modern Jewish History,* pp. 192–93.

116. For Reform in general, see Jewish encyclopedias; also S. Freehof, *Reform Jewish Practice and its Rabbinical Background,* and D. Philipson, *The Reform Movement in Judaism,* rev. ed., Cincinnati, 1930, reprinted 1967. American Reform is more liberal than European; Liberal and Progressive Judaism is the European equivalent of American Reform Judaism.

117. Joseph Carlebach (an orthodox opponent of Reform), "Architektur der Synagoge," *Jeschurun* XVI, #3–4 (1929), pp. 109–31, criticized Reform seating arrangements for this reason, among others.

118. A family memoir records a hops merchant, Marx Tuchmann, who directed the building of the small 18th-century synagogue at Uhlfeld (M. Richartz, *Jüdisches Leben in Deutschland. Selbstzeugnisse zur Sozialgeschichte 1780–1871,* New York, 1976, p. 242). This rare document about Jewish participation in building may mean only that he was chairman of a building committee. A military engineer, Lewin Holländer, is a possible can-

didate for architect of the synagogue of 1694 in Altona; see Wolf, *Mitteilungen,* neue Reihe I, Heft 1 (= VIII, Heft 15) (1905), pp. 46–47. In Szeged, Jews were carpenters and builders in the 1870s, and by 1901 there are supposed to have been more than 5,000 Jewish masons and carpenters. For Szeged, see *Jewish Chronicle,* July 29, 1877, p. 5; for Rumania, see Wolf, *Mitteilungen* V, #1, Heft 9 (1902), p. 48. For the numerous building craftsmen in Vilnius ca. 1880, see J. Rülf, *Drei Tage in jüdisch-Russland,* Frankfurt am Main, 1882, pp. 40ff. Jews also helped to build churches in Vilnius at that time. For Jews in building crafts in eastern Europe in the 19th century, see Wolf, *Mitteilungen,* neue Reihe I, Heft 1 (= VIII, Heft 15) (1905), p. 43.

119. For court and government architects who designed synagogues, see Appendix I.
120. Even in the 20th century, most of Erich Mendelsohn's clients were Jewish.
121. Wolf, *Mitteilungen,* neue Reihe I, Heft 1 (= VIII, Heft 15) (1905), p. 48 mentioned Israel Daniel Itzig, building administrator in Berlin at the end of the 18th century; a government architect (*Regierungsbaumeister*) named Sachs, active 1792–1842; and royal building inspector Wilhelm Ney, whose father was Jewish. In England, George Basevi was a prominent architect, converted from Judaism. None of these converts designed synagogues.
122. For Jewish architects in France, see Appendix I.
123. Archives nationales F 19 11120. This petition had no known outcome (R. Weyl and F. Raphael, *Les juifs en Alsace. Culture, société, histoire,* Toulouse, 1977, p. 148 [Collection Franco-Judaica, 5]).
124. *Jewish Chronicle,* Sept. 16, 1898, p. 23.
125. E. Jamilly, "Anglo-Jewish Architects and Architecture in the 18th and 19th Centuries," *Jewish Historical Society of England, Transactions* XVIII, 1958, pp. 127–41, and idem, "Synagogue Art and Architecture," in *A Century of Jewish Life, 1870–1970,* London, 1971, pp. 75–91. For Mocatta, see also obituary in *Jewish Chronicle,* May 5, 1882, pp. 4, 9; J. Lever, ed., *Catalogue of the Drawings Collection of the Royal Institute of British Architects,* vol. L–N, London, 1973, s.v. Mocatta; V. D. Lipman, *Three Centuries of Anglo-Jewish History,* Cambridge, 1961, p. 74; A. S. Diamond, *The Building of a Synagogue,* London, 1970, p. 7; H. M. Colvin, *A Biographical Dictionary of British Architects, 1600–1840,* rev. ed., 1978, and Wischnitzer, *Architecture,* p. 294, nn. 34–36.
126. For English Jewish synagogue architects, see Appendix I.
127. F. Voigt in *Allgemeines Künstler-Lexikon,* ed. U. Thieme and G. Becker, s.v. Rosengarten; Wolf, *Mitteilungen,* V, #1, Heft 9 (1902), p. 48; R. Hallo, *Kasseler Synagogengeschichte,* Kassel, 1932, passim.
128. *AZJ* XV (1851), p. 252. He claimed to have made synagogue architecture his particular task, but he did not say which ones he actually built.
129. For German Jewish synagogue architects, see Appendix I.
130. For Austro-Hungarian Jewish synagogue architects, see Appendix I.
131. For his synagogues, see Appendix I, Jewish architects in Austria-Hungary. His publications on synagogue architecture include: *Deutsche;* "Alte Almemorgitter," *Ost und West* XVII, #5/6 (1917), cols. 157–62; "Die alte Synagoge in Kurnik," *Zentralblatt der Bauverwaltung* XXXVI, #49 (June 17, 1916), pp. 341–42; "Die Beeinflussung jüdischer östlicher Sakralkunst durch Prager Vorbilder," *Jahrbuch der Gesellschaft für die Geschichte der Juden in der Čechoslovakischen Republik* VI (1934), pp. 457–69; "[Die Juden in der Kunst] . . . und in der deutschen Baukunst," *C.-V. Zeitung* VI, #31/32 (August 5, 1927), p. 463; "Die Synagoge als Mittelpunkt jüdischen Gemeindelebens," *Festnummer zum Ordenstage. Grossloge für Deutschland VIII U.O.B.B.,* October, 1928, pp. 155–58; (with D. Herzog) "Die Synagoge in Bruck a. M.," *Monatsschrift für Geschichte und Wissenschaft des Judentums* LXXXI (1937), pp 443–44; "Ein neues Synagogen-Bauprogramm," *Die Kirche. Zentralorgan für Bau . . . von Kirchen* XII (1915), pp. 75–78; "Historische Baudokumente jüdischer Wande-

rung in Böhmen und Mähren," *Jahrbuch der Gesellschaft für die Geschichte der Juden in der Čechoslovakischen Republik* VII (1935), pp. 399–410 (371–82 in Czech edition); "Jüdische Sakralkunst in Schlesien," *Menorah* IV, #5 (1926), pp. 273–78; "Neuere Forschungen über kirchliche Verteidigungsbauten," *Die Denkmalpflege* XXIII, #7/8 (1921), pp. 56–59; "Ostjüdische Sakralkunst und ihre Ausstrahlungen auf deutsches Gebiet," *Monatshefte für Kunstwissenschaft* XI, #5 (1918), pp. 135–38; "Restauration der alten Pinkas-Synagoge in Prag," *Denkmalpflege und Heimatschutz* XXVI (1924), pp. 35–36; "Synagogen-Kirchen in Schlesien," ibid. XXXI (1929), pp. 35–38; *Synagogenspuren in Schlesischen Kirchen* (Schriften der Gesellschaft zur Förderung der Wissenschaft des Judentums, 41), Wrocław, 1937; "Vergessene Sakralbauten in Westböhmen," *Technische Blätter, Zeitschrift des Deutschen Polytechnischen Vereins in Böhmen* L (1918), pp. 7–14.

132. Daniele Jessurun (repaired synagogue), Ettore Luzzatto (president of technical committee), both of Trieste. Giuseppe Sullum (president of the technical committee), synagogue of Milan, 1892.
133. For German and Austrian architects of this period, see Appendix I.
134. B. Zevi, *Erich Mendelsohn, Opera completa,* Milan, 1970, p. 122 (Biblioteca della rivista *L'architettura, cronache e storia,* 1). Mendelsohn is also said to have designed the youth home of the Essen community, finished in 1931; it had no synagogue (see H. Schröter, *Geschichte und Schicksal der Essener Juden,* Essen, 1980, pp. 124–25).
135. "Neue Arbeiten von Arch. Ing. Otto Eisler," *Forum* VI (1936), pp. 126–27.
136. For Dutch Jewish synagogue architects of this period, see Appendix I.
137. For Hungarian Jewish synagogue architects of this period, see Appendix I.
138. Competitions included those for synagogues at Augsburg, 1911; Berlin, 1888, 1907, 1929, 1957; Cologne, 1894; Dessau, 1904; Dortmund, 1896; Düsseldorf, 1901; Essen, 1908; Kaliningrad (then Königsberg), 1892–93; Antwerp, 1923; Brussels, 1869; Amsterdam, 1934; Strasbourg, 1952; Vienna-Hietzing, 1924; Szeged, 1898; Žilina, 1927–28; Liverpool, 1872; London-Reform, 1867.
139. For Christian architects of synagogues who enjoyed distinguished local or international reputations, see Appendix I.
140. W. Boesiger, ed., *Richard Neutra, Buildings and Projects,* Zürich, 1951, p. 193, a drawing for the Vienna-Hietzing competition, dated 1924.
141. For Hasidic synagogue pictures, see Jewish encyclopedias; community memorial books; the *Entsiklopedia shel Galuyot* [Encyclopedia of the Diaspora]; Abramovitch, *Vanished World;* E. Vinecour and C. Fishman, *Polish Jews. The Final Chapter,* New York, 1977; *Pinkas ha-Kehillot* [Encyclopedia of Jewish Communities], Jerusalem, 1969–80; see these sources under names of towns which were seats of famous Hasidic leaders, e.g., Belz, Bobowa, Góra Kalwaria, Lyady, Kock, Ruzhin, Rymanów, Sadgura. At Sadgura, the leader's court included a prayer hall that held a thousand people; it had paintings of fruits and flowers executed by Jewish Russian artists. The rabbi and his family, however, said most of their prayers in adjacent oratories, only entering the large hall for the principal prayers that must be said with a quorum; see H. Gold, ed., *Geschichte der Juden in der Bukowina,* Tel Aviv, 1958, vol. 1, p. 100.
142. Wischnitzer, *Architecture,* pp. 159–60; H. Rosenau, "German Synagogues in the Early Period of Emancipation," *Publications of the Leo Baeck Institute, Yearbook* VIII (1963), pp. 214–25. Excellent photographs in Eschwege, *Die Synagoge in der deutschen Geschichte,* pp. 90–91.
143. E. Jamilly, "The Architecture of the Contemporary Synagogue," in C. Roth, ed., *Jewish Art,* col. 758. A photograph at YIVO, New York, shows the exterior with the curved part encased in a rectilinear outer shell.
144. J. J. van Agt, "De synagoge van Maastricht en de Synagogen elders in Limburg," *Scolae judaeorum. De joden in Limburg*

en hun Synagogen, Maastricht, 1967, pp. 25–47; Maastricht: pp. 25–31; Meerssen: pp. 31–33.

145. F. Feuchtwanger, "Die bildenden Kuenste im juedischen Kultus," *Ost und West* III, #5 (1903), cols. 337–38, proposal for hexagonal synagogue with bimah in the center. There was a 19th-century octagonal synagogue at Weissensee in Austria, executed in a stripped Romanesque style, and the older synagogue of Floss in the Upper Palatinate (1815) is an elongated octagon, illustrated in Grotte, *Deutsche,* p. 93. The Floss synagogue survived the war, but needs repair.

146. A. Valdenaire, *Friedrich Weinbrenner. Sein Leben und seine Bauten,* 2nd ed., Karlsrühe, 1926, pp. 61–65; Hammer-Schenk, "Untersuchungen," pp. 317–24; idem, *Synagogen,* pp. 235–40; Hallo, *Kasseler Synagogengeschichte,* p. 49, called this synagogue one in pharaoh's clothing built by a student of Rome who had worked on the restoration of Strasbourg's Gothic cathedral.

147. Hammer-Schenk, *Synagogen,* pp. 37–57 (for Klenze, esp. pp. 54–55).

148. Wischnitzer, *Architecture,* pp. 194ff.; idem, "The Problem of Synagogue Architecture," *Commentary* III, #3 (1947), pp. 233–41; Hammer-Schenk, "Untersuchungen" and *Synagogen,* passim; J. Carlebach, "Architektur der Synagoge," pp. 109–31; M. Eisler, "Bau und Einrichtung der Synagogen," *Jüdische Rundschau,* 1946, #4/5, pp. 29–35; "Die jüdische Baukunst," *AZJ* XXXIII (1869), *Beilage* to #37, Sept. 14, 1869, pp. 753–54.

149. *Centralblatt der Bauverwaltung* VI (1886), pp. 256–58.

150. On the Governor's order, *AJYb* 1910–11 (1910), p. 143; on the religious teacher's school, ibid., 1911–12 (1911), p. 157. A milder but more effective order about a synagogue's appearance came from Kaiser Wilhelm, who disapproved of J. Otto Kerwien's Romanesque design of 1899 for the Potsdam synagogue; accordingly, the design was revised and the synagogue was built in 1901–3 in the "post-Frederician" (i.e., late baroque-rococo style) which the Kaiser preferred for public buildings in his residential town. See: R. Kaelter, *Geschichte der jüdischen Gemeinde zu Potsdam. Gedenkschrift,* Potsdam, 1903; "Potsdam," *Beilage* #26 to *AZJ* LXVII (June 26, 1903), p. 2.

151. Berlin - Oranienburgerstrasse, Vienna-Tempelgasse, Leipzig, Budapest-Dohány Street.

152. Central-plan synagogue: "Early Christian" style—Trieste; Romanesque—Hamburg synagogues by A. Rosengarten, Györ, London-Upper Berkeley Street, Strasbourg 1898; Moorish—Florence, Prague-Dušní Street; "Byzantine"—Augsburg, Trenčin; florid eclectic—Aszód, Kunszentmárton, Subotica; Egyptian—Frankfurt am Main-Westend (with other styles); Gothic—Dortmund, Bielefeld.

153. K. Döhmer, *"In welchen Stil sollen wir bauen?" Architekturtheorie zwischen Klassizismus und Jugendstil,* Munich, 1976, p. 42 (Studien zur Kunst des neunzehnten Jahrhunderts, 36). Since Stier's brother Gustav built a Reform temple in Berlin, Wilhelm surely included Jews in his remarks.

154. London, United Synagogue Archives, Minutes Book, Dec. 12, 1867.

155. *Revue générale de l'architecture et des travaux publics* XXII (1865), text to pls. 43–48.

156. *Synagogen in Berlin, Zur Geschichte einer zerstörten Architektur,* eds. V. Bendt and R. Bothe, Berlin, 1983, Catalogue #13.

157. I. Löw, "Glasmalereien der neuen Synagoge in Szegedin," *Mitteilungen der Gesellschaft für jüdische Volkskunde* VII, Heft 13 (1904), pp. 37–39.

158. R. Klapheck, *Die neue Synagoge in Essen a.d. Ruhr, erbaut von Professor Edmund Körner,* Berlin, 1914 (Sonderheft d. *Architektur des XX Jahrhunderts,* 13).

159. H. Rosenau, *A Short History of Jewish Art,* London, 1948, p. 58, fig. 52. Before 1915, the Cracow/Kazimierz High Synagogue had pictures of Noah's ark and Jacob's offering, according to Grotte, *Deutsche,* pp. 50–51.

160. R. Margittay, "Haldoklo Temető, Haldoklo Templom," *Múlt és Jövő* #1, 1938, p. 16.

161. R. Grünfeld, *Ein Gang durch die Ge-*

schichte der Juden in Augsburg. Festschrift zur Einweihung der neuen Synagoge am 4 April, 1917, Augsburg, 1917, pp. 79ff.

162. For Egyptian style in synagogues, see also Hammer-Schenk, *Synagogen,* pp. 58–71 for individual buildings other than Munich's and Frankfurt's Compostellhof, and pp. 71–85 for the evaluation of Egyptian style; Wischnitzer, *Architecture,* pp. 161, 183–85; see also below, Canterbury, Ramsgate, Scandinavia. Egyptian details were found in the following synagogues: Altona-Kleine Papagoyenstrasse capitals as renovated in 1832; Efringen-Kirchen; Frankfurt am Main-Compostellhof doorway; Frankfurt am Main-Westend interior ornament; Munich 1824–26 column capitals; Ramsgate ark frame; Rödelheim; Strasbourg-rue Ste.-Hélène ark frame; Trieste ark frame; details of competition entries for Kassel ca. 1836 and Rome, 1889. For the Egyptian revival in general, see N. Pevsner and S. Lang, "The Egyptian Revival," *Architectural Review* CXIX (May 1956), pp. 242–54.
163. "Die neue Synagoge in Cassel," *Allgemeine Bauzeitung* V (1840), pp. 205–6.
164. Egyptian forms were used rarely if ever between ca. 1840 and ca. 1890. Moorish and Byzantine were the Eastern modes preferred then. Renewed interest in Egyptian style may be due to dissatisfaction with Moorish, to the ancient associations of Egypt that suited a classical revival ca. 1900, and to Egyptian heaviness and mass, seen in other styles on much public architecture around 1900.
165. See P. Frankl, *The Gothic,* Princeton, 1960, pp. 89–93, 417, 511; Hammer-Schenk, *Synagogen,* p. 234. The Houses of Parliament competition, for example, specified that entries had to be in an English Gothic or Tudor style. Exceptional observers who understood that Jews had used the Gothic style in the Middle Ages included Goethe, who visited the synagogue remains at Eger and noted in the 1820s that it was built "in the good old times of German architecture" (M. Waldman, *Goethe and the Jews: A Challenge to Hitlerism,* New York and London, 1934, p. 145), and Wilhelm Lübke who knew about Gothic synagogues in Prague and Passau (Hammer-Schenk, *Synagogen,* p. 233). It is amusing to read the remarks of Joseph Jacobs, historian of his Canterbury synagogue, who thought that Gothic was a Christian style to be avoided in favor of Canterbury's Egyptian building (*Narrative of the Erection of the New Synagogue at Canterbury,* 1851, MS in London, United Synagogue Archives, typed copy at Canterbury City Library). The general identification of Gothic with Christianity made it necessary for the few Jewish synagogue planners who wanted to use Gothic to defend their choice emphatically; see below, nn. 206–9.
166. For *Rundbogenstil* and Romanesque in German architectural theory and its application to synagogues, see Hammer-Schenk, *Synagogen,* pp. 165–75, 217–32; idem, "Opplers," pp. 101–13; A. Rosengarten, *Die architektonischen Stylarten,* Braunschweig, 1857, p. 346. One source of confusion between Romanesque or *Rundbogenstil* and Byzantine was the use in northern Europe of Italian Romanesque or pre-Romanesque models such as S. Vitale in Ravenna (cf. Dresden, exterior). A foreign Romanesque could be used for "exotic" people. The London-Upper Berkeley Street temple is not English Romanesque in style, and the United Synagogue Archives contain the architect N. S. Joseph's analysis of foreign round-arched styles to be used for the London-Central Synagogue.
167. Vilnius-Choral; Antwerp, 1893.
168. See below, Hannover; also Strasbourg, 1898, Cologne-Roonstrasse, et al.
169. G. Riesser, *Verteidigung der bürgerlichen Gleichstellung der Juden gegen die Einwürfe des Herrn Doktor Paulus, 1831,* (*Gesammelte Schriften,* ed. M. Isler, Frankfurt and Leipzig, 1867, vol. 1, p. 133), dismissed those who constantly reminded Jews that their ancestors had migrated to Germany. The Jews whom he represented "were born here and because we are natives we have no pretension to a home anywhere else." In short, "we are either Germans or we have no homeland." At the cornerstone-laying

ceremony for the Hamburg-Oberstrasse synagogue in 1930, the address included this statement: "We German Jews find this sense of being rooted [in German soil] especially strong in these times when [Nazis] want to contest our right to a German home." This did not mean abandoning Judaism or concealing the differences among religions and religious buildings. The importance of style as an indicator of social position was mentioned also by K. Prellwitz, "Eine Synagoge von Friedrich Adler," *Innen Dekoration* XXVIII (1917), p. 348.

170. The Worms synagogue has been rebuilt. The other buildings are: Rome, a house in vicolo dell'Atleta identified as a synagogue to Ferdinand Gregorovius in the mid-19th century; Bury St. Edmunds, Moyses Hall; Lincoln, Jews' Court.

171. Rosengarten: Kassel, Hamburg-Kohlhöfen, Alte und Neue Klaus. Oppler: Hannover, Bleicherode, Wrocław. Hirsch: Lyon. Aldrophe: Paris-rue de la Victoire, Versailles. L. Lévy: Baden-Baden, Strasbourg-Quai Kléber. (Hammer-Schenk, *Synagogen,* pp. 355–57 explains Lévy's earlier Moorish synagogues as having been built before anti-Semitic attitudes had taken firm hold.) Wolffenstein and his Roman Catholic partner, Wilhelm Cremer: Kaliningrad, Berlin-Charlottenburg Schulstrasse (now Behaimstrasse), Berlin-Lützowstrasse, Berlin-Lindenstrasse, Berlin-Spandau, Poznań, Dessau; competitions for Dortmund and Essen. J. Hoeniger, the Berlin Jewish community architect, and his partner Sedelmeier (religion unknown): Berlin-Rykestrasse, Levetzowstrasse. Artilleriestrasse; competitions for Dortmund, Poznań, Berlin-Lützowstrasse, Frankfurt am Main-Israelitische Religionsgesellschaft. For these synagogues, see Hammer-Schenk, *Synagogen,* passim, and E. Meyer, "Wilhelminische Synagogen von Cremer und Wolffenstein," *Architectura* X, #2 (1982), pp. 169–84.

172. For the evaluation of Byzantine style in relation to German synagogues, see Hammer-Schenk, *Synagogen,* pp. 223–24.

173. *De Vrijdagavond* IX, #23 (Sept. 2, 1932), p. 354. The synagogue mixed Romanesque, Moorish, and other styles, in fact. See J. S. da Silva Rosa, "Bij het 25-jaarig bestaan van Groningens Synagoge," ibid., VIII, #2 (April 10, 1931), pp. 24–26. Stylistic terms continued to be imprecise.

174. Basel, Dvůr Králové nad Labem, Hamburg-Bornplatz, Inowrocław, London-Lauderdale Road, Marburg, Rome, Strasbourg-Quai Kléber, Szeged, Trieste, Vienna-Humboldtgasse, et al. The *style* of these buildings was not necessarily Byzantine.

175. That is why criticism of the untraditional idea of dome-building at Berlin and Nuremberg had so little effect. Domes appear in the examples cited in n. 174 above and, among many other cities, at Augsburg, Berlin-Prinzregentenstrasse, Bratislava-Reform, Bydgoszcz (1854), Cologne-Glockengasse, Katowice, London-Liberal, Poznań, Vienna-Leopoldgasse.

176. See above, n. 155. His sources were apparently European and Romanesque, not Eastern. This is another case of imprecise use of stylistic terms.

177. *Der Architekt* VIII (1902), p. 7, pls. 15, 16. This is one of the first massive, smooth-walled, low-domed modernized Byzantine synagogue designs, along with that of Franz Brantzky for Düsseldorf (1900); see Hammer-Schenk, *Synagogen,* fig. 334. As these designs were published, they may have influenced executed and projected designs for synagogues at Essen, Augsburg, Offenbach, Vienna-Hietzing, etc.

178. Berlin-Oranienburgerstrasse, Leipzig, Vienna-Tempelgasse, Bradford-Bowland Street, Florence, Sofia, Vilnius-Choral, Leningrad, Lida, Minsk, Odessa-Great, Bratislava-Reform, Opava, Prague-Jerusalémská Street, Debrecen, Keszthely, Luduş, Bytom, Łódź-Old Town.

179. See above list in n. 178, and Besançon, Prague-Dušní Street, Dresden, interior.

180. See above, nn. 178 and 179. Also Frankfurt am Main-Börneplatz, Karlovy Vary, Moscow (originally), Rotterdam-Botersloot, Vienna-Leopoldgasse, Wiesbaden.

181. See below, Vienna-Tempelgasse, which

inspired dozens of synagogue facades, especially—but not only—in the Austro-Hungarian lands. See also *Allgemeine Bauzeitung* XXIII (1858), pp. 14–16 for Förster's explanation of his use of the style.

182. A. Rosengarten, *A Handbook of Architectural Styles,* London [1878], p. 485.

183. Hammer-Schenk, *Synagogen,* pp. 80, 259–61 for Ingenheim (dedicated 1834), Kirchheimbolanden (dedicated 1835), and Speyer (dedicated 1837).

184. "Die Synagoge zu Dresden," *Allgemeine Bauzeitung* XII (1847), p. 127, pls. 105–7.

185. Hammer-Schenk, *Synagogen,* pp. 251–58 for the evaluation of Islamic styles in German theory. See also H. Künzl, "Zur Aufnahme islamische Architekturstile im Synagogenbau des 19 Jahrhunderts," *Zeitschrift der deutschen morgenländischen Gesellschaft, suppl. III, 2. XIX Deutscher Orientalistentag, 1975, Vorträge,* ed. W. Voigt, 1977, pp. 1626–31; Wischnitzer, *Architecture,* pp. 198–214.

186. Förster designed Vienna-Tempelgasse (1853–58), Budapest-Dohány Street (1854–60), and the synagogue at Miskolc (*Allgemeine Bauzeitung* XLI [1876], p. 15, pls. 16–18). Zwirner designed Cologne-Glockengasse (1856–61). Earlier Moorish synagogues include those of Kaiserslautern (ca. 1847), Altdorf in Baden (ca. 1850), Heidenheim in Franconia (ca. 1850) by Eduard Bürklein (*Allgemeine Bauzeitung* XIX [1854], pp. 389–91), Paris-rue Notre Dame de Nazareth, interior remodeling by J. A. Thierry (1850–52); Dresden (see below, Dresden).

187. *Allgemeine Bauzeitung* XXIII (1858), pp. 14–16, pls. 230–35.

188. *Jewish Chronicle,* Dec. 16, 1859, p. 7.

189. The Hungarian poet Ferenc Kazinczy (1759–1831) connected Gothic and Saracenic when he said that early Renaissance architects liked the Arab taste but that Palladio had dispensed with everything that reminded people of Gothic; see A. Zádor, "Palladianism in the Eclectic Architecture of Hungary," *Acta Technica Academiae Scientiarum Hungaricae* LXXVII, #1–4 (1970), p. 129 n. 9; also Hammer-Schenk, *Synagogen,* pp. 250–58, esp. for Hittorff and other authorities. For the entire question of Gothic revival and its association with "Saracenic" architecture, see P. Frankl, *The Gothic,* pp. 364ff.

190. G. Stamp, "British Architecture in India, 1857–1947," *The Royal Society for the Encouragement of Arts, Manufactures, and Commerce. Journal* CXXIX, #5298 (May 1981), pp. 358–79. There are parallels between the exterior of the Berlin-Oranienburgerstrasse synagogue and the Bombay Municipal Building by J. W. Stevens (1883–93) or the Board of Revenue offices in Madras by R. F. Chisholm, but direct connections between synagogues and Indian buildings are unlikely.

191. Hammer-Schenk, *Synagogen,* pp. 251–58, 308–9, p. 628 n. 878; C. Schnaase, *Geschichte der bildenden Künste,* vol. 3, 2d ed., part 1, Düsseldorf, 1869, pp. 404, 474, 487, 491.

192. Moorish-style synagogues show that those Jewish clients accepted an identification with the East. For German examples, see Hammer-Schenk, *Synagogen.* A Belgian, apparently Jewish, wrote in *L'Echo du parlement* (June 27, 1869) that designs making synagogues look local were unsuitable to both the nature of a synagogue and the Jewish heritage. Romanesque, a Christian style, evoked the Crusades when Jews had been persecuted. As for Moorish, "Is the art of the caliphs suited to the religion of the Prophets?" He hoped for a style evoking the *ancient* Near East. In Britain, where Jews were tolerated more generously, the English Jewish architect N. S. Joseph wrote on Dec. 19, 1867 that "Gothic architecture is scarcely admissible, being essentially Christian in its forms and its symbols; and Classic architecture . . . [is] Pagan Architecture. . . . For an ecclesiastical edifice like ours the Moresque seemed to me to be that which recommended itself on the score of its dignity, its Eastern origin, its elasticity of adjustment to internal requirements, its econ-

omy of space, and even economy of material" (*Report #1, Central Branch Synagogue. Report of the Building and Finance committees ... 2nd February, 1868,* p. 13, in United Synagogue Archives, London). The Jewish author of a book on a major Liverpool synagogue noted with satisfaction the remarks published in the *Liverpool Mercury* on Sept. 11, 1857: "The character of originality pervades the building, which renders it an object of great attention" (P. Ettinger, *Hope Place in Liverpool Jewry,* Liverpool, 1930, p. 60). The idea of capturing public attention seems to have appealed to congregations which sponsored unusual-looking synagogues, even though the *Liverpool Mercury*'s remarks could be interpreted unfavorably also. A Jewish writer, S. Foà, wrote of the Moorish style "with which the Semitic genius affirmed itself in architecture, necessarily without the aid of figural painting or sculpture" ("Il cinquantenario del Tempio Israelitico a Torino," *Torino. Rassegna mensile della città* XIV, #3 [March 1934], p. 36). C. Caselli, "Il tempio israelitico di Vercelli del comm. G. Locarni," *L'ingegneria civile e le arte industriali* XIV (1899), p. 8 praised the design based on Egyptian (Mamluk) buildings of the 14th and 15th centuries, the period of the apogee of architecture in Egypt, in Caselli's opinion. No explanation was given for the use of this style at Vercelli in the 1890s.

The infrequent Renaissance-style synagogues in northern Europe may have been meant to suggest secular architecture to avoid imitating churches. Among them are synagogues in Liberec and Vienna-Turnergasse by Karl König, Frankfurt am Main-Börneplatz by Siegfried Kusnitzky, and Manchester-Cheetham Hill Road Great and New by Thomas Bird.

193. N. M. Gelber, "The Sephardic Community in Vienna," *Jewish Social Studies* X (1948), pp. 359ff. A. von Zemlinsky, *Geschichte der Türkisch-israelitischen Gemeinde zu Wien,* Vienna, 1888, esp. p. 11.

194. C. McCorquodale, "A Tuscan Alhambra," *Connoisseur* (London) CCVI, #830 (1981), pp. 272–75.

195. ". . . ob es nicht angemessen erscheint, die neue Synagoge in einem dem israelitischen Kultus entsprechenden Stile etwa dem maurischen, als in dem vorzugsweise für christliche Kirchen zur Anwendung kommende gothischen Stile auszuführen" (Protokolle der kurfürstlich-hessischen Regierung der Provinz Hanau, Nov. 6, 1865). See: R. Stahl, *Geschichte der Nauheimer Juden. Festschrift zur Einweihung der neuen Synagoge,* Bad Nauheim, 1929, p. 20 (*Bad Nauheimer Jahrbuch* VIII, #9/12); Hammer-Schenk, "Untersuchungen," p. 326 with further references. The plans were changed and the synagogue was dedicated in 1867. The Bonn Reform synagogue also avoided the difficulties of looking Christian, see H. Maertens, "Die Synagoge zu Bonn," *Deutsche Bauzeitung* XXIV (April 19, 1890), p. 192. These are two of many examples.

196. Letter of Dec. 1881, "50 Jahre Grosse Synagoge Reitbahn, 1887–1937," *Jüdisches Gemeindeblatt (Danzig)* X, #1 (Aug. 30, 1937), pp. 1–2. Kusnitzky designed the Frankfurt am Main-Börneplatz synagogue in Renaissance style but it had a bulbous Moorish cupola. A Christian writer praised A. Schmidt's synagogue in Munich for avoiding the foreign-looking Moorish style: H. von Berlepsch, "Architektonisches aus München, II: Die neue Synagoge," *Zeitschrift für bildende Kunst* XXIII (1888), pp. 234–37. O. Herbenová, in discussing the Moorish remodeling of the Dušní Street synagogue in Prague which was decorated using Islamic Spanish models for ornament, wrote of it as a setting for the Thousand and One Nights: "Španělská synagoga," in *Zidovská ročenka 5721,* Prague, 1960, p. 113. Rosengarten thought that the only virtue of Islamic architecture for Jewish use was its common avoidance of figural ornament: "Die neue synagoge in Cassel," *Allgemeine Bauzeitung* V (1840), pp. 205–6.

197. B. Levy, "Causerie parisienne. L'orphélinat-les nouveaux temples-la Fondation Bischoffsheim," *Archives israélites* XXXV

(1874), pp. 395–400.

198. Edwin Oppler, who knew that they existed, argued that the Prague and Worms synagogues were older and more complete, suggesting that if one wanted models from the past one could find them close to home. He did not advocate copying those, either, but rather creating modern buildings in an authentic German style within the German state. See *Leben und Schicksal. Zur Einweihung der Synagoge in Hannover,* 1963, p. 193, and Hammer-Schenk, "Opplers."

199. Girault de Frangey, *Monuments arabes et mauresques de Cordoue, Séville, et Grenade,* Paris, 1837; Patricio de la Escosura, *España artística y monumental,* Paris, 1842, vol. 1, pp. 44–45, 71–72.

200. *Jewish Chronicle,* June 13, 1873, p. 177. The architect was Edward Salomons.

201. Wischnitzer, *Architecture,* pp. 208–9; V. Stassov, "Po povodu Postroiki sinagogi v Sant Peterburge," *Yevreiskaia Biblioteka* II (1889), pp. 435–53.

202. *Builder* XXX (Jan. 20, 1872), p. 49.

203. Spacerowej (formerly Promenaden, Kosciuszko) Aleja. The synagogue remains were destroyed after 1945.

204. Other synagogues with Gothic elements include the following. In Austria: Vienna-Müllnergasse, Neudeggergasse, and Schmalzhofgasse, all by Max Fleischer between 1884 and 1906. In Czechoslovakia: Bardejov ca. 1808; České Budějovice by Fleischer, 1888; Městečko, ded. 1811; Pelhřimov by Fleischer, late 1890s; Prague-Altschul, ca. 1837; Prague-Meisel, remodeled by Alfred Grotte, 1893–1905; Velké Meziříčí by August Prokop, 1867. In France: Oberschaeffolsheim. In Germany (West and East): Bückeburg, ded. 1866; Fulda, 1859; Fürth by A. Reindel after 1831; Eldagsen by Bösser, 1866–68; Göttingen, 1897; Hadamar, 1842; Krefeld, 1902, remodeled by J. Reck; Ladenburg, ded. 1832; Oedheim, 1860s; Regensburg, 1837–41. In Great Britain: Leeds; Pontypridd by Lloyd, 1895. In Hungary: Devecser; Hatvan. In the Netherlands: Aalten; Amersfoort, 1842; Borne; Buren; Culemborg; Emmen, 1878; Gennep; Haarlem, 1841, 1896; Harderwijk; Harlingen, 1877; Heusden; Kampen; Oldenzaal, 1880; Schiedam; Veghel; Zutphen, before 1879; Zwolle, before 1860. In Poland: Poznań-New. The Coburg synagogue kept the old Gothic forms of the St. Nicholas Chapel when the chapel was converted into a synagogue in 1873. On Gothic elements at Karlsruhe, 1798ff., see Hammer-Schenk, *Synagogen,* pp. 235–40. Most of the Dutch buildings and the Pontypridd synagogue look like modest chapels.

205. For Fürth, see below, and Hammer-Schenk, *Synagogen,* pp. 243–46. For Prague: Hammer-Schenk, *Synagogen,* pp. 246–47; J. Heřman and M. Vilímková, *Die Prager Synagogen,* Prague, 1970; O. Herbenová, "Španělská synagoga," pp. 108–9; V. Sadek, "La synagogue réformée à Prague (la 'Vieille école') et les études juives au cours du 19ème siècle," *Judaica Bohemiae* XVI, #2 (1980), pp. 119–23. For Regensburg, see Hammer-Schenk, *Synagogen,* pp. 247–49, and I. Meyer, *Zur Geschichte der Juden in Regensburg,* Berlin, 1913.

206. *Jewish Chronicle,* Sept. 5, 1851, p. 384. In Beilen in the Netherlands, the mayor and the parson took up a collection to help build a synagogue in 1855: Gans, *Memorbook,* p. 476. For Solihull, see *AJR Information* XXXII, 1977, p. 3. The mayor of Lingolsheim in Alsace set up a subscription fund and a Protestant minister took up a collection in 1861 to build a new synagogue: *Jewish Chronicle,* Oct. 11, 1861. The Leiden synagogue was reconstructed with money sent in part by individual Christians: *AJR Information* XXXIII (June 1975). A Catholic lent most of the money for the new synagogue at Olesno at exceptionally low interest: H. E. Weigert (1819–1905), "Meine Lebensgeschichte bis 1895," in M. Richarz, ed., *Jüdisches Leben in Deutschland. Selbstzeugnisse zur Sozialgeschichte 1780–1871,* New York, 1976, p. 319. A student choir from the University of Münster in Westphalia toured the United States after the Second World War to raise money to help rebuild the synagogue in that city: P. Spiegel, *Festschrift zur Weihe der neuen Synagoge in Münster/Westf.*

[Münster], 1961, p. 38.

207. "Über Synagogenbauten," *Zeitschrift des oesterreichischen Ingenieur-und Architekten-Vereines* XLVI, #8 (May 4, 1894), pp. 253–58.

208. *Zentralblatt der Bauverwaltung* XIV (1894), pp. 178–79.

209. Hammer-Schenk, *Synagogen,* p. 444. The desire not to look obviously different, (i.e., eccentric) was surely a factor in the decision of Bochum's Jews to demolish the towers which had given a bizarre appearance to the 19th-century synagogue. Jews in Hamburg in 1856 also were nervous about being too obvious, see Hammer-Schenk, *Synagogen,* p. 190.

210. "Wie baut man Synagogen?" *AZJ* LXV, #10 (March 8, 1901), pp. 115–17.

211. Dortmund dedication ceremony: *Dortmunder Zeitung,* June 6, 1900. Krefeld: E. Stockhausen, "Zur Geschichte der jüdischen Gemeinde Krefelds im 19 Jahrhundert," and D. Hangebroch, "Emigriert-Deportiert. Das Schicksal der Juden in Krefeld zwischen 1933 und 1945," both in *Krefelder Juden,* ed. G. Rotthoff, Bonn, 1980, pp. 69, 142–45 (Krefelder Studien, 2).

212. Hangebroch, "Emigriert-Deportiert," esp. pp. 142–45. The Krefeld refacing of 1902 in an eccentric mixture of late-Gothic decorative stonework and round-arched forms may have been meant to suggest an early German Renaissance style; photograph in Eschwege, *Die Synagoge in der deutschen Geschichte,* p. 107.

213. J. Heřman and M. Vilímková, *Prague's Synagogues,* pp. 53, 56. The Jews were caught between their inclination toward German culture and the pressure of rising Czech cultural awareness.

214. Budapest-Ujlak, Zsigmond (now Leo Frankel) Street: Heller and Vajda, *The Synagogues of Hungary,* p. 24 and figs. 373–74.

215. Haarlem: photo at YIVO. Other Dutch synagogues: photograph files at the Rijksdienst voor Monumentenzorg.

216. Jews of German birth showed little eagerness to associate with their Eastern, especially Yiddish-speaking, coreligionists even after 1945; see M. Elovitz, "The Wiesbaden Synagogue," *Reconstructionist* XXXII (Dec. 9, 1966), p. 20, and P. Arnsberg, *Neunhundert Jahre "Muttergemeinde Israel", Frankfurt am Main, 1074–1974,* Frankfurt, 1974, p. 193. As for French-born Jews, Rabbi Israel Lévi of Paris said that French rabbis would not accept the foreign-born orthodox Rabbi Herzog at the rue des Tournelles synagogue, and that preaching done in a foreign language would not fail to have repercussions on the entire Jewish community (Consistoire Israélite archive B-95. Commission du 4ème arrondissement, 1913, May 20). Rabbis at the June 4, 1913 meeting would have allowed Polish orthodox rabbis only on consistorial commissions dealing with ritual. One J. Zébaume wrote on June 4, 1913, that the consistory should leave immigrants to care for their own poor. These attitudes naturally led to the formation of separate congregations and to the building of separate synagogues. See below, Paris-rue Pavée.

217. The literature on these subjects, too vast to be cited here, confirms my summary remarks. See, for example, M. Kreutzberger and I. Foerg, eds., *Leo Baeck Institute. New York. Bibliothek und Archiv. Katalog,* vol. 1, Tübingen, 1970. Works on Jewish history, sociology, Jewish-Christian relations, anti-Semitism, and the origins of the Holocaust may be consulted.

218. See above, n. 169 for Riesser. Insistence on patriotism served Jews well in their relations with the Kaiser and local rulers, but it also expressed their sincere yearning for full integration. In 1842, the Hamburg-Poolstrasse Reform synagogue dedication included a song with these words: "We are German with the closest ties. The Temple expresses itself clearly: A truly German house of God." This warded off remarks that the building seemed foreign. See G. Salomon, *Kurzgefässte Geschichte des neuen israelitischen Tempels in Hamburg während des ersten 25 Jahre seines Bestehens,* Hamburg, 1844, p. 137. The synagogues that reflect this attitude include those of Berlin-Fasanenstrasse, Cologne-Roon-

strasse, Düsseldorf, Hagen as remodeled with twin towers, Poznań (then Posen), Strasbourg (then Strassburg)-Quai Kléber.

219. H. Hammer-Schenk, "Aesthetische und politische Funktionen historisierender Baustile in Synagogenbau des ausgehenden 19 Jahrhunderts," *Kritische Berichte, Mitteilungen des Ulmer Vereins für Kunstwissenschaft* II, #2/3 (1975), pp. 14–15.

220. Barcs, Budapest-Rumbach Street, Carei, Cluj, Fadd, Hlohovec, Prešov, Senica, Székesfehérvár, Szekszárd, Vrbouce. Elsewhere: Łowicz, Bucharest-Choral.

221. Photograph collections at YIVO and Leo Baeck Institute, New York; at Państwowy Instytut Sztuki, Warsaw; encyclopedias and community histories. Examples include: Prague-Jerusalémská Street, Leningrad-Great, Lida, Łódż-Old Town, Minsk. In the West, see comparably vigorous (or coarse) synagogues in Rotterdam-Botersloot and Luxembourg. The Warsaw-Tłómacka Street synagogue in classical-baroque style was exceptional.

222. See below, Florence, Milan, Rome, Turin.

223. On worship declining in the home, see W. Tachau, "The Architecture of the Synagogue," *AJYb* XXVII, 1926–27 (1926), p. 172.

224. The faintly oriental designs might reflect the influence of Zionism. T. Herzl's *Der Judenstaat* was published in 1896. It was one response to the continuing problem faced by Jews who understood how unwelcome many Christians found Jewish efforts to integrate. Published accounts of buildings do not make this connection, however. The massive style with its medieval or classical variants can be seen in architectural periodicals of Germany and Scandinavia in the period ca. 1885–ca. 1914. For Nijmegen, see B. deBreffny, *The Synagogue,* New York, 1978, pp. 180–85. R. Ziegler designed an unexecuted synagogue for Berlin in a fussier version of the massive style; see *Berliner Architekturwelt* XIV (1912), pp. 325–27.

225. For these synagogues, see references in S. Waetzoldt, ed., with V. Haas, *Bibliographie zur Architektur im 19 Jahrhundert. Die Aufsätze in den deutschsprachigen Architektur-Zeitschriften 1789–1918,* vol. 3, Nendeln, 1977, pp. 1603–20, and Hammer-Schenk, *Synagogen.*

226. E. Hiller, "Über den modernen Synagogenbau," *Ost und West* VI, #1 (Jan. 1906), cols. 29–36, esp. col. 31.

227. "Neubau der Westend Synagoge, Frankfurt am Main," *Deutsche Bauzeitung* XLV, #62 (1911), pp. 535–36; "Die Westendsynagoge in Frankfurt am Main," *Neudeutsche Bauzeitung* VII (1911), pp. 365–76; "Die Westend-synagoge in Frankfurt am Main," *Der Baumeister* IX, #7 (1911), pp. 73–80.

228. J. DeLange, "Ontwerp voor Synagoog te Antwerpen," *Jubelalbum van het Kring voor Bouwkunde 1900–1910,* Antwerp, 1910, pp. 73–77. I owe this reference to Alfred E. Willis.

229. Three windows are illustrated in Eschwege, *Die Synagoge in der deutschen Geschichte,* p. 130.

230. For Belz: *AZJ,* Nov. 6, 1914. General destruction of Jews and their monuments: *AJYb* 1915–16 (1915), pp. 226, 268–69; 1916–17 (1916), p. 117. Among the distinctive wooden synagogues lost in the years 1914–18 were those of Jedwabne, Ozery, and Śniadowo; see C. Aronson, "Les synagogues en bois du XVIIe et du XVIIIe siècle en Pologne," *Gazette des Beaux-Arts* sér. VI, XVI (Dec. 1936), pp. 233–44. G. Lukomski, "The Wooden Synagogues of Eastern Europe," *Burlington Magazine* LXVI, #382 (1935), pp. 14–21 said that those of Jabłonów, Nasielsk, and Narów were also destroyed, but one must use all his writings with caution. (Narów may be Narowla; there is no town now in Poland spelled Narów.)

231. Staszów and Prushkov: *AJYb* 1915–16 (1915), pp. 263, 260; Snekshni: ibid., 1916–17 (1916), p. 199.

232. Fastov, *AJYb,* 1920–21 (1920), p. 281.

233. J. Rothenberg, "Synagogues in the Soviet Union. A Report to the Institute of East European Jewish Affairs, Brandeis University," typescript, March 1966. S. Lightman, ed., *The Jewish Travel Guide,* London, 1980, lists addresses for syn-

agogues in 46 localities in the U.S.S.R.

234. École nationale supérieure des Beaux-Arts. *Les concours d'architecture de l'année scolaire* X (1918–19), pls. 3–18.

235. J. Lever, ed., *Catalogue of the Drawings in the R.I.B.A.,* s.v. Landauer.

236. Illustrated in Heller and Vajda, *Synagogues of Hungary,* figs. 448, 449, 454. See illustration there of Pozsony (=Bratislava), fig. 20, and see below, Bratislava.

237. Photographs at YIVO, New York.

238. See below, Amsterdam: 1928–38.

239. London-St. John's Wood Road, 1925 by E. Joseph: *Architectural Review* LVIII (Nov. 1925), pp. 198–201. Paris-rue Copernic, 1922–24: P. R. Roland Marcel, *A Guide to Jewish Monuments in France,* Paris [1937], pp. 18–19. Berlin-Prinzregentenstrasse by A. Beer, 1930: Bendt & Bothe, vol. 1, pp. 60–64, 148–55.

240. London-Willesden Green by Landauer, Wills, and Kaula, 1936–38: *Architectural Review* LXXXIII (May 1938), p. 243, *Architects' Journal,* April 14, 1938, pp. 617–19, and Lever, ed., *Catalogue of the Drawings in the R.I.B.A.,* s.v. Landauer, drawings dated 1936. Liverpool-Greenbank Drive by A. Ernest Shennan, 1936–38: *Architecture Illustrated* XVI (April 1938), pp. 90–97. R. Joseph projects: Leo Baeck Institute Archives, R. Joseph Collection. Zürich-Freigutstrasse: M. Eisler, "Neue Synagoge," *Menorah* VIII, #11/12 (Nov.–Dec. 1930), p. 549. See also the stripped Carpentierstraat synagogue in The Hague-Bezuidenhout by Jacob Baars, 1938; a design for a synagogue at Antwerp by Josef Frank, *Menorah* VII, #11/12 (Nov.–Dec. 1929), p. 557; and London-Shepherd's Bush, *Builder* CLVII (July 14, 1939), pp. 67–68.

241. For Žilina, see below. War memorial "Heroes' Temple": see Heller and Vajda, *Synagogues of Hungary,* figs. 445–47. The "Heroes' Temple" is very close to the design by Béla Lajta for an unexecuted synagogue in Budapest: *Der Architekt* XVIII (1912), pl. 79.

242. Rosenthal: H. Herkommer, "Kirchliche Kunst der Gegenwart," *Deutsche Bauten,* 1930, #6/7, p. 48. Mendelsohn: B. Zevi, *Erich Mendelsohn, Opera completa,* p. 122. Neutra: W. Boesiger, ed., *Richard Neutra. Buildings and Projects,* p. 193. Amsterdam-Obrechtplein: see below, Amsterdam 1928–38: Rotterdam: D. Hausdorff, *Platenatlas van drie en halve eeuw geschiedenis van de joodse gemeente in Rotterdam van 1610 tot ca. 1960,* Baarn, 1978, p. 72. Plauen: see below, Plauen. By this time, Landauer was persuaded that the First World War had given a reason to build anew and express new life, and that contemporary language had a duty to form content: W. Goldberg, ed., *Blätter zur Erinnerung an die Weihe der Synagoge Plauen i/V* [Plauen], 1930, pp. 25–28. Berlin-Klopstockstrasse: Hammer-Schenk, *Synagogen,* figs. 468, 493–95.

243. Brno: "Neue Arbeiten von Arch.-Ing. Otto Eisler," *Forum* VI (1936), pp. 126–27. Paris-rue J. Lacroix: M. Zahar, "Une synagogue à Belleville," *L'amour de l'art* II (1931), pp. 254–55. London-Hendon United: deBreffny, *Synagogue,* pp. 194–95. Other comparable synagogues include: Bad Nauheim and Hamburg-Oberstrasse (see below, Hamburg); Hove-Liberal ("Synagogue. Edward Lewis," *Architectural Review* LXXXV [Jan. 1939], pp. 36ff.); R. Joseph's design of 1934–37 for a pavilion convertible from an exposition pavilion to a permanent synagogue (Leo Baeck Institute, New York, Archives, R. Joseph Collection). The argument about looking different continued long after 1918.

244. Hammer-Schenk, *Synagogen,* pp. 524–28 for painted decoration in German synagogues during the 1920s.

245. *Encyclopedia Judaica,* 1971, for individual communities. A. Diamant, *Zerstörte Synagogen vom November 1938. Eine Bestandsaufnahme,* Frankfurt am Main, 1978; R. Thalmann and E. Feinermann, *Crystal Night, 9–10 November 1938,* New York, 1974; A. Kober, "Jewish Communities in Germany from the Age of Enlightenment to their Destruction by the Nazis," *Jewish Social Studies* IX, #3 (1947), pp. 195ff.; A. Charim, *Die toten Gemeinden,* Vienna, 1966; Z. Baker, "Bibliography of Eastern European Memorial

Books Updated and Revised," *Toledot* III, #2–3 (1979–80), pp. 7–42.

246. R. Feder, "Religious Life in Terezín," *Terezín,* Prague, 1965, pp. 52–53; Heller and Vajda, *Synagogues of Hungary,* p. 191 for Bergen-Belsen's, built largely by Hungarian Jews; Z. Szajkowski, *Analytical Franco-Jewish Gazetteer, 1939–1945,* New York, 1966, pp. 202, 210, 280 for French camps. A watercolor by the late Czech-born artist, Norbert Troller, showing a vaulted casemate fitted with an ark in Terezín, is in the collection of the Leo Baeck Institute, New York.
247. Szajkowski, *Analytical Franco-Jewish Gazetteer,* p. 206, citing the catalogue of the exhibition "Les juifs dans la lutte contre Hitler," 1965, p. 26.
248. For the stable at Verdun, ibid., p. 229. In Hungary: P. Meyer, *Jews in the Soviet Satellites,* Syracuse, 1950, p. 398. Laundry: Berlin-Pestalozzistrasse. Garbage dump: Celle, Wischnitzer, *Architecture,* pp. 148–49. Brothel: Belgrade-Kosmayska Street. Prison for deportees: Bordeaux-rue Ste. Catherine, 1944, F. Ambrière, *Guide religieux de France,* Paris, 1967, pp. 973–74.
249. This has also been done to convert churches to new uses, e.g., London-Bedford Park Suburb.
250. U. Nahon, *Holy Arks and Ritual Appurtenances from Italy in Israel,* Tel Aviv, 1970 (Hebrew), recapitulating Nahon's earlier publications on this subject.
251. For Jewish synagogue architects after 1945, see Appendix I.
252. France: Fontainebleau, Sarcelles, Massy, and Antony (photographs at Consistoire Israélite office, Paris, courtesy of M. Bronner); Paris-Abrabanel ("Synagogue à Paris," *L'architecture d'aujourd'hui* XXXVI, #12 [Apr.–May 1966], pp. [92–93] for the winning project by Heaume and Persitz, and ibid., Oct.–Nov. 1966, p. 30 for Neumann and Hecker's unsuccessful proposal); "Centro comunitario e sinagoga a Parigi," *L'architettura* XXVIII (June 1982), pp. 408–16. England: Hove-Palmeira Avenue; of the London-Romford synagogue a critic wrote that it looked like a converted air-raid shelter and had a flat roof that let in the rain. It obviously projected something other than a universal-abstract image; see *Jewish Chronicle,* July 10, 1964. See also London-Smith Terrace, Leeds-Moortown Road. Eire: Dublin-Terenure. West Germany: Dortmund, Trier. Netherlands: Rotterdam. Italy: Milan as rebuilt. Spain: Madrid. For Dublin, Leeds, Dortmund, Trier, and Rotterdam, see Wischnitzer, *Architecture,* pp. 248–76.
253. Villeurbanne's synagogue has, at least, a distinctive history. It was built in 1963–64 with some money supplied by the Conference on Jewish Material Claims Against Germany and more funds and volunteer labor donated by a German Protestant youth group, Aktion Sühnezeichen, who hoped to expiate the evils of their parents' generation.
254. I am glad to thank Murry Cohen, Philip Creme, Alexander Flinder, Maureen Gilbert, Jane Leaver, Bernhard Leitner, and Rachel Wischnitzer for taking photographs for me or lending me plans and pictures.
255. See below, Essen.
256. Wischnitzer, *Architecture,* p. 262, fig. 234.
257. See below, Žilina and Vienna-Hietzing.
258. See below, Livorno.
259. Wischnitzer, *Architecture,* pp. 250 and 262, figs. 224 and 234. There are photographs also at the offices of the *Allgemeine unabhängige . . . Wochenzeitung* newspaper office and the Zentralrat der Juden in Deutschland, both in Düsseldorf; I am grateful to Messrs. Spiegel, Sachser, and Levy there.
260. G. Swet, "The Jewish Religion in Soviet Russia," in G. Aronson et al., eds., *Russian Jewry, 1917–1967,* New York, 1969, pp. 215–16. Rothenberg, "Synagogues," pp. 6–8 lists all known extant synagogues as of 1965. See also L. Shapiro, "Russian Jews after Stalin," in Aronson, ed., *Russian Jewry,* pp. 452–55.
261. D. J. Elazar, ed., *Balkan Jewries Today,* Jerusalem and Philadelphia, 1974.
262. E.g., Samuel Halevi Abulafia (Toledo), Mordecai Meisel (Prague), Moses Montefiore (Ramsgate), Abraham Oppenhei-

mer (Cologne), the father of Moses Isserles (Cracow), Jacob Neuschatz (Iaşi), I. Landau (Paris).

263. D. Cohen, "Une page d'histoire des juifs de Marseille au XIXe siècle. La construction du temple de la rue Breteuil (1874)," *Revue des études juives* CXXXV, #1–3 (1976), pp. 78–79.

264. See below, Florence, Turin.

265. Rabbi of Mainz quoted in S. Salfeld, *Blätter zur Erinnerung an die Einweihung der neuen Synagoge in Mainz,* Mainz, 1913, p. 18.

266. Roman Catholicism was the established religion before 1905. Dr. Jonathan Helfand, author of studies on 19th-century French Jewry, confirms this identification of "synagogue" with something exotic and questionable. Italian synagogues also were known as temples, and the change in terms from "scuola" to "tempio" was noted by Bachi, "Appunti," p. 36. English Jews based appeals for equality on their similarity to Christian denominations outside the established Church of England (T. Endelman, *The Jews of Georgian England,* Philadelphia, 1979), although they did not normally use the word *temple.*

267. *AZJ,* Oct. 10, 1913, pp. 484–85; Cohen, "Une page d'histoire . . ."; *Jewish Chronicle,* Sept. 30, 1887. Others who expressed sentiments like Geiger's included Jews at Leipzig in 1854 (quoted in W. Haller, "Der Tempelbau," *Aus Geschichte und Leben der Juden in Leipzig,* Leipzig, 1930, pp. 56–57), and the Grand Rabbi of Metz in 1913 (*Archives israélites* LXXIV [Oct. 2, 1913]).

268. Cohen, "Une page d'histoire . . . ," p. 80.

269. E. Bassi, *Architettura del sei e settecento a Venezia,* Naples [ca. 1962], p. 118. See also a visitor to Worms who wrote about its "eastern" appearance in *The Builder,* 1867, as noted below, s.v. Worms. See also the writer for the *Illustrirte Zeitung* on the Frankfurt am Main-Israelitische Religionsgesellschaft synagogue of 1853, below, s.v. Frankfurt am Main.

270. I. Zangwill: edition published in New York, 1892, vol. 2, p. 317; L. Hatvany-Deutsch, *Bondy Jr.,* New York, 1931, p. 227 (originally: *Bondy jr. Ein Roman,* Munich, 1929): "Then the synagogue loomed before them in the mist like a double-headed dragon, with its red brick and its two towers. The uprights of the iron railings in front stood there like rigid sentries with halberds."

271. July 5, 1971. For Karlsruhe, see also *AZJ,* July 16, 1971.

272. *Strasbourg. La Synagogue de la Paix,* Strasbourg, 1958, p. 75. Similarly, in prewar years: Rabbi Löb at Osnabrück, 1906, cited in K. Kühling, *Die Juden in Osnabrück,* Osnabrück, 1969, p. 74; F. Engel, "Der Jude and die deutsche Kultur," *C-V Zeitung* VI, #31–32 (Aug. 5, 1927), pp. 436–37; Frankfurt am Main, Westend Reform synagogue, 1910, was described in a local newspaper as expressing the Jews' attitude that they were "Treudeutsch und jüdisch allezeit" (faithfully German and ever Jewish), see *Kleine Presse,* Sept. 29, 1910. Paris, rue Gaston-de-Caillavet Liberal synagogue, described in I. Schein, "Centro comunitario e sinagoga a Parigi," *L'architettura* XXVIII (June 1982), p. 410.

273. A selection of ideas on religious attitudes to be expressed in synagogue architecture (without architectural prescriptions) may be found in: J. Klein, *Was lehrt uns das Gotteshaus? Predigt bei der Einweihung der neu erbauten Synagoge der israelitischen Gemeinde in Czempin, 17 September, 1861,* Wrocław, 1861; E. Mihaly, "Jewish Prayer and Synagogue Architecture," in R. Gordis and M. Davidowitz, eds., *Art in Judaism,* New York, 1975, pp. 53–63; J. Carlebach, "Architektur der Synagoge," *Jeschurun* XVI, #3–4 (1929), pp. 109–31, esp. pp. 114–25.

Selected Examples

Introduction

The synagogues discussed in the following pages represent architectural and historical conditions in many parts of Europe at many periods. Readers who want to know about additional synagogues will find information in the references cited in the Bibliography and in community histories, copies of which are available at major Jewish research libraries. In some cases, especially with regard to destroyed eastern European synagogues, no reliable information exists.

The short essays in this section have been grouped under nine broad headings:

Austria-Hungary and the Balkans
Eastern Europe and the U.S.S.R.
France and Belgium
Germany and Switzerland
Iberian Peninsula
Italy
The Netherlands
Scandinavia
United Kingdom

In making these groupings, I have sometimes observed cultural tendencies rather than present national boundaries. For example, the synagogues of Wrocław are discussed under Germany rather than Poland because the city was Breslau, Germany, at the time the synagogues were built. Žilina and London-Reform are found with Hamburg's Oberstrasse and Poolstrasse synagogues respectively, because the Czech and British examples add to the accounts of the German buildings. The synagogues of Trieste were built under Austrian rule, but since the Jewish cultural tendencies there were neither purely Austrian nor purely Italian, it seemed convenient to leave Trieste under the heading of its present country. Belgium has been grouped with France because the Jews of both countries had a consistorial governance in the nineteenth century, and because their synagogues often had neo-Romanesque stylistic features. Switzerland accompanies Germany, because the Swiss synagogues discussed here were formerly in Baden, Germany, before the borders changed, and they represent small-town synagogues of the eighteenth and nineteenth centuries as found both in Germany and Switzerland. Synagogue builders in the Balkan states had political and cultural ties to their counterparts in Austria and Hungary, and it seemed unnecessary to put the one exception, that of Samokov in Bulgaria, into a separate section.

Austria-Hungary and the Balkans*

Lower Austria and Burgenland: Medieval Synagogues

Near the eastern border of Austria and the western edge of Hungary are remains of medieval synagogues, those of Hainburg, Korneuburg, and Sopron. Another, now destroyed, was built nearer Vienna, at Mödling. The area was hospitable to Jewish settlement during the late Middle Ages, before the expulsion of Jews in 1420–21, and again in the eighteenth and later centuries. Both medieval and nineteenth-century synagogues survive, some now classified as official historic monuments.

Hainburg

The small stone building traditionally identified as a synagogue in the medieval street, known as Jews' Street, leading west from the marketplace has not been used as a synagogue since 1420 (Fig. 18). Alterations make its original form uncertain. A ritual bath on the same plot of land and the reputed former existence of a hand-washing basin reinforce the association with a synagogue.

Remaining are an octagonal stone tower topped by a pointed cover, and an adjacent rectangular chamber of which the wall nearest the tower is made of the same masonry as the tower. The tower has no windows, and is thus likely to have sheltered the ark. An entry in the Catholic parish book for 1830 records that the octagon contained pictures of Abraham, Isaac, and Jacob. While this supports a connection with Judaism, there are no other figural images known on medieval ark walls, and the images may well have postdated 1420. An octagon added to a rectangle, and an octagonal ark chamber are unique in synagogue architecture, as far as we know. Nevertheless, the numerous Jews in late medieval Hainburg included merchants and a moneylender, so that the community may have had enough money and confidence for architectural experimentation.

Figure 18. Hainburg, medieval synagogue, exterior.

Korneuburg

In this town north of Vienna, Jews were active as traders in agricultural products and salt. Their rectangular synagogue, probably of the fourteenth century, lies in the center of the town, a block away from the main square (Fig. 19). It has not been used as a synagogue since

*A discussion of the Žilina synagogue may be found under Germany, Modern Geometric Synagogues.

Figure 19. Korneuburg, medieval synagogue, exterior.

the fifteenth century, and its roof is apparently of the baroque period, but the fabric was in generally good condition in 1980. The synagogue, whose external measurement is 13.2 m. by 10.5 m. (L. Moses gave dimensions as 11.6 m. by 9.4 m., evidently internal measurement), is made principally of rough stone. Better-cut local stone is used on door and window frames and at the centers and ends of the long north and south walls, probably to ensure the stability of the vaults. The synagogue was originally vaulted with two four-part ribbed groin vaults, as one can tell from traces of ribs in the walls.

Figure 20. Mödling, medieval synagogue, interior.

The nearly rectangular plan was therefore similar to plans of the Miltenberg and Sopron-Uj Street #11 synagogues. The height of the original facade is given by the surviving plaster cornice. The Korneuburg synagogue has tall, pointed windows partly filled in with brick; a pointed-arched door was later blocked. Steps led down from the entrance to the level of the prayer hall. Remains of steps visible in 1932 were interpreted as leading to a women's section in a gallery, but this is far from certain.

After it was taken from the Jews in 1421, the structure became a flour mill and a silo; a loft floor and loading door were added to serve these purposes. The remains of steps may have been related to some of the synagogue's later functions, such as a hayloft and a pharmacist's storeroom. The present owners, intending to turn the building into a gargage, cut off 2 meters at the top of each wall. At that time, the historic monuments authorities stepped in and placed the building under their protection, expecting to convert it into a house.

Mödling

To judge from the architectural forms preserved in a drawing made in 1875, the now-destroyed synagogue of Mödling was a room at least two bays long, covered with four-part ribbed groin vaults over squarish bays (Fig. 20). The vault rib profiles suggest a date in the late thirteenth century at the earliest; the building cannot postdate the expulsion of Jews in 1420-21.

It is hard to tell from the freehand drawing whether the building was slightly wider in its northern than in its southern part. The floor level originally may have been lower than it was when the drawing was made, so that the vault corners would not have seemed to press down upon the occupants of the synagogue. The proportion and location of windows on the east also suggest that the original floor was lower, as the two small and deeply set trilobed windows and a central round window are surprisingly far down on the wall.

The changes could have been made after the expulsion of 1420-21. The new owners used the building for some Christian purpose, for they installed a crucifix on the north wall opposite an entrance on the south. The entrance shown in the drawing is an unmolded recess cut perpendicularly into the south wall, three steps above the floor. The link between doorsill and flooring is effected by a crude wooden ladder. While it is likely that the synagogue floor lay below the doorsill (so that prayer could come "out of the depths"), it is hard to imagine a congregation that was able to afford a vaulted masonry synagogue but not proper and safe steps. The south entrance must therefore postdate 1421.

Figure 22. Sopron, Uj Street #11, street view in 1981.

Sopron

The Jews of Sopron were documented there from the early thirteenth century until their expulsion in 1526. During those years, they erected two synagogues nearly facing each other along the Jews' Street (known since 1440 as Uj, or "new," Street). Both have been uncovered during the past generation—the synagogue at #11 identified in the mid-1950s and that at #22–24 in the mid-1960s. The synagogue at #22–24 of ca. 1300 is earlier than the one at #11 of ca. 1350. Each stands in the rear portion of its building lot, the one at #22–24 closer to the street (Fig. 21). The entrance to each lies between two later houses, with #11 approached under the archway to the courtyard of the house which forms an almost solid block along the street front (Fig. 22). The synagogues are both oblong structures of masonry, about 6 m. by 9 m., with thick plastered walls, stone paving, ribbed groin vaults, small windows placed high on the walls, an ark recess on the eastern wall (probably with steps leading up to the ark recess), and one or more women's annexes (Figs. 23, 24). The women's areas, added after the men's prayer halls were built, are connected to the latter by slit openings. The purpose of extra niches on the eastern walls is unknown.

Figure 21. Sopron, Uj Street #22–24, exterior in 1981.

Figure 23. Sopron, Uj Street #22–24, interior to ark in 1981, with modern bimah.

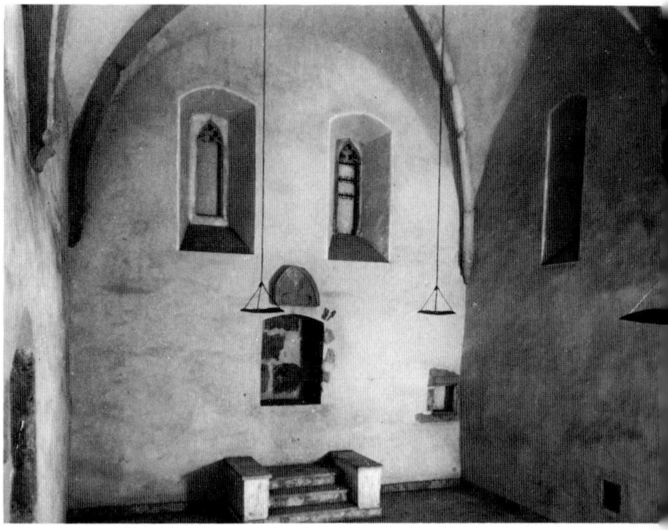

Figure 24. Sopron, Uj Street #11, interior.

The older synagogue at #22–24 had carved vines and foliage in the triangular tympanum over its modest rectangular ark niche. Polylobed tracery filled the tympanum over the entrance door from the vestibule on the north; fragments of the traceried ark niche tympanum also have been uncovered. The synagogue has relatively long windows on the eastern wall, one on either side of the small round traceried window over the ark.

The most significant architectural differences have to do with the vaulting. While both have ribbed groin vaults resting on wall brackets, the earlier vaulting scheme had three such vaults with two auxiliary ribs added to the eastern and western webs. These ribs link the apex of the vault with the western and eastern walls and provide a kind of canopy over the ark. The vaults at #22–24 are more elegant in their profiles than are the quadripartite vaults at #11. The latter synagogue, a simpler two-bay room, is similar in size, plan, and vaulting to the synagogue of Miltenberg, where there was also a windowless north wall and a comparable ark. Uj Street #11 has a plan and vault design which also may be compared to the nearby Korneuburg synagogue.

At the present time, the building at #22–24 is a historic site and museum, while #11 Uj Street awaits restoration.

BIBLIOGRAPHIES

HAINBURG

G. Dehio, *Handbuch der deutschen Kunstdenkmäler,* 2 Abteilung: *Oesterreich,* II, ed. D. Frey, K. Ginhart, et al., Vienna and Berlin, 1935, pp. 185, 188.

R. K. Donin, *Die Kunstdenkmäler der Stadt Hainburg,* Vienna, 1931, pp. 45–46 and fig. 29.

L. Moses, *Die Juden in Niederösterreich,* Vienna, 1935, p. 131.

———, "Synagogenbauten und deren Reste in Niederösterreich," *Unsere Heimat. Monatsblatt des Vereines für Landeskunde von Niederösterreich,* n. F. V, 1932, #10, pp. 297–307, esp. pp. 302–4.

J. Pick, *Jüdisch-geschichtliche Stätten in Wien und in den österreichischen Bundesländern,* Vienna, 1935, p. 44.

N. B.: Moses, *Juden in Niederösterreich* . . . , contains brief remarks on synagogues at Neunkirchen (p. 141) and others—mainly of the 17th century—at Bockfliess, Michlstetten, Nieder-Absdorf, Schönbühel, Tribuswinkel, and Wolfstal.

KORNEUBURG

Files at the Bundesdenkmalamt in the Hofburg, Vienna.

J. Pick, op. cit., p. 46.

F. Zeissl, *Geschichte der Stadt Korneuburg,* vol. 1., Korneuburg, 1959, pp. 73ff.

I owe much information to Dr. Wolfgang Schleidt, Dept. of Biology, University of Maryland, who seems to have inspired efforts to preserve the building.

MÖDLING

K. Giannoni, *Geschichte der Stadt Mödling,* Vienna, 1905.

SOPRON

F. David, *A soproni ó-zsinagóga,* Budapest, 1978, including J. Sedlmayr, "A Soproni ó-zsinagóga helyreállítása," (A Magyarországi zsidó hitközségek monografiai, 8, ed. S. Scheiber).

I. Feuer, "Magyarországi középkori zsinagógák az általános európai fejlődes tükrében," *Magyar Izraelita Országos Kommittee, Evkönyv* 1971/1972, pp. 43ff.

R. Hootz, *Kunstdenkmäler in Ungarn. Ein Bildhandbuch,* Berlin, etc., 1974, pp. 434–35.

J. Nagypál-Kiss, "Die Rekonstruktion der Stadt Sopron/Ungarn," *Bauwelt* 1978, Heft 40, pp. 1502–5.

M. Pollak, *Die Geschichte der Juden in Ödenburg,* Vienna, 1929 (= translation of Hungarian ed., 1896).

S. Scheiber, "Une synagogue médiévale à Sopron," *Revue des études juives* CXVIII (1959–60), pp. 79–93, esp. pp. 84–91.

J. Sedlmayr, "Középkori zsinagóga helyreállitása," *Magyar Epitömüvészet,* 1977, #4, pp. 48–53.

———, "14 Század eleji zsinagóga helyreállitása Sopronban," *Müemlékvédelem* XXII, #1 (1978), pp. 10–18.

Bratislava

Bratislava, a famous seat of orthodoxy, was the leading Jewish center in Slovakia. Its yeshivah was renowned, and the Talmudic scholar, Moses Sofer, who served as Bratislava's chief rabbi from 1807 to 1839, helped to lead the opposition to Reform. A Reform congregation, organized as late as 1872, held services in converted buildings until Dezsö Milch designed a striped, twin-towered synagogue built from 1893 to 1895 (Fig. 25); by 1927, Reformers had a second synagogue and two schools. Nevertheless, orthodoxy dominated Bratislava's Jewish life, and in 1927 the orthodox maintained eleven synagogues, six oratories, six schools including the yeshivah, and eleven houses of study.

Figure 25. Bratislava, Reform synagogue, 1893–95, facade.

Figure 26. Bratislava, orthodox synagogue, 1862–63, facade.

The Jews of Bratislava erected many synagogues between 1335 and 1923. Between 1335 and 1425 they had to move their homes and their synagogues three times. Part of the 1335 building may survive in the walls of the Ursuline church. A synagogue is mentioned in 1439 near the city hall, in a quarter where the Jews were then concentrated. This structure remained in the hands of the Jews until they were expelled or fled from the city in 1527, following the defeat of the Hungarians by the Ottoman Turks at the Battle of Mohács (1526). The city acquired the building in 1539 and turned it into a mill, which suggests that the synagogue had no distinctive form to prevent its conversion into a utilitarian structure.

Jews lived near the city at the foot of the castle hill for the next century and a half under the protection of the Pálffy counts; they were confined in a ghetto enclosed within the town in 1712. Two years later, Count Nicholas Pálffy allowed the Jews to have two synagogues, one in a room of a Christian-owned building on the castle hill and one elsewhere, in an inconspicuous building which was renovated in 1783. The Jews bought the building on the hill in 1716 and remodeled it. They purchased neighboring houses during the course of the eighteenth century and in 1783 had enough space and money for a comprehensive renovation and enlargement. The renovated building burned in 1796, but by then there were many private synagogues and prayer gatherings. A generation earlier, in fact, the synagogue congregation had had trouble assembling a quorum for prayer, and had tried to close the private assemblies in order to concentrate all the men in the main synagogue.

In the 1830s, there were eight synagogues, all located around the same street. Sigmund Mayer, who grew up in Bratislava at this period, wrote that the larger the building and the longer its services lasted, the more prestige it had.

Orthodox Synagogue

The increasing Jewish population needed more synagogue space, and in 1862–63 the community replaced the principal synagogue on the castle hill with a large plastered masonry building designed by Ignatz Feigler (Figs. 26, 27). The architect proposed something quite different from the modest houses and rented rooms where the Jews had been praying. He designed a building with two thin side towers and a central tower crowned with a cupola. Because this scheme was derived from church architecture, several influential rabbis rejected it and called for changes. The chief rabbi agreed to attend the dedication only if the central cupola were removed. Demolition began in haste one night, giving rise to a legend that the offending part had disappeared by miraculous means. The synagogue, as a result, looked less like a church and more like a fortress with a Moorish-ornamented flat-topped tower—another inappropriate image for a synagogue. Feigler may have drawn his original inspiration from the recently completed synagogue at Cologne, which had a striped facade with strong horizontal accents, arcaded cornices, and a domed tower behind the facade. The turrets at Cologne looked less

Figure 27. Bratislava, orthodox synagogue, interior.

like church bell towers, however, and nothing about that synagogue gave an ecclesiastical impression. Feigler also may have known about the domed and turreted Berlin-Oranienburgerstrasse synagogue which was then being built (see Figs. 182–184). A synagogue design closely related to the original one at Bratislava was built at Prešov, where the majority of the community rejected orthodoxy and was less worried about making a church-like impression.

The massive synagogue rose behind a gateway trimmed with bulbous domes. Around three sides of the interior ran two tiers of balconies on thin iron supports. Broad windows and chandeliers of both baroque and contemporary design lit the prayer hall. The bimah, a raised platform surrounded by iron railings, occupied a large amount of space in the center. The triple-arched and domed ark had geometric and plant decorations in vivid colors, which—with the ark's heavy horizontal cornice—must have been meant to suggest something Solomonic-Assyrian-Moorish-Eastern. The rest of the decoration mixed Islamic with medieval. Perhaps the architect meant to create a type of Jewish Gothic by adding details of an Eastern, exotic style. The bimah rails had Gothic tracery; the window tracery suggested both Moorish and Gothic forms; the iron gallery supports ended in brackets recalling some thin columns at the Alhambra (a favorite source of synagogue design after Semper used it at Dresden); and the gallery grilles and ceiling paintings were Moorish in detail.

Heydukova Street

After 1918, under the new Czechoslovak republic, some orthodox Jews moved into a new district and sponsored a competition for the design of a synagogue on Heydukova Street. Artur Szalatnai of Bratislava won the prize, and his synagogue opened in 1923. The *Deutsche Bauzeitung* praised his ability to blend traditional, practical, and personal elements in his building.

The south side of the asymmetrical site faces a narrow street of no distinction, and the architect designed a facade that was neither so startling as to be obtrusive nor so reticent as to be nondescript (Fig. 28). Yellow ochre plastered surfaces matched others in the city, and thus fitted the synagogue into the area. Under a horizontal cornice, a row of seven square piers—two attached to the terminal walls—distills the essentials of the classical Doric portico. Ornament is confined to the two moldings that substitute for capitals on the piers and to stylized floral forms in the metopes of the frieze. Flat-topped ground floor windows and round-headed upper floor windows with circular and angular mullions gave a modern Moorish touch to the windows and forecast traditional designs inside. The traditional elements make this building different from those with the unadorned planes, cubes, and delicately thin walls of the International Style, such as that of Plauen at the end of the decade (see Figs. 156, 157). The Bratislava building did, however, use modern technology, being made of reinforced concrete. The details were produced from artificial stone, including the facade piers, gallery, window grilles, and water basin in the vestibule.

Figure 28. Bratislava, Heydukova Street, 1923, facade.

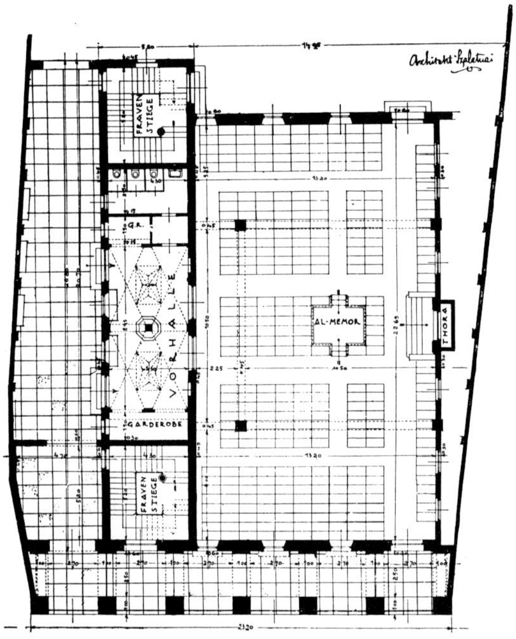

Figure 29. Bratislava, Heydukova Street, plan.

Men enter the prayer hall directly from a door at the southeast, and women use the southwest door to reach the southern staircase to their galleries (Fig. 29). An arch at the southwest corner opens on a narrow passage to the vestibule at the west side of the prayer hall. A vestibule fulfills the Talmudic admonition to enter the synagogue by two doors, but here the vestibule loses some of its function because it is tucked out of the way. In the center of the vestibule a thick column rises from a water basin. The hand-washing basin is customary in synagogues, but this curious and rather clumsy combination is not. It may have been meant to give an exotic cast to the entrance area.

Beyond the vestibule lies the prayer hall, wider along the north-south than along the east-west axis (Fig. 30). The room does not seem to stretch out laterally because galleries on three sides create the impression of a square room. The women are physically and visually separated from the men, following orthodox tradition.

Also in accord with orthodox practice, the bimah stands in the center of the inner square—here, exactly in the center. It is a raised platform enclosed within a metal railing and sheltered by a metal canopy with pointed arches. The design recalls late medieval and Renaissance bimahs in central and eastern Europe, such as that of the Altneuschul at Prague. It may also be based in part on a design by Hugo Gorge for Vienna-Hietzing in 1912, which was published in 1918, close to the time of Szalatnai's project (see Figs. 49, 66). The bimah is more imposing than the ark which is flat and therefore reticent. Candlesticks and other images used in late-Renaissance painted wooden synagogues in eastern Europe adorn the triumphal arch on the ark wall. A tall and narrow window zigzags upward from the center of the ark cornice to the ceiling, its colored glass representing stylized flowers. The attempt to design a modern ark wall and the originality of the window design show that Szalatnai wanted to establish a setting for orthodoxy in modern society, just as his clients seem to have wanted to do in their own lives.

Figure 30. Bratislava, Heydukova Street, longitudinal section.

The gallery railings and the window mullions show the same intention. They are faintly Middle Eastern in design, but Szalatnai did not copy old forms directly. Appropriate associations for the strictly orthodox congregation are introduced with a contemporary taste for smooth surfaces, pure lines, and clear geometric shapes. In this respect, Szalatnai's synagogue is parallel to the contemporary church at Le Raincy by Auguste Perret. There, a modern building material—reinforced concrete—produced tall, thin elements like those of a Gothic church, and formed a pierced outer wall with inlaid glass recalling medieval window patterns.

Szalatnai's thoughtfully conceived building survived the Second World War, but most of its congregation did not; by May 1942, all the Jews were believed to have been deported or to have gone into hiding. At war's end, remnants of the community and other refugees rehabilitated the vandalized Reform synagogue, providing bimah and gallery arrangements suited to the orthodox, but later the building was demolished. Another synagogue was turned into a television studio. The ark from the destroyed orthodox synagogue on the castle hill is now at yeshivah Hekhal Pressburg in Jerusalem; there it has been refinished in a dark wood color to suit a generation that does not think of Islamic designs and Jewish orthodoxy as having much in common. In Bratislava itself, a small Jewish community still exists, served by a rabbi who officiates in the synagogue of 1923. Funds do not seem to be available to assure the perfect maintenance of the building.

BIBLIOGRAPHY

"Bauten aus der Slowakei," *Deutsche Bauzeitung,* Oct. 1929, pp. 705–9.

A. Charim, *Die toten Gemeinden,* Vienna, etc., 1966.

Encyclopedia Judaica, 1971, s.v. Pressburg.

H. Gold, ed., *Die Juden und die Judengemeinde Bratislava in Vergangenheit und Gegenwart,* Brno, 1932, esp. S. Krauss, "Pressburger Synagogen," pp. 91–98; see also pp. 114, 136.

A. Grünhut, *Katastrophenzeit des slowakischen Judentums. Aufstieg und Niedergang der Juden von Pressburg,* Tel Aviv, 1972.

I. Heller and Z. Vajda, *The Synagogues of Hungary. An Album,* eds. R. Braham and E. Farkas, New York, 1968, p. 11, figs. 3, 218, 219, 420.
Jewish Encyclopedia, s.v. Pressburg.
"Neubau eines jüd.-orth. Tempels in Bratislava. Arch. Artur Szalatnai," *Forum* I (1931), pp. 109–11.
Universal Jewish Encyclopedia, s.v. Pressburg.
S. Hacohen Weingarten, *History of the Jews of Bratislava. Arim va-imahot be-Yisroel,* ed., Y. L. Hacohen Maimon (Fishman), vol. 7, Jerusalem, 1960.

I am grateful to Ludovit Dojč and Štefan Šlachta for photographs, information, and assistance, and to Robert and Sarah Kaiser Hyams for current information.

Bruck an der Leitha

The synagogue at Bruck an der Leitha, not far from Vienna, was built in 1915 to meet an urgent need rather than to satisfy the slowly developing requirements of an existing community. The Austrian officials charged with caring for the refugees from war-ravaged towns in Galicia provided well-conceived housing, clinics, kindergartens, and religious facilities. As the refugees streamed westward, government workers directed them to special new settlements, knowing that Vienna and other major cities could not cope with a mass of Galicians who were unfamiliar with urban life. The Jews, who were kept apart from Christian refugees to minimize intergroup friction, were settled outside Mikulov, in Pohrlitz, and in Gaya in the autumn of 1914, and at Bruck an der Leitha in the winter of 1914–15.

Housing, often in long barracks-like structures divided into family units, was at least marginally adequate. The social and educational buildings were sensibly built with locally available wood, and the architects took pains to provide good natural light and ventilation. The religious facilities had a more imposing and stabilizing character because the planners foresaw that the refugees might remain even after the war ended and the buildings might then become permanent.

The buildings erected for both Jewish and Christian worshippers recalled the simple geometric wooden structures of their homelands farther east and would have been familiar and comforting to their users (Fig. 31). Rectilinear shapes were varied by the strongly slanting roofs, as in older eastern European religious buildings (see Fig. 12). The architects used a double sheathing of wood covered with creosote on the exterior. The insides were painted with traditional designs, such as six-pointed stars, that could easily be executed with stencils (Fig. 32).

The synagogue at Bruck was an almost square box extended on the east by an ark recess flanked by rooms for community needs, and on the west by a vestibule (Fig. 33). Three pairs of wooden piers divided the main space, helped support the roof, and delimited the women's galleries on the north and south. The galleries had high barriers which suited the orthodox worshippers. The reader's desk, on a

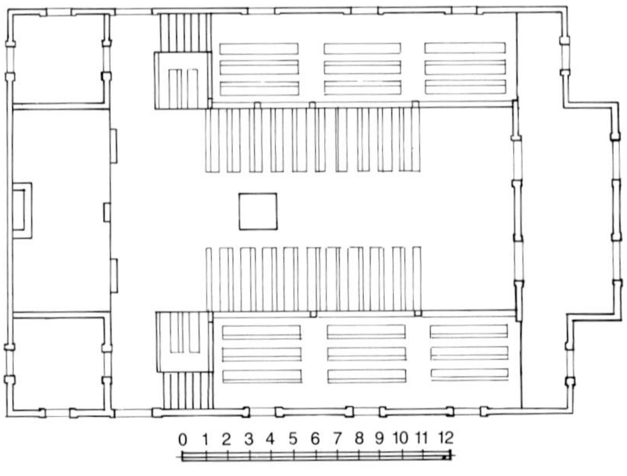

Figure 31. Bruck an der Leitha, 1915, plan.

Figure 32. Bruck an der Leitha, exterior.

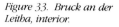

Figure 33. Bruck an der Leitha, interior.

slightly raised bimah enclosed by a simple railing, stood in the center of the building, also following orthodox practice. Light entered the room through long, banded clerestory windows and through round-arched windows and doorways set in polygonal-headed frames. The austerity and economy were disguised successfully by such touches as the varied window openings, the sloping wooden buttresses on the exterior, and the delicate and neat ornamental bands painted on the light-colored interior.

The architects, mainly from government building departments in the nearby regions, included a few from the Imperial Ministry of Works. The unknown designer responsible for the synagogue at Bruck was a person of taste and good judgment: The synagogue combined hints of older Galician tradition with the delicate clarity of early modern architecture to provide an exceptionally satisfying and economical refuge for those whose lives and spirits needed sensitive and practical help.

BIBLIOGRAPHY

AJYb, 1916–17 (1916), p. 116.

H. Fischel, "Bauanlagen der Staatlichen Flüchtlingsfürsorge," *Der Architekt. Monatshefte für Bau und Raumkunst, mit der Beilage 'Die bildenden Künste'* XXI (1916–18), Heft 1/2, pp. 15–24. (This is *Der Architekt* XXI, as well as *Die bildenden Künste* I.)

Bucharest

Bucharest has long been the preeminent city of Rumanian Jews. Despite a host of civil disabilities imposed on them, Jews migrated to the vicinity of the town, where, until the nineteenth century, they were confined to a suburb. Some of the synagogues are known only through accounts of their destruction, but from about 1800 onward they multiplied in number in order to serve a rapidly increasing population. From a supposed figure of about one thousand Jews in the city in 1800, the population grew to about six times that in 1860, just before Bucharest became the capital of the newly formed Kingdom of Rumania in 1861.

Harsh laws of the first half of the nineteenth century affected poor and rural Jews more severely than they did the urban Jews, who achieved comparative prosperity. As early as 1818, Bucharest's Sephardic Jews petitioned successfully for permission to build a new synagogue. The Jewish population also included those born locally, as well as Russians, Prussians, and Austrians, with some adhering to traditional and others to Reform Judaism. Most of them were served by small synagogues. The impetus to erect larger ones in Bucharest may have come, as it did in Iaşi, from population pressure and from the undignified spectacle of synagogue members accosting passers-by and inviting them to help form a *minyan* in synagogues too small to have ten reliable quorum members. In 1837, the tailors' synagogue congregation discussed plans to build a new house of worship. During the later 1840s and 1850s, impressive synagogues rose in Vacareşti, Bucharest's Jewish quarter, reflecting the varied origins and degrees of orthodoxy in the population.

Sinagoga Mare

In 1845, several congregations merged to form the Great (Mare) Synagogue, built in 1845–47 to the design of the congregation's leaders. This large building was damaged by vandals and repaired in the mid-1860s. It was remodeled or rebuilt in 1903, had the ark wall moved farther to the east in 1909, received electric lighting in 1915, and underwent a more thorough renovation in 1931–32. Gherson M. Horowitz (1882–1942) decorated it with rococo-style ceiling paintings in 1936. Fascists damaged it severely in the early 1940s, but repairs were made after the Second World War and the building has been restored in recent years.

The form we see is apparently that of 1903–9. The synagogue is built of brick covered with stucco designed in Renaissance forms, including a rusticated basement, drafted "masonry" above, and pilasters separating the bays and parts of the facade. The exterior articulation suggests a basilican plan; the eclectic but sober interior has a nave flanked by galleried aisles, a recess for the ark at the east, and ample lobed and polychromed arches crowning the openings of the galleries onto the nave.

MaLBiM Synagogue

In 1848, the orthodox Jews erected a synagogue, now named in honor of a learned rabbi known as MaLBiM (1809–79). As rabbi of Bucharest (1858–63) and other cities, he was a vehement opponent of Reform. The synagogue erected by his sympathizers is ornate, with Moorish motifs and tracery combined with details in other styles. Perhaps here, as elsewhere, a style unlike the more restrained form of other synagogues was selected in order to make known the special interests of the congregation. Its present appearance surely postdates 1848 and even 1864, the construction date given in one source. The synagogue was renovated in 1904, when the style may have been introduced, and again in 1928.

Templul Unirea-Sfanta

In 1850, two years after the MaLBiM Synagogue opened, the tailors' congregation inaugurated its new building, known as the Unirea-Sfanta or Holy Union Synagogue. The plan with a nave and galleried aisles may go back to 1850, but the present height, the use of iron supports for two levels of galleries, and the tall, lobed arch leading to the ark suggest the date of 1906, when the synagogue was remodeled or rebuilt. The cheerful facade has red and cream-colored stripes and a mixture of Moorish, Byzantine, and Romanesque details—all still common in eastern Europe at the start of this century. The interior, four bays long, is decorated with colorful and exuberant ornament, including stylized plants and six-pointed stars which reach a crescendo of lobes, circles, and multiple cornices above the ark. The bimah and ark are near each other at the east. Although damaged by

Figure 34. Bucharest, Choral Temple, 1864–66, facade in 1981.

the fascist Iron Guard in 1941, the restored synagogue has been the seat of the Jewish Historical Museum since 1978, housing ritual objects and other materials.

Choral Temple

One synagogue that has preserved its mid-nineteenth-century appearance is the Choral Temple, ceremonially inaugurated in June 1860, but actually constructed in 1864–66 and repaired in 1867 after rioting vandals injured it in 1866 (Figs. 34, 35). The building was put up by a predominantly German-Austrian congregation, the group most susceptible to the Reform ideas embodied in the ritual used. For their clients,

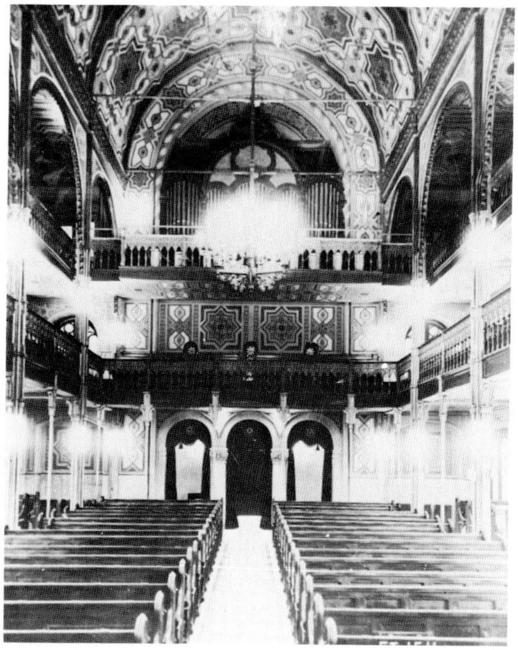

Figure 35. Bucharest, Choral Temple, interior to entrance.

the architects Enderle and Freiwald adopted Ludwig von Förster's design for the large Vienna-Tempelgasse synagogue of 1855–58 (see Fig. 64). The Bucharest congregation had begun to plan for a new synagogue in 1857 and was alert to the new design created by a prominent architect who worked for the Austrian government. By using so recent a model, the Bucharest Reform congregation showed its cultural links to German-speaking and more progressive parts of Europe, and displayed its own modern outlook in both architecture and religious practice. The chief synagogue of the imperial metropolis was easy to copy in the provinces, because Förster had published drawings and a description of it in his own *Allgemeine Bauzeitung*.

After renovation in 1932 by the architect I. Leoneanu (who also built the community library in 1933), the synagogue again fell victim to extensive vandalism, perpetrated by the Iron Guard, but the building was repaired after 1945 with the help of international Jewish charitable organizations. Now the seat of the Chief Rabbi of Rumania, it is kept in order with contributions from the Rumanian government. Architectural preservation is meant to show the world that Rumanian Jews are treated well, even though the majority have chosen to leave the country since the end of the Second World War.

By 1861, there were twenty-nine other synagogues in Bucharest, and later there were over seventy in Vacareşti. One was the main Sephardic synagogue, now an empty brick shell, which had Byzantine ornamental details as if to proclaim the Turkish origin of many of its members. The tiny Zisu Synagogue still nestles in a small garden across the street from the Unirea-Sfanta Synagogue. Some of the remaining houses of worship are hard to find, since street names in the Jewish district have disappeared from recent detailed maps of Bucharest. In 1961–62 there were forty-two synagogues in the city, but only twelve in 1977, and four of these were damaged in the earthquake in March of that year.

Although Jewish life is still intense, especially in the towns of northeast Rumania around Fălticeni and Dorohoi, and although the Federation of Jewish Communities of the Socialist Republic of Rumania maintains synagogues, religious schools, kasher restaurants, and even health-resort homes, it is unlikely that more synagogues will be needed. In 1889, before the annexation of additional territory but before the mass emigrations, the Jewish population of Rumania was estimated at about 267,000; during the 1920s, Greater Rumania had about 760,000–800,000 Jews; in 1977, there were only about 40,000 remaining.

BIBLIOGRAPHY

AJR Information, Aug. 1978, p. 7.

"Centenarul Sinagogii Mari," *Revista Cultului Mozaic* XIX, #111 (Dec. 1, 1964).

Federation of Jewish Communities of the Socialist Republic of Rumania, *Jewish Life in Romania in 1978,* Bucharest, n.d.

M. A. Halevy, *Comunitatile evreilor din Iaşi şi Bucureşti,* I, *Pana la 1821,* Bucharest, 1931.

———, *Monografie istorica a Templului Coral din Bucureşti,* Bucharest, 1935.

———, *Sinagoga mare din Bucureşti,* Bucharest, 1931.

———, *Templul Unirea-Sfanta din Bucureşti,* Bucharest, 1937.

G. Levenson, "Revisiting the Little Tailors' Synagogue," *Jewish Digest* XXIV (July–Aug., 1979), pp. 75–78.

Y. L. Hacohen Maimon (Fishman), ed., *Arim va-imahot be-Yisroel,* vol. 4, Jerusalem, n.d., pp. 207–9.

I. Niemirower, *Ochire asupra istoriei comunitații israelite din Iaşi,* Bucharest, 1907, esp. p. 30.

Pinkas ha-Kehillot [Encyclopedia of Jewish Communities], *Rumania,* Jerusalem, 1969, pp. 44ff.

N. L. Porter and D. B. Rostovsky, *The Roumanian Handbook,* London, 1931.

S. Savin, "Pictorul-decorator al Sinagogii Mari," *Revista Cultului Mozaic* XIV, #200 (Feb. 1, 1969), p. 5.

———, "Vecchi sinagogi din Bucureştiul de altadata," *ibid.,* XI, #149 (Nov. 1, 1966), p. 3.

I am indebted to Edward Sullivan and Ellen C. Schwartz for photographs and to Berta Barasch for translation.

Budapest

Jews have had a long history within the modern limits of Budapest, attaining special distinction in the nineteenth century. As the historian Arthur J. May expressed it, "so much of the [city's] progress was due to the energy and initiative of the Jewish population" that the united city of Buda and Pest was "not uncommonly referred to as a 'Jewish creation.' "

Buda–Medieval Synagogues

In Buda, on the right bank of the Danube, Jews enjoyed a generally tranquil existence from the mid-thirteenth century to about 1490, with persecution and temporary expulsions confined mainly to the years 1360–64. From ca. 1251 to ca. 1360, a synagogue stood in the southern part of the castle district. After 1364, the synagogues were built in the northern part, in the present Táncsics Street, where modern excavators uncovered traces of a synagogue of ca. 1400–61 at #26 and of another (1461–1526) at #23. The older building is another example of a two-naved synagogue of the type known at Worms, Prague-Altneuschul, Regensburg, and Cracow/Kazimierz-Old. The Buda synagogue was unusually large, reflecting the royal protection and charters offered to the Jews who were royal financiers. The remains of the building include an entrance adorned with Gothic piers bearing sixteenth- or seventeenth-century Hebrew inscriptions and Jewish symbols, and a western wall with the contours of a blocked window between the women's and men's areas. Excavations of 1964–65 uncovered 19 m. of the northern wall and determined building dimensions of about 19 m. by 9 m. and a height between 7.5 and 8 m. The building was vaulted and its interior walls were probably plastered. The pavement lay below street level, as it did in the approximately contemporaneous synagogue of Tomar. There were three bays in each nave, either originally or after 1541, when the Jews returned to this building after being expelled in 1526. After 1541, the dimensions were 26.5 by 10.7 m. The women's area adjoined the men's on the south and was connected to it by windows. On the same side opened a large entrance arch to the men's section. Later, a wooden roof replaced the vault. The building suffered damage from shells in sixteenth- and seventeenth-century sieges of the city, and the remains have now been covered by an apartment house.

Obuda

When Jews were forbidden to live in Buda, they moved north to Obuda where, from ca. 1712 onward, Countess Zichy, a local noblewoman, offered protection and houses for rent in an enclave near the river. A synagogue was built by 1737 on the site of the extant Obuda synagogue at the northern end of Lajos Street; the architect was Mátyás Nepauer.

The extant building of 1820–21, apparently using parts of the older one, was the work of András Landherr, who secured the job because a competitor's design was judged to be less sturdy and more costly (Figs. 36, 37). Landherr's, costing about 130,000 Viennese florins, was not well built either, and it required repair in 1865 and in 1900. During the First World War, the government requisitioned copper from the roof. During the Second World War, a perpendicular crack appeared in the ark wall, and that nearly brought down the whole synagogue. Repairs were made in 1947, but the much diminished community could not maintain the synagogue adequately. By the late 1970s, the near ruin passed into the hands of a television company which rehabilitated the exterior, except for the ark wall, which had to be destroyed.

The remains of the neoclassical synagogue are still handsome. The building has a six-columned temple facade fronting a four-bay rectilinear prayer hall. On the sides, two storeys of round-headed windows open between pilasters that divide the exterior into bays. The synagogue was unclassically asymmetrical, with a staircase annex on the north and galleries only on the north and west; Landherr built only the west and south walls. Several details—for example, the leaf-like forms left and right of a clock in the pediment, the pilaster strips and scrolls that replaced the original pediment decoration probably in 1865, the three storeys of windows on the facade, and the corner quoins—also were not archaeologically pure. Nevertheless, references to the shape and portico of a classical temple gave dignity to both secular and religious buildings around 1820.

The ark sheltered its twenty-eight Torah scrolls under an arched opening beneath an entablature. Above that, a high, arched field contained the tablets of the Law which seemed to float in the center of a circular window, a baroque stylistic feature. Embracing the ark and arched field was a framework composed of columns on unusually high bases, a tall entablature, and a round arch; painted draperies, apparently made of plaster, descended from the top of the framework. The ensemble looked like a modernized eighteenth-century eastern European ark composition, with its often awkward proportions, bold frame, and ornamental protuberances at the sides. It may have come

Figure 36. Budapest-Obuda, 1820–21, exterior in 1981.

from the preceding Obuda synagogue. The bimah, more up to date in style, was a platform framed by tall Egyptian obelisks which here implied the Jews' long existence and their origin somewhere in the vicinity of the eastern Mediterranean.

The location of the bimah in the center, and the lower level of the main room floor compared to that of the vestibule floor, were orthodox and traditional elements maintained even after the congregation became conservatively Reformed (Neolog) following the death in 1831 of the staunchly orthodox rabbi, Moses Münz. The modern-minded Jews of Obuda espoused the Hungarian national cause in 1848, had sermons delivered in alternate weeks in Hungarian and German, and closed the ritual bath because, in the words of a former resident of Obuda, "it wasn't that kind of neighborhood." Ironically, opportunities brought about by modernization diminished the Obuda community throughout the nineteenth and early twentieth centuries, as many Jews moved to the new commercial areas across the river in Pest.

Pest–Orczy House

Jews traditionally had not been allowed in Pest, where craftsmen and small merchants mistrusted a minority that was protected by royal

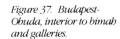

Figure 37. Budapest-Obuda, interior to bimah and galleries.

and noble employers. They were admitted as residents first in the 1780s when they were confined to several streets. They had a synagogue at Király Street 1340/12r and small prayer houses in private dwellings. Their center of activity—and the location of the synagogue—was the Orczy House, a large building with several wings, named after its noble owners. In 1826 or 1829 the Jews established there a larger, galleried orthodox synagogue with almost six hundred seats, designed by Lőrinc Zofahl; within a decade they had built a slightly Reformed temple on the first floor (a galleried basilica in classical style, also by Zofahl, 1830). They also built a Jewish Hospital (1840–41).

Jews prospered in commerce and manufacturing as civic leaders fostered business in an effort to increase the wealth and relative stature of Hungary within the Empire. Since neither the untrained masses nor the unwilling aristocracy could be called upon in large numbers to practice commerce, the Jews filled the gap, sometimes as nominal directors and as deputies for noble shareholders. The Hungarian ethnic element also was eager to gain allies in Magyarization efforts, and many Jews accepted any invitation into national circles.

Pest–Dohány Street

By 1843, the Jews in Pest had grown so numerous that they needed a new synagogue, but disputes about ritual orthodoxy diverted funds from the controversial synagogue to a Jewish school while the population continued to increase. One writer declared that Jews had been leaving country towns for the big cities like rats deserting a sinking ship. The occasion for his remark was the opening in 1859 of the huge twin-towered synagogue in Dohány Street, which seats about three thousand people and is now the largest synagogue remaining in use in all of Europe (Figs. 38, 39).

One of the forces responsible for the realization of this synagogue project was Löw Schwab, community rabbi from 1836 until his death in 1857. To strengthen community cohesion, he closed a Liberal Reform congregation that had flourished from 1848 to 1852, and in 1853 he superintended a compromise between the orthodox and the Neolog Jews so that plans could be made for united community synagogue buildings. The compromise allowed for a service in Hebrew and unabridged ritual, but it permitted a (male) choir, low gallery parapets, vernacular sermons, and an organ.

The congregation sought the most famous architects available. The first plans were made in 1848 by József Hild, a prominent neoclassicist, but that revolutionary year was not calm enough to allow building and the Jews were not yet sufficiently united. An eclectic designer, Frigyes Feszl, with two associates, Gerster and Kauffer, made new plans in 1850 for a tall, domed, and richly ornamented central-plan building recessed behind two-storey wings along the street, but these were not executed, either. After the compromise of 1853, the eminent Viennese architect, Ludwig von Förster, won a design competition. Employing Förster

Figure 38. Budapest, Dohány Street, 1854–59, facade.

Figure 39. Budapest, Dohány Street, interior to ark.

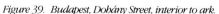

assured the Jews of a work acceptable to the public, since the architect had been officially appointed to help redesign parts of Vienna and had secured the commission for the Moorish-style Vienna-Tempelgasse synagogue (see Figs. 63, 64).

The Budapest competition committee of forty-five members chose Förster's project, also in the Moorish mode, because they believed it had a purely oriental style to which elements of the Temple of Solomon were successfully united. Franz Xaver Kempf, a contemporary historian of the building, felt that in style and size (55m. × 26m. × 26 m.) the synagogue was close to the Temple, suiting a people over five thousand years old. He related the towers to Jakhin and Boaz. Wisely choosing not to press the comparison too far, he admitted the similarity of various details to such secular buildings as the Moorish Alhambra in Granada, the Alcázar of Toledo, and to unspecified parts of Holyroodhouse Palace in Edinburgh.

Like the Vienna-Tempelgasse synagogue, this one in Budapest had a brick exterior that looked thin and sharply defined. The bricks were specially molded and set on a red stone foundation. With the gilded cupolas, the stone and terra-cotta trim, and wrought and cast iron from the mines of Archduke Albert himself, the synagogue presented a warmly colorful impression, while it introduced brick to Budapest as a suitable facing for monumental architecture.

Unfortunately, as funds ran out, the interior was finished in cheaper materials and never received the intended decorations. Förster quit the job, leaving Hild in charge—Hild having supervised the masonry work earlier. Hild left in 1856. Ignác Wechselmann, the Jewish superintending architect, completed the work with the help of Károly Schumann and the supervision of an eight-member building committee. The ark area was nevertheless executed in materials of high quality; it was designed by Feszl, perhaps after the other prominent architects had left the project.

Compared with the Vienna synagogue, that of Budapest had a larger lot and a more conspicuous situation on a wider street; the Budapest lot was enlarged in the 1920s to hold a community house, a garden, and the small Heroes' Temple war memorial synagogue. The greater visibility of the facade at Budapest allowed Förster to use simple round windows rather than the lobed shapes that helped to emphasize the Vienna facade on its narrow street. The octagonal towers of Budapest, over 41 m. high, would have been hard to see in the Viennese street, but they were effective accents in the Budapest cityscape. Both synagogues have linear rather than sculptural detail, including patterned or striped masonry, geometric window tracery, and some interlaces and delicate cusps. Large round-arched windows in both synagogues and in their community houses were filled with tracery based on Gothic patterns but using round rather than pointed forms, cusps in some arches, and pierced window screens. All this created a kind of Moorish style that might have been seen as "Jewish Gothic."

The tall and thin characteristics of both Moorish and Gothic architecture appeared inside both of these double-galleried, apsed basilican synagogues. Slender iron piers with gilt capitals supported the galleries and flat ceilings, and candelabra and chandeliers were built into the iron framework. Both synagogues had round, cusped arches defining the nave bays; those at Budapest were over 12 m. in diameter, springing from iron piers of about 0.75 m. in diameter. Both had round arches leading to the ark area, with those in Vienna embellished by cusps. Both had flat walls and ceilings with painted decorations, though the patterns were far more elaborate at Vienna, where more money was available. Both had painted or glazed roundels on the eastern wall.

The principal differences between the synagogues included the larger size of the Budapest building and the focal wall design. At Vienna, the flat eastern wall was framed by a painted strip of Moorish decoration which contained the painted roundel above triple stilted arches around the ark. Tablets of the Law linked the stilted arches with the roundel. At Budapest, there is an architectural composition in several planes: a gabled framework with a stilted arch enclosing the Torah scrolls; a pierced screen of Moorish-Gothic design filling the remaining width of the ark opening, behind which were a square drum and bulbous cupola over the scrolls niche itself; organ pipes flanking the cupola; and finally the eastern wall plane with its round window. The three-dimensional character of this area, and the use of a large cupola and screen above and around the ark, show the style of Feszl, who is best known for his Vigadó concert hall, a building based on Viennese sources overlaid with an astonishing mix of forms including Moorish and Gothic. The screen and cupola of the Budapest ark inspired later followers, such as that of Berlin-Oranienburgerstrasse, while the simpler interior and exterior compositions at Vienna had many other imitators.

The Budapest and Vienna synagogues reveal the greater self-confidence of Jews in these cities during the 1850s, when at last they were able to commission buildings with conspicuous street fronts in a supposedly Jewish style. The large buildings manifested the commercial success and full urbanization of many Jews at the time.

Förster published the Vienna synagogue in his *Allgemeine Bauzeitung* and omitted the Budapest synagogue, no doubt only because it was not executed entirely to his design. The style was an equivalent of Gothic but it showed the oriental "national" origin of Jews within the multicultural Austro-Hungarian lands in an age of increasing nationalism. Of course, this made the Jews appear more oriental than European, and one wonders what conflicting messages it offered to Theodor Herzl, founder of modern Zionism, who lived next door to the Budapest synagogue and celebrated his bar mitzvah in it.

Pest–Rumbach Street

The urge toward modernity in religion did not suit everyone. When the religious compromise was achieved in Budapest in 1853, the participants agreed to build orthodox synagogues as well as synagogues for those who wished to keep whatever mix of tradition and modernity they had followed earlier; the latter group used what were known as "status quo" synagogues.

The synagogue of 1869–72 is one example of a "status quo" synagogue. It is interesting as an early work of the Viennese architect Otto Wagner, who won the commission in a competition of 1869 and sent a sepia interior perspective of it to the Paris Universal Exposition of 1878. He was then only twenty-eight years old, had had only seven small jobs on his own, and had not found his distinctive direction.

This is one of the rare synagogues to recall the shape of the polygonal, domed Islamic monument known as the Dome of the Rock in Jerusalem, said to be on the site of the Temple (Figs. 40, 41, 42). Logically there is no reason to make a "little sanctuary" look like the Islamic replacement for the great sanctuary, but Wagner's clients probably preferred significant associations to logic. At about the same time, Károly Benkö designed for Győr a domed, square synagogue whose exterior resembled that of Dresden's. Inside, however, the galleries formed seven sides of an octagon. Surely Benkö had the Temple in mind, for against the round window of the eastern wall he set an ornamental motif of a facade with three parts and heavy flat cornices, which Förster had earlier associated with the Temple facade. Both Benkö and Wagner had models—in Dohány Street and in Vienna—for their use of Islamic forms and allusions to the Temple; perhaps they thought they were improving upon Förster's ideas, which had no basis in archaeology. Wagner had studied with Förster, and we may assume that he studied and criticized his teacher's work on the same kind of unusual building.

Wagner's synagogue has additional rectangular bays about 5 m. wide and 3.5 m. long at the east and west, and a vestibule. The plan, then, is not identical with that of the Dome of the Rock, and the facades of the buildings are different. Wagner designed a tripartite composition with a higher center and lower sides, varying Förster's design for Vienna. A decorative cornice with little minaret-like turrets breaks the horizontals of the cornice line. Plastered brick with polychrome surface patterns differentiates

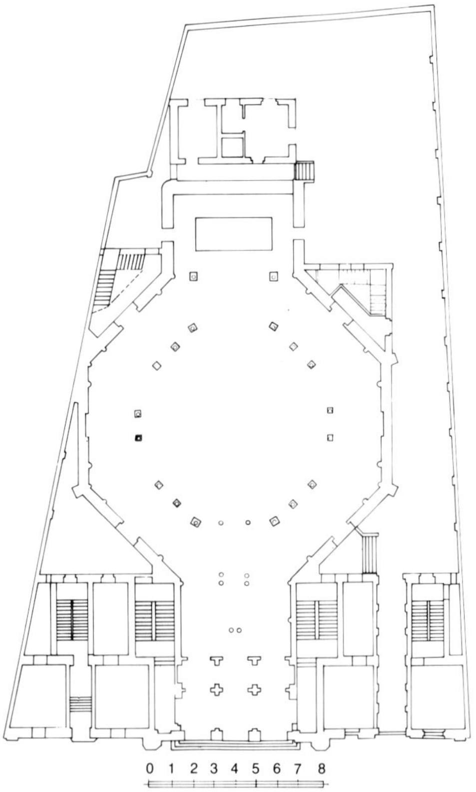

Figure 40. Budapest, Rumbach Street, 1869–72, plan.

Figure 41. Budapest, Rumbach Street, interior to ark.

Figure 42. Budapest, Rumbach Street, facade in 1981.

the ground floor from the upper storeys. Openings include a triple-arched portal with cusped and stilted arches, and a triad of arches enclosing two upper storeys marked by paired windows. This composition combines elements of the Vienna and Berlin-Oranienburgerstrasse synagogues.

Wagner and Mór Kallina, the construction supervisor, had drawings ready by July 1870. Their building stands on an irregular lot on a narrow street where the land cost only 50,000 förints. The building extends about 21 m. along the street front and about 32 m. into the lot. It is disposed on its site asymmetrically, leaving open space for light and ventilation on all sides and for a courtyard protected from the street. Between the street front and the first bay is an open, three-domed vestibule with offices and functional rooms on either side of the western bay and vestibule. At the far end of the octagon, beyond the ark bay, are small rooms for the rabbi and cantor, and others for storage.

The main interior space, the octagon, measures 18.95 m. from corner to corner. There are 1,160 seats, 786 of them for men. The core of the octagon is separated from the galleried aisles by eight major iron piers defining the corners of the octagon, and two smaller piers between them which are set slightly closer to the core. The major piers extend at gallery level into wide, round, cusped arches, also made of iron. Above the galleries runs a clerestory. Light also enters through large round windows in each gallery bay and through a lantern in the sloping polygonal roof above the octagon; the lantern stands above the rectangular metal bimah, which occupies the center of the octagonal space. Small-patterned painted ornament based on "Moorish" sources covers many surfaces and gives an exotic impression in the gaslight.

The postwar Jewish population of Budapest made little use of this synagogue, and the matter of its sale and possible demolition was discussed even before part of the ark end collapsed in 1980. Repairs would cost millions of förints, and so it is unlikely that the synagogue ever will be used again. If this synagogue is destroyed, the Jews of Budapest will still have over thirty synagogues of several degrees of orthodoxy, but local Jewish cultural history and the legacy of Otto Wagner will be diminished.

BIBLIOGRAPHIES

BUDA

I. Feuer, "Magyarországi középkori zsinagógák az általános európai fejlődes tükrében," *Magyar Izraelita Országos Kommittee, Evkönyv* 1971/1972, pp. 43ff.

F. Grünvald, "A Buda-várhegyi zsinagóga es zsidó temető helye török idökben," *Jubilee volume in honor of Prof. Bernhard Heller,* ed. A. Scheiber, Budapest, 1941, pp. 164–69 (not consulted).

M. Papp, "Baudenkmäler im mittelalterlichen Judenviertel der Budaer (Ofner) Burg," *Acta Technica Academiae Scientiarum Hungaricae* LXVII, #1–4 (1970), pp. 205–25.

S. Scheiber, "La découverte d'une synagogue médiévale à Sopron," *Revue des études juives* CXVII (1959–60), pp. 79–93.

L. Zolnay, "Középkori zsinagógák a Budaj várban," *Budapest Régiségei* XXII (1971), pp. 271–84. I owe this reference to Nicholas Ehrenfeld.

———, "Nagy jelentőségű feltárási munka a vár lakone gyedében," *Budapest* IV (Apr. 1966).

OBUDA, PEST

AJYb LXXVIII (1978), p. 460.

Allgemeine illustrirte Judenzeitung (Pest) I, Sept. 6, 1860 (interior view).

AZJ Sept. 19, 1859.

A. Büchler, *A Zsidók története Budapesten,* Budapest, 1901.

[?] Calm, "Ein Sonnabend in Pest," *Jüdisches Volksblatt* (Leipzig) VII, #37 (1860), pp. 146–48; #40 (1860), pp. 157–59.

"Concurrenzpläne für die Synagoge der Leopoldstadt in Budapest," *Der Architekt* V, #5 (1899), p. 39 and pls. 45, 65.

[?] Csetenyi, "Az őtvenes évek sajtója es a zsidó kerdes," *Emlekkönyv néhai Dr. Kohn Sámuel,* Budapest, 1941, pp. 83–112.

Die Neuzeit V, #42 (Oct. 20, 1865), p. 494; XII, #44 (Nov. 1, 1872), pp. 488–89.

Encyclopedia Judaica, 1971, s.v. Budapest; Obuda.

R. Fehérváry, T. Guzsik, and M. Kalmár, "A Budapesti VII. Kerületi, Rumbach utcai zsinagoga," (typescript), Budapest, Müszaki Egyetem, Építés-Mérnöki Kar, 1980.

I. Friedmann, "Der Bau des Pester israelitischen Kultus-Tempels," *Illustrirtes israelitisches Jahrbuch für Ernst und Scheiz,* 1859–60, pp. 1–7.

A. Fürst, "Die Judenviertel Budapests," *Menorah* VII, #7/8 (1929), pp. 385–92.

H. Geretsegger and M. Peintner, *Otto Wagner, 1841–1918,* Salzburg, 1964, p. 211.

F. Grünvald and E. Namenyi, "Budapesti zsinagógák," bound with Katona, see below.

I. Heller and Z. Vajda, *The Synagogues of Hungary. An Album,* eds. R. Braham and E. Farkas, New York, 1968.

Jewish Chronicle, Aug. 8, 1856.

Jewish Encyclopedia, s.v. Alt Ofen; Budapest.

Jüdisches Lexikon, s.v. Budapest.

J. Katona, *A 90 éves Dohány utcai Templom,* Budapest, 1949, esp. pp. 4–16.

F. X. Kempf, *Geschichte und Bau der israelitische Cultustempel,* Budapest, also summarized in *Wiener Bauindustrie-Zeitung* IX (1891–92), pp. 279–80.

A. J. May, *The Hapsburg Monarchy 1867–1914,* Cambridge, Mass., 1951.

Pinkas ha-Kehillot [Encyclopedia of Jewish Communities], Jerusalem, 1976, esp. pp. 136, 207 (for bibliography).

F. Pogany, *Budapest Müemlékei* II (*Magyarország müemléki Topografiája. VI Kotet*), Budapest, 1962, pp. 424–29 with full Hungarian bibliography on the Obuda synagogue.

M. Pollák, "Zsidó templomépítés Magyarországon a XIX századtól a mai napig," *Evkönyv kiadja. Az izraelita magyar irodalmi Társulat 1934* (= *Az Izraelita Magyar Társulat Kiadvanyai LVI, Evkönyv*), 1934, pp. 191–206.

J. Sisa, "A Rumbach utcai Zsinagóga, Otto Wagner Ifjúkori Alkotása," *Ars Hungarica,* 1982, #1, pp. 43–49.

H. Sochurek, "Matzoh, Wine, Salami—and Piety—Still Flavor This Wartime Ghetto," *Smithsonian,* Aug. 1979, pp. 64–73, 118.

A. Unger, "Denominations in Contemporary Jewry," *Reconstructionist* XXXII (Feb. 18, 1966), pp. 22–28.

E. Vadász, "A Pesti Zsidó templom első ötven éve," *Magyar Zsidó Szemle,* 1909, pp. 193–227, esp. pp. 198–211.

A. Zador, J. Rado, *A klasszicismus építészete Magyarországon,* Budapest, 1943, pp. 83, 87, 154–57.

K. Vazquez, print of Obuda synagogue before exterior alteration, Budapest Historical Museum.

Plans of Rumbach Street synagogue prepared in 1968.

I am glad to thank Sándor Scheiber, Ilona Beneschofsky, the staff of the Historical Monuments Service in Budapest, Fruma Mohrer, and John Ritter for various important favors offered to me.

České Budějovice

Medieval Synagogue

In the medieval Jews' street of this Bohemian city, there stood a house about 5 m. by 6.5 m. large and about 7 m. high that was used as a synagogue before the expulsion of Jews in 1506. It was a groin-vaulted masonry building supported in part by four buttresses. The main entrance opened in the north wall, while in the south wall a wide opening may have led to a neighboring house, perhaps the rabbi's. On the south interior wall were painted ornaments in two registers, alternating five-petaled roses and six-pointed stars below a dividing stripe, and above it black designs which may have imitated a tapestry. Just over the stripe ran an inscription from Psalms, one often associated with three other inscriptions from the same source that are known in other synagogues. The other walls may also have had ornamental painting.

This modest building served the first Jewish settlement in the town, which lasted from the fourteenth century to 1506. After 1506, the Jews had the right only to attend markets (1538ff.); they had no synagogue until residence restrictions were removed during the revolutionary year of 1848. After that, they grew rapidly in number, prospered, assimilated culturally, and embraced Reform. The synagogue they built between 1885 and 1888 was designed in a medieval style—Gothic—but it had nothing to do with the medieval predecessor because the old remains came to light only after 1888, and, in any case, the nineteenth-century congregation needed a different kind of building.

Figure 43. České Budějovice, 1888, exterior.

Reform Temple

The new synagogue captures our interest because it looked like a Gothic church (Figs. 43, 44, 45). It was not the only synagogue in Europe in Gothic style, but it was the most obviously church-like structure erected for Jewish worship during the nineteenth and twentieth centuries.

In 1885, the Jews acquired a site of 4,200 square meters from the city, and engaged Max Fleischer, a Jewish architect working in Vienna, to design the building. The synagogue was made of red brick outside and yellow brick inside. It had a twin-towered facade; a groin-vaulted nave about 26 m. long by about 11 m. wide and 11 m. high; and low, vaulted aisles only 4.5 m. high. There were no galleries, so that the interior resembled that of a Catholic church rather than a Protestant one or a recent synagogue. Other church-like features included the buttresses sloping over the aisle roofs, gables over the north and south side windows, slim towers with sharp, slender spires and pinnacles, and a Gothic-style ark framed in oak. The synagogue even had a barrel-vaulted apse; it was nearly 5 m. deep, had a flat east end, and painted patterns on the walls.

Figure 44. České Budějovice, plan.

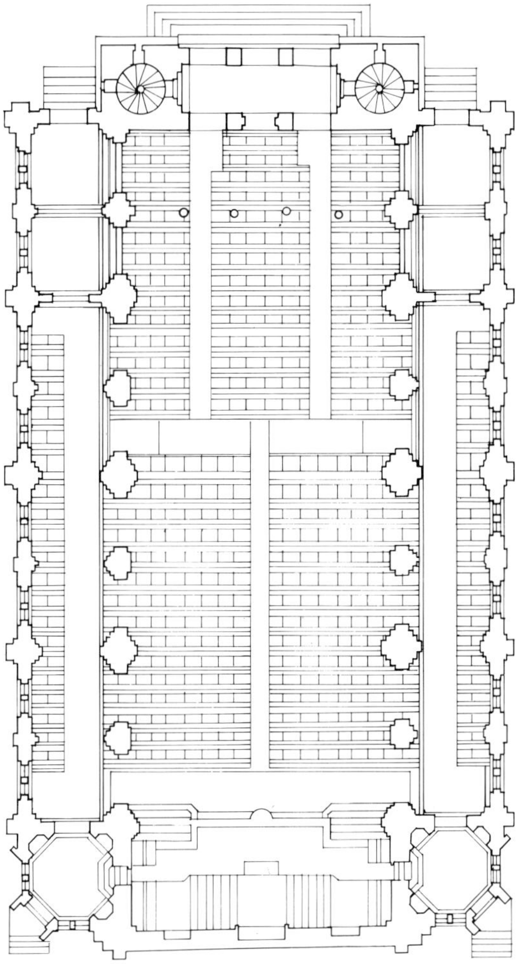

Figure 45. České Budějovice, interior to ark.

The exterior of the synagogue closely resembled that of the twin-towered church of St. Brigitta in the Brigittenau (XX) district of Vienna, designed by Friedrich von Schmidt with whom Fleischer had studied and to whom he was devoted personally. The distinguished antecedents of the Viennese church include neo-Gothic designs by K. F. Schinkel, such as a twin-towered church published in a lithograph of 1812. The architect of the České Budějovice synagogue was more interested in making his synagogue resemble other nineteenth-century buildings for worship than in developing a specific Jewish or local tradition. Fleischer addressed a meeting of architects in the capital in 1894, defending the use of a style so "Christian" as the Gothic in Jewish buildings. He pointed out that Jews always had used the prevailing architectural style. If religious architecture in the late nineteenth century was often Gothic, religious architecture commissioned by Jews could be, too. If Gothic style was the one best suited to evoking thoughts of the divine, all religions ought to use it. Moreover, he said, one could obtain a handsomer building at lower cost by erecting a brick Gothic building than by using any other combination of styles and materials. In a speech in 1884, explaining his partly Gothic synagogue in the Schmalzhofgasse in Vienna, he said that Gothic was the only style suited to the use of brick in buildings where one wanted a suitable character. (The cost of brick was particularly low in České Budějovice because the local prince promised to sell the facing bricks to the congregation at a low price. Of course, the congregation found it prudent to use brick, though that did not prevent the synagogue's final cost from exceeding the estimate.)

In his speeches, Fleischer presented Jews and their buildings as ordinary Austrian people and structures: Anyone noticing that a synagogue was Gothic should also remark upon the religious denomination of every other Gothic building. By such arguments, Fleischer used style to promote the acceptance of Jews in society.

The congregation evidently shared the architect's aims. Upon seeing his earlier synagogue in Vienna, the community leaders asked Fleischer for a Gothic building. The congregation was so Reformed that the women no longer sat in galleries but on the men's level; the only "gallery" was the organ loft, where female choristers sang. The ostensible reason for the absence of women's galleries was an appeal to local tradition: The old building erected about forty years earlier had been too small and too modest to have galleries, and the women sat behind the men. In the new building, which was intended for about six hundred people, galleries would have given the women better sight lines (a point Fleischer denied) and greater proximity to the ark, but the women remained downstairs, as in a Catholic church. Fleischer maintained that galleries injured the religious character of a building, were less secure and convenient than seats on the main level, and were warm and poorly ventilated, especially in the evening when gaslights were used. The rationalizations hardly dispel the impression that the Jews were almost hoping to be mistaken for local Catholics, not just accepted as fellow citizens—although that, too, was important to them.

The dedication speeches included a remarkable number of patriotic sentiments. This must have been a matter of some urgency for Jews living in the Hapsburg Empire in the late nineteenth century. It had never been easy to integrate all the ethnic and religious groups within the imperial territory. The Jews in particular felt pressured as the political life of the capital became infected by anti-Semites, eventually including the mayor, Karl Lueger. Urban Jews were also highly visible scapegoats, having recently become prominent in several fields that gave them substantial public exposure, such as retailing, medicine, and the law. At the same time, poverty-stricken Jews from Austrian Galicia were emigrating in vast numbers. The spectacle of wretched, Yiddish-speaking, small-town folk passing through the major cities was taken as "evidence" of disloyalty by those who failed to understand these emigrants' desperate condition. It is no wonder that Fleischer, a culturally assimilated middle-class Jew, tried to suggest through his buildings that most Jews were, or would have wanted to be, Austrians like other Austrians, Bohemians like other Bohemians. The Jews were not to be special and different, suitable objects of discrimination and scorn. Didn't they, after all, worship the same God, and in similar buildings?

Fleischer thereby went beyond Rosengarten, Hirsch, Aldrophe, and Oppler, Jewish architects who earlier had recommended the use of Romanesque styles for synagogues. For the older architects, Romanesque had seemed the best way to suggest Jewish roots in Germany and France when the other style choices were classical, Moorish, or Gothic, denoting pagan, Islamic, or Christian, respectively. Fleischer wanted Gothic to be everyone's religious style.

The public in České Budějovice responded well to suggestions of fraternity, for racial anti-Semitism was not yet as virulent there in 1888 when the synagogue was dedicated as it later became when Fleischer spoke to the Viennese architects in 1894. Indeed, the municipality of České Budějovice had sold the synagogue lot to the Jews at a low price, and leading citizens attended the dedication on September 5, 1888. They were reported to have enjoyed the organ prelude and to have listened to the addresses, including one by the architect, who said he was glad that no construction workers had been injured during the building campaign.

Perhaps a few of the Christians who attended the ceremony were still alive on June 5, 1942, when Nazis set off an explosion that ruined the synagogue. The site is now an empty space covered with grass. Of the few Jews who lived in the town after 1945, most were old people. The young ones tended to baptize their children in hopes of saving them from social problems later in life—a different kind of assimilation, surely, from that envisioned by Max Fleischer and those for whom he designed a synagogue in the Gothic style.

BIBLIOGRAPHY

A. Charim, *Die toten Gemeinden,* Vienna, etc., 1966, pp. 23–27.

"Die neue Synagoge in Budweis vom Architekten Max Fleischer in Wien," *Der Bautechniker* XI, (1891), pp. 249–51, 260.

Encyclopedia Judaica, 1971.

H. Gold, ed., *Die Juden und Judengemeinde Böhmens in Vergangenheit und Gegenwart,* Brno, 1934, pp. 44–48.

Hammer-Schenk, *Synagogen,* pp. 433–38, and nn. 961–75 on Fleischer and his synagogues elsewhere.

E. Hiller, "Betrachtungen über den modernen Synagogen," *Ost und West* VI (1906), cols. 28–36, esp. 35–36.

R. Huyer, *Zur Geschichte der Judengemeinde in Budweis,* n.p., 1911.

Jewish Encyclopedia, s.v. Budweis.

"Neue Art von Synagogenbau in Budweis," *Wiener Bauindustrie Zeitung* V (1888), p. 604.

Oesterreichische Wochenschrift, Sept. 7, 1888, p. 571; Sept. 21, 1888, p. 605; May 18, 1894, pp. 392–97 reprinting Fleischer's address, "Über Synagogenbauten," *Zeitschrift des oesterreichischen Ingenieur und Architekten Vereins* XLVI (1894), pp. 253–58, Taf. VIII, IX.

Dubrovnik

In the past, on the Balkan peninsula, there were probably a good many small synagogues like the one remaining at Dubrovnik which is the sole survivor of the type. Located in the narrow alley in the center of the ghetto, the synagogue occupies the upper floor of a building distinguished from its neighbors by a polished wood door and brass knobs and by the odd combination of window shapes—ogee-arched on the second level under one semicircular and two rectangular windows (Fig. 46). The lower floors house the community offices, a sensible arrangement used in other constricted ghettoes. The Dubrovnik synagogue is also like others in that it is connected to the neighboring house; for centuries, the house has belonged to the Tolentino family, which takes care of the synagogue.

The Dubrovnik synagogue owes its significance to its age, its interior form, and its position as a survivor in its area. Although the synagogue is said to date back to 1352, this must refer to the year of the first recorded services, which were always Sephardic. The Jews surely had a synagogue in 1408 when they received legal status in the city. Perhaps the synagogue was located in the present building, but the form of the present prayer hall goes back to 1652.

Unlike other extant European synagogues, this one is an oblong room divided internally by a transverse wall pierced by three arches (Fig. 47). The bimah here, a large platform with

Figure 46. Dubrovnik, exterior, drawing ca. 1965.

Figure 47. Dubrovnik, interior to bimah in 1985.

a balustrade of wooden slats and nineteenth-century lamps at the corners, passes through the arched wall, extending east of it toward the ark and west of it into the rear section of the room. We do not know how the congregation was organized hierarchically or how the ceremonies were conducted, so we do not know why the room was arranged in this way. Some Sephardic synagogues in North Africa, one in Tblisi, and some in the Holy Land also are divided by arched walls, and there may be links among them.

The synagogue has been refurbished several times since 1652 and probably does not preserve its original appearance. The ark, with its applied Corinthian columns with twisted shafts, appears to be of eighteenth-century date. It is exuberant in form and provincial in execution. Above the ark, two scrolls meet in the center, forming an arch; the scrolls rest on blocks above the ark cornice. This arch, or the gilt-lettered tablets of the Law which they frame, may not be coeval with the ark. The ark is in imperfect condition, partly because Emilio Tolentino sawed it apart during the Second World War so that he could hide it. He thus saved it, together with the Torah scrolls and lamps. The bimah received its present form in the nineteenth century, and the blue ceiling painted with gold stars may also be a nineteenth-century invention, since restored. The dates of the dark wood wall panels and of all the chandeliers are not known. Just over a century ago, the women's gallery was added at the back of the room, providing airier accommodation than the former badly ventilated galleries behind the side walls (a feature also in Italian synagogues). The galleries had to be entered through the Tolentino house because there was no stairway in the synagogue building; this, too, is known in other old synagogues. The irregular fenestration indicates several building campaigns, but the details of the building history were lost along with the community records during the Second World War.

The synagogue managed to survive a massive earthquake in 1667 and the Second World War.

Owing to a population loss of 80 percent among Jews during the war years, and to subsequent emigration of other Jews, there is seldom a quorum of ten men. Tourists come to a building reminiscent of others in the Mediterranean and Adriatic borderlands, with plastered masonry, thick-walled lower storeys and foundations, and some sloping buttress walls outside. Inside, they see ritual objects and some fine old fabrics. These, however, are components of a memorial and a museum, no longer an active synagogue at the heart of an old and vibrant community.

BIBLIOGRAPHY

Evrejski istorijski muzej. Zbornik I, 1971.

Jewish Chronicle, May 16, 1862 (lists Jewish population as 60).

Jewish Historical Monuments in Dubrovnik (pamphlet), Dubrovnik, n.d.

B. Laitin, "The Old Synagogue of Dubrovnik," *Chicago Jewish Forum* XXIII (1965), pp. 270–74.

Savez jevrejskih opština jugoslavije, Spomenica, Belgrade, 1969.

C. Spencer, "The Sephardim of Yugoslavia," *Le judaïsme séphardi* n.s. III (Feb. 1954), pp. 110–11.

L. Tagliacozzo, "Dubrovnik: Il suo tempio; il suo ghetto," *Ha-Tikwa* XXXII (1980), pp. 6, 8.

I am grateful to Gordon Fellman for information about the building.

Prague

The synagogues of Prague's Jewish quarter met a fate different from that of most other synagogues under German control. Instead of destroying them, the occupying government intended to turn them into museums for the promotion of anti-Semitism. On display were to be objects looted or requisitioned from other Bohemian and Moravian Jewish communities. The project had ironic consequences: It preserved objects that otherwise would have been destroyed. They are now in the Czech State Jewish Museum, which is housed in several of the surviving synagogues. One of these, the Altneuschul (Fig. 48), is the oldest functioning synagogue in Europe (the Worms synagogue having been destroyed and rebuilt). The other synagogues date from ca. 1500 to ca. 1930.

Altneuschul

The curious name of *Altneuschul,* "Old New Synagogue," is explained by the fact that there was an Altschul, or Old Synagogue, in Dušní Street until the 1860s, when it was demolished and replaced. There was also a Neuschul, or New Synagogue, in another Jewish settlement nearby. When an even newer synagogue was erected later, the second synagogue became the "Old New Synagogue."

There were originally two separate medieval Jewish settlements in Prague, one on each bank of the Vltava River. They were probably on the edges of the outer baileys of Prague Castle and the Vyšehrad castle. By the mid-thirteenth century, these settlements were moved to the right-bank area now called the Old Town. Situated near the river, the Jewish quarter experienced repeated disastrous floods. Inundations in 1771, 1784, 1845, 1862, and 1890 so badly damaged the synagogues that the water levels of nineteenth-century floods were marked on the walls of the Altneuschul; the synagogue was said to have held 5 feet of water in 1845. In this wretched location, the two original settlements maintained their independence as well as their synagogues.

For centuries, the Altneuschul has captured the interest of artists, scholars, and laymen (Fig. 49). The Czech artists Josef Mánes and Vilém Kandler executed drawings of it before 1843 which give us a good idea of the interior before the restoration of 1883 (although Mánes was more reliable than Kandler). Sir George Gilbert Scott drew details of the architecture and furnishings in 1847. Jewish visitors to Prague invariably visited the synagogue and described its evocative gloom and decrepitude. Sentimental tourists and credulous natives believed they saw on its walls the blood of pogrom victims of 1389, who actually were murdered in the Alt-

Figure 48. Prague, Altneuschul, ca. 1280, exterior of east end in late 19th century.

schul. They were told that the walls had never been whitewashed, out of respect for the martyrs' bloodstains. They believed that the two central columns were reminders of Jakhin and Boaz and that the splayed windows—seen in many other medieval buildings—recalled those of Solomon's Temple. They often recounted the legend of a dove which hovered over the synagogue, protecting it from flames during a fire. A romantic interest in the rabbi of Prague, Jehuda ben Bezalel Loew, who is supposed to have invented an artificial man, the Golem, enhanced the appeal of a synagogue building associated with the remote past.

The synagogue is a grayish stone structure composed of a double-naved main room for men and annexes used as a vestibule on the south and as women's areas on the north and west (Fig. 50). The two-naved plan, known earlier at Worms and Regensburg, probably came to Bohemia from Germany along with migrating Jews; Christian builders would have been familiar with the plan from monastic refectories, chapter houses, and chapels.

The building as we know it may unite the two oldest usable synagogue buildings (Fig. 51). Recent scholarship suggests that the south annex to the synagogue is actually a remodeled single-naved synagogue of 1230–40, while the larger, double-naved prayer hall connected to it is a building of the last quarter of the thirteenth century. The evidence for this hypothesis rests

Figure 49. Prague, Altneuschul, interior to ark, painting by Josef Mánes, 1843.

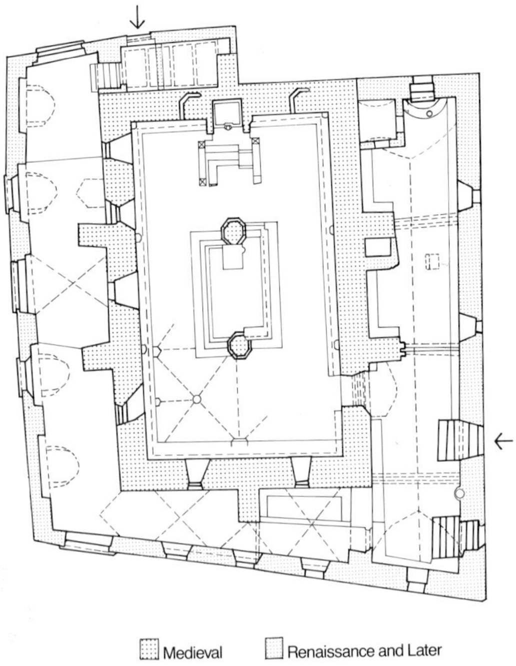

Figure 50. Prague, Altneuschul, plan, with five-part vaulting shown in one bay.

Figure 51. Prague, Altneuschul, south annex, ca. 1240, interior in 1981.

on several points: (1) The annex is longer than the two-naved prayer hall, a length which would have been unnecessary had the annex been meant as a vestibule for the double-naved building; (2) The annex's pointed barrel vault is not independent of the double-naved building's structure, but rather passes behind the buttresses of the south wall of the double-naved building. Milada Vílímkova observed, "It looks as though the buttresses have been walled up at the base and then built up from the springing [of the annex's vault arches]"; (3) The south portal of the two-naved building was obviously cut into an existing vault, so that at least part of the south annex antedated the two-naved building; (4) The vault is of a type known in Bohemia before 1250; (5) A stone column with carved letters referring to a cantor is attached to the east wall of the south annex; the column would have been part of a bimah. Moreover, there is a walled-up door in the east wall of the south annex, which may be the original location of the ark. The ark and bimah could have been installed by 1250.

Later tradition records the use of the south annex as a synagogue for those who came to pray before regular worship hours.

The synagogue's plastered walls are over a meter thick, and are decorated with late-Gothic brick gables on the short west and east ends. The two-naved main room measures about 14.3 by 8.7 m., and about 9.3 m. high. Two octagonal piers resting on socles separate the naves, each of three bays. Between the two piers there is ample space for the bimah, which therefore occupies the central position in the synagogue. The ark stands at the eastern focal point.

The piers hold groin vaults with five ribs, an arrangement that has been interpreted in several ways. Some consider it an attempt to avoid a cross form. This is unlikely, however, because synagogues elsewhere have four ribs, and because the ribs of a vault look only remotely like the Latin or Tau crosses associated with Jesus. Moreover, five-ribbed vaults are known in other religious buildings, both Christian and Jewish, including the monastic refectory at Maulbronn and the north transept of the church at Kolín.

Others interpret the arrangement as a means of differentiating the sides of a synagogue from its more important center, an aesthetic decision of which the architects of this building appear to have been capable. A third interpretation sees it as a means of emphasizing the symbolic number of twelve windows—ten divided between the north and south walls, and two on the west. There is one window for each of the twelve tribes of Israel, each in a vault web of its own. There are difficulties with this hypothesis, however. For one, the western bay has five ribs but only one window—though this could have been done to keep the vaulting uniform. Also, we do not know the extent to which Jews of this time were interested in number symbolism in architecture. There are, to be sure, twelve vine shoots for the twelve tribes on the late-thirteenth-century tympana of the ark and southern entrance doorway, but this need not mean that the architects coordinated aspects of structure and lighting with aspects of ornament. On the other hand, there is no other available explanation for the omission of the sixth window of the north and south walls.

The major vault ribs rest on semicircular shafts that run down the wall to intersect a cornice about 2.4 m. above the floor. The fifth rib rests on a console at the height of the capitals of the wall shafts. The vaults have been damaged, with the ribs separated from the webs at some points by as much as 8 cm. The capitals are now partly damaged, and few retain their original beauty. Those on the south are more delicately carved. Many corbels are now merely rough protuberances, but those on the two central piers are finer in design, as are the bosses at the vault rib intersections. There was evidently a master at work together with some less talented assistants.

The synagogue has other windows in addition to the twelve matched ones already discussed. The two round ones in the east wall are said to be from the sixteenth or seventeenth century. Nineteenth-century views already show a small rectangular window in the center of that wall. Most of the light came originally from candlesticks set along the walls over the seats, replacing earlier candle-holding spikes (the windows were largely for ventilation); metal reflectors enhanced the candles' light. Chandeliers hung from the ceiling and on hooks extending from the bimah. Most of the chandeliers known now are of eighteenth- and nineteenth-century date and have been electrified with white glass bulbs; others were looted by the Nazis during wartime. Josef Mánes's drawings record most accurately the appearance of the light fixtures in ca. 1840.

The large bimah probably was erected when repairs were made to the synagogue after a pogrom in 1483. It consists of a stone platform sunk slightly below floor level, supporting a wrought-iron grille with ogee arches and perpendicular compartments. At the top of the grille are the long hooks for chandeliers and finials in the form of covered cups and stars of David. The northern portion is a restoration of the eighteenth century, the original having been stolen during a period of Jewish exile in 1745–48. Cinnabar-colored decorations in the Empire style, added to the top of the bimah, were removed in the 1883 restoration.

The ark base is slightly sunken under the present floor but its doors are approached by five steps. The ark composition consists of a framework of limestone pilasters with grape leaves in relief, resting on corbeled plinths probably dating to the seventeenth century; upon it rests a triangular Gothic pediment with vine carvings in the tympanum. Much of the ark was reworked in restorations of 1883–87 and 1920; Josef Mánes's preparatory drawings for his watercolor painting show the appearance of the ark ca. 1840. The modern restorations strengthened the limestone pilasters and removed ornamental accretions and the infilling that had blocked the Gothic stone tracery on the parapet beside the steps to the ark. The uppermost moldings of the pediment still do not fit perfectly and some of the framing moldings are crude in design. The original carved and gilded wooden door of the ark, destroyed in the eighteenth century, was replaced by the present iron one after 1784. The parapet had four obelisk-shaped candle holders, of which three remain.

The synagogue has other old furnishings, including stone benches on the north and south walls (now covered with wood); a huge red damask flag given by the crown to the Jews in the eighteenth century, reputedly for their help against the Swedes in the Thirty Years' War; and wooden seats which have been distributed along the walls and on the north, south, and west of the bimah. They have been in this position since about 1840 at least, and reflect a far older pattern of placing seats around the bimah, but in their present Gothic-arched form they date from the restoration of the 1880s. Reading stands are movable; there is nothing of the one-directional arrangement of furniture seen in Reform temples. J. J. Schudt noted in the eighteenth century that the synagogue had an organ, an extraordinary addition to a synagogue, but it was played only to herald the Sabbath, not on the Sabbath itself. Originally, the walls had polychrome ornament, but this was covered by whitewash in 1618.

Annexes surround the prayer hall. The southern annex, now the vestibule, lies several steps below street level, with the prayer hall floor a few steps below that. The original entrance was apparently on the north side of the part that projects beyond the prayer hall walls at the west, the present access from the south being a later addition. In the vestibule are seventeenth-century safes. There are also low stone parapets which now hold candles but which could also have been used as seats. We have noted the traditional use of this vestibule for prayer and study; it now contains documents and photographs concerning Jewish history. The entrance portal from the present vestibule to the synagogue lies in the western bay. It consists of a stone doorway with several moldings. The molding just inside the outer torus has spherical stylized plants; farther down, leaves mark pseudocapitals on the outermost torus, which is thereby made to resemble a door jamb column. Over this doorway is the second beautiful tympanum carved with vine leaves and grapes hanging from shoots that emerge from twelve roots. Such ornamental forms are known also in Christian buildings in Bohemia, Saxony, and Silesia, although this one refers to the twelve Jewish tribes. The pointed window near this entrance portal at the west is a replacement of the 1880s for an earlier round window.

The western annex, for women, is a barrel-vaulted hall lit by three windows at the west. Several details suggest an early-seventeenth-century date: characteristic profiles of the two groined lunettes that penetrate the vault, the simplicity of the lunette over the central window, and the simple framing of the three windows with their interwoven bars of Renaissance form. The annex is low and impressive. By itself, it could not hold all the women of the congregation, and so a northern annex also was provided. An eastern annex was removed in 1908 when the present entrance was opened. When the number of women worshippers later declined and could be contained in the northern annex, the western one became a Polish-rite oratory (as reported in 1868) and a house of study (as reported in 1933).

The northern annex was built in 1731 to replace an older northern annex which was about to collapse, threatening the stability of the entire synagogue. The new annex, said in an inscription to have been rebuilt from the foundations to the roof, may have used some of the older masonry. A groin vault and lunettes corresponding to the windows interrupt the barrel vault. The women looked into the prayer hall through four small slits like the two of the western annex. The little holes and the constricted space, about 3 m. wide, reveal the position of women in older synagogues. The floor level of the annexes is higher, suggesting that women's prayer need not come "out of the depths."

The Altneuschul as we see it now is not, then, wholly medieval. To the original single-naved part and subsequent two-naved synagogue were added fifteenth-century gables and late-Renaissance annexes. The original wall paintings disappeared under the interior whitewash of 1618. Restorations occurred in 1883–87, 1921–27, and in 1966–67, with minor alterations in the 1890s. In the restoration of the 1880s Joseph

Mocker and Emanuel Brand purged the interior of rococo and Empire decorative additions. They replaced the decrepit east gable by a copy, repaired the interior cornice, replaced damaged vault ribs, gables, and bosses, strengthened the pilasters around the ark, installed new seats, and repaired the entrance portal. The structural repairs took only one year, but work on the ark went on until 1887.

In the 1890s and the first decade of the twentieth century, the municipality demolished slums in the old Jewish area, a measure that affected mainly Jews who were too poor to have moved elsewhere after 1848, when they were free to do so. The city officials laid out new building lots and widened streets in the area. They built Pařížská Street on the east side of the synagogue, thereby depriving the building of its original setting in the heart of a densely built community. A public fountain and a low wall enclosing a small courtyard at the east of the synagogue were taken down at this time. The synagogue received new entrances, electric lighting in the annexes, and new flooring in the main hall to replace the old floor destroyed in the flood of 1890.

The restoration of 1921–27 affected the ornament more than the structure; central heating was installed at this time, too. A locally well-known sculpture restorer, Jindřich Čapek, restored many of the details. It was either then or in 1883 that most of the details were recut. Nineteenth-century images by Josef Mánes and others show the consoles in their original condition. During the Nazi occupation, František Zelenka, an architect and poster designer, made plans for the present repaving in red brick, for replacing some of the (stolen) chandeliers, and for installing electric lights along the cornice.

In 1966–67, J. Bušek, an architect working for the state building restoration institute, made the plans for the recent new furnishing, insulation, lighting, and window glass, and for repairing the heating system and south annex vault masonry. The building is now better equipped to receive thousands of museum visitors. It has, however, only a tiny congregation.

Pinkas Synagogue

Other synagogues in Prague have had complex histories, too, and much has been published about them, especially by scholars associated with the State Jewish Museum. The Pinkas Synagogue, the other medieval example, was built as a private synagogue of the prominent Horowitz family. It is noteworthy especially for the net vault over its single-naved main space. The vault probably dates from 1519, as, no doubt, did the original Gothic ark and Gothic-Renaissance bimah. In the early seventeenth century, probably between 1607 and 1620, the master builder Judah Coref de Herz vaulted the vestibule on the south and the ground floor women's section, built the women's gallery, and remodeled the exterior. The bimah, damaged in the flood of 1771, received a rococo frame in 1798; it still survives. Nineteenth-century remodeling included regularizing the floor levels and opening large arches between the women's and men's areas. Christian Czechs argued successfully for its preservation when plans were made around 1880 for clearing the ghetto. František Richter, the civil engineer who was the building administrator in the 1920s, found the old bimah parapet and stone desk. Recommendations for further restoration languished on community officials' desks until 1938. On the walls of this synagogue are now painted the names of over 77,000 Czech Jews who were murdered by the Nazis.

Altschul

The Altschul, or old synagogue, in Dušní Street antedated the pogrom of 1389 in which it was damaged. Its ruins constituted the shell of a new synagogue for Iberian Jews who sought refuge in Prague in the 1490s. The Portuguese rite was used there for many years. Jews of oriental origin worshipped in it during some periods. Between the sixteenth century and the demolition of this synagogue in 1868, the building was remodeled several times. The Reform Ashkenazic rite was introduced in 1837, and the synagogue was then generally known as the Temple. This congregation introduced neo-Gothic furnishings, tracery, and vault ribs, apparently in order to look religious in the Gothic style then associated by Christians with the loftiest religious sentiment.

A new central-plan synagogue of 1867–68, by Vojtěch Ignác Ullmann, was neo-Romanesque—by then the usual assimilationist style—although it had some Moorish details. An alternative design for the interior was made in 1873 by Josef Niklas, and executed in the 1880s by Antonín Baum and Bedřich Münzberger under the direction of Guido Bělský, a masterbuilder. It is entirely Moorish, perhaps to recall the Iberian and oriental cultural roots of this congregation, and to reflect the Jews' desire to express a specific self-image, at least indoors.

Later Synagogues

Later synagogues in Prague included: the late-sixteenth-century High Synagogue in the Jewish Town Hall, built probably by Pankrác Roder with funds from the benevolent magnate, Mordecai Meisel, and graced by a decorative vault design which emphasizes the center of the room; a smaller room in the Town Hall which was formerly used for prayer; the synagogue of 1590–92, named for Meisel who financed its construction by Judah Coref de Herz (it was later rebuilt in 1691 and 1893–1905); the Klaus Synagogue, finished in 1694, enlarged in 1883–84, and partly rebuilt in 1910; the Great Court Synagogue of 1627, financed by Jacob Basevi, the first Jew of Prague to be ennobled; the baroque "Gypsy" synagogue, demolished together with the Great Court during urban renewal around 1900; the synagogue in the Vinohrady district, built in 1893–98 by Wilhelm Stiassny and Ludwig Richter and demolished in an air raid; the Emperor Franz Josef Jubilee Synagogue in Jerusalémská Street by Stiassny and Richter, erected in 1906 on the sixtieth anniversary of the Emperor's accession to the throne to accommodate 1,500 worshippers displaced by urban renewal; the Smichov synagogue of the beginning of the second half of the nineteenth century (1863?), rebuilt in the 1930s, and now used for a secular purpose. The Altneuschul and Jubilee synagogues are the only two in which services are held at the present time.

BIBLIOGRAPHY

On the Altneuschul and other synagogues in Prague: *Allgemeine Bauzeitung* LI (1886), pls. 46–48, for Julius Deutsch's drawings of the Altneuschul.

Allgemeine illustrirte Judenzeitung (Pest) II, #15 (Apr. 12, 1861), cover engraving of Altneuschul ca. 1860.

"Ancient Synagogues of Central Europe," *Builder* XXV (Jan. 5, 1867), pp. 9–10.

E. Bachmann, *Ein spätstaufische Baugruppe in mittelböhmischen Raum,* Brno and Leipzig, 1940, esp. chap. 2, "Die Prager Synagoge," pp. 40–55. (Kunstgeschichte in Sudeten und Carpathienländer, ed. K. Swoboda, 3).

V. Benda, *The State Jewish Museum in Prague,* Prague, n.d.

B. Foges and D. J. Podiebrad, *Alterthümer der Prager Josefstadt,* Prague, 1862.

Grotte, *Deutsche.*

———, "Die Beeinflüssung jüdischer östlicher Sakralbaukunst durch Prager Vorbilder," *Jahrbuch der Gesellschaft für die Geschichte der Juden in der ČSR* VI (1934), pp. 457–69.

J. Heřman and M. Vílímkova, *Die Prager Synagogen,* Prague, 1970, pp. 22–37.

R. Iltis, ed., *Jewish Studies. Essays in Honor of the Very Reverend Dr. Gustav Sicher,* Prague [ca. 1955], esp. pp. 45ff., 62ff.

———, *Tisič Let. Thousand Years. Tausend Jahre,* Prague, 1969.

A. S. Isaacs, "The Story of the Synagogue," *Architectural Record* XX, #6 (Dec. 1906), pp. 474–75.

Jewish Chronicle, Feb. 16, 1855; June 1, 1855; Jan. 17, 1868; Oct. 16, 1868; Sept. 26, 1890.

A. Kisch, "Die Synagogen Prags. I. Die grossen Synagogen," *Jahrbuch für die israelitischen Cultusgemeinden Böhmens,* Prague, 1893, pp. 85ff.

Krautheimer, *Mitt. Syn.,* pp. 202–11.

J. Kreppel, *Juden und Judentum von Heute,* Zurich, 1925; p. 752 discusses other Prague synagogues extant ca. 1925.

J. Lion and J. Lukas, *Das Prager Ghetto,* Prague, 1959.

M. Lowenthal, *A World Passed By,* New York, 1933,

esp. pp. 339, 342–43.
J. Mánes, drawings for a watercolor of 1843, National Gallery, Prague, Graphic Collection.
P. Meyer et al., *The Jews in the Soviet Satellites,* Syracuse, N.Y., 1953, pp. 141–42.
F. M. [Mikowec], "Prag und seine Baukunst," *Allgemeine Bauzeitung* X (1845), pp. 15–38, esp. pp. 22 for Altneuschul and 23 for Altschul; see also pl. 637 for depiction of Altneuschul by Mertens.
F. B. Mikowec, *Alterthümer und Denkwürdigkeiten Böhmens* (vol. 2 with W. Zap), Prague, 1865, vol. 1, pp. 163–67, vol. 2, pp. 97–100.
Monuments of Jewish Culture in Prague and Czechoslovakia, [Prague?, n.d. (1930s)].
Z. Muenzer, "Die Altneu Synagoge in Prag," *Jahrbuch der Gesellschaft für die Geschichte der Juden in der Čechoslovakischen Republik* IV (1932), pp. 63–96. (Also in the Czech edition of this periodical: *Ročenka Společnosti pro dějiny židu v Československé republice.*)
O. Muneles, *The Prague Ghetto in the Renaissance Period,* Prague, 1952.
E. Poche, "Něčo o staronové synagoze v Praze," *Kalendář česko-židovský* (Praha), 1929–30, pp. 123–27.
——— et al., *Praha středověká. Čtvero Knih o Praze,* Prague, 1983 (not consulted).
M. Popper, "Beiträge zur Geschichte der Juden in Prag," *Monatsschrift für Geschichte und Wissenschaft des Judentums* XXXVIII (1894), pp. 371–79, 414–21, 467–72.
V. Ryneš, "L'incendie de la synagogue du faubourg du château de Prague en 1142," *Judaica Bohemiae* I, (1965), pp. 19–24.
J. J. Schudt, *Jüdische Merkwürdigkeiten,* Frankfurt and Leipzig, 1714–18, Buch IV, cap. 14, paragraph 3, p. 218.
O. Schürer, *Prag. Kultur, Kunst, Geschichte,* Vienna and Leipzig, 1930.
G. G. Scott, drawings of 1847, in Royal Institute of British Architects Drawings Collection, Book 11 (new number) or 27 (old number). I owe this information to Mosette Glaser Broderick.
M. Vílímkova, "Seven Hundred Years of the Old-New Synagogue," *Judaica Bohemiae* V (1969), pp. 72–83.
Wischnitzer, *Architecture,* pp. 52–54, 78–81, 215.

On synagogues other than the Altneuschul specifically:
AJYb LXXVIII (1978), p. 452.
A. Deutsch, *Die Zigeuner, Grossenhof, und Neusynagogen in Prag,* Prague, 1907 (not consulted).
———, "Pražské synagogi," *Věstnik židovske naboženské obce v Praze* I, #5 (1934), pp. 1ff.
A. Grotte, "Restauration der alten Pinkas-Synagoge in Prag," *Denkmalpflege und Heimatschütz* XXVI (1924), pp. 35–36.
Hammer-Schenk, *Synagogen,* pp. 246–49.
O. Herbenová, "Vysoka synagoga," *Židovská ročenka 5722,* Prague, 1961, pp. 45–49.
———, "Španělská synagoga," ibid. 5721, Prague, 1960, pp. 108–13.
D. Kaufmann, "La synagogue de Mardoché Meisel et Jacob Segré," *Revue des études juives* XXI (1890), pp. 143–45.
W. Klein, *100 Jahre Verein für geregelte Gottesdienst der Israeliten in der Altschul in Prag,* Prague, 1937.
V. Sadek, "La synagogue réformée de Prague (la 'Vieille École') et les études juives au cours de la 19ème siècle," *Judaica Bohemiae* XVI, #2 (1980), pp. 119–23.
H. Volavková, *Schicksal des jüdischen Museums in Prag,* Prague, 1965.
——— et al., *The Pinkas Synagogue,* Prague, 1955.
———, *Zmizela Praha, 3. Zidovské město Pražské,* Prague, 1947.

I am glad to thank E. Pařík and E. Lukeš for their exceptionally helpful assistance.

Samokov

The synagogue embellishes a town of about 13,000 people located in southwestern Bulgaria, where Sephardic Jews from Sofia, Dupnitsa, and Salonica settled in the seventeenth century. Between the world wars about 8% of Samokov's population was Jewish. The building shows how Jewish needs were wedded to local artistic forms, and offers an example of the preemancipation town synagogue in a little-known part of Europe. This synagogue plan was probably like others in the Balkans, but the chances are that it was atypically large and atypically well designed. It was built in 1858 under the comparatively permissive rule of the Ottoman Turks, before Bulgaria became independent in 1878, and although less grand than a mosque or church, it was allowed to be attractive (Figs. 52, 53).

Figure 52. Samokov, 1858, exterior.

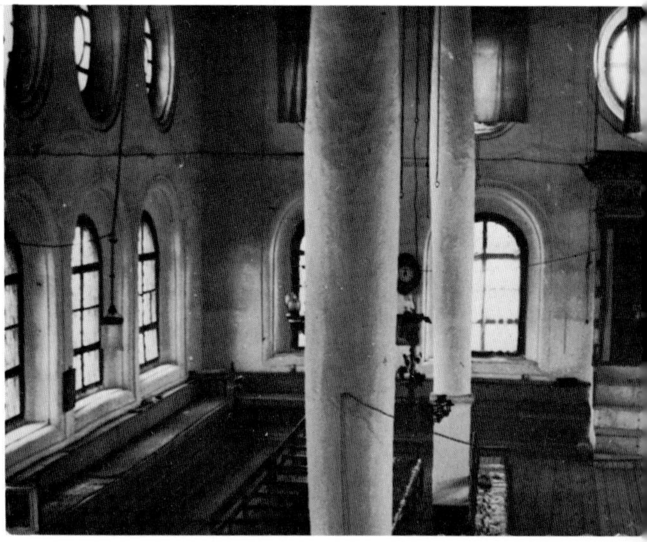

Figure 53. Samokov, interior to ark.

The oblong synagogue has an ark at the east, the entrance on the north side along the street, and a western annex housing two storeys of galleries. The gently pitched roof unites the nearly cubic prayer hall and the annex. Unlike the usual small-town synagogue, this one has a distinctive exterior, with ground floor arched entrances and windows and elliptical windows on the upper level, at the height of the upper gallery inside. The center of the seven-bay northern facade is marked by a circular window of larger diameter than the three windows on either side of it. The arch and window reveals and the salient cornice at the top of the flat white wall have painted floral and foliate designs. There are small leaf scrolls in the reveals, and bouquets of flowers between the windows. The main door also had floral ornament around it originally. The decoration exemplifies the artistic style associated with the Bulgarian "Renaissance" or nationalist movement of the mid-nineteenth century, and particularly with the Samokov school. The motifs are treated with the exuberance and strong color that characterize good folk art, and a sophisticated sensibility coordinated the ornamental painting and the architecture. Spiral and leaf forms reinforce the curves on the window reveals, and a blue band emphasizes the finality of the cornice.

This style is not associated only with Jewish monuments. The somewhat earlier Bayraki Mosque in the same town was decorated in a similar style. That the Jews could use it too is due to several circumstances. The Jews in Samokov in 1858 were still in the same position as were those of earlier periods in many western European countries—able to build in the only locally available style, one used by Jews, Moslems, and perhaps by Christians. That they were able to employ skillful artists is probably due to the wealth and prestige of the local Jewish families who paid for the building, including three members of the charitable Arie family of industrialists who lived nearby and who had at least one of their houses decorated in a similar manner.

Inside the synagogue are more scrolls and bouquets. These emphasize the architectural moldings less clearly than the decorations of the exterior do, although they are handsome in themselves. Along the rear (west) wall of the interior is a fine display of blue and gold bouquets under round arches that continue the design of the windows and entrances on the other walls. Scrolls recalling those of the exterior appear on some ceiling moldings, but the ceiling is embellished mainly with geometric and Islamic designs, arranged in sunburst patterns typical of Bulgarian ceilings elsewhere. The combination of decorative forms does not look Moorish, as did such central European synagogues of the time as those of Leipzig or Budapest-Dohány Street. Instead, the ensemble at Samokov reflects local traditional design, which includes white walls with simple windows and niches set off by bold color, and ornament like that of the Samokov mosque. The Samokov synagogue may not, then, have been decorated by Jewish artists.

The architecture also differs from earlier, four-pillared eastern European synagogues which seem at first to have similar plans (see Figs. 76, 81, 85). The Samokov synagogue has four internal wooden supports delimiting a square in the center of the prayer hall, but they are not linked to form a tabernacle as they were in some eastern European synagogues of the late sixteenth through the early nineteenth century. The supports at Samokov are tall and slim, allowing for convenient sight lines around them. They hold an ornamental paneled and recessed ceiling with inscribed circles and squares alternating inside the central square panels, while square and rectangular panels alternate around the perimeter of the room. The bimah stands not under the central panel but near the west wall, as was usual in Mediterranean-area synagogues. The axial arrangement of ark, columns, and bimah precluded the mystical illumination or sense of religious climax found in the Ashkenazic four-pillared synagogues.

The airy four-support building type at Samokov is in use today in Istanbul in synagogues built by Balkan Jews, such as the Yambol synagogue. It is not yet possible to define the connection between the Balkan Sephardic synagogues and the four-columned synagogue at Tomar in Portugal (see Fig. 186), but Jews expelled from the Iberian peninsula in 1492 and 1496 settled in the Balkans and in Turkey.

To their credit, the Bulgarians managed to save almost all their Jews during the Nazi period. On the other hand, the government encouraged Jewish emigration to Israel, and an overwhelming majority of Jews had left their native country by 1950. The present government, officially atheist, maintains synagogues in Sofia and Samokov as national cultural monuments, although various reports tell of the Samokov synagogue being used as a warehouse or local museum.

BIBLIOGRAPHY

El Correo de Vienna, Feb. 14, 1870 (not consulted).

A. Rashkovska, "The Arie Painted Houses in Samokov," ibid., V (1970), pp. 149–53 (in Bulgarian with English summary).

———, "The Synagogue in Samokov," *Social, Cultural, and Educational Association of the Jews in the People's Republic of Bulgaria. Annual.* III (1968), pp. 175–79 (Bulgarian with English summary, pp. 213–14).

V. Tamir, *Bulgaria and Her Jews: The History of a Dubious Symbiosis,* New York, 1979, esp. pp. 57, 64.

T. Zlatew, *Bulgarski natzionalna arkhitektura,* Sofia, 1955, pp. 82–84.

I am grateful to Milka Bliznakov for translating the Bulgarian material and to Mark Epstein for photographs of synagogues in Istanbul.

Szeged and Sofia

The synagogues of Szeged in Hungary (1899–1903) and Sofia in Bulgaria (1903–9) represent characteristic examples of a synagogue plan that was widespread in Europe at the turn of the twentieth century. It was based on a Greek cross or a polygon with a dome or cupola over the crossing, usually with the main entrance and vestibule at the west. At the east (or in a western vestibule wing) may be offices for the rabbi and cantor, robing rooms, and a choir room. The corners between the arms of the cross, or the diagonals of the polygon, may be filled in with seats, stair towers, cloakrooms, or offices. While Greek-cross and other central plans had been used in the previous generation, never before had the decoration been as lavish and eclectic. Details differed in each synagogue, but the taste for large amounts of ornament from varied sources can be seen in synagogues as far apart as those of Sofia, Braşov, Subotica, Rome, Dortmund, and Bielefeld, all with comparable plans. This was the last generation of abundant eclecticism in synagogue design; even historicizing buildings erected after 1918 had stripped surfaces and restrained silhouettes.

Szeged

Szeged was one of Hungary's largest cities around 1900. Its main synagogue lay, like its Viennese ancestor, on a boulevard called the Ring. Surrounded by a garden, the synagogue occupies an entire block of about 9,900 square meters. The conspicuous location and size must be related to a law of 1896 that granted equality to all religions in Hungary. By this time, Jews had earned a significant place in expanding Hungarian cities, as they had been largely responsible for commerce in many cities of the Hapsburg Empire.

This building, for 660 men and 550 women, relieved pressure on the earlier synagogue of 1843 in Hajnoczy Street, built by Henryk and József Lipovszky (Figs. 54, 55). Rectilinear, gabled, and articulated by pilasters and other classical forms outside, the older building was a galleried basilica inside. It had wide and relatively low arches on the ground floor and gallery level, a central bimah (of which four stubby columns remain; they were apparently decorative, unlike the earlier four-columned tabernacles supporting Polish synagogue vaults), and an ark niche with paired columns.

Figure 54. Szeged, Hajnoczy Street, 1842–43, exterior.

Figure 55. Szeged, Hajnoczy Street, interior to ark.

The new synagogue was different, inside and out. It was the result of one of the era's frequent design competitions, this one held in 1898. Ten Hungarian architects entered, vying for a prize of 3,000 crowns, which represented 1 percent of the anticipated total cost. The jury included architects from Budapest and Vienna as well as Szeged, revealing the earnest purpose with which the Jewish community undertook the project. They bought or gave prizes to four designs, and the first two prize-winning entries were published in the Viennese periodical, *Der Architekt.*

The second-prize entry, by Marczell Komor and Deszö Jacob, had sinuous gables leading to the central cupola. The design converted traditional Gothic curves into freer, swooping lines echoing those of the *art nouveau*. The synagogues of Bielefeld and Dortmund, both by Eduard Fürstenau, and those of Aszód and Subotica share similar forms, perhaps because the German designs had been published in time for the Hungarian architects to have seen them; Subotica's synagogue of 1901 was in fact designed by Komor and Jacob. At Szeged, however, a design by Lipót Baumhorn was executed (Figs. 56, 57).

Baumhorn designed at least twenty-four synagogues, more than any other known European architect. His energetic eclecticism and taste for the obvious apparently recommended him to a wide clientele. His synagogue styles changed from thin and uninteresting ones to a more robust and confident manner. At Szeged, his clients had the money to pay for a big cupola, for vaults instead of flat ceilings, and for large amounts of carved decoration. Moreover, the community rabbi was the learned Immanuel Löw, who as a botanist also saw beauty in details. The architect and rabbi worked closely together, achieving the aesthetic goals apparently shared by many Hungarians of all backgrounds at that time. The streets of Budapest itself are lined with buildings of the same period which, like the Szeged synagogue, show a joyful efflorescence of form and decoration.

On the exterior, the synagogue reveals its plan clearly. The cross arms are marked by large gabled ends with arched windows above gabled portals, and by separate rooflines. The longer roofline of the western arm indicates the western vestibule. Towers above the northwest and southwest corner rooms terminate the facade. Sloping roofs tilt up to the cupola with its girdle of triple-arched gables, traceried dome, and terminal lantern. The ornament includes familiar Romanesque motifs and more inventive but heavy-handed Gothic-inspired tracery and ribs linking portals and windows. The profusion of towers and ornaments and the multiple layers of the cupola give a festive character to the exterior. The desire for display is evident in the high dome, with tracery surely derived from that on the most famous synagogue cupola, in Berlin-Oranienburgerstrasse. The Szeged dome has a double shell, with the outer one considerably higher than the one visible inside the prayer hall.

The interior again combines Romanesque and Gothic with a few Moorish details to decorate a galleried basilica. The longitudinal emphasis given by the east-west file of supports, and the focus on the east, contradict the centralizing effect of the cupola. If the congregation had been orthodox, the bimah would have stood in the center with the dome appropriately above it. This was a Neolog congregation, how-

Figure 56. Szeged, 1899–1903, exterior.

ever, and thus the dome simply covers some seats. All the seats face the grandiose ark-and-bimah composition. Organ pipes fill the apse vault, leading the eye eastward beyond the marble ark screen with its arches, panels, tracery, and openwork dome above the Torah niche.

The barrel and groin vaults, dome, thick marble columns and square piers, Moorish cusped arches, and trilobed arches would attract attention on their own. But Rabbi Löw also had Baumhorn include inscriptions and images which made all the parts of the building meaningful in a literal-minded way. In the dome pendentives are large roundels with cobalt blue letters, and where the pendentives' supporting piers meet the gallery parapet, other inscrip-

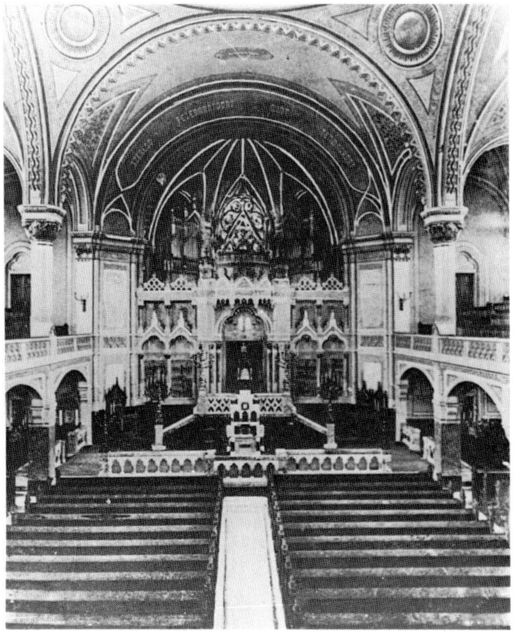

Figure 57. Szeged, 1899–1903, interior to ark.

tions refer to essential tenets of Judaism such as respect for parents, charity, and Torah study. On the metal ark door, the hyssop plant symbolizes spiritual purity. Vaults above the side aisles have symbols taken from the Pentateuch and from Prophets. The cupola, 10 m. in diameter, is made of blue glass with gold stars, alluding to heaven. Windows along the north and south sides show the Jewish cycle of feasts; the images for Passover, for instance, include papyrus, the sea, and chicory flowers representing the bitter herbs eaten at the Passover meal. Some windows also contain inscriptions. Images recalling Jewish history, including cult objects from the Temple, fill the choir windows and main door. The Jerusalem Temple appears in a window at the entrance, and below it is a glass panel showing the "little sanctuaries" of Szeged—the old synagogue and the newly built one. Rabbi Löw's exhaustive published account of all the symbols probably inspired the banal images in colored glass windows that disfigure many synagogues, rarely attaining even the level of conscientious artistry and intellectual endeavor found in Szeged.

The Szeged synagogue survives in a country where there are still thousands of Jews, recalling an energetic and optimistic period in Hungarian Jewish history.

Sofia

Jews of Greek and Roman culture are said to have settled in Bulgaria in the fourth or fifth century; in the period from the fourteenth through the sixteenth century came substantial numbers of Iberian, German, Hungarian, and French Jews. Additional Jews came in the eighteenth century to practice commerce. There were separate synagogues for followers of different rites, but around 1900, the Sofia community of about eight thousand was primarily Sephardic. The constitution of Turnovo (1879) promoted freedom and legal equality. Some Jews prospered, even though most were poor and suffered discrimination in matters such as education and land ownership, with the Ashkenazim usually the most disfavored. At the turn of the century, the degraded old Jewish-gypsy-Turkish quarter in central Sofia was razed and the ethnic communities obtained new and separate residential areas. In 1901, the Jews of Sofia employed a chief rabbi for the first time in about a decade, and two years later they began to plan a new chief synagogue (erected 1905–10). The site was that of an earlier, smaller synagogue, perhaps built after 1826 when Sultan Mahmoud II allowed all religious groups to erect places of worship if they did not compete visually with mosques. To this site, adjacent Jewish-owned lots were added.

Several synagogues, including the four-pillared Cahal de Francos, had been demolished during a street-widening program of the 1890s, and the last Greek synagogue closed in 1881, but the new congregations found substitute prayer rooms. The new synagogue was probably not needed, as small groups already were established in their new premises and not all Sofia Jews followed the Sephardic rite proposed for the new synagogue. Zionists said that while Jewish schools were inadequate, it would be wasteful to indulge in building. Although part of an existing synagogue suffered fire damage

Figure 58. Sofia, 1905–10, exterior in 1929.

in 1904, the building could be repaired; in any case, the fire postdated plans for the new building (Figs. 58, 59).

Apparently seeking a monument to their leadership, three men maneuvered the new synagogue into existence: Ezra Tadjer and Abraham Davichon (also Doyun or Deutsch) Levi, each a community president, and a Mr. Ben Bassat. They were among the few rich Jews who had good connections at court, where the ruling prince employed a Jewish court sculptor, Boris Schatz. Friedrich Grünanger, the Viennese Christian architect selected to design the synagogue, was also known to the court, for during his years in Bulgaria (1879–1905), he had designed for Sofia, Razgrad, and Shumen the royal residences, a major insurance company building, and the Dukhovnaia seminary. Good connections probably account for the Jews receiving permission to locate the synagogue in central Sofia on its own block near the Alexander Nevsky Cathedral, the former cathedral, the mosque, and the central covered market.

Levi's memoirs record his desire to erect in Sofia a synagogue like the "Turkish"—that is, Balkan Sephardic—one in the Zirkusgasse of Vienna, built in 1885–87 by Hugo von Wiedenfeld. The plan of both synagogues is that of a domed octagon inscribed in a square (Fig. 60), with curved niches in the four corners of the Sofia synagogue. The Viennese building lies in the rear of a courtyard, is much smaller, and has thin and planar walls embellished with Moorish decoration. By contrast, the Sofia synagogue stands open to view on all sides, is among the largest Sephardic synagogues in Europe (1,170 seats), and has more robust and eclectic decorations. Levi may simply have wanted an elaborate building and left to the architect the job of providing one, whether or not it was similar to the Viennese building. Improvement of the Jewish school waited while the synagogue budget

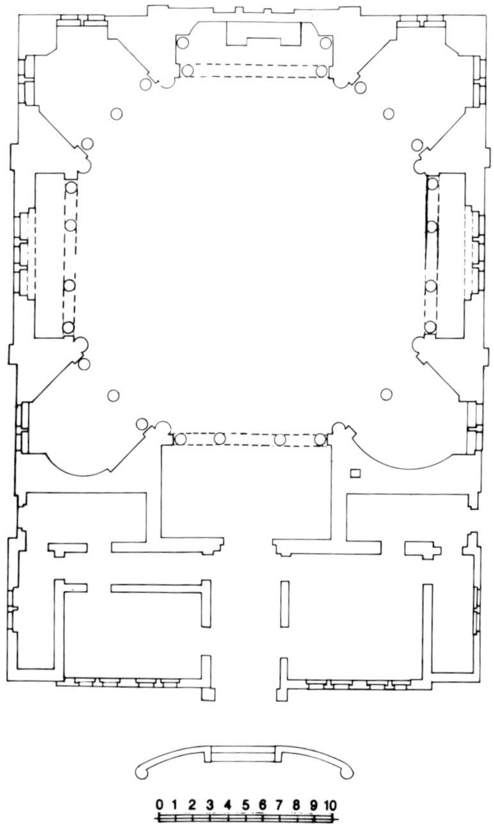

Figure 59. Sofia, interior to ark.

Figure 60. Sofia, plan, slightly modified in execution.

rose from 120,000 to 438,000 leva.

Like the Szeged synagogue in its general plan and in the elaboration of each facade, the Sofia synagogue also resembles that of Szeged in the elaboration of its detail. The style of the Szeged synagogue was hard to define: *Der Architekt* called it an original mixture of English, Gothic, and oriental, while Sándor Balint, a modern writer, described it as Arabic-Moorish-Mediterranean. But the Sofia synagogue did not, in the end, resemble the synagogues of Szeged or Vienna; it has a plan probably derived from Byzantine rather than indigenous European or Islamic sources. Grünanger's early works in Bulgaria had used the Austrian neo-Baroque style, but by about 1900, Bulgarian architecture responded to a nationalist spirit by developing a style based on Byzantine sources, and Grünanger's synagogue was part of this trend. It has cusped and stilted arches and little turrets based on Islamic models; striped and rusticated surfaces and long thin windows of the sort seen on other contemporary Bulgarian buildings, such as the Orthodox Synodal Palace; window tracery that freely develops exceptionally heavy Gothic tracery; and a squashed dome that may trace its ancestry indirectly to the Paris Opera House. The building makes its appeal through enthusiastic elaboration. Many of its decorative elements have parallels in architecture elsewhere in Bulgaria and in Russia at the turn of the century, and it is possible that the Sofia synagogue was meant to seem authentically indigenous, rather than exclusively Jewish or exotic. Nonetheless, Grünanger designed a building different in plan from the basilican Orthodox cathedral, and different in exterior appearance from the low-domed, smooth-walled mosque. It is not certain that all its details were executed to his design, as he left Bulgaria in 1905.

The Bulgarian Jews, who enjoyed a certain amount of official benevolence, welcomed the king to the dedication ceremonies on September 23, 1909, when he gave money for the relief of the Jewish poor. Unfortunately, the synagogue had an effective life of only about forty years, owing to mass Jewish emigration after 1948. Today, there are at most six thousand Bulgarian Jews left. Those who remain in Sofia are now mostly aged and without a rabbi. Their large synagogue, damaged in an earthquake in 1977, was repaired at government expense and designated a landmark. The Jews now hold services in humbler quarters beside the large synagogue, in a room not crowned by a dome but held up by a stovepipe.

BIBLIOGRAPHIES

SZEGED

S. Balint, *Szeged Városa,* Budapest, 1959, pp. 93–95, 128, 230–31.

Der Architekt V (1899), pls. 86, 92.

I. Heller and Z. Vajda, *The Synagogues of Hungary. An Album,* eds. R. Braham and E. Farkas, New York, 1968, pp. 24–26, figs. 380–415.

I. Löw, "Glasmalereien der neuen Synagoge in Szegedin," *Mitteilungen der Gesellschaft für jüdische Volkskunde* XIII (1904), pp. 37–39.

Z. Nagy and I. Papp, *Szeged* (Városkepek-Müemlékek Szeged), Budapest, 1960, p. 230, figs. 155, 156.

G. Somogyi and J. Gerle, "Baumhorn Lipót zsinagógái," *Évkönyv. Kiadja a Magyar Izraeliták Országos Képviselete,* ed. S. Scheiber, 1979/1980, Budapest, 1980, pp. 355–65.

SOFIA

AJYb LXXXIII (1983), p. 230.

O. Alcalay, "Bulgaria," *European Judaism* II (Winter, 1968-69), pp. 26–33.

Entsiklopedia shel Galuyot, ed. A. Romano et al., Jerusalem-Tel Aviv, 1967, vol. 10, cols. 283, 959.

S. Gergov, *Bulgaria,* Sofia, 1974, p. 106.

Jewish Chronicle, Oct. 1, 1909, p. 7.

Jewish Encyclopedia, s.v. Bulgaria.

H. Kamm, "A Sephardic Service in Bulgaria: Worshippers are Mostly Aged," *New York Times,* May 18, 1975.

London Times, Sept. 29, 1909, p. 12.

P. Meyer et al., *The Jews in the Soviet Satellites,* Syracuse, N. Y., 1953, pp. 559–75.

Meyers Reisebücher, *Turkei, Rumanien, Serbien, Bulgarien,* 7th ed., Leipzig and Vienna, 1908, pp. 46, 50.

S. Mezan, *Les juifs espagnols en Bulgarie,* Sofia, 1925, pp. 12–16, 67, 74–75.

"Short Notes on the Past of the Bulgarian Jews," Sofia, n.d. (leaflet available at the Sofia synagogue).

E. Singer, "Die Juden in Bulgarien einst und jetzt," *Menorah* V, #10 (Oct. 1927), pp. 607–10.

P. Stoyanov, ed., *Churches and Religions in the People's Republic of Bulgaria,* Sofia, 1975, pp. 72–75.

A. Tadjer (also Tadger, Tadja, Tadzher), *Notas historicas sorve los judios de Bulgaria* (also published as *La historia de los judios de Bulgaria y de la Comunidad de Sofia*), Sofia, 1932.

V. Tamir, *Bulgaria and Her Jews: The History of a Dubious Symbiosis,* New York, 1979.

YIVO photograph collection.

I am grateful to Mark Epstein for consulting Tadjer's book for me and providing illustrations.

Vienna–Seitenstettengasse

At the beginning of this century, Vienna was home to a Jewish population of about 200,000, including unusually large concentrations of Turkish, Galician, Balkan, and Hungarian Jews. Synagogues proliferated to accommodate regional groups, gradations of orthodoxy, and craftsmen in special industries who formed their own congregations. The stylistic range in Viennese synagogues encompassed neoclassicism (Seitenstettengasse), Moorish (Tempelgasse), a free mixture of massive *art nouveau* with Romanesque and Gothic detail (Pazmanitengasse), and timid modernistic (Hietzing-Eitelbergergasse). Of all these synagogues, numbering about sixty during the mid-1930s, only one survived tne Second World War. That was the oldest, the "Tempel" in the Seitenstettengasse in central Vienna.

It took a long time for the Jews to increase sufficiently in number and status to commission this building. There had been Jews in Vienna since the late twelfth century; the first synagogue, in St. Stephen's parish, was mentioned in a document of 1204. Later thirteenth-century documents refer to this or other synagogues, and documents of 1406 and 1420 refer to the burning of synagogues. The document of 1420 describes the synagogue on the Judenplatz as having a men's prayer hall, a women's section linked to the men's by a window, movable seats, and an area where oil was stored. In 1421 came the expulsion or burning of the few Jews who had not died during the pogrom of the previous year.

After the official expulsion, only a few Jews managed to return to Vienna, where they practiced medicine or trade. Most were itinerants who had to stay in special Jewish inns where religious services probably were conducted. Gradually, the imperial court found it financially expedient to let certain rich Jews live in the city—seven families ca. 1550 and thirty-one people in ca. 1599 (probably fewer than seven families). By 1614, there were forty-four Jewish households. There were two synagogues. One, apparently closed in 1620 but perhaps reopened in 1623, was in Sterngasse. Another, authorized in 1603, was built by Veit Munk, leader of the local privileged Jews.

The Jews were, however, removed to the Leopoldstadt district across the Danube in 1625, where the Jewish population multiplied several times before it was again expelled in 1670. During this period there were two public synagogues, one on either side of the Grosse Pfarrgasse, as well as at least two private ones. Loeb Maor Katon (alias Leo Lucerna), a physician who was also a rabbi, owned one of these private synagogues; it had three windows in each of four directions and was thus probably squarish. The learned Zechariah Halevi (alias Zechariah Mayer) either owned another or helped to found the newer, larger public synagogue, which was worth twice as much money as the older one. In any case, a synagogue associated with this man was converted into the St. Leopold Parish Church (which was shortly replaced by a new church), while another synagogue became the St. Margaret Chapel in 1675. The expelled Jews migrated mainly to Moravia, Prague, Bratislava, and Franconia, where synagogues sometimes had to be expanded to house the newcomers.

The 1670 expulsion was not final, either, for we hear of newly privileged Jews again in the eighteenth century. A synagogue was established ca. 1715 in the house of the Wertheimer family, where it existed until 1817. A visitor in 1735 reported his estimate of eight hundred Jews in the city, all with official privileges or connections to the court. At that time, there were eight synagogues—seven Ashkenazic and one Sephardic—all in private houses. The Sephardic Jews were said to have come from Timisoara and to be Turkish subjects. As such, they were governed by rules applicable to Turks rather than to Jews, according to an Austrian-Turkish treaty of 1730. They were therefore allowed to have a prayer room at 307 Ringmauer and later to dedicate a synagogue on April 9, 1778, although it was only a room in a building in Obere Donaustrasse. When this burned in 1824, a new synagogue was set up at 321 Grosse Hafnergasse, later renovated and replaced in 1867–68 for the eighty-five Sephardic families then in the city. As the congregation increased, its leaders had the architect Hugo von Wiedenfeld design a larger new synagogue in the Moorish style in Zirkusgasse, which was dedicated on September 17, 1887.

The Ashkenazic Jews worshipped in private houses, and only a public prayer room in Sterngasse, meant for travelers and attended by poor Jews, was available for community worship. In 1811, the condition of this synagogue was described as dark, damp, and below ground level, "more like a prison than a house of God." Perhaps this condition was lamented extra loudly because for a year the congregation had been asking for a new building.

By a decree of Emperor Francis I dated February 8, 1811, these Jews were allowed to set up a prayer room in a building that they bought in the Dempfingerhof (formerly Pempfingerhof) in the Katzenstieg. It was only permitted as a source of funds for an institution to benefit the Jewish sick and needy. This synagogue was dedicated on September 11, 1812.

It became the central community synagogue

when existing private ones were closed in 1817, but the demand for seats soon outstripped its capacity. The repressive Emperor Francis would not allow them to enlarge the synagogue, erect a new one elsewhere, or let the local Reform Jews establish their own synagogue. In order to get a larger building where their new ideas might have some influence, some of the Reform leaders resorted to a ruse. They let it be known that the existing building had been poorly built and was in danger of collapse. Before anyone could check the facts, the ringleader, Michael Lazar Biedermann, arranged for scaffolding to cover the building and had the synagogue dismantled. Even the malevolent emperor could not deny the Jews a place to worship, and plans for a new building were carried further. In 1823, the community leaders solicited architects' designs. At a meeting on October 26, 1824, they selected those of Josef Kornhäusel (1782–1860), who worked in the Empire-Biedermeier transitional style and was an architect to the crown and to Prince Liechtenstein (Figs. 61, 62). Perhaps the Jewish leaders thought that his prestige and contacts would reduce the chances of having the Emperor or the police object to the design. At the synagogue, Kornhäusel was assisted by *Stadtbaumeister* Jacob Heinz and *Stadtzimmermeister* Mathias Jacks.

Figure 61. Vienna, Seitenstettengasse, 1824–26, plan drawn by Josef Kornhäusel.

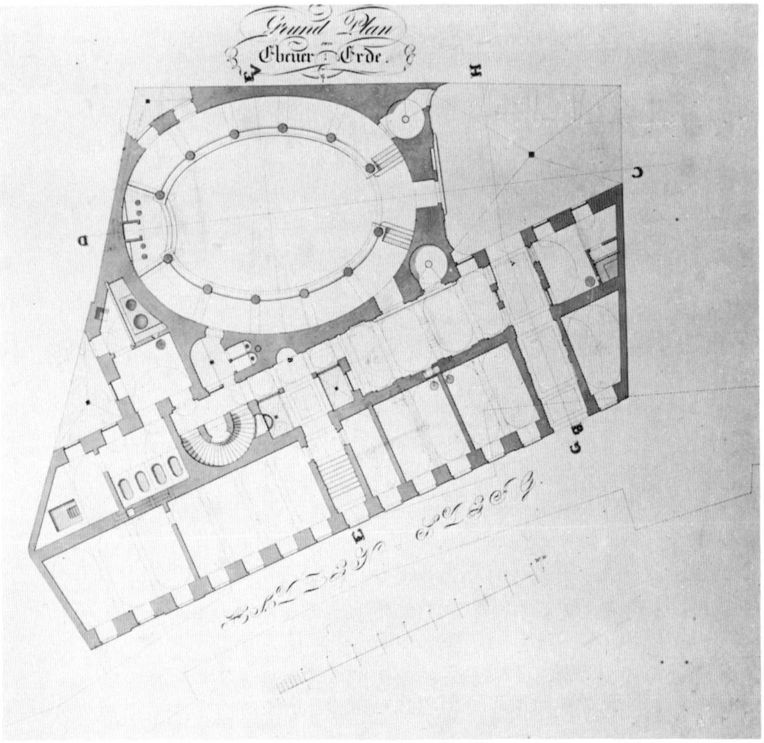

A later critic thought that a building in the fashionable contemporary style was important for the self-image of a Jewish community whose youth was increasingly being baptized. Another found it a sign of Reform consciousness, assimilating not to Christianity but to ideals of universal humanity. Another believed that an *à la mode* design was adopted in order to erase memories of the ghetto. The leaders active in obtaining the new building were, after all, the wealthy, assimilated Jews who were strongly attracted to the aesthetic refinements of the new Reform movement. The synagogue was dedicated on April 9, 1826, to the accompaniment of music by the Christian composer, Jacob Drechsler, who was *Kapellmeister* at St. Stephen's Cathedral. The cantor, Salomon Sulzer, and the Reform-oriented rabbi, Isak Noah Mannheimer, had asked other eminent composers, including Beethoven, to compose music for that occasion, and later Sulzer obtained from Schubert a setting for Psalm 92. Sulzer was as eager to reform synagogue music as the rabbi was to alter the service.

The authorities refused to let non-Catholic religious buildings be visible to the public, and thus the synagogue is wedged between two five-storey apartment houses which conceal it from the street. It is rusticated on its lower floor, smooth above, and looks like many secular buildings of its city and period, characteristic of its time in all but function. The main room is oval, framed by twelve unfluted Ionic columns bearing two tiers of galleries (Fig. 63). A dome, originally adorned with delicately scaled trellis-like designs, covers the room and admits abundant light through the lantern in its center. A glazed lunette in the vault above the entrance door gave additional illumination, as did chandeliers and sconces at the level of the bottom of the lower galleries. An aisle runs outside the columns, beneath the galleries; originally these auxiliary spaces were less brightly lit than they are now and were more clearly distinguished from the central space. High screens over the gallery parapets originally separated the women from the men. All the women were, however, allowed at least a partial view of the ark, because the bays on either side of the ark originally had no galleries and seats. The ark extended only to the perimeter wall and did not project like an apse on the exterior. It was framed by Doric pilasters bearing round arches. Above it, the tablets of the Law were surrounded by semicircular rays which echoed the form of the arches below and corresponded to the lunette across the room at the entrance. The simple, red-draped bimah was located at the east below the raised ark, following the Reform members' preference. Accordingly, all the men's seats were arranged in long pews to face the east. The choir, located in the center of the upper gallery, faced the congregation.

The building's oval shape, combining the longitudinal axis toward the east with the centralizing pull of the dome and lantern, might have better suited an orthodox than a Reform synagogue. There was no reason for a Reform synagogue to emphasize the center, but perhaps Kornhäusel used the form for aesthetic reasons. He seems to have had the Pantheon in mind—a temple to all the gods, later a church of the Virgin and all martyred saints, and now a temple in which ideals of universal tolerance and fraternity with other faiths could be implied. The inner ring with dark outer areas, the dome with a central light source, the lunette over the entrance door corresponding to the ark composition opposite, are all elements derived ultimately from the Pantheon. The secular idea of the Pantheon as a hall of fame for eminent men reduced the pagan-Christian associations of the Roman building and made it more acceptable as a model for any kind of building, including a Jewish one. To be sure, Kornhäusel may also

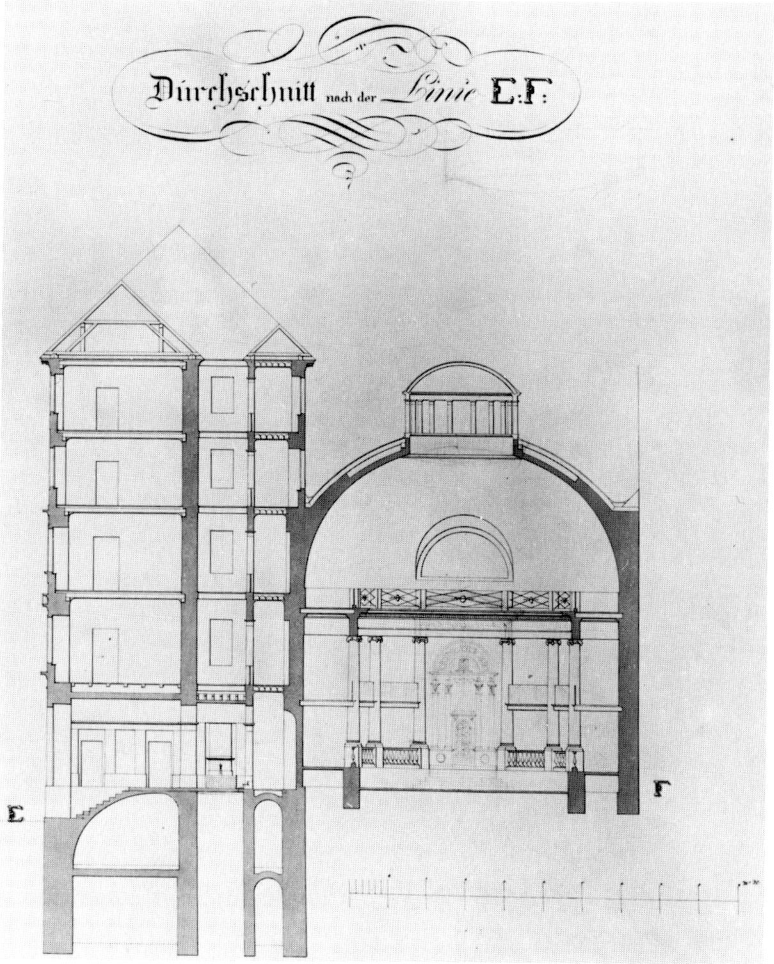

Figure 62. Vienna, Seitenstettengasse, cross section drawn by Josef Kornhäusel.

have been influenced by secular models, such as the theaters or the Winter Riding School in the Palace.

Between 1895 and 1904, the synagogue was remodeled by Wilhelm Stiassny, a Jewish architect who designed several synagogues including one for a Polish congregation in Leopoldgasse (1893). He extended the galleries of the Seitenstettengasse synagogue to the ark and removed the screens above the gallery parapets. The upper gallery railing was modified when vertical bases that had held candelabra above ten of the twelve Ionic columns were

Figure 63. Vienna, Seitenstettengasse, interior to ark in 1904, painting by F. Ranzenhofer.

removed (probably because new lighting made them superfluous). The lights at the base of the galleries also were eliminated in favor of lamps hung in the intercolumniations and on the perimeter wall. These modifications changed the spatial definition from that of a light, central-domed cylinder contrasting with a dark perimeter ring to a unified space with a single oval form interrupted by columns and galleries. After wartime vandalism and near destruction, Professor Otto Niedermoser renovated the synagogue, restoring in 1963 the original design of bases and railings and candelabra in the upper galleries. By keeping Stiassny's lighting arrangements—except for placing electric lights under the lower gallery instead of on the perimeter wall and using simple fixtures—Niedermoser preserved Stiassny's spatial effects. He redesigned the ceiling with gold stars and a gold circle of flames around the lantern, introduced alternating rays and smooth plaster above the ark, redesigned the lunette and pilasters around the ark, and covered the perimeter walls with wood veneer.

The synagogue nevertheless retains its original outlines and more than enough of its form to give us a good idea of the taste of the assimilated, Reform-minded Jews of Vienna. The only signs of the building's dedication to Judaism were the tablets of the Law. Although Jews did not receive equal civil rights until 1867, the synagogue had no exotic elements to show their separateness from the Christians of Austria. Apparently, the Jews were left free to have the synagogue that they were willing to pay for, as long as it did not attract attention to itself as something alien (subversive). The emperors may well have worried about the ethnic diversity in their country, or about the problems of national unity at a time when the memory of Napoleon was still vivid. But as long as the Jews supported the crown, and as long as they were willing to withdraw into unobstrusive buildings and adhere to the taste and styles around them, there was no harm in allowing them to erect a handsome synagogue.

BIBLIOGRAPHY

R. Blaha, *"Der Innenraum der Synagoge, Wien I. Seitenstettengasse, 4.,"* thesis, Vienna, 1977.

E. Brody, "Schubert and Sulzer Revisited: A Recapitulation of the Events Leading to Schubert's Setting in Hebrew of Psalm XCII, D. 953," *Schubert Studies: Problems of Style and Chronology,* eds. E. Badura-Skoda and P. Branscombe, Cambridge, 1982, pp. 47–60.

L. A. Frankl, *Zur Geschichte der Juden in Wien,* Vienna, 1853.

N. M. Gelber, "The Sephardic Community in Vienna," *Jewish Social Studies* X (1948), pp. 359–96.

H. Gold, *Geschichte der Juden in Wien, Ein Gedenkbuch,* Tel Aviv, 1966.

M. Grünwald, *Vienna,* Philadelphia, 1936.

Hammer-Schenk, *Synagogen,* pp. 160–62 and n. 378.

H. Herzmansky, *"Josef Kornhäusel. Eine Künstler-*

monographie," diss., Vienna, 1964, esp. pp. 258ff.
S. Husserl, *Gründungsgeschichte des Stadt-Tempels,* Vienna and Leipzig, 1926.
Menorah, 1926, special issue: *100 Jahre Wiener Stadttempel.*
H. Rotter and A. Schmieger, *Das Ghetto und die Wiener Leopoldstadt,* Vienna, 1926.
K. Schubert, ed., *Studia Judaica Austriaca VI. Der Wiener Stadttempel, 1826–1976,* Eisenstadt, 1978, esp. N. Vielmetti, "150 Jahre Stadttempel. Bilder und Dokumente," pp. 91–102 with bibliography.
S. Spitzer, "Das Wiener Judentum bis zur Vertreibung im Jahre 1421," *Kairos* XIX, 1977, #2, pp. 134–45.
B. Wachstein, *Die ersten Statuten des Bethauses in der Inneren Stadt,* Vienna, 1926.
R. Wagner-Rieger, *Wiens Architektur im 19 Jahrhundert,* Vienna, 1970, p. 17.
G. Wolf, *Geschichte der Juden in Wien (1156–1876),* Vienna, 1876.
———, *Vom ersten bis zum zweiten Tempel. Geschichte der israelitischen Cultusgemeinde in Wien (1820–1860),* Vienna, 1861.

I am grateful for information and many courtesies to Nikolaus Vielmetti, Bernhard Leitner, W. Kitlitschka, the Austrian Photographic Library staff, and Jewish community officials in Vienna.

Vienna–Tempelgasse

In 1849, the Jews of Vienna welcomed the official constitution of Emperor Francis Joseph I, which stated that "the enjoyment of civil and political rights does not depend upon religious confession." Since the rights of residence and land ownership and the practice of all legal trades came within the scope of this document, the Jews could live anywhere they wished in Vienna. Those who had been there illegally could declare their presence openly. Thus, the official Jewish population of Vienna, which was 3,739 in 1846, increased to 9,731 in 1850 and to between 14,000 and 15,000 by 1854 (even though many of their rights were revoked between 1853 and 1867).

From 1846 onward, the Jews needed more synagogue seats for the High Holy Days. They remodeled the Seitenstettengasse synagogue to provide more seating in 1849, when they were allowed to form an official community organization, but this did little to solve the problem. Vienna gained another synagogue in 1852 by annexing a suburb, but that did not increase the existing stock of seats. A few prayer rooms were dedicated in 1853 to serve the overflow population, and at least one of them was orthodox, in contrast to the Reform tendencies of the official community. At last, in 1853, community officials concluded four years of talks about building a new synagogue and opened a subscription toward the cost of a new large synagogue in Wällisch-(later Tempel)gasse in the Leopoldstadt, the II District of Vienna, where most Jews lived. The rite was to be like that at Seitenstettengasse, so that the Jewish community could attest to its legally required religious unity.

The design was entrusted in 1853 to Ludwig von Förster (1797–1863), an architect who had helped plan the modernization of Vienna since 1839. Presumably the community liked his work; they certainly would have found it wise to hire an architect with good government connections. By April 1854, he had drawn plans, and the following month the Emperor granted permission to build. The cornerstone-laying ceremony occurred in 1856 and the dedication services were held on June 15, 1858.

Förster situated the synagogue in the center of its irregular oblong site so that it could enjoy air and light on all sides and yet be adjacent only to property held by Jews (Fig. 64). It is indicative of the Jews' legal progress that the facade could be seen from the street; it no longer had to be hidden in a courtyard like the Seitenstettengasse synagogue's entrance.

The architect now had to face the problem of the image that the facade should present, and he took his inspiration from the Temple of Solomon. He created a tripartite facade with a higher center section, perhaps because the Temple could have been visualized in this way

Figure 64. Vienna, Tempelgasse, 1853–58, exterior, lithograph by R. van Alt.

from the Biblical descriptions supplemented by newly discovered Assyrian remains. Förster compared his vestibule, a three-part division of the prayer hall into nave and galleried aisles, and ark recess to the plan of Solomon's Temple. He said that the minaret-like turrets flanking the central section of the facade were evocations of Jakhin and Boaz, the Temple's famous columns, and he pointed out that the cornerstone itself had come from the Holy Land. He even examined archaeological excavation reports from the Middle East, in order to come as close as pos-

Figure 65. Vienna, Tempelgasse, interior to ark in 1904, painting by F. Ranzenhofer.

sible to ancient Hebrew architecture. (The reports he mentioned, however, were written about Nineveh, not Jerusalem!)

Believing that the ancient Jews and Arabs shared geographical affinities, he imitated Islamic ornament and that of ancient Near Eastern monuments. Each section of the facade had a quatrefoil window over a large round-arched opening, the central one serving as the entrance. Heavy cornices at the top of each section contrasted with slim turrets at the corners. Palm designs on the interior walls, cusped arches, geometric ceiling designs, the tracery over the entrance, and multicolored tiles in the vestibule were among the many details taken from Islamic models.

Slender Moorish columns could be imitated well in cast iron, and Förster used this material to support the galleries (Fig. 65). The thin columns allowed the women to have an almost unobstructed view of activities on the main floor. Synagogues here and elsewhere were among the chief early users of cast iron that was not disguised as stone.

The ark niche was framed by several slim columns supporting an arch under a horizontal cornice. A rose window provided additional light above the ark, and fulfilled the requirement for an opening at the east. The bimah stood in a balustrade of vaguely Moorish arches in the center of the men's level.

These designs became well known after Förster published and explained them in his own architectural periodical, the well-respected *Allgemeine Bauzeitung*. Synagogues in Bucharest and Iaşi in Rumania were modeled upon it, as were others including those of Duren, Łowicz, Giessen, and, in part, Stockholm.

This synagogue was significant as a monument to Jewish community growth, and to legal and social change. The fact that the congregation did not use the organ for which Förster had made room showed that the more liberal Jews wanted to come to terms with the more orthodox. The building also exemplified Christian thinking about Jewish ethnicity and history in the context of nineteenth-century architectural ideas which required almost every group to have its "own" expressive style. The use of the style here may have been meant only to characterize, but not isolate, the Jews, since the parish church of Insdorf (1846) had Islamic ornament in the choir, but Islamic decoration remained rare in churches, while it became common in synagogues.

Jewish immigration to Vienna continued, and by 1859, the year after the Tempelgasse synagogue dedication, there were so many recent orthodox arrivals that they established their own synagogue. After the 1867 constitution guaranteed most rights to Jews, synagogues proliferated. By 1938 there were about sixty, including seven community synagogues using the Seitenstettengasse rite, twelve community orthodox synagogues, a Turkish-Sephardic rite synagogue, Hasidic synagogues, and modest premises used for prayer. The Tempelgasse synagogue remained the most conspicuous, surviving a fire in 1917 and benefiting from repairs completed in 1921. On Crystal Night, November 9–10, 1938, twenty-four of the freestanding synagogues were destroyed or badly damaged; the more modest synagogues all succumbed by 1945. A fragment of the Tempelgasse office building survived the war, but the ruins of the synagogue itself were cleared away. Förster's watercolor drawing for the facade has recently been brought to light and is exhibited at the new Jewish Museum in Eisenstadt.

BIBLIOGRAPHY

L. von Förster, "Über Synagogenbau," *Allgemeine Bauzeitung* XXIV (1859), pp. 14–16, pls. 230–35.

———, "Über Synagogenbau," *AZJ* XXII (May 31, 1858), pp. 314–15.

Hammer-Schenk, *Synagogen,* pp. 182–83, 302–6, and n. 711.

Jewish Chronicle, July 18, 1873.

I. Oehler, "Geschichte des Leopoldstädter Tempels in Wien," *Zeitschrift für die Geschichte der Juden* I (1964), pp. 22–27.

Oesterreichischer Ingenieur-und Architekten Verein, *Wien am Anfang des 20 Jahrhunderts,* Vienna, 1906, vol. 2, p. 89.

M. Paul, *Technischer Führer durch Wien,* Vienna, 1910, pp. 281–82.

"Verzeichnis der am 9 und 10 November 1938 von den National-Sozialisten zerstörten Tempelobjekte." List prepared of freestanding buildings, available at Jewish community headquarters in Vienna. (Sixteen such synagogues in Lower Austria, eleven in Burgenland, and nine elsewhere in Austria fell victim to the vandals.)

R. Wagner-Rieger, *Wiens Architektur im 19 Jahrhundert,* Vienna, 1970.

G. Wolf, *Vom ersten bis zum zweiten Tempel. Geschichte der israelitischen Cultusgemeinde in Wien (1820–1860),* Vienna, 1861.

Vienna–Hietzing

The synagogue of Hietzing, the XIII District of Vienna, represents a type of small suburban synagogue that became increasingly common in the twentieth century. It is of special interest because several designs for it, made between 1912 and 1924, have been preserved. We also have contemporary analyses by an architect, Hugo Gorge, and by Austria's foremost critic of Jewish art and architecture, Max Eisler.

In 1877, the many Jewish residents of Vienna who summered in Hietzing welcomed an offer by the Jewish Baron Königswarter to use his villa temporarily for prayer meetings. Thirty-five years later, the Jewish population of Hietzing had grown large and prosperous enough to want a permanent building for year-round use, and in 1912 the community sponsored a design competition. Among the entrants were Rudolf Perco, Ernst Lichtblau, and Hugo Gorge, all of Vienna and probably all Jewish. The competition program evidently specified that the building lot was nearly square, that certain community rooms were required, and that the bimah had to be in the center of the prayer hall; all the projects now known agreed in these respects.

Perco proposed a monumental structure, a distant descendant of the Pantheon, flanked by domestic-looking wings containing the community rooms. His "Pantheon" had, instead of a columnar porch, a triple-arched entrance with a long row of tall and narrow windows above it, the entire composition crowned by a pediment with only a star of David to suggest the building's use.

Lichtblau designed a flat-roofed building, with the sanctuary shifted to the right of the lot to allow for a single community building at the left side. It looked like an apartment house interrupted at the right by three long rectangular windows with modified triangular hoods, but there were stars of David encased in round openings on the walls. In this building, also wider than long, the bimah was more obviously relegated to the center, because there were seats attached to it on the east side.

Gorge published his drawings and his comments on them in 1918 (Fig. 66). Max Eisler endorsed them warmly, as they corresponded to Eisler's own taste for simplicity in architecture and conservatism in religious practice. Gorge designed a solid rectangular prism faced in random-cut stone, with four rectilinear entrances and thin, acutely pointed triangles projecting from the roofline. His earlier designs for the facade included a salient balcony on angular brackets, arrangements of small windows, and denser forms at the roofline, but in all he revealed a constant taste for rectilinear simplicity. He associated his forms with ideas of universality and brotherhood. Inside the wall, he designed an open courtyard. Its high, smooth walls were broken by rectilinear windows that linked the sanctuary and courtyard visually. They also lit the women's gallery and the space below it, as well as service rooms on the street side. In the center of the courtyard, Gorge placed an unusually large fountain. The principal entrance lay along the main axis from the street. The ark, however, did not terminate the axis, but lay at right angles to it, because Gorge believed that worshippers should not be able to see the ark until they had entered the synagogue. This recalls the arrangements of vestibules on the north and south sides of medieval

Figure 66. Vienna-Hietzing, project for interior by Hugo Gorge, 1912.

synagogues. The rectangular prayer hall was slightly longer on the east-west axis, and the axial direction was further emphasized by blocking any visual expansion to the south, where the wall was divided into two storeys, the upper one for women. A drawing of the interior, in close to its definitive form, showed smooth, white-plastered walls, large, square-paned rectilinear windows with thin, flat curtains over them, a checkerboard floor, and a late-medieval-style ceiling with small longitudinal beams interrupted by large crossbeams. Arches rose from the floor to a height well above the women's heads, and a substantial parapet hung in front of the arches; a later design provided for a single pier to support the women's gallery. The seats were to have been starkly upright and arranged in rows facing the bimah, as they were in medieval synagogues. The bimah design echoed medieval examples such as that of the Prague Altneuschul, with a platform surrounded by an iron cage from which projecting horizontals carried light fixtures (see Figs. 49, 71). It occupied the center of the building and commanded attention, because Gorge believed that the starting point of any synagogue must be the permanent core of Jewish worship: the communication of Holy Writ and the reading of the Torah. An even older tradition was embodied in the ark, a freestanding peak-roofed chest placed against, but not in, the eastern wall. This was meant to recall the portable ark in the wilderness, described in Exodus. It also reflected the archaeological reports of early synagogues that lacked ark niches or apses, and of the portable ark in the early synagogue. Gorge provided clearly defined aisles, a court, and garden spaces, and designed folding doors to accommodate traditional processions and ceremonial activities such as those associated with weddings, the feast of Tabernacles, and the new-moon ceremonies. His planning balanced sentiment and tradition with their expression in simple modern forms. The clear geometry, the smooth walls and overall planarity of the elements, the delicate metalwork, and the occasional use of craft forms (as on the stonework of the facade) reveal his connections to contemporary design in the Josef Hoffmann circle in Vienna, and they show his belief that Judaism was not a mystical religion but one based on rationality.

To the regret of Max Eisler, Gorge's design was not built, either in 1912 or following a second competition for Jewish architects in the spring of 1924. (No doubt the war and its aftermath had delayed any earlier resumption of synagogue planning.) Gorge submitted a modified version of his earlier design, but only won second prize. The third prize went to Fritz Landauer of Munich, who submitted a design related to that of his Augsburg synagogue of over a decade earlier. Two of his surviving proposals show a cross-shaped central plan, one with a low Byzantine dome and the other with a

Figure 67. Vienna-Hietzing, project for exterior by Fritz Landauer, 1924.

steeply pitched cupola recalling a tent hidden under a smooth exterior dome with a lantern. (Gorge had already criticized cross plans and domes for setting the officiant apart from the congregation, which went against Jewish tradition.) Landauer's actual competition entry showed a pitched roof over a rectangular room within thick walls pierced by a triad of triangle-headed windows (Fig. 67). Projecting from it were the ark recess and adjacent spaces, the vestibule, and other community rooms. The main sanctuary looked like a modernized fortified synagogue, with its heavy walls, pitched roof, buttresses or pilaster strips, and corbel table, but the triad of tall windows gave the fortress a slightly ecclesiastical air. No wonder Landauer did not win the competition; he seems to have been unsure of what he wanted to express.

The most famous competitor was Richard Neutra, who from his new home in the United States submitted a design in the International Modern Style, labeled "Die Neue Welt [new world] Tempel" (Fig. 68). His sanctuary was a long, low building occupying one side of the lot. The community building of smooth, stark rectilinear forms was perpendicular to it along another side, and a walled garden filled the remainder of the site. Long, white expanses of entirely untraditional architecture struck Max Eisler as being "American" and unsuitable; probably the title made Eisler think of America, although to our eyes the project recalls the German work of Erich Mendelsohn and seems perfectly suitable.

The judges, who included Josef Hoffmann and three Viennese Jewish architects, gave first prize and the building commission to the least profound architectural thinker, who produced the most superficially pretty design (Fig. 69). This was Arthur Grünberger, a Viennese architect who had moved to California. He designed a two-storey oblong box with another box projecting to accommodate the main entrance and vestibule. Steps on either side, sheltered by porches, led to the upper floor. The synagogue was modern in having a simple form and flat surfaces covered with smooth plaster. The frame of the main door was merely a salient molding rather than anything suggestive of Jakhin and Boaz. But the simple clarity of the basic forms contrasted with the upper parts of the

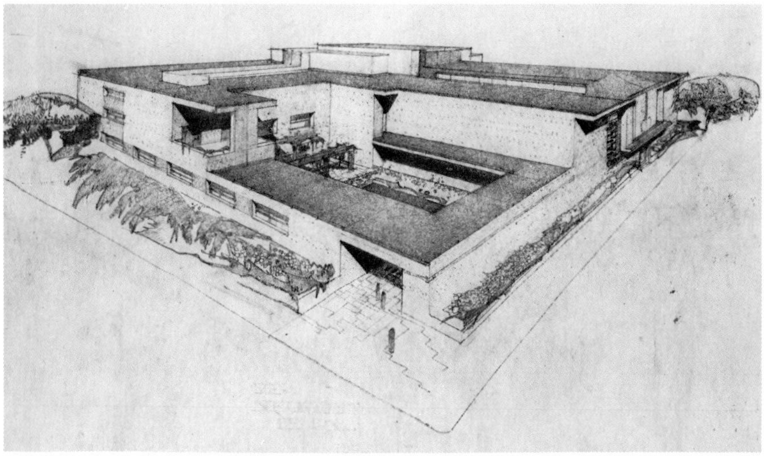

Figure 68. Vienna-Hietzing, project for exterior by Richard Neutra.

synagogue. The tops of the walls and porches were adorned with alternating curves and small angular peaks, creating a scalloped effect. This rhythm changed on the exterior of the upper storey, where Grünberger designed a kind of large corbel table or pseudo-attic made of alternating large curves and thin, downward-tapering niches. Windows with three lobes and three points occupied the space under the large curves. The effect of several rhythms of curves and points was that of Arabic writing. This gave an exotic cast to the simple "modern" building and tied this synagogue to earlier historicist examples in Vienna, especially the Moorish examples in Tempelgasse, Leopoldgasse, and Schopenhauerstrasse. An attic with blank arcades was, however, also a feature of certain synagogues in eastern Europe, such as those of Cracow/Kazimierz-Old, Lutsk, Zholkva, and Lyuboml (see Fig. 11). The reference to old eastern

Figure 69. Vienna-Hietzing, facade in 1930.

European synagogues added a sentimental note. (After all, the worshippers were living in the pleasant inner suburbs of Vienna between the world wars, not in embattled city-border areas of seventeenth-century Poland.) The combination of crisp white walls and an ornamental topping made the building look flimsy and trivial. It would have looked even more trivial if the fancy windows designed for the competition had been executed. The plan was more innocuous than the style. A vestibule flanked by a weekday synagogue and by offices, with the women's gallery above these rooms, led to a square sanctuary with smooth walls, a beamed ceiling, a central bimah, and an elevated ark.

All this effort had an impact of short duration, because the Nazis destroyed the building. Nevertheless, thanks to the many projects made for the Hietzing synagogue, we have a broader knowledge of synagogue planning before and after the First World War. Moreover, some of Gorge's ideas lived on in Artur Szalatnai's synagogue for the orthodox Jews of Bratislava (see Fig. 30), which shows its architect's attempt—perhaps under Gorge's inspiration—to blend simple architectural forms with traditional arrangements.

BIBLIOGRAPHY

W. Boesiger, ed., *Richard Neutra, Buildings and Projects,* Zurich etc., 1951, p. 193.

M. Eisler, "Beispiel fur Laien und Vorstehen von Gemeinden. Zum Synagogenbau," *Menorah* VIII (1930), p. 85.

———, "Die Wettbewerb um einer Wiener Synagoge," *Oesterreichs Bau-und Werkkunst* II (1925–26), pp. 1–7.

H. Gorge, "Ein Synagogenentwurf," *Der Architekt* XXII (1918–19), pp. 133–40.

Hammer-Schenk, *Synagogen,* pp. 508–10.

Jewish Chronicle, July 29, 1877, p. 13.

J. Lever, ed., *Catalogue of the Drawings in the Royal Institute of British Architects, Drawings Collection,* London, 1973, vol. L–N (for Landauer). Drawing Ran 15/E/15 may have been made originally for Augsburg.

"Tempel in Wien. Wettbewerb," *Zentralblatt der Bauverwaltung* XLIV (1924), pp. 166, 415.

N.B. The Oesterreichische Nationalbibliothek photographic service label gives the building to Adolf Jelletz; perhaps he was Grünberger's supervising architect, resident in Vienna.

Eastern Europe and the U.S.S.R.

Cracow

The synagogues of Kazimierz, the eighth ward of Cracow but once a suburban town, are even now the goals of Jewish visitors. Pilgrims come to the synogogue named for Moses Isserles, (known as ReMO), the great sixteenth-century legal authority, and to the Old Synagogue, which has been made into a Jewish museum. The synagogues embody the history of an important center of traditional Jewish culture and of Kabbalistic lore, of Jewish law, and of Jewish self-government in the years when Cracow was the seat of the Little Poland district within the Jewish Council of the Four Lands.

Other synagogues remain in the Jewish quarter, although most of them are used now for secular purposes. One is a sculpture workshop, another an apartment house; a third is too decrepit to use. These and others reflect Jewish history under the Nazis and under the postwar Polish government.

The first recorded Jewish settlement in the Cracow area dates from 1304, and a synagogue is first mentioned in 1356. Polish kings found Jews useful for stimulating commerce, and after a pogrom in Prague in 1389, Bohemian Jews came to Cracow. Charters established their right to have a synagogue. At first, most Jews lived in Cracow proper, but after a catastrophic fire in 1494 that led to shifts in land tenure, they were removed to an existing Jewish settlement in Kazimierz.

Old Synagogue

The expelled Jews must have established a place for prayer soon afterward, unless they crowded into existing synagogues. Legend takes the foundation date of the Old Synagogue back to the fourteenth century, but there were not then enough Jews in Kazimierz to warrant building the largest medieval two-naved synagogue known to modern research (17.7 m. × 12.4 m.). In 1469, two synagogues had been closed in Cracow when the Jews were forced to move elsewhere; nevertheless, as Jews continued to live in Cracow for another quarter-century, there must have been other synagogues available there after 1469, making a large synagogue in Kazimierz superfluous.

In its present form the Kazimierz building is considerably later than the Altneuschul of Prague, and the Bohemian Jews may not have transmitted its plan, although both have two naves of three bays each. Two-naved buildings existed in Poland since the thirteenth century (monastic chapter house at Koprzywnica), and fourteenth-century examples include the convent chapel at Cracow and churches at Stopnica and Wiślica. The columns at Kazimierz are 60 cm. in diameter, compared to 85 cm. at Prague, and the walls are thinner than those of the Altneuschul, showing a more advanced understanding of statics. The Kazimierz building, while taller in absolute measurement (10.15 m. compared to 9.7 m. at Prague), appears to be broader, as is characteristic of Renaissance buildings. The height-to-width proportions are 10.15:17 m. at Kazimierz and 9.7:14.3 m. at Prague.

The Old Synagogue at Kazimierz probably postdates 1494, when the Jews were confined to this area. It may not have been built immediately, for the Jews must have needed houses first and may have thought themselves in too precarious a position to risk building a large and permanent masonry synagogue. The Old

Synagogue could have been built before 1519, as a document records a dispute between the Polish-born and the Bohemian Jews for possession of an "old" synagogue, but we cannot be sure that this is the building now known by that name. Much of what we see today is of ca. 1570 and later, the product of repairs made to a building that was damaged by fire in 1557. A few earlier details survive, such as the four-part ribbed groin vaults and vestiges of wall shafts which were replaced by corbels on three interior walls.

The architect of the work done ca. 1570 is said to have been Matteo Gucci, an Italian who worked elsewhere in the Cracow area. A pre-1570 building might have had a gabled roof, salient masonry buttresses, pointed-arch windows, different capitals, and other interior details. The present building has a horizontal roofline, formed by the arcaded attic that is typical of the Renaissance in Poland (Fig. 70). The capitals are ring-molded and the windows round-headed; the ark and bimah have Renaissance forms.

At Kazimierz, as in other one- or two-naved synagogues, the bimah asserts itself because of the fine polygonal and canopied wrought-iron cage enclosing the elevated platform (Fig. 71). Plans made in the early twentieth century showed the bimah slightly off center, but even ReMO did not say that one had to determine dead center mathematically. The ark steps rise between two low wall spurs, as at the Prague Altneuschul.

A painting of 1865 shows movable seats and lecterns rather than fixed wooden benches. The synagogue had many bronze chandeliers, and the German commandant of the area during the Second World War thought so highly of them that he moved them to his own residence. By the early twentieth century, there were painted inscriptions and arcades in relief on the north wall and painted inscriptions on the south annex walls. Most of these fittings were common to hundreds of other synagogues from the sixteenth to the nineteenth century.

Other aspects of the Old Synagogue that are

Figure 70. Cracow, Old Synagogue, after 1494, exterior ca. 1570 in 1981.

Figure 71. Cracow, Old Synagogue, interior to ark in 1981.

Figure 72. Cracow, Old Synagogue, women's section, after ca. 1600, interior in 1981.

Figure 73. Cracow, ReMO Synagogue, 1556–57, exterior in 1981.

comparable to those elsewhere are the lowering of the main hall's floor level below grade, either for symbolic reasons or to obtain more interior height; the addition of vaulted women's galleries and other annexes of the seventeenth through the nineteenth century (Fig. 72); and the surrounding of the synagogue by gable-roofed, vaulted annexes, dating from the seventeenth to the nineteenth century.

The Old Synagogue was restored in 1773 and reconstructed in 1889. The government funded conservation work in 1913 and again in 1936 under Professor Hendla. Between 1940 and 1945, the synagogue lost its roof, vaults, furniture, windows, and library collections, and its courtyard was used for Nazi executions. Postwar restoration, begun at the initiative of a member of the Polish Parliament, Dr. Bolesław Drobner, ended in 1959, after which the building became a museum of Jewish history and culture under the aegis of the city historical museum. The Parliament declared it an official historic monument, one of three Polish synagogues so designated. In May 1982, despite the ostensible controls of martial law, burglars ransacked the building and stole objects of ritual art.

ReMO Synagogue

While the more imposing Old Synagogue stands along the now-demolished ghetto walls at one end of a plaza-like extension of Szeroka Street, the main thoroughfare of the Jewish quarter, the more revered ReMO Synagogue is tucked away in a court off the street, at the edge of the principal Jewish cemetery (Fig. 73). This was a private synagogue built in 1553 under a special royal dispensation by Israel Isserles, chief of the Cracow Jewish community and father of Moses Isserles (ReMO, 1520–72). The son was the head of the local yeshivah, a member of the community legal court, and—most important—author of commentaries on the legal treatises by Jacob ben Asher and Joseph Caro. The 1553 synagogue, possibly made of wood, burned down but was rebuilt in masonry in 1556–57. It stood intact until the Nazis burned it in 1940. Reerected after the war, it is still used for prayer and study although no one is employed to care for its trunks full of decaying books and Torah scrolls.

This is believed to be the first Polish masonry synagogue of Renaissance style. It is a plain rectilinear building with a north side vestibule and a courtyard. Battered buttresses on the exterior of the main prayer hall reveal the presence of vaults inside. The main space, being small, needs no internal supports. The windows are set high in the wall, as usual, and most likely for the usual reasons—stability of the walls, reduction of window-breaking and vandalism, desire to avoid distraction to worshippers. The large lunettes at the east and west ends probably were added later. The bimah, a wrought-iron cage, was rescued during the war. The ark resembles that of the Old Synagogue. Pairs of stubby Corinthianesque pilasters flank it, and there are abundant floral carvings and finely crafted doors with carvings in relief. The steps to the ark are bordered by an iron handrail apparently of the nineteenth century. While the building is not distinctive architecturally, it is important for its associations with the learned ReMO. About fifteen people usually worshipped there during the mid-1970s, but orthodox Jews come on pilgrimages from a broad geographic area, and two hundred people crowd it almost beyond capacity on the High Holy Days.

Smaller Synagogues

In the confined Jewish quarter of Kazimierz were other synagogues, some of which are extant though not now used for religious purposes. The High (Wysoka) Synagogue at Jozefa Street 38, of either ca. 1595 or 1633, is a masonry building with sloping buttresses outside and vaults inside which rise from wall pilasters. It had a modest ark with elaborately carved side pieces of a type common in eighteenth-century Poland, and figurative paintings of Bible passages including Noah and the ark, Moses receiving the tablets of the Law, and the Babylonian exiles' harps hanging from the trees.

The Popper Synagogue was built beside the ghetto wall in 1620 by Wolf Bocian (alias Popper), the richest Jew of his time. Inside its plain-stuccoed, thick, and buttressed masonry walls were figurative murals painted by Leon Schenker between the world wars.

The Kuppoh Synagogue was built with community funds ca. 1600 (or ca. 1647). It is long and low in proportion and has a women's gallery; the men's and women's entrances are at either end of the long south wall.

Other venerable synagogues included a little one on a small hill, Reb Aron's *kloyz* on Jozefa Street, Rabbi Nathan Shapiro's *shtibl,* and the Isaac Synagogue in Izaaka Street.

Synagoga Postepowa

A more modern building is the nineteenth-century eclectic Tempel, or Synagoga Postepowa, in Miodowa Street 24. Its rather flat facade is imposing because of its size and its copious, though uncoordinated, ornament, with friezes of Romanesque and Gothic arches and Gothic quadrilobes creating different rhythms from those of the varied window openings. It represents the taste of Cracow's assimilated Jews, who looked to central European ideas of style and self-image—not exactly Christian, but not exotically Islamic. The dark main sanctuary still is used on High Holy Days. It is a galleried five-aisled basilica with an apse. The ornament mixes Romanesque and Moorish elements, and is painted primarily in red, blue, and brown. The quality of design is not distinguished, but the unrecorded architect added plenty of decorative detail. This, with the colored glass windows, accentuates the difference between nineteenth-century synagogues of this type and the traditional plainer ones in the nearby streets. When government authorities disputed the Jews' right to retain this building in the mid-1960s, fifteen men undertook to worship there, constituting the legally required number to keep the building's status as a synagogue.

Isaac Synagogue

Of all the old synagogues, the Isaac Synagogue is the most important architecturally (Figs. 74, 75). It was a private foundation by Isaac Jacobowicz (died 1673), banker to King Władisław IV under whose patronage the synagogue was planned in 1638–44. The design is attributed to Francesco Olivieri, another Italian who worked for eminent Poles. This synagogue, like all the

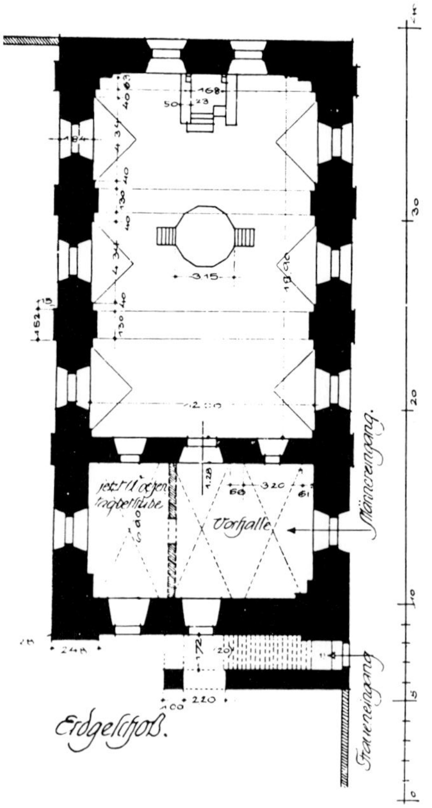

Figure 74. Cracow, Isaac Synagogue, 1638–44, plan.

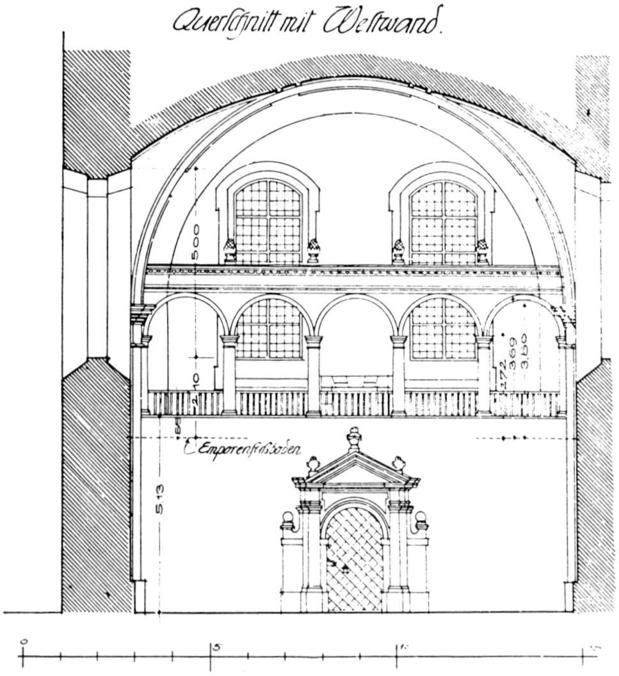

Figure 75. Cracow, Isaac Synagogue, cross section to gallery over entrance.

others surviving in Cracow, was made of masonry. Its gabled roof covered a barrel-vaulted main room 16.9 m. by 12 m. in size. An exterior porch sheltered stairs leading to the upper-floor women's gallery, evidently a later addition; the handsome Renaissance screen in front of the gallery fits awkwardly into the side walls and vaults, and thus must postdate the building construction. The bimah had a magnificent polygonal wrought-iron canopy, while the ark was heavy and classical in detail; of the ark, only the marble frame and the tablets of the Law remain today. Before the ark steps stood an iron grille with a triumphal arch in the center. This may have been added during the reconstruction of 1857. At a date now unknown, landscapes of Hebron, Jerusalem, and Machpelah were painted on the walls. An Eternal Light on the eastern wall, segment-headed windows in the vault lunettes, and an imposing door with rusticated jambs and a pediment were other details executed at various times. Although the building was well cared for until the Nazi period, having been restored in 1935–36, it suffered badly under the German occupation. It now houses a sculpture workshop, in which only remnants of the ark and fragments of Hebrew inscriptions reveal its original use.

Cracow, then, preserves even in its converted buildings a rich collection of synagogues of three major types. The Old Synagogue retains a medieval two-naved plan. The ReMO, High, Kuppoh, and Isaac synagogues are typical single-room, vaulted buildings of the late sixteenth to the early nineteenth century: simple in form; apparently light in color and better supplied with natural lighting than were older buildings; covered with painted Hebrew inscriptions as their principal but not exclusive interior ornaments; lit by bronze chandeliers; graced by a central polygonal bimah under a wrought-iron canopy; and provided with an ark recess within the eastern wall. If the furnishings shown in old photographs did not all date from the Renaissance, they nevertheless represented the types of furnishings needed in the buildings. Finally, the Tempel exemplified the historicist eclectic style, and the interest in designing facades so as to establish the modernized Jews' public posture, which characterized the later nineteenth century throughout Europe.

BIBLIOGRAPHY

AZJ VII (Feb. 11, 1843), p. 84.

M. Bałaban, *Historia żydów w Krakowie na Kazimierzu 1304–1868,* vol. 1, Cracow, 1931.

———, *Przewodnik po żydowskich zabytkach Krakowa,* Cracow, 1935.

———, "Von Ghetto zu Ghetto," *Menorah* V, #5/6 (1927), pp. 347–52.

———, *Zabytki historyczne Żydów w Polsce,* Warsaw, 1929.

M. Borwicz, *1000 ans de vie juive en Pologne,* Paris, 1955.

S. Czerpak, *The Old Synagogue of Cracow,* Cracow, n.d.

B. deBreffny, *The Synagogue,* New York, 1978, pp. 110–17.

L. Dobroszycki and B. Kirshenblatt-Gimblett, *Image Before my Eyes,* New York, 1977.

Grotte, *Deutsche.*

———, "Die Beeinflussung jüdischer östlicher Sakralbaukunst durch Prager Vorbilder," *Jahrbuch der Gesellschaft für die Geschichte der Juden in den ČSR* VI (1934), pp. 457–69.

H. Kamm, "Martial Law Turns Cracow into Hotbed of Apathy," *New York Times,* June 2, 1982, p. 2.

A. Kubiak, "Żydowska architektura zabytkowa w Polsce," *Żydowski Instytut Historyczny. Biuletyn.* Parts I and II, 1953, pp. 122–71; III, 1953, pp. 73–96 (= Rozdz. II, 1953, pp. 137–42).

Y. L. Hacohen Maimon (Fishman), ed., *Arim va-imahot be-Yisroel,* vol. 2, Jerusalem, n.d., pp. 352–54.

New York Times, Nov. 28, 1976, X, pp. 1ff.

E. Vinecour, *Polish Jews. The Final Chapter,* New York, 1977.

F. H. Wettstein, *Quellenschriften zur Geschichte der Juden in Polen,* Cracow, 1892 (Hebrew).

Wischnitzer, *Architecture,* pp. 54–56, 107–8, 111–12.

———, "Mutual Influences between Eastern and Western Synagogue Architecture from the 12th to the 18th Century," *YIVO Annual,* reprinted in J. Gutmann, ed., *The Synagogue,* New York, 1975, pp. 265–308.

Four-Pillar Tabernacle Synagogues

Before the Holocaust, eastern Europe had many synagogues, built both in wood and in masonry, of the late sixteenth through the early nineteenth century. Impressive because of their mass and size, the masonry synagogues might be dignified or mysterious or even charming internally. A small number survived German invasion and the depredations of local anti-Semites, because they were too hard to destroy or could be useful. Today, most of the remaining masonry buildings are cultural facilities; a few are historic monuments, and others serve private secular uses (see Appendix II).

Many masonry synagogues had rectangular plans, with women's galleries over a western vestibule or appended to the north and south sides of the building. They had cloister vaults or barrel vaults with penetrations above the windows. Examples include the cloister-vaulted synagogue at Chroučovice in Czechoslovakia, and the barrel-vaulted Isaac Synagogue in Cracow/Kazimierz.

Other eastern European masonry synagogues had square plans, sometimes with added annexes. Their thick walls were sometimes supported by massive exterior buttresses, as at Zholkva and Szydłów. Some had a tower, possibly for use in time of military crisis, as at Lutsk, Lesko, and Pinsk. A synagogue had a battlemented roof if it was supposed to help fortify the town, as at Lutsk, Leshnev, Lyuboml, or Gusyatin. Those with decorative attics took them either from fortresses or from Polish Renaissance town halls, as at Belz, Przemyśl, Brody, or Lukov; the civic building comparison was appropriate because the synagogue was the center of the Jews' self-governing activities.

These square buildings had several types of interior arrangements. One was a large open room in which everyone could see and hear clearly, as at Zamość, Szydłów, and Szczebrzeszyn. This was true especially if the bimah was only a cage-like construction with thin iron framing as at Zamość, or a small stone kiosk as at Szydłów.

Another interior arrangement had the ceiling supported on four columns or piers that formed a central bay, usually smaller than the other ceiling bays, as at Vilnius-Great, Druya, Ostrog, Kremenets, Mikulov (winter synagogue), and Podivin. More distinctively, the four columns could be joined to form a tabernacle over the bimah, as at Leshnev, Lutsk, Lukov, Mikulov (old), Novogrudok, Przeworsk, Rzeszów (both synagogues), Rymanów, Slonim, and Zmigrod. Three examples—the synagogues of Lublin, Łańcut, and Pinsk—suffice here to describe the type. (See also L'vov and Vilnius below.)

Lublin

Lublin is significant because of its large Jewish population, its service as a political center of Polish Jewry during the late Renaissance, the learning of its famous rabbis, and because a synagogue there is believed to have been the first of the type with four piers clustering around the central bimah. The city was representative of others in the location of its Jewish settlement, in the number and types of its synagogues, and in the tragic fate suffered by its Jews and Jewish quarter after 1939.

A Jewish settlement near Lublin is documented in 1336, when Jewish migration to Poland was becoming substantial. While the Christian townsfolk retained the privilege—known elsewhere—of forbidding Jews to live within the town walls, the Jews were relegated to the nearby village of Piaski Żydówskie. As others did elsewhere, these Jews lived under the direct protection of noblemen who encouraged them to settle on their own land to transact business which could be kept at least partly independent of the town's commercial activity. By the late fifteenth century, some Jews lived at the foot of the castle hill outside Lublin. When Jews began to filter into the town in the mid-sixteenth century, they rented space in buildings owned by the clergy and nobility because these premises were free of the burghers' direct jurisdiction. Synagogues, however, were not built in the city but out of town in the Podzamcze ("below the castle") area, the chief Jewish settlement. This district increased in size from the late fourteenth to the late sixteenth century, just when Lublin became the chief commercial center between the Vistula and Dnieper rivers. The first formal synagogue was built on land purchased in 1557 from a Jewish physician. In 1567, a privilege approved the construction of a synagogue and a yeshivah on that site. Several years later, a second, smaller synagogue was built adjacent to the first one and sheltered by the same roof. In 1636 or 1638, a third synagogue, named for Hersz Doktorowicz, was inaugurated on the upper floor of a building located a few steps from the Jews' Gate of the city, toward which the expanding Jewish settlement had spread. We do not know what any of these synagogues looked like because they were burned in 1656 by Russians who captured the city and set fire to the Jewish quarter.

It is possible, however, that the principal synagogue of the area was the first of the many eastern European synagogues to have four central supports around the bimah. The post-1656 synagogue on the site shows this arrangement (Fig. 76); it lay adjacent to a smaller and oblong one, as did the original two synagogues, and these buildings retained the names of the previous synagogues. (The larger one was called the MaHaRSHaL Synagogue.) Perhaps the Russians destroyed the interiors but not the structural masonry of the synagogues. Moreover, the Lublin synagogue type became widespread in Poland a generation later. As Lublin was the seat of rabbis who held legal jurisdiction over Jews in a wide area, and the seat of a Jewish council (the Council of the Four Lands) which regulated Jewish affairs from the late sixteenth through the mid-eighteenth century, a building

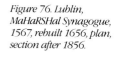

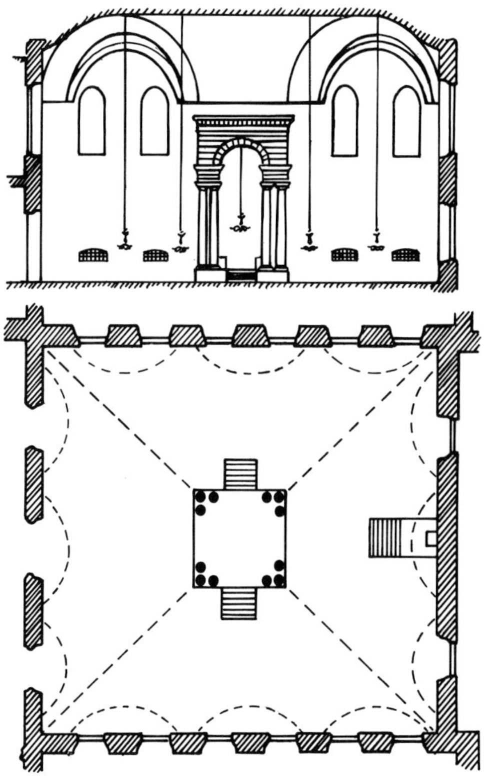

Figure 76. Lublin, MaHaRSHal Synagogue, 1567, rebuilt 1656, plan, section after 1856.

type which originated in Lublin may have been adopted in other towns. The type is known at Przemyśl (1592–95), but a significant architectural innovation is more likely to have been created for Lublin.

The Lublin synagogue, as rebuilt after 1656, is said to have been able to hold three thousand worshippers. Almost square in form, it had thick walls pierced by round-headed windows. If the exterior resembled that of other Polish synagogues of the period, it was plastered and whitewashed or painted. The building was more interesting inside than out. It had nine groin-vaulted bays, the central one smaller than the others. The center bay vault groins rested on the top of a square tabernacle held on four corner supports, each of three Corinthian columns. The columns stood on a platform that also held the bimah table between the clustered supports, under the center of the tabernacle. Readers ascended to the bimah by steps on the north and south sides of the platform.

The distinctive feature of this plan is the placement of the central supports close to each other, creating a small and therefore tightly focused central bay. The plan is known over a considerable geographic region, for example at Lutsk, Pinsk, Slonim, and Novogrudok in the Volhynia-Lithuania region north and east of Lublin, as well as at Rzeszów-New Town and Opatów in Galicia to the south. This is different from a related type of four-pillared central plan—known at Vilnius-Great, L'vov-Suburban, Druya, and Ostrog—in which the bays are more nearly equal (see Figs. 85, 93).

Perhaps the four triads of columns supporting the bimah tabernacle in Lublin were nineteenth-century inventions. The synagogue was damaged by a disastrous fire in 1856, when the adjacent synagogue, the eighteenth-century house of study, the ritual bath, and other community facilities also burned. All the buildings had to be reerected several years later, and new details may have been introduced at that time. The historian Majer Bałaban thought that the windows were too large for the seventeenth century, and the exterior as it was rebuilt suggested to him more a concert hall than a venerable synagogue.

The plan, however, is characteristic of the seventeenth century, not the nineteenth. The chairs facing the bimah rather than the east also preserved old customs. The women's galleries at the north and west reflect seventeenth-century *ad hoc* planning rather than the better integrated planning for women's seating that was usual in large synagogues of 1856 and later. Moreover, the presence under one roof of a large synagogue, a smaller one, and two small guild or fraternity synagogues reflects old traditions born of necessity.

The adjacent synagogue, known as the MaHaRaM, was also of a type known in the seventeenth century in both masonry and wooden synagogues. It was a single-naved building in which two-thirds of the space was reserved for men and one-third for women. The areas were separated by a low wall above which arches helped to support the flat ceiling. The bimah stood in the center surrounded by a bronze grille between carved corner posts. If the synagogue was reduced to ashes in 1856, the bimah surrounds, the gleaming metal lamps, the menorah, and other objects must have been nineteenth-century products unless older ones were rescued or donated.

The guild synagogues in this building were smaller rooms of no architectural pretension. The town had many such modest premises. The carters had a synagogue near the main one, and named it the Saul Wahl Schul after a man who is famous in Jewish legend for having been king of Poland for one night. The bimah of this synagogue was polygonal, with a bimah canopy held on simple cylindrical supports. The tailors, business clerks, and coppersmiths each had their own synagogues. Another small one was called the Parnasschul because it had been founded by a distinguished synagogue elder (a *parnas*). The Podzamcze area was described as being thick with synagogues and houses of study, and the nineteenth-century Jewish settlement in the Old Town inside the walls was well supplied with other houses of prayer and learning. The large number of Jews did not mean that they and their institutions were welcomed by the entire Christian population. As late as 1913, one synagogue was closed on the pretext that it was too near a church.

An irony of fate brought the Jews back to Piaski Żydówski. About 45,000 Jews were assembled there and in Lublin in 1941 by the Nazis, who shipped them later to slave labor or death camps. The Podzamcze quarter was annihilated as well; it is now a level, paved, empty open space. Although several thousand Jews, including many from Soviet territories, settled in Lublin after the war, most of them left in 1946–50 and nearly all the rest departed during the anti-Semitic wave of 1968.

Pinsk

Another impressive four-pillared masonry synagogue was built in 1640 at Pinsk, a city now in the Belorussian S.S.R. This building was about 30 m. wide and 27 m. long, including annexes

Figure 77. Pinsk, 1640, exterior, west and north sides.

on the north, west, and south (Fig. 77). The men's prayer hall measured about 16 m. by 18 m. internally, and was about 9 m. high. The exterior was plastered and the annexes, if not also the main hall, were made of brick. The thick walls contained round-headed windows. A parapet of triangular gables may once have enhanced the roof cornice, but by the 1930s it had been removed, leaving a clumsy band of rectangles instead. The annexes included a vestibule at the west; women's areas at the north and south, built over basements; and a cylindrical tower at the northwest corner, apparently

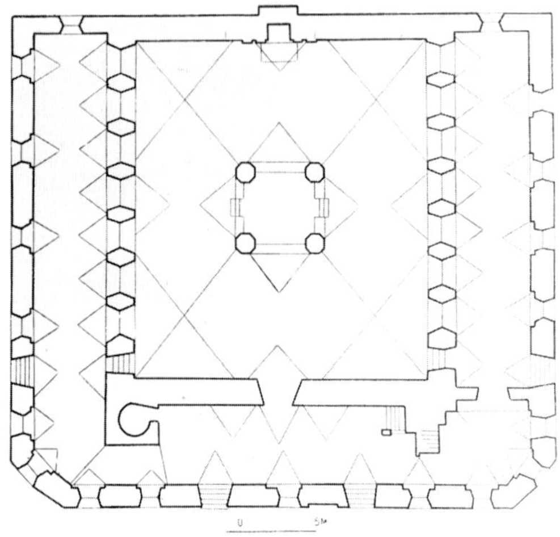

Figure 78. Pinsk, plan.

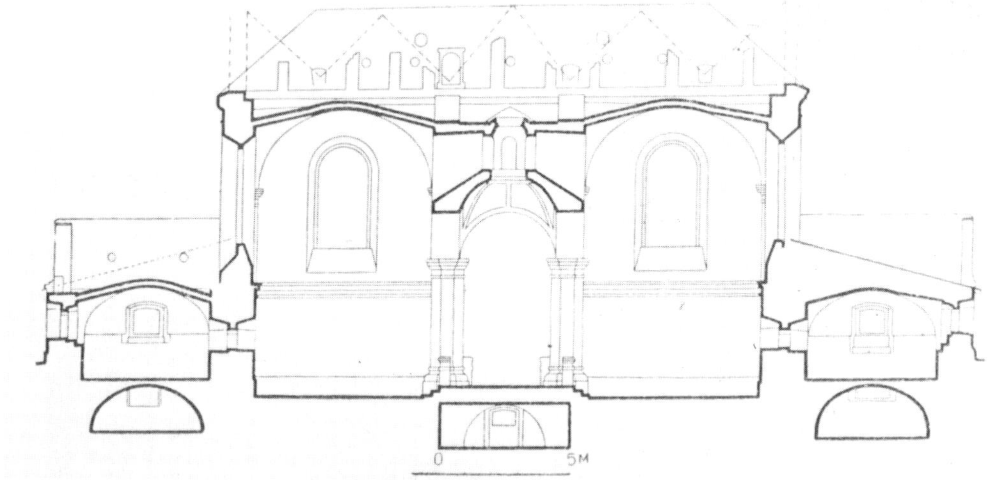

Figure 79. Pinsk, section.

antedating the western vestibule that encased the tower's lower parts (Fig. 78). Annexes also housed trade guild rooms, particularly for butchers and others (perhaps goldsmiths) who did work important to Jewish ritual, and a robing room which could have been used by the rabbi for other purposes.

Inside, the synagogue was barrel vaulted with penetrations and groin vaults at the corners (Fig. 79). Four octagonal compound piers held a cupola with a lantern framing the bimah. The ark stood in front of a small rectangular recess in the thickness of the eastern wall; this was the usual design rather than the protruding niche or apse common in western Europe. Among the furnishings was a large Hanukkah lamp, about 2 m. wide and about 1.6 m. high, set on a stone socle about 1.3 m. high; such objects were introduced in the seventeenth century. A fire damaged the synagogue in 1923, but by 1932 it had been rehabilitated by an architect named Saposznik. The bimah became a simple platform with a low metal railing, and the window over the ark was transformed into a round opening. The ark—with two levels of classical columns and cornices with tendril and leaf decoration—the four piers, and all other visible surfaces were painted with ornaments mixing Moorish interlace and Renaissance motifs of various periods. They were all rendered in bright colors with strident dark and light contrasts.

Around the synagogue, and dominated by it, was a neighborhood of modest dwellings and houses of study; this cityscape could be seen elsewhere, too, as in Kielmy and Panevėžys. Casualties of anti-Semitism and war, all these synagogues and community buildings have been destroyed.

Łańcut

The Lublin-MaHaRSHaL and Pinsk synagogues have been destroyed. No satisfactory photographs of the former exist, but some idea of these buildings may be gained by examining a synagogue of the same general type and of the seventeenth or eighteenth century which survives at Łańcut in southeastern Poland.

This masonry building, about 18 m. by 15 m. in size, stands just outside the grounds of the residence of Count Potocki, under whose aegis the Jews lived in the town (Fig. 80). The structure has a simple plan, with a vestibule and a side room on the entrance side and a main hall beyond. Women sat above the vestibule, and reached their gallery by an external stairway. The exterior and interior surfaces are plastered.

Upon descending several steps from the vestibule, one sees the unusually light main prayer

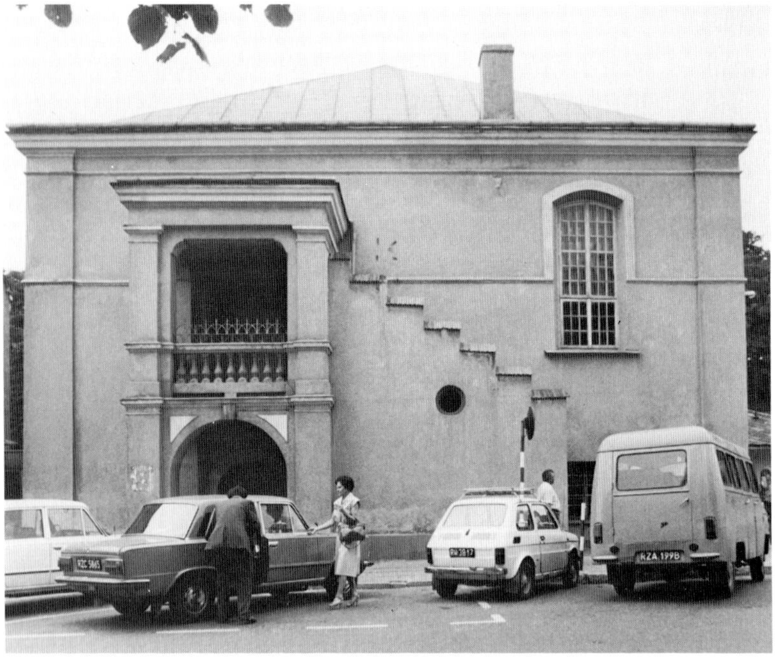

Figure 80. Łańcut, 17th century(?) with 18th-century redecoration, exterior, west side, in 1981.

Figure 81. Łańcut, interior to ark in 1981.

hall (Fig. 81); perhaps the Jews felt secure enough with the count's protection to have larger-than-usual windows. In the center stand four thick polygonal pillars. The vaulting system is more complex here than it was at Lublin. At Łańcut, the vaults are not continuous. The synagogue is divided into eight bays around the central tabernacle. The four bays at the cardinal points have barrel vaults with interior surfaces resting on the tabernacle. The corner bays are groin vaulted. Arched bands separate the barrel vaults from the groin vaults. The ornamental features include decorative plasterwork and paintings on the vaults as well as on the necking and capitals of the four pillars. Cornices, shallow, arched niches on the walls, and a pediment beside the ark recess may also have been made of plaster, possibly at a date different from that of the tabernacle decoration. The synagogue, as restored in 1896 and redecorated in 1909–10, had a cement floor and paintings of the zodiac and musical instruments mentioned in Psalms; these paintings were executed by Jewish artists from Łańcut and nearby Rzeszów. The sole record of the eighteenth-century appearance of the interior is recorded in a watercolor which distorts the spatial impression. It was painted after 1786 by the Polish scenic-view painter, Zygmunt Vogel (alias Ptashek, 1764–1826).

The synagogue still gives a good idea of the spatial arrangement of the tabernacle type of synagogue. The congregation had room in which to circulate, or in which to arrange seats north and south of the bimah. Compressing the bimah in the center of the room intensified its importance, for it became both a canopy of honor and a structural member; without the tabernacle and its supports, the building could not have been as long and wide as it was. Thus the tabernacle was related to the entire building as well as to its heart. With the bimah raised on a platform under the canopy, everyone understood its elevated status in physical as well as metaphoric terms.

The Łańcut synagogue met a happier fate than did the Lublin multiple-synagogue building, although the Jews of Łańcut were exterminated just as ruthlessly. The synagogue suffered some fire damage early in the Second World War but was repaired soon afterward, either before the extermination program began or by the Germans, who used the building as a grain depot. In 1956, the town council proposed to destroy the building, as there was no longer a Jewish community in Łańcut and the building was in poor condition. A physician, Dr. Stanisław Bałicki, persuaded the council to preserve the structure as a museum of Jewish antiquities, and to sponsor an exhibition in it to mark Łańcut's six-hundredth anniversary. His motives for preserving the building included his affectionate memory of murdered Jewish friends and his knowledge of local history in which Jews had been important, having constituted 45 percent of the town's population in 1880. Moreover, he believed that the crimes against the Jews had to be recorded and made evident. In collaboration with Jan Micał, head of the cultural department in the Rzeszów district of which Łańcut forms a part, Dr. Bałicki tried to obtain 200,000 złotys for building restoration. The government actually allocated 124,000 to secure the structure and replace the ornament. Much of the work had been done by 1981, and the restored interior with its delightful pastel colors and decorations was scheduled to house an exhibit of Judaica. The vestibule is to receive the Jewish gravestones retrieved from German street-paving operations, which used the stones. If the building can be maintained properly, it will continue to represent a socio-political and architectural history that is all but obliterated elsewhere.

BIBLIOGRAPHY

R. Abramovitch, *The Vanished World,* New York, 1947.

M. Bałaban, *Bibliografia historii żydów w Polsce . . . , 1900–1939,* Warsaw, 1939.

———, *Bóżnice obronne na wschodnich kresach Rzeczpospolitej. Studia historyczne,* Warsaw, 1927 (not consulted, but content is similar to that in "Wehrhafte . . ." below).

———, *Die Judenstadt von Lublin,* Berlin, 1919.

———, *O warownych bóżnicach w Polsce,* Warsaw, 1929 (not consulted).

———, *Skizzen und Studien zur Geschichte der Juden in Polen,* Berlin, 1911.

———, "Von Ghetto zu Ghetto," *Menorah* V, #6/7 (1927), pp. 347–62.

———, "Wehrhafte Synagogen in den östlichen Randgebieten der polnischen Republik," *Menorah* V, #6/7 (1927), pp. 369–76.

———, *Zabytki historyczne Żydów w Polsce,* Warsaw, 1929.

M. Borwicz, *1000 Ans de vie juive en Pologne,* Paris, 1956 (for pictures).

Das Bukh fun Lublin, Paris, 1952 (not consulted).

D. Davidowicz, *Bate keneset be-Polen ve-Hurbanim,* Jerusalem, 1960.

B. deBreffny, *The Synagogue,* New York, 1978, pp. 105–28.

L. Dobroszycki and B. Kirshenblatt-Gimblett, *Image before my Eyes,* New York, 1977.

Entsiklopedia shel Galuyot, Lublin, ed. M. Blumenthal and M. Korzen, Jerusalem, 1957.

Z. Gostynski, *Les pierres racontent,* Paris, 1973 (for pictures).

Grotte, *Deutsche.*

———, "Neuere Forschungen über kirchliche Verteidigungsbauten," *Die Denkmalpflege* XXIII, #7/8 (June 8, 1921), pp. 56–59.

M. Grünwald, "Was geschieht für den jüdischen Kunstdenkmäler in Polen?" *Menorah* VIII, #5/6 (1930), pp. 261–63.

A. Heppner and I. Herzberg, *Aus Vergangenheit und Gegenwart der Juden und der jüdischen Gemeinden in den Posener Landen,* Poznań, 1904–8.

B. Hoffman, ed., *Toyznt Yor Pinsk; geshikhte fun der shtot, der yidisher yishev,* New York, 1941 (Yiddish and English).

P. Juckoff-Skopau, *Architektonischer Atlas von Polen (Kongress-Polen),* Berlin, 1921 (Beiträge zur polnischen Landeskunde, Reihe B, Band 8).

A. Kubiak, "Żydowska architektura zabytkowa w Polsce III," *Biuletyn Żydowski Instytut Historyczny* 1953, #6-7, pp. 122–71, #8, pp. 73–96.
G. K. Lukomski, *Jewish Art in European Synagogues,* London, 1947, and articles drawn from the book in *Journal of the Royal Institute of British Architects,* 1935, *Burlington Magazine,* 1935, *Revue de l'art ancien et moderne,* 1937, etc. (N.B.: texts are full of errors; use these publications mainly for pictures, although some are mislabeled.)
Piechotka, pp. 9–34.
B. Postal and S. Abramson, *The Traveler's Guide to Jewish Landmarks in Europe,* New York, 1971.
H. Schultze, "Zwei jüdische Kultbauten in Polen," *Zentralblatt der Bauverwaltung* XL (Nov. 1920), pp. 557–60, and letter by A. Grotte, p. 615.
A. Shulman, *The Old Country,* New York, 1974 (for pictures).
A. Szyszko-Bohusz, "Materialny do architektury bóżnici w Polsce," *Prace komisji Historii Sztuki* IV, #1 (1927), pp. 1–25.
N. Tamir, ed., *Pinsk. Sefer edut ve-Zikkaron le-Kehilot Pinsk-Karlin,* Tel Aviv, 1966–73 (Hebrew and Yiddish, not consulted).
W. Tatarkiewicz, "Typ lubelski i typ kaliski w architektur ze koscielnej XVII wieku," *Prace komisji historiji sztuki* VII, #1 (1927), pp. 23–60.
E. Vinecour and C. Fishman, *Polish Jews. The Final Chapter,* New York, 1977.
M. Walzer and N. Kudish, *Łańcut. Hayeha ve-Hurbana shel kehila Yehudit,* Tel Aviv, 1963 (Hebrew, Yiddish, English).
Wischnitzer, *Architecture,* pp. 107–24.
———, "Mutual Influences between Eastern and Western Synagogue Architecture from the 12th to the 18th Century," *YIVO Annual of Jewish Social Science* II–III (1947–48), pp. 25–68, reprinted in J. Gutmann, ed., *The Synagogue,* New York, 1975.
———, "Starynnaia sinagoga v Lutzke,"*Novy voskhod,* January 1913, pp. 47–54.
———, "Synagogen im ehemaligen Königreich Polen," in S. J. Agnon and A Eliasberg, eds., *Das Buch von den polnischen Juden,* Berlin, 1916, pp. 89–105.
S. Wojciechowski, "Gmina żydowska w Lublinie w XVI w.," *Biuletyn Żydowski Instytut Historyczny* 2(4), Warsaw, 1952, pp. 204–30.
Zabytki sztuki w Polsce, Inwentarz Topograficzny, vol. 1, part 1, Warsaw, 1939.
S. Zajczyk, "Architektura barokowych bóżnic murowanych w Polsce," *Biuletyn Naukowy. Zaklad Architektury Polskiej i Historii Sztuki Politechniki Warszawskiej,* June 1933, pp. 186–95.

L'vov

In L'vov, one of the great centers of Jewish population in eastern Europe, Jews had lived under the protection of the Polish crown since the fourteenth century. A Jews' street is recorded in 1387 inside the city walls, while a settlement in the suburb called Cracow existed in 1352. The suburb also had a Karaite settlement until 1457. The city and suburban communities had separate synagogues, ritual facilities, and charitable institutions.

The Jews in L'vov endured commercial and personal harassment during the late Middle Ages and early Renaissance, but until the mid-sixteenth century, the kings, who valued the commercial skills of the Jews, looked the other way when new synagogues were established or enlarged. In the mid-sixteenth century, however, the Polish crown acceded to the demands of Roman Catholic church authorities who wanted to limit the number of synagogues according to the rules of canon law. Nevertheless, the Jews were allowed to repair damaged buildings under canon and secular law, and therefore rebuilt the Old (or Great) Synagogue inside the city walls in about 1580, after it had burned down in 1571.

TaZ Synagogue

Exceptionally important Jews sometimes received permission to build private (rather than community) synagogues. Their privileges exempted them from the laws of 1571, which stated that Jews who bought land for any purpose could be forced to give it up in case of a municipal defense emergency. The privilege operated in favor of Isaac Nachmanowicz, a financier to the king who allowed him in 1581 to buy from the city a site which could never be requisitioned by the city magistrates. Isaac failed, however, to secure the local archbishop's approval for construction of the private syn-

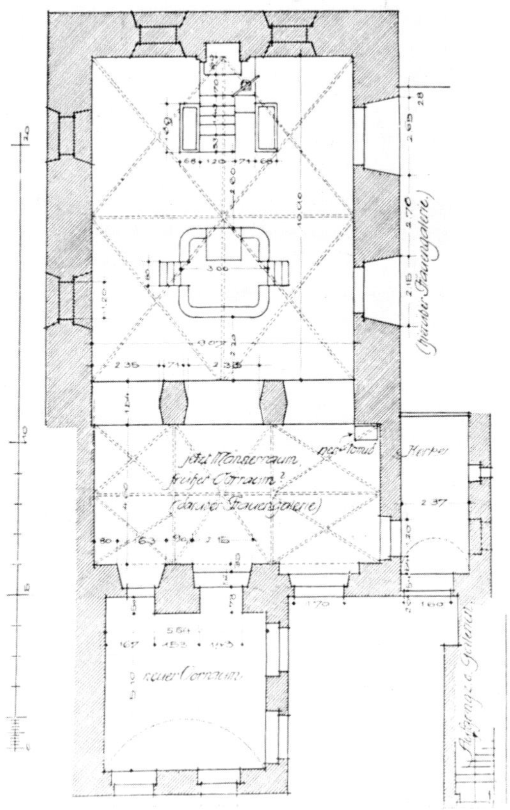

Figure 82. L'vov, TaZ Synagogue, 1582, plan.

Figure 83. L'vov, TaZ Synagogue, cross section to east.

agogue which he completed in 1582 (Figs. 82, 83); this made the Jesuits all the more eager to expropriate the "illegal" building a generation later.

Isaac is supposed to have employed a Swiss architect, Paolo Romano from Chiamut in the Grisons, who built civic and Christian religious buildings in L'vov at this time, and who might have worked for a Jew who was closely associated with the crown. Isaac was also the president of the Council of the Four Lands. The synagogue was therefore generally known by his name, although it was later called the TaZ Synagogue after the treatise *Ture Zahav* by the seventeenth-century Talmudist David ben Samuel Halevi. It is sometimes called the Golden Rose Synagogue because of a legend that one of Isaac's daughters, Rose, saved the building from expropriation.

The masonry building proved to be typical in some ways and unique in others. Like many synagogues, it had at first a single, partly sunken, men's area and no women's annex. It was also typically thick-walled, with small windows high up. Its decorative style was characteristic of religious and secular buildings in society at large. It was unusual in having an axial arrangement of annex and main room, although that may have been dictated by the land available for building. Its unusual squarish shape might have been chosen because the architect was imbued with Renaissance cultural ideas favoring the use of central plans in religious architecture, but the plan is not a perfect square, nor is it likely that a Christian architect would have designed for Jews a building which was supposed to be ideal for Christians. The Jews probably wanted a shape that suggested communal gathering rather than hierarchical linear arrangement, and the result was governed in part by the architect's ability to vault a room of a given span.

The principal room was about 10.9 m. by 9.07 m., covered by four groin vaults. Ribbed vaults, conservative in the 1580s, were used perhaps

Figure 84. L'vov, TaZ Synagogue, annex toward men's prayer hall.

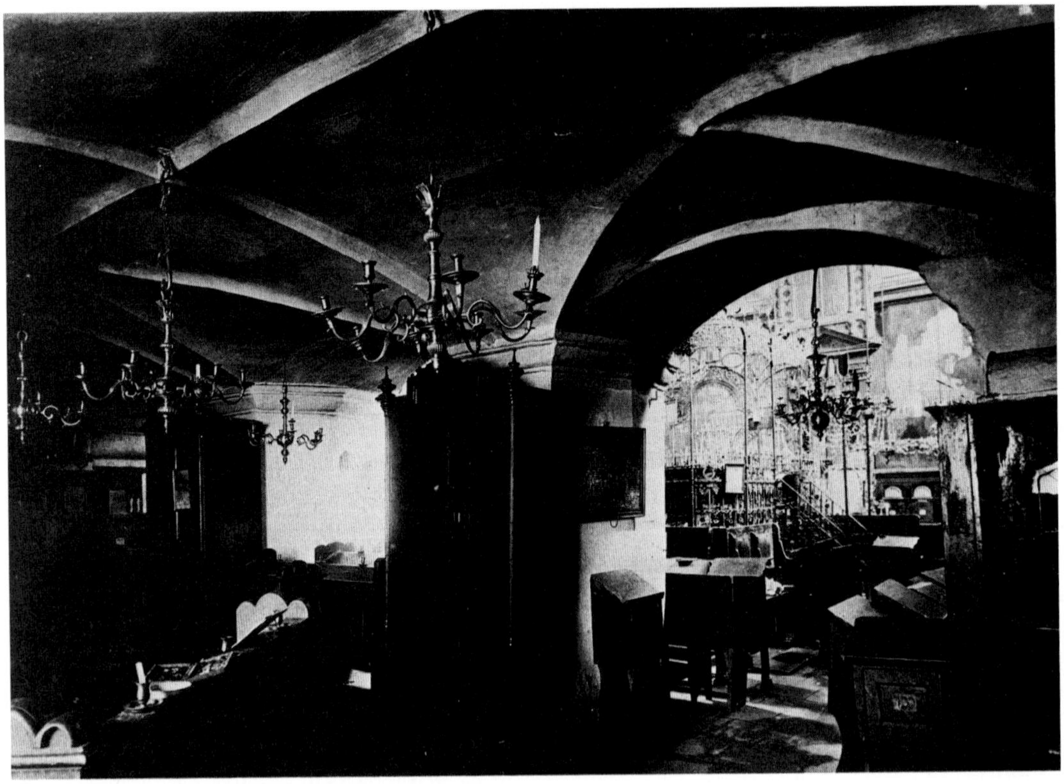

because the local builders lacked skill in modern construction; or because architects were reluctant to make Jewish buildings resemble recent Christian ones; or because the patrons themselves had conservative tastes. The bimah of Isaac's synagogue stood not under the crown of the vault but slightly to the west, within an iron grille elaborately wrought with a design of rampant lions. The ark resembled a Renaissance pedimented altarpiece or aedicula. Either originally or during one of the later restorations, the columns and the narrow arch around its doors were given ornamental patterns, perhaps in carved stucco. Renaissance shapes appeared also in the brackets below the vaults and in the wood revetment (possibly a later addition) on the lower parts of the walls.

Only the main prayer hall remained in its original condition. In 1587, Isaac and his wife bought additional land on which their son Mordecai built an addition to the synagogue to provide an entrance unhindered by the private construction which originally stood close to the door. Under Mordecai's supervision, and later as well, the original entrance was modified to provide a room about 5.1 m. by 4.6 m. with additional seating for men and a women's gallery above (Fig. 84). This new room appears to have altered the architectural design of the original entrance door. Another women's gallery was erected on the south side of the main prayer hall near a room added to serve as a jail. A new tunnel-like corridor, including steps, led to the women's galleries.

The building was repaired several times: in 1611 after a temporary confiscation by the Jesuits; again, after a pogrom and a raid in 1664; perhaps during the eighteenth and nineteenth centuries; and in this century following Russian depredations in 1915 and a pogrom shortly after the armistice in November 1918. At various times, chandeliers, wall sconces with hammered metal reflectors (one of which had a human figure in relief), and painted votive tablets were added to the main room, and an Eternal Light in a wooden niche was installed in the vestibule. The ark was restored and freshly gilded shortly before 1933.

Nearby, an entire synagogue center grew up over the years. In a single street lay the Isaac Nachmanowicz Synagogue, the Great Synagogue of about 1580 (demolished 1797, rebuilt 1801) using a plan with four central pillars, the Tailors' Synagogue, the house of study, the community school, and the ritual bath. The crowded ghetto was maintained by official decree until 1867 when the Galician Jews were finally able to own property and live where they wished; part of it was torn down in 1907.

Suburban Synagogue

Outside the city walls, in the Cracow suburb, a fire destroyed the old synagogue in 1623. In 1624, the Jews concluded an agreement with the city magistrate specifying the structure and location of the replacement erected in 1632–33. This masonry synagogue had a western vestibule a step or two above the main room, whose dimensions were about 19.3 m. by 20.1 m. by 19.2 m. The main room had a nine-bay plan supported by four octagonal pillars, each over a meter thick, defining the central bay (Fig. 85). The pillars stood farther apart than those at Lublin, Łańcut, and Pinsk. Women's annexes on the north and south were added later. The western vestibule contained stairs, a pillory, and guild rooms.

Attached to the interior face of the western (entrance) wall of the main room, a boys' choir gallery rose 4.15 m. on fifteen steps (Fig. 86). This was one of the unusual features of the building, as was the location of the pillory in the east wall of the vestibule. Typical of eastern Galicia were the setting of the Eternal Light in a closed niche on the west wall of the main room, and the row of ornamental arches below the window zone (Fig. 87).

The main impact of the room came from the impressive central area. In the central bay, the

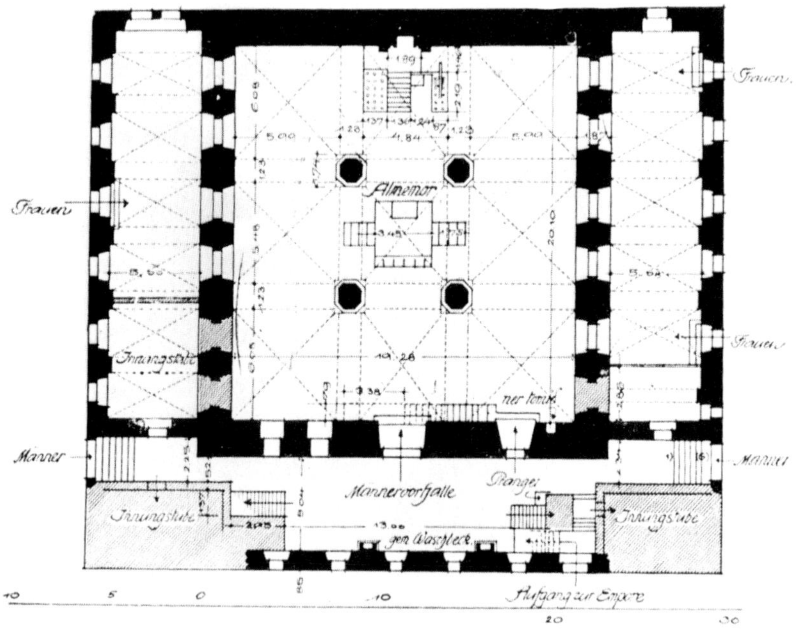

Figure 85. L'vov, Suburban synagogue, 1632–33, plan.

four octagonal pillars permitted light to pass but they nevertheless framed the bimah. Because the bimah was not confined by a tabernacle, it could be a traditional platform surrounded by a wrought-iron grille. The pillars carried the groin vaults, which were divided into bays by flat arches.

On the outside, the rectilinear structure had thick walls and smooth whitewashed surfaces which produced the impression of sturdy strength. At some time the building may also have been fortified.

Over the years, the congregation modified the interior and the furnishings. The windows may have been enlarged during a period of peace when fortifications and narrow windows seemed unnecessary. The Eternal Light must have been framed originally in the seventeenth century but was partly destroyed, perhaps in 1664. In 1844, a Reform rabbi, Abraham Kohn, attempted to introduce innovations in a congregation whose leaders were then assimilating to German culture; in fact, a separate Reform synagogue was built and dedicated in 1846. Kohn's tenure lasted only four years, however, for a

Figure 86. L'vov, Suburban synagogue, interior to western choir gallery.

Figure 87. L'vov, Suburban synagogue, longitudinal section to north.

traditionalist assassinated him in 1848. Either in Kohn's time or later in the century, new wooden benches made the interior look more formal and sound much quieter, since fixed seats eliminated the noise of movable chairs and reading stands.

The Jewish population increased in L'vov during the period of Austrian rule (1772–1914), when it was the main city of Austrian Galicia. Nevertheless, the large synagogue did not have to be greatly enlarged or replaced because the Great Synagogue inside the walls had already been expanded in 1801. Moreover, some of the new arrivals in town were Hasids who set up their own *shtibl* in 1820, adding six more by 1838. In 1869, the city had fourteen synagogues and eighty prayer rooms.

When the city returned to Polish rule after the First World War, a deadly riot erupted against the Jews. In November 1918, the Great Synagogue was burned and the Suburban synagogue plundered. The latter was the only Jewish structure left standing in its entire neighborhood. The community managed to survive, however, and later increased until there were about 109,500 Jews in L'vov in 1939. Between March 1942 and January 1943, approximately 97,000 Jews were murdered there or sent to slave labor and death camps. Of those deported, it is said that only about 150 survived.

The synagogues perished along with the population, and in 1959 the Ukrainian government which ruled the city after 1945 closed a synagogue formed by returnees and refugees after the Second World War. The militia even dispersed the private *minyanim* in 1969, leaving few physical remains of the once active Jewish presence in L'vov. A playground now occupies the site of the TaZ Synagogue.

BIBLIOGRAPHY

AJYb, 1919–20 (1919), pp. 252–53.

M. Bałaban, *Historia lwowskiej synagogi postepowej* (not consulted).

———, *Skizzen und Studien zur Geschichte der Juden in Polen,* Berlin, 1911.

———, "Von Ghetto zu Ghetto," *Menorah* V, #6/7 (1927), pp. 347–52.

———, "Wehrhafte Synagogen in den östlichen Randgebieten der polnischen Republik," *Menorah* V, #6/7 (1927), pp. 369–76, esp. pp. 372–73.

———, *Żydzí Lwowscy na prełomie XVI i XVII wieku,* L'vov, 1906 (Monografie z Historyi żydów w Polsce, 3).

"Ben Ami," *Between Hammer and Sickle,* Philadelphia, 1967, pp. 60–67.

M. Borwicz, *1000 ans de vie juive en Pologne,* Paris, 1956, pp. 183, 201.

S. Buber, *Anshe Shem,* Cracow, 1895, reprint ed., Jerusalem, 1967–68, pp. 9–22 (Hebrew).

J. Caro, *Geschichte der Juden in Lemberg von den ältesten Zeiten bis zur Theilung Polens im Jahre 1792,* Cracow, 1894.

B. deBreffny, *The Synagogue,* New York, 1978, pp. 114–18.

S.. Dubnow, *History of the Jews in Russia and Poland,* vol. 1, Philadelphia, 1916.

Encyclopedia Judaica, 1971, ad loc.

Entsiklopedia shel Galuyot, L'vov, ed. N. M. Gelber, part 1, Jerusalem, 1956.

Grotte, *Deutsche.*

Jewish Encyclopedia, ad loc.

Jüdisches Lexikon, ad loc.

M. Lowenthal, *A World Passed By,* New York, 1933, pp. 364–67 (with some incorrect information and legendary material).

Y. L. Hacohen Maimon (Fishman), ed., *Arim va-imahot be-Yisroel,* vol. 1, Jerusalem, n.d., esp. bibliography on pp. 342–44.

Wischnitzer, *Architecture,* pp. 109, 117, 120, 141.

Moscow and Leningrad

The history of the Great synagogues of Leningrad and Moscow shows the position of the richest and most privileged Jews in czarist Russia.

Leningrad

As late as 1846, the Jews of Leningrad (then Saint Petersburg) were not organized, because they were subject to harsh residence restrictions in the capital. Three synagogues mentioned in 1859 were probably in soldiers' barracks; L. M. Rothschild mentioned a synagogue in each of four barracks in 1856. When certain classes of Jews obtained the right to live in the city in 1868, a legal synagogue was at last established, and five other premises for prayer were known at the time. About a thousand Jews had this right because they were useful in large-scale business, banking, and railroad building, and they worshipped in a building on the Small Lion Bridge that had opened in 1865. Poorer Jews, such as retired soldiers, tradesmen, or illegal residents, met for prayer privately. Gradually, the legal residents won the privileges of having a community rabbi and community administration, and of holding New Year services.

In 1869, while Czar Alexander II was still benevolent toward Jews (partly to assimilate them culturally), he granted permission to build a synagogue to hold all the legal Jewish inhabitants, both temporary and permanent, who then numbered about five thousand. This may be the synagogue, perhaps of the 1870s, that survives at the rear of the lot of the present main synagogue. Behind a late-nineteenth-century iron gate, a three-storey, tripartite facade of brick is adorned mainly by pointed arches over the windows and door of the ground floor, and a heavy cornice like that of Stockholm's synagogue (see Fig. 237). The center of the building, covering the nave, curves back to the aisle facades. Windows in the upper storeys indicate that the interior is a galleried box; iron piers support the galleries.

According to Vladimir Stassov, a prominent art critic who was friendly toward Jews, the community had neither the site nor the money for building a monumental synagogue. If, however, the richest Jews had wanted to do so, they could have built a synagogue with their resources alone, and the fact that the community was able to afford a larger new building a few years later indicates that the members would have been able to pay for one earlier. A site could generally be found if the government tried honestly to find one. Perhaps the truth was that the government was uncooperative, and there may also have been internal dissension among the Jews themselves. Stassov could hardly have written about such things in a Jewish magazine published under government censorship.

By 1873, the Jews and the government had agreed on a site for a synagogue fronting on Lermontov Street, but five years passed before the congregation received permission to buy the land. The site was obtained through the exertions of Baron Horace Günzburg who, with other rich Jews, gave money for construction. One condition governing the land acquisition was that the synagogue site be at least seven hundred paces from the nearest church. A more important condition was that all other synagogues be closed, but the new building capacity, variously recorded as 1,200 or 2,000, could not have held all the city's Jews. Thanks again to Baron Günzburg, small local synagogues continued to exist, if not legally then with the acquiescence of the authorities who ignored rules that were meant to concentrate Jews in as few places as possible to ensure their supervision. The government also had a financial interest in regulating synagogues, since buildings containing religious institutions were exempt from taxes; strict officials tried to prevent houses and even inns from being used for prayer.

The new Leningrad synagogue was meant to be dignified, but as usual, everyone found it hard to decide what Jewish architecture ought to look like. Few models were available in Russia. The synagogues in Odessa were designed in odd mixtures of neo-Romanesque and other styles; the Warsaw-Tłomacka Street synagogue was neo-Renaissance; and few of the other large eastern European synagogues for the wealthy middle classes had been built by 1878.

Stassov apparently influenced the local Jews by his article, which was probably written and discussed in the 1870s, although published in 1889. Since his goal was to have art provide a sense of national identity, and since he thought that the Jews constituted a nation different from that of Russian Christians, he tried to inform himself about Jewish-related arts. He concluded that Byzantine ornament could be used in synagogues because early Christians in the eastern Mediterranean had learned much from ancient

Jewish architecture. Moorish architecture, however, might be more suitable because Arabs were even closer to Jews. He believed that Arabic-Jewish cultural interchange had made Moorish building distinctive in the overall picture of Islamic art, and he pointed to the two medieval synagogues of Toledo as showing the connections clearly (see Figs. 181, 184). No doubt he reached this conclusion because he could see published views of the beautiful Spanish buildings but none of ancient Jewish architecture!

Despite Stassov's limitations, his opinions were significant historically because he connected the use of Moorish architecture in modern synagogues with the *Jewish* buildings of medieval Spain. His remarks about the buildings of a bygone privileged Jewish élite whose financial and commercial skills were important in a Christian country surely were read with interest by Russian Jews who were in the same position.

Stassov was too realistic to recommend building a copy of a medieval Spanish synagogue. Instead, he looked for inspiration to nineteenth-century synagogues in the Moorish mode which had been erected in Western cities such as Leipzig (1855) and Berlin (1866). The German examples were especially suitable models in the age of the Three Emperors' League (an Austro-Hungarian-Russian alliance, 1872–87) and the Russian-German alliance (1887–90). The Berlin-Oranienburgerstrasse synagogue impressed him more than all others, and he thought that the interior was one of the most beautiful creations of the century (see Figs. 122, 124). He was less enthusiastic about the exterior, finding it too much like an apartment house with a dome on top, but three pages devoted to that synagogue called his readers' attention to the beauties of a domed building with Moorish or other Islamic ornament.

Stassov's prestige, and the security to be gained by following a renowned Christian's advice, were so appealing that the community accepted a suggestive oriental design of 1879–83 produced by Professor Ivan I. Shaposhnikov of the Academy of Arts and by his assistant, Lev I. Bachman, who had been the first Jew to gain admission to the school (Figs. 88, 89). The design suited the prosperous upper middle class, which, like its counterparts in Berlin and Vienna, felt increasing confidence despite lingering civil disabilities and elected to show its confidence by using a distinctive style. The new synagogue also had hints of colorful late-Byzantine architecture, and that style would have connected Jews to the current Russian national Romantic movement in architecture, suggesting that Jews also could be part of the larger nation. Nevertheless, a German-Moslem oddity is unlikely to have increased fraternal feelings between Christians and Jews, however well-intentioned Stassov and the architects were.

The Leningrad synagogue has a domed central section and two lower projecting wings. The center of the facade resembles an Islamic gateway, with a stilted opening in the center and turrets rising over the ends of the cornice. The cross-in-square plan of the interior is known in Islamic and Byzantine architecture; Rachel Wischnitzer cited the school mosque as one such building type. The reeded dome on a drum with canted corners was inspired by a mosque of the Mamluk period in Cairo. None of these design elements appears in the Spanish medieval synagogues, but as Jewish and Islamic architecture were supposed to be closely related, the architects felt free to use features of all Islamic buildings.

The exterior has cream-colored stuccoed masonry walls above a stone basement. The walls have beveled courses, carved capitals, and moldings of both decorative and imitation-structural form. Window and door openings are stilted, lancet-shaped, round-headed, circular, and rectangular. The interior, a galleried basilica, has an inlaid vestibule floor, an apse with the ark set under a dome, and intricately patterned nave ceiling panels. The interior would have been more elaborate but civil authorities demanded changes in design. The congregation succeeded in installing a squarish wedding room, lavishly decorated in blue and gold with Islamic capitals and a mosaic floor with plant ornament.

Figure 88. Leningrad, 1880s–1893, exterior in 1969.

Figure 89. Leningrad, 1880s–1893, interior, detail of ark area.

Despite the importance to Russian commerce of the rich Jews who sponsored the synagogue, the work was delayed by hostile officials. The building, begun in the 1880s, was opened only in 1893. By that time, there were 15,000 Jews officially in the city, a number far greater than the synagogue's capacity.

In 1905, the government lifted residence restrictions under pressure from recently formed opposition parties. In that year, there were synagogues in the Moscow and Simion sections, and prayer houses in four other parts of the city. In 1909, Hasids received permission to build a separate synagogue, and the first Reform congregation (with Sunday services!) was founded.

Two years later, the community inaugurated the extant synagogue at the Jewish cemetery; it is now used only as an impressive funerary ceremonial hall in place of an earlier and smaller one in fourteenth-century French Gothic style. I. G. Gevirts, a Jewish architect, prepared the new building's design; he had already designed two prayer houses, the cemetery administration buildings, and family tombs within the burial ground. In plan, the synagogue is a longer version of the 1893 synagogue. Its elevation is simpler, more geometric, and modern. A low-pitched, smooth, green dome, slightly pointed at the top, rests on a square, blind-arched and slit-windowed tan drum which rises above a massive facade. Gray stone blocks flank lighter stonework around the four-centered entrance arch. Receding wings have blind arcading along the sides. Low walls enclose an arcaded forecourt, where Hebrew inscriptions run above pointed arches that are supported by Islamic capitals held on slender, short columns. The front gateway has massive rectilinear and stepped gateposts, reinforcing the impression of weighty geometric form. There is a faint suggestion of venerable tombs in the Holy Land, or even of Assyrian ruins. Comparable simplified Middle Eastern forms were introduced into synagogue design elsewhere at this time and shortly afterward, as in Sarajevo, Augsburg, and in projects made for Budapest by Siegfried and David Jonas and by Béla Lajta.

Moscow

Until the relatively humane Alexander II became czar in 1855, no Russian Jewish subjects were allowed to live permanently in Moscow. They could only visit the city for two weeks at a time, and had to live in an establishment owned by a Christian who made available a prayer room, a ritual slaughterer, and a cantor. Within a few years of ascending the throne, however, the czar rescinded some of the residence restrictions, and a synagogue was chartered in 1861. Samuel Poliakov, a railroad magnate, paid 100,000 rubles for a synagogue which was under construction in 1868. Contemporaries called it magnificent, and high government officials attended the consecration ceremonies on July 1, 1870. The czar, however, grew increasingly hostile toward Jews, and terrifying pogroms spread rapidly after he was assassinated in 1881.

The synagogue of 1870 did not suffice for Moscow's Jewish population and eventually the Jewish élite secured permission to erect the present Great or Central Synagogue in Arkhipova Street, which opened in 1891. The building, smaller than the main synagogue in Leningrad, was built and remodeled under such adverse circumstances that it is more a monument to politics and survival than to art.

Figure 90. Moscow, Arkhipova Street, 1891, exterior (Photograph by JESSE ZEL LURIE*).*

The neoclassical facade has a four-columned, triangular-pedimented temple front projecting slightly in front of wings faced with plaster imitating drafted masonry (Fig. 90). The building originally had a dome crowned outside by a six-pointed star, but hardly had the dome been built than the congregation was forced to demolish it. Conspicuous display of Jewish identity and public position displeased the authorities, who were cunning enough to let the Jews pay for a costly dome before making them pay for tearing it down. The synagogue was closed and the rabbi banished for daring to ask for its reopening. The Jews then had to remodel the building into a Jewish trade school, but the authorities closed that, too, and made the Jews remodel the trade school into a religious school. Perhaps the government hoped that the costs of all this work would ruin the congregational treasury, but proceeds from a bequest paid the bills for construction and demolition.

As we see it now, the synagogue retains its imposing facade, which relates the structure to other neoclassical public buildings in Moscow and Leningrad, and perhaps to the Tłomacka Street synagogue in Warsaw. From a vestibule, glass doors lead into the prayer hall—a galleried box with a raised apse for the ark (Fig. 91). Galleries on three sides rest on square piers which are sheared at the corners. As the magnates of Russian Jewry who paid for the building tended to be modern in outlook and interested in Hebrew *belles lettres* rather than in Hebrew as a language of traditional religion, they may have asked for the wooden parapets on the women's galleries that we see now, rather than for the high grilles found in orthodox synagogues. The men occupy fixed benches facing east. The ark has framing columns and a gabled superstructure. Around it, in the apse, murals of stylized plants and symbols give a faintly exotic cast to this otherwise simple interior.

The Jewish population of Moscow rose to

Figure 91. Moscow, Arkhipova Street, interior to ark (Photograph by JESSE ZEL LURIE*).*

about ten thousand by 1895. The Jews had to pray in five oratories, located in soliders' barracks and in private houses from which they were forbidden to move—a rule that allowed Christian landlords to raise the rents unconscionably. The Great Synagogue reopened in 1906, after the political changes brought about by the 1905 Revolution. Hasids received a permit to open a separate synagogue in 1908, and the Reform congregation was founded in 1909. Under the Soviets, synagogues in Moscow and elsewhere were closed, although the Great Synagogue has been restored and is kept open to placate critics of Soviet policy. It is a meeting place on major Jewish holy days for those who want to affirm their identity as Jews.

Two other synagogues now exist in wooden structures in the Maryino Roshcha and Cherkizovo districts, and another synagogue is located in Malakhovka, a nearby locality. The building in Maryino Roshcha is a gabled box made of wood painted light blue. Closed and half-hidden behind a barrier, it looks like an ordinary, if rather large, vernacular building with its shuttered windows and decorative wood appliqués. In 1974, the government shut down a synagogue that opened in 1932 in Tomilino, a suburban town southeast of Moscow. This continued the well-known Soviet practice of closing synagogues wherever the local Jews are afraid to protest or cannot do so effectively.

BIBLIOGRAPHY

AJYb, annual reports for the situation of Jews in these cities.

AZJ XLII (Oct. 29, 1878), pp. 696–97; LVII (July 28, 1893), Beilage, p. 3. (Oct. 6, 1893), Beilage, p. 3.

Jewish Chronicle, Nov. 14, 1856, p. 798; March 18, 1859, p. 7; Aug. 7, 1868, p. 6; May 20, 1870, p. 2; Sept. 16, 1870, p. 5; March 28, 1873, p. 771; March 22, 1878, p. 11; Oct. 25, 1878, p. 10.

Jüdisches Lexikon and *Universal Jewish Encyclopedia* have photographs of the cemetery synagogue, s.v. St. Petersburg or Leningrad.

B. W. Kean, *All the Empty Palaces,* New York, 1983, p. 7.

L. Kochan, *The Jews in Soviet Russia since 1917,* London and New York, 2d ed., 1972, esp. J. Rothenberg, "The Jewish Religion in the Soviet Union," pp. 40–68.

I. Levitats, *The Jewish Community in Russia, 1844–1917,* Jerusalem [1981].

B. Pinkus and A. A. Greenbaum, eds., *Russian Publications on Jews and Judaism in the Soviet Union, 1917–1967. Bibliography,* Jerusalem, 1970.

L. R. Rosenberg, *Jews in the Soviet Union. An Annotated Bibliography, 1967–1971,* New York, 1971.

St. Petersburg Imperial Academy of Fine Arts, *Yearbook of the Society of Architects-Artists,* #6 (1911) (Russian).

V. V. Stassov, "Po povodu postroiki sinagoga," *Yevreiskaia Biblioteka* II (1889), pp. 463–73.

Wischnitzer, *Architecture,* pp. 208–9.

Yevreiskaia Entsiklopedia, s.v. Moscow; St. Petersburg.

I am glad to thank Ethel Hirsch, Leon Gordon, Dina Abramowicz, Pamela Sharpless, Valentina Berezhina, and Aline Isdebsky-Pritchard for photographs, references, and translations.

Vilnius

The Great, or City, Synagogue in Vilnius could have laid special claim to the title of "Little Sanctuary," because Jews called Vilnius itself the "Jerusalem of Lithuania." The city was famous among Jews for the learning of her rabbis, especially Elijah ben Solomon Zalman (1720–97), called the Vilna Gaon (Eminence). An interest in secular knowledge also became noticeable in Vilnius by the 1820s. The renowned Strashun Library stood at the entrance to the main synagogue complex. Booksellers sold their volumes in its courtyard, surrounded by several synagogues. Historians, poets, and journalists wrote in Hebrew, while Yiddish writing also flourished. The YIVO (Yiddish Scientific Institute) was founded in Vilnius; its rescued archives and photographs are now housed in New York City.

Serious scholarship enhanced religious devotion. Before the Second World War, there were said to be 122 synagogues in the city and forty more small prayer rooms or houses of study where prayers were offered. Even in 1860, when the city's population was smaller, there were said to be a hundred places of worship. Most of them were small, undistinguished outside, and simply furnished. There were some early-twentieth-century paintings in the premises used by the painters' association, but the chimney sweeps, tailors, butchers, Hasids, and other groups had simpler quarters.

Several of the religious buildings were more impressive, such as the Gaon's *kloyz,* sometimes called a synagogue (built in 1758 as the Gaon's house, altered or rebuilt as a synagogue ca. 1800, rebuilt in 1868). This two-storeyed gabled building had sober, free, classical detail adorning a facade opened with low arches on the ground floor and five taller and wider ones on the upper, principal, floor. The "Old Synagogue," or *kloyz,* dated erroneously by legend to 1440, probably was erected in its final form in the eighteenth or early nineteenth century. In plan, it was double-naved, like the medieval synagogues at Worms and Prague-Altneuschul. But this "synagogue" was primarily a house of study, and its two thick Tuscan columns may have been used simply to enlarge the meeting space rather than to imitate an older architectural form. The ark was in the center of one long wall so that a reader on the bimah could see it close at hand with no columns to block the view. The large Reform temple of 1904, housing a congregation organized in 1848, had a broad-arched central section sheltering Romanesque portals between striped brick wings. Inside, in the vaulted and galleried hall with free Romanesque decorative forms, the bimah stood near the fanciful "Moorish" ark. There were even two Karaite synagogues: the old one of 1894, which was a simple whitewashed building with geometric ironwork in round-headed windows; and a new one of 1911 in the nearby town of Zvieriniets, with coarse Moorish-inspired ornament.

The most important of all was the Great Synagogue, a handsome example of the four-pillared plan (Fig. 92). Some writers date it to 1573. It was much enlarged, or perhaps rebuilt, around 1633 when the Jews received a residence privilege including the right to erect a synagogue. It may have been injured in an anti-Semitic assault in 1635, and in 1640 the Jewish tailors' guild provided durable iron gates to guard an entrance to the building complex in which the synagogue stood. Perhaps the synagogue known to our century was actually built after 1661, when the Jews returned to the city after an exile of several years' duration; this date is closer to that of other four-pillared synagogues. It may have been redecorated or

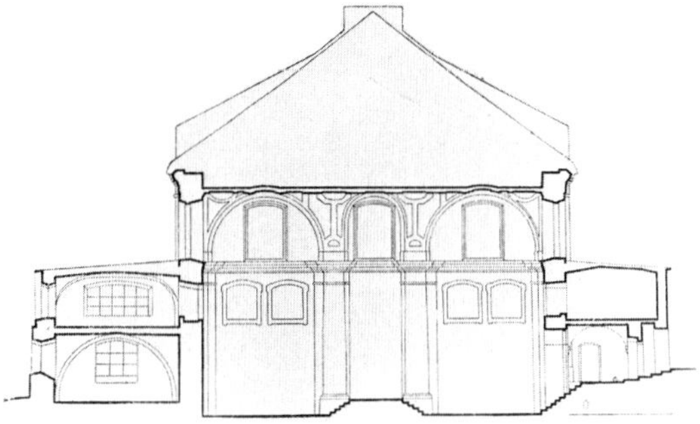

Figure 92. Vilnius, Great Synagogue, ca. 1633–48(?), after 1666(?), section.

Figure 93. Vilnius, Great Synagogue interior, painting by Francizsek Smuglewicz, ca. 1800.

partly remodeled in the late seventeenth century. No adequate documents have been preserved concerning the date or architect.

The synagogue lay a few steps below street level in a remarkable courtyard that sheltered the Old Synagogue as well as the Gaon's *kloyz* and other religious and community buildings. The courtyard was a small open space entered through metal gates at each end, tucked between streets inhabited almost entirely by Jews. Around the court stood fourteen synagogues and houses of study—in the 1880s there may have been thirty—the ritual bath, the neighborhood well and fountain (which were the only places where Jews were allowed to obtain water), the kasher slaughterhouse, community offices, and the Strashun Library. While most of the minor synagogues were simple oblong rooms, the Great Synagogue was comparatively tall—about five storeys in height—and measured 22.5 m. by 21 m. inside the main room. Surrounding buildings concealed most of the exterior, but a gable rose above the lower structures. In ca. 1800, a Russian-style multilevel wooden gallery was added to the gable, perhaps as an access route to the newly built women's annex. Later, in the nineteenth century, another annex in coarse provincial Renaissance style was added on this side.

In the vestibule there was a pillory until the early twentieth century—a common feature of many eastern European synagogues associated with the rabbinical court.

The prayer hall was groin vaulted, with windows high up in the walls (Fig. 93). Four massive Tuscan columns surrounded the bimah. The bimah's elaborate superstructure resting on twelve columns is said to have been the gift of the scholarly Rabbi Judah ben Eliezer (alias YeSoD, d. 1762). Paneled designs appear to have been added in the nineteenth century to the lower parts of the walls and to the vaults. These embellishments, while sufficiently simple and classical to harmonize with the four pillars, clashed with the bimah and ark. The latter were more sumptuously decorated with moldings, relief carvings, broken cornices, and other elements of late rococo style, and their scale was smaller than that of the building itself. Around 1800, before the paneled decorations were applied and when the interior surfaces were plainer, the stylistic clash was less obvious because the rococo furnishings relieved the stark and sturdy forms of the building itself.

The sense of force and drama within the synagogue is conveyed by a painting of ca. 1800 by Francizsek Smuglewicz (1745–1807), in which the building overwhelms the worshippers. Borrowing a trick of Piranesi, the artist reduced the scale of the figures and their reading desks while retaining the real scale of the architecture. He intensified the light at the bimah and near the ark, exaggerated the number of steps leading to the bimah which lent dramatic stature to the reader's platform, and used deep shadows and tonal contrasts to enhance the appearance of mystery. The mood has little to do with accounts of the learned, anti-Hasidic, anti-mystical character of Judaism in Vilnius. Perhaps the Christian painter thought of Jewish services as akin to the mysteries of the *Magic Flute.*

The Great Synagogue survived the Second World War as a gutted ruin, a state common to any Jewish buildings that were not completely destroyed. When the Soviet government incorporated Lithuania into the Soviet Union, its officials razed the entire synagogue courtyard and replaced the religious buildings with apartment houses. The Gaon's *kloyz* was burned during the infamous Doctors' Trial in 1952. The Soviet rulers turned the Jewish cemetery into an athletic field and tried to obliterate as many traces as possible of the 56,000 or more Vilnius Jews who had formed over 40 percent of the city's population between the world wars. Guidebooks and art books dealing with the city omitted any mention of Jewish buildings. The Choral (Reform) Synagogue, a galleried basilica in mixed Romanesque and Moorish style, is the only one standing; it is not used as a synagogue, and the few Jews left in Vilnius have only a single, shabby building for prayer—a little sanctuary indeed.

BIBLIOGRAPHY

AZJ XXXVI (Sept. 10, 1872, and Sept. 24, 1872), p. 794.
M. Bałaban, *Die Judenstadt von Lublin,* Berlin, 1919, p. 107 n.6 to Chap. 12.
———, "Von Ghetto zu Ghetto," *Menorah* V, #5/6 (1927), p. 351.
I. Cohen, *Vilna,* Philadelphia, 1943.
M. Grossmann, *Yidishe Vilna,* 1925 (not consulted).
I. Levitats, *The Jewish Community in Russia, 1844–1917,* Jerusalem, [1981].
M. Lowenthal, *A World Passed By,* New York, 1933, p. 374.
H. Lunsky, *Me ha-geto ha-Vilnai* [Vilnius], 1921, esp. pp. 48–70 (not consulted).
Y. L. Hacohen Maimon (Fishman), ed., *Arim va-imahot be-Yisroel,* vol. 1, Jerusalem, n.d. pp. 141–75.
Piechotka, p. 31.
L. Ran, *Jerusalem of Lithuania,* New York, 1974.
J. Rülf, *Drei Tage in Jüdisch-Russland. Ein Cultur- und Sittenbild,* Frankfurt am Main, 1882, esp. pp. 108–9.
P. Weber, *Vilna. Eine vergessene Kunststätte,* Vilnius, 1917.
Wischnitzer, *Architecture,* pp. 119, 123–24.
———, "Mutual Influences between Eastern and Western European Synagogue Architecture in the Eighteenth Century," *YIVO Annual of Jewish Social Science* II-III, 1947–48, p. 41.
Yevreiskaia Entsiklopedia, s.v. Vilnius (Vilna).

Volpa

The synagogue of Volpa in Belorussia was the most beautiful of all the wooden synagogues known in eastern Europe, with the spectacular multitiered roofline and corner pavilions characteristic of northern Polish examples (Fig. 94).

It was erected in a town of no special importance in Jewish history, but Volpa was characteristic of many eastern European localities in that the Jews had been expressly invited by the noble family that owned the town. The princely

Figure 94. Volpa, early 18th century, exterior, west side.

Sapieha family wanted Jews to foster commerce on the family's behalf, even in territory where most Christian inhabitants were hostile to Jews.

The synagogue's first serious investigator, Alois Breier, thought it was built in the mid-seventeenth century, but Kazimierz and Maria Piechotka proposed an early-eighteenth-century date. The region around the city of Grodno, including the town of Volpa, experienced an economic surge in the late eighteenth century, and it is no doubt due to the increase in prosperity that the Jews could afford to restore (or redesign) the roof in 1781 and to pay the taxes probably exacted in return for the privilege. Prince Sapieha may even have let his chief carpenter work for the "prince's Jews" on the roof project. Court carpenters designed other brilliant wooden structures—Roman

Catholic and Orthodox churches, and pavilioned manor houses, to name the two types closest to the wooden synagogues.

Situated on a road running north-south, the Volpa synagogue was shielded from traffic by a picket fence. The Jewish quarter does not appear to have been crowded, for a farm adjoined the synagogue on the east. In this prosaic setting, the building made its impression thanks to the graceful rhythm of the three curving tiers of roof over the men's prayer hall, continued laterally in the bell-shaped, two-tiered roofs of the corner pavilions and frontally in the sloping roofs of the women's annexes and vestibule. Its proportions were satisfying and its silhouette extraordinary, even among comparable synagogues such as those of nearby Grodno and Zabłudów.

Small details emphasized the major features of the exterior. In the central gable were two tiny applied columns, marking the center and culmination of the facade and alluding perhaps to Jakhin and Boaz. The two-storey corner pavilions were made more delicate and more expansive by their graceful arcaded and balustraded balconies. The vertical stiffeners of the horizontal boarded walls punctuated the walls rhythmically and set the ark apart from the side areas of the eastern wall.

Inside, the centrality of the primary space was reinforced by the squarish shape and intensified by the spectacular wooden vault which bounded upward in three coved tiers (Figs. 95, 96). The architect anchored the bottom of each tier by enclosing it in a balustrade. Then he allowed the cove to spring upward. As one tier followed another, the designer reduced the height of the balustrades and the width of the openwork carved-board decorations. This adjustment produced the illusion of a vault much higher than it was. One scholar, Zygmunt Gloger, estimated the height at 30 m., whereas it was in fact only 14 m. Four wooden pillars increased the effects of height and centrality, by rising to help support the octagonal cupola, which was the fourth and concluding tier of the vault. In the center of the cupola, a pendant tied the vaulting boards together, while pointing back down to earth.

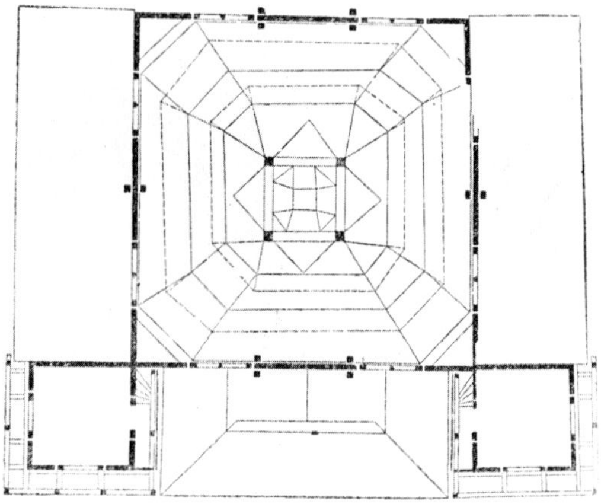

Figure 95. Volpa, plan at first cornice level.

Decorative forms enhanced the technical means used in building the synagogue. Pendentives eased the visual transition from the square walls to the octagonal vaults, but they also helped to prevent the buckling of walls under the pressure of the roof. In addition, they supported part of the two further storeys of scaffolding which carried the roof framework. The balustrade and the openwork boards marked the point where the horizontal beams of the framework tied the roof to the boards, forming the ceiling tiers. Each tier was inscribed into one truss of the hammerbeam roof, so that structure complemented its interior reflection. The four central supports emphasized the bimah and formed a canopy high above it, while they held the canopy. Even if the four pillars were inspired by masonry prototypes, they were appropriately reinterpreted here.

The bimah known in the twentieth century was a polygonal enclosure (Fig. 97). Paneled piers encasing the four central supports of the cupola articulated the four principal angles; between them stretched triads of arches held on thinner supports. Sustaining the arcade was a parapet, paneled at a level just above the seating ledge which surrounded the bimah, and decorated with strapwork grilles above the panels. The bimah terminated in a cornice and had no canopy, unlike most Ashkenazic bimah structures antedating Reform influence. Either the canopy or open scrolls were removed because

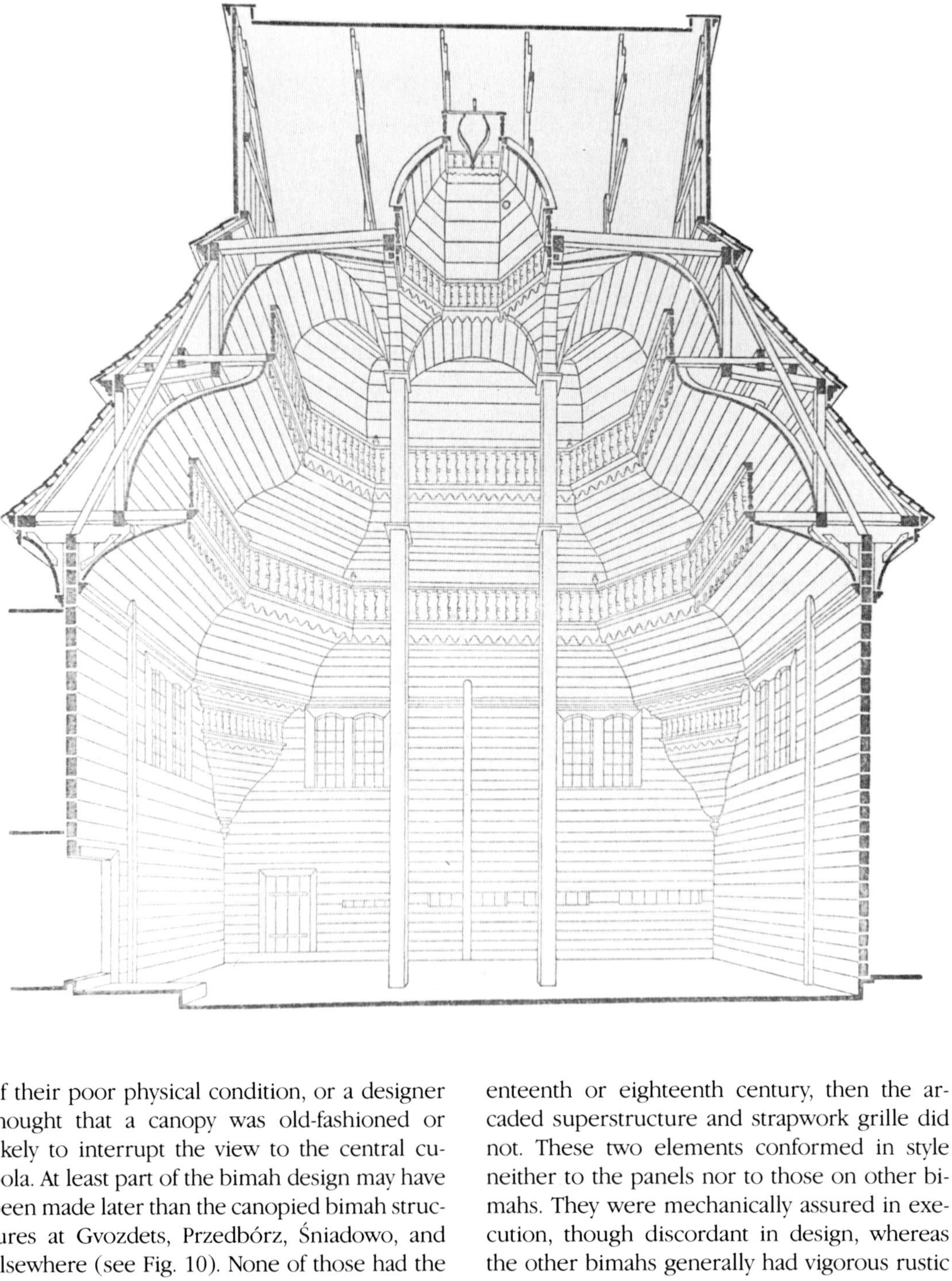

Figure 96. Volpa, elevation.

of their poor physical condition, or a designer thought that a canopy was old-fashioned or likely to interrupt the view to the central cupola. At least part of the bimah design may have been made later than the canopied bimah structures at Gvozdets, Przedbórz, Śniadowo, and elsewhere (see Fig. 10). None of those had the heavy panels and decorative designs, the strapwork, or the slender arcade of Volpa's bimah. If the paneling at Volpa dated from the late seventeenth or eighteenth century, then the arcaded superstructure and strapwork grille did not. These two elements conformed in style neither to the panels nor to those on other bimahs. They were mechanically assured in execution, though discordant in design, whereas the other bimahs generally had vigorous rustic execution of designs composed of familiar and coordinated elements. Wooden balustrades were major ornamental features of the bimah

Figure 97. Volpa, interior to ark.

at most of the synagogues mentioned, but balusters were seen at Volpa only on the railings of the steps to the bimah platform. Can the strapwork have replaced a balustrade? (A bimah with panels under a balustrade, and with no canopy was known also at Grodno.) The arches and their moldings looked like sophisticated versions of folk art forms and profiles rather than the real thing. They were far removed from the Russian-style arches on the exterior corner pavilion balconies. How much of the Volpa bimah, then, was conceived along with the architecture?

The synagogue was certainly redecorated and at least partly refurnished in the nineteenth or early twentieth century, when the bimah could have been remodeled. Perhaps the synagogue once had vivid folk art paintings with the plant forms and symbolic animals seen at Khodorov, Gvozdets, and other Polish and eastern European examples, and at the German synagogues painted in the 1730s by Eliezer Sussmann. If so, the paintings were removed and replaced by painted imitation-marble wainscoting and oriental silk. This work probably was done during a period when Volpa's Jewish leaders put a strict interpretation on the prohibition against images of living things, even symbolic ones. The paintings at Khodorov had imitated oriental fabric, but the painted hanging at Volpa had a Moorish-revival character rather than the appearance of a provincial but genuine oriental cloth as copied by a folk artist.

The baroque ark, on the other hand, was a splendid creation. It was 10 m. high and 4.5 m. wide, and it stood at the head of five steps. It was abundantly decorated with vine scrolls and plants tangled on the half-columns beside the ark door, swirling in ornamental projections left and right of the half-columns, and climbing between the central attic and two turrets at the attic level. The ark decoration included carved animals and animal heads, eagles, flowers, urns, a central boss, Hebrew letters, and openwork boards and balustrades. A seven-branched lampstand carved in relief under painted Hebrew inscriptions filled the ark door. The ark resembled other multistoreyed arks with side projections, being decorated with symbolic plants, animals, columns, and turrets. Examples are known at Grodno and Janów Sokólski (where the related designs are more sober), Berlin-Heidereutergasse, and elsewhere.

The synagogue at Volpa in its final form had fewer inscriptions than several other wooden synagogues, but among the inscriptions was one distributed across several medallions. It was a prayer for the government of the relatively liberal Czar Alexander II. The assassination of this ruler in 1881 led to pogroms against Jews, which frightened many of them into leaving for western Europe and the Americas. The emigration from a number of small towns, combined with the enforced impoverishment of many of the Jews who remained, contributed to the physical decline of Jewish religious buildings. Several wooden synagogues had simply collapsed of old age and lack of repair by the start of the present century. Those wooden synagogues that survived despite emigration and lack of resources fell victim to plunderers and vandals in 1914–18 and to even more depraved attacks after 1939. By 1945, not one wooden synagogue stood in all of Poland, Lithuania, Belorussia, or the Ukraine.

BIBLIOGRAPHY

J. Bartyš, "Materiały do budownictwa drewnianego i do struktury społecno-zawodowej ludności żydowskie w Strykowie w XVIII wieku," *Biuletyn żydowski instytut historyczny* #9–10 (1954), pp. 89–96.

M. Bersohn, *Kilka słów o dawniejskych bóżnicach drewnianych w Polsce,* Cracow, 1895–1903.

A. Breier, M. Eisler, and M. Grünwald, *Holzsynagogen in Polen,* Baden bei Wien, 1934.

D. Davidowicz, *Synagogues of Poland and their Destruction,* Jerusalem, 1960 (Hebrew).

M. Einhorn, ed., *Wolkovisker Yizkor Bukh,* New York, 1949, vol. 2, pp. 614–21.

Z. Gloger, *Budownictwo drzewne i wyroby z drzewa w dawnej Polsce,* vol. 1, ser. 1, Warsaw, 1907, pp. 22–53.

Grotte, *Deutsche,* esp. pp. 7, 9, 48–67.

K. Mokłowski, *Bóżnice drewniane na terenie woj. białostockiego, woj. białostockie. Przeszłość i zabytki,* Białystok, 1928.

Piechotka, pp. 21–22, 37, 40–43, 209, and figs. 257–72.

Wischnitzer, *Architecture,* pp. 125–47.

Plans and photographs are found at: Academy of Art, Polish Institute of Science, Warsaw; Jewish Historical Institute, Warsaw; Polytechnical Institute, Warsaw; YIVO, New York.

Warsaw

For centuries, the Jews in the Warsaw area were restricted to the suburb of Praga, and other occasional settlements were short-lived. Only gradually was there a selection of professionally or commercially useful Jews who were allowed to settle in Warsaw itself. Their number increased at the end of the eighteenth century and under the Napoleonic Duchy of Warsaw, when German Jews were admitted and allowed to open a synagogue in 1802 in Danilowiczowa Street, where they added German sermons to traditional services. (Their later synagogue, with a cupola near the facade, was modeled loosely on the Berlin-Oranienburgerstrasse synagogue.) Some rights gained under the Duchy were rescinded after 1808, and it was only in 1862 that Jews received substantial residence, property, and commercial rights. From this time onward, Warsaw became the chief Jewish population center in Poland, with 90,000 Jews in the mid-1870s, augmented by migrants from farther east who were victims of pogroms after 1881. Between 1882 and the Nazi period, Jews always constituted at least a third of Warsaw's population.

By 1851, there were five synagogue districts.

The main synagogue stood in Wierzbowa Street, but it was damaged by the Russian soldiers who suppressed the Polish Revolt of 1863.

Tłomacka Street Synagogue

From 1871 to 1926, an energetic group of culturally assimilated men assumed community leadership. They incorporated the Praga community into that of Warsaw, to the benefit of the suburban Jews, whose synagogue and cemetery and ritual bath were in a sorry state. They also set a building committee to work on proposals for a large synagogue in central Warsaw. The Jews must have felt confident in doing so, because of the new rights granted in the 1860s, and because their leaders' modern orthodoxy pleased the government, which wanted to promote assimilation.

After disagreements between the community leaders and the first contractors, Leandro Marconi (1834–1919) became the architect; he was the son of a better-known Italian architect who had migrated to Poland earlier in the nineteenth century. Plans made in 1874 were executed in 1875–77 at a cost of 300,000 rubles, which were given by those few culturally assimilated Jews who could afford to contribute and by at least one benevolent Catholic who sent fifty rubles for the synagogue and fifty more for the poor. The Governor General of Poland attended the consecration in 1878, opening the main portal at the start of the ceremonies, in official approval of the atypically assimilated and wealthy Jewish leadership.

The synagogue lay recessed from Tłomacka Street (Fig. 98). Its situation provided perspective for those approaching a grand building meant to seat eleven hundred people. The facade comprised a central section with low recessed screens linking the center to slightly projected terminal pavilions. Behind the screens, courtyards used for open-air ceremonies flanked the side walls of the building, and the courts gave access to the community offices at the far end of the synagogue. The terminal pavilions housed a caretaker's apartment and toilets, among other facilities. The central section facade had a pedimented porch of Corinthian columns between paneled bays and crowned by a triangular pediment. Behind the facade was a low-domed vestibule (Fig. 99). Beyond that lay a space used as a weekday synagogue, covered by a square drum carrying a ribbed cupola. Then came the seven-bay, galleried nave. Talmudic scholars influenced the decision to situate the ark at the south rather than the east, reasoning that Warsaw was north rather than west of Jerusalem.

The design was as far as it could be from the 450 modest Hasidic and traditional prayer rooms that dotted the Jewish district by 1926. This classicizing building—with its porticoed central section, dome, receding wings, and projecting terminal elements—descended from such buildings with similar arrangements as the church of St. Charles Borromeo in Vienna (1716–37) and the Palace of Justice in Brussels (1866–83), which was one of the most conspicuous public buildings of Marconi's time. The porch and dome of the facade trace their ancestry to the Pantheon in Rome. Marconi would not have needed to copy any of these potential sources, because the general compositional principles were well known and widely accepted. Their very familiarity made them useful for Jews who wanted to assimilate culturally with the Christian population, especially as a classicizing style was associated with the imperial government in Moscow.

The plan had an important feature in common with one notable synagogue, that of Oranienburgerstrasse in Berlin (see Figs. 122, 123). In both, the main dome covered a subsidiary space, the weekday synagogue, so that the dome would be seen easily from the street, and thus manifest the building's importance. The people who sponsored these two synagogues wanted to distinguish their buildings from the religious structures of humble, traditional Jews and from those of Christians as well. Their idea of a dome was closer to the dome of the Paris Opera than to anything Eastern. It looked remarkably secular, usually an indication that the Jews wished to avoid imitating a church or looking exotic, preferring a synagogue that would not clash with public buildings.

Figure 98. Warsaw, Tłomacka Street, 1874–77, exterior.

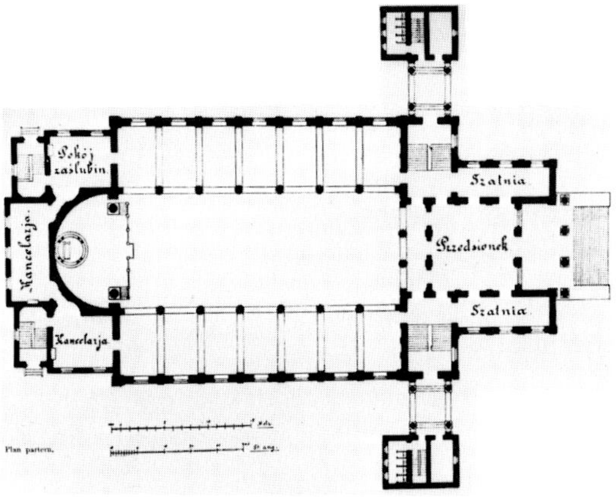

Figure 99. Warsaw, Tłomacka Street, plan.

Figure 100. Warsaw, Tłomacka Street, interior to ark.

Inside, the nave and apse of the main prayer hall extended more than 38 m. (Fig. 100). The hall was about 28 m. wide. Many details of this galleried basilica were classical—the coffered-apse half-dome, the unfluted Corinthian columns of aisles and galleries, the two huge dark-veined marble columns (Jakhin and Boaz) at the apse entrance—but the overall effect, with its mix of medieval and Greco-Roman elements, was eclectic.

The liturgy remained orthodox, but the interior arrangements approached Reform practice. The eleven hundred men's seats faced the ark, which dominated the bimah. The apse included a choir loft for the (usually) all-male choir. Low gallery railings allowed women to see and be seen. There was an organ, even though it was not played on the Sabbath. Former residents of Warsaw remember that in the 1920s the synagogue's rabbi, Samuel Poznański, translated the prayer book into Polish, to be used by the assimilated gentlemen who wore top hats to religious services.

Nozyk Synagogue

At the Nozyk Synagogue, men wore more ordinary hats, for neither they nor the synagogue building wished to make a grand public impression (Figs. 101, 102). This synagogue, now the only one in Warsaw, was financed privately by Zelman and Ryfka Nozyk, a childless couple who left it in their will to the Jewish community. They had it built in 1898–1902 to the design of an architect whose name is no longer known, but in 1893 a synagogue—this one?—had been designed for Warsaw by a Jewish person from Moscow, perhaps Lev Bachman. The synagogue rises on an off-street site, and presents an unremarkable facade of mixed medieval and classical details. Smaller than the Tłomacka Street synagogue, the Nozyk Synagogue is over 19 m. long, over 15 m. wide, and almost 12 m. high to the crown of the nave's ribless groin vaults. Its facade rises about 15 m. to the peak of its

Figure 101. Warsaw, Nozyk Synagogue, 1898–1902, exterior, north side, in 1981.

gable. Like the Tlómacka Street synagogue, it is a galleried basilica with an apsidal ark recess—in this case, flat-ended. The Nozyks surely were not eager to imitate the earlier synagogue, nor, indeed, were most of Warsaw's Jews. Because they were pious and poor, they had even less to do with the magnates of Tłómacka Street than did the rich Nozyks.

The style is mainly Romanesque with alternating square piers and columns supporting the galleries. The segmental arches, parapet ornament, and other details were common to nineteenth-century buildings. An octagonal, cloister-vaulted canopy shelters the bimah.

The Nazis saw to it that the Tłómacka Street synagogue's visual message of assimilation would not endure. After liquidating the Warsaw ghetto, they blew up the synagogue in mid-May 1943, and demolished all other synagogues except the Nozyk. Among these were the syn-

Figure 102. Warsaw, Nozyk Synagogue, interior to ark in 1981.

agogues of the Zionist Ohel Moshe and Moriah congregations, founded in 1885 and 1908 respectively. The Nozyk Synagogue was turned into a stable but at least it was left standing. It received a preliminary rehabilitation in 1949. It is now an officially designated historic monument, restored under the architects Hanna Szczepanowska and Eva Dziedzic between 1975 and 1983. Offices and guest rooms were built onto the ark end of the building.

The Warsaw congregation now has only two hundred members, as most of the city's Jews died during the Second World War. Survivors and postwar immigrants from the east left Poland following pogroms in 1946–47 and two waves of official anti-Semitism in the late 1950s and 1960s. The remaining group of mostly aged people worships without a rabbi in a tiny apartment next door to the synagogue.

BIBLIOGRAPHY

Arim va-imahot be Yisroel, vol. 3, *Warsaw,* by D. Flinker, Jerusalem, 1948.
"Briefe aus Russland," AZJ LVII (Sept. 29, 1893), p. 461.
Encyclopedia Judaica, s.v. Warsaw.
Entsiklopedia shel Galuyot. Warsaw, ed. J. Grunebaum, Jerusalem, 1953–73.
I. L. Grosglik, "Nowa synagoga w Warszawie," *Izraelita* XIII, #38 (1878), pp. 301–4.
C. S. Heller, "Poles of Jewish Background—The Case of Assimilation without Integration in Interwar Poland," *Studies in Polish Jewry,* ed. J. A. Fishman, New York, 1974, pp. 242, 276.
Israelietische Nieuwsbode, Oct. 25, 1878, p. 1, Nov. 1, 1878, p. 2.
T. S. Jaroszewski and A. Rottermund, "Leandro Marconi," *Polski Słownik Biograficzny,* XIX, Warsaw, 1974.
Jewish Chronicle, Oct. 4 and 22, 1863; July 11, 1873; Aug. 24, 1877; Nov. 1, 8, 15, 1878.
Jewish Encyclopedia, s.v. Warsaw.
J. Schatzky, *De geshikte fun Yidn in Varshe,* vol. 3, New York, 1953, pp. 150–71.
———, "Institutional Aspects of Jewish Life in Warsaw in the Second Half of the 19th Century," *YIVO Annual of Jewish Social Science* X (1955), pp. 9–44.
Universal Jewish Encyclopedia, s.v. Warsaw.
Yevreiskaia Entsiklopedia, s.v. Warsaw.

I am grateful to Leon Jolson for photographs, to Samuel Mozes for suggestions and introductions, to Aharon Kashtan and Michael Schudrich for information, to representatives of the Jewish Community, Jewish Historical Institute, the National Institute of Art, and the Historic Monuments Service in Warsaw for expert help offered immediately.

France and Belgium

France: Medieval Synagogues

Remains of medieval synagogues are scattered throughout much of France, from Rouffach in Alsace to Carpentras in the southwest. The examples mentioned here indicate the nature of many of the known pre-Renaissance synagogue remains in France and northwestern Europe.

Rouen

The Jewish community of Rouen, concentrated in the rue aux Juifs, flourished during the twelfth century. An eighteenth-century plan of the Jewish quarter shows a squarish masonry synagogue with thick walls, narrow windows, and a curved projection at the east, no doubt meant to hold the ark (Fig. 103). The building had a tower rising above other buildings in the Jews' street, although the tower would not have rivaled in height the tower of any local church. The synagogue stood on the south side of the Jews' street, where this building appears on the plan.

The synagogue plans and descriptions were analyzed by Norman Golb, who determined that the main prayer hall for men was about 8 m. by 5.3 m., and about 6.5 m. high, with walls about 2 m. thick. The construction was of dressed stone, but about 2 of the roughly 3 m. of masonry that were below grade level were of uneven stonework. Small windows opened on the south and west. Perhaps there was another opening at the east, toward Jerusalem, unless the Jews of Rouen considered Jerusalem to lie more to the south. Above the main room rose another room, with a vaulted ceiling painted in fresco; remains of paint were still visible in 1820, above a ceiling added at a later date.

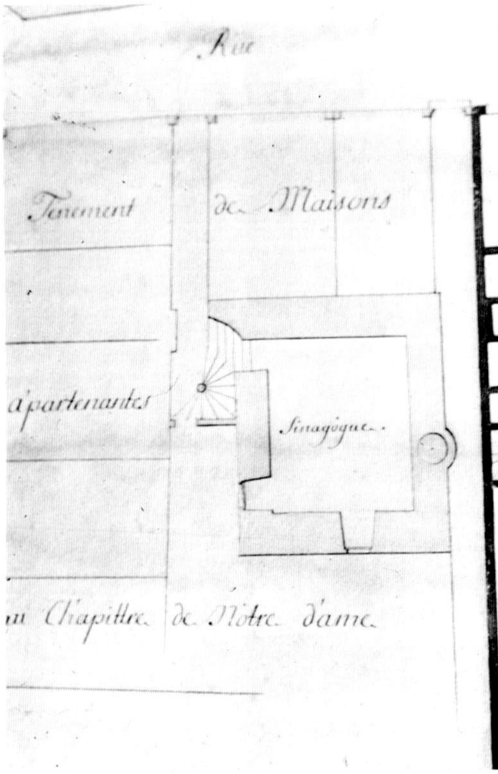

Figure 103. Rouen, medieval synagogue, plan, drawn in 18th century.

In 1976, excavators working in the forecourt of the Palace of Justice at Rouen unearthed well-cut stone walls of a rectangular building datable between ca. 1097 and 1116. The structure measures 14.14 m. by 9.46 m. on the exterior, but the 1.60 m. wall thickness reduces the interior measurement to about 11 m. by 6.3 m. The walls survive to a height of about 4 m. in some places, although the remains are now below the modern street level; about 2 m. were below the medieval street level. The building had at least two storeys originally, and the lowest storey had windows only on the north. A stair tower of cramped dimensions rises at one corner of the building.

Hebrew graffiti on the walls, and information about the medieval Jewish quarter available in old descriptions of the city, support the identification of this imposing structure as one built for Jewish use. While Bernhard Blumenkranz believes that it was a synagogue, Norman Golb believes that it was the house of study that served the large number of Jewish scholars recorded later in twelfth-century Rouen. An old description of the city identifies the house of study as lying on the north side of the Jews' street, as this building does. Since there are no other plans or remains of Norman synagogues of so early a date, and none of any monumental houses of study, debate about the identification of this Jewish monument may continue until the scholars are able to reconcile their views.

Draguignan

The synagogue, probably of the thirteenth century, was built into the corner of a square tower of the city ramparts, a position—close to the walls—that was well known in other towns. The remains consist of the ground and first floors of the 23 m.-long facade and a vaulted room inside. The finely cut stone facade has four arched openings on the ground floor, arranged symmetrically, with the two center bays being wider. There are four twin windows on the first floor, but they have been blocked. The squarish room inside has a curious vaulting arrangement: The four arches meet in the center; their thrusts are deflected to the walls by other arches. If the bimah and ark lay at opposite ends of the room, the designer may have left the center free in order to improve sight lines. As the synagogue has a longer north-south axis, a central pier would have further reduced the visual impressiveness of the east-west axis, which is more important from a liturgical point of view. The building has not been used as a synagogue for centuries, perhaps since 1481, the probable date of the Jews' expulsion from the town.

Mende

The remains are not those of the principal medieval synagogue, but they indicate that this synagogue had more than one storey. An arched and molded door leads from the street to a courtyard, with some pointed and some round arches sustaining galleries above. A rectilinear basement was either the women's synagogue or the ritual bath—perhaps the former if ventilation holes in the barrel vault connected the men's and women's areas. The building antedates 1306, when it was confiscated.

Trets

The facade alone survives of this twelfth-century synagogue. The two-storey facade, 12 m. wide and 8 m. high, has two arched portals on the ground floor, 3.3 m. and 2.5 m. wide, with large keystones. The upper floor has two Romanesque twin-arched windows with the arches separated by a small column. Stringcourses run below these windows.

BIBLIOGRAPHIES

ROUEN

B. Blumenkranz, "Un ensemble synagogal à Rouen: 1096–1116," *Académie des Inscriptions et Belles-Lettres. Comptes rendus des séances de l'année 1976,* Paris, 1976, séance of Dec. 3, 1976, pp. 663–87.

———, "La synagogue à Rouen (env. 1100)," *Archives juives* XIII (1977), pp. 37–44.

———, ed. *Art et archéologie des juifs en France médiévale,* Toulouse, 1980 (Collection Franco-Judaica 9), containing on pp. 231–303: M. Bayle, "Les monuments juifs de Rouen et l'architecture romane"; B. Blumenkranz, "La synagogue de Rouen"; G. Duval, "Découverte, conservation, et présentation de l'édifice juif d'époque romane de Rouen"; D. Halbout-Bertin, "Rapport sommaire de la fouille."

G. Duval, "Découverte d'un monument hébraïque roman," *Les monuments historiques de France,* 1977, #4, pp. 13–16.

R. Eder, "In France, Ancient Site Yields to a Parking

Lot," *New York Times,* Aug. 1, 1982 (on the nearby house of a rich Jew).
N. Golb, "Exceptionnelle découverte à Rouen: les vestiges d'une école hébraïque du XIIe s.," *Archéologia* #129 (April 1979), pp. 8–33.
———, "The Forgotten Jewish History of Mediaeval Rouen," *Archeology* XXX (1977), pp. 254–63, 314–25.
———, "Localisation de l'ancienne académie juive et de la synagogue monumentale," *Les monuments historiques de France,* 1977, #4, pp. 17–19.
———, "Nature et destination du monument juif découvert à Rouen," *Proceedings of the American Academy of Jewish Research* XLVIII (1981), pp. 101–76, with further bibliography.

DRAGUIGNAN

B. Blumenkranz, "Le sauvetage de la synagogue de Draguignan," *L'Arche* #76 (May 1963), pp. 48–51.
Bulletin de la Société d'Études Scientifiques et Archéologiques de Draguignan XLIII (1940–41), meeting of May 6, 1941.
Équipe de recherche "208," "Inventaire archéologique," *Art et archéologie des juifs en France médiévale,* ed. B. Blumenkranz, Toulouse, 1980, pp. 332–35 (Collection Franco-Judaica 9).
File in Ministry of Culture, Caisse Nationale des Monuments Historiques, Paris.

MENDE

A. Lunel, "La synagogue de Mende," *L'Arche* #87 (April 1964), pp. 38–39.
M. Pinzuti, "Les juifs du Gevaudan," *L'Arche* #112 (June 1966), p. 27.
J. Sabbath, "Plaidoyer pour la synagogue de Mende," *L'Arche* #112 (June 1966), pp. 24–27.

TRETS

File in Ministry of Culture, Caisse Nationale des Monuments Historiques, Paris.
A. Lunel, "L'ancienne synagogue de Trets," *L'Arche* #120 (Feb. 1967), pp. 42–43.

Carpentras and Cavaillon

Visitors who enter the synagogues of Carpentras and Cavaillon in southern France are invariably surprised to see prayer halls that seem to be charming rooms in a local mansion. Remodeled in 1741–44 and 1772–74 respectively, the synagogues have wood paneling with classical and rococo motifs that would have been at home in Parisian salons a generation before the styles were absorbed in these provincial towns. The rooms suggest anything but the mystical power of the contemporary four-pillared and wooden synagogues in eastern Europe. The comparison shows that there is no standard mood in Jewish religious architecture.

These French synagogues are unusual in other respects, for they are the only survivors of a group of synagogues located in the Comtat Venaissin and the territory of Avignon. Because these areas were papal possessions from the thirteenth century until the French Revolution, the Jews there were not affected by the expulsion of Jews from France decreed by the French king in 1394. Jewish communities established at various times—by the thirteenth century at Carpentras, in the fifteenth at Cavaillon—were distributed around the Comtat Venaissin until 1624, when a papal decree restricted them to the towns just mentioned, to L'Isle-sur-Sorgue within the Comtat, and to Avignon outside it. This regulation led to the destruction of existing synagogues elsewhere, as had occurred at Noves and Bedarrides during an earlier expulsion of 1322, and probably led to Jewish migration to the four authorized towns. Known collectively as the *Arba'ah Kehillot* (Four Communities), these isolated communities developed a distinctive local liturgy and culture, with a special prayer book, dialect, holiday food, and synagogue plans.

The buildings were nondescript externally, located in cramped Jewish quarters, known as *carrières* in French, to which the Jews were confined in the fifteenth century. The Carpentras *carrière,* perhaps the worst, had about 160 families living within a perimeter of 72 m. by 55 m. between 1746 and 1758, and a quarter of the families received charity. One consequence of the crowding was that—as in Frankfurt and Venice—the ghetto houses grew to seven and eight storeys, so that when seen from afar, ironically, the *carrière* of Carpentras was the most imposing part of town.

Carpentras

A synagogue was established near the ramparts of Carpentras, probably in the thirteenth century. In 1322, when the Jews were expelled from various localities in the Comtat, the Carpentras synagogue became the site of a church dedicated to the Virgin. When the Jews returned in 1343–44, they moved to their permanent location in the town center. The 1344 synagogue, in a house rented from a local notary, was allowed on condition that it not be higher or bigger than the pre-1322 building, which was just under 14 m. long and just under 8 m. wide and high. The 1344 synagogue was a bit less than 10 m. by 8 m. by 8 m. When the lease expired in 1367, a new synagogue was allowed providing it was no larger than the previous one. For this privilege the Jewish community had to give the bishop six pounds of spices and money as well as extra payment each time a synagogue seat changed hands. The synagogue of 1367 included a men's area perhaps originally no larger than the present bimah gallery, with the women accommodated in a room underneath it. A matzah bakery and ritual bath were located in two basement levels. These premises were all superimposed rather than distributed around a courtyard because there was no space in the *carrière* for them to spread. Until the eighteenth century, the women's areas at Carpentras and Avignon—and surely elsewhere—were linked to the men's only by a small square opening in the floor of the men's space, near the ark, so that the women could see the Torah when the scrolls were removed or replaced. In 1599, Thomas Platter, a Swiss visitor, described a women's separate service in Hebrew mixed with the vernacular, led by a blind rabbi in the dark subordinate women's space at Avignon. Haim Joseph David Azulai, an eighteenth-century visitor, said that in the Comtat Venaissin, women's prayers were recited in the vernacular. Since in 1808 the fifty-eight Jewish adults at Cavaillon included twenty-two women, all illiterate, one may suppose that women in the *Arba'ah Kehillot* had never been expected to participate in the synagogue services by reading the prayers in Hebrew.

In 1677, the Carpentras synagogue was in ruinous condition and was repaired. Repairs were made again in 1730, this time to a raised area or tribune, referred to as the former men's synagogue. It seems, then, that by this time, the synagogue was raised in height to about 16.3 m., making the area that once had held all the men into a blocked-off appendage of the principal, taller space. Documents suggest that the synagogue then had some wall paneling and a small eastern window opening rather more like an air hole than a proper window, and that the tribune received light from an octagonal cupola or lantern because it was still separated from the new, taller, main men's area and could not benefit from the lighting in the latter.

By 1741, when the community had grown to 752 individuals, the old synagogue was thoroughly decrepit. Permission was obtained to remodel the building (Figs. 104, 105). A local civil engineer, Antoine d'Allemand, was chosen as the architect. He had just designed an aqueduct and the town hall, and was rumored to be a freemason, which may mean that he was more open than the average man to the idea of working with non-Catholics. The Jews obtained approval to extend the synagogue toward church property at the east and to insert two adequate windows on that side. The building also was extended on the north and south sides. The remodeling produced a vaulted room, 15.7 m. by 8.7 m., located above the former women's synagogue, which was abandoned. The men sat on benches around walls lined with wooden panels and grilled arches separated by fluted Tuscan pilasters below a Doric frieze and a terminal balustrade. The painted wooden ark, raised on a low platform at the east, is framed in panels of carved stucco and set off by iron railings. It is more elaborate in style than the

Figure 104. Carpentras, remodeled 1741, interior to ark (Photograph by DANIEL FRANCK, *Paris).*

Figure 105. Carpentras, interior to bimah (Photograph by DANIEL FRANCK, *Paris).*

sober wall paneling elsewhere in the room, and may be of a different date.

At the west rises a tribune or balcony, 9.5 m. by 6.3 m., supported on fluted Tuscan columns and extending into a recess in what was, perhaps, the area of the original men's synagogue, which now forms part of the enlarged main space. Upon this balcony stands the bimah table with thin columns rising from each corner to support scrolls that meet in the center. This little tabernacle echoes with a faint whisper the design of Bernini's canopy over the high altar at St. Peter's in the Vatican, a canopy whose columns are said in legend to look like those in the Temple of Jerusalem. We do not know whether Antoine d'Allemand ordered this as an allusion to the pope who ruled Carpentras, or whether it was simply a design popular for tabernacles at the time. The elevated bimah is known in Italian synagogues, such as those of Ancona, Pesaro, and Venice, and Jews of the *Arba'ah Kehillot* had closer ties to the Jews of Italy than to those elsewhere. The balcony also holds seats for the synagogue officials and three seven-branched candlesticks, two of the Napoleonic period and one of the Restoration period.

Women sat in grilled enclosures raised a bit above the men's floor level. On the south, a balustraded gallery rises above the grilled women's area. As it is not enclosed it may, if meant for women, be later than the grilled area below it. In 1858, part of a ruined house at the north was bought to provide a tribune there as well.

At the floor level of the bimah and the side galleries, the synagogue is wider and longer than it is at the men's floor level. It is 18.9 m. by 9.7 m., about 62 feet by 38 feet.

A singular feature of the Carpentras and Cavaillon synagogues is a niche placed several feet above floor level near the ark, containing a small chair about half a meter high, called the Chair of Elijah. It was placed near the ark during the circumcision ceremony, which the prophet Elijah, protector of children, was invited to attend. In other synagogues, larger benches or chairs usually are kept in storerooms when not in use. The chairs in the Comtadin synagogues, however, are always on display and are too small to be sat upon so they must have been ceremonial or symbolic. Their meaning is uncertain, although it may be connected to the empty throne, awaiting the coming of its owner, which is seen in various contexts in earlier Jewish and Christian art. The bishop's cathedra at St. Peter's in the Vatican is elevated on the focal wall. Is it conceivable that the Comtadin synagogues contain references to the seat of authority of the pope who ruled the *Arba'ah Kehillot*?

A terrace on the roof at the northeast was used for ceremonies of the new moon and for building the booth at the Sukkot festival. This location saved space and assured privacy.

The mid-eighteenth-century work, planned and executed primarily between 1741 and 1744, did not end quickly. Litigation dragged on, and authorities investigated charges that the synagogue was taller than several churches. Church authorities wanted the building reduced in height, pointing out that the Jews had sunk to their subordinate station in society through their own fault, and should be obliged to look as lowly as they were. The synagogue's east windows were blocked but later unblocked, the main room was reduced in size, and the authorities ordered the west (bimah) tribune sealed from the rest of the room. The disputes terminated only with the Revolution, or shortly before if the date of 1784 on the tablets of the Law near the ark celebrates accord between Jews and Christians.

During the Revolution, the synagogue was closed and, like other places of worship at the time, was despoiled of its precious metal, carved woodwork, chandeliers, and precious fabrics. While the building served as a Jacobin clubhouse, the costly objects went to a government warehouse, destined to be sold or melted down. Nevertheless, the Jews repossessed the synagogue in 1800; three of the present lighting fixtures date from the seventeenth century and may be original furnishings that were given back.

The post-Napoleonic period brought few fundamental changes, despite several restorations and modifications. In 1885, a new entrance was made in the rue de la Juiverie, supplementing the one from the Place de la Juiverie. In 1865–91 and later, demolition of the old ghetto produced the present plaza with the Town Hall on one side. In 1900, the synagogue was restored at the initiative of the rabbi of Avignon and a Jewish layman. In 1923, the woodwork was painted dark brown, except for that of the ark area, which was painted to imitate marble. In the following year, the government proclaimed the building a historic monument, leading to further restoration in 1929–30. In 1936, the roofs, already in bad condition in 1923, were repaired, as were the water pipes. Between 1950 and 1953, the masonry as well as the interior were repaired. Some of the funds came from Louis Schweitzer of New York, who owned a local industry. The French government also supported this work. In 1970, when the community had only a few elderly survivors, 150 Jews from North Africa were relocated in the town and they now provide a congregation for the building.

Figure 106. Cavaillon, 1772–74, exterior (Photograph by ROGER-VIOLLET, *Paris).*

Cavaillon

Cavaillon's synagogue is a smaller, stone-faced building. The first synagogue erected on the site near the town ramparts in 1499 is the core of the present one built in 1772–74 under the direction of Antoine Armelin and his son Pierre, master masons of Cavaillon (Fig. 106).

The building bridges a street at the entrance to the *carrière,* so that the interior had to be reached by an exterior stairway, moved to its present position in 1901 to allow better circulation in the street. The stairs lead to a balcony with a carved portal giving access to the men's area. During the fifteenth century, the women sat on the ground floor, but in the present synagogue they occupy a turret (with a lintel dated 1754) projecting from the body of the synagogue on the north side. The interior, about 9 m. long, 7.2 m. wide, and 8.3 m. high, is paneled in wood with rococo decorations at the top of each panel (Fig. 107). More than any other feature, it is the cheerful, domestic-scale woodwork that gives the Comtadin synagogues a disconcertingly secular appearance. At Cavaillon there are shells, fruit baskets, leaves, and festoons, the work of Jean-Joseph Charmot, a sculptor from L'Isle-sur-Sorgue.

The ark extends into a niche, the land needed for this extension having been bought in 1773. The purchase suggests that the earlier ark may have been a chest inside the room, as was usual before the eighteenth century. The bimah here, as in Carpentras, stands on a balcony held on fluted Corinthian columns, and it is enclosed by a fine wrought-iron grille. In the center of the balcony is a bimah table of undulating oval form supporting four columns from which hang carved curtains painted light blue. Garlands of roses twist around the columns.

Apparently, the work done here by fine local craftsmen was well enough appreciated to attract a municipal donation of five hundred francs for urgent repairs in 1853. In 1864, a house that concealed the entrance side of the synagogue was torn down, and the sustaining wall under the entrance balcony was rebuilt. In

1876, the city bought and demolished a part of the building adjacent to the synagogue on the north, so that the turret is now visible. In 1901, the entrance stairs were moved. As of 1922, all the paneled and sculptured woodwork was painted sea green with gilded highlights, and the pretty synagogue gained historic monument designation in 1924. This stimulated the repair of the roof in 1928 and a general restoration in 1930. In 1950, André Dumoulin, who later published a book about this building, discovered older synagogue fragments, including two sixteenth-century tabernacle doors showing the fruits and flowers of Sukkot, but with the virtual disappearance of the congregation there was no one to use these appurtenances. A scales-maker set up his workshop illegally on the ground floor in 1952 but, as he was in an official historic monument, he was forced to leave. In 1961 and 1963, the north facade was cleaned and damaged parts of the entrance balcony were replaced.

Both synagogues had a matzah bakery and ritual bath in the immediate vicinity. At Carpentras, one reaches the dimly-lit cellar bakery from a courtyard at the south. The room contains a preparation table donated by a pious woman in 1652. In the sub-basement lies the ritual bath in a cold and gloomy rock-cut chamber. In 1886 a more comfortable bath was provided elsewhere. At Cavaillon, the ritual bath is in a small court off the main Jewish street, twelve steps down in a vaulted cellar 4 m. long, 2 m. wide, and 5 m. deep. The bakery below the synagogue now houses a museum of Judeo-Comtadin history.

Figure 107. Cavaillon, interior from bimah gallery to ark (Photograph by DANIEL FRANCK, *Paris).*

BIBLIOGRAPHY

F. Ambrière, ed., *Guide religieuse de la France,* Paris, 1967, pp. 595–96, 632.

Archives Nationales, File F 11120.

L. Bardinet, "Antiquité et organisation des juiveries du Comtat Venaissin," *Revue des études juives* IV (1880), pp. 262–92.

———, "Documents relatifs à l'histoire des juifs dans le Comtat Venaissin," *Revue des études juives* VII (1883), pp. 139–46.

J. Bauer, "Les troupes du Maréchal de Belle-Isle et les juifs du Comtat Venaissin, 1746–58," *Revue des études juives* XXVII (1893), pp. 263–68.

B. Blumenkranz, *Histoire des juifs en France,* Toulouse, 1972, pp. 203–5.

——— and Monique Lévy, *Bibliographie des juifs en France,* Toulouse, 1974 (Collection Franco-Judaica).

T. Brun, *Les juifs du Pape à Carpentras,* Carpentras, 1975.

H. Chobaut, "Les juifs d'Avignon et du Comtat et la Révolution française. Fin des Quatre Carrières (1787–1800)," *Revue des études juives,* n.s. I (= CI) (Jan.–June 1937), pp. 5–52; n.s. II (= CII) (July–Dec. 1937), pp. 3–39.

———, "Notes archéologiques sur Cavaillon," *Mémoires de l'académie de Vaucluse,* XXXIII (1933), pp. 48–51.

J. de Dianous, "Les communautés juives du Comtat Venaissin et de l'état d'Avignon d'après leurs statuts (1490–1790)," summarized in *Positions des thèses de l'École Nationale des Chartes,* 1938, pp. 31–36; 1939, pp. 53–59.

A. Dumoulin, *Un joyau de l'art judaïque français. La synagogue de Cavaillon,* Paris, 1970.

Équipe de recherche "208," "Inventaire archéologique," *Art et archéologie des juifs en France médiévale,* ed. B. Blumenkranz, Toulouse, 1980 (Collection Franco-Judaica 9), pp. 321–23.

Files of the Caisse Nationale des Monuments Historiques.
H. Gross, *Gallia Judaica.* Paris, 1897, reprint ed., Amsterdam, 1969, Carpentras, pp. 605–13; Cavaillon, pp. 538–40.
P. Lavedan, "Les synagogues de Carpentras et de Cavaillon," *Congrès archéologique de France* CXXI (1946), pp. 307–11.
I. Loeb, "Les juifs de Carpentras sous le gouvernement pontifical," *Revue des études juives* XII (1886), pp. 34–64, 161–235.
M. Lowenthal, *A World Passed By,* New York, 1933, p. 111.
A. Lunel, "Les synagogues comtadins," *L'Oeil,* #4 (Apr. 15, 1955), pp. 14–17.
R. de Maulde, *Les juifs dans les états français du Saint Siège au Moyen Âge,* Paris, 1886.
A. Mossé, *Histoire des juifs d'Avignon et du Comtat Venaissin,* Paris, 1934.
Thomas Platter d.J., *Beschreibung der Reisen durch Frankreich, Spanien, England, und die Niederlaende, 1595–1600,* Basel and Stuttgart (1968), p. 128.
C. Roth, "Jüdische Brauche im Comtat Venaissin," *Menorah* V, #4 (1927), pp. 256–60.
———, "The Liturgies of Avignon and the Comtat Venaissin," *Journal of Jewish Bibliography* I, (1938–39), pp. 99–105. Addenda by A. Marx refer to liturgical studies.
Z. Szajkowski, "Die Geshikhte fun Karpentraser Beis Keneses in 18ten Jahrhundert," *YIVO-Bleter* XXIII (1944), pp. 149–52.
———, "Synagogues during the French Revolution, 1789–1800," *Jewish Social Studies* XX (1958), pp. 215–31, esp. pp. 220, 224.
Wischnitzer, *Architecture,* pp. 69–75.

Paris

The Jewish presence in Paris is documented intermittently from the sixth century onward. During the Middle Ages, there were synagogues in the Jewish districts on the right and left banks as well as on the Ile de la Cité where the famous flower market was later established. We know of a twelfth-century synagogue there, a building 8 m. wide and 31 m. long, which Philip Augustus expropriated in 1182 and gave to the Bishop of Paris who transformed it into the church of St. Mary Magdalen. The Jews were expelled from and readmitted to Paris regularly between that date and their definitive expulsion in 1394. During their years of residence, they erected new synagogues in the rue de la Tacherie and the rue du Franc-Mourier. For almost four hundred years after 1394, there were no publicly acknowledged synagogues in Paris and there were no Jews known as such in Paris during the fifteenth and sixteenth centuries. After about 1720, Avignonese and Sephardic Jews from Bordeaux settled in an area centering on the rue St. André-des-Arts, while Ashkenazic Jews from Metz settled in a poorer area on the right bank near Les Halles, worshipping in inns where they set up illegal prayer rooms. Only in 1788 was there a publicly acknowledged synagogue, established by the Ashkenazic Jews in rue Brisemiche.

Two years later, the Sephardic and Avignonese Jews received full citizenship rights, a year before Ashkenazic Jews received them in 1791. This enabled all Jews to build synagogues freely, and we know of four in 1792: in rue Brisemiche, rue des Petits-Champs, rue St. Martin, and rue du Renard. During the Reign of Terror, the Jews had to pray secretly in a cellar, but afterward they were able to reopen the earlier synagogues or establish new ones.

Under Napoleon, in 1808, the Jews in France and in all the territories ruled by France were organized into regional consistories which received tax revenue to help build synagogues. The government tried to limit the number of synagogues, and because the large synagogues needed large congregations to assure their financial stability, the consistory directors supported government efforts to keep down the number of separate prayer rooms.

Rue Notre Dame de Nazareth

By 1815, the Paris consistory governed about two hundred Sephardic, a hundred Avignonese, and 2,400 Ashkenazic Jews who worshipped in five synagogues and several smaller prayer rooms. When the landlord of the rue St.-Avoye synagogue declined to renew the lease, the

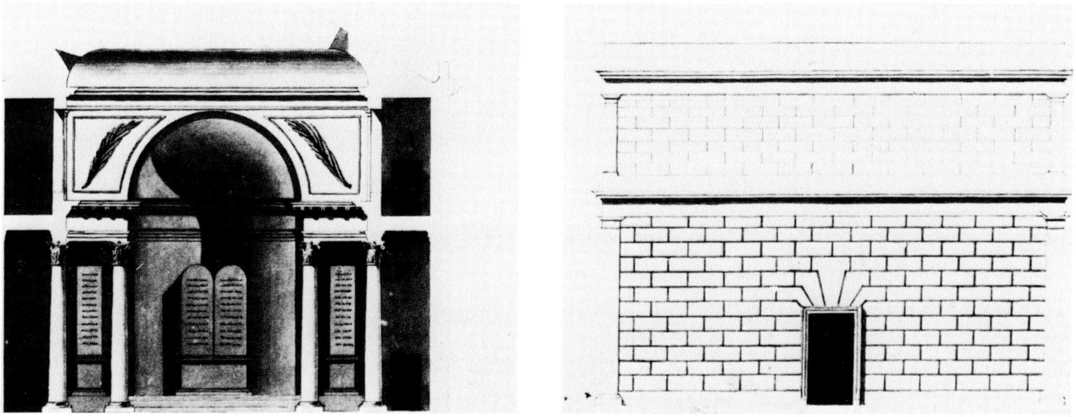

Figure 108. Paris, rue Notre Dame de Nazareth, 1819, facade and cross section drawn by J. P. Sandrié and Jacob Silveyra.

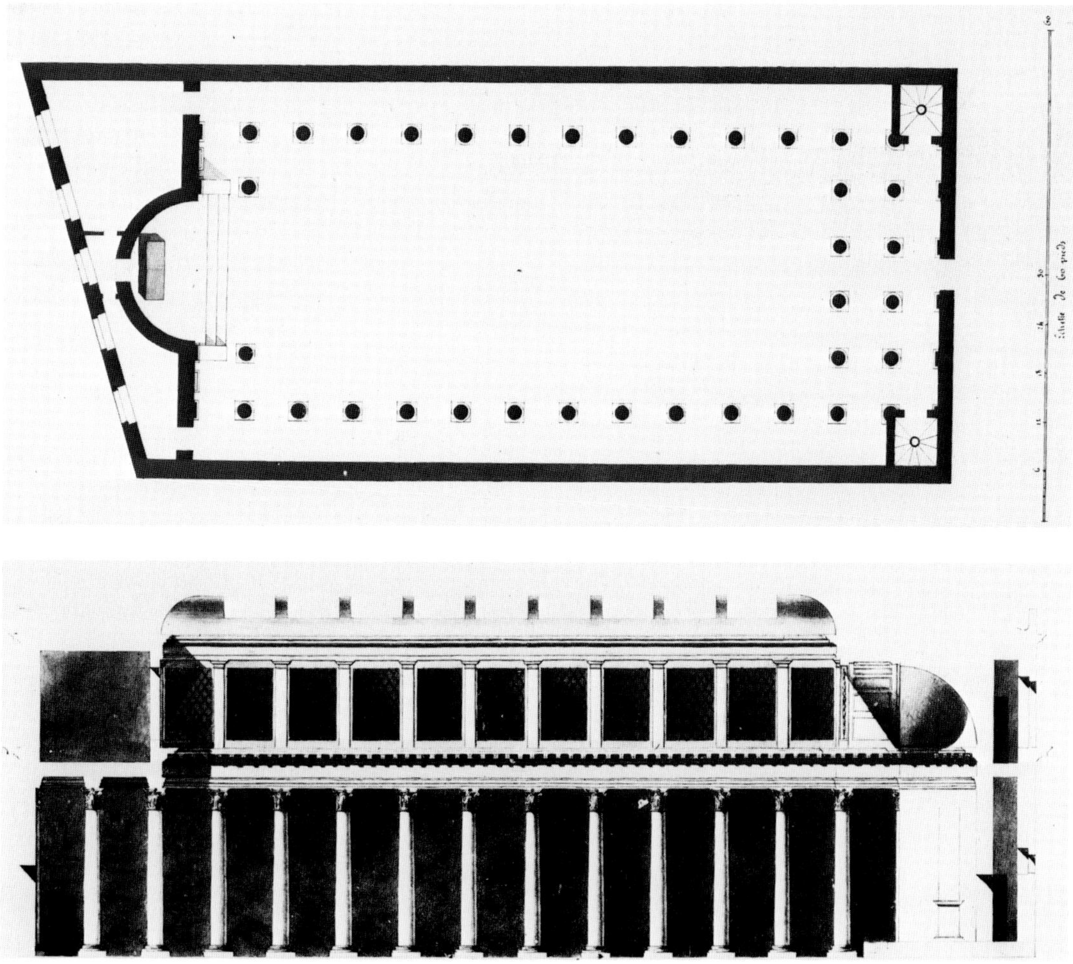

Figure 109. Paris, rue Notre Dame de Nazareth, plan and longitudinal section drawn by J. P. Sandrié and Jacob Silveyra.

Jews made plans for a new synagogue in 1817 and bought land for it in 1818. In 1819, building began on a large public Ashkenazic synagogue for a thousand worshippers in rue Notre Dame de Nazareth (Figs. 108, 109). Its designers were J. P. Sandrié, a Christian of Belgian origin, and Jacob Silveyra (1785–?), whose Portuguese name and Bordeaux birthplace suggest that he was a Sephardic Jew or a descendant of one—especially as he was one of the architects of a Sephardic synagogue established with private funds in rue Lamartine (1851).

The consistorial synagogue was a handsome galleried basilica, inaugurated in 1822. It was about 33 m. long and 16 m. wide (105 × 50 Parisian feet), including the outer walls. Tuscan columns carried the galleries and stood beneath Ionic pilasters between the screens in front of the women's galleries. A triumphal arch framed the simple ark recess, crowned by large tablets of the Law. Light entered through windows cut into the barrel vault in every other bay. Only a few details modified the chaste severity of the room. There were lyre-shaped lamps suspended between the columns, fronds in the spandrels of the ark-recess arch, and thin iron railings in a repetitive Gothic lancet design around the ark and the bimah. The bimah stood near the center of the room. Adjoining a column near the bimah was a cylindrical pulpit for the sermons that were introduced into the somewhat modernized service. The arrangements were close to those of the Ashkenazic Great Synagogue in London of 1790–91 (see Fig. 245). With the newly acquired civil rights in the early nineteenth century, synagogues comparable to that of Paris were built in Bordeaux and Bayonne for Sephardic Jews, and in Munich and London-Great St. Helen's for Ashkenazic Jews.

The pace of building could not keep up with the Jewish population of Paris. Moreover, in 1850, Jewish leaders pointed out in a letter to the Prefect of Paris that the 1822 synagogue was in ruinous condition and could not possibly serve the city's 15,000 Jews. Plans for a new synagogue had, in fact, been initiated in 1849, and Gottfried Semper submitted a design to one of the Rothschilds, hoping in vain to obtain the commission for a large new synagogue. But during the next few years only the Sephardic synagogue of 1851 in the rue Lamartine and a private chapel at 44 rue de la Victoire (1852) opened to more than tiny groups.

Enlargement of the 1822 building was effected by the architect J. A. Thierry (1794–1863), who finished the Jewish hospital in 1852, when the altered synagogue reopened. He created mixed Romanesque-Byzantine-Moorish forms with some Egyptian-inspired features crowning the facade, showing that the French Jews, like those elsewhere at this period, were willing to announce their separate identity. Baron de Rothschild had sent Thierry to Italy in 1850 to seek a suitable model for rebuilding the synagogue, but the architect evidently came back without good ideas, for his cheaply executed eclectic designs were criticized in the next generation as being vulgar, like the ornament of a "café-concert Alcázar." At least one of his economies was practical—his use of iron construction—but as was customary at the time, he concealed the iron with masonry. With only 1,200 seats, the synagogue was immediately inadequate, for there were almost 25,000 Jews in Paris in 1858.

Rue de la Victoire

In 1859, the consistory officials wrote again to the Prefect of Paris about the crowded conditions and the need for subventions to finance a new synagogue. They in fact built two. One, replacing the private synagogue at 44 rue de la Victoire, became the seat of the Grand Rabbi and the Consistory of Paris. The other, in the rue des Tournelles, serving the older Jewish quarter in the fourth arrondissement, was designed by a Christian, M. E. Varcollier, an official district architect. The decision to build two large structures was greeted with general acclaim, but at least one community leader said that it would have been preferable to build ten small synagogues like the one that had just been set up in the Rothschild Orphanage, and not everyone believed there were enough worshippers to justify the rue de la Victoire synagogue. The consistory had found that two large sites would cost less than many small ones, and in any case the officials had a public presence to maintain.

The rue de la Victoire building was supposed to have a mixed Ashkenazic and Sephardic rite to unite both groups, but discussions on that subject ended in 1874, and the synagogue remained Ashkenazic. Daniel Osiris Iffla, a prominent Sephardi, then paid much of the cost of a nine-hundred-seat Sephardic synagogue in rue Buffault, designed by Stanislas Ferrand and opened in 1877.

The rue de la Victoire synagogue lies on a relatively narrow street (Fig. 110). Jewish officials had hoped to have the facade on the somewhat more conspicuous rue St.-Georges, from which one now enters the community offices, but the empress's confessor, reputedly a converted Jew, did not want the building to be visible on a well-used thoroughfare, so the congregation had to put up with the resulting incorrect orientation of the ark. Nevertheless, the synagogue and the community buildings were large, covering about 85 percent of a site of 2,400 square meters. In 1874, the year of the synagogue's dedication, a Jewish writer claimed that its nave-width of 17 m. was second only to that of the church of La Madeleine in Paris. Its nave height from floor to vault is 28.1 m., higher than that of Noyon cathedral. The synagogue is 44 m. long from the entrance to the sanctuary.

The site, synagogue, and community buildings at rue de la Victoire cost 3,260,000 francs, or 1,557 francs per square meter of covered surface. By comparison, the cost of a slightly earlier Roman Catholic church, St. Augustin (1860–71) by Victor Baltard, cost 5,700,000 francs or about 2,000 francs per square meter. The large rue des Tournelles synagogue (1861–76) cost only 840,000 francs, or about 840 francs per square meter.

The synagogue facade recedes about 3 m. from the street line. Narrow side bays flank a broad central section with a recessed open

Figure 110. Paris, rue de la Victoire, 1861–74.

porch, two rows of windows above it, and a large curved gable. The curved gable as a crowning feature can be traced back several decades (for example, to the chapel of St. Ferdinand, 1843, by Fontaine and Lefranc); it may have been inspired by Byzantine churches such as the twelfth-century Kalenderhane Camii in Istanbul, and it is known in some Italian Renaissance churches, although these are less like the synagogue than are the other examples just mentioned. The synagogue facade inspired later ones including those of rue des Tournelles and rue Buffault in Paris, and others in Florence and Nancy.

Beyond the porch is a vestibule from which one reaches stairways to the galleries and congregational meeting rooms. The prayer hall is a galleried basilica with widely spaced supports which bear round arches (Fig. 111). On the gallery supports are relatively short Romanesque piers which carry taller and slimmer half-columns in the same style, a set of proportions comparable to that of the London New Synagogue (1838 by John Davies), the Berlin-Heidereutergasse as remodeled in 1856, and others. The combination of expansive arches and two tiers of supports lends to the Paris synagogue an impression of openness combined with solidity. Domes over the gallery bays, as seen from the barrel-vaulted nave and through the round arches of the gallery, create a strong but lively play of curves, an effect which compensates for the pedestrian quality of the detail.

The vaulted ark recess resembles a raised choir. Twelve windows there, made by Husson, Lefèvre, and Oudinet, are inscribed with the names of the twelve tribes of Israel, and five round windows contain the names of the books of the Pentateuch. The most elaborate decoration, reserved for the ark niche, includes marble columns framing the entrance, an iron grille near the steps leading to the ark, enamel ornament on the wall, and colored glass, a Rothschild gift, in the two windows.

At the entrance to the ark recess stood a small organ and seats for the choir, while just below the choir were seats for the synagogue

Figure 111. Paris, rue de la Victoire, interior to ark in 1980.

and consistorial officials. The bimah is now near them, at the ark end of the nave, but older plans and descriptions show it closer to the center of the nave. The elaboration of the ark end and the moving of the bimah exemplify the arrangements in European synagogues touched, however lightly, by Reform, and more firmly by businesslike, worldly ideas of orderliness and efficiency.

Also characteristic of consistorial synagogues in France was the separation of the sexes but the absence of high grilles. Originally, women occupied the aisle galleries and another gallery over the entrance. At present, the women sit in the ground floor aisles except during High Holy Days when enough men attend services to fill the aisle seats. A second gallery in front of the organ accommodated impoverished men for whom there was no room downstairs. The organ, too, is a feature of synagogues affected by the Reform movement.

The architect of the synagogue and community house was Alfred Philibert Aldrophe (1834–95), a Jew who worked mainly for the government on international expositions (1855, 1862), and who became a Chevalier of the Legion of Honor. The consistory employed him to make preliminary plans for the synagogue in 1861, and he drew up the later ones for the community buildings in 1867. He exhibited views of the rue de la Victoire synagogue at the Vienna Exposition of 1873. For Jewish clients, he designed the Rothschild Orphanage, the house of Gustave de Rothschild, and the synagogue at Versailles (1886), also financed by the Rothschilds. In addition, Aldrophe is said to have had something to do with the design of the consistorial synagogue in the rue des Tournelles.

Aldrophe understood commonsense requirements. A contemporary critic praised him for having provided an open porch recessed from the street, so that people could be deposited from carriages in a sheltered area during inclement weather; that would be of particular interest to female wedding guests who would worry about their appearance! Aldrophe designed convenient staircases to the galleries and offices above the porch. He provided a cloakroom and a wedding reception room that could be converted into a weekday synagogue. His courtyard is roofed with a metal and glass canopy that serves as a tabernacle at the Sukkot festival. The synagogue has space to hold five thousand people sitting and standing; fourteen entrances provide easy access and unobtrusive exits during the day-long High Holy Day services.

Aldrophe chose Romanesque rather than Moorish style because Romanesque admitted large, bare surfaces and little ornament. A good job of Moorish decoration would have required ornamenting every surface and cutting capitals and moldings in unfamiliar shapes. Perhaps the local Jews also wanted to avoid the taint of exoticism and the danger of building another "café-concert Alcázar." Moreover, neo-Romanesque style was used for the prominent Parisian churches of St. Ambroise and St. Augustin in the 1860s, when the synagogue was first proposed. A Romanesque synagogue would thus be fashionably French without being Gothic French. A sturdy Romanesque style with interior building parts in comparable proportions was adopted in the 1860s by two other Jewish architects—Abraham Hirsch at Lyon and Edwin Oels Oppler in his church-like synagogues at Hannover and Wrocław. The architects may have known about each other's designs and might even have been personal acquaintances, as Oppler had studied in Paris.

Aldrophe guided his buildings through a protracted construction period. Work was interrupted several times, most notably by the Franco-Prussian War and the Commune. Indeed, at the synagogue dedication in September 1874, the Grand Rabbi, Zadoc Kahn, proclaimed the building to be "proof that . . . France . . . has the right to take off its mourning clothes and celebrate anew the feasts of the spirit, of art, and of religion." The building, he said, would affirm the idea of all religions living in harmony. Although that harmony was not always evident, particularly when the building was bombed in October 1941, the synagogue—restored and rededicated—bears witness to the stolid strength of the Parisian Ashkenazic Jewish "establishment." At the present time, when the consistory is no longer state-affiliated, when over a third of the Jews in metropolitan Paris are Sephardic from North Africa, and when fewer than 40 percent of French Jews attend synagogue services regularly, the centrality of this synagogue has been diminished. All the same, it has kept its place as the great ceremonial synagogue and the most representative architecture of Jewry in the French capital, serving Ashkenazim in the main building and Tunisian and Egyptian congregations in the weekday synagogue or other rooms of the consistorial buildings.

BIBLIOGRAPHY

P. C. Albert, *The Modernization of French Jewry,* Hanover, N.H., 1977, esp. pp. 220–21.

Archives israélites XXV (1874), p. 552.

Archives Nationales F 19, 11119.

Association Consistoriale Israélite de Paris, A A 6, Régistre des procès-verbaux 1874–1881; synagogue picture file.

J. Baissac, "Historique des synagogues israélites de Paris," *La voix de la vérité,* Aug. 20, 1851.

Benoît Lévy, "Causerie parisienne. L'orphélinat-Les nouveaux temples-La fondation Bischoffsheim," *Archives israélites* XXV (1874), pp. 395–400.

D. Bensimon, "Socio-Demographic Aspects of French Jewry," *European Judaism* XII, #1 (1978), pp. 12–16.

E. Brault, *Les architectes par leurs oeuvres,* Paris, 1893, vol. 3, p. 20.

Encyclopedia Judaica, s.v. Paris.

P. Girard, *Les juifs de France de 1789 à 1860,* Paris, 1976.

A. Halphen, *Recueil des lois, décrets, ordonnances . . . concernant les israélites depuis . . . 1789,* Paris, 1851.

E. Haymann, *Paris judaica,* Paris, 1979.

Inventaire général des oeuvres d'art appartenant à la ville de Paris, Paris, 1886.

Jewish Chronicle, Feb. 15, 1850, p. 151.

Jewish Encyclopedia, s.v. Paris.

"Le temple israélite du rite portugais," *Moniteur des architectes,* n.s. XII (1878), cols. 25–27 and pl. 10; for the 1852 synagogue, ibid. XIX (1853), pp. 220–27.

R. Marcel, *A Guide to Jewish Monuments,* Paris [1931].

F. Narjoux, *Paris. Monuments élévées par la ville 1850–1880. Édifices religieux,* Paris, 1883.

D. Philipson, *The Reform Movement in Judaism,* rev. ed., New York, 1931, p. 427.

L. Poliakov, "A Conflict between the German Army and Secret Police over the Bombing of Paris Synagogues," *Jewish Social Studies* XVI (1954), pp. 253ff.

H. Rosenau, "Gottfried Semper and German Synagogue Architecture," *Publications of the Leo Baeck Institute. Year Book* XXII (1977), pp. 237–44.

Z. Szajkowski, *Franco-Judaica. An Analytical Bibliography,* New York, 1962.

I am grateful to Roger Kohn, archivist, and MM. Linke and Bronner at the Consistoire offices, and Jonathan Helfand for information about Paris Jewry.

Rue Pavée

The synagogue in rue Pavée is the only one in pure *art nouveau* style (Fig. 112). One might expect such a design to have been made for liberal, assimilated Jews who sought the latest fashion in worship and in design, but it was built in 1911–13 for Yiddish-speaking recent immigrants to Paris from Russia and Rumania.

The rue Pavée is located in a working-class Jewish district, now partly gentrified but still home to tenements, kasher butcher shops, and small prayer rooms. The synagogue was meant to provide a consolidated house of worship to replace a group of small synagogues for the

Figure 112. Paris, rue Pavée, 1911–13, facade in 1985.

Polish Ashkenazic rite; this was not the modernized orthodox Ashkenazic rite used in synagogues of the Consistoire Israélite, the official religious agency before the law of 1905 separated church and state. Prior to that year, ritual dissidents were relegated to small private prayer rooms established with contributions given in addition to government religious taxes which supported only the state-connected consistorial synagogues. The rue Pavée synagogue would hardly have been possible until after 1905, when all religious contributions could go where the donors chose to send them.

The building in rue Pavée was the first strictly orthodox synagogue built in Paris after 1905, and the first large synagogue for the eastern European immigrants who had been coming to the city in large numbers. That they were not offered, and did not ask for, the underutilized consistorial synagogue in nearby rue des Tournelles was due to tension between the adherents of the now-private consistory organization and the immigrant group. The consistory, in its new nongovernmental form, had recently voted to admit to its membership only those Jews who had lived in France for ten years, with foreign-born Jews not to exceed a quarter of the membership. These rules were established by native French Jews, mainly of Alsatian origin, who did not speak eastern Yiddish. The consistorial archives and contemporary articles in the Jewish press contain abundant evidence of the antipathy felt by some of these culturally assimilated burghers toward the immigrants. The poverty of the newcomers, their inelegant appearance, and their use of Yiddish were felt to threaten the fragile social position and the charity funds of the native Jews.

The consistorial synagogues of Paris, Lyon, and Marseille, had been essentially Romanesque in style, as Gothic, classical, and Moorish had been rejected by most French consistories (and government supervisors?). The associated congregations at rue Pavée could not use the unacceptable styles, and surely did not want to use the Romanesque which the hostile consistory favored. Their only option was to use something entirely new, and they commissioned a remarkable building, far handsomer than the usual neighborhood synagogue, which might be a converted apartment (rue Saulnier), a converted warehouse (rue Ambroise Thomas), or a synagogue in a rear courtyard (rue Cadet). The leaders at rue Pavée were evidently prepared to adopt such new art forms in their new French home as did not interfere with essential aspects of religion. The well-established journal, *Archives israélites,* said that the airy and spacious new building would attract youth who had no taste for the older, cramped synagogues where they had been worshipping; perhaps a modern French style was chosen in part to help keep the interest of young Jews who might be tempted to stray from the faith along the secular byways of Paris.

It is not clear why the congregation employed Hector Guimard as their architect, although he was well known in Paris at the time. He was married to a woman of Jewish descent, née Adeline Oppenheim; she may have had some influence on the commission, in that Guimard was not obviously anti-Semitic. We do not know how closely she was linked to the Jewish community. The Guimards' marriage was solemnized in a church, but they emigrated when the Germans occupied France. A certain Mr. I. Landau probably chose the architect, as he was the major contributor to the building fund and countersigned the drawing for the facade. It is possible that the Russian Jews wanted to avoid the best-known Jewish architect of the period, Emmanuel Pontrémoli, because he had recently built a consistorial synagogue at Boulogne-sur-Seine in a more traditional style.

The architect faced the difficult task of making a synagogue for about a thousand people on a narrow, oblique plot in a narrow street. His ideas had to be modified at least twice, as we see from a drawing of the facade. Guimard sacrificed a few feet of space in order to set the building back from neighboring houses, which almost seem to squeeze the synagogue into its tall, bowed shape. The curving facade gives the building immediate distinctiveness and introduces the sinuous motion that characterized Guimard's style. The four-and-a-half-storey fa-

Figure 113. Paris, rue Pavée, interior to ark in 1980.

cade might sooner belong to an apartment house than to a traditional religious structure (it does contain residential quarters for the staff). The center of each storey is emphasized by closer-set and more numerous windows than are found in the recessed side bays. The entrance door is modest. There is no rose window. The top of the facade has only a curving contour rather than an elaborate cornice. The feature of greatest interest on the street front is the design of the openings, which undulate with an assured rhythm calculated to prevent disturbance of the modest dignity of the facade. Crisp, biting metalwork window grilles contrast beautifully with the whitish reinforced concrete of which the building was constructed.

The plan includes the rectangular galleried prayer hall and a vestibule (Fig. 113). From the vestibule one has access to the hall, galleries, a Talmud Torah school, offices, community rooms, and the stairs up to the apartments. At the ark end of the prayer hall, an enormous window attracts the eye and supplies natural light which is not available at the sides where the walls abut neighboring buildings. Guimard also provided skylights in the ceiling, as well as metal candelabra around the bimah and metal electric lamps with glass fixtures shaped like compact flames. The lamps project from slender piers which hold the two levels of galleries that were needed to accommodate the entire congregation. The reinforced concrete is partly disguised by markings on the piers that recall the edges of stone blocks. The suggestion of the traditionally noble material, stone, in the practical and space-saving material, concrete, represented a sensible compromise on the architect's part; he was not, after all, creating a building meant chiefly to express modernist theory about the frank expression of the nature of materials. Ornamental metalwork, one of Guimard's specialties, appears on the gallery railings, the bimah, the windows, and elsewhere in a wide variety of patterns. A characteristic detail is the design of the seat backs in a wave pattern. Although local tradition connects this form with the waves of the Red Sea, Guimard may simply have wanted to enliven the monotonous rows of seats and did so, as usual, with curves.

The building is not Guimard's masterpiece, but some flaws were unavoidable. If the interior proportions are cramped, stressing vertical extension, it is due to functional requirements. Although on a narrow site, the synagogue had to hold about a thousand people, with the women separated from the men. Guimard thus was forced to design a narrow-naved building bordered by aisles beneath several tiers of galleries. If the style shows a slackening of the architect's earlier brilliant snap and tension, the style chosen may be all the more appropriate for a house of worship than for a private house or Métro station. By this time in any case, advanced French architects were moving toward more sober forms, sometimes tinged with the historicist coloration that *art nouveau* had shunned. A few critics have even found hints of neo-Gothic here in the abundantly glazed facade and in the slender interior proportions.

In 1941, on the day before the holy day of Yom Kippur, the synagogue was severely damaged by a bomb during an anti-Semitic demonstration led by an egregious Fascist. On that occasion, six other Parisian synagogues suffered damage, including the large consistorial synagogues in rue Notre Dame de Nazareth, rue de la Victoire, and rue des Tournelles, as well as the Liberal synagogue in rue Copernic. The damage was repaired after the war when the remaining Jews could conduct public services again, and when new immigrants came from eastern Europe.

In addition to serving the needs of worshippers, the synagogue now is an attraction on walking tours offered by groups interested in urban architecture and historic preservation. When attention was given to the rich urban fabric of the Marais area, the synagogue facade and roof were included among the official Monuments Historiques of France.

BIBLIOGRAPHY

Archives de la Seine, série v.o., s.v. 10, rue Pavée. Francine Haber provided this reference.
Archives of the Consistoire Israélite, Paris.
R. Culpepper, *Guimard. 1867–1942,* Paris, 1971.
F. L. Graham, *Hector Guimard,* New York, 1970 (36-page bibliography).
C. Krinsky, "Hector Guimard's Art Nouveau Synagogue in Paris," *Journal of Jewish Art* VI (1979), pp. 105–11.

Antwerp and Brussels

The Jewish communities of Belgium's chief cities began to flourish in the early nineteenth century. The first public nineteenth-century synagogue in Antwerp was a building in the Paardenmarkt where an apartment house now stands. The second was the fifteenth-century church of St. Salvator in Grote Pieter Potstraat, a building that had been secularized earlier and then rented in 1846 to the Jews, who received financial aid from the magistracy of the city.

Brussels–Rue de Bavière

In Brussels, Jews lived near the city walls from about 1300 onward, occupying a district below the castle of the dukes of Brabant. Their synagogue, at the corner of the rue des Sols and the rue des Douze Apôtres, was converted in 1436 into a Christian chapel, a common occurrence at that time. The modern Jewish settlement had begun by the seventeenth century, and a medieval house in rue Ravenstein served as the synagogue. The first nineteenth-century public synagogue in Brussels that was more than a rented house was a structure in the rue de Bavière, built in 1702 and used as a butcher shop and a theater and concert hall before an architect named François Coppens made it a synagogue. It was a three-storey oblong building with a gabled facade and a giant order of Tuscan pilasters linking the second and third floors. The long prayer hall had a gallery at the entrance side and several auxiliary rooms, an attic, and a basement housing community offices and the concierge's apartment. The primarily Ashkenazic community, governed by an official consistory, acquired the building in 1834 shortly after Judaism was granted equal status with other religions. This meant that Jews could obtain state subsidies for maintaining a house of worship. At the dedication ceremony, the rabbi said that the building was larger and more beautiful than any the congregation had used earlier.

By about 1850, the synagogue was in irreparably poor condition. Moreover, it could not

Figure 114. (opposite) Brussels, rue de la Régence, 1872–78, facade (Photograph by ROGER-VIOLLET, *Paris).*

hold the growing population on the High Holy Days, when there were too many worshippers for the two hundred available seats. The community leaders began to think about a new and larger synagogue, but in the early 1860s, the Minister of Justice and other government officials refused to recognize the consistory as having the legal capacity to rent or buy property. They could hardly dispossess the Jews from the existing synagogue, especially as state money had been used to obtain it, but they could prevent them from having a larger building anywhere else until a law of 1871 established the consistory's rights. Perhaps the difficulties made the Jews all the more eager to build a new synagogue to signify their presence.

In the meantime, Christian visitors reported that the rue de Bavière building did not have even fifty Jews present for Sabbath worship, and that there were Jews in the city who were actually in their shops rather than in the synagogue on the Lord's day of rest. If this was so, the community leaders may have hoped to bring religion back to errant members of the congregation by building an attractive synagogue.

Brussels–Rue de la Régence

In 1868, the consistory persuaded Jewish subscribers to purchase for 150,000 francs a site in the rue des Marais and asked for permission to build—in effect, asking for the definitive resolution of the consistory's status. The site, however, was both too small and too far from the center of the city to satisfy all the congregation's needs; apparently it had been obtained so that subscribers could see action being taken with their money, and to show the government that they were serious about erecting a new synagogue. The consistory announced a building design competition in 1868, to be evaluated primarily by architects and engineers rather than by Jewish laymen. The synagogue was to seat 450 men on the ground floor and 250 women in galleries, with thirty choir members in a loft. The competition terms specified a meeting room for two hundred people, a wedding room, a minister's robing room, and a caretaker's apartment—all characteristic of the carefully organized modern synagogues erected in large Jewish settlements after about 1840. The cost was not to surpass 225,000 francs.

Although none of the fifteen entries fulfilled the program, three winners were proclaimed. The commission went to one of them, Désiré DeKeyser (d. 1897), a Christian architect who was gaining attention for his work, which included a variety of buildings in central Brussels, a fashionable Channel resort hotel, and the funeral vehicle of King Leopold I.

The architect did not, however, build where he had expected to build. Owing to the deficiencies of the rue des Marais site and to the promise of government subsidies once the legal status of the consistory was defined, the consistory decided to obtain a site in the rue de la Régence. In this street are such structures as the Roman Catholic church of Notre Dame des Sablons, an important Protestant church, the Palace of Justice, and the Museum of Fine Arts. The consistory officials, boldly linking the synagogue to these august companions, declared that it was "urgent" to endow the Belgian capital with a synagogue in harmony with the city's recent beautification.

DeKeyser rallied to the new demands, and by November 1872 he had designed the building that we know today (Fig. 114). Even then, things did not proceed smoothly. In 1874, the Royal Monuments Commission criticized the plans because it felt Romanesque style was too Christian to be used by Jews. That the Jews had avoided Gothic with its commonly accepted Christian connotation made no impression on the commissioners. The proposed design, they said, failed to suggest the oriental origin or the great antiquity of the Jewish religion (traits which some people might understand as being foreign and outmoded). A contemporary journalist writing in *L'Echo du parlement* felt that Romanesque recalled the terrors inflicted on the Jews during the Crusades; he preferred something evoking the ancient Near East. The commissioners agreed that the best sources

were the orient and ancient Hebrew architecture. Someone must have persuaded them that DeKeyser had designed the correct details because news reports said that DeKeyser had taken his Romanesque details from central Syrian monuments of the first to seventh centuries A.D., in which the decorative principles were strikingly like those found in monuments of the Holy Land.

No doubt, the Jews understood that the commissioners were telling them to make their buildings different from other Belgian buildings, and that their efforts to assimilate would not be welcomed by some influential members of the majority culture. It is easy to see why the rabbi worked into his dedication sermon the idea that monotheism promotes the unity of all men and not their division into opposing groups who hate those unlike themselves. He also expressed profound happiness that some Christians had helped to promote the synagogue building project.

Not all Belgians were favorably inclined toward the Jews and their synagogue. Roman Catholic clergy stayed away from the dedication ceremonies, while Protestant and government representatives attended. Because no local organist would play at the dedication, the congregation had to import an organist from Paris.

The synagogue's stone facade is related to the Frankfurt am Main synagogue facade of 1860, although DeKeyser changed the details, and to the Paris synagogue of 1861–74 (see Fig. 110). With the cupola originally designed for it, the synagogue would also have recalled the even more recent synagogue of Nuremberg. The Brussels synagogue has a three-storeyed, gabled central section flanked by slightly recessed four-storeyed towers which conceal low glass-covered passages running along the north and south sides of the building. The ornamental features of the facade include a rose window and an aedicula housing the tablets of the Law at the peak of the dwarf-arcaded central gable. In the vestibule, stairs lead to the women's galleries and to the wedding room and weekday synagogue, which are actually in the annexed community building.

Inside the main prayer hall, wide-arched bays in the 25 m.-high nave precede the raised apse. The creamy white nave contrasts strongly with the lavish apse. The apse is covered with rich, warm-colored ornament including paintings in the semidome representing the Mosaic tablets, the candlestick, and other sacred objects. Twenty-five windows have glass painted by an artist from Bruges, Henri Dobbelaere, with references to Mount Sinai, the ancient ark, religious principles, and religious leaders. The iconographic program was executed imperfectly because the Christian artist, ignorant of Hebrew, put the wrong texts to the images. The present rabbi, however, has reconstructed the program which reveals the nineteenth-century community's desire to avoid extremes either of traditional observance or of Reform. Inside, the bimah stood just below the ark platform rather than in the center; the galleries for women, on three sides of the room, had no high grilles; and there was a choir and organ loft above the western women's gallery—all revealing the impact of Reform on a community that generally respected tradition. The elaborate wooden ark, originally tripartite and flat-topped, recalled the facade of the Tempelgasse synagogue in Vienna of 1858 (see Fig. 64); later, a domed superstructure was added. In its general style and in the demeanor of its congregation, the Brussels synagogue resembled the recently built rue de la Victoire synagogue of Paris.

A prominent Jewish mining engineer, Georges Montefiore-Lévi, directed the synagogue construction in 1875–78. The consistory spent about 900,000 francs on the synagogue, the community administration building next door, the furnishing, and the decoration. The result was "one of the most successfully carried out buildings of modern Brussels," according to a writer for the *Builder*.

Antwerp–Bouwmeesterstraat

At Antwerp in 1888 or 1889, Ernest Stordiau, a Christian, designed a synagogue for the corner of the rue des Architectes (Bouwmeesterstraat) and the rue des Peintres, to be financed in part with a state subsidy of 50,000 francs. When Stordiau left to work in Luxembourg, the congregation commissioned Joseph Hertogs to prepare another plan, with costs estimated in 1891 as 220,000 francs. This building opened in 1893 (Fig. 115). While the preceding synagogue had been long and narrow with a gallery over the entrance door—described by a visiting English rabbi as "perfectly free from pretension"—the new one looked more obviously exotic. It was modeled loosely on earlier domed and turreted Moorish-style synagogues, such as that of Nuremberg (1874). The Antwerp building has a tripartite twin-towered facade with a recessed central section containing a rose window under a stilted arch, a porch like an Islamic gateway, and oriental cupolas over the western bay and towers. Behind this facade is the galleried nave, lighted by windows with Moorish tracery. The building has limited artistic merit, but it is imposing and different in style from the Brussels synagogue. The Jews of Antwerp may have accepted directions from government officials, or may have wished to emphasize their difference from the Jews in Brussels, who were less traditional in their social and religious conduct.

Figure 115. Antwerp, Bouwmeesterstraat, 1891–93, facade in 1982.

Antwerp–Hovenierstraat

For the Sephardic congregation that belonged to the same official and state-supported Jewish community in Antwerp, Joseph DeLange, a Jewish architect, erected a Romanesque-Byzantine eclectic synagogue in Hovenierstraat which was dedicated in 1913. In style it was less elaborate, "more dignified, soberer in decoration," and less exotic than the 1893 synagogue, for DeLange had evidently come to see disadvantages in the "restless and fantastic styles used almost everywhere until recently in buildings meant for Jewish worship." As the congregation traced its ancestry to the Ottoman Empire rather than to medieval Spain, the oriental elements in the building were meant to suggest the Middle East; this had motivated the same stylistic choice at the Turkish congregational synagogue in Vienna (1887).

Antwerp–Oostenstraat

Adherents of the Russo-Polish rite, organized into a separate community, called Machsike Hadass, commissioned a synagogue in 1910 from Jules Hofman, another Jewish architect, but as its completion was interrupted by the First World War, the building, designed in 1911–13, was not used for regular services until 1918 (Fig. 116). The congregation included ultraorthodox members and was close to certain Hasidic groups. It was thus even more devoted to a traditional eastern European self-image than was the orthodox congregation in

Figure 116. Antwerp, Oostenstraat, 1911–13, facade in 1982.

the 1893 synagogue. Nevertheless, the architect could not have designed the Machsike Hadass synagogue in the same exotic style as that used by the government-sponsored community synagogues, because similar buildings would have suggested a nonexistent harmony between the two synagogue groups. It would have been even less appropriate to house the Machsike Hadass in a Romanesque building of the type used by the westernized Brussels congregation. The solution, as at rue Pavée in Paris, was found in new forms—flat exterior walls divided into storeys, like a commercial building with larger windows on the lower floors. It was articulated mainly by its window rhythms, which were small and repetitive above boldly curving cavities crossed by rectilinear mullions, characteristic forms of the *art nouveau*. Little turrets with cupolas at the ends of the cornice, and small details of the cornice itself, were mere allusions to the past; the overall image was that of an unassuming, conservatively contemporary building. Its message can be interpreted as suggesting the external modesty that might cloak a rich interior community life. Those who attended the house of study in this building described the atmosphere as restful and aristocratic, unlike that of other ultraorthodox and Hasidic houses of study and synagogues. Perhaps the building's style was intended as a quiet rebuke to the showier synagogue of 1893.

Antwerp–Van Den Nestlei

The Antwerp Jewish population grew rapidly, from about 8,000 in 1900 to about 35,000 by 1927. The city was a major embarkation point for emigrants to America, but many prospective emigrants found jobs in Antwerp's diamond industry which burgeoned after diamonds were exploited in South Africa. The official community—which benefited from state subventions as church groups did—had 1,200 members by 1928, and needed additional Ashkenazic synagogues. A brick synagogue meant for a thousand worshippers was built in Van den Nestlei in 1929, following a competition held in 1923 for Jewish architects. The results reflected the polite conservatism among Antwerp's Jews. Joseph DeLange and Germain Debré each submitted designs based on that of Essen's synagogue, which had been completed only a decade earlier. Their designs shared second prize in the absence of a first-prize winner. Like the Essen synagogue, the Antwerp designs had a central plan preceded by a vestibule between low towers and approached by steps compressed by the towers. DeLange received the commission and completed the building in 1929. His use of varied window forms and checkered and salient brickwork related the building to other early-twentieth-century architecture in the Low Countries (see Figs. 229, 230). The building has been remodeled in recent years, to its aesthetic detriment.

Among the other competitors was Josef Frank, who proposed a simple, compact, and planar building which, because it evoked historic precedent, was different in spirit from works in the contemporary nascent International Modern Style. Receding rectilinear forms, resembling an ancient Near Eastern ziggurat, crowned the main space, and two awkward round-headed protuberances rose above the cornice over each of the twin entrances, recalling the tablets of the Law. An architect identified as Grünberg (probably Arthur Grünberger who won the Vienna-Hietzing competition in 1924) proposed a more complex ziggurat. Seven receding slabs constituted the main part of the building, and six-pointed star-shaped windows lit the slabs. In front of the ziggurat, a two-storey vestibule terminated in turrets. Much of the vestibule's surface was covered with Moorish fretwork. This proposal managed to be both grandiose and frivolous. Further variety appeared in a more serious and monumental design by an architect named Löffler, perhaps the Hungarian-born architect who converted a warehouse in Paris into the "Rashi" Synagogue in the 1930s. Löffler suggested a domed cylinder set into the site behind cylindrical turrets which formed an entranceway; they also served to terminate the multistorey secular buildings which the architect designed along the streets bounding the site. As in the Vienna-Hietzing competition, the proposals showed a wide variety of approaches to synagogue design in the early 1920s. They all incorporated some references to Judaism or the East, but the designs cleared away some of the complexity of earlier plans and decoration.

The synagogue as built represented a community of increasingly assimilated Jews who remained conscious of their heritage while living as practical businessmen. They would have been as unlikely to accept the collective ideals advanced by some of the International Modernist avant-garde as to commission the showy design by Grünberger.

Antwerp's principal synagogues survived the war and are in use today. Belgian Jews continue to worship in buildings of several plans and styles, including tiny Hasidic assembly rooms and a Liberal synagogue in the Brussels suburb of Forest. The designs reflect the variety in Jewish life in a small and culturally diverse country.

BIBLIOGRAPHIES

BRUSSELS

J. Apers, A. Hoppenbrouwers, and J. Vandenbreeden, *Bouwen door de eeuwen heen: Urgentie-Inventaris van het bouwkundig erfgoed van de Brusselse agglomeratie,* Ghent, 1979, p. 150.

Archives israélites XXXIX (1878), pp. 594–95.

AZJ XXXII (1869), "Die jüdische Baukunst" pamphlet *Beilage* to #37, Sept. 14, 1869, pp. 753–54, reprinted from *L'Écho du parlement,* June 27, 1869.

Builder XXXVIII (May 22, 1880), pp. 637, 641.

Bulletin des Commissions Royales d'Art et d'Archéologie XIII (1874), p. 208, XVI (1877), p. 238.

C. Daly, "Concours pour Bruxelles," *Revue générale de l'architecture* XXVI (1868), col. 22, XXVII (1869), col. 253.

Encyclopedia Judaica, 1971, s.v. Brussels.

Jewish Chronicle, Jan. 7, 1859, p. 2, Jan. 14, 1859, p. 7.

Jewish Encyclopedia, s. v. Brussels.

La Grande Synagogue de Bruxelles. Contributions à l'histoire juif de Bruxelles, 1878–1978, Brussels, 1978, esp. T. Gergely, "Naissance d'une synagogue," pp. 77–94, and M. Kahlenberg, "Textes et ornements symboliques de notre synagogue," pp. 95–100.

Mariano, "Une cité juive en démolition," *La Ligue des architectes et des artisans du bâtiment* IV (1910), pp. 129–30.

Société centrale d'architecture de Belgique, *Exposition nationale d'architecture, 1883, Catalogue,* Brussels, 1883 (competition entries by D. De Keyser and by L.-J.-L. Delhaye).

ANTWERP

Bulletin des Commissions Royales d'Art et d'Archéologie XXIV (1885), p. 310, XXVII (1888), p. 14.

L. de Barsée, "De Bouwkunst in de XIXde eeuw," *Bouwstoffen voor de Geschiedenis van Antwerpen in de XIXde eeuw,* Antwerp, 1964, pp. 238–66, esp. p. 261 (for Hertogs) and p. 264 (for Stordiau).

J. DeLange, in *Jubelalbum van de Kring voor Bouwkunde 1900–1910,* Antwerp, n.d., pp. 73–76.

De Vrijdagavond, Oct. 9, 1931, p. 19; Oct. 30, 1931, p. 75.

Encyclopedia Judaica, 1971, s.v. Antwerp.

J. Frank's drawing, *Menorah* VI, #11/12 (1929), p. 557.

J. Gutwirth, "Antwerp Jewry Today," *Jewish Journal of Sociology* X, #1 (1968), pp. 121–37, esp. pp. 128–29. (An earlier version is "Le judaïsme anversois aujourd'hui," *Revue des études juives* CXXV, #4 [Oct.–Dec. 1966].)

Jewish Chronicle, Aug. 29, 1890, pp. 7–8.

Jewish Encyclopedia, s.v. Antwerp.

J. d. L[ange], "Eene nieuwe Synagogue," *De Bouwgids. Maandschrift voor Huis & Haard* V, #8 (Aug. 1913), pp. 139–42 (for Hovenierstraat Sephardic synagogue).

K. Liberman, "La découverte d'une synagogue secrète à Anvers à la fin du dix-septième siècle," *Revue des études juives* C (1935), pp. 36–48.

A. Marinower, ed., *Eeuwfeest van de israelitische gemeente Antwerpen 1876–1976,* n. p., n. d.

F. S. "François Coppens," *Journal des Beaux-Arts* XV, #7 (1873), pp. 57–58.

E. Schmidt, *Geschiedenis van de Joden in Antwerpen,* Antwerp, 1963.

S. van Aerschot et al., *Bouwen door de eeuwen in Vlaanderen: Stad Antwerpen,* Ghent, 1979, vol. 3, pp. 565–66.

B. Vanhove, "De Art Nouveau Architectuur in het Antwerpse: een doorsnede," thesis, Rijksuniversiteit, Ghent, 1978, pp. 26, 33.

Alfred E. Willis most generously offered bibliographic and archival material, including: Archives générales du Royaume, Brussels, inventaire 178, Beaux-Arts, #73 (Antwerp), #417 (Brussels); Inventaire 227, Rijkscommissie voor Monumenten en Landschappen, 3216/2/#23 (Antwerp).

Germany and Switzerland*

Berlin–Heidereutergasse and Ansbach

The Heidereutergasse synagogue in Berlin (1712–14) and the synagogue at Ansbach in Franconia (1744–46) exemplify eighteenth-century synagogues built by privileged Jews. They are typical in being single-naved and vaulted, with a gallery only at the end opposite the ark. These descend from single-naved medieval synagogues such as those of Poznań, Prague-Pinkas, Rouffach, Miltenberg, and Sopron (see Fig. 24). The later buildings, however, are more completely organized, with vestibule, gallery, vaults that emphasize the center of the room, and long windows that admit abundant light. The examples in Berlin and Ansbach are perhaps the most attractive of the type, probably because their architects were conscious of working for a group protected by the local ruler; the architect at Ansbach, Leopold Retti, worked for the margrave, who was being paid handsomely by the congregation so that they could have a synagogue big enough to hold them all.

Both buildings were erected in part to resolve feuds between proprietors of earlier, private synagogues—feuds that did not ease relations between the rulers and "their" Jews. In each case, the decision to build a new synagogue led to resentment among those whose prerogatives had been reduced, or among those who had to pay for someone else's privileges—a common occurrence in the history of European synagogue building. These synagogues, like many others, were products of the personal and religious oppositions and compromises found in small, inward-turning communities whose members knew each other all too well.

*Included in this section under Hamburg–Poolstrasse (Reform temple) is a discussion of the related building in London–Upper Berkeley Street, and under Modern Geometric Synagogues, a discussion of the Žilina synagogue.

Berlin–Heidereutergasse

The synagogue in Berlin was built about forty years after the definitive settlement of Jews in the city (1671). Michael Kemmeter of Regensburg, a Christian architect, built it on a center-city site not far from the church of St. Mary, on land which had been owned by the bishops of Havelberg. The synagogue occupied part of a large courtyard hidden from the street by the house of a government official (Fig. 117). The synagogue was a substantial one, apparently about 10 m. high, made of masonry covered with stucco, and crowned by a peaked roof with dormers. Five tall, round-headed windows filled the eastern wall, and six more lighted the north and south walls. A rusticated main portal and a door to the right of it led to the main floor where the men's area was located, while women entered by a modest door in the west bay of the north side and climbed interior stairs up to the gallery.

The main room was oblong and tall, although the engraver of a view of the interior exaggerated its height and proportion (Fig. 118). About half of each wall seems to have been given over to the long windows. The ceiling's coved panels rose to a slightly depressed elongated octagonal panel which emphasized the center of the room, where the large bimah was placed. Each of the pews along the central axis could seat

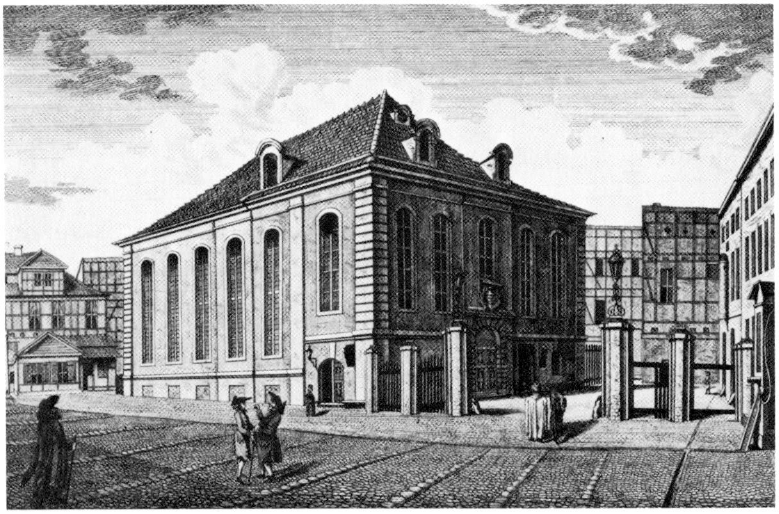

Figure 117. Berlin, Heidereutergasse, 1712–14, exterior in ca. 1795, etching by F. A. Calau.

Figure 118. Berlin, Heidereutergasse, interior in ca. 1720, engraving designed by A. M. Werner.

only about three or four men because the squarish bimah took up so much room. The bimah lacked a canopy but had seats attached to its western side, a feature familiar from the bimahs at Prague-Altneuschul, Metz (pre-1845), and Volpa (see Figs. 49, 97). The ark was tall and lavishly carved with two tiers of columns and undulating cornices; dense foliage projecting at each side recalled earlier German church altarpieces and (later?) arks in Polish synagogues such as Gąbin and Volpa, or examples elsewhere such as Pečky in Bohemia or Conegliano in the Veneto. The general impression given by the interior was, however, far from that of the densely decorated, emotionally demanding Polish synagogues. The building in Berlin had the bright, clear, and straightforward appearance of a Protestant church.

The handsome synagogue was too small to hold the ever-increasing number of Jews who settled in Berlin. Some of the pressure on the synagogue was relieved by the conversions to

Christianity that occurred in noticeable numbers during the late eighteenth and early nineteenth centuries. Around 1820, and then after about 1830, some Jews abandoned the community synagogue for Reform prayer rooms which were succeeded in 1846 by the first large Reform temple. But the old community synagogue remained badly overcrowded, and fruitless plans for a new one were laid in 1841 and in 1846–47. The Jews hoped to build a new synagogue near the Garnisonkirche, not far from the Heidereutergasse. The king granted permission for the use of this site, but then withdrew his approval, supposedly because the worshippers of one religion would disturb those of the other religion. He offered instead an unsuitable site far to the southeast, out of the heart of town and away from the center of Jewish residence. Political and financial turmoil then prevented any synagogue building project from being resumed for several years. When it was taken up again, in 1853, the Jews still lacked a new site, and therefore decided to remodel the old building. They engaged a Protestant architect, Eduard Knoblauch, who did the work in 1853–56 and later designed the Oranienburgerstrasse synagogue and the Jewish hospital. He added anterooms, galleries, and pews, and changed the decorative style to an eclectic classical-Romanesque mixture which was in fashion around 1855. This work was altered in 1881 by the creation of a vaulted apse behind the ark, and the extension of the galleries along the side walls. The windows were also modified to take account of their interruption by the new galleries. In 1891, the synagogue was repainted, completing a transformation which made the building unrecognizable as the structure of 1712–14.

The Heidereutergasse synagogue was the only one in which religious services were permitted after the outbreak of war in 1939. Services were, in fact, held there until 1943. The synagogue itself was bombed in later air raids but survived in poor condition—as did a remnant of the pre-Nazi-era congregation. The East Berlin city government was said to be thinking about rebuilding the structure, but the future is not likely to bring an increased demand for synagogue services in addition to those now available at a restored synagogue in Rykestrasse outside the city center.

Ansbach

A happier fate awaited the synagogue at Ansbach, which was saved from the Nazis when the mayor staged a false fire in the building, duping the vandals who surely planned to destroy it on Crystal Night. Although the number of Jews remaining in the town is not even large enough to form a *minyan,* the building itself was restored after the Second World War and is, at least, a monument to a vanished population.

The small synagogue is about 16 m. long and about 12.5 m. wide (Figs. 119, 120, 121). It contains a main room for the men, a vestibule at the west with a gallery above it, and a stairwell projecting southward into the synagogue court-

Figure 119. Ansbach, 1744–46, exterior.

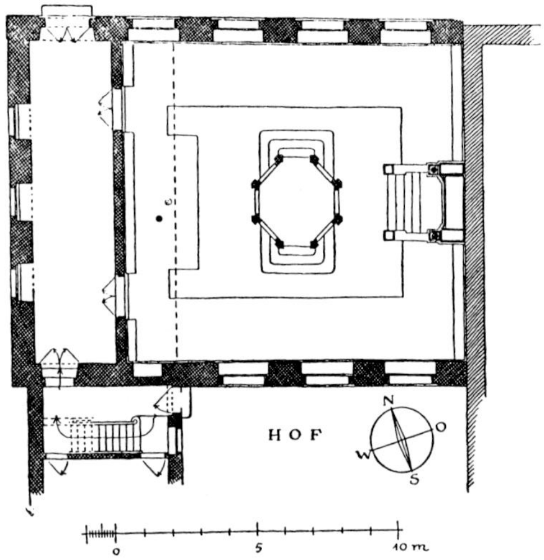

Figure 120. Ansbach, plan.

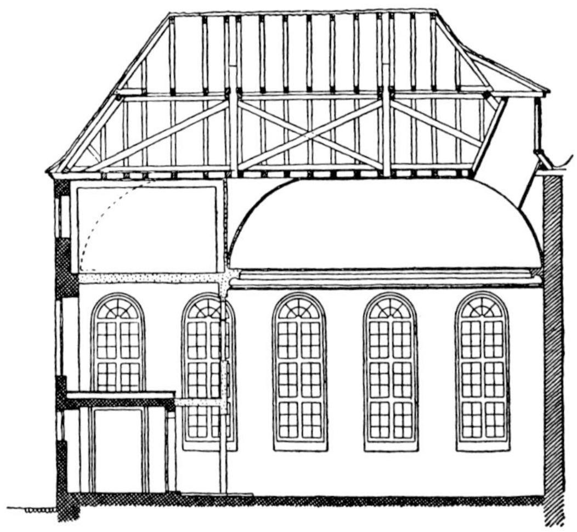

Figure 121. Ansbach, longitudinal section.

yard. The exterior wall surfaces are covered with light-colored stucco and punctuated by pilaster strips between large round-headed windows, four on each side of the men's area and one on each side of the vestibule. A double-pitched roof covers a coved ceiling. The main entrance is located in the north side, in the western bay, but neither at the portal nor anywhere else on the outside of the building is there conspicuous ornament. It is likely that Leopold Retti had orders to provide a design that was handsome enough to make sponsors of the synagogue willing to pay for its cost but not so noticeable as to lend unnecessary prestige to the Jews.

The contemporary interior furnishings are more elaborate than we might guess from a view of the exterior. The octagonal bimah stands on a step in the center of the room and has a railing made of solid pillars alternating with openwork grilles of wrought iron. On each pillar stands a twisted column, decorated to imitate marble, holding a gilt capital. Above the octagonal cornice, white and gilt urns mark the corners. The ark is raised on steps and is embellished by twisted columns which flank the ark doors. Imitation marble is used here and on the bimah. The twisted columns, generally popular in the late seventeenth and eighteenth centuries (after Bernini used them on the altar canopy at St. Peter's in the Vatican), had special meaning in synagogues, for smaller columns of the same form, now in the crossing at St. Peter's, were believed since medieval times to have come from Solomon's Temple. Additional decoration is provided by the tablets of the Law flanked by lions in the tympanum of the ark, and by the lighting fixtures, some of which are original eighteenth-century candelabra.

The clarity and crisp lightness of the design, and the smooth white walls relieved by the richness of the furnishings, make this an especially attractive synagogue. The overall sobriety of the building, though not its furnishing style, persisted in synagogue architecture well into the nineteenth century, until historicist styles took the lead about a century after the Ansbach synagogue was completed.

BIBLIOGRAPHIES

BERLIN

AJR Information, July 1978, p. 10.

Archives israélites XXXV (1874), p. 360 (on 1818 remodeling).

AZJ, 1846, 1847, 1853, 1855.

Bendt & Bothe, esp. vol. 1, pp. 22, 24, 27, 72–75; vol. 2, pp. 77–78.

R. Borrmann, *Bau-und Kunstdenkmäler von Berlin,* Berlin, 1893.

L. Geiger, *Geschichte der Juden in Berlin,* Berlin, 1871, esp. vol. 1, pp. 22ff., vol. 2, pp. 46ff.
Hammer-Schenk, *Synagogen,* p. 31 and n. 4.
Jewish Chronicle for 1846, 1847, 1853, 1855.
Krautheimer, *Mitt. Syn.*

ANSBACH

Encyclopedia Judaica, 1971, s.v. Ansbach.
G. P. Fehring, *Bayerische Kunstdenkmale II: Stadt und Kreis Ansbach,* Munich, 1958, pp. 24–25.
S. Haenle, *Geschichte der Juden im ehemaligen Fürstenthum Ansbach,* Ansbach, 1867, pp. 141–46.
"In der Synagoge gehen wieder die Lichte an," *Fränkische Landeszeitung,* Feb. 10, 1962.
F. Scholl, *Leopold Retti, markgräflich Ansbachscher Baudirektor,* Ansbach, 1930, esp. pp. 81–82.

Berlin–Oranienburgerstrasse

Only a ravaged shell survives of what was once one of Europe's most important synagogues, indeed, the largest synagogue in the world when completed in 1866 (Fig. 122). As one of the first large buildings in Germany to exploit the possibilities of iron construction, and lit by ingenious methods of gas lighting, the synagogue won praise for integrating art with technology.

The fact that the Jews could build a synagogue that was as visually impressive as a church, located in central Berlin and on a street rather than a lane, marked a significant victory. As late as 1847, the idea that a synagogue might face the street was considered remarkable; by the mid-1850s, Christians had accepted the idea. At the dedication ceremony, Count Bismarck and Baron Wrangel heard a sermon expressing satisfaction with the Jews' condition in 1866.

The size of the building bore witness to the migration of Jews to the Prussian capital from German and Slavic villages. The impressive appearance reflected the wealth of the richest Jews, who bought shares to finance the construction costs, which reached about a million thalers. This was one of the first synagogues to have an externally conspicuous cupola, and the fact that the cupola was bulbous and gilded shows that the leaders of Berlin Jewry wanted their building to make a strong impact on the cityscape, as if to proclaim their newly won rights. Ironically, the gleaming dome and the red-striped yellow brick and brown stone facade—constrasting with the pale plastered buildings ubiquitous in Berlin—gave some observers the idea that Jews were exotic and never to be considered entirely German. For Jews elsewhere, however, the Oranienburgerstrasse synagogue symbolized improved status. For that reason, in addition to its aesthetic appeal, it influenced the design of other synagogues for culturally assimilated congregations, including those of Bratislava, Chernovtsy, and Leningrad (see Figs. 25, 88).

Additional synagogues were already in demand when this synagogue was initiated, the Jewish population in Berlin having increased by 10,000 between 1839 and 1859. Only the Heidereutergasse synagogue and eight small oratories served 16,000 Jews. Meeting halls had to be rented for the High Holy Days in the autumn, to accommodate those who could neither afford nor obtain synagogue seats. The construction of a Reform temple in 1853–54 and the enlargement of the Heidereutergasse synagogue in 1856 offered little relief.

After daring to reject an inconvenient location offered by government supervisors, the congregation settled on a city-center block occupied among other buildings by Jewish and Roman Catholic hospitals. The lot had an awkward shape, with narrow frontage on the street and a shift in axis as it extended into the block. In order to have the widest choice of solutions to problems caused by the site, the community leaders sponsored a design competition, one of the earliest for any kind of building in Germany. Judges from the Berlin Architects' Association found that no entry satisfied the criteria perfectly, and eventually the commission went to one entrant, Eduard Knoblauch (1801–65), who had been a consultant on site selection and competition program preparation. This Protestant architect, a pupil of Schinkel and a leader

of the Berlin Architects' Association, built private mansions, the Russian embassy, the Jewish hospital, and the Heidereutergasse synagogue enlargement; the Oranienburgerstrasse synagogue was his most successful achievement.

The first spade of earth was turned in May 1859, while Knoblauch was still busy reworking the plans to suit community leaders' demands that their offices be relocated. The architect satisfied them quickly, and building continued at a satisfactory pace so that the shell and some interior work were completed by 1862. Knoblauch, however, became ill in that year. He entrusted the job to his friend, August Stüler, who executed most of the interior decoration, but both architects died in 1865. Shortages of material, especially iron, during Prussia's wars with Denmark and Austria delayed the dedication of the synagogue until 1866. Knoblauch's assistant, Hähnel, supervised the completion and executed some of the ornament; he had helped to make preparatory studies and was associated with the building from its inception. Another architect, W. Schwedler, took charge of the interior vaulting and its iron supports.

The synagogue has several sections, following the long bent axis into the depth of the lot (Fig. 123). On the Oranienburgerstrasse, the facade consists of a recessed center with a triad of entrance arches resting on polished granite columns and flanked by square towers advancing to the street line. A small cupola crowning each tower reached a height of about 34 m. (100 Berlin feet). Over the entrance arches and the vestibule behind them, was the boardroom. The huge dome, about 50 m. (160 Berlin feet) high, covered the vestibule. It did not cover the prayer hall because that lay so far back in the lot that a dome above it would have been invisible from the street.

In the vestibule, the top-hatted gentlemen of the congregation checked their umbrellas with an attendant. A fountain provided a small jet of water for those who followed the tradition of washing hands before attending services. Side doors led from the vestibule to staff apartments and meeting rooms. Most importantly, the vestibule disguised the shift in the axis of the lot, enabling a visitor to enter about 30 degrees to the left of the axis of the rest of the building. This could be accomplished with a graceful rather than an awkward transition because the vestibule was twelve-sided and the centralized shape disguised the sudden shift in direction. Along the new axis lay an anteroom, the weekday synagogue, and then the main prayer hall.

The prayer hall, a galleried basilica, measured about 57 m. in length, about 40 m. in width, and about 23 m. in height (188 × 126

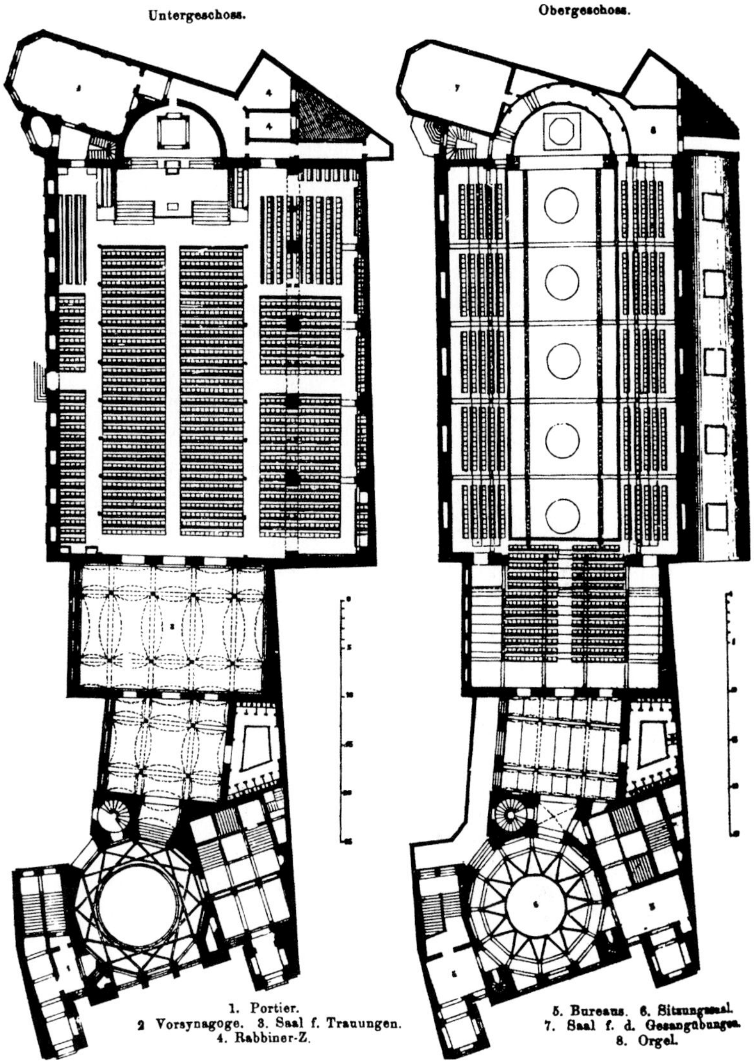

Figure 122. (opposite) Berlin, Oranienburgerstrasse, 1859–66, facade.

Figure 123. Berlin, Oranienburgerstrasse, plan.

× 87 Berlin feet). The apse, as wide as the nave, contained the ark and room for the choir and organ (Fig. 124). The room held over three thousand people, including about twelve hundred women in the galleries. Because the building lot widened at this point, there was room on the south to enlarge the men's seating area by the equivalent of another aisle. Old prints and photographs offer no hint of this because the nave elevations were made identical, to give the impression of symmetry.

Within the brick perimeter walls, most of the structure in the prayer hall was composed of iron, glass, and brick, some of it covered by plaster. The galleries and ceiling were made of iron, a material well suited to a room in which good sight lines and the easy flow of sound are essential. The compressive strength of iron allowed the erection of large galleries on thin piers and thin hemispheric domes under the seats. Other important synagogues already had used iron to reduce visual obstructions and to save masonry and money (e.g., Semper's synagogue at Dresden and Förster's at Budapest-Dohány Street and Vienna-Tempelgasse; see Figs. 130, 39, 65). The iron design at Berlin was bolder, however, and the wide arches over the nave created an unusual and grand effect of great openness. The variety of arches—segments and half-segments spanning the nave, low arches under the galleries, broad stilted arches framing the galleries and apse, and pointed arches for some windows—gave an impression of inventive richness and frank impurity of style. The synagogue was described as Moorish by sponsors and architects, who found the Alhambra a good model for slender columns and rich "oriental" decoration. As the Alhambra had no suitable dome, the architect borrowed the form of the "Indian" dome on the Royal Pavilion at Brighton! A writer for the orthodox periodical, *Der Israelit,* asked acerbically why there was not a Jewish rather than a Moorish synagogue, preferably with a traditionally Jewish prayer book and ritual.

Everyone agreed, however, that the technical means used to achieve exotic effects were extraordinary. The lighting and ventilating systems were integrated by methods said to have been used earlier for theaters in Paris. The technique employed a layer of clear window glass on the outside of the building, and one of brilliantly colored glass inside. Ventilating ducts between the layers carried away heat and fumes from gaslights that were installed in the same space. Placing gaslight behind a screen of colored glass allowed glowing light of great intensity and rich color to enhance the interior, but it prevented the gaslight from causing the usual glare and excessive heat. Large skylights in the nave and apse ceilings admitted daylight, but at night gas jets were turned on at skylight level to provide light from above. Breezes on the roof would not extinguish the gas jets because a protective reflector slid over the jets and skylights when the gas was turned on.

The modernity of the technical fittings and the splendor of the results accorded with the Reform ritual and the self-image of the congregation's leaders. The bimah stood just west of the ark; most of the men's seats faced east; the women's galleries had no grilles; and there was an organ, hidden behind a screen in the apse. The prosperous and assimilated congregation wore formal evening dress to the dedication ceremonies. An orthodox visitor commented that "in size and splendour this new Jewish Temple unquestionably eclipses the Temple of Solomon. . . . It is in the display of wealth involved in building this structure that the Jews can show what power they possess, and the pride of which it is the expression is even stronger than the internal hatred of the two sects of Jews [Reform and orthodox] whose united money built it." In the anti-Reform *Jewish Messenger* of New York, a correspondent wrote that "the world sees this temple . . . bearing itself above the most pretentious churches, and concludes involuntarily—there must be something in Judaism. . . . It interprets the new sentiment of Israel reasserting her supremacy and the acknowledgement of the multitude. Otherwise, the synagogue were a failure—for it were difficult to discern devoutness of bearing

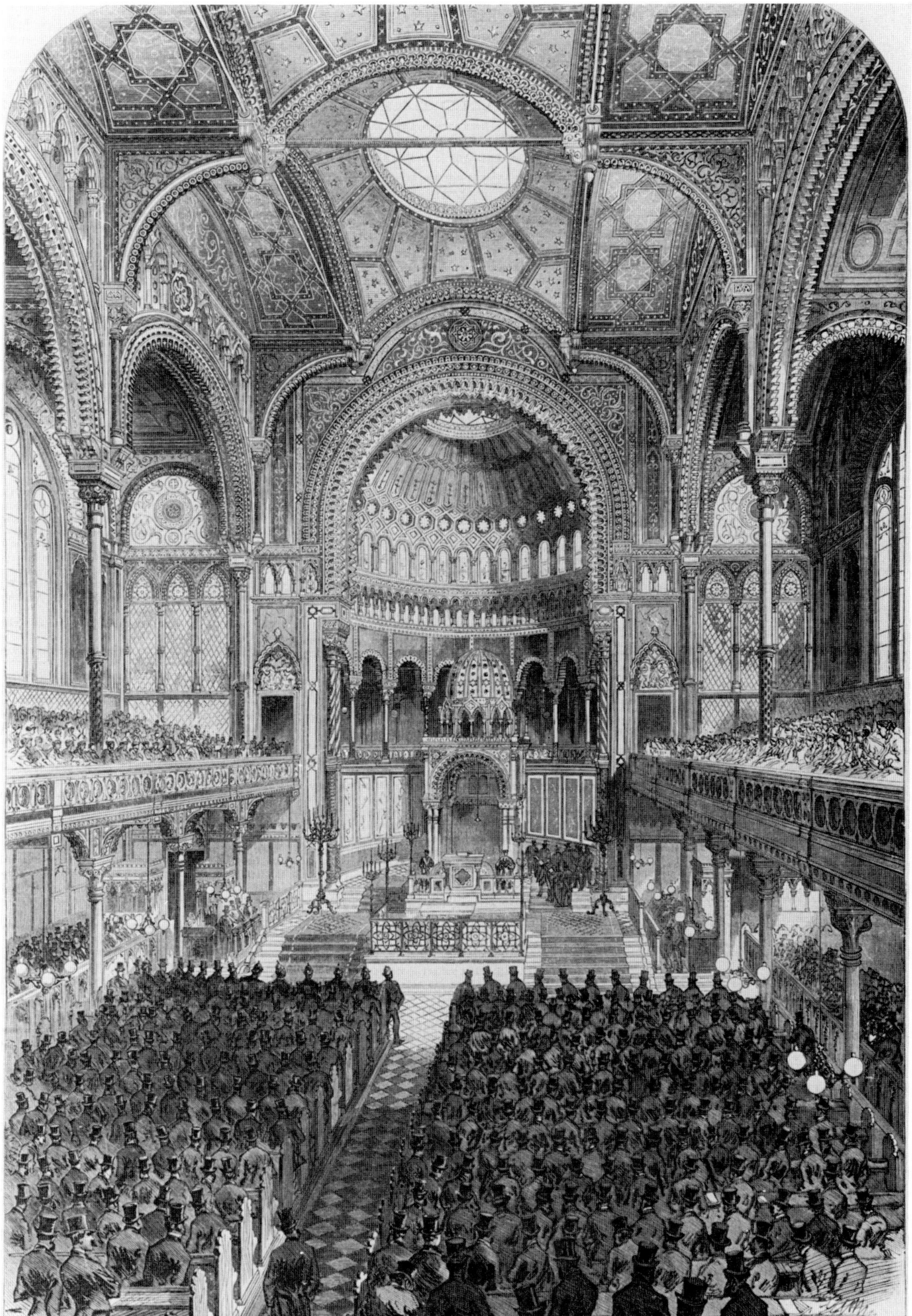

Figure 124. Berlin, Oranienburgerstrasse, interior to ark in 1866.

reflected upon the worshippers as a result of contemplation or association."

The grand synagogue, then, was a brilliant ambiguity. It showed in its technical provisions something of the imagination and entrepreneurial and scientific taste that distinguished many members of the Berlin Jewish community from the Enlightenment to 1933. It revealed the taste for Reform and modernity and cultural assimilation among Berlin Jewry, which had lost many young people to the social and political appeal of Christian conversion. It expressed the optimism and confidence that characterized Jewish Berliners for another sixty-five years after the dedication date. But it hinted, too, at *nouveau riche* love of display, which aroused the scorn of the pious and the hatred of those who sought an excuse for being anti-Semitic.

Vandals who regarded the Jews of Berlin as an inferior oriental race set fire to the "Moorish" Oranienburgerstrasse synagogue on Crystal Night in 1938. Much of what was left was damaged further in an Allied fire-bombing. The synagogue, representing the achievements of modern technology and civilization, remains as a skeletal presence beside the Jewish community office building in East Berlin.

BIBLIOGRAPHY

Bendt & Bothe, esp. vol. 1, pp. 27–36, 87–98; vol. 2, pp. 78–80, with rare prints and photographs on pp. 7, 14, 28, 30–36.

Der Israelit XI, #40/41 (Oct. 5, 1870), p. 751.

Hammer-Schenk, *Synagogen,* esp. pp. 284–96.

———, "Untersuchungen," pp. 399–413, 424, 427.

G. Knoblauch, "Die neue Synagoge in Berlin," *Zeitschrift für Bauwesen* XV (1865), col. 273, XVI (1866), cols. 3ff., 32ff., 481–86, XVIII (1868), cols. 3ff. and pls.

M. Kreutzberger and I. Foerg, eds., *Leo Baeck Institute. New York. Bibliothek und Archiv. Katalog* vol. 1, Tübingen, 1970, s.v. Berlin.

H. Künzl, "Zur Aufnahme islamischer Architekturstile im Synagogenbau des 19 Jahrhunderts," *Zeitschrift der Deutschen Morgenländischen Gesellschaft,* Supplement III, *2. Deutscher Orientalistentag 1975, Vorträge,* ed. W. Voigt, Wiesbaden, 1977, pp. 1626–31.

P. Wallé, *Die neue Synagoge zu Berlin,* extract from *Der Bär,* vol. 12, 1884.

H. Zopf and G. Heinrich, *Berlin-Bibliographie bis 1960 in der Senatsbibliothek Berlin,* Berlin, 1965, pp. 358–60. (Veröffentlichungen der Historischen Kommission zu Berlin beim Friedrich Meinecke Institut der Freien Universität, 15: Bibliographie, Band I.)

Buchau am Federsee

The story of the synagogue at Buchau in southwestern Germany is one that could be repeated about many other European examples. The last synagogue there, opened in 1835, was a handsome building with the unusual feature of a bell tower, but it was like synagogues elsewhere in many ways. The building was erected outside the main Christian settlement. It replaced earlier prayer rooms set up in premises that were evidently used also as dwellings. It could be a separate and attractive structure only after the Jews received local citizenship or other legal rights. Its style was common to many buildings of its time and place. Christians designed and constructed the synagogue. Adjacent lay community offices, a school, and the officiants' residence. The synagogue was destroyed in 1938, and the congregation members either emigrated or fell victim to the Nazis.

Documents concerning the Jews of Buchau go back to the late fourteenth century, but we cannot tell whether or for how long they were permanent residents or numerous enough to form the quorum needed for the establishment of a synagogue. We have better documentation for the Jews in Buchau from 1577 onward. They received protection (sometimes from secular and sometimes from religious officials) alternating with expulsion and readmission to town, a pattern that characterized the history of vulnerable Jewish groups all over Europe. By about 1700, however, their position stabilized. They worshipped in a prayer room on the top floor of a three-storey house in the Jewish quarter. In 1938, traces of the ark were still visible on the eastern wall between a pair of windows that admitted only limited light. A coffered ceiling covered the room, which lacked other architectural features of note. A prayer room was established slightly later in another house, but repeated building alterations had made the synagogue's arrangement untraceable by the late 1930s. In the last third of the eighteenth century, a more imposing room was fitted up for prayer. This room, like the earliest known of Buchau's synagogues, occupied the top floor of a house in the Jewish neighborhood; the rabbi or other Jews would have occupied the rest of the three-storeyed building and attic. The oblong prayer hall had a door in one corner, wide plank flooring, plastered walls, and a pretty wooden ceiling with flowers painted in the square and slightly recessed panels, and similar decoration on the inner face of the door. When some of the hinged ceiling panels were open, the room became an outdoor booth used at the Sukkot feast. The usual ground-level booth would have exposed participants to the cold and fog of autumn in Buchau.

The community grew larger in the 1750s, and obtained permission to open a separate building for synagogue use in the Jews' street. Small and visually undistinguished like many synagogues, it was a vernacular building of no special "Jewish" character apart from the grilled women's gallery. The synagogue could be heated, which suggests that it was also used as a house of study. A meeting room adjacent to the prayer hall enlarged the synagogue's capacity, but by 1824 serious overcrowding inconvenienced the congregation. Fortunately, the Buchau Jews received citizenship rights in 1828, and could now build what they wished, free of the onerous special laws that had formerly governed them.

In 1833, the community leaders decided to replace the old building and its courtyard where weddings were held. They bought a lot so situated that the synagogue's facade would be on a fairly broad street, not hidden behind a community house. They purchased the property from a local nobleman, apparently still finding it easier to deal with those who protected them in return for financial benefits than to deal with ordinary Christian townsmen. The Jews obtained additional land for the community office and rabbi's house. Two years later, the local prince's construction superintendent, a certain Baur, produced a building plan based upon that of Munich's neoclassical synagogue of 1824–26. The building committee approved, making allowance for local conditions that required modifications. Congregation members paid most of the cost of about 15,800 florins by buying seats and making special donations. About 5 percent of the cost came from King William I of Württemberg and Prince Maximilian of Thurn and Taxis. Donations to religious buildings were common obligations of rulers, and many noblemen knew the value of being decent to the Jews who had stimulated commerce and prosperity in their lands. As the Buchau community, with its dependent community of Kappel, then had about 875 Jews—the largest concentration in Württemberg—the rulers may have found it particularly fitting to subsidize the Buchau synagogue.

Pilaster strips and connecting horizontal moldings divided the rectilinear, triangular-gabled facade of the Buchau synagogue into three vertical compartments, each with a door indicating the nave and aisles inside (Fig. 125). Over each door was a hood molding and a round-headed window above. This arrangement, and a double row of round-headed windows on the building's sides, revealed the two-storey interior elevation. Behind the masonry between the doors and windows was the gallery between the storeys. A semicircular window in the facade gable lit the attic. The design was clear and the form smoothly plastered. Other facades of the same general style are known as far away as Szeged (see Fig. 54) in Hungary and Włodawa in Poland. The Montefiore synagogue at Ramsgate shares the general aesthetic seen at Buchau—a predominant classicism with a few Egyptian details around the ark to suggest the (presumably Egyptian-style) Temple of Solomon (see Figs. 252, 253).

The interior was a galleried box with a flat ceiling under a broad and high gabled roof (Fig. 126). The Munich synagogue had a coffered

Figure 125. Buchau am Federsee, 1833–35, facade.

Figure 126. Buchau am Federsee, interior to ark.

barrel vault, but Buchau's Jews settled for a simpler and cheaper ceiling. Oaken Tuscan columns, stuccoed to imitate marble, supported the gallery. Broad window openings had simple molded surrounds. The mood was not dour, however, because the building was spacious and well lit. A stately curve forming an apse-like ark recess introduced a note of variety. Paired columns framed the wide opening for the ark doors, a three-part design that echoed the broader nave and narrower aisles. The color, mostly white with touches of blue and gold, sustained the impression of refined simplicity. This was a synagogue characteristic of the country-town counterparts of the culturally assimilated Jews of London, Paris, Bordeaux, Munich, Copenhagen, and Wrocław—all of whom worshipped in buildings of similar plan and style by the time the Buchau synagogue was constructed (see Figs. 108, 109, 175, 176, 177, 235, 236).

The impression given by synagogues of the Buchau type is one of dignity and restraint. This would not be remarkable if we were dealing with Christian, especially Protestant, buildings. But the Jews had often been seen as odd foreigners. Now, however, Jews with citizenship rights began to be more easily accepted in civic life. They no longer had to live only in Buchau's Jewish quarter. The synagogue on the public street had a facade like that of a modest church. The Jewish leaders and the secular authorities even agreed that the synagogue should have a short bell tower with a clock so that the building would not look like a humble creation beside the handsome churches of the town. The synagogue here, as elsewhere in the years between about 1815 and 1840, marks an important change in the status of Jews. This was clear to other Jews. Those of Pflaumloch asked in 1841 for the plan and for information about the synagogue's cost, as they hoped to imitate it. The Jews of Lengnau did the same when they wanted to improve their eighteenth-century building, although the synagogue there was not built as a literal copy of Buchau's.

BIBLIOGRAPHY

Gesellschaft zur Erforschung jüdische Kunstdenkmäler, Notizblatt 33 (1933), for photographs.

F. Hundsnurcher and G. Taddey, *Die jüdische Ge-*

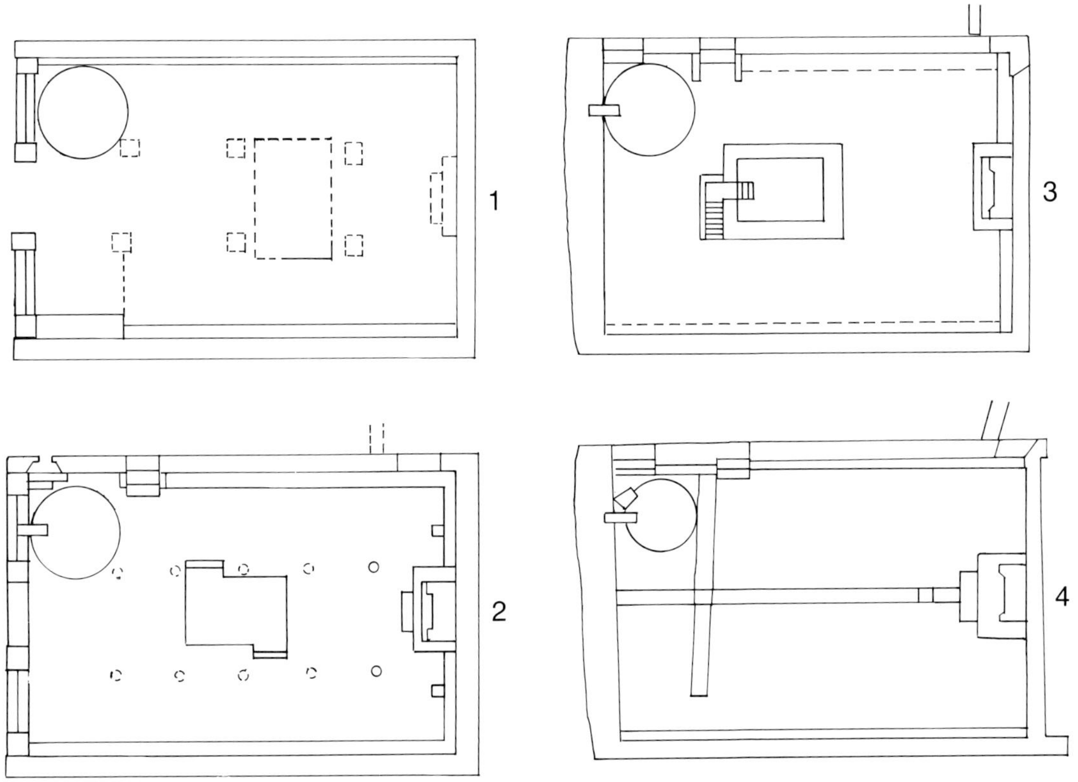

Figure 127. Cologne, medieval synagogue, (1) ca. 1000–96, (2) 1096–ca. 1280, (3) ca. 1280–1349, (4) 1372–1426.

meinde in Baden, Denkmale, Geschichte, Schicksale, Stuttgart, 1968 (Veröffentlichungen der Staatlichen Archivverwaltung Baden-Württemberg, 19).

J. Mohn, *Der Leidensweg unter dem Hakenkreuz,* Bad Buchau, 1970.

P. Rieger, ed., *Jüdische Gotteshäuser und Friedhöfe in Württemberg,* Stuttgart, 1932 (Soncino-Gesellschaft der Freunde des jüdischen Buches, 12).

The most important sources of information are in the Moritz Vierfelder Collection in the Archives of the Leo Baeck Institute, New York. The collection contains abundant photographic documentation.

Cologne

Medieval Synagogue

Medieval synagogue remains are most numerous in German-speaking areas, perhaps because archaeologists there have been more active than elsewhere. The Cologne synagogue was excavated in the late 1950s, in the heart of the city near the cathedral, where aerial bombing during the Second World War destroyed the later buildings on the site, ironically making excavation easier (Fig. 127). The remains showed four stages of development within the same walls of about 9.2 m. by 14.5 m. The first stage lasted from ca. 1000 to 1096 when Crusaders damaged the building. The second stage, from 1096 to ca. 1280, ended with a remodeling. The third stage lasted until 1349, when there was a pogrom and expulsion of the Jews. The fourth lasted from 1372, when the Jews were readmitted, until 1426, when the synagogue was converted into the Town Councillors' chapel.

The first synagogue may have had a nave and aisles, an entrance to the nave at the west, a freestanding ark at the east, a central bimah, benches lining the walls, a brick pavement sunk slightly below street level, and a circular well in the northwest corner of the property. After 1096, the synagogue may again have had a nave and aisles, then separated by perhaps five pairs of cylindrical wooden piers. The two columns nearest the ark have been excavated, leading Otto Doppelfeld, the archaeologist, to postulate the existence of others; Otto Böcher, the leading authority on the Worms synagogue, thought that the two columns could have been part of an unidentified ark construction. The ark was associated with some sort of projection of about 1.5 m. into the room from the east wall and raised three steps above new flooring. The increased dignity of the ark and the larger size of the new bimah may have inspired the design of a new entrance near the west end of the north wall, as from there the bimah would not block the view of the ark for those entering the prayer hall. Openings on the west wall, an annex (for women?) on the northeast, and raised, broader benches were other changes introduced at this time. A written record mentions stained glass showing a lion and a serpent, embellishments later removed. The remodeling of this synagogue is dated ca. 1280 because fragments of finely carved decorative sculpture were discovered in a storage space for disused sacred objects beneath the bimah; these leaves and birds, apparently from the bimah, may have been carved by the sculptors of the Cologne cathedral capitals of ca. 1270. The Jewish community flourished at this period, for we know also of a new women's area and of a community festivities building (Tanzhaus), and enlargement of the synagogue courtyard. After the fourteenth-century expulsion and readmission, the synagogue received a more radical alteration. A new masonry wall of now unknown height divided the main space into two long and narrow parts. It seems to have had nothing to do with vaulting, as the outer walls could not have sustained masonry vaults, so that the ceiling must have been made of wood. The post-1372 plan cannot be well understood, and we have no other two-naved synagogues with dividing walls rather than dividing pillars.

Werkbund Exhibition Synagogue

The city of Cologne had synagogues at least intermittently since late Roman imperial times, and that of Roonstrasse (1899) in late Romanesque style even survived the Second World War. But the most recent synagogue in the city was the one with the shortest life—the model synagogue erected only for the Werkbund exhibition in 1914 (Fig. 128).

Fairs and exhibitions often include small prayer facilities whose sponsors may be religious groups, sellers of religious objects, or countries with state religions. The Deutscher Werkbund's Cologne exhibition of 1914 had Protestant, Catholic, and Jewish chapels in the architecture and landscape section, built as examples of the good design and of the artistic-industrial cooperation the Werkbund was set up to promote. Friedrich Adler (1868–1942), a Jewish craftsman and architect active in Munich and Hamburg, who had redesigned the Laupheim synagogue between 1900 and 1910, designed the exhibition synagogue and its vestibule. Peter Jessen, author of the official

Figure 128. Cologne, Werkbund Exhibition Synagogue, 1914, interior to ark.

catalogue for the exhibition, admired the synagogue far more than the churches, and pronounced it an exemplary achievement of the Werkbund.

The vestibule walls were covered with colored tiles, some plain and some with relief rosettes. A side entrance to the vestibule and the twin doorways to the synagogue hall had ceramic tiles with vine and floral reliefs framing the openings. Above the paired doors stretched a wide ornamental frieze, also made of ceramic tiles in relief. Hexagonal shapes in the center panels were probably allusions to the star of David, but the designs had no other obvious symbolic references.

Thick curtains separated the vestibule from the prayer hall. The main room was proportionately high for its length and had slender compound piers sustaining the coved ceiling. These supports stood near the outer walls, leaving space for an aisle around the center space and for a gallery over the aisles. The galleries, bowing outward, looked like boxes at the theater. The bimah and ark joined in a single composition to make a model synagogue for Reform Jews—the assimilated people who were likely to be at the exhibition. The bimah railing curved in a wide arc, complementing the broad half-dome in which Adler set the ark. The eastern walls were covered with panels of foliate and lattice designs, remotely resembling fourteenth-century ornament in synagogues at Toledo and Córdoba, but the architectural forms, the building proportions, the colored glass windows showing Jewish symbols, and the organ behind ornamental panels had nothing to do with Moorish models. A ponderous chandelier hung from the center of the ceiling, illuminating the craftsmanship of the contractors and the Jewish ritual artifacts on display in vitrines. The moderately progressive design, with its long and simplified compound piers, the use of materials that could be produced in molds and by machines, the semiabstract ornament, and a gentle interplay of spaces aroused the interest of Peter Jessen and lay visitors.

To those who think of the 1914 exhibition as the site of advanced experiments in glass, concrete, and purified architectural form, Jessen's evaluation of Adler's synagogue may be surprising. The vestibule and prayer hall have dense and vaguely historicist forms, and the main room appears from photographs to have been spacious in size but slightly stuffy in feeling. This was not congenial to Bruno Taut's Glass House or Walter Gropius's Model Factory, also designed for the same exhibition; nevertheless, there were more traditionally evocative buildings than avant-garde structures at the exhibition, and the synagogue fit in comfortably.

The design was not used for any later synagogues, and Adler is not known to have received subsequent synagogue commissions. We may regret that the efforts of architect and craftsmen endured for so short a time, but this synagogue's expected demise was more acceptable than the Nazis' wanton destruction of Cologne's permanent synagogues.

Twenty-three years later, after the Nazis had come to power, another German Jewish architect, Rudolf Joseph, proposed an exposition synagogue, but this one was to be more than an example of modern design. Joseph, exiled in Paris, hoped that a Jewish pavilion at the International Exposition of 1937 in the French capital could be an information center about Judaism and Jews, to counteract Nazi and anti-Semitic propaganda. The exposition building would be made with a frame of permanent materials but filled with lightweight walls and partitions, so that at the end of the fair the frame could be moved to a site where a new synagogue was needed and be rebuilt with stronger walls. This would spread the cost of the pavilion between the exhibition sponsors and a congregation, reducing the financial burden on both and filling two needs simultaneously. The various designs that Joseph proposed were all simple and geometric, symmetrical in plan, and in harmony with the half-hearted modernism of the Paris exposition architecture. His suggestions were not adopted, nor were they taken up for the New York World's Fair of 1939–40 when Joseph, then resident in America, proposed them again. These circumstances contrast poignantly with those under which Adler had presented his synagogue so optimistically a quarter-century earlier in Cologne.

BIBLIOGRAPHY

Deutscher Werkbund, *Jahrbuch 1915: Deutsche Form im Kriegsjahr. Die Ausstellung Köln, 1914,* pp. 64–65.

O. Doppelfeld, *"Residenzen Gottes". Die ältesten Synagogen von Köln,* Cologne, 1959 (Schriftenreihe der Kölnischen Gesellschaft für christlich-jüdisch Zusammenarbeit, Heft 4).

K. Prellwitz, "Eine Synagoge von Friedrich Adler, Hamburg," *Innen Dekoration* XXVIII (1917), pp. 348–57.

Rudolf Joseph Collection, Leo Baeck Institute (New York), Archives.

Schwäbische Zeitung, April 28, 1978, "Laupheimer Nachrichten."

There were synagogues in the 1906 crafts exhibition in Dresden, and at the religious art exhibition in Stuttgart, 1930.

Dresden

In a city long home to anti-Semitic tendencies, one would not have expected to find an innovative synagogue designed by an important architect in a conspicuous location. But that is what the Jews of Dresden were given in 1838–40 by Gottfried Semper, one of the most important German architects of the ninteenth century. When Nazis burned the synagogue in 1938, they deprived their Jewish and Christian countrymen of an original and significant achievement.

Jews had been expelled from Dresden in 1430. Some trickled back in the next few centuries, but in 1838 not even a thousand lived in all of Saxony. Of these, 631 were clustered in Dresden, worshipping in several private prayer rooms.

A moderate Reform rabbi, Zecharias Frankel, came from Bohemia at the end of 1835. Believing that factionalism could be tempered by uniting all Jews in one congregation, he addressed himself to the problem of securing a synagogue. In it he hoped to promote "progress, piety, and decorum" by regularizing the synagogue service and by introducing German prayers and sermons. These measures were meant to increase understanding and devotion and to remove the temptation to gossip, smoke, and wander in and out during services. The changes had the effect of fostering cultural assimilation, a goal dear to public officials who largely for this reason gave the Jews permission to form a community in 1837 and to build a synagogue.

The community called on the Protestant architect Semper; there was at the time hardly a Jewish architect in Europe, and by employing a local Christian who was a professor at the architecture faculty of the Dresden art academy the Jews formed a bridge to the surrounding community (since architects usually do not bite the hand that feeds them). Besides, Semper had liberal political attitudes.

Early drawings for the synagogue show that Semper thought of a plan much like the executed one but different in elevation. At first, he designed an oblong, apsed building with a single- or twin-towered facade. East of it was a short and relatively narrow bay, which could be heated for use as the winter or weekday synagogue; following this was a large square bay for the main prayer hall, and an apse for the ark. A cloister vault covered the center of the square bay, but Semper could not decide whether to make the tent-like roof above the vault rise to the height of the tower(s) or whether to lower it and thereby allow the facade to dominate both the front and the side elevations. In either case, the building would have looked like a compact church in a style combining several round-arched forms of the past. It would not have been visually distinctive because other German architects of the time were designing religious, especially Protestant, buildings in a generally similar manner. It would have suggested that Jews were more fully integrated into the surrounding society than

Figure 129. Dresden, 1838–40, exterior, north side.

they actually were.

The design was not realized, however, either because the congregation or the government hesitated to have a synagogue that approached Christian types so closely, or because the Jews could not afford a masonry building with high towers and a lofty vault. As executed, the facade had a flat-topped central portion and low towers. The side elevations were equally geometric and simple, with towers, winter synagogue, large square prayer hall, and cupola articulated by vertical moldings, buttresses, and changes in plane (Fig. 129). Semper restricted external ornament to corbel tables on the walls and towers, a dwarf arcade at the top of the cupola drum, and a six-pointed star at the top of the cupola. Allusions to early Christian, Byzantine, and Romanesque architecture were meant to be functional as well as aesthetic. Semper advocated round-arched styles in galleried buildings, because galleries would interrupt the long pointed windows that helped to make Gothic buildings distinctive. The geometric clarity testified to the good taste of the architect. For their part, the Jews may have feared that lavish external display would attract unwanted attention. As their funds were limited, they may have been pleased with a simple and economical exterior.

Simplicity could show their polite lack of aggressiveness, and the clear articulation of building parts suggested that no arcane or subversive rites were taking place inside. The style, massive to suggest venerable models such as S. Lorenzo in Milan or S. Vitale in Ravenna, and ornamented to suggest German roots and government-approved status, fit an ancient people who were established in Germany but who had an exotic heritage.

The exterior would have prepared a visitor for the central plan. Semper preferred central plans for Protestant churches where reading and preaching were important, as they were in synagogues. The style of the interior, however, was surprising, for there Semper emphasized the Jews' oriental background (Fig. 130). The design incorporated such Byzantine forms as the domed square and the galleried nave (the latter also known in Romanesque architecture), and it employed decorative motifs taken from Moorish sources, especially from the Alhambra at Granada; the capitals, for instance, are close to those of the Patio of the Lions, and the cupola may be related to the Room of the Two Sisters. Semper took great pains with the details, designing such fittings as the candelabra and the Eternal Light. This exemplified his own teaching, in which he advocated the serious study of appropriate older art forms and the coordination of both architectural and decorative elements. His wall and vault decorations were small-scale designs of plant and geometric forms painted in subdued colors. The central cloister vault was blue with a design of rays recalling descriptions of heaven.

The sumptuously decorated interior gave no sign of having been built as economically as it was. The first designs for the synagogue had envisioned the construction of stone arches supporting the galleries, but in the final design they were made of wood. At least some were replaced or reinforced later with stone. The cloister-vaulted cupola was to have been made of masonry, but the second design provided for a wooden one of about 25-m. diameter. The effect was what was wanted, rather than consistency of structure. The central plan and slender piers ensured that all worshippers could see and hear clearly. The bimah stood nearer to the ark than was traditional, and grilles were never installed on the galleries, both indications of Reform influence, but there was no organ until 1870 because two rich contributors had stipulated that there be neither an organ nor a choir.

As a practical building, the Dresden synagogue was successful. Semper arranged entrance doors on the south side—the side with adequate space—to lead to the winter and the main synagogues. He provided three hundred seats for men on the ground floor and two hundred for women in two levels of galleries. A thousand worshippers could be accommodated if half of them stood, and that number attended the dedication ceremonies in 1840. The winter synagogue, a resting room, an area for kasher food preparations, and the synagogue caretaker's apartment all were included. Nevertheless, some Jewish periodicals criticized the cost, 30,204 thalers, and questioned the need for a conspicuous edifice when worship could be conducted more modestly.

Inside and out, the building conveyed ambiguous messages about the ways in which Jews saw themselves in relation to the surrounding society. The exterior must have satisfied both those Jews and Christians who wanted the Jews to appear more German, to speak modern German, and to change their separate, impoverished condition. The building was not hidden in a back courtyard on an unhealthy site, but was visible near the Gondelhafen and the later Bruhl Terrace, thereby acknowledging the Jews' existence. Religion, properly conducted, was seen by the conservative government as supporting the established order. It is understandable that Dresden's Jews felt insecure enough to accept a design that suggested they were almost German in public and perhaps something else in private. If there was a sharp divergence between exterior and interior, the congregation must have accepted the contemporary idea that architecture was national and racial in character. Just as the British Houses of Parliament were rebuilt in a style considered British at about this time, the Jews began to look for styles through which to establish their character and position in society. At least they were not being forced to assimilate entirely, nor to seem completely alien. They were only partly assimilated to the general society, and Semper's synagogue revealed their situation.

The synagogue design was influential, although there were few close imitations of it. Its exterior and that of Kassel were both published in the architectural press and in prints, and they fostered interest in Romanesque style for synagogues. The Dresden interior surely provided the model for the use of Islamic ornament in synagogues. Especially in the first years after the granting of full civil rights to Jews in united Germany (1871), and later when Jews emphasized that they took these rights for granted despite the rise of anti-Semitism, designs of this mixed type reappeared (see Figs. 41, 42, 212, 213), revealing the aspirations of those who tried to balance the realities of being both Jewish and European.

BIBLIOGRAPHY

AZJ II, June 22, 1838 (letter frm Dresden by B. B.), Aug. 23, 1838; III Jan. 8, 1839, Feb. 13, 1839.

R. Bruck, "Gottfried Semper," *Der Baumeister* I, #8 (1903), pp. 85–86.

Deutsche Bauzeitung XIV (1880), p. 3 for Semper's obituary.

A. Diamant, *Chronik der Juden in Dresden,* Darmstadt, 1973.

"Die Synagoge zu Dresden," *Allgemeine Bauzeitung* XII (1847), p. 127, pls. 105–7.

M. Fröhlich, *Gottfried Semper. Zeichnerische Nachlass im Besitz der E.T.H. Zürich,* Basel and Stuttgart, 1974, pp. 74–75, cat. #99-1-1 to 4.

C. Gurlitt, *Beschreibende Darstellung der aelteren Bau und Kunstdenkmaeler des Koenigreichs Sachsen,* Heft 21-23, Dresden, 1903, p. 296.

Hammer-Schenk, *Synagogen,* pp. 308–47.

———, "Untersuchungen," pp. 179–213.

A. Lévy, "Notes sur l'histoire des juifs de Saxe," *Revue des études juives* XXV (1892), pp. 217–34.

F. Löffler, *Das alte Dresden, Geschichte und Bauten,* 5th ed., Frankfurt, 1966, pp. 136, 377.

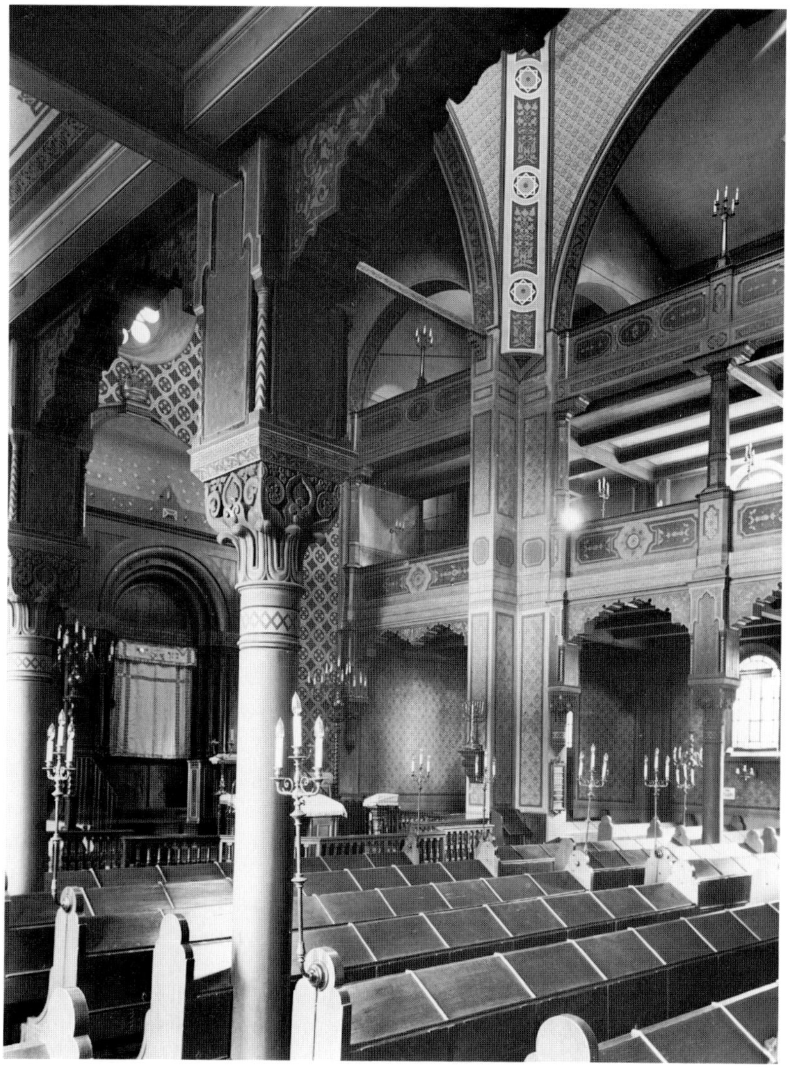

Figure 130. Dresden, interior to ark.

H. Rosenau, "Gottfried Semper and German Synagogue Architecture," *Publications of the Leo Baeck Institute. Yearbook* XXII (1977), pp. 237–44.

H. Semper, *Gottfried Semper. Ein Bild seines Lebens und Wirkens,* Berlin, 1880, p. 14.

Endingen and Lengnau

The synagogues of Endingen and Lengnau are among the few extant small-town synagogues, and they are exceptional in having escaped willful damage by vandals or wartime destruction. They are among the small number of Switzerland's religious buildings of any faith that are still in virtually unaltered nineteenth-century condition. They testify to the existence of Jewish life in one corner of a country in which few Jews were permitted to live after their expulsion from the larger cities in the fifteenth century. The nineteenth-century synagogues also bring to mind their eighteenth-century predecessors, the only two synagogues within the modern borders of Switzerland from the mid-eighteenth to the early nineteenth century. Pictorial documents record three stages of their design.

These synagogues owe their existence to the fact that they were built in an area that did not always belong to Switzerland, but was part of the margravate of Baden, where some Jews had been documented in the fifteenth century and again in the first half of the seventeenth; the first record of Jews in Lengnau dates from 1622 and in Endingen, 1678. Most of the Jews were from the Rhineland, to judge from their names, but others were of Polish origin. In 1766, however, the 108 Jewish families in Baden were confined to Endingen and Lengnau, which lay on the main route between the fair towns of Baden and Zurzach; here, it was expected, they would be useful in commerce.

Eighteenth Century

The Jews of Endingen and Lengnau already had synagogues and a jointly maintained cemetery, and thus the newcomers could be accommodated in community institutions. Before 1750, when the Lengnau synagogue was dedicated, and before 1764 in Endingen, the Jews had worshipped in rented buildings, of which Endingen's, at least, was in poor condition by 1754. Johann Caspar Ulrich, an antiquarian and clergyman of Zurich, said that it might more properly be called a Jewish stable than a synagogue. The description fits the tiny box recorded in an old photograph; it had a gabled roof and external wooden stairway. Of no physical distinction whatever, it was typical of many country synagogues. The interior appearance survives in a drawing Ulrich made during his travels in search of information about Jews and Judaism (Fig. 131). The prayer hall was barrel vaulted, with a balustrade and grilles delimiting the women's section on the south and west. The men, in the principal area, stood wrapped in their prayer shawls at movable reading stands set in irregular lines long the north, south, and east. A table, no doubt used during religious study sessions, stood in front of the women's balustrade on the south wall. The other furnishings were more elaborate. The ark at the east contained several Torah scrolls. The congregation enclosed them inside wooden doors secured with ornamental metalwork set in a frame with twisted columns at the sides—recalling those at St. Peter's in Rome, which were said to come from the Temple in Jerusalem; surmounting the columns were rampant lions on either side of a cartouche. (Similar ark compositions are known in other eighteenth-century synagogues, and a Bavarian example is preserved in the Jewish Museum in New York City.) The bimah was a hexagonal cage apparently made of wood, and decorated with turned balusters, carved leaf forms on the cornice, round finials at the corners, and some peaked terminal features added to the east and west side cornices. Sconces for candles projected from at least one side of the bimah. Additional light came from chandeliers suspended from the wooden barrel vault by chains; the more elaborate ones hung closer to the ark. In addition, there were round-headed windows containing panes of bull's-eye glass, and a lobed window in the center of the eastern wall. The eastern wall windows were asymmetrically disposed, with the south side window given more generous space between the ark and the south wall and the ark correspondingly pushed toward the north. This was done apparently because the women's section lay along the south and had its own windows and chandeliers; the southern window on the eastern wall illuminated the men's area.

Apart from the spacing of windows, the Lengnau synagogue was much like that of Endingen, and comparable to other eighteenth-century vil-

Figure 131. Endingen, interior in ca. 1754, drawn by Johann Caspar Ulrich.

Figure 132. Lengnau, interior in ca. 1754, drawn by Johann Caspar Ulrich.

Figure 133. Lengnau, exterior in ca. 1754, drawn by Johann Caspar Ulrich.

lage synagogues such as those of Bechhofen, Ellrich am Sudharz, Horb, and Rechnitz, although details and decoration differed (Fig. 132; see Fig. 13). At Lengnau, the synagogue had an octagonal wooden bimah with seats around the base. A pulpit stood adjacent to it. The ark had twisted columns and rampant lions, but the columns were stubbier in proportion and there was a carved wooden or plaster curtain motif above the lions and cartouche. Iron spikes to hold candles rested on a parapet beside the steps to the ark. The men used movable reading stands lit by many-branched chandeliers. A women's gallery extended on the west and south, with an extra window on the south side of the east wall to light it.

The Lengnau synagogue appears in Ulrich's drawing as a simple rectilinear building with a peaked and slightly concave roof (Fig. 133). It was about 18 m. by 15 m. with walls about 8.4 m. high made of timber filled with masonry and plastered over. Ulrich showed the exterior surface as entirely plain, but the artist J. I. Holzhalb depicted quoins at the corners in a book he published in 1768 discussing Jewish history and Judaism. There may have been improvements in the years between 1750 and 1768, because Holzhalb claimed to have made the drawing of the building on the spot. The synagogue had a porch leading to men's and women's doors, and three round-headed windows on the entrance side, on the south.

The Endingen synagogue as rebuilt in 1764 was more elaborate, with exterior walls divided into bays by smooth borders in relief, apparently made of the plaster that covered the entire rectangular building under its double-pitched roof. A porch stretched over the whole western side, with doors to the men's area and apparently to a gallery; the exterior had round windows on the second storey which could have lighted an upstairs gallery. The attractive building influenced the design of the Randegg synagogue of ca. 1800, located near Konstanz in the German-Swiss border area, and that of Hohenems in the Vorarlberg, to which Endingen was connected by a well-used trade route.

Nineteenth Century

As one consequence of the French Revolution, the southernmost part of Baden became part of Switzerland, the canton of Aargau. The Jews of Endingen and Lengnau did not acquire equal rights as citizens until 1876. Nevertheless, they increased in number in both towns, and by 1834 the Endingen Jews needed a new synagogue because the old one was decrepit and probably too small for a Jewish population that in 1850 reached its peak of 1,515 individuals in both towns combined. No one foresaw the migration to cities that occurred during the last third of the century, making small-town synagogue building projects superfluous. Being no more prescient than anyone else, the Jews of Lengnau and Endingen erected new synagogues in 1846–49 and 1850–52, respectively. The former was designed by Ferdinand Stadler (1813–70) who had studied in Darmstadt and Karlsruhe where one of his teachers was Friedrich Eisenlohr (who worked on the Mannheim synagogue of 1855). Stadler was particularly active in designing churches and government buildings. The Endingen synagogue was designed by Caspar Joseph Jeuch (1811–95), trained in Munich, who designed primarily secular works, a few churches, and urban sanitation and renewal projects in Baden.

The Lengnau synagogue cost 44,000 francs, 150 percent of the estimate. To make up the deficit in construction funds, the cantonal government rather grudgingly granted about 2.5 percent of the cost. The result was a synagogue of 91 by 55 local feet (about 29.5 m. × 17 m.), set back from the street on a low platform. Its three-part facade reflects the nave and galleried aisles inside (Fig. 134). The higher center bay terminates in a gable crowned by the tablets of the Law at a height of about 21 m. The inspiration for this design, including corbel table ornament (now lost) and two storeys of tall, round-headed windows with circular ones above them, comes from the Kassel synagogue of 1839 (see Fig. 164). That synagogue incorporated conspicuous borrowings from church design and Romanesque style, and Stadler's training would have made him sympathetic to it.

The elevation apparently descends from that of the Kassel synagogue, although that one had an arched ceiling while the nave ceiling of the Lengnau synagogue forms three sides of a polygon (Fig. 135). The Swiss building is a galleried basilica with a low ground floor and a higher arcaded gallery floor. Simple grilles stretch under the gallery arches on three sides, running from one slender pier to another. Overall, the style is fine-lined, as is characteristic of many buildings of the 1840s, and the details are Romanesque and classical, that is, *Rundbogenstil.* The polygonal bimah stands near the ark, a location motivated here apparently by the need to install more seats rather than any need to satisfy Reformers. In general, the Lengnau synagogue is more measured and stately in its rhythms, while the forms at Endingen spring together in a daintier and livelier way.

The Endingen synagogue of 1850–52 also had a tripartite facade, combining a basilican and a temple front, without classical details (Fig. 136). Instead of a pediment, Jeuch placed a stepped gable at the summit of the facade. It recalls the stepped gables of Gothic and later vernacular buildings, as well as Jeuch's church facade designs for Basel and Leuggern, but here the proportions are squat rather than elongated. Perhaps Jeuch tried to make the synagogue recall other religious buildings, while keeping it different enough to be distinctive. As

Figure 134. Lengnau, 1846–49, facade.

Figure 135. Lengnau, interior to ark.

Figure 136. Endingen, 1850–52, facade.

Figure 137. Endingen, interior to ark.

his design for the town church of St. Elisabeth's, Basel, is more elaborate, with its tall tower, than his design for a village church in Leuggern, Jeuch probably thought that there were appropriate modes of design to suit specific classes of buildings. He arrived at a simple, non-Gothic mode for the Jews of a small town.

The synagogue is 29.5 m. by 19.5 m. in exterior measurement, larger than Lengnau's. Like the latter, it has a rectilinear plan with a projecting apsidal niche for the ark (Fig. 137). It is a galleried basilica with wide arches at the women's gallery level on three sides of the interior. The supports are so thin that they must be made of iron. The nave ceiling is segmentally arched. The nineteenth-century decorations are in Moorish style, but some window frames, candelabra, an oil lamp, charity boxes, textiles, and some seats came from the former synagogue in the town. The congregation had, in fact, intended only to remodel the old building until consultants warned them that the foundations could not support an enlarged building. Cantonal government officials, sympathetic to the Endingen Jews' request for a subvention, granted 2,500 francs for a total of about 46,000 francs needed to rebuild. Later, they praised the construction as well as the honorable intentions of the Jews who could not have foretold the need to build an entirely new synagogue on the old site, and who had made financial sacrifices to build it and the adjacent school (which cost 26,000 francs).

Since the nineteenth century, an arched and partly glazed partition has been added between the vestibule and the main hall at Endingen, and both synagogues were partially electrified. The Lengnau facade is now painted in uniform tones rather than the original contrasting colors of its wall and its moldings, and it has also lost some of its ornament. All the same, the synagogues look much the way they did originally and are now officially listed as sites of regional significance. Endingen was restored in 1933 and 1952 by an architect named Schneider from Ennetbaden, and in 1976 both buildings were surveyed and studied by Ernst Guggenheim of Zurich, who pointed out grave structural problems. The Swiss central and cantonal governments have agreed to furnish about a third of the projected 5,200,000-franc cost of restoration, and additional funds are being solicited from other donors. Asking the local Jews will not suffice: Whereas in 1850, the thousand or so Jews of Endingen constituted a third of Swiss Jewry, today there are not even ten Jewish families in both towns combined.

BIBLIOGRAPHIES

ENDINGEN AND LENGNAU

E. Guggenheim, *Restauration Synagogen Endingen und Lengnau,* Zurich, 1976.

F. Guggenheim-Gruenberg, *Die Juden in der Schweiz,* Zurich, 1961 (*Beiträge zur Geschichte und Volkskunde der Juden in der Schweiz,* Heft 7).

S. Guggenheim-Weil, "Restauration der Synagogen Endingen und Lengnau," *Neue Zürcher Zeitung* July 22/23, 1978, #168, p. 29.

E. Haller, *Die rechtliche Stellung der Juden im Kanton Aargau,* Aarau, 1901.

Hammer-Schenk, *Synagogen,* p. 548, n. 20.

J. C. Ulrich, *Sammlung jüdischer Geschichten,* Basel, 1768, pp. 166, 271, 296–97.

A. Weldler-Steinberg, *Geschichte der Juden in der Schweiz: vom 16 Jahrhundert bis nach der Emanzipation,* 2 vols., Zurich, 1966–70, esp. vol. 2.

F. Wyler, *Die Staatsrechtliche Stellung der israelitischen Religionsgenossenschaft in der Schweiz,* Glarus, 1929.

BECHHOFEN, ELLRICH, HORB, RECHNITZ, ET AL.

D. Davidowicz, *Wandmalereien in alten Synagogen,* Hameln and Hannover, 1969.

K. Lohrmann, ed., *1000 Jahre Österreichisches Judentum. Ausstellungskatalog (Österreichische Jüdische Museum,* Eisenstadt 1982 [Studia Judaica Austriaca, 9]).

Wischnitzer, *Architecture,* with further references.

Nikolaus Vielmetti and the late H. W. Janson kindly provided references to the works by Lohrmann, Guggenheim, and Guggenheim-Weil.

Essen

Steelerstrasse

When the synagogue at Essen was completed in 1914, architects and critics lavished praise upon it: They found the building expertly adapted to its location in the city and to a difficult site; it was appropriate visually to the expression of its spiritual purpose; the essence of its architecture lay in its space-forming mass, not in petty details. They also commended the architect for creating suitable details, not mere copies of historic shapes. They believed that Germany had a synagogue—at last—that did not look like a transplant from the medieval orient. The local

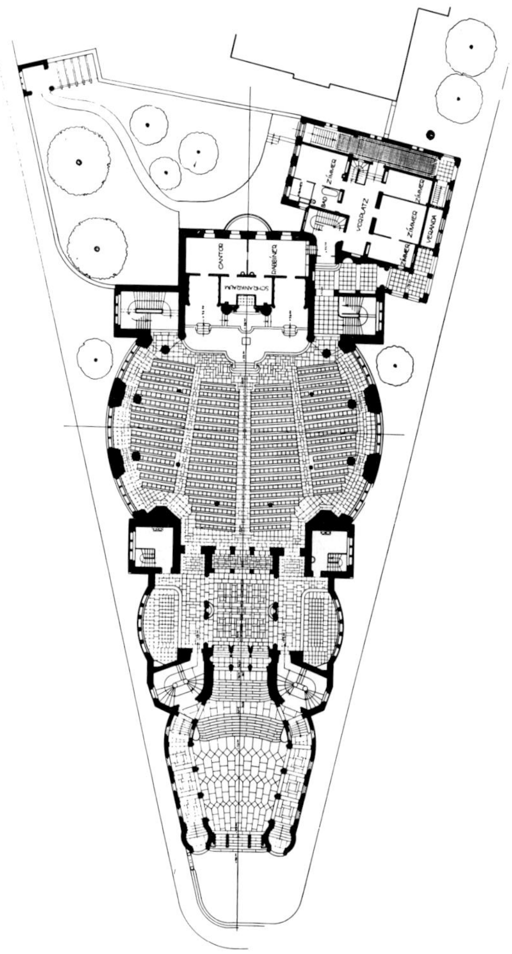

Figure 138. Essen, Steelerstrasse, 1908–14, plan.

Figure 139. Essen, Steelerstrasse, exterior before 1938.

rabbi, Dr. S. Samuel, who actually thought that the Moorish orientalism of medieval Spanish synagogues was suited to modern times, nevertheless felt that the synagogue justified his belief that a Christian architect who understood his commission could fulfill Jewish needs. A tour organized by the Deutscher Werkbund in 1914 found the synagogue to be a highlight of the visit to Essen. Critics suggested that this might be the first really modern synagogue, even the first modern building!

The number of Jews in Essen, never more than 1 percent of the total population, increased after the Ruhr became industrialized in the nineteenth century. The enlarged community needed a bigger synagogue than the existing one, which was only about 19 m. long and 13 m. wide. A prominent Jewish banker, Isaac Hirschland, was on good terms with the mayor and secured his approval to buy the site of a villa on a conspicuous corner. The Jewish community sponsored an open design competition in 1908 and received seventy-two entries. First prize went to a local architect, Edmund Körner (1875–1927); Otto Kühlmann of Berlin submitted a second-prize entry which looked a good deal like the winner's presentation in general plan and elevation.

Körner designed well for a site shaped like an irregular triangle with its apex at the west but sloping upward toward the east and north (Fig. 138). The western end, with the synagogue portal, faced the heart of the city on a corner from which the Steelerstrasse, a wide street with trolley tracks, left the city through the Steele Gate en route to the suburb of that name (Fig. 139). A forecourt followed, using some of the expanding triangular area. At the wide far end of the forecourt, steps ascended to a vestibule flanked by corridors leading to staircase turrets. Beyond that lay a commodious lobby, marked on the exterior by a broad gable. The lobby wall along Steelerstrasse maintained the building lines along this built-up street. The undulating straight and curved walls of the synagogue, followed by the lower but straight walls of the community house, gave the street some visual variety as well. Körner placed the garden on the northeast, making good use of the irregular leftover space. (The synagogue and forecourt occupied about 2,400 of the 3,000 square meters available.)

The architect alternated gently curving walls (courtyard turrets; facade and portal) with sturdy verticals and strong diagonal rooflines. Then he countered the concave curves with the convexity of the main dome, crowning the round main space. He lightened the impression of mass with turrets and carefully designed ornaments in stone and metal. The design must have satisfied Rabbi Samuel, who had written that in synagogue projects an architect should be careful not to ruin the streetscape with an oddity. He may have been pleased that here an impressive building ascended in compact masses from the entrance to the eight-sided dome on a square drum in a manner that was stately and not at all bizarre.

Körner accommodated the slope of the site by raising the prayer hall twenty-eight steps above the narrow west end. The steps were grouped at the forecourt entrance, the main door, and inside between rooms, to make the rise gradual and to reinforce the sense of ascent toward the ark. Elevating the main level allowed room under the rabbi's and cantor's rooms east of the ark for a basement to house the weekday synagogue, meeting areas, and a library.

The problem of noise along Steelerstrasse was handled to some extent by the thick walls, their thickness emphasized by rough-surfaced masonry. The construction material—used for walls, arches, most floors, and ornamental work such as the ark—was mainly limestone. Brickwork helped to sustain the largest arches inside,

Figure 140. Essen, Steelerstrasse, interior before 1938.

and reinforced concrete was used for foundations, balcony supports, and most ceilings and domes.

These materials also serve aesthetic purposes. The rough stone entrance sets off the smooth curves and surfaces of the forecourt arches. The facade's roughness and mass are relieved by the sinuous curves of the smooth entrance steps and by the dignified metal portals. The lobby has straight lines and flat surfaces, and there are neoclassical aspects to the rigid geometry and coffered ceiling, providing a contrast to the prayer hall. In the latter, the sense of compact enclosure given by curving forms contrasts with the lofty spaciousness and play of light over surfaces of blended colors and sparkling gold mosaic (Fig. 140). The effects of space and color culminate at the east, around the ark and bimah, which are close together, following Reform practice. Resonant sound from the city's largest organ and from a musicians' gallery around the inner oculus of the double dome would have enhanced the sensuous visual effects.

Körner's handsome design reflected others of the same generation. From his teacher, Johannes Otzen, the young Körner had learned about the suitability of centrally planned buildings for Protestant worship, and he understood that this plan could be applied to Reform temples. From Cremer's and Wolffenstein's synagogue of Poznań—which opened in 1908, the year of the Essen competition—Körner could have taken the turrets flanking a forecourt, the facade gable, and the idea of a dome. From earlier architects, such as Robert Curjel and Karl Moser in Germany and Ferdinand Boberg in Sweden, Körner could have learned about compact masses and rough masonry relieved by linear stone moldings and plaques. From the synagogue of the Israelitische Religionsgesellschaft, then under way at Frankfurt am Main, Körner could have understood the Jews' interest in a free and modern style that had some connection to civic and Christian architecture (see Fig. 144).

The Essen synagogue, like others of the time at Frankfurt am Main and Bamberg, has interpenetrating forms rather than the clearly articulated building elements that Cremer and Wolffenstein used. And it has one of several early-twentieth-century synagogue rotundas (others were at Augsburg, Mainz, and Offenbach) (see Fig. 16). Körner shared the belief of his colleagues at the Darmstadt Artists' Colony (which he joined in 1911) that an architect must concern himself with every element in his building, although he did not know when to stop designing ornament. The broad sweep of his balconies, for instance, was vitiated by their decoration, and every door panel and colored glass windowpane has banal symbolic meaning. The ornament itself was, at least, inventive, based loosely on classical and Mesopotamian ideas to indicate the Jews' ancient and oriental heritage.

Rabbi Samuel had written in 1908 that an Eastern style would suggest the golden age of Jewry in medieval Spain, where synagogues were designed in Moorish styles (see Figs. 181, 184). This connection to Spanish Jewry had been discussed by a Christian art critic, V. Stassov, earlier in connection with the Leningrad synagogue, but it is not known to have been linked to the actual design of synagogues. Rabbi Samuel did not, however, like all the building details that were usual in Moorish synagogues. An older synagogue in Essen (Gerswidastrasse), built by *Bauinspektor* Spannagel in 1869–70, had onion domes, but Rabbi Samuel thought that onion domes suggested the Greek Orthodox church. He did not like cross plans, either, which he associated with Christian buildings. He must have been ready for Körner's suggestion—but not imitation—of a Byzantine dome, and for faintly oriental medallions, subtly fused colors, and golden glints. These, however, had no connection to the Jewish monuments of medieval Spain. The forecourt and some of the ornament nevertheless evoked memories of something eastern: the Temple of Jerusalem.

All this invention, care, and craftsmanship nearly fell victim to the Nazis on Crystal Night in 1938, but Körner's structure proved so solid that it would have been too costly to demolish it. The interior was devastated, however, and after the war the two-hundred-member Jewish community was too small to repair a building meant for four thousand people, or to use its twelve hundred seats economically. The city bought the building, allowing Jews to send fragments of it to New York City where the Habonim Synagogue built a memorial of its pieces. The building became a museum of industrial art, preserving only the shell but not the forecourt, which gave way to a street-widening project. On the steps of the museum stands a sarcophagus under tangled barbed wire, with an inscription stating that 2,500 local Jews lost their lives between 1933 and 1945. Some Jews were unhappy about the modern use of the building, and about the inscription which said nothing about how the lives were lost. When a fire broke out inside the museum in 1979 and the displays were removed, some members of the Jewish community successfully petitioned for the building to become a memorial rather than a secular museum.

Figure 141. Essen, Ruhrallee, 1959, exterior.

Ruhrallee

In 1959, the community dedicated a new synagogue and community center of vastly different form. This one, too, was designed by sympathetic Christian architects, Dieter Knoblauch and Heinz Heise, who won an interfaith competition and who also built the West Berlin Jewish Community Center in Fasanenstrasse (1957–59), replacing a demolished synagogue. The site for the new Essen synagogue was that of the prewar Jewish youth center designed by Erich Mendelsohn (1931).

Although the architects studied books about ancient synagogues in the Holy Land and about the Steelerstrasse synagogue, they created something different—a hemispheric sanctuary to express the essence of the oldest monotheistic religion (Figs. 141, 142). On one side is a rectilinear entrance and on the other a gently curving community center which provides a formal transition between the surprising hemisphere and the preexisting buildings of the neighborhood.

The hemisphere and other simple shapes conform to the taste for geometry then much in favor among architects. But the hemisphere had special appropriateness in Essen and on this site, for Mendelsohn had won acclaim for the Park Synagogue in Cleveland (1946–52), which has a hemispheric dome. Knoblauch's and Heise's hemisphere is purer in form, for it descends to the ground, whereas Mendelsohn's rose above walls.

It is ironic that Mendelsohn-in-Essen, followed by Mendelsohn-in-Cleveland, should have returned thus in spirit to Essen. (Coincidentally, much of the money to build the youth center came from America.) In turn, Körner's synagogue in Essen may have influenced the domed and turreted Tifereth Israel Synagogue in Cleveland (1924, by Charles R. Grieco), one

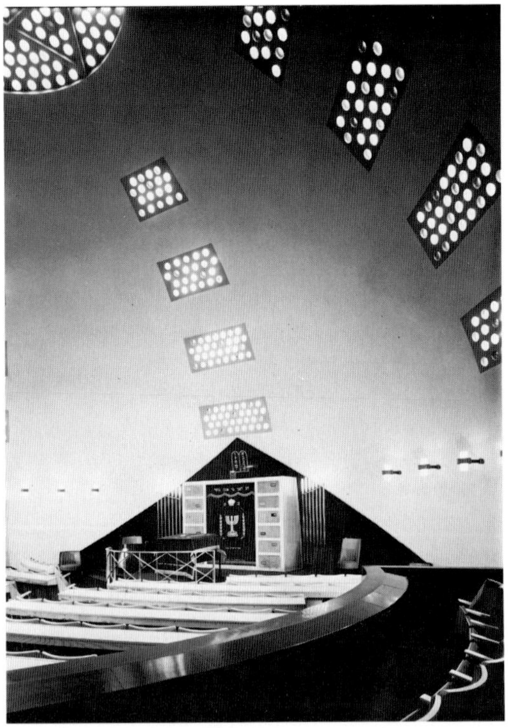
Figure 142. Essen, Ruhrallee, interior to ark.

of the earliest massive, stone-faced, low-domed synagogues in America.

The interior of the new Essen synagogue juxtaposes triangular and circular forms. The ark is a rectangle framed by a triangle that may evoke the Tent in the Wilderness. Rows of windows—round openings in a rectangular frame—curve up to the top of the concrete dome. The center of the dome is lighted by a round window with a six-pointed star motif based on a circle, a hexagon, and triangles.

The differences between the pre- and postwar Essen synagogues offer further ironies. The massive Steelerstrasse building, too solid to be blown up, revealed the firm confidence of a community that was in fact to be blown away. The thinner, delicate forms of the postwar construction, with even the concrete hemisphere perched on the ground like an inflatable structure, and made more ephemeral by its light-reflecting copper cladding, hints at the fragile nature of Jewish existence. On the other hand, the city has an officially benevolent policy toward Jews, who may well use the new synagogue for a long time. This building, with its encompassing form, can express universal values accepted by architects and laymen of all faiths.

BIBLIOGRAPHY

Berliner Architekturwelt XXI (1919), p. 349 (for O. Kühlmann's project).

G. Biermann, review of R. Klapheck book, *Der Cicerone* VI (1914), p. 667.

O. Brattskoven, "Edmund Körner," U. Thieme and F. Becker, eds., *Allgemeines Lexikon der bildenden Künstler.*

E. Cohn, "Die neue Synagoge in Essen," *AZJ,* Nov. 22, 1913, pp. 558–60.

Hammer-Schenk, *Synagogen,* pp. 480–87. N. 1044 refers to other published projects.

R. Klapheck, *Die neue Synagoge in Essen a.d. Ruhr, erbaut von Professor Edmund Körner,* Berlin [1913] (*Architektur des XX Jahrhunderts,* 13 Sonderheft).

R. Klopfer, "Rudolf Bitzan," *Moderne Bauformen* VIII (1909), pp. 226–28 with Bitzan's project, also published earlier. Cf. Hammer-Schenk, *Synagogen,* n. 1044.

D. Knoblauch and H. Heise, "Ein Gotteshaus ist fertig," in H. Elkan, ed., *Festschrift zum Weihe der neuen Essener Synagoge,* Essen, 1959, pp. 20–22.

W. Kornick, "Die neue Synagoge in Essen-Ruhr," *Neudeutsche Bauzeitung* XI (1915), pp. 33–34.

H. Künzl, "Zur Dekoration der Essener Synagoge von 1911–1913," *Das Münster am Hellweg* XXIX, #2 (Feb. 1976), pp. 17–30.

A. Müller-Frauenfeld, "Vom Synagogenbau," *Deutsche Bauhütte* XIV (1910), pp. 216–17 (including A. Schiffer's project).

"Neue Synagoge mit Gemeindezentrum in Essen," *Der Baumeister* LVIII (1961), pp. 100-105.

S. Samuel, "Von der Ausstellung jüdischer Bauten und Kultusgegenstände zu Düsseldorf," *AZJ,* July 31, 1908, pp. 369–70.

H. Schröter, *Geschichte und Schicksal der Essener Juden,* Essen, 1980.

Wischnitzer, *Architecture,* pp. 256–59.

Frankfurt am Main–Israelitische Religionsgesellschaft

The growth of Reform tendencies caused grave concern among the orthodox. The strong statements made by impassioned rabbis on behalf of traditional practice reached the ears of a faithful audience. Spurred on by their deep beliefs, orthodox members of official communities that had espoused Reform developed organizations and prayer meetings of their own, even though this meant paying dues to the community in addition to assessments for their private prayer rooms, ritual baths, and schools.

One such orthodox group was the Israelitische Religionsgesellschaft of Frankfurt, founded in 1848. Although it could not secede from the existing community until 1876, this dynamic group continued to attract adherents and was an important influence on the growth of the worldwide Agudath Israel orthodox organization, founded in 1912.

By 1848, the growing Jewish population of Frankfurt was cramped in its existing synagogues. One of these was a building erected in 1711, a modified reconstruction of a synagogue of ca. 1462; it was single naved and groin vaulted, and it had a three-storey annex for women on the north. The other was a galleried box erected for Reformers in 1810 in the Compostellhof; its austere entrance door had an Egyptian coved cornice, and the interior gallery supports had Egyptian palm capitals.

The Religionsgesellschaft, eager to build its own synagogue, secured building funds from members of the devoutly orthodox Rothschild family, on condition that the congregation follow an orthodox rabbi, as they were fully prepared to do. They called Samson Raphael Hirsch, who served from 1851 to 1888 and who attained an international reputation.

In 1852–53, the group built its first synagogue in the eastern part of the Jewish district. The building seated 250 men and 200 women (although this may have been its capacity after an enlargement with loud Moorish decoration in 1874–75). The original architect was a local practitioner, J. W. Renk, who designed a squarish plan with galleries on three sides and a bimah in the center. Although the west side of the synagogue fronted on the street, it was not given a door. Christians in 1853 would have found a street-side entrance impudent, while the Jews might have found it imprudent.

The west side did receive artistic treatment, but it looked more like the east end of a church than the west facade of any religious building. Perhaps just as important was its freedom from any hint of Reform tendencies. The three-part division of the west wall reflected a flat apse and aisle ends. The center part had no door but only a large arched window above a stretch of wall with accentuated masonry (an allusion to the Wailing Wall in Jerusalem?). Above them were large windows in rectangular frames with emphatic horizontal cornices; Harold Hammer-Schenk likened the sides of the composition to the lower storeys of church towers designed for a group that would not have wanted—or been allowed—to have church towers. All the window tracery was slender and fine with tall, thin lights capped by lobed circles. The style of the windows looked more Gothic than anything else. Nevertheless, a contemporary journal, the *Illustrirte Zeitung,* called the windows Arabic-Byzantine, exemplifying a common tendency to find orientalism in Jewish buildings even when it wasn't there.

This synagogue did not suffice for a congregation that had grown to more than ten times its original size by 1900. Fortunately, by that time, the ghetto no longer existed, and the Jewish group was able to obtain a building site in a suburban area in the east end.

The synagogue design competition in 1904 received 129 proposals. The range is suggested by designs of architects based in Berlin, published in the *Berliner Architekturwelt.* Joseph Reuters and Karl Friedenthal won first prize with a massive but uncoordinated design with Assyrian, Early Christian, and Romanesque features and a huge, smooth, and lightly pointed dome. Another aesthetic failure was the neobaroque design of Otto Kühlmann, who also proposed a large cupola, this one smooth and hemispheric atop a drum filled with round-headed windows separated by paired columns. Wilhelm Freiherr von Tettau suggested a more unified and consistent low-domed design with massive geometric building forms relieved by delicate geometric ornament in the manner of the school of Otto Wagner in Vienna. Semicircular turrets at the entrance recalled Jakhin and Boaz.

The commission went to the third-prize winners, Peter Jürgensen and Jürgen Bachmann, whose most famous building is the Schöneberg Town Hall in West Berlin, but who were well known for other secular buildings and for Protestant churches with massive towers.

The architects had to put a correctly oriented rectangular building on a trapezoidal site, preferably without making a jagged gap in the street line. They filled the street front with a twin-arched screen bordered by two buildings with similar facades but different lengths, thus solving the problem in a functional and attractive way (Figs. 143, 144). The two buildings were gabled oblong boxes with bands of small-paned windows directly under the gables and round openings placed off center below the windows. Rachel Wischnitzer connected the style to contemporary English use of simplified and recombined forms of late-medieval vernacular domestic architecture, a tendency influential in Germany at this time. The details at Frankfurt need not have come from England, for the old Judengasse (Jews' Street) at Frankfurt had gabled houses with strips of small-paned windows and rectangular openings in the gables.

At the far end of the courtyard lay the gray limestone synagogue, a twin-towered gabled building with a higher gabled nave visible over the peak of the facade. The merging of the contours of the towers and facade was a common but still rather new design idea, as were the height and thinness of the vertical tower recesses and the rectilinear tracery descending from the small-windowed gable over the round window of the facade. Some aspects of the facade were less up to date, such as the arched entrance portico with arches between bays of a

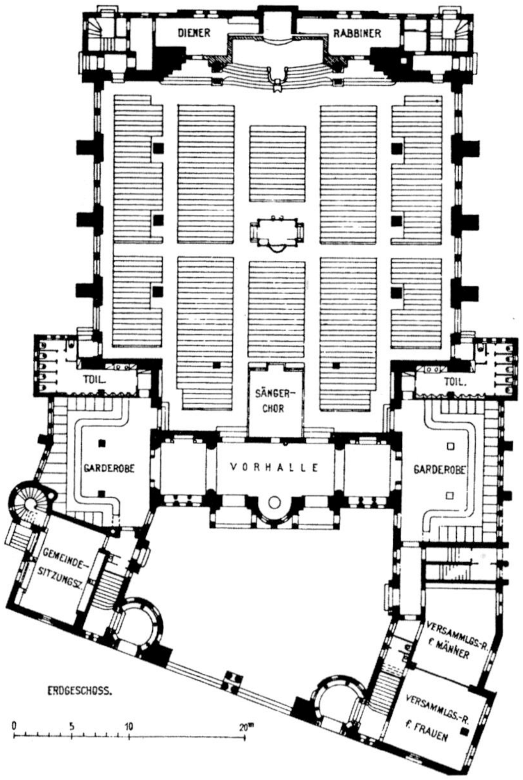

Figure 143. Frankfurt am Main, Israelitische Religionsgesellschaft, 1904–7, plan.

colonnade, but they did not alter the overall impression.

The synagogue facade looked remarkably church-like with its towers and gable and porch, but it did not look like a traditional church and was therefore acceptable. The congregation was used to worshipping in a church-like building anyway, and for it the combination of medieval and modern ideas was a good one. The medieval references alluded to the Jews' long residence in western Germany and suggested the venerability of religious tradition to which this congregation adhered. The modern elements showed that a traditional religion did not have to cling to traditional architecture for its expression in modern times. Local Jewish historians tried to define the style but could only decide on "forms of the early Middle Ages with weak echoes of Byzantine in oriental modes."

The synagogue was a galleried basilica with a slightly flattened barrel-vaulted ceiling penetrated by the round arches over the women's

Figure 144. Frankfurt am Main, Israelitische Religionsgesellschaft, exterior.

gallery, which ran around three sides of the interior (Fig. 145). The gallery rested on low, square piers, and squat columns above the piers held the vault. The galleries ended where a depressed rounded arch stretched across the nave, opening to the wide ark recess. The ark was framed in reddish brown marble and had bronze doors between decorative shafts. Sweeping over this composition was a smaller depressed arch with a horizontal cornice above it holding the superstructure of the ark. On either side of the ark composition, a column alluded to Jakhin and Boaz. The white marble bimah stood in the center, balancing the more richly colored ark composition. For the Shavuot holiday, a webless groin vault was erected on poles at the four corners of the bimah and foliage was twined around the vault ribs. The vaulted ceiling had large and small circular ornaments, arranged in rows but suggesting stars and planets by their great number and wide spacing. With good practical sense, the designers used some of the "planets" to disguise ventilation openings in the ceiling.

The effects of mass, textural contrast, and subdued exoticism were seen in several other synagogue designs before the First World War, including those by Fritz Landauer before he moved to England, and Edmund Körner's for Essen (see Figs. 67, 140). The atmosphere in these synagogues was unusual and enclosed, and yet part of the contemporary architectural scene. Contemporaneity dominated outside, and exoticism inside. The Frankfurt competition program had even specified that no oriental forms were to be used on the exterior. Here,

Figure 145. Frankfurt am Main, Israelitische Religionsgesellschaft, interior to ark.

Figure 146. Fürth, synagogues of 1615–16 (right) and 1697 (left), exterior.

as at the classical-outside/Egyptian-inside Reform synagogue in the west end of Frankfurt (1907–10), the nationalistic small businessmen who belonged to the Israelitische Religionsgesellschaft could show that they were "Treudeutsch und jüdisch allezeit"—faithfully German and ever Jewish.

BIBLIOGRAPHY

P. Arnsberg, *Die Geschichte der Frankfurter Juden seit der französischen Revolution,* vol. 2, Darmstadt, 1983, pp. 21–43.

———, *Neun hundert Jahre "Muttergemeinde Israel", Frankfurt am Main 1074–1974,* Frankfurt am Main, 1974.

Arnsberg Collection, Frankfurt Stadt–und Landesbibliothek (copy at Leo Baeck Institute, New York).

Berliner Architekturwelt IX (1907), pp. 167–68, 299.

Der Baumeister VI, #2 (1907), pp. 13ff. (with abundant illustrations).

Deutsche Bauzeitung XL (1906), p. 538.

A. Freimann and F. Kracauer, *Frankfort,* Philadelphia, 1929.

Hammer-Schenk, *Synagogen,* pp. 117–18, 462–65 (on both old and new Religionsgesellschaft synagogues).

———, "Untersuchungen," pp. 157–61 (on old Religionsgesellschaft synagogue).

H. O. Schembs et al., eds., *Bibliographie zur Geschichte der Frankfurter Juden, 1781–1945,* Frankfurt am Main, 1978, pp. 261–69.

Thieme-Becker, *Künstler-Lexikon,* s.v. Jurgensen.

Zentralblatt der Bauverwaltung XXIV (1904), pp. 319, 420.

Fürth

The oldest synagogue in Fürth near Nuremberg exemplified several tendencies in synagogue building. It was built in 1615–16 and dedicated in 1617, about a decade after enough Jews had settled in Fürth to form a quorum of ten men (Fig. 146). They must have been optimistic about further growth and about their own security, because they spent a good deal of money on a masonry building. The optimism was justified, since the government of the city was subject to three separate overlords whose rivalries kept any one of them from having full control over the Jews. Thus, while nominally subject to one prince, the Jews were able to obtain a building site and building permission from church officials. As canon law contained strictures against building new synagogues, we may conclude that the church was exercising the same local independence that secular authorities did when there was a good reason—usually financial—to accommodate Jews. Following the pattern in many other localities, the synagogue stood at the edge of town, at what was then the southern border. Uncharacteristically, it rose on elevated ground, a location favored in Jewish law but seldom obtainable. The building lay in a courtyard which by ca. 1700 contained a second, half-timbered, synagogue built in 1697 and known as the Kahlschul, the ritual slaughterhouse, and Jewish-owned houses on two sides. In other words, it was part of a type of enclave, or Schulhof, found in many other towns at this time. The synagogue was oriented, as usual.

Four years after the first synagogue's dedication, Count Tilly, commander of the Catholic allies in the Thirty Years' War, requisitioned the building for a jail. This suggests that the synagogue had stout walls, few doors that could be used for escape, and either very small or very high windows. The fact that in 1634 Croatian troops used the building as a horse stable suggests that the main space was close to grade level and that there were few steps into it. It is not clear whether the synagogue then had a projecting ark niche or a projecting vestibule or a women's section in a side wing, as these features do not appear on seventeenth-century prints. A nineteenth-century plan, however, shows that all the walls and buttresses had the same thickness, which suggests that they were built at the same time. We know that some work was done in 1692 but we do not know what it was. As the forms of the ark and bimah recall those of such Nuremberg Renaissance monuments as the Peller House of the early seventeenth century, they may also date to ca. 1617, or to some unrecorded mid-century rehabilitation following the end of the Thirty Years' War, rather than to 1692.

In any case, prints of 1705 show the ark niche, north-side men's vestibule, and south-side women's annex (Fig. 147). The synagogue was then T-shaped, with entrance bays at the west end forming the cross bars and the body of the building extending eastward. The main part was nearly square, 14.96 m. by 14.60 m., divided into a main men's area about 9 m. wide and the two-storey women's annex in a parallel aisle. A wall pierced by segment-headed grilled openings divided the men from the women. Exterior buttresses supported groin vaults over both sections. The vaults rested on consoles inside, ending well above the level of the candle shelf on the north wall. Groin vaulting was archaic at this time, used only exceptionally by patrons interested in recalling traditional styles. At the Fürth synagogue, and in 1711 at Frankfurt am Main, groin vaulting seems to indicate the Jews' conservative attachment to traditional building forms, perhaps to honor their fathers, or to differentiate their buildings from those of most Christians. It is hard to insist on the second alternative, because the segmental windows, Renaissance furnishings, and entrance details were similar to those seen in Christian buildings of the time.

Figure 147. Fürth, interior of 1615–16 synagogue in 1705.

The prints show other interior features: large metal chandeliers; barriers running north-south separating lines of men who stood at their individual prayer desks; other prayer desks and long benches backed up on the north and south walls; steps which were used at weddings leading from the women's section down to the men's; a long table at the west, probably for group study; the sober classical men's entrance door frame perhaps added in 1692.

As the congregation was well known for its orthodox traditionalism, it is not likely that the building underwent dramatic changes during the eighteenth century. In the late 1820s, however, breezes of Reform wafted through the Fürth community, fanned by the local government which felt that orthodox practices hindered the integration of the Jews with the general population, creating impediments to commerce and to the smooth functioning of municipal bureaucracy. The Reformers became dominant and summoned a rabbi who suited them. Immediately after his installation in March 1831, Rabbi Loewi initiated the synagogue remodeling, expressing his wish to modernize and Germanize both the services and the conduct of his congregation. The architect was a Christian, Albert von Reindel, then director of the Nuremberg art gallery and art

Figure 148. Fürth, interior of 1615–16 synagogue in 1832, engraving by G. C. Wilder.

school, and no doubt the rabbi had his public prestige as much as his talent in mind. When the work was finished, the citizens of Fürth could admire a building with abundant Gothic ornament for the sake of assimilation (Fig. 148); a bimah without a framework set near the Gothic-style ark for assimilation and modernity and more seating room; orderly pews for the sake of decorum; galleries and added windows, to integrate the women in the modern manner; and a greater degree of cleanliness than the old, crowded synagogue had maintained.

Here and at the Altschul in Prague, we see that in the 1830s it was possible and even desirable for Jews in some towns to use the Gothic style to express their willingness to approach the majority culture. But the Gothic style scarcely showed on the outside, and there was therefore no risk of offending those who might resent the Jews' use of a style associated with Christianity.

No adequate pictures or written descriptions remain of the synagogue after a further remodeling in 1863 which lengthened the building toward the west and introduced a northern aisle with a gallery, new vaulting, new stonework, and Gothic decorations outside. The slaughterhouse was torn down at this time. The Kahlschul was removed just about a decade before Crystal Night, 1938, when Nazi vandals brought to ruin everything else in the old Schulhof, leaving the Jewish orphanage synagogue as the lone survivor of the eight prewar synagogues of Fürth.

BIBLIOGRAPHY

Aus alter und neuer Zeit. Illustrierte Beilage zum Israelitisches Familienblatt, Hamburg, #82, Sept. 8, 1927, *Beilage* to #36, p. 652.

Hammer-Schenk, *Synagogen,* pp. 243–46.

———, "Untersuchungen," pp. 234–38.

Krautheimer, *Mitt. Syn.,* pp. 243–48.

H. Mahr, "Die Fürther Hauptsynagoge," *Fürther Heimatblätter* n.F. XVI, #6 (1966), pp. 121–37. I am grateful to Professor Krautheimer for this reference.

J. Toury, "Types of Jewish Municipal Rights in German Townships. The Problem of Local Emancipation," *Publications of the Leo Baeck Institute. Yearbook* XXII (1977), pp. 57–58.

Wischnitzer, *Architecture,* pp. 81, 94.

I am grateful for assistance to Stadtbibliothekar E. Ammon, Fürth.

Hamburg–Poolstrasse, and London–Upper Berkeley Street

The main Reform temples of Hamburg and London represent the religious architecture of two significant Reform congregations.

Each Reform congregation is free to adopt as many Reform practices as it wishes. Although there is no fixed type of building for this group of synagogues, the domed square was considered inappropriate for a temple with an eastern bimah. The central dome in such a building seems to demand something important under it, namely, the bimah. (In Reform temples, where the bimah is moved to the east, a central dome apparently substitutes for a steeple as an architecturally representative and conspicuous element.) Many Reform temples therefore are galleried basilicas with an eastern apsidal recess. Synagogues built originally for orthodox ritual were converted for Reform use by removing the high grilles that concealed the women, moving the bimah eastward, and making all seats face the east.

In 1817, sixty-five Jewish men in Hamburg founded a Reform association. It was to help modern German-speaking Jews maintain their faith by making services both more intelligible through increased use of German, and more orderly by following an organ and a trained choir. The number of rich and educated Jews was proportionately greater among the Reformers than within the orthodox community, but the Reformers never broke away; in fact, as years went by, they reintroduced traditional elements into their prayer books. Nevertheless, they wanted to set up a separate house of worship, which they did first in the Brünnenstrasse in 1818.

Hamburg–First Reform Temple

The Brünnenstrasse temple, designed by Heinrich Gottfried Krug, was a flat-ceilinged, galleried box holding 142 men on the main floor and 107 women in cantilevered galleries without grilles. The room received light from two storeys of rectangular windows on the south. A gallery on the west accommodated the choir and organ. Framing the ark, a classical aedicula composed of engaged Ionic columns carried a horizontal cornice enclosing an arch which sprang from the top of the wall molding at gallery height. Most seats faced east, but those for the elders stood parallel to the side walls, facing the draped pulpit-like bimah which stood in a balustraded enclosure extending into the seating space. The bimah was thus not united with the ark in a single composition at the east, as it had been in the earlier, more radical Frankfurt am Main-Compostellhof Reform temple of ca. 1815.

Hamburg–Poolstrasse

The Reform association grew and in 1840, when it had about eight hundred members, it obtained city officials' permission to erect a new building. The congregation commissioned a stucco-covered brick temple seating 350 men and 290 women. It was built in 1842–44 to the design of Johann Heinrich Klees-Wülbern, the Christian architect of the ceremonial hall at the Jewish cemetery (1838) and the Jewish hospital (1841–43).

The Hamburg Reform Jews were sensitive to the image they presented to both orthodox Jews and Christians. Reformers acknowledged their differences from the Christians, but they wanted to be regarded as Germans rather than as outsiders. Reform Jews wisely emphasized their sincere patriotism at a time when the king regarded departures from any religious tradition as likely to accompany radical political ideas. At the ceremonial cornerstone-laying ceremony in October 1842, on a patriotic anniversary, the congregation sang a hymn declaring its close German bonds and its belief that the temple was "a genuinely German house of God," able to link the Judaism of the orient with that of the German occident.

The new building occupied an inconspicuous site, as was usual at the time. It lay on the interior of a lot, hidden behind a four-storey building and reached only through an alley. A path led to a single door for men and women; in older synagogues, women had used a secondary side entrance. The facade was a tall, gabled rectangle flanked by thin turrets that looked more Gothic in style than anything else (Fig. 149). Vertical moldings ran high up the wall, turning into a semicircular arch that formed the dominant facade motif. The arch framed the top of a rose window which had a six-pointed-star tracery design. The semicircular arched portal opened under a pediment flanked by vertical moldings. The combination echoed the larger forms of the entire facade but the portal details were closer to the Renaissance than to the Middle Ages.

The design was original in synagogue architecture, perhaps by intention so as to express the new aspects of Reform, but the facade was close to designs for Gothic revival chapels of the preceding two decades in Germany and even in England. The familiar elements were

Figure 149. Hamburg, Poolstrasse, 1842–44, facade.

tokens of Germanness, while the unfamiliar combination of ingredients and the details such as the tracery star of David and the tablets of the Law atop the gable proclaimed that this was a building for the Jews—"West und Osten schön verbinden," as the hymn said.

Inside, the temple was a galleried basilica with a vaulted but flattened nave ceiling (Fig. 150). It was about 23.7 m. long, 22 m. wide, and 17.3 m. high. An apse housing the ark opened at the east below a semicircular window. The apse was framed by concentric arches held on Romanesque supports and was surmounted by a cornice decorated with Middle Eastern cren-

Figure 150. Hamburg, Poolstrasse, interior to ark.

ellations. The faint exoticism of this composition was part of a thoroughly eclectic design including Romanesque gallery supports, a ceiling with thin-ribbed quadripartite vaults, and paneled patterns on the low gallery parapet and in front of the ark and bimah (which were united in one composition).

All these forms shared the thin-planed lightness, linearity, low relief, and delicate ornamentation that generally characterized architecture in these years. A galleried basilica with an apse and most seats facing east was also common in Christian religious buildings. The eclectic and exotic stylistic elements, however, marked the building as belonging to a special group. If this combination is what the Jews wanted, they did not realize that the temple looked less German than they supposed and thus more foreign than they hoped. When a Jewish architect, A. Rosengarten, moved to Hamburg and built three orthodox synagogues there during the 1850s, he designed Romanesque buildings. In so doing, he made the orthodox appear to be more completely assimilated Germans than the Reformers! Ironically, some walls of the Poolstrasse survived the Nazi terror, while the Romanesque synagogues all succumbed.

The Poolstrasse temple was not strong enough in style to exert much influence, but the facade arch may have inspired the dominant exterior motif of the synagogues at Stuttgart (1861, by G. A. Breymann and A. Wolff) and Nuremberg (1870–74, by Wolff). In general, however, north German synagogues did not follow the unusual style of the Poolstrasse temple. Later large synagogues were designed in Romanesque (Hamburg-Bornplatz, Kaliningrad), German Renaissance (Gdańsk), and north German brick Gothic styles (Lüneburg). Through architecture, the Jews, who had no medieval roots in this area, attached themselves all the more obviously to their fellow Germans.

London–Upper Berkeley Street

The Poolstrasse temple may, however, have been one model for the London Reform temple of 1866–70 in Upper Berkeley Street. This building was the successor to neoclassical buildings that had accommodated the British Reform congregation after its establishment in 1840, first set up in Bruton Street in a converted Protestant chapel (redesigned 1841, consecrated January 27, 1842) and then in Margaret Street in 1849, on a site that could not be extended when the congregation increased. The London temple of 1866–70, designed by Davis & Emanuel, has a facade with a tall semicircular entrance arch under a peaked gable, flanked by thin strips of wall, as at the Poolstrasse temple (Fig. 151). The London building lacks the little turrets, but the architects added a dwarf-arcaded cornice, more ornament, and a triple-arched portal, reflecting the greater architectural elaboration common in the 1860s.

The London plan is also different from that of the three-aisled Poolstrasse temple. It is related to the earlier London Reform building in Margaret Street by David Mocatta, a Sephardic

Figure 151. London, Upper Berkeley Street, 1866–70, facade in 1982.

Jew who had joined the Reform group. He designed a square prayer hall seating 350 worshippers with galleries held by Ionic piers on three sides and arches rising from gallery level to the ceiling where a central lantern admitted light. The 1866 London plan is even closer to Rosengarten's Kohlhöfen orthodox synagogue of 1857–59, with galleries on three sides of a central domed bay and four smaller cupolas in the corners (Fig. 152). The London plan may also be related to the domed square plans of Gottfried Semper at Dresden and Gustav Stier in Berlin (Reform Temple, Johannisstrasse, 1853–54), but those had no corner cupolas. Davis & Emanuel could have found information about all these buildings erected for culturally assimilated Jews in the *Illustrirter Zeitung* (Kohlhöfen), in prints (Berlin), and in the *Allgemeine Bauzeitung* (Dresden), among other sources. The English architects must have been at least curious to know about Reform temples in Hamburg and Berlin, as those were the most influential centers of Reform. They might have been interested in Semper's plan, as he was well known in England because of his sojourn there. Rosengarten's work should have been of special interest for he was Jewish and was an authority on architecture, having published his widely read textbook, *Die architektonischen Stylarten* in 1857.

A combination of Reform and orthodox German design suited the religious position of London's Reform congregation. The Ashkenazic Jews of Britain were then predominantly of German rather than eastern European origin. The English congregation was, however, less liberal than the German ones, and had not intended to secede from the orthodox community. Also, the Reform and orthodox Jews were social equals in England; it was not a question of the rich and educated abandoning the orthodoxy of their less-favored fellow Jews so as to promote their own political emancipation or social acceptance. Consequently, the Reform Jews of England had no need to commission either more or less "English"-looking buildings than did the orthodox Jews. It was, then, reasonable for architects to produce, and for competition judges to choose, a design linking Reform and orthodoxy—Poolstrasse and Kohlhöfen, so to speak. As Hamburg's Reform Jews themselves had been moving back toward aspects of traditional Judaism, the references to Hamburg rather than to Berlin or Dresden were particularly appropriate.

The London synagogue design was selected in a limited competition in which the other participants were the well-known Christian architects C. R. Cockerell and Wyatt Papworth and the Jewish architect, Hyman Henry Collins. The eminent Christian architect, P. C. Hardwick, was a consultant to the building committee, as was

David Mocatta.

The prayer hall is 70 feet square, with five hundred seats on the ground floor and several hundred women's places in the galleries. The corner piers are clustered and massive; thinner ones support the galleries between the corners. The supports are made of polished red Devonshire marble veined with gray, and they have white capitals—part of a sober but richly varied color scheme. The ark, pulpit, and bimah are now united in a single composition at the east, with organ pipes forming a backdrop for the domed ark and the arched screens to conceal the choir on either side of it; originally, the bimah stood in the center of the room under the dome. The ark and screen arrangement, like a Roman fastigium but not in a classical style, is an innovation of this period. It is also seen at Collins's excessively lavish Chatham Memorial Synagogue near Rochester (1866–69) and later at Strasbourg, Szeged, and elsewhere. At London, the design has Byzantine stilted arches and Italian Romanesque inlaid ornament similar to that used on the polygonal pulpit nearby.

Geometric and floral designs on the brightly colored windows were created by A. F. Usher. Originally, the painted wall decorations used only geometric forms, but in the 1920s, new decorators applied arabesque ornament in rust and ochre tones.

Figure 152. London, Upper Berkeley Street, interior to ark in 1982.

BIBLIOGRAPHIES

HAMBURG

K. Goldenberg, "Der Kultus und Profanbau der Juden. Erläutert an Hand von Hamburg-Altona-Wandsbek," diss., Dresden, Technische Hochschule [ca. 1922], pp. 4, 55–57 (copy at Staats- und-Universitätsbibliothek, Hamburg).

M. Haarbleicher, *Zwei Epochen aus der Geschichte der Deutsch-Israelitisch Gemeinde in Hamburg,* Hamburg, 1867, esp. p. 178.

"Hamburg. Sefardische und aschkenasische Tradition," *Allgemeine unabhängige jüdische Wochenzeitung* XV, Sept. 2, 1960, p. 3.

H. Hammer-Schenk, *Hamburgs Synagogen des 19 und frühen 20 Jahrhunderts,* Hamburg, 1978. On Poolstrasse, see pp. 14–21, essentially identical to the related pages in *Synagogen.*

———, *Synagogen,* pp. 146–64, with further bibliography for Poolstrasse and Kohlhöfen.

H. Krohn, *Die Juden in Hamburg, 1800–1850,* Freiburg, 1967 (Hamburger Studien zur neueren Geschichte, 9).

———, *Die Juden in Hamburg, 1849–1919,* Hamburg, 1974 (Hamburger Beiträge zur Geschichte der deutschen Juden, 4), with excellent bibliography.

J. Lehmann, *Gemeinde Synagoge Kohlhöfen, 1859–1934,* Hamburg, 1934.

D. Leimdörfer, "Zum hundert-jährigen Bestehen des Tempels," *Festschrift zur 100-jährigen Bestehen des israelitischen Tempels in Hamburg, 1818–1918,* ed. D. Leimdörfer, Hamburg, 1918.

Y. L. Hacohen Maimon (Fishman), *Arim va-imahot be-Yisroel,* vol. 2, Jerusalem, n. d.

G. Salomon, *Kurzgefasste Geschichte des neuen israelitischen Tempels in Hamburg,* Hamburg, 1844.

Wischnitzer, *Architecture,* pp. 240–42.

LONDON

Builder XXV (1867), pp. 515, 577, 613; XXVIII (1870), p. 789.

A. S. Diamond, *The Building of a Synagogue. A Brief History,* London, 1970.

A. Galliner, "Our Synagogue. Reflections on the Interior of the West London Synagogue," *The Synagogue Review* XXVI, #10 (June 1952), pp. 289–93.
"Inauguration of the West London Synagogue of British Jews," *Builder* VII (1849), p. 307 (Margaret Street synagogue).
"120th Anniversary of the West London Synagogue," *Jewish Chronicle,* June 7, 1963, pp. 23–26.
Print made during the 1880s, kept at the West London Synagogue.
Royal Institute of British Architects, Drawings Collection, s.v. Mocatta, David, Box U 17/2 (1–16) labeled "St. Helen's Synagogue" but actually drawings for the Margaret Street synagogue. Cf. J. Lever, ed., *Catalogue of the Drawings of the Royal Institute of British Architects,* London, 1973, vol. L–N, pp. 78–79.
S. Sharot, "Reform and Liberal Judaism in London, 1840–1940," *Jewish Social Studies* XLI (1979), pp. 211–28.

BERLIN-JOHANNISSTRASSE

AZJ, Oct. 10, 1913, pp. 487–88.
Beṇdt & Bothe, vol. 1, pp. 25–26, 67, 82–86.
Deutsche Bauzeitung XIV (1880), pp. 519–21 (for Stier obituary and plan, section, and facade of the temple).
Hammer-Schenk, *Synagogen,* pp. 163–64.

Modern Geometric Synagogues

The synagogues of Hamburg-Oberstrasse, Plauen, and Žilina exemplify a current of taste in the years around 1930 in which geometric shapes and large stretches of plain wall reflected forms found also in other types of buildings. The similarities reveal that certain Jews in many parts of Europe embraced progressive aspects of design. Reform and Liberal Jews, eager to assimilate in society, saw themselves as intellectually progressive and sought to express their attitude with new architectural styles. Orthodox congregations built in comparable styles either because they saw no contradiction between traditional faith and mere clothing of a current type, or because the new forms suggested universal values while providing few distractions from prayer.

Hamburg–Oberstrasse

At Hamburg, the Liberal Reform congregation, though a minority, had sustained itself well enough to need a successor to the temple in Poolstrasse, an inner-city street from which the Jews were then moving. The old location was believed to be one cause of the small attendance at services. Paradoxically, the Reform rabbi claimed in 1908 that the Poolstrasse temple was too small—no doubt only on High Holy Days; looking for other excuses to build, he said that it had inadequate emergency exits. The congregational leaders, hoping to entice members into more regular attendance, decided to erect a temple nearer to the new Jewish neighborhoods and collected money for it before the 1914–18 war began. Postwar inflation annihilated the building fund, but a building commission constituted in 1927 amassed enough money to buy a city-owned site in the Harvestehude district and to sponsor a design competition in 1929. The known competitors were all Jewish—this may have been a competition limited to Jewish architects—but both Jews and Christians were later employed in the construction and decoration, as Jewish commentators noted with satisfaction.

The three prizewinning entries and three others are still known. They indicate the variety of ideas for synagogue design in the late 1920s, especially when they are set beside designs for other contemporary synagogues at Plauen in Saxony and Žilina in Czechoslovakia. The first-prize winner, Felix Ascher, and the third-prize winner, Robert Friedmann, eventually joined to produce a rectilinear main block set back from the street, with projecting lower blocks (housing the weekday synagogue, community rooms, and office) to the left and right (Figs. 153, 154).

This design is close to two unpremiated designs submitted by Wilhelm Haller and Fritz Landauer, and to a design by Leo Nachtlicht for an unexecuted synagogue in Berlin-Klopstockstrasse. One of Landauer's two entries, a project labeled "Abraham," also had rectilinear blocks with the center one recessed, smooth walls, long window strips, and a round window with

Figure 153. Hamburg, Oberstrasse, 1929–31, facade in 1985.

a Jewish motif in the tracery. Ascher's first-prize entry was rectilinear as well, with a projecting vestibule along the whole facade, and exterior stairs encased in each end of the projecting vestibule, the vestibule's roof giving access to gallery level doors. The door and window openings were all rectangular strips, except for a window in the center in the shape of a six-pointed star.

Landauer's interiors for both his "Abraham" and his "Thora" projects were straight-lined and smooth-surfaced, the former emphasizing width and the latter being taller and thinner in proportion (Fig. 155). The interiors were animated by the light admitted through long strips of windows on the north and south. Friedmann's and Haller's interior designs included curves, perhaps to suggest congregational brotherhood, or the universality of God in the vault of heaven. Friedmann's drawing showed a cylindrical space with a gallery curving around most of the cylinder, and a dome radiant with light above. Haller placed his vault above an oblong room and decorated its lower surfaces with a network of crossing ribs, giving a lighter but less coordinated impression. The block-like geometric forms are comparable to those of Gusti Hecht's and Hermann Neumann's competition-winning entry for Berlin-Klopstockstrasse (1929), N. Liaskowski's competition entry for Zurich (ca. 1929), and—even earlier—Arthur Szalatnai's orthodox synagogue at Bratislava (1923) (see Fig. 28). The heavy, curved interiors recall massive prewar synagogues such as those of Augsburg, Görlitz, Mainz, and Offenbach (see Fig. 16), as well as the contemporary synagogues at Berlin-Prinzregentenstrasse and Žilina.

The Hamburg competition entries were stripped of older stylistic associations, and this conformed to postwar progressive taste, but only one design, Landauer's "Thora," was allied to the International Style of the leading spirits of modernism such as Le Corbusier and Mies van der Rohe. The "Thora" facade was a simple rectangle with a ground floor marked by three

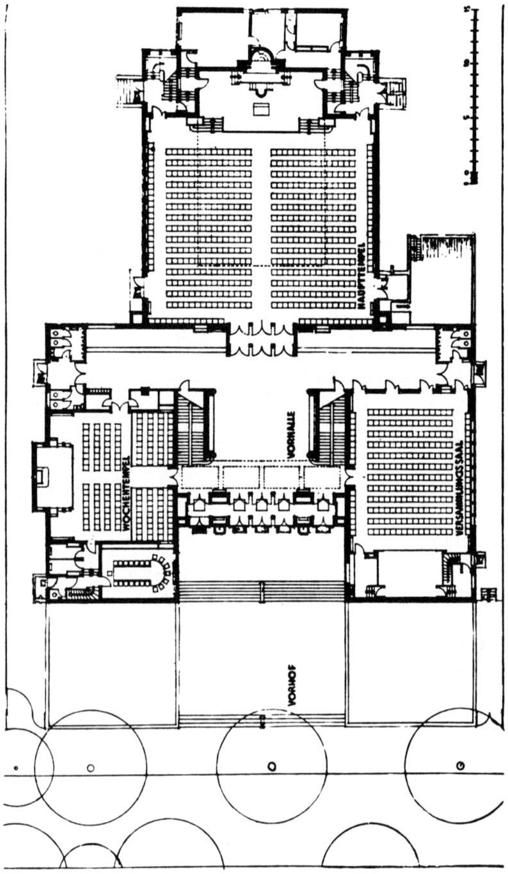

Figure 154. Hamburg, Oberstrasse, plan.

Figure 155. Hamburg, Oberstrasse, project "Abraham" by Fritz Landauer, 1929.

squarish windows, and the upper floor by a long strip of windows and a circular window with the star of David motif. A staccato rhythm of two levels of small oblong windows near the squarish ones on the lower floor indicated offices and community rooms. The free arrangement of windows, made possible by concrete-framed and steel-framed construction, exemplifies the flexible window design espoused by International Style architectural leaders of the 1920s. In their work, and in the "Thora" project, the wall appeared thin rather than massive, again showing the possibilities inherent in modern construction.

Plauen

Landauer had already used a similar form and the same technical means at his community center and synagogue building for the Reform (principal) congregation at Plauen (1928–30). This was one of the purest International Style synagogues ever built, with an exterior that echoed Le Corbusier's Citrohan house erected at the Weissenhof housing colony at Stuttgart in 1927 (Fig. 156). As he did at Hamburg, Landauer designed a simple oblong box which united community activity and religious practice, and used a steel frame and thin walls, with windows giving the principal ornamental effects. At Plauen, the main entrance was merely a break in the ground floor wall, and one passed through freestanding piers of prismatic form rather than between imitations of Jakhin and Boaz.

Under the influence of the new social and architectural climate of the late 1920s, Landauer departed from the massive, somber, and thick-walled forms he had used at Augsburg and had proposed for Vienna-Hietzing (see Fig. 67). He felt that the war had given people reason to build in a new way, and that this new architectural language could help to shape the content—in this case, the religious impression—of a building. He wanted to use technological developments to create forms interpreting Germany's postwar life. He clearly identified all parts of his building, and achieved expressive

Figure 156. Plauen, Reform synagogue, 1928–30, exterior.

Figure 157. Plauen, Reform synagogue, interior to ark.

effects mainly by manipulating architectural elements rather than by adding oriental details. He intensified the verticality of the roughly 10 m.-wide interior by lowering the galleries and raising the clerestory windows to exaggerate the distance between them and thereby make the room seem dramatically taller than it was (Fig. 157). He adjusted light effects, brightly illuminating the seats and creating a gentle twilight near the dark wood ceiling. He focused the congregation's attention at the east by elevating the ark and bimah composition, by having Professor Lois Gruber of Munich paint and incise symbols on the ark recess walls, and by pitching the floor slightly to allow worshippers at the west end to see the ark and bimah clearly.

Allying synagogues with the new International Style allowed Landauer and his clients to associate themselves with up-to-date culture in the Weimar Republic, in which Jews hoped that they were comfortably established, although anti-Semitic riots erupted in Plauen during and after the First World War. The star of David outside, and the delicate ark recess ornament inside, affirmed group identity within a universal context. The Plauen synagogue identified its users more forthrightly than did the competition entry for the Berlin-Klopstockstrasse synagogue submitted in 1929 by P. L. Wiener and his partner, Jaretzki, which resembled Le Corbusier's villa at Garches of 1926–27 and had nothing to mark it as a synagogue—the idea of universally applicable building forms here brought to an extreme.

Anti-Semites could interpret the new architectural style as a manifestation of unwelcome internationalism and loyalty primarily to people outside the Fatherland (i.e., to "international Jewry" and radical causes). Their fanatic nation-

Figure 158. Žilina, Neolog synagogue, 1928–30, exterior before 1939.

alist response to these new forms is most clearly illustrated by a retouched photograph of the International Style housing group at the Weissenhof in Stuttgart in which the white, flat-roofed buildings are shown surrounded by Middle Eastern figures and camels, giving a Semitic, non-German character to buildings which looked like the Plauen synagogue. A few years later, Landauer himself had to seek refuge in England.

Žilina

The Jews of Žilina in Slovakia, who followed the moderate Reform of the Hungarian Neolog type, also commissioned a synagogue in 1928. It was completed in 1931, to the design of Peter Behrens of Berlin, under the supervision of a Jewish architect, Zigo Wertheimer. The synagogue was related to the Haller and Friedmann designs for Hamburg in that it was domed, and, like the Ascher design, had a facade composed of two horizontal blocks (Fig. 158). The Žilina design, however, was lighter and more open inside than the two domed projects for Hamburg, and more traditional in feeling. It had more varied materials outside and more details abstracted from historic styles. Despite the fact that Behrens had earlier influenced Le Corbusier, Mies, and Gropius, his synagogue had little in common with International Style work, except for an emphasis on simple geometric forms and the use of reinforced concrete to produce them.

The Žilina synagogue stands on a long slope with a north-south major axis. Behrens used the ends of the site for an entrance platform reached by broad steps on the south, and for a paved court on the north (Fig. 159). He filled the entire east-west axis with the synagogue. The building is a rectangle containing vestibules on the north and south, rabbi's and cantor's and other auxiliary rooms in the corners of the plan, and on the north a narrow wing housing the plain rectilinear weekday synagogue. The rectangular prayer hall gives the impression of containing a square, because a dome of 16-m. diameter is inscribed within a square held on four piers in the northern two-thirds of the interior (Fig. 160). Slender reinforced concrete piers hold the low-fronted galleries as well as the dome, which rests on a cornice above the piers. The apex of the dome rises 17.6 m. above the floor. The bimah stood east of the center. The ark frame had a stepped design at the sides, either to recall the stepped corners of the exterior cornice, or to make an ark design of geometric elements in a modern manner. Fine materials embellished the ark, but the rest of the synagogue is made of simple and economical materials. The walls were decorated only with painted stripes of terra-cotta on white, and the dome's inner face had intersecting gold lines forming a large and a small six-pointed star. Triads of windows on each side light the galleries, while single windows in the corners of the building light the auxiliary rooms and corridors. The organ and choir loft rise above the ark. Four hundred and fifty men on the main floor and three hundred women in the gallery met in a synagogue whose structure and simple shapes were as clear as the vernacular prayers and sermons.

The exterior is more complex, but the varied materials clearly identify the building components. The ground floor, faced in stone, has a central entrance and side wings that wrap around to the east and west sides of the building. The eastern wall below the window level also is faced in stone to mark the presence of the ark inside. The upper walls, plaster-faced, end in parapets stepped up at the corners; originally, a thin staff topped by a six-pointed star rose at each corner. The exoticism of this cornice line is reinforced by the copper-covered

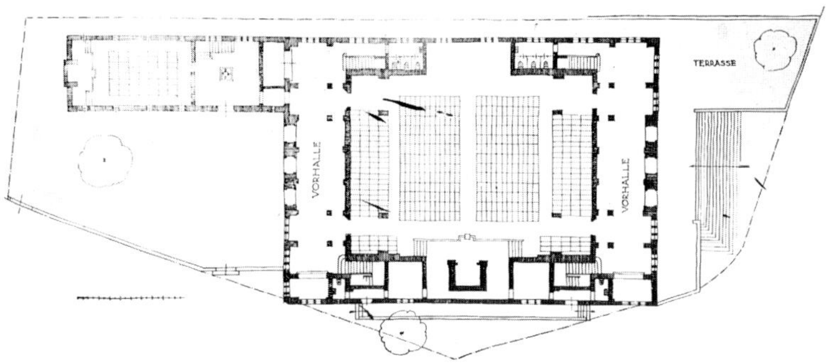

Figure 159. Žilina, Neolog synagogue, plan.

Figure 160. Žilina, Neolog synagogue interior before 1939.

dome and its star-topped staff. Perhaps the domed, squarish forms and the stone facing referred to architecture in Jerusalem. The Žilina design may be criticized for being too fussy in detail for its elemental forms and too monumental for the congregation of a small city.

Behrens was selected in a limited competition to which Josef Hoffmann also had been

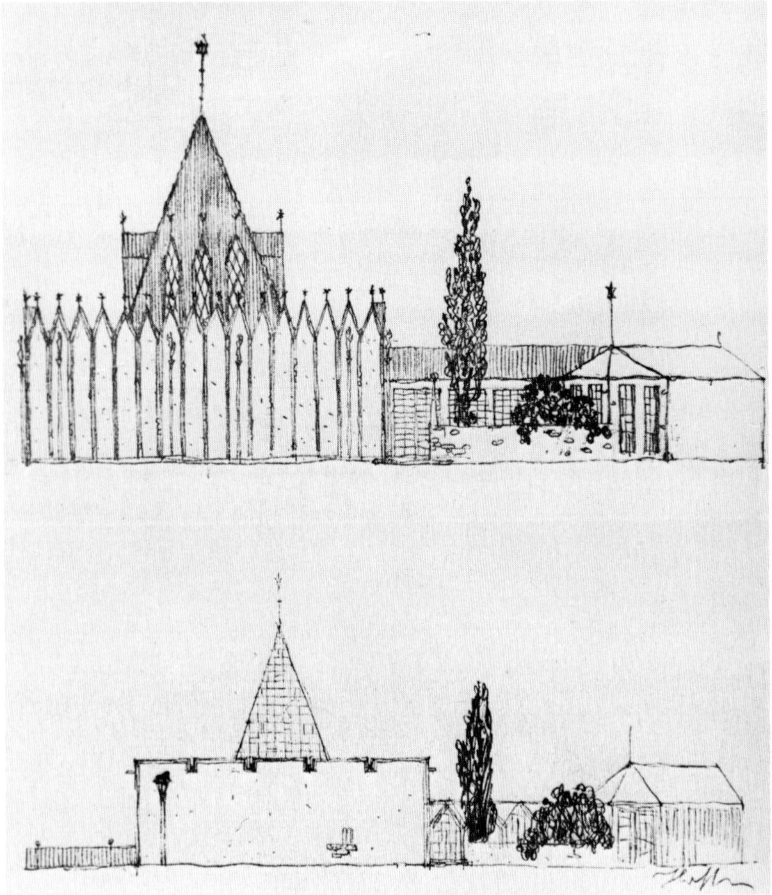

Figure 161. Žilina, projects by Josef Hoffmann, 1928.

invited. Eight of Hoffmann's sixteen drawings for the synagogue were published by Max Eisler, the Jewish art critic and champion of restrained modernism. Hoffmann at first proposed a rectilinear building bearing a hemispheric dome, because the congregation had specified a dome in its competition rules. Then Hoffmann thought of a rectilinear building with a patterned surface and a tall drum with pointed windows topped by an elongated curved cupola. Next came a series of designs with rectangular plans, gabled or crenellated walls, and a tent-like pitched roof rising in the center above the prayer hall (Fig. 161). Finally, he devised a temple-fronted broad building and a building with several wings, both covered by wide, tent-like roofs. Some of Hoffmann's designs must refer to the Tent in the Wilderness. His drawings may be derived from proposals made for the Vienna-Hietzing synagogue, especially those by Hugo Gorge who had won Eisler's praise earlier for a similar form and idea. That Hoffmann had his eye on the earlier competition is also suggested by the cornice of curves and triangles he proposed for one of his tent plans, a detail that evokes the executed synagogue at Hietzing.

The third competitor was Lipót Baumhorn, the Hungarian architect who designed the elaborate eclectic synagogue at Szeged and—alone and with his son-in-law György Somogyi—some twenty others as well. Baumhorn's style had become much more restrained since the turn of the century, but he always used exotic or historic forms, although we do not know if this was true of his design for Žilina, which was not published.

The designs that we know suggest that the Jews felt sufficiently at ease in the new Czechoslovak Republic to express their special history. The orthodox congregation in Košice erected a domed and faintly Middle Eastern synagogue, too, at about the same time. Even in Hungary, where there were occasional anti-Semitic outrages, the Budapest Jews built a war memorial "Heroes' Chapel" behind the Dohány Street synagogue. The chapel is a cube covered by a smooth hemispheric dome, enhanced by Middle Eastern details. These modern but exotic designs show that the Jews expected and were expected to have a special image. It would probably never have occurred to Behrens or the other architects to design a church in an oriental mode, even though Jesus himself had lived in the Holy Land.

These designs, linking rectilinear and curved elements, have basic forms in common with more conservative synagogues of the same years. London's Liberal Synagogue (St. John's Wood Road, by Ernest M. Joseph, a member of the congregation, dedicated 1925) is a distant descendant of the Pantheon, which combined rectilinear and domed areas. The London building has a heavy Ionic hexastyle porch of Portland stone in front of a brick, domed octagonal prayer hall. The Liberal Jews accommodated themselves to Western culture by using forms with well-known connotations of universality. Smooth plastered walls and a minimum of moldings reflect the taste for the general rather than the sectarian. The ark recalls that of Amsterdam's Sephardic synagogue, but the Dutch ark, too, had used classical forms rather than any exotic ones.

The Neolog synagogue in Košice (1927) was another descendant of the Pantheon, and its form probably had a similar motivation. The Liberal synagogue in Berlin-Prinzregentenstrasse (1930, by Alexander Beer) had a porch with a gabled roof above it and a domed rotunda behind, also recalling the Pantheon. The drive toward assimilation was so strong in this congregation that men and women sat together if they were married, and the prayer hall could be used for secular purposes when an iron curtain was lowered in front of the ark.

Overall, the picture of synagogue architecture around 1930 was one in which elemental forms, smooth walls, and modern construction were evident in many parts of Europe. Synagogues built soon afterward in London-Hendon United, Paris-rue J. Lacroix, and Brno continued to use contemporary forms and materials. Most of the designs emphasized cubic solidity, as did many conservatively modern, stripped-classical buildings of the period; it was this solidity that implied the Jews' desire to confirm their rightful presence in the new political divisions of postwar Europe. Neither these hopes nor all the central European synagogues survived. The Plauen synagogue is gone. The damaged Žilina synagogue was restored and converted into the *aula magna* of the local university. When the Nazis found the effort of blowing up the Hamburg synagogue too costly, it survived to be remodeled in 1950 for use as a broadcasting studio.

BIBLIOGRAPHIES

HAMBURG

Der neue Tempel. Zu seiner Einweihung am 30 August 1931. Gedenkblatt des Hamburger Familienblattes.

M. Eisler, "Neue Synagogen," *Menorah* VIII, #11/12 (Nov.–Dec. 1930), pp. 541–49.

H. Eulenberg, ed., *Robert Friedmann,* Berlin and Leipzig, 1930.

Gemeindeblatt der Deutsch-Israelitisch Gemeinde zu Hamburg, #7, July 10, 1929, #8, Aug. 12, 1929, #11, Nov. 10, 1930.

Hammer-Schenk, *Synagogen,* pp. 534–40, notes, and bibliography, pp. 651–52.

H. Hipp, *Harvestehude. Rotherbaum,* Hamburg, 1976, pp. 82–83 (Arbeitshefte zur Denkmalpflege in Hamburg, 3).

J. Lever, ed., *Catalogue of the Drawings Collection of the Royal Institute of British Architects,* London, 1973, vol. L–N. Landauer drawings Ran 15/F 8–20 (two projects for the synagogue).

"Liberal Jewish Synagogue at Hamburg," *Architects' Journal* LXXXIX (April 20, 1939), pp. 660–63.

A. and V. Marg, *Hamburg–Bauten seit 1900,* Hamburg [ca. 1971], fig. 65 and text.

M. Reimann, *Neue Werke. Wilhelm Haller,* Berlin, etc., 1930, p. 12.

ŽILINA

P. J. Cremers, *Peter Behrens,* Essen, 1928, pp. 103–5.

"Die neue Synagoge in Žilina," *Forum* I (1931), pp. 280–82.

M. Eisler, "Die Synagoge in Sillein," *Menorah* IX, #11/12 (Nov.–Dec. 1931), pp. 525–31.

———, "Entwürfe für eine Synagoge," *Menorah* VII, #2 (Feb. 1929), pp. 86–95.

Peter Behrens (1868–1940). Gedenkschrift mit Katalog aus Anlass der Ausstellung, Pfalzgalerie Kaiserslautern, Akademie der Künste, Berlin, etc., 1966/67, pp. 104–5 for preliminary drawings by Behrens.

PLAUEN

A. Diamant, *Chronik der Juden in Dresden,* Darmstadt, 1973, pp. 150–51.

W. Goldberg, *Blätter der Erinnerung an die Weihe der Synagoge Plauen i. V.,* [Plauen], 1930.

Hammer-Schenk, *Synagogen,* pp. 532–34, 651, nn. 1137–39 and 1108 for Plauen and for Berlin-

Klopstockstrasse project (fig. 468).
"Israelitisches Gemeindehaus mit Synagoge in Plauen i. V.," *Baugilde,* 1932, #7, pp. 359–60.
F. Landauer, "Jüdische Kultbauten von Heute," *C.–V. Zeitung* X, #27 (July 3, 1931), pp. 341–42.
J. Lever, loc. cit.

BRNO

"Neue Arbeiten von Arch. Ing. Otto Eisler, Brunn," *Forum* VI (1936), pp. 126–27. Vladimír Šlapeta kindly provided this reference.

LONDON-LIBERAL

Le Rayon (Paris), Jan. 15, 1923, pp. 10–12; April 15, 1932, pp. 11–12.
"The Liberal Jewish Synagogue, St. John's Wood Road, London," *Architectural Review* LVIII (Nov. 1925), pp. 198–201.

I thank Mr. John Levinson, ex-Secretary, for a helpful interview.

PARIS-BELLEVILLE, RUE JULIEN-LACROIX

M. Zahar, "Une synagogue à Belleville," *L'Amour de l'art* II (1931), pp. 254–55.

The Caisse Nationale des Monuments Historiques has information stating that Germain Debré, architect of this synagogue, also designed a synagogue in La Varenne-St. Hilaire. I am grateful to Mme. Marie-Thérèse Berger for her assistance.

ZÜRICH

M. Eisler, "Neue Synagogen," *Menorah* VIII, #11/12 (Nov.–Dec. 1930), p. 549.

For the entire period, see Wischnitzer, *Architecture,* pp. 231–47 and Hammer-Schenk, *Synagogen,* pp. 503–41.

Hannover

The early history of the Jews in Hannover is typical of that of Jews in many other cities. Documented in the city in the early fourteenth century, they were subjected to expulsions and readmissions after extortionate payments; to laws against living in the burghers' area, the Old City, although they could live in the nobleman's New City; to a conversion sermon preached in the synagogue (1588); to prohibitions against owning real estate (until 1847); and to other kinds of discrimination. Synagogues are mentioned in documents of 1499, 1535, 1584, 1588, 1590, 1609, 1613, 1688, 1703, and 1741; all seem to have been rooms in houses, or premises in the rear court of a building. A new brick synagogue was built in 1826–27, still on a rear lot, behind the community house which faced the street. As was usual at that time, it was designed in classical style, as a galleried basilica. The building had a wooden barrel vault, a shallow rectilinear niche at the east for the ark, Doric columns supporting the galleries, and gallery parapets with glazed arched openings divided by Ionic fluted pilasters. A simple enclosure of metal and wood surrounded the bimah. Apart from the glass-fronted galleries, this synagogue was not appreciably different from others of the 1820s and 1830s.

After 1847, and especially in the 1850s, Jews left country towns for cities including Hannover. At that time, the old synagogue became overcrowded. In 1861, the community leaders decided to build a new one, and the next year they gave the commission to the Jewish architect Edwin Oels Oppler. Oppler, who had studied in Paris with Viollet-le-Duc, also had studied brick architecture and Gothic forms in Hannover, following a contemporary local tendency. He was already familiar with the synagogues of Kassel, Cologne, Dresden, Hamburg, and Berlin (see Figs. 164, 129, 149, 122). To prepare himself further for this commission, he traveled with a banker who must have been on the building committee and went to Frankfurt, Mainz, Mannheim, Stuttgart, Munich, Vienna, and Budapest (see Figs. 64, 38).

The architect objected to the Moorish forms in many of these buildings, several of them finished during the previous ten years. Oppler himself was so culturally assimilated that he even received commissions from the local aristocracy, and he neglected to have the synagogue contractor stipulate that no work be done on the Sabbath. Oppler was obviously not one to accept the suggestions of Christian architects—Semper, Zwirner, von Förster—that the Jews should use Moorish style. Moorish, he wrote in 1863, "has not the slightest relationship to Jewry." In 1865 he wrote, "The German Jew wants above all to be a German, he struggles and suffers for equalization with his Christian brothers, can and should he then isolate himself by means of his house of God, without any ritual basis [for doing so]?" Oppler chose instead to follow the older German Jewish synagogue architect, Rosengarten, who chose Romanesque as the style best suited to Jewish history and Jewish aspiration. Oppler believed that the oldest surviving synagogues, those of Prague and Worms, were originally Romanesque (see Figs. 48, 49, 170, 171). The German Jew who wanted to build in a German style could therefore use Romanesque, as it belonged to the Jewish, as much as to the Christian, past.

Oppler cited as good examples of Romanesque synagogues the buildings at Dresden (more or less Romanesque, but only on the outside), Kassel (Rosengarten's most Romanesque design), and Pest (i.e., the Dohány Street synagogue, which is not Romanesque but which has round arches and the twin towers often seen in churches). His clients had asked for a conspicuously beautiful building, and the Budapest synagogue inspired thoughts of grand size, while the Dresden synagogue suggested a model setting and an integrative style on the exterior. The architect himself lamented that many synagogues were half hidden, and he welcomed the chance to design one that lay open to view on all sides.

We must conclude that Oppler had a perfectly clear idea of the Romanesque forms he really wanted, because his synagogues at Hannover and Wrocław (see Figs. 177, 178), his designs for synagogues at Nuremburg, Munich, and Karlovy Vary, and his later synagogues at

Figure 162. Hannover, 1862–70, exterior.

Świdnica, Hameln, and Bleicherode show none of the inconsistencies we would expect if Oppler had mixed elements of the Budapest, Dresden, and Kassel synagogues. On the contrary, the synagogue of Hannover shows the careful blending of the most eminent Rhenish Romanesque cathedrals with the most eminent Parisian neo-Romanesque church, that of St. Augustin, begun in 1860 (Fig. 162). Copies of modest medieval two-naved synagogues in Worms and Prague were not what he or his clients had in mind.

From St. Augustin, he borrowed the basic elements of his facade—steps leading to a triple-arched entrance, a low arcade above it, and a rose window above the arcade, all sheltered under a shallow arch and crowned by a triangular gable. From the same source, he may have taken the curved ribbed dome. The extensive plain surfaces and the polygonal turrets may have come from any of several Rhenish churches (at Hannover, the turrets housed the toilets and the chimneys for the heating system). The polygonal drum, and the gables at the base of the dome probably were inspired by the dome and drum added to Charlemagne's Palatine Chapel at Aachen. The use of brick, and the more insistent verticals of the transept facades, may have come from local sources and the local interest in traditional regional materials and styles.

The plan is independent of St. Augustin and of the medieval synagogues. It is a domed Greek cross, modified by the addition of a semicircular apse, aisle bays in the western projection of the cross, and a vestibule (also used as a weekday synagogue) at the west. Domed central plans already had been used in synagogues which Oppler admired—at Dresden and on two occasions in Hamburg in designs by Rosengarten—but they were square rather than cruciform and had different domes. At Dresden, the dome was covered by a polygonal drum and peaked roof, and the cupola at the Hamburg-Kohlhöfen synagogue was too small to be compared with Hannover's. The apsed Greek cross and the dome at Hannover appear, therefore, to be based on church prototypes, as in early-sixteenth-century plans for St. Peter's in Rome, or Pavia Cathedral.

If these relationships were made consciously—and it is hard to see how an architect could fail to recognize them—it does not necessarily mean that the architect wanted to make synagogues into churches or vice versa. Oppler had different reasons for doing what he did. He had criticized other architects for failing to match the purpose of a synagogue to its form, for failing to coordinate the interior and the exterior, and for failing to build from the inside out. By adopting a central plan for his building, with the bimah placed below the dome, he emphasized the centrality of communal prayer in Judaism. The galleries and the prominent ark

Figure 163. Hannover, interior to entrance.

on a large and lavishly decorated platform also lent the interior a strong eastward emphasis (Fig. 163). By expressing the dome both outside and inside, he related the interior and the exterior, just as the strong horizontal divisions along the outer walls revealed the presence of two storeys inside. By using a plan which had salient arms on all four sides, Oppler was able to retain the central plan which was well suited to orthodox Jewish needs, while presenting four interesting sides to passers-by outside; this was of great importance in the first large, freestanding synagogue in Germany.

The spectacular appearance of the Hannover synagogue led to Oppler's later commissions for Romanesque synagogues and to commissions for the Jewish cemetery ceremonial hall (1866) and the Jewish school (1875) in Hannover. His works became models for later architects who wanted to show that their clients were loyal patriots who happened to be of the Jewish faith. Loyalty did not help the Jews of Hannover after 1933, for the synagogue was vandalized and later destroyed.

Only in 1960–63 could the small postwar Hannover Jewish community erect a new synagogue. Designed by Hermann Guttmann of Frankfurt, the structure of parabolic plan forms part of a community center.

BIBLIOGRAPHY

P. Eilitz, *Leben und Werk des königlichen hannoverschen Baurats Edwin Oppler,* Hannover, 1971 (*Hannoversche Geschictsblätter* n. F., XXV, #3–4), esp. pp. 135–36, 164–67, with archival references.

H. Hammer-Schenk, "Opplers," pp. 101–13, with further bibliography and documents.

———, *Synagogen,* pp. 203–13.

———, "Untersuchungen," pp. 261–72.

Jewish Chronicle, June 23, 1865.

L. Lazarus, "Die Synagoge zu Hannover," *Mitteilungen der Kulturvereine in Hannover* XXXIII, Nov. 1958, pp. 1–4.

Leben und Schicksal. Zur Einweihung der Synagoge in Hannover, Hannover, 1963.

Kassel

The synagogue in Kassel is significant to the present history because it was among the first to be built in the *Rundbogenstil,* a mixture of classical and Romanesque forms that became a favorite style of synagogue architecture in the nineteenth and early twentieth centuries. Documents and drawings, some now lost, recorded the opinions of its architects, its clients, and its government supervisors.

Jews in the area of Kassel had been restricted to a suburb in the sixteenth and seventeenth centuries. Only a few lived in the city in the next century, and they were mostly court factors who could afford private synagogues. As the Jewish population grew, worshippers needed a public synagogue and in 1754 one was built that looked like a house, behind another house.

In 1771, the *Landgraf* asked the Jews to move and, quite exceptionally, offered to let them choose a new site. By 1775, they had bought land and engaged Heinrich Christoph Jussow, son of the then-extant synagogue's designer, who made a drawing for a new building probably in 1781. This had a porch with a triangular gable in front of a rotunda crowned by a tall drum and a cupola. It would have been too conspicuous to suit some Christians and its north-south orientation would not have suited the Jews. The new structure was therefore not executed and the Jews remained where they were.

With the absorption of Kassel into the Napoleonic Kingdom of Westphalia in 1807, the Jews received equal rights and retained most of them after the restoration of earlier governments. When Napoleon introduced consistories to supervise religion, the right to erect synagogues in certain towns formed part of the law. Some rich Jews in Kassel worried about the cost of a new building, and some hesitated to alter the existing pattern of seat tenure. Others feared that a new building would pave the way to Reform: Kassel's consistorial synagogue had opened in 1809 with German sermons, some German prayers, and confirmation ceremonies, and in 1810 a Reform temple had opened in Seesen. Although the Jewish population in 1822 far outstripped the capacity of the decrepit old synagogue, another building project fell through because too few people agreed to pay for it. In 1827, the government finally closed the old synagogue as unstable, but even then the rich members opposed new building plans. The following year, community officials at last resolved to build a new structure risking the defection of the rich, who in the end remained within the congregation.

The *Landgraf* proposed a site on which the synagogue would terminate a vista. Making a synagogue so conspicuous—so equal, one might say—was intended not strictly for the congregation's benefit; it also would have created a fine urban accent in a ruler's seat, as at Karlsruhe earlier. The Jews demurred—which must have been hard to do—explaining that the site lay too far from the homes of worshippers who would have to walk to it on the Sabbath. In fact, the site was really a negligible distance from the one they later accepted. A keen analyst of the documents, Harold Hammer-Schenk, suggests that the Jews declined because they were still too nervous about being conspicuous. They may have been reluctant to accept a building of bizarre style which the princely architect might design for the site so as to give his patron a delightful oddity.

When the government offered a satisfactory site, the Jewish community leaders asked for the architectural services of August Schuchardt, a government architect (*Oberlandbaumeister*) who had been offered the job earlier. Schuchardt's appeal may have been enhanced by the fact that he was a supervisor of the Jewish architect A. Rosengarten, who was trained in the government building service; perhaps the Jews really were hoping to employ the latter through Schuchardt, as they did eventually.

Between late 1830 and 1832, Schuchardt prepared several drawings, of which one was for a galleried basilica. This building type, familiar since the seventeenth century, here was accompanied by references to the galleried box synagogue of Munich built in 1826 by J. B. Métivier, known from a detailed publication. The Kassel project had Doric columns and a barrel vault, and was described as being cheap to build. The bimah was to have been in the center.

The design had to be submitted to the local buildings department where the director (and until 1831 also court architect), Conrad Bromeis, prepared his own proposals. Bromeis had been a student of Jussow, who designed the 1781 project, but there is no visible link between the designs.

The government officials in charge of religious buildings preferred an Egyptian design. Bromeis therefore submitted one that recalled certain reconstructions of the Temple, but he did so against his will. He found no connection between the Egyptian and German climates, and no ties between Egyptian architecture and the real Temple of Solomon. He also referred to the backward image of Egyptian art, as compared with progress made by the Greeks toward ideal beauty. He admitted that Egyptian buildings looked durable, but that was the only appropriate feature of the style. Schuchardt in turn pointed out the stylistic impurity of Bromeis's design, its consequent lack of strength and character, and the inappropriateness of using a style associated with slavery. If the Jews shared with Arabs a history of wandering, their architecture should not look durable and Egyptian. As to the Temple connections, Schuchardt reminded his readers that the Temple was made of wood, not stone. Another opinion came from *Oberbau-Ingenieur* Kühnert who said that in such an enlightened time, when Jews were less oppressed, they should not use a style associated with a dark period in their history. Moreover, as Jews and Christians believed in the same God, their architectural expressions should not be widely differentiated. All these critics preferred classical style as representing progress and beauty, rather than what they called dark feelings and unregulated fantasy; besides, the elegant handling of conventional classical style could enhance their own reputations as men of taste.

The designs made by these and others were set aside, to the congregation's apparent relief. In May 1833, new designs satisfied the community's requirements of being oriented and liturgically suitable, accommodated to the budget, and appropriate to the character and history of the religion. The last qualification meant that they did not want an oriental or Egyptian design. Christianity also had originated in the East; the Jews felt that not just Jewish buildings but Christian as well should be designed in oriental and exotic modes. They did not want a style associated with polytheism, or a style used in a culture devoid of an alphabet. Besides, the Jews mentioned emphatically that their history was substantially Western, not Eastern.

The *Landgraf,* whose residence had an Egyptian salon, clung to his idea of decorating his city with something unusual. In 1834 he asked his current court architect, Julius Eugen Ruhl, to create another design. This one had a helmet-domed round entrance bay flanked by towers in front of a two-bay hall with an apsed ark end, all decorated with motifs taken from Islamic architecture. The Jews dared to demur once more, saying that this did not look like the

Figure 164. Kassel, 1836–39, exterior, steel engraving designed by I. Rohbock.

style of a patriotic group. Fortunately for them, Bromeis did not like the design, either.

The community really wanted a design by (Schuchardt and) Rosengarten, and they refused alternatives until they received permission to build what they wanted (Figs. 164, 165). Erected in 1836–39, the synagogue was a four-bay galleried and barrel-vaulted basilica with a central bimah, a western vestibule flanked by stair turrets, and a semicircular apse for the ark with service rooms for the rabbi and cantor on either side. The architects referred to it as being in the *Rundbogenstil.*

The exterior looked more Romanesque with its flat-topped staircase bays flanking a gabled center part; three storeys of round-headed windows (the top row circular); a round-arched frieze under the cornice; and color contrasts in the yellowish white stone walls, red stone borders around openings, and yellow gray buttresses. The interior was based on the scheme of an early Christian galleried basilica and gave a neoclassical impression, but the octagonal piers and many other details did not come from an ancient source.

To the Jews, this was the style of modernity and moderate assimilation. It avoided Egyptian exoticism, classical paganism, and the churchly associations of Romanesque and Gothic. Rosengarten said that the style gave a solemn and uplifting effect. While the synagogue did not look exactly like anything else in Kassel (which may have satisfied the ruler), it did not look entirely out of place. A three-part facade with a slightly salient entrance bay and round-arched and circular openings was also familiar in some older synagogues, such as that of Sulzbach; one had only to bring the style up to date.

Rosengarten's article on the synagogue in the *Allgemeine Bauzeitung* of 1840 is the first account of a synagogue written by a Jew. His illustrated analysis of what a synagogue should be and what the problems were in synagogue design gained wide circulation. The building in Kassel inspired others, such as those of Mannheim, Marburg, Linz, Prešov, and Jihlava. Its general interior disposition may have influenced the Reform temple at Hamburg-Poolstrasse (see Fig. 150).

Rosengarten himself went on to design three synagogues at Hamburg in the 1850s, all demolished now, but his polychromed *Rundbo-*

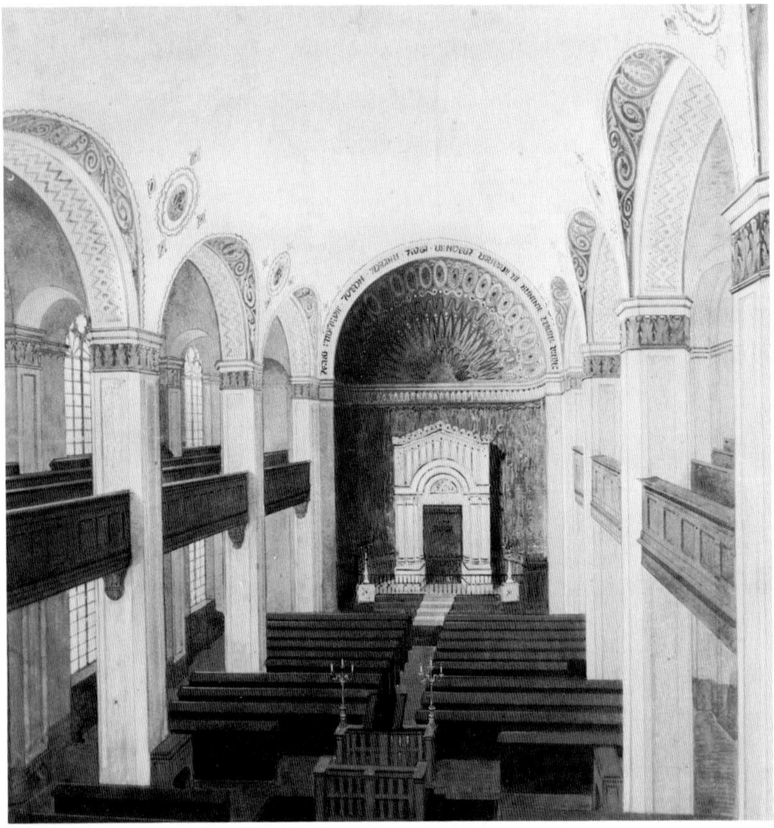

Figure 165. Kassel, interior to ark as redecorated ca. 1928.

genstil may still be seen at the domed chapel and adjacent buildings of the Schröderstift in Hamburg.

The Kassel synagogue received its last redecoration, simplifying the painted ornament, only about a decade before the historic structure fell victim to Nazi vandalism.

BIBLIOGRAPHY

Encyclopedia Judaica, 1971, s.v. Jacobson.

R. Hallo, *Geschichte der jüdischen Gemeinde Kassel.* I. *Kasseler Synagogengeschichte,* Kassel, 1931.

Hammer-Schenk, *Synagogen,* pp. 87–113. N. 244 transcribed the opinions of 1833 in the Stadtarchiv, Marburg.

______, "Untersuchungen," pp. 114–54.

Rosengarten, "Die Synagoge in Cassel," *Allgemeine Bauzeitung* V (1840), pp. 205ff.

Seesen

The synagogue at Seesen was the first to have its interior arrangements established for Reform Judaism.

When Napoleon created the Kingdom of Westphalia, the French administrator introduced a consistory in 1808 to supervise religious activity and to promote the Jews' integration into society. The authorities wanted only to foster cultural assimilation, not to alter religious fundamentals. The governing officials chose the consistory president from among the assimilated and prosperous Jews of the region. They selected Israel Jacobson (1768–1828), a financier who thought of Napoleon as the emancipator of the Jews and who in 1806 had written a letter to Napoleon and a treatise on this theme. Jacobson believed his people should improve their position in the Diaspora rather than preserve a separate, downtrodden existence while awaiting a return to the Holy Land. To promote his ideas, he had founded a school for Jewish children in Seesen in Lower Saxony as early as 1801. The curriculum was mostly secular and vocational, not Talmudic, and in this sense was similar to earlier secular schools established by Jews in Berlin, Wrocław, and Dessau. By 1804, Christian parents also expressed interest in having their children attend Jacobson's school, and he admitted pupils from the local, largely Protestant population—a step that brought him nearer to his goal of Jewish-Christian fraternity. As religion was an essential part of nineteenth-century education, and as ideas about synagogue reform could more easily be introduced in a children's service than in a community synagogue, Jacobson commissioned a synagogue within his school grounds. He knew that a partly German service already had been introduced in the Jewish school in the consistorial seat at Kassel. Jacobson's building was begun in 1805, but the name of the designer and the building documents were lost by the start of the twentieth century.

The synagogue, like many small-town synagogues, was designed in a local vernacular style (Figs. 166, 167). The rectangular, half-tim-

Figure 166. Seesen, Jacobson School Synagogue, 1805–10, exterior.

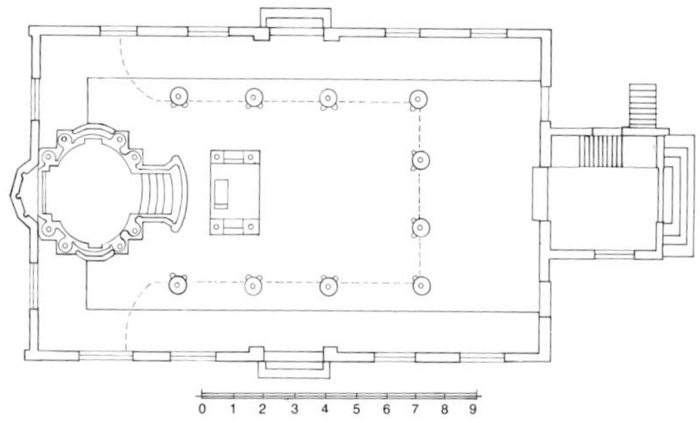

Figure 167. Seesen, Jacobson School Synagogue, plan.

bered, and shingled building had a tiny ark recess at the east and a vestibule and steps to the gallery at the west. The curving roof held rounded dormer windows that recalled late baroque architecture, and the synagogue has been compared to the local St. Andrew's church of 1695–1702. But the synagogue bore evidence of its real date in the neoclassical columns at the north doorway, the balustrated belvedere on the roof, and the interior balcony, ark, and bimah. Empire taste appears also in the white-painted galleries on white columns crowned with gold capitals, all surmounted by a blue ceiling. It was appropriate to use a French-inspired style in a building erected by the president of the French-inspired consistory, although Gallic neoclassic forms were found in other early-nineteenth-century buildings in Seesen.

The simple, clear style of straight lines and clear directions expressed Jacobson's aims. In this synagogue and in the others established in the Kingdom of Westphalia, he wanted to promote the understanding of religion by offering a German sermon and a choir and organ to make singing more uniform and thus more intelligible. Congregation members were no longer to pray at individual speeds, creating a pious cacophony unlike the sound of Protestant services. No longer would there be any excuse for gossiping or indifference, because the principal language would be the one that everyone knew rather than the Hebrew that was little known by assimilated Jews. Perhaps Jacobson thought of himself as a Jewish Luther wishing to bring reformed religion to people in their own language. The synagogue dedication ceremony was even known as the Festival of the Jewish Reformation. Protestant practices influenced Jacobson in other ways as well. His desire for uniform prayers uttered by a leader and followed by an orderly congregation sitting in a well-equipped building reflects his observation of contemporary Protestant services. He placed the bimah near the ark, subordinating it to the ark, even though a canopied tabernacle supported on eight classical columns stood above the bimah. The bimah's significance was deemphasized further by the raised pulpit that stood just behind it; the pulpit was used for sermons in German offered by the lay and religious leaders. The pulpit and ark arrangement probably was influenced by the Christian pulpit and altar. The organ, an extraordinary piece of synagogue furniture, was another object imported from churches. (It took a local organ maker about three-and-a-half years to construct, and it may have caused the long delay in dedicating the synagogue.) Once it was played, it set off intense scholarly debate about its propriety in a synagogue, fostering many congregational schisms in towns throughout Europe. Another church-inspired innovation was the introduction of bells. They were unique at that time in synagogues, and remained anomalous. At Seesen, they may have been by-products of the need to have heavy weights attached to the works of a clock located in a dormer of the roof, but if Jacobson had not wanted bells he could have had something else attached to the clockworks.

To be sure, Jacobson did not think of his synagogue as a church, but as the only temple that the Jews could expect to see within their lifetimes. He referred to the Seesen building as a temple in the Diaspora, but for him this must have had a different meaning from that given to the temporary "little sanctuaries" found in Córdoba and other cities where the Jews hoped for a return to Jerusalem. To confirm the local heritage of the Seesen temple, Jacobson even called it the "Jacobstempel," in honor of his father who had lived in Halberstadt rather than in the Middle East. As the word *temple* was used also for Huguenot churches, and as Jacobson could think of himself as a reformer, he may have found the term especially appropriate for his own building, where two columns stood at the entrance door, the descendants of Jakhin and Boaz at Solomon's Temple.

In July 1810, the Seesen synagogue was dedicated with festive ceremonies, an address by Jacobson, and a banquet for several hundred people given at his expense. Christian and Jewish lay and religious dignitaries attended. The organ music swelled. Students sang. Two months later, the Westphalian consistory promulgated rules for synagogue worship that followed Jacobson's principles of decorum and procedure. The cantor's voice alone was raised in parts of the liturgy that had formerly been open to congregational participation. Secular announcements were no longer permitted, making the synagogue a house of prayer more than a house of assembly. Certain types of detailed text exegesis were eliminated as being petty and tedious, and services were shortened to the length of Christian ones.

But Jacobson and the consistory did not continue their activities in Seesen for long. In 1813, the Kingdom of Westphalia came to an end. Its collapse meant the end of the consistory and of Jacobson's privileged status. He departed for Berlin, where he set up a temple in his house; by 1817 sixty-six members had joined it. The enlarged congregation later worshipped in the home of Jacob Herz Beer, a banker, and at one time it included 435 members, almost all from prosperous and assimilated families. Reform temples in Berlin and elsewhere were sometimes closed by authorities at the behest of orthodox leaders who feared a loss of members from their own synagogues, but Reformers eventually won the right to maintain separate premises. Important Reform congregations were found in Hamburg, Kassel (where Reform services were held as early as 1809 but without Jacobson's purpose-built architectural setting), Frankfurt am Main, and London (see Figs. 149–152).

In Seesen, Jacobson's school continued to function, but by the early twentieth century its synagogue was only a museum. It was reduced to ashes by the Nazis. Nevertheless, its memory lives on among Reform Jews and among the Christian students and teachers of the school which became the successor to Jacobson's foundation.

BIBLIOGRAPHY

Z. Asaria, *Die Juden in Niedersachsen,* Leer, 1979, pp. 444–53 and bibliography, p. 650.

G. Ballin, "Die Jacobson-Schule in Seesen. Ein Beitrag zu ihre Geschichte," *Tausend Jahre Seesen. Beiträge zur Geschichte der Stadt Seesen am Harz, 974–1974,* Seesen, 1974, pp. 349ff.

———, *Geschichte der Juden in Seesen,* Seesen, 1979, esp. pp. 35–39.

Encyclopedia Judaica, 1971, s.v. Jacobson.

"Feyerliche Einweihung des Jacobson Tempels in Seesen," *Sulamith* III, Bd. L, #5 (1810), pp. 298ff., esp. pp. 309, 314.

N. Friedland, *Zur Geschichte des Tempels der Jacobson-Schule,* Seesen, 1910.

Hammer-Schenk, *Synagogen,* pp. 149–52.

———, "Untersuchungen," pp. 14–15.

J. Marcus, *Israel Jacobson, The Founder of the Reform Movement in Judaism,* Cincinnati, 1972.

M. A. Meyer, *The Origins of the Modern Jew: Jewish Identity and European Culture in Germany, 1749–1824,* Detroit, 1967, pp. 132–36.

D. Philipson, *The Reform Movement in Judaism,* rev. ed., Cincinnati, 1930 (reprinted with introduction by S. B. Freehof, New York, 1967), esp. pp. 12–15.

K. Steinacker, *Die Bau und Kunstdenkmäler des Herzogtums Braunschweig.* V. Band. *Die Kunstdenkmäler des Kreises Gandersheim,* Wolfenbüttel, 1910, pp. 337ff.

Worms

The synagogue we are able to visit today is a faithful reconstruction of the one that was burned and bombed between 1938 and 1945 (Fig. 168). That building was the oldest medieval synagogue of which there were remains above ground; only the ancient synagogues of Ostia and Stobi are both certainly older. The structure at Worms was distinguished on many counts: its age; its position in the Rhineland where Jews were well established in Mainz, Cologne, Speyer, and Worms itself; and the fine craftsmanship of its carved details.

Jews were first documented in Worms around the year 1000, and the first known synagogue was completed in 1034. It was the gift of Jacob ben David and his wife, Rachel, one of the many pious, childless couples who have sponsored synagogues. It lay in the interior of a lot in the Jewish street and stood west of the later synagogue, which was the one extant in 1938. The east wall of the earlier synagogue was replaced by the longer west wall of its successor. A small courtyard may have been located along its north side. Like some synagogues elsewhere, including the earliest one at Cologne (see Fig. 127), the Worms synagogue is likely to have had a 3:2 proportion, measuring 46 by 32 local feet (about 13.8 m. × 9.6 m.). It was rectangular, unvaulted, and oriented. It may not have had a projecting niche to house the ark.

The first Worms synagogue is believed to have been badly damaged by rioters in 1096 and 1146, when Crusades aroused anti-Semitic

Figure 168. Worms, 1174–75 and later, facade before 1938.

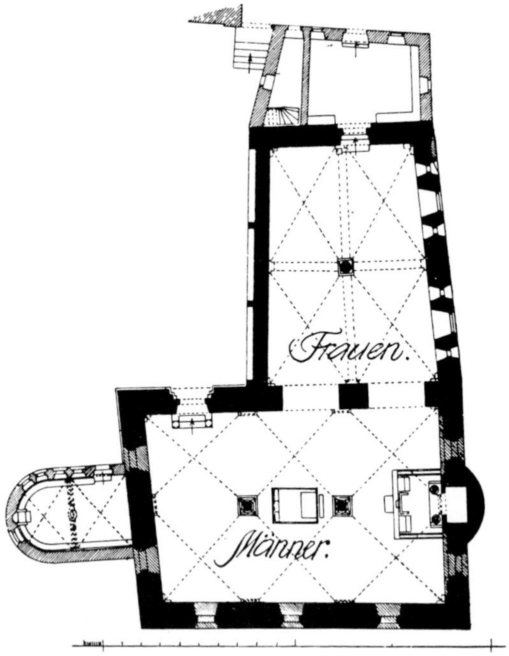

Figure 169. Worms, plan after 1841.

Figure 170. Worms, interior of men's prayer hall between 1847 and 1938.

fervor, and in 1174–75 it was entirely rebuilt. The date is given by a lost inscription copied in 1559 and by a chronogram on the abacus of one of the interior columns. This building was close to 3:2 in proportion—18 m. by 12.4 m. in maximum dimensions—but it was not a rectangle in plan because the eastern wall was realigned. This was done probably to orient the focal wall accurately, following careful calculation of east made at the spring equinox. The synagogue in modern times lay below grade, but that was due to the rise in the street level over the centuries; the men's prayer hall was not sunken originally.

The sandstone building was plastered and perhaps painted. It had two aisles, each of three groin-vaulted bays supported on two monolithic columns along the center axis (Fig. 169). This is the earliest known two-naved synagogue plan, antedating those of Regensburg, Prague-Altneuschul, and Cracow/Kazimierz-Old (see Figs. 4, 50, 71). The main door lay on the north side, and its carved leaf and geometric decoration recalls that on portals at Worms cathedral, indicating that the synagogue sculpture was the work of Christian craftsmen. Another small door opened at the south. The west wall, forming one side of the original synagogue courtyard, had an oculus 24 cm. in diameter, which was probably used before clocks became common to check on whether the sun had set to start the Sabbath. A niche for the Torah scrolls protruded on the east, a feature known at the medieval synagogues of Speyer and Frankfurt am Main. The windows may have looked like the round-headed pair preserved from the Speyer synagogue. The vaults were probably four-part groin vaults with flat arch bands between them. The central columns had capitals of two different designs, which are early examples of an Alsatian capital type used in this area, and which also are close in style to carving at the cathedrals of Worms and Fritzlar (Fig. 170). Details of the capital ornament sufficiently resemble pomegranates and chains to suggest that the two columns were meant to recall Jakhin and Boaz. Oil lamps were affixed to the capitals, and other light came from the candles

Figure 171. Worms, interior of women's section, 1212–13, between 1847 and 1938.

Figure 172. Worms, interior of men's prayer hall in ca. 1830, view to ark with bimah of 1623–24.

arranged on a cornice around the wall. We know nothing about the appearance of the ark or the bimah at this period.

Little remained, even before 1938, of the synagogue of 1174–75 other than the plan, the stone columns, and portals, for the building was remodeled and nearly demolished several times. The first modification was the addition of a women's section in 1212–13 (Fig. 171), the gift of Meir ben Joel and his wife, Judith. This was a trapezoidal room covered by four groin vaults that rested on a central column. (The capital of this column has been preserved; after its removal from the synagogue, it was used to support the washing basin at the Jewish cemetery.) The column could stand in the middle because there was no bimah in the women's section to occupy the center. There was no ark either, as the women did not have a complete and separate synagogue service. We know that in the thirteenth century, women led other women in prayer. Their section was linked to the men's prayer hall by five small windows and a door in the common wall. Light entered the women's section through other round-arched windows and oculi in the eastern wall. The entrance lay at the north through a handsome molded portal which was sheltered by a vestibule added in 1620–30.

During the Black Death (1348–50), the Christians of Worms blamed the Jews for the plague, expelled the "culprits" from the city, and damaged the synagogue so badly that only about 3 m. of the men's synagogue walls stood above ground in some places. In 1355, however, the Jews returned to Worms and began to rebuild. They retained the old plan but added pointed-arched windows in the west, south, and east, and they opened oculi as well. The vaults were rebuilt and new polygonal waterspouts drew off rainwater. The courtyard was moved to the area bounded by the north wall of the men's area and the west wall of the women's area. New arched niches sheltering seats lined the women's-area wall and the wall opposite. This well-appointed courtyard remained a center of community life into the nineteenth century.

Inside the synagogue, the ark probably kept its old form but was given new details. It may have had a pointed-arch outline containing two doors shaped like twin-pointed arches. The ark received new grilles for the doors; the grilles were used in later arks and have survived. If the later bimah was close in form to the medieval one, we may suppose that the fourteenth-century bimah was a square stone cage with tracery designs in several horizontal registers (Fig. 172).

In another pogrom, in 1615, vandals badly damaged the synagogue, demolishing the vaults and reducing the northern wall of the men's area to 2.7 m. above ground level. After 1620, the women's area vaults and the central column were replaced, the new Tuscan column remaining until 1942. In the men's area, masons built the groin vaults, which lasted until 1942, and opened three round windows in the north wall. More brick was used in the reconstruction than had been used earlier, and it could be seen around these windows. The ark niche was repaired. Among the rectangular niches that were built into the walls at this time, one at the west of the small south door held the Eternal Light. Before the nineteenth-century introduction of gas and electric lights, the Eternal Light was kept in a masonry niche near the door to shield it from extinguishing drafts and to reduce the danger of fire (this was done elsewhere, too).

The ark and bimah survived the pogrom, though probably not without damage, since craftsmen executed new ones. According to Otto Böcher's reconstruction from extant fragments, the ark was an aedicula raised on three steps. It had an arched opening under a cornice with leaves carved in relief. Above were an attic with reliefs of three crowns and a triangular pediment containing a carved crown. On either side of the opening, arched spandrels contained reliefs of dragons. All these are images known in other Jewish art. To the left and right rose pilasters decorated with vine scrolls, stubby pilasters and scrolls above the cornice, and little obelisks on either side of the pediment. The ark had clumsy proportions. It is not hard to see why it was replaced during the next remodeling (1704–5) by a simpler classicizing ark. This one had fluted columns and a broken pediment, but retained the obelisks and crown reliefs of the 1620 ark. The bimah of 1621 remained a square stone cage and was designed in two bands of trefoiled Gothic arches over two levels of balustrades, a mixture of modernity with tradition (and old fragments?) that is known in other artistic circles, the best known being that of the Jesuits who commissioned a number of Gothic churches in German-speaking countries during the baroque period. The bimah, about 3 m. on each side, occupied most of the space between the two columns and it rose well over a tall man's height. The 1704–5 ark survived until the Nazi period, but the bimah was demolished in 1842.

The most substantial alteration of the 1620s was the construction in 1623–24 of a small apsed and vaulted room west of the men's prayer hall (Fig. 173). Known as the Rashi Chapel, it had nothing to do with the medieval scholar of that name who studied for a time in Worms, and it was not a chapel but a house of study. This annex was, like the bimah and much of the synagogue work of this time, the gift of a rich man, David Oppenheimer.

Invading French soldiers all but destroyed Worms in 1689 and used the roofless men's area as a stable. Only the women's section retained its vaults, and everything but the bimah and columns needed repair or replacement when the Jews could attend to their synagogue in 1699. This accounts for the new ark of 1704–5 and other new elements: a cornice for candles, vault consoles, transverse arches in the women's section, and a roof spanning the men's and women's areas, which earlier had been roofed separately. During the seventeenth and eighteenth centuries, donors gave elaborate metal candelabra. Some of these had incongruous ornaments such as figures of Zeus or the imperial eagle, probably because they were stock products of the period.

Some renovation was undertaken in 1816, but the really significant changes occurred in 1841–42. At that time, city architect Obenheimer opened two wide pointed arches to link the women's area to the men's (although the women remained behind wooden grilles until 1847), and several alterations increased the emphasis on the ark at the expense of the bimah. The large bimah gave way to a puny replacement, a podium enclosed by a low metal railing. Synagogue leaders explained that they

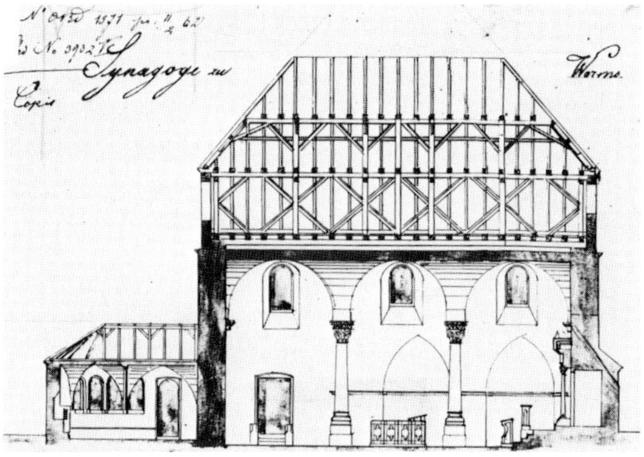

Figure 173. Worms, longitudinal section after 1847.

wanted the old bimah removed to increase seating capacity and to obtain a symmetrical seating arrangement. They wanted readers at the bimah to be heard, and needed to give synagogue officers a good view of the congregation so as to maintain order more easily. New seats lined up to face the east. The Eternal Light was taken out of its niche and hung in front of the ark, adding another attraction to the east end. All these changes show the influence of assimilation to external Christian culture and the parallel influence of Jewish Reform. The impression given by the synagogue may have seemed more German or church-like to the Jews, but a visitor in 1866, evidently writing on the basis of his preconceptions, said that the building presented an "Eastern appearance" because of the rich contrast between the sculptured capitals and the plain piers—a contrast that is neither oriental nor occidental.

Repairs to the synagogue before 1938 preserved its nineteenth-century form. The Rashi Chapel had to be almost entirely rebuilt in 1854–55 and all its walls were newly constructed then, presumably copying the older ones. Having abandoned a plan of 1862 to demolish and replace the old building, the congregation refurbished it in 1866 and removed old whitewash. In 1876 and 1877, part of the western wall of the courtyard with its seating niches was taken down. The congregation installed a gallery, later used as an organ loft. They bought and renovated a community house.

By this time, the dominance of Reform had led the orthodox eastern European Jews of Worms to move to a small new synagogue a block away, while the German orthodox Jews met in the "Mannheimer Schul" established in 1840 in a private house by a scholar named Moses Mannheimer, who disapproved of Reform.

In 1926, restorers removed thick layers of whitewash from the two column capitals in the men's area and painted them in primary colors. They framed the Romanesque oculus in brick. They altered the heating and ventilating and electrical installations. This was done while the Jews of the Rhineland and vicinity felt themselves to be integral members of the German nation and permanently at home there. Twelve years later, vandals burned the synagogue on Crystal Night, November 9–10, 1938, and in 1942 blew up much of what was left. American bombs demolished the rest in 1945.

After the war, the city museum personnel assembled architectural remains and reerected the synagogue, using as many fragments as possible. Several of the former Jewish community buildings also were repaired, including the community house and the ritual bath. There was some thought of restoring the entire Jewish street with all its buildings. As there are few Jews in Worms and its environs, opinions differ even among Jews on the wisdom of complete rebuilding. There is no doubt, however, that the scholars and archaeologists and builders at Worms have done excellent and humanely motivated work.

BIBLIOGRAPHY

O. Böcher, *"Die alte Synagoge zu Worms,"* diss., Johann-Gutenberg-Universität zu Mainz, Worms, 1960, published in *Der Wormsgau. Zeitschrift der Kulturinstitute der Stadt Worms und des Altertumsvereins Worms,* Beiheft 18.

Böcher's text forms pp. 11–154 of E. Roth, ed., *Die alte Synagoge zu Worms,* Frankfurt am Main, 1961.

To the extensive bibliography in Böcher's publications, may be added:

"Ancient Synagogues in Central Europe," *Builder* XXV, #1248 (Jan. 5, 1867), p. 9.

Aronius, *Regesten,* p. 65.

H. R. Huttenbach, *The Destruction of the Jewish Community of Worms, 1933–1945. A Study of the Holocaust Experience in Germany,* New York, 1981.

Isidor Kiefer Collection, Leo Baeck Institute, New York, Box 1, folder "Synagoge Worms," esp. "Vortrag betr. Synagoge: 1841. Ein Wendepunkt in der Baugeschichte unserer alten Synagoge," esp. pp. 15–19; "Verbesserung der inneren Einrichtung . . . , 15 März, 1841"; "Almemor-Abbruch 1841 II." Folder "Geschichte der Juden in Worms," esp. Kiefer, "Die Juden in Worms. Ihre Bauten und Geschichte."

M. Lowenthal, *A World Passed By,* New York, 1933, pp. 275–85.

J. Maier, *Das Judentum von der biblischen Zeit bis zur Moderne,* Munich, 1973, pp. 480–81.

Rashi Association, *Reports,* 1977.

G. Stein, "Die Juden und ihre Kultbauten am Oberrhein bis 1349," *Zeitschrift für die Geschichte des Oberrheins* CXVII (1969), pp. 333–55.

Wischnitzer, *Architecture,* pp. 45–49.

For one of many declarations by Jews of their affiliation with Germany between the two world wars, see A. Kober and E. Moses, *Aus der Geschichte der Juden im Rheinland: Jüdische Kunst und Kunstdenkmäler* (*Rheinischer Verein für Denkmalpflege und Heimatschütz, Zeitschrift,* XXIV [1931], Heft 1), Düsseldorf, 1931, p. 89.

Wrocław

At its apogee around 1920, the Jewish community of Wrocław, then Breslau, numbered about 23,200 people and ranked as the third largest Jewish center in Germany. There were two large community synagogues and eight private ones. There were also synagogues in the Reform theological seminary, the Jewish hospital, and the Jewish old-age home. Private prayer rooms accommodated special groups, such as those who favored specific liturgies, hailed from the same town, or belonged to the same fraternal lodge. The wide architectural range included the Landschule in the local vernacular manner, the stately, classical Storch Synagogue, the neo-Romanesque New Synagogue, and the simplified Byzantine-Romanesque hospital oratory. The architects included two well-respected men, Karl Friedrich Langhans at the Storch Synagogue, and Edwin Oels Oppler, the Jewish architect of Hannover, at the New Synagogue.

Jews were recorded in and near Wrocław from the twelfth century onward. A document refers to a synagogue in 1270, and there were at least two in 1349, when the synagogues were confiscated and the Jews ejected from the city on suspicion of having caused the Black Death. As was often the case after an expulsion, the Jews were allowed back soon afterward, no doubt because commerce had suffered during their absence. They built another synagogue near the city walls in an undesirable quarter—as was also often the case. They were expelled and readmitted several times until their definitive expulsion in 1453, when they were accused of having stolen the host from a church; this was a frequently used pretext for banishing Jews and confiscating their property. For a century afterward, Jews were generally absent from the city, although nearby, in Brzeg Dolny, they established a long-lived community. They settled in Wrocław officially only after the 1630s when the government hoped to promote trade with eastern Poland by allowing some Jewish merchants to remain after the trade fairs ended. A few other Jews with special privileges joined them. Their synagogues had to be small; most were organized by people from the same area. In 1695 there were seven synagogues, and in 1701, ten. One was the private synagogue of a privileged Jew from Hamburg, but others were known by names such as the Glogauer, Kalischer, Krotoschiner, Lemberger, and Lissaer, serving congregations from towns now called Glogów, Kalisz, Krotoszyn, L'vov, and Leszno. Other synagogues were organized by people from elsewhere in Silesia and from Bohemia and Moravia.

The Landschule mentioned in 1741, which may have developed from an earlier one of

1695, was the principal synagogue before the nineteenth century. It seated 150 men and, quite unusually, an equal number of women; the congregation came from Silesia, Bohemia, and Moravia. The Landschule, destroyed sometime before 1926, was located in the Poköyhof, a court invisible from the street, as usual; the courtyard was the site of the main Jewish merchandise depot. The government did not permit the building to look like a religious edifice. The Landschule had two principal storeys under its tall double-pitched roof. The synagogue was on the upper floor, reached by staircases for men and women which led to an open gallery outside the prayer hall. The two staircases set close together were the only indication that this was not an ordinary utilitarian building.

Frederick the Great enforced more comprehensive regulation of the Jews, and from the 1740s until the Hitler period, they did not have to fear arbitrary expulsion. Despite limits to the number of Jews officially allowed in the city, there were many exemptions from the rules. In 1776 there were almost two thousand Jews in Wrocław. Some of the earlier congregations united and others were formed, especially by immigrants from Lithuania and Volhynia (e.g., the Sklower Schul).

Storch Synagogue

The growing Jewish population included many who were influenced by the Enlightenment, especially among the city's wealthier citizens. In 1780, several of them formed a fraternal organization, the Gesellschaft der Brüder, dedicated to ethical and philanthropic purposes. They took over a building which had earlier held other synagogues, and *Bauassistent* Johann Gottlieb Eik redesigned it. The synagogue was dedicated in October 1796. The Christian owner of the building kept raising the rent, while the Jews kept increasing in number, so the fraternity decided to build a new synagogue and in 1819 obtained a government permit. The government hoped that by allowing the construction of one large building, the diverse small synagogues could be closed, allowing Jewish activities to be watched more closely. Although the Glogauer Synagogue leaders protested, because the lease on their recently built synagogue had ten years to run, and other Jews were afraid that the government would require a new ritual—no doubt Reform—the new synagogue's promoters obtained some property on which there was a building called "Zum weissen Storch," which gave its name to the synagogue later erected there. Wearisome quarrels about the purchase terms delayed construction of the building until 1827–29, when a Jewish merchant who had owned part of the land built the Storch Synagogue at his own expense and rented it to the congregation. The design had been made around 1820 by Karl F. Langhans, son of the architect of the Brandenburg Gate in Berlin and later famous in his own right as a theater designer. A Jewish painter, Raphael Moses Abraham Biow (1773–1836), adorned the interior, but his decorations were lost during a remodeling.

The imposing three-storey neoclassical building of plastered brick has five-bay facades on the east and west (Figs. 174, 175). A giant order of fluted Corinthian pilasters divides the three central bays, while a triangular pediment connects them. Long, round-headed windows fill the four side bays. The central western bay contains the main door, and the eastern central bay has an ark niche under a circular window. On either side of the east facade are auxiliary bays, probably for stairs and robing rooms, lighted on the north and south sides by three storeys of round-headed windows. The general design of a pilastered facade was already familiar from the Hamburg-Bäckerstrasse synagogue, but the details at Wrocław differed. The latter also has a small lantern over the center of the interior, which, though visible outside, does not resemble a dome. Indeed, this synagogue has nothing to make it look traditionally Christian or "religious" on the exterior.

Inside, the Storch Synagogue has two storeys of galleries on three sides, and an additional gallery on the east side which was probably the choir loft (Fig. 176). As we see it now, the building seems to reflect a mid-nineteenth century

Figure 174. Wroclaw, Storch Synagogue, ca. 1820, 1827–29, exterior, west side in ca. 1981.

Figure 175. Wroclaw, Storch Synagogue, exterior, east side in ca. 1981.

remodeling. Low, broad arches were introduced to help support the galleries; perhaps their original cylindrical piers became unstable. Square pillars with truncated pyramidal capitals bearing trefoil ornaments rise from the upper gallery parapet to the ceiling. They, too, may have been introduced in the later remodeling. On the simple molded gallery parapets are irregularly placed vertical bands of plant or interlace ornament. The color scheme was originally white and gold. The ark, now without its frame and with its niche destroyed, once looked like a wooden altarpiece, with columns bearing lotus capitals beside the opening. The congregation accepted some identification with Egypt inside the synagogue, where the Egyptian details were private allusions to ancient and separate traditions; similar details also were introduced by the architects, with congregational approval or acquiescence, at Munich and Frankfurt am Main-Compostellhof. The exterior, however, suggested that the orthodox congregation included German-speaking people who

Figure 176. Wrocław, Storch Synagogue, interior to ark in ca. 1981.

could assimilate culturally to the surrounding Christian community.

Reform Temple

The tendencies to cultural assimilation led some of Wrocław's Jews to espouse Reform, and Abraham Geiger, a Reform rabbi, served there from 1838 to 1863 in a difficult relationship with the local orthodox rabbinate. A Reform theological seminary opened in 1854. The Reform congregation commissioned its own synagogue from Oppler, who had been planning a new, large synagogue at Hannover since 1862 (see Figs. 162, 163). For both cities, he produced monumental synagogues that resembled Rhenish Romanesque cathedrals, but with nearly central plans rather than Latin crosses. Wrocław's was erected from 1866 to 1872; no doubt some delays were caused by Prussia's wars of the time (Figs. 177, 178). Oppler hoped to design synagogues that would make the Jews look German. He used Romanesque to remind people that Jews had used the style during the Middle Ages, and were European rather than an exotic people. Nevertheless, Oppler's imposing domed brick edifice had so little in common with other buildings in Wrocław that it looked unusual anyway. It was injured by vandals in November 1938, and was demolished eventually. A police department parking lot later occupied the site.

Jewish Hospital Oratory

Among the other places for prayer in Wrocław was the hospital oratory, located on the Jewish hospital's central axis and easily reached by the principal staircases (Fig. 179). The building and oratory were designed in 1899 by the Herold firm in Berlin, which won first prize in a design competition. It was completed in 1903 under the direction of architects in Wrocław, R. and P. Ehrlich and Otto Finster. It was a good example of a prayer room in an important community institution, the kind of facility that was often built but seldom mentioned because it lacked the permanent congregation of a formally constituted synagogue.

The room was a simple rectangle, more broad than long. It had smooth walls and a smooth ceiling, three windows on the ark wall, pairs of thin columns flanking the ark, and a simple bimah table. Women sat on the same level as the men. The decorative style was modernized medieval. Separating the women's area north of the main space was a parapet holding a triple-arched arcade resting on short Romanesque columns with cubic capitals. The dado paintings around the entire room included geometric leaf and round floral forms. The side windows of the men's section had twin round-arched windows under a large circular opening; the twin windows had arts-and-crafts floral designs, perhaps roses of Sharon. These details evoked the distant past somewhere between the Rhine and the Jordan, smoothed and stylized in a manner congenial to modern artistic movements. The only discordant elements were six fancy metal chandeliers and the rays in the circular window over the unimposing ark. The oratory overall was close in taste to the synagogues of Trieste (1912) and Essen (1913), and its style was up to date in its day (see Figs. 140, 208).

Figure 177. (opposite) Wroclaw, Reform temple, 1866–72, exterior.

Figure 178. Wroclaw, Reform temple, longitudinal section.

Figure 179. Wrocław, Jewish Hospital Oratory, 1899, interior to ark.

The Storch Synagogue was the only one left standing after the war. It survived because would-be arsonists were told not to risk burning down Christian-owned buildings near it. In 1945, when the city came under Polish rule, displaced persons came there and constituted one of the largest Polish postwar communities. Following the 1967 Arab-Israeli fighting, vandals damaged the building. After 1968, when nationalistic, anti-Semitic outbursts were attributed to government instigation, the Jewish population emigrated from Wrocław. While the Storch Synagogue survives and is officially designated a historic monument, its condition is poor—its windows broken, its walls sometimes used for anti-Semitic graffiti. The Jewish community is too small to make the government eager to restore and maintain the building adequately. The remaining Jews worship in a small room in the old rabbinical seminary building near the Storch Synagogue. Both the Jewish community and the Storch Synagogue are crumbling with age.

BIBLIOGRAPHY

L. Burgemeister and G. Grundmann, *Die Kunstdenkmäler der Provinz Niederschlesien: Die Kunstdenkmäler der Stadt Breslau, III. Die kirchlichen Denkmäler der Altstadt (Fortsetzung) und des erweiterten Stadtgebietes. Die Friedhöfe,* Wrocław, 1934, pp. 157–58.

P. Eilitz, *Leben und Werk des königlichen hannoverschen Baurats Edwin Oppler,* Hannover, 1971, pp. 167–69. (Hannoversche Geschichtsblätter, n.F., XXV, 3–4).

Encyclopedia Judaica, 1971, s.v. Breslau.

A. Grotte, "Jüdische Sakralkunst in Schlesien," *Jüdische Kultur in Schlesien,* special issue of *Menorah* IV, #5 (May 1926), pp. 273–78, esp. p. 274.

Hammer-Schenk, "Opplers," pp. 101–13.

———, *Synagogen,* pp. 56–57, 213–17.

———, "Untersuchungen," pp. 284–88.

A. Heppner, "Zur Jahrhundertfeier der Storchsynagoge am 23 April 1929," *Breslauer jüdisches Gemeindeblatt,* VI (April 1929), pp. 1–2.

——— and B. Brilling, "Breslauer Synagogen," *ibid.,* VIII (Dec. 1931), IX (May 1932), IX (July 1932).

E. Hintze, ed., *Katalog der vom "Verein jüdisches Museum Breslau" . . . veranstalteten Ausstellung: Das Judentum in der Geschichte Schlesiens,* Wrocław, 1929, p. 22 #64–66, pp. 23–24 #72, p. 32 #117–19.

Jewish Encyclopedia, s.v. Breslau.

H. Kamm, "Polish city, once German, retains only trace of vibrant Jewish life," *New York Times,* Dec. 4, 1973.

L. Klasen, *Grundrissvorbilder. XI. Gebäude für kirchlichen Zweck,* Leipzig, 1889, p. 1469 and fig. 1941.

"Respekt vor der Vergangenheit," *Allgemeine unabhängige jüdische Wochenzeitung* XXXII, Sept. 9, 1977.

E. Sandberg, G. Reinbach, and P. Ehrlich, *Das israelitische Krankenhaus zu Breslau. Denkschrift,* Wrocław, 1904.

M. Silberstein, *Zeitbilder aus der Geschichte der Juden in Breslau,* Denkschrift, Wrocław, 1904.

Universal Jewish Encyclopedia, s.v. Breslau.

Before 1945, the following images existed (present whereabouts unknown): Landschule, in Stadtliche Vermessungsamt; Sklowerschule, in collection of photographer Klette; Storch Synagogue lithograph, in Schlesisches Museum für Kunstgewerbe und Altertümer; drawing of synagogue existing in 1746, in City Library.

I am most indebted to Olgierd Czerner for photographs.

Iberian Peninsula

Toledo

Enchanting to the traveler, fascinating to the historian and architect, the two surviving medieval synagogues of Toledo are among the most memorable in Europe. Though very different in plan and decoration, both nevertheless reveal the convergence of Jewish, Christian, and Islamic factors in the art and culture of the city. Their form and decoration characterize a period when the local Jews and Christians spoke a language that was partly Arabic, and when Jewish documents were in Arabic but written in Hebrew characters.

"Santa María la Blanca"

The five-aisled synagogue is a monument with a unique form and an incomplete history. It is an irregular quadrilateral, between 26 and 28 m. long and between 19 and 23 m. wide (Fig. 180). At the eastern end are three Renaissance apses which were not part of the building when the Jews owned it; there is no documentation of the original east end.

The plain brick exterior is as unprepossessing as that of most Islamic religious buildings of the same period in Spain. Some stone courses alternate with the brick courses; plaster covers some of the brick. The masonry techniques found in the building were common in Toledo. Most of the window openings and one of the two present door openings may have been later additions; the wooden doors themselves date from 1923.

The interior is far more impressive. Twenty-four octagonal piers of brick now separate the five unequal but parallel aisles; eight-and-a-half partial piers are attached to the walls (Fig. 181). The piers support twenty-eight horseshoe arches which rise to a ceiling 12.5 m. from the floor of the nave, about 10 m. in the inner aisles, and 7 m. in the outer aisles. A ring of glazed tiles instead of a plinth or sculptured base surrounds the inner piers at the bottom. The handsome capitals, made of hard plaster, have carved pine cones and foliate forms separated by decorative interlace.

The outer aisle walls are plain, but the wall ornament of the three inner aisles is the glory of the building (Fig. 182). It consists of plaster spandrel decoration with horizontal friezes above. In all the spandrels there are circles of exquisite vines which flank circular medallions containing fine and varied plaster designs. A second level of the central nave, between the

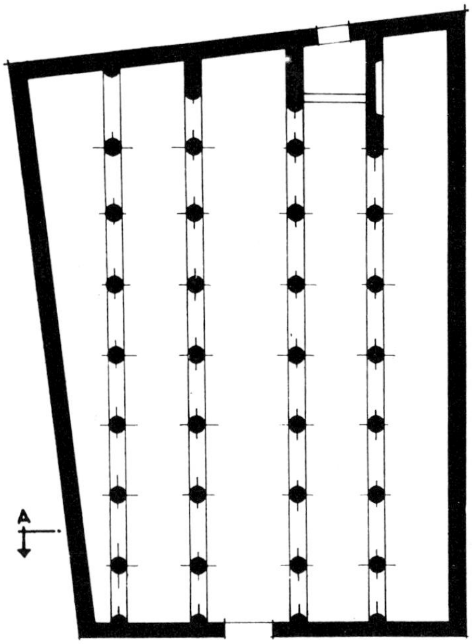

Figure 180. Toledo, "Santa María la Blanca," 13th century (?), plan.

Figure 181. Toledo, "Santa María la Blanca," interior in 19th century before 1842, lithograph.

spandrels and a frieze of cusped arches, contains three bands of ornament. Narrow friezes in the lower and upper parts of the intermediate zone have intersecting triangular fields with shells in the center, immediately above each spandrel medallion. Between these decorations stretches a band of plaster, now blank, which may once have contained inscriptions. Above this zone runs a frieze of lively angular vertical and diagonal designs in squarish fields. In the inner flanking aisles, a narrow frieze with blank plastered spaces is punctuated above the spandrel medallions by square plaques containing reliefs of shells.

The wooden *artesonado* ceiling has twin transverse beams creating ceiling bays which span two bays of the arcade below. Its profile in the center bays slopes upward at the sides to a flat ceiling over three side aisles. The sloping sides meet at a peak; over the narrowest and most irregular aisle, the ceiling has a single slope. The entire ceiling, and perhaps the sloping roof, may be later inventions rather than restored originals; Otto Czekelius, an architect who examined the building about fifty years ago, suggested that there were originally double-pitched roofs over clerestories that illuminated the three inner aisles, and that the building had open timber roofs rather than the ceilings which now block the upper parts of the walls. Rachel Wischnitzer, on the other hand, thought that Spanish authorities must have limited the number of windows here as they did elsewhere, and she thought that double-pitched aisle roofs were found only on buildings with aisles of equal height.

Figure 182. Toledo, "Santa María la Blanca," interior, detail of ornament.

There may have been a women's gallery, which Czekelius thought was at the western end of the building. He suggested that openings in the interior of the west wall connected the men's and the women's sections, and that brackets, of which remains survive in the west wall, supported the gallery. In addition, he believed the present west wall to be merely a blocking-in of the building portions that remained after the demolition of the gallery.

The synagogue must have had an ark niche or chest. The form of the bimah and the seating arrangements are also unknown, as is the original appearance of the floor, which is now tiled in two patterns that may date only from a restoration.

The plan of the building is puzzling. There is no other extant five-aisled synagogue on the European continent. In North Africa, however, there are examples of synagogues with several aisles divided by columns. Tunis has two. They are not as old as the building in Toledo, and they differ from the axial arrangement seen in Toledo in that their rows of columns cross the main axis, which need not be the longer one.

Attempts have been made to link the Toledo synagogue's plan to the *diplostoon* arrangement of the ancient synagogue of Alexandria, but scholars debate whether a *diplostoon* plan is one with an aisle within an aisle or one with a gallery above an aisle. There is no known connection in any case between medieval Toledo and ancient Alexandria, where the synagogue had been destroyed in the early Christian period, long before Toledo's synagogue was built.

A five-aisled plan provides a wider and thus more impressive building on a lot of limited length, but the interior supports interfere with visibility and to some extent with good acoustics. They divide the synagogue into loosely defined compartments, thereby dissipating some of the desirable communality which is an objective implied by the establishment of a *minyan*.

It is not possible to say why the five-aisled plan was adopted. Just as the Islamic horseshoe arches and the decoration with inscriptions and ornament may have been executed by Moorish craftsmen, the plan, too, suggests Islamic influence since mosques often have many aisles. Perhaps the synagogue was erected on the foundations of an earlier mosque or was a mosque converted to a synagogue. Another possibility is that the patron wanted the largest and widest possible synagogue with abundant ornament inside. Styles mixing Islamic and Christian artistic ideas were common at this time and even later in Spain.

We are uncertain of the building's date and patron, and we do not know whether the craftsmen were Moslems, Jews, or Christians. Closely comparable dated examples from the same area do not exist to help us. The date of ca. 1205, which is accepted by many modern scholars, comes from circumstantial evidence. An elegy written after a massacre of Jews lists the synagogues of Toledo and names the "new" synagogue among the greatest of them. The "Santa María la Blanca" synagogue is clearly a noteworthy one, so that it was reasonable to identify the "new" synagogue with it. Since "new" did not necessarily mean "recent" but merely "newer" than older synagogues mentioned in the same elegy, scholars first looked in available documents for a suitable patron of thirteenth- or fourteenth-century date. When they learned that the other extant Toledan synagogue is documented to the mid-fourteenth century, and when they saw that the decorative style of the "Blanca" synagogue is both different and earlier, they sought a thirteenth-century patron. They found one in Joseph ben Meir ben Shoshan (= Yucef Abenxuxen), who died in 1205 and whose epitaph, recorded in a fifteenth-century manuscript, mentioned his having built a synagogue. A Provençal visitor of 1204 recorded information about him but said nothing about a synagogue. Joseph would certainly have had the money and position necessary for the patronage of an elaborate synagogue, as he was the son of a finance minister (*almoxarife*) to Alfonso VIII of Castile (ruled 1158–1214). Joseph, if he *was* the patron of this building, might have restored an earlier building which had been damaged by fire or vandalism, perhaps during an anti-Jewish uprising that occurred in 1180. This might account for its curiously irregular plan.

The synagogue is closer in style to twelfth-century monuments in Morocco—the Tinmal (1153) and Kutubiyya (ca. 1150) mosques in Marrakech—than to any others elsewhere; it could have been executed in a style similar to these precedents some years later in the Spanish "provinces," while Joseph was alive. A wooden tablet found in Toledo with the inscription, "Its ruins were raised up in the year 4940"[= A.D. 1180], may refer to this synagogue and to a restoration in that year.

Some scholars prefer to date the ornament in the second half of the thirteenth century. In their view, the piers and probably the capitals could antedate the plaster decoration on the walls between the aisles. L. Torres Balbas suggested stylistic similarities between the plaster work here and at the convent of Las Huelgas in Burgos of about 1275, but the resemblances to the twelfth-century mosques are far more specific. They include the moderate size of the ornament; the scale of the ornament in relation to that of the building; the combination of light, open, vegetable ornament against a blank background and denser, geometric forms; and inscriptions located in separate fields rather than integrated in the ornament.

The synagogue was drastically altered after its construction. It was taken from its Jewish owners in 1405 or 1411, following a series of anti-Jewish manifestations in Toledo and elsewhere in Spain. St. Vincent Ferrer may not have instigated the confiscation, as has been alleged, although he was certainly an enemy of the Jews. The building was made into a church dedicated to St. Mary of the Snows, and is still known as Santa María la Blanca. From 1554 to about 1600, it served as a convent for reformed prostitutes. In connection with its use as a church, the building received the three apses that we now see, and the steps ascending to the central apse. This construction entailed the demolition of the original east end. By about 1600, there was apparently an insufficient supply of penitent women but the convent could not be opened to ordinary novices because of restrictions in the foundation charter. The convent closed and the building became a humble oratory. By 1790–91 it seems to have become an *ad hoc* shelter for derelict people. It was used for lodging after 1791 for a few years. A sensitive visitor, Don Vicente Dominguez de Prado, *intendente* of the royal armies and general of the province of Toledo, resolved to restore the building to a decent use, even if not to the service of religion. He had the building made serviceable in 1798 so that it could become a depository for royal treasury goods. The former synagogue came to more general attention in 1842, when the first volume of *España artística y monumental* appeared with handsome illustrations of it. Six years later, the decaying building was declared a national monument, and in 1856 it experienced a more far-reaching restoration under the architect Francisco Enríquez Ferrer. At this time, almost all the capitals were completely recut under the direction of the sculptor Ceferino Díaz, and the plasterwork was restored. Only a few wooden ceiling brackets appear to have evaded the restorers' tools; the reworking limits our ability to distinguish medieval hands and styles and perhaps even precise dates.

The building's origin and form may be puzzling, but the restored remains still captivate us. The unfamiliar style conjures up a distant past and exotic associations. The many aisles suggest endless depths and imply the presence of many fellow worshippers. The white-painted piers stand out sharply in the half-light, and lead the eye in a heavy but bounding rhythm toward the east. The sensations are not specifically religious, given the absence of a current congregation and even of the furnishing needed for synagogue worship. The hard, mechanical work of the restorers, and the heavy hand of the modern whitewasher are all too evident, although they cannot obscure the fundamental beauty of the ornament. In the sensations it inspires—of mystery and of distance from its creators—this building enlarges our experience of the surroundings that have been considered desirable for Jewish worship in the past.

"Nuestra Señora del Tránsito"

In contrast to the earlier synagogue at Toledo, the synagogue built by Samuel Halevi Abulafia in about 1360 has a simpler form and a simpler history. This synagogue, too, has an unadorned exterior of brick and stone, pierced by small windows in the upper walls and by a door, in this case on the south side. The belfry is a later, Christian, addition (Figs. 183, 184). Inside, the synagogue is a single-naved hall, about 23 m. long, 9.5 m. high, and 12 m. wide. On the east, three niches in the lower thickness of the wall were recesses for the Torah scrolls which must originally have been protected by wooden doors. High above, two windows open toward Jerusalem. A women's gallery on the north side forms the second storey of an annex. The lower part of the annex incorporates remains of an eleventh- or twelfth-century building. Another

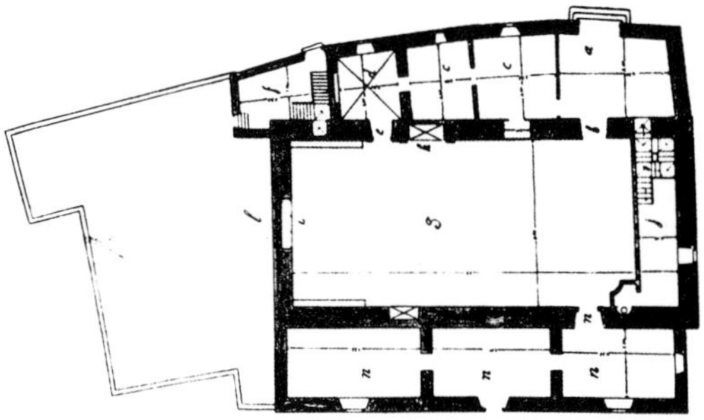

Figure 183. Toledo, "Nuestra Señora del Tránsito," ca. 1350–60, plan.

annex lies at the south. A room on the west which held archives has been demolished. Other additions to the building are a plain doorway to the north annex and on the south wall a Renaissance tomb recess and a Renaissance door leading to the eastern end of the north annex.

The ornament of the prayer hall includes a dedicatory inscription recording the foundation of the building by Abulafia, who was finance minister and advisor to King Pedro the Cruel of Castile (ruled 1350–69). Abulafia apparently built this as a private synagogue, rather than as a general Jewish communal facility, since there was an entrance to the synagogue from his (now destroyed) house. The proud tone of the inscription also suggests his private ownership. Pride preceded a fall in his case, for he was executed at his royal master's orders in 1360 or 1361, soon after his grand, spacious synagogue was completed.

The ornamental plasterwork is of exceptional quality. It is arranged in fields which underline the shape of the room, as is customary in Mudéjar design. On the east wall are three rectangular panels under the horizontal attic with its row of arches and twin windows in the center (Fig. 185). The central panel is slightly higher than the adjacent ones, and has relief ornament in diamond-shaped fields. The center is further emphasized by the three-arched former ark repository. The ornament of the side panels is curvilinear, in a design resembling the pomegranate pattern. There is a dedicatory plaque at the base of each side panel.

Figure 184. Toledo, "Nuestra Señora del Tránsito," interior to ark in ca. 1880–ca. 1960.

Figure 185. Toledo, "Nuestra Señora del Tránsito," detail of east wall ornament, condition in ca. 1880–ca. 1960.

The plasterwork on the side walls below the frieze has been destroyed. Each frieze and attic band is kept distinct with its own ornament—filigree interlace bosses, cusped arches, Hebrew script, tendrils and leaves, heraldic shields. They tie together the walls of the vast room without interfering with the panel designs of the east end. Geometric panels dividing a wall clearly into primary and subordinate fields are seen also at the small fourteenth-century synagogue in Córdoba. There, however, the plasterwork in the tiny room is flatter and more geometric and linear in form. It still shows the framed fields, dense, small-scaled and repetitive patterns, delicate lines, cusped arches, and diagonal compartments which we see in the Tránsito synagogue, and it is certainly the product of the same century; it was dedicated in 1315. The plasterwork originally was painted in both buildings, but most of the color and the gilt which once adorned some of the lettering and details are gone.

The *artesonado* ceiling at Toledo is of a type known elsewhere and, though much restored, it is a beautiful work of construction. Five pairs of beams span the width of the room, dividing it into six bays. Each bay is covered by a wooden framework in which the components slant upward toward a flat ceiling in a lattice design running along the center of the interior. Ivory inlays form geometric patterns on the wooden framework. Inscriptions on the ceiling come mainly from passages in Exodus, I Kings, I Chronicles, Psalms, Isaiah, and Habakkuk. No one has discovered the specific idea that they were intended to illustrate.

After the Jews were expelled from Spain in 1492, King Ferdinand granted the building to the Order of Calatrava. These monastic knights transformed it into the church of San Benito. By the late eighteenth century it was no longer a priory church of the order but a mere oratory dedicated to Nuestra Señora del Tránsito, and during the Napoleonic period it was used for military purposes. The building attracted the attention of philologists and antiquarians for its many plasterwork Hebrew inscriptions, in addition to Abulafia's dedication. The inscriptions were copied first in 1752 by Francisco Pérez Bayer in his manuscript *De Toletano Hebraeorum Templo,* published first in 1795 by Don Juan Josef Heydeck in his *De ilustración de la inscripción hebrea que se halla en la iglesia de Nuestra Señora del Tránsito,* and published again by the Real Academia de la Historia in 1799. Debate raged among scholars who found fault with one or the other of the readings. Sufficient attention was drawn to the inscriptions and plasterwork that the government decided to clean and repair the building when it was deconsecrated and designated a national monument in 1877. The building could not be restored to its original state, because no one knew then or knows now what it looked like or how it was furnished. Instead, the first restorations (1880–83, under Don Francisco Isidori y

Ronda; 1905, under Don Arturo Mélida) preserved the tombs of the Knights of Calatrava in the center of the room and the knights' wooden choir stalls along the north and south walls. They cleaned the Renaissance tomb and doorway on the south, and removed an internal gallery and a Christian altarpiece with its crowning canopy.

The building remained in this condition until the 1960s, when the Spanish government made the building into a Jewish museum. New restorers removed the choir stalls and tombs, except for the one on the south wall and an immured tomb chest on the north wall. The plasterwork of the east wall received a new backing to prevent further decay due to moisture and structural instability. New fabric now covers the other walls, and the plaster ornament was repaired. The floor pavement was restored, including a rectangle of glass mosaic at the east with geometric designs. If the mosaic antedates 1492, it may mark the location of the ark. The north annex houses inscriptions relating to Spanish Jewry, books, ritual objects, and other items which constitute a small Sephardic Museum. A synagogue service celebrated this new and more suitable use of the building. It was the first one held in such a public fashion since the expulsion of Jews from Spain in 1492; services conducted in the interim were held in private buildings which had to be owned by individuals, not by a Jewish community acting as a corporation. Not long after the rededication of the Abulafia synagogue, the Spanish government modified some of its restrictive religious laws so that Jews could hold services openly wherever they were needed. Government representatives attended the dedication of a new synagogue in Madrid, and there are other functioning synagogues in Barcelona and Ceuta. The Abulafia synagogue, however, has no regular congregation, although many visitors come to see the building and its fine details.

At the present time, the synagogue, clean and cavernous, looks like the official monument it now is. Its beauty lies in its spacious grandeur, its ornament, and its associations of history and sentiment, rather than in a specific aura of sanctity and faith. Its refinement and amplitude remind twentieth-century visitors of the eminence and culture of the most fortunate among the Spanish Jews who lived during the medieval "golden age" of Sephardic Jewry.

BIBLIOGRAPHIES

F. Cantera y Burgos, *Sinagogas de Toledo, Segovia, y Córdoba,* Madrid, 1973.

———, *Sinagogas españolas,* Madrid, 1955.

R. Singerman, *The Jews in Spain and Portugal. A Bibliography,* New York and London, 1975, esp. entries 1032–34, 1044–1103, 2654–69, and s.v. Cantera y Burgos.

Publications postdating the extensive bibliographies in the books cited above are:

E. Ashtor, *The Jews of Moslem Spain,* Philadelphia, 1973, esp. p. 326.

B. Pavón Maldonado, "Una problema arqueológico en la sinagoga de El Tránsito," *Sefarad* XXVI, #1 (1976), pp. 141–44.

P. Riera Vidal, *The Jews of Toledo and their Synagogues,* Toledo, 1975.

Note: The principal early modern description of the synagogues is in P. de la Escosura, *España artística y monumental,* vol. 1, Paris, 1842, pp. 44–45, 71–72 with lithographs opposite pp. 44 and 71 which inspired later views. For other important early descriptions and illustrations, see J. Amador de los Rios, *Toledo pintoresca,* Toledo, 1845, and M. de Assas, "Antiga sinagoga hoy iglesia de Santa María la Blanca," *Monumentos arquitectónicos de España,* vol. 7, Madrid, 1878.

CÓRDOBA

Singerman, op cit., entries 548–67.

L. Torres Balbas, *Arte almohade. Arte nazarí. Arte Mudéjar,* Madrid, 1949 (Ars Hispaniae 4).

NORTH AFRICA

H. Basset and H. Terrasse, *Sanctuaires et forteresses almohades,* Paris, 1932, esp. pp. 185, 187 for monuments comparable to Santa María la Blanca.

J. Pinkerfeld, *The Synagogues of North Africa,* Jerusalem, 1974, esp. pp. 5–8 (Hebrew).

Tomar

The synagogue at Tomar is isolated geographically and formally, a unique record of synagogue architecture in pre-expulsion Portugal.

The small building stands in what was once the Jews' street in a part of the town which was enclosed by gates, as in a ghetto. A document referring to the former synagogue as a square, vaulted building on that street confirms the identification, although the structure has no other clear signs of its old function.

As we see it now, the entrance opens on the north in a facade with windows and doors that postdate the expulsion of the Jews from Portugal in 1496–97. Archaeologists have uncovered some walls of an eastern annex and the original ogee-arched entrance on that side, near the north end. Inside, the prayer hall is nearly square, about 9.5 m. by 8.2 m., with a longer north-south axis (Fig. 186). The pavement lies about 0.5 m. below street level and three modern steps lead down to it; either the floor was lowered for symbolic purposes or the street level has risen in five centuries, or both may have occurred. The groin vaulting rests on four thin cylindrical piers forming a square bay in the center of the room (Fig. 187). The supports stand on bases and bear capitals with three different designs. The vaults also rest on eight brackets, whose forms may be vestigially antique, retained elsewhere by Moorish craftsmen, rather than incipiently Renaissance. The vaults and pillars form a nine-bay plan, but there is no apparent connection between the nine-bay scheme seen here and four-pillar and nine-bay plans of Poland (see Figs. 76, 78, 85). At Tomar, the vaults are virtually identical and there is no attempt to group the four central supports around a central bimah. Perhaps the bimah at Tomar did not even stand in the center, but rather in the wall opposite the (surely freestanding) ark, as is customary in Sephardic synagogues. The vaults also differ from those of eastern Europe in that they are bisected so as to emphasize the four central vaults rather than a single central one. We cannot tell whether the scheme at Tomar has any connection with the four-column, centrally emphatic Sephardic synagogue type seen later in the Balkans (Samokov [see Fig. 53] and Sofia-Cahal de Francos), in Gibraltar, and in the Hamburg-Kleine Papagoyenstrasse synagogue of 1682; Iberian Jews settled in the Balkans after their expulsion from the Iberian peninsula, while others later settled in Hamburg and Altona. Relations between the Tomar synagogue and small Islamic religious structures are hard to specify, but some connection may exist.

It may be, however, that Islamic craftsmen worked at the Tomar synagogue. The evidence is sketchy, but the synagogue seems to be one of a circumscribed group of mid-fifteenth-century monuments, including the crypt at the Collegiate Church of Ourem and the Founders' Chapel at Batalha, which are all different in style from most Portuguese architecture. The work at Ourem was sponsored by Fernando, second duke of Bragança, who is known to have been on good terms with the Moors, and in whose time the Jewish quarter existed in Tomar. Documents record craftsmen with Moorish names at the Convento do Cristo in Tomar. And a capital, vestigially Ionic and of Moorish execution, is kept in the Museu Arqueológico of Santarém. Such evidence as there is, then, hints at the possibility of the Tomar synagogue interior

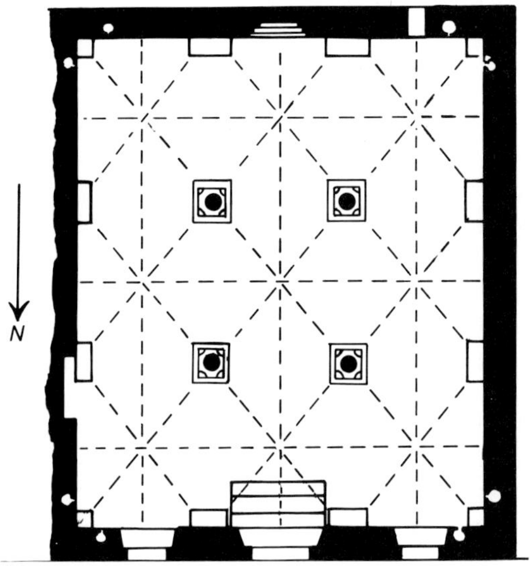

Figure 186. Tomar, ca. 1460(?), plan.

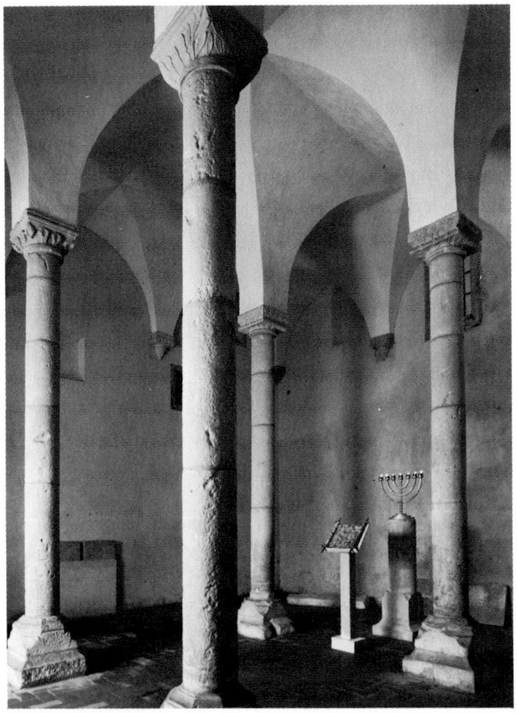

Figure 187. Tomar, interior.

being of about 1460, perhaps designed by someone of Moorish background and training.

We know nothing about the original furniture or decoration of this synagogue. Whatever there was disappeared when the building became a prison. (This fate also befell the Guimarães synagogue after 1497 and perhaps that at Oporto.) Later, the Tomar synagogue became a chapel dedicated to St. Bartholomew.

Examinations of the building revealed a storage area, perhaps a repository for damaged Torah scrolls and ritual objects no longer fit for use. Scholars also have found vases which may have been used to enhance acoustic properties, following a practice recorded in ancient times by Vitruvius. The synagogue is, however, too small to require amplification of the human voice within the main room.

Although there has been no congregation here for half a millennium, the building has been treated with respect in this century. Samuel Schwarz, a Polish mining engineer who lived in Portugal, bought it and later gave it to the Portuguese government to be used as a Portuguese-Jewish museum. It was dedicated in late 1939 with an expression of strong antiracist sentiments by a representative of the Portuguese government. In 1942, when so many synagogues in central and eastern Europe had been turned to ashes, the building was cleaned and repaired. It stands in good condition today, a puzzling but valuable witness to a lost culture.

BIBLIOGRAPHY

F. A. Garcez Teixeira, *A antiga sinagoga de Tomar,* Lisbon, 1925.

J. M. Santos Simões, *Tomar e a sua judaria,* Tomar, 1943.

S. Schwarz, *Projecto de organização de um museu luso-hebraico na antiga sinagoga de Tomar,* Lisbon, 1939.

Italy

Ancona

The synagogues of Ancona, typical of many in Italy before emancipation, provided settings for the city's long-enduring Jewish life. Jewish settlement in Ancona dates back to the fifteenth century at least, and a synagogue is mentioned in a document of 1498. After 1532, when Ancona came under papal control, Levantines including Jews were welcomed to support the commerce of the town. Under Pope Paul III (1534–49), Jews expelled from Spanish territories in southern Italy found refuge in Ancona. Paul IV (1555–59), however, instituted a ghetto and the community was allowed to have only one synagogue, even though adherents of different rites had earlier been allowed to have separate synagogues. Those buildings were not destroyed, so that the Jews had to pay taxes on the former synagogues even though they could not use them. At least they were allowed to remain in the city when Pius V (1566–72) prohibited Jewish residence in the Papal States, except in Rome, Avignon, and Ancona. After 1585, under Sixtus V (1585–90) and his successors, the Jews fared slightly better. When the Confraternity of San Rocco requisitioned the Italian-rite synagogue beside their church for a hospital, it relocated the Scuola Italiana to the site later known as the Piazza 3 Aprile and paid for a new building there.

Scuola Italiana

This synagogue was like many in Italy that served Spanish-, Levantine-, and Italian-rite congregations from the sixteenth to the early twentieth centuries (Figs. 188, 189). It was a rectangle, 12.2 m. by 6.4 m., in a structure having no identifiable character on the outside. The ark at the east countered a bimah raised on a high platform at the west. The vaulted room received light from two storeys of windows along the north and west sides, a central skylight, and, later, a matched set of electric chandeliers. Grilles concealing the women's area filled sections of the south wall opposite the windows in the north wall; the floor of the women's section seems to have been raised over the level of the men's floor, as was the case in many other Italian synagogues. Long wooden benches stood on the east-west axis, and the central aisle between them kept the space free between the high bimah platform and the elaborate ark with its twisted and straight columns, pediment, carved doors, and rococo entrance arch. The length of the room, typical of Italian synagogues, dramatically extended the perspective, placing added emphasis on the bimah and the ark.

The plan was efficient and egalitarian. The elevated bimah allowed the entrance door to nestle beneath the platform, and the underside of the platform provided the effect of a tiny vestibule or lower space in which one could pause before continuing into the higher space of the rest of the room. The seating arrangement ensured that if a worshipper could not easily hear the words uttered at the distant end of the room, he could all the more easily hear the words uttered at his own end. Since each end was equally important, everyone was in a desirable seat.

This synagogue was closed in 1932 for an urban redevelopment project and was demolished in 1933. The municipal authorities promised to build a new Italian-rite synagogue, and the ark and the rococo arch were saved for use in the new structure.

Figure 188. Ancona, Scuola Italiana, ca. 1600(?), interior to ark.

Figure 189. Ancona, Scuola Italiana, interior to bimah.

Scuola Levantina

The other principal congregation in Ancona was that of the Levantines, whose first synagogue was established during the first half of the sixteenth century (Fig. 190). Its plan was similar to that of the Scuola Italiana, although its dimensions of about 17 m. by 5.5 m. made it longer and narrower. Like the Scuola Italiana and most Italian synagogues up to the late nineteenth century, it was designed in a Renaissance style, with round-headed windows alternating with rectangular panels (or pilasters), a vaulted ceiling, and a lantern serving as ventilator and skylight. Dado plaques seem to have been added later, since their shape did not conform

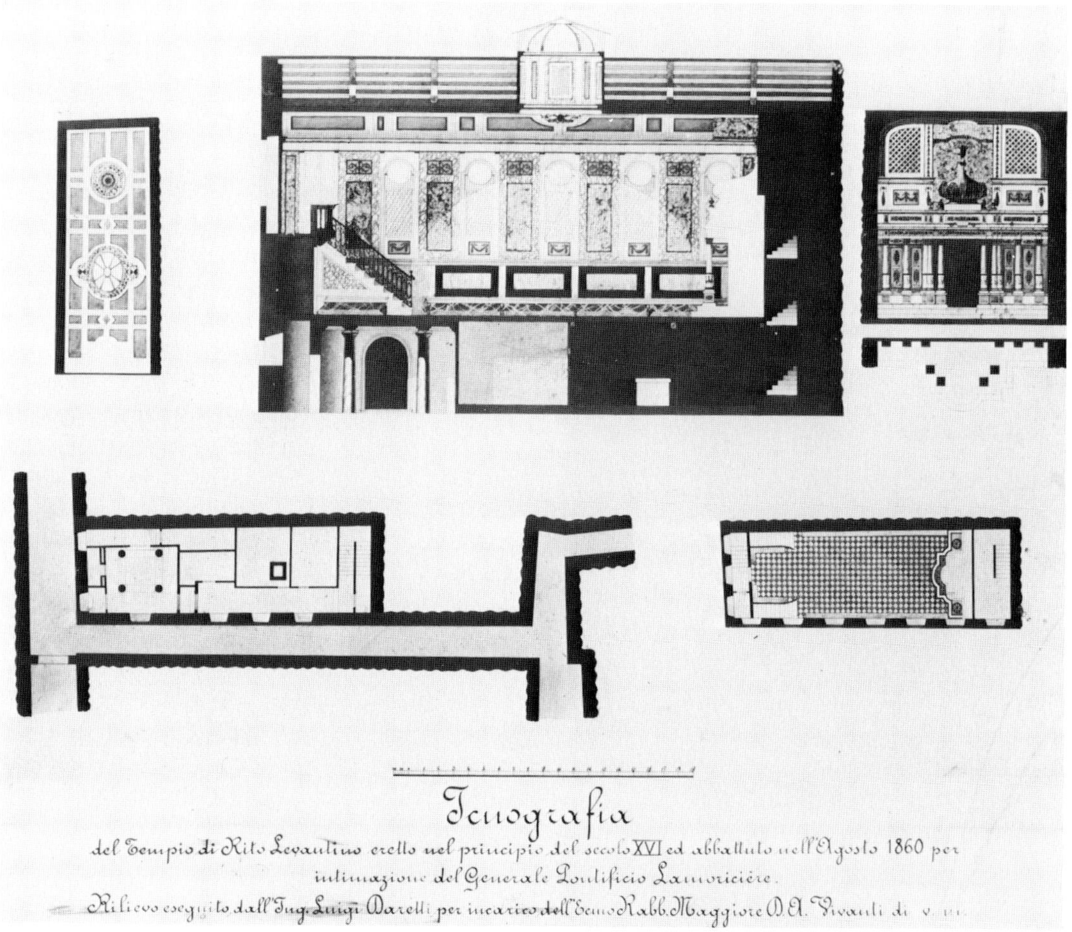

Icnografia
del Tempio di Rito Levantino eretto nel principio del secolo XVI ed abbattuto nell'Agosto 1860 per
intimazione del Generale Pontificio Lamoricière.
Rilievo eseguito dall'Ing. Luigi Daretti per incarico dell'Ecmo Rabb. Maggiore D. A. Vivanti

Figure 190. Ancona, Scuola Levantina, 16th century and later, ceiling plan, longitudinal section, cross section, site plan, prayer hall (upper storey) plan.

to the rhythm of the wall divisions above them. The ark stood on three steps and projected about 2.5 m. into the room. Its columns, cornices, and curves alternating with straight sections made it resemble a church altarpiece. The bimah, as in the Scuola Italiana, had no canopy but drew attention because of its elevated position and its access stairs, which stretched into the room for several meters. Women were accommodated behind grilles, apparently behind and above the ark on either side, as well as along the north, possibly in an annex built in the adjacent structure. Although few women were expected to attend synagogue services, those who did could not easily have seen the activities in the men's area, and if seated at the eastern end, they could not have seen the Torah scrolls being removed from or placed in the ark.

The fate of this building illustrates the treatment of Jews in the Papal States in 1860. Although the ghetto walls of Ancona had come down during a popular uprising in 1831, in 1855 the Jewish quarter was still a small and crowded area with narrow streets. The inhabitants lacked light, air, and hygiene; were subject to illegal baptism (and subsequent separation from their Jewish families); and were unable even to bury their dead during the daytime lest they "offend" others by their rituals and prayers. Under these oppressive circumstances, they had no recourse when the papal general

Figure 191. Ancona, Scuola Levantina, 1874–79, interior to ark in ca. 1970.

demolished the synagogue in 1860 in order to free the site for military use. The Jews requested, but never obtained, monetary compensation for the destruction, and had to erect a new synagogue at their own expense. The foundation stone for this building was laid in 1874; it opened in 1879.

A few months after the synagogue demolition, Ancona had become part of the Kingdom of Piedmont, and in 1861, part of the Kingdom of Italy. This gave the Jews virtually all civil rights, including the right to build places of worship. The new Scuola Levantina was a stately room, squarer in proportion and taller than the former synagogue (Fig. 191). It had round-headed arches on each wall with marble panels between them, and round-arched windows in the lunettes of the vault. The furnishings included the ark taken from the demolished synagogue, long benches along the principal axis, and chandeliers and wall sconces that were probably gaslit originally. The bimah stood on a platform at the west end. The women occupied spaces behind grilles on the north and south walls. The dignified correctness and amplitude of this room suggest that the congregation wished to demonstrate its rightful place within the modern and enlightened order of things in the new kingdom while retaining the traditional bipolar arrangement of ark and bimah as a sign of fidelity to Jewish tradition.

The synagogue was restored in 1935, not long before some of Ancona's Jews understood the wisdom of leaving an increasingly anti-Semitic environment; some who remained were deported or murdered in the early 1940s. Like many other towns where Jews had been numerous at the turn of the twentieth century, postwar Ancona became a city with a small, steadily diminishing Jewish population. Many young Italian Jews went to Israel, as did most of Ancona's synagogue ritual art. An eighteenth-century ark has gone to the synagogue at the University of Tel Aviv, and a seventeenth-century ark is now in the Hekhal Yacov Synagogue in Bat Yam. Despite these losses, which paradoxically may ensure the preservation of Jewish artifacts, Jewish life in Ancona survives—as it did not in many other localities. In the old ghetto area, in Via Astagno, the Levantine and Italian congregations occupy two prayer halls in the Scuola Levantina.

BIBLIOGRAPHY

Archives israélites XXXV (1874), p. 95.

C. Ciavarini, *Memorie storiche degli israeliti in Ancona,* 2d ed., Ancona, 1898.

R. Elia, "Ricordi del tempio di Ancona," *Scritti sull'ebraismo in memoria di Guido Bedarida,* Florence, 1966, pp. 71–75 (not consulted).

Encyclopedia Judaica, 1971.

Jewish Chronicle, Feb. 16, 1855, Jan. 1, 1869.

E. Loevinson, "Gli ebrei dello stato della Chiesa nel periodo del risorgimento politico d'Italia," *Israel. La rassegna mensile,* 2 ser. IX, #11–12 (1935), pp. 542–63, esp. 542–50.

A. Milano, "Immagini del passato ebraico. Ancona," ibid., XXXIII, 1967, pp. 165–66.

Nahon, *Arks.*

Pinkerfeld, pp. 33–35.

Casale Monferrato

The synagogue of Casale Monferrato is one of the few surviving synagogues in Piedmont, where once there flourished many small Jewish communities. It represents a group of synagogues in which a local rite, the "APAM" rite of Asti-Fossano-Moncalvo, was celebrated in the Duchy of Monferrato after the Jews settled there in the fifteenth century. Its external appearance and situation are typical of synagogues within an old streetscape. It resembles synagogues elsewhere in northwestern Italy, such as those of Carmagnola, Mondovì, Cherasco, Moncalvo, and the oldest ones in Turin.

The present building occupies the site of a house and courtyard which the Jews rented in 1595. It lies in the heart of the traditional Jewish quarter and later ghetto, in a street now named for a Jew, Salomone Olper. Buildings there had modest facades because of custom and economical planning, and because more fully articulated designs could hardly have been appreciated on so narrow a thoroughfare. Many synagogues in Europe were situated in similar streets, if not hidden in a rear courtyard (see Figs. 7, 46).

In most European synagogues of the Renaissance period, the main entrance door did not open from the street, owing to the Jews' concern for their security and to laws in many places which forbade allowing the sound of Jewish prayer to reach Christians' ears. At Casale, the worshipper entered the synagogue by walking through a narrow passage to a courtyard and then through a covered vestibule-corridor to the door at the west, opposite the ark. The men's area was about 16.5 m. long and less than half that in width; the door, bimah, and ark lay along the short axis. Unlike other synagogues of the time, this one had a women's gallery when it was first set up, but the women's space was still separated from the men's. The women occupied rooms on the south and west which rested on the walls of the ground floor offices and vestibule corridor—an arrangement used during the next three centuries in many synagogues that were set up in existing buildings.

The distribution of ancillary rooms was also a common one. Community offices, well, ritual bath, school, and storage rooms were disposed around the courtyard in an irregular and asymmetrical but apparently functional manner. The rabbi's apartment, for instance, was conveniently connected to the school. The women's sections could be entered directly from some of the Jewish-occupied houses around the courtyard as well as from the synagogue vestibule. The storeroom for lights and oil was isolated from other rooms to reduce the hazard of a fire which might break out there.

A synagogue plan of 1599 shows that the seating arrangements were similar to those seen in a plan made in 1663, just after the Jews obtained permission to buy the site. The 1663 plan also shows the furnishings, in schematic form. The number of men had increased, perhaps to over five hundred, so that four benches running east to west were installed in the empty space between the bimah and the seats along the short side walls. The small ark was raised on several steps, decorated by columns and a semicircular pediment, and flanked by seats for the eminent men of the community. The bimah, apparently polygonal, had a raised platform and surrounding railings. The slender supports at the corners of the bimah held a canopy. It probably had complex curves which the draftsman of the seating diagram had no need to include. Other bimahs of the sixteenth through the early nineteenth century had such elaborate canopies; a surviving example is at Carmagnola. The seating diagram also shows two immense standing candlesticks flanking the bimah; similar objects were known elsewhere, as at Pinsk. In 1684, one Samuel Isaac gave two green ornaments, which must be the stucco reliefs (now colored brown) showing Hebron and Jerusalem. They face each other on the side walls near the ark.

In the second half of the eighteenth century, Casale's Jewish population increased, partly because of migration from nearby towns. The enlarged congregation of 130 families needed more synagogue accommodation, and a new

Figure 192. Casale Monferrato, interior as remodeled in 1853–66.

section for the poor was built on the south side above the women's area. More room for women was provided on the north. The women sat in two rows, facing each other as the men did, not necessarily facing the grilles into the men's space; the grilles were thus ventilators and sound transmitters rather than merely screens to hide the women from the sight of the men. We do not know where else this disposition of women's seats was found, but at Avignon, Carpentras, and Worms the women were so completely separated from the men that they had their own services and preachers.

The Casale synagogue experienced other changes in the eighteenth and nineteenth centuries. In the 1760s, a new pulpit was installed on the west wall and in 1787 came the installation of a new ark. These furnishings survive (Fig. 192). The ark is a tripartite structure with fluted Corinthian columns framing the central section, and elaborate carving on the frieze and cornice. The wood paneling, originally painted white, was darkened in 1850 to express sorrow at the death of King Carlo Alberto, who had granted emancipation to the Jews in 1848. In 1866, the ark received its side panels and lavishly carved attic. The pulpit commanded attention with long brackets and sweeping curves. The octagonal bimah in the center of the room had longer sides to emphasize the east-west axis. The reader stood at the intersection of the east-west and north-south axes. A plan of 1808, however, shows the bimah slightly farther west, with its west side directly under the easternmost end of the ribs of the cloister vault. The vault itself was three bays long on the north-south axis, with the ark and bimah occupying the center bay and the congregational seats placed under the side bays and the coves. The synagogue retained this form until the mid-nineteenth century, although more benches were added in the side bays and in 1823 the floor was renovated.

Between 1853 and 1866, when emancipation was secure, the Jews modified the building. They left the walls, ark, pulpit, and restored mural inscriptions but altered the bimah, seating arrangement, and ceiling. In a new spirit of optimistic modernity—now that traditional persecution was unlikely—they created a new entrance hall closer to the street. They placed the entranceway on the north, below the women's gallery that had been added on that side earlier. The new hall made the old south corridor superfluous and so it was suppressed, lengthening the synagogue on the south side. Only a narrow passageway remained there, leading to the western corridor-vestibule and the courtyard beyond that to the west. Worshippers no longer entered from the courtyard, which lost significance as a social and community center; the synagogue building became primary. With the synagogue now enlarged along its north-south axis, and with the number of ceiling bays increased to four, the ark and bimah no longer occupied the center bay of a three-bay plan. This awkward situation was remedied by moving the ark to the south wall and having the long axis and the four ceiling bays reinforce a new axial direction. To those who pointed out that the ark now lay in the south rather than in the east (where a fresco of Jerusalem had been painted to mark the direction of prayer), the community leaders could respond that the synagogue was actually oriented to the southeast, so that either the eastern or the southern side could be considered the one facing Jerusalem. The seats were thereupon changed from the concentric pattern so as to face the ark. The bimah was moved immediately north of the ark, forming a coordinated group like that seen in Reform temples, but here probably motivated by the factor of convenience in directing prayers from fixed benches. The congregation favored the seating change for another reason which reveals a new spirit of fraternity and modernity: They wished to abolish the segregated seating areas for the poor, which they now regarded as a shameful thing for the community to have tolerated. Now the poor were to come down from the top floor to join their fellows on the main floor, and the arrangement of benches and the ark-bimah coordination at one end made room for more seats downstairs. (The old southern section for poor men became an apartment and the northern section became a storage area.) When these alterations were made, the interior walls were straightened and the synagogue was widened toward the west. These more orderly and "church-like" changes seem to have caused little comment in Italian towns where Jews had recently become emancipated and where they longed for close relations with their Christian neighbors.

The Jewish population of Casale diminished slowly, as its members emigrated to cities in the late nineteenth and early twentieth centuries. The population of about 700 to 800 (130 families) in the eighteenth century dropped to about 300 people in 1860. Because of this, the space allotted to women after the 1860s sufficed—two storeys of rooms at the north and south ends, hidden from view by carved and gilded screens. The winter synagogue, a room in a community building, was more often used by the men.

The dwindling population found it hard to maintain the synagogue, although a heating system was added in 1900. This equipment was incorrectly installed, however, and it emitted soot which damaged the stucco work and inscriptions. Eventually, the roof began to leak, and German troops inflicted willful damage in 1945, by which time there were only twenty-five Jews left in Casale. Nevertheless, the building was restored to its 1860s condition in 1968 under the direction of Pietro Vignoli of Alessandria, with the help and supervision of the Superintendent of Monuments in Turin. Workmen repaired the gilded stucco and painted surfaces, so that their colors now catch the light from the east and west windows. Without a congregation, however, the synagogue is more a historic monument than a house of worship. It incorporates a museum of Jewish art in the former women's galleries, and it has an archive and a library of about six hundred books, mainly of eighteenth-century date. It has been host to concerts of Jewish music since 1976. The Italian-Jewish collections are second only to those of the Jewish museum in Rome, and together the museums commemorate Jewish life in north and central Italy, in a small community and in a metropolis.

BIBLIOGRAPHY

AJYb LXXVIII (1978), p. 401.

L. Angelino, "La sinagoga di Casale, Museo dell'arte religiosa ebraica," *Piemonte vivo,* 1970, #5, pp. 18–25.

G. Avigdor, "La sinagoga di Casale," *Studi piemontesi* I, #1 (1972), pp. 94–96.

D. Cassuto, "History of a Synagogue," *Scritti in memoria di Umberto Nahon,* ed. R. Bonfil et al., Jerusalem, 1978, pp. 176–95, with further bibliography (Hebrew).

Encyclopedia Judaica, 1971, s.v. Casale.

S. Foà, "Appunti d'archivio di storia ebraica monferrina," *Israel. La rassegna mensile* 2 ser. XV, #3 (1949), pp. 113–21.

———, *Gli ebrei nel Monferrato nei secoli XVI e XVII,* Bologna, 1965 (reprint of 1914 edition).

A. Milano, "Immagini del passato ebraico, XIV: Casale Monferrato," *Israel. La rassegna mensile* 2 ser. XXXIV, #3 (1968), p. 119.

Nahon, *Arks,* for information on synagogue appurtenances in Casale and vicinity, including Saluzzo, Acqui, Moncalvo, etc.

L. Ottolenghi, *Breve cenni sugli israeliti casalesi e sul loro sacro Oratorio,* Casale, 1866 (not consulted).

Pinkerfeld, pp. 31–33.

C. Roth, *The History of the Jews in Italy,* Philadelphia, 1946, esp. pp. 343, 519.

A. Segre, *Memorie di vita ebraica: Casale Monferrato, Roma, Gerusalemme, 1918–1960,* Rome, 1979.

Sincere thanks to Victoria Newhouse, Isabelle Hyman, and William Krinsky for obtaining photographs and articles, and to Moshe Barasch for translations.

Florence

Individual Jews may have lived in Florence before 1437, but only in that year did they establish a community. Their commercial experience made them welcome, and although they suffered from occasional serious persecutions and expulsions, and from the customary animosity of Christians, they were better off in Florence than in many other cities of Europe. They lived in a ghetto near the Old Market and built their synagogues in the prevailing local style. In 1859, when Tuscany was incorporated into the Kingdom of Sardinia, the Jews received full and long-lasting rights as citizens.

When Florence became the capital of Italy (1864–70), the Jewish community was eager to show its patriotism and its new equal status by adorning the city with a beautiful synagogue. A rich man named Daniele Levi left funds in his will for the synagogue, and even though Rome had replaced Florence as the national capital well before the building was begun, the Levi bequest was used for its intended purpose. Work began on the building in 1874 and was nearly finished in 1880; the dedication took place in 1882.

The designers were three Florentine architects, Mariano Falcini (1804–85), Vincente Micheli (1830–93), and Marco Treves (1814–98), of whom only Treves was Jewish. Falcini was the city's chief of civil engineering works and concerned himself usually with post offices, hospitals, and the like; Micheli designed public works such as hospitals, theaters, and bridges. Neither man had any experience in synagogue design and little, if any, in church building, but Treves had designed the classical-style synagogue at Pisa (opened in 1863). Jews had often chosen, or had been told, to employ important municipal building personnel, and this architectural team was unusual only in that it included a Jew, a man all the more unusual because he was also a professor of architecture, as Micheli was.

The synagogue occupies an area of over 50 m. by 25 m. and stands free of other buildings on a site that was, in the 1870s, on the "fashionable outskirts" of the city (Fig. 193). It faces west

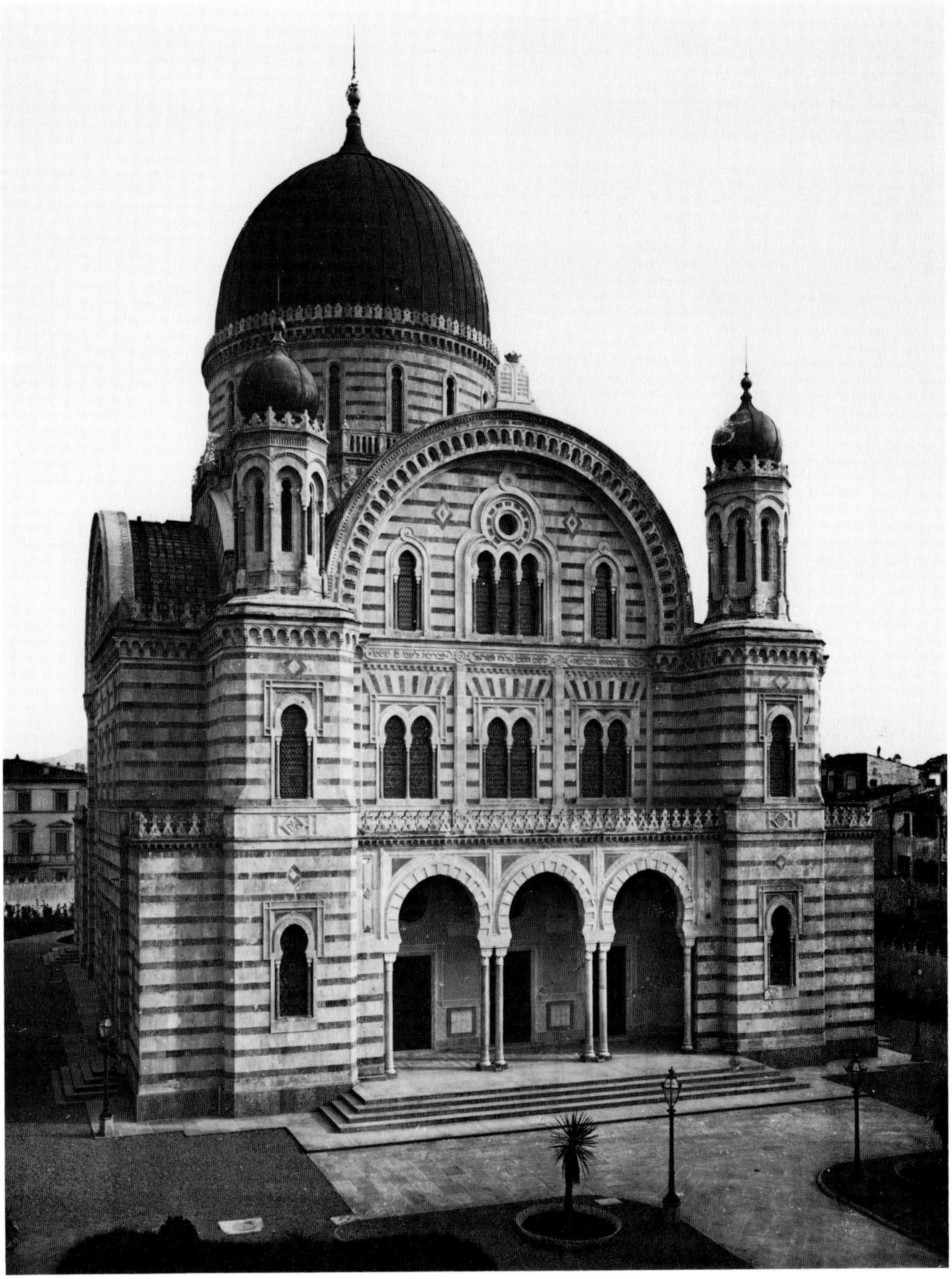

Figure 193. Florence, 1874–82, exterior.

Figure 194. Florence, interior to ark.

and has a front garden in which the community planted palms and other oriental vegetation. On the facade, turrets flank a tan-and-rose-striped flat wall with an entrance porch at ground level, and a curved gable at the top. The plan, a domed Greek cross, has a western vestibule for stairs and cloakrooms, with robing and synagogue administration rooms on either side of the apse on the east. In the richly colored prayer hall, many lobed arches culminate in the grand curves of the central cupola (Fig. 194). The surface decoration is a carpet-like display of polychrome small-scale patterns of Islamic derivation. Galleries stretch over three arms of the Greek cross, yielding at the east to an apse that houses the ark and the pulpit; it is raised on low steps and looks like the *minbar* of a mosque. The bimah is closer to the center of the building, even though the congregation followed the Italian rite which, in earlier and smaller synagogues, usually located the bimah at the west. But the central bimah in this synagogue, which is neither small nor traditional, comes from Ashkenazic practice, as do other features of the Florentine synagogue. Its builders claimed to have taken the design from Spanish and Egyptian examples (meaning Islamic), which they "modified and adapted to the times, needs, and place." But the fundamentals of the design—domed Greek cross, galleries in the cross arms, towers bordering the facade, round gable, borrowings from Islamic sources—all reflect ideas found in Ashkenazic synagogues in northern Europe. They were the most imposing and therefore the most obvious models for a community that wanted to display its new status through architecture. Besides, they already were synagogues and thus were more readily adaptable as models than mosques or secular buildings would have been. The domed Greek cross was known, for instance, at Wrocław and London in the 1860s (see Figs. 151, 152, 177, 178). The prominent dome in the Islamic taste was familiar from the synagogue of Cologne (1861). The synagogue at Leipzig (1855) had horseshoe arches and other Moorish details, as did many other synagogues erected between those of Dresden (1840) (see Fig. 130) and Florence itself. The huge, round facade gable was seen in the main synagogue in rue de la Victoire, Paris (1874), a city where Treves had worked (see Fig. 110). Small minaret-like towers were erected in Vienna (1858) and Budapest-Rumbach Street (1872) (see Figs. 42, 64). In short, if the Florentine architects looked at architecture periodicals and consulted interested Jewish travelers, they could easily have conceived their synagogue on the basis of readily available northern European buildings. The architects avoided Spanish plans and used Egyptian buildings only as models for the dome. Eduardo Vitta, a member of the synagogue building committee, said that the silhouette of the cupola recalled that of mosques and the tombs of the caliphs in Cairo. Although he did not explain why Egyptian sources were chosen, it must have been because Mudéjar

Spanish-Jewish monuments, that is, the then-extant synagogues of Toledo, Córdoba, and Seville, did not have domes and there were no appropriate models at the Alhambra.

Why did the Jews of Florence, patriotic as they were, choose a Moorish style of any kind? In 1870, when the new synagogue was still in the discussion stages, the leaders of the Italian Jewish communities sent an address to King Victor Emmanuel asserting their loyalty to the new Kingdom of Italy and their intention of "remembering only when in our temples of worship that we are Israelites." But the exotic synagogues of Vercelli, Florence, Rome, Turin, and Genoa suggest that the Jews wanted to remember that they were Israelites even when they approached their synagogues, not just when they were inside them. Given that municipal building officials accepted these unusual buildings, and that the king praised the Jews of Florence for having embellished their beautiful city, government authorities seem to have acknowledged the Jews as a people who were supposed to be seen as different. Centuries of exclusion from being fully equal Italians had left their mark on the self-perception of the Jews, who chose to be separate though equal, and on their fellow citizens' perception of them.

The three architects did their technical work well. They inserted service areas for building maintenance; covered the dome in long-wearing copper and secured it with iron chains; saved money on the basement and applied some of the savings to the tan travertine and red granite of the facade; provided an elevator to lift the infirm to the women's gallery; and selected a height for the gallery grilles that allowed the women a sense of participation while at the same time preventing the building from resembling a theater.

The confidence of Florence's Jews was shattered temporarily during 1942–44 when Mussolini applied "racial" laws far more severely than he had been inclined to do earlier. After the war, the community repaired the damage done by bombs and vandals. Only the tragic flood of 1966, which came not long after a renovation, has caused further damage to the building; the flood waters rose to 10 feet inside and gravely damaged the furniture, scrolls, and books.

The community was much diminished after the war, with about 1,250 Jews in 1970 compared to 2,730 in 1930. Although the postwar congregation was augmented by migrants from other regions, deaths now outnumber births and some young people emigrate to Israel and elsewhere. Remnants of destroyed earlier Florentine synagogues also have been moved to Israel; these include a nineteenth-century ark now in the Yad Giborim Synagogue in Ramat Gan, and alms boxes in the corridor exhibition area of the Italian Synagogue in Jerusalem. Today Florentine Jews worship in the Grand Synagogue and also in oratories for Italian and Sephardic groups located in Via delle Oche.

BIBLIOGRAPHY

AJYb LXVIII (1966), p. 345.

Bachi, pp. 25–46, esp. pp. 37–38.

P. A. Bigazzi, *Firenze e contorni. Manuale bibliografico,* Florence, 1893.

E. Brault, *Les architectes par leurs oeuvres,* Paris, 1883, vol. 3, pp. 396, 398.

Builder XXXVIII (May 22, 1880), pp. 632–33.

U. Cassuto, *Gli ebrei a Firenze nell'età del Rinascimento* (Pubblicazioni del R. Istituto di Studi Superior i Pratici e di Perfezionamento in Firenze. Sezione di filosofia e filologia), Florence, 1918, esp. pp. 216–18.

Encyclopedia Judaica, 1971, s. v. Florence.

R. Gottheil, "Les archives juives de Florence," *Revue des études juives* LI (1906), pp. 303–17; LII (1906), pp. 114–28; and corrections by U. Cassuto, *La rivista israelitica* III (1906), pp. 133–36, 171–76.

Jewish Chronicle, Aug. 30, 1878.

C.L.V. Meeks, *Italian Architecture, 1750–1914,* New Haven and London, 1966, p. 268.

Nahon, *Arks.*

C. Roth, *The History of the Jews in Italy,* Philadelphia, 1946, p. 492.

E. Vitta, *Relazione a corredo del rendiconto dei lavori eseguiti per la contruzione del Tempio Israelitico di Firenze,* Florence, 1883.

Livorno

Renaissance Synagogue

The Jewish community of Livorno was one of the most fortunate and prosperous in the world for the two centuries between about 1600 and 1800, and its principal synagogue was one of the handsomest in Europe. After its destruction during the Second World War, a new synagogue of far different character was built to replace it.

Jews and Marranos achieved their enviable position in the city because they were available in large numbers just when the grand dukes of Tuscany needed them to promote commerce in Livorno during the sixteenth century. The Jews had been expelled from Spain and Portugal in 1492 and 1496, and Marranos were subject to the unwelcome scrutiny of inquisitors who were inclined to accuse them of heresy and lapses of faith. In Livorno, however, various privileges were offered to foreign traders during the 1540s, and in 1593 Grand Duke Ferdinand I promulgated a comprehensive privilege called the "Costituzione Livornina" which appealed to a wide range of foreign merchants, with Jews at the head of the list. The text offered residential and commercial rights, and article 20 allowed Jews to have a synagogue along with protection from violence to their persons and possessions. (A synagogue may already have been set up in 1591 or 1592 on the ground floor of a building in the heart of town.) By 1604, the Sephardic Jews joined a second building to their first synagogue, and in 1605 added a third to the first two. Eventually, the synagogue moved and expanded to an upper floor.

Ferdinand also tried to attract French and Italian Jews. This time, he allowed the settlers not merely to use the first synagogue but also to construct new ones of their own, even though most community resources still went to the Sephardic synagogue.

When, in 1640, their population exceeded 1,000, the Jews petitioned the government for permission to enlarge the principal Sephardic synagogue, presumably by extending it into contiguous houses. A visitor in 1657 did not describe the synagogue in detail, but reported that women sat in an enclosure all around the room.

The community included about 3,500 members by the 1690s. Officials who were elected in 1693 to supervise the synagogue and its furnishings decided once again that the building was too small and that the ark was both small and decrepit. They asked to be allowed to unite another adjacent building to the synagogue, and they surrounded three sides of the large prayer hall with galleries above a round-arched arcade (Fig. 195). The names of those who gave money in 1701–17 for the columns and arches and the dates of their donations were inscribed on the gallery parapets. For a time, the women of the donors' families sat directly behind their inscriptions, but this practice was later abandoned because it caused resentment. In 1716, a traveling priest who visited the synagogue noted that the women dressed in black *à la française* and wore pearls and jewels to the services. The men wore black clothing in the style of Florence or Genoa, and they crowned their costumes with wigs. The rabbi wore a long red robe, a prayer shawl, and a hat.

Modifications to the community offices, rabbinical courtroom, and ritual bath also were

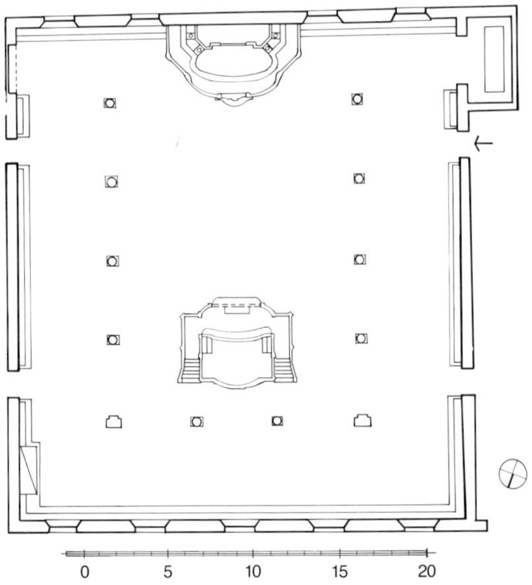

Figure 195. Livorno, Renaissance synagogue, plan after 1693.

Figure 196. Livorno, Renaissance synagogue, interior as remodeled in 1787–89.

undertaken around 1715, but only in 1740 did the sculptor Isidoro Baratta from Carrara prepare designs for a marble ark. He won the commission over two competitors and received the approval of the grand duke's architects and engineers. The ark, composed of four columns supporting a heavy, scrolled and garlanded pediment, was installed formally in 1742. In that year, Baratta was asked also to prepare models for the bimah. A bimah design by David Nunes, vice-chancellor of the Jewish community, became the choice of the building commission in 1743, although Nunes was told to use some of Baratta's ideas. The bimah, installed in 1745, was a polygonal platform of marble within a balustraded enclosure. Both ark and bimah were heavy, curvilinear, and colorful, like much of the secular Italian furniture of the time (Fig. 196). Each asserted itself strongly against the architecture, focusing the worshipper's attention on the religious activity rather than on the handsome arcaded setting for it.

Several earthquakes during the eighteenth century made the community fear for the stability of the synagogue. The loads were apparently too great for the lower walls and foundations. In 1787, the Jews employed the architect Ignazio Fazzi to take care of the structural needs and then to add an extra women's gallery above the earlier one. He supported the ceiling on a scaffolding with enormous trusses and beams (felled in the woods of Camaldolese monks) and managed to complete the work, including an enlargement of the bimah enclosure, by 1789. The building then reached its most glorious stage with three stately tiers of arches, graceful gallery grilles, many large windows, and imposing furnishings. The hall measured 25.8 m. by 28.2 m., with wide intercolumniations between some of the piers. The regularity

Figure 197. Livorno, Renaissance synagogue, facade of 1875.

of the arched rhythms acted as a foil for the abundant ornament, the gold-lettered inscriptions, the wood revetment of the lower walls, and the solid furnishings. There was no other synagogue of this form, although the Sephardic synagogue of Amsterdam exuded a comparable air of spacious grandeur and assurance (see Figs. 227, 228).

When the port suffered a blockade during the Napoleonic wars, and later when it lost its special privileges as a free port, Livorno and its Jews lost much of their wealth. In 1799, the Jews had to melt down some of the synagogue's precious metal lamps and other fittings to meet French demands, and later had to spend a good deal of money to obtain new ones. In a gesture of self-affirmation, they remodeled the synagogue in 1846–48 to bring it up to date without making fundamental changes. Decorators altered some of the eighteenth-century ornament by substituting Jewish symbols for the earlier foliage, and they introduced some enormous chandeliers. They enlarged the bimah enough to accommodate a choir, and raised the height of the ark by inserting new material between the capitals and the pediment. By 1863, red curtains covered the windows. In 1875, a wealthy donor supplied lavish new doors for the ark, 2.25 m. high and 1.36 m. wide, inlaid with wood, mother-of-pearl, and silver cut into plant forms. Much later, in 1903, the community installed what was described as an "excellent" organ made by the Tronci firm in Pistoia; part of the first gallery was given over to it.

More noticeable changes were made to the exterior in 1875 (Fig. 197). Urban renewal demolitions created a small plaza beside the synagogue. This exposed the rear of the building to public view, and made the rear facade on Piazza Nuova (now Benamozegh) the most visible side. Luigi Bosi, a local architect, covered the wall with white marble; he placed columns around the portal, introduced some Jewish symbols, and designed moldings around the existing window openings to put a fine face on the unanticipated "main" facade. Colored glass was inserted in the windows in 1915, done to the design of an art professor, Alberto Calza Bini, who worked with the firm of DeMatteis in Florence. The adjacent community house also required some architectural modifications at this time. Later, in 1927 when buildings in Via Cairoli, an access street, were torn down for sanitary reasons, an uninteresting third facade was created, but it had no substantial effect on the cityscape.

Although competing synagogues had earlier been discouraged by Jewish community leaders and by the government, Livorno had other, more modest synagogues and prayer rooms in the nineteenth and twentieth centuries. One of the oldest was near the church of St. Anthony. They all succumbed to a combination of Allied bombing and Fascist vandalism.

Postwar Synagogue

The wartime murder and postwar migration of Jews left the Livorno community far smaller than it had been. The survivors needed a synagogue, but not one as large as the destroyed building. The community and the government (which paid most of the construction costs) therefore decided to erect an entirely new and smaller building, with a small Sephardic oratory in the basement, rooms for community activities, a rabbi's residence, and other practical spaces.

The synagogue, dedicated in September 1962, is more than purely utilitarian, although considerations of utility underlay its planning. Rising boldly above the mundane materiality of its surroundings, on an irregular site bounded by wide streets, it demands to be noticed (Fig. 198). One critic emphasized that this was not an American-style community center but an affirmative statement of Jewish existence. The dramatic form and modern materials proclaim the survival of the Jews into the present, and suggest the forward-looking vitality of the Livorno community. To the critics, and surely to this community, the new synagogue suggested strength rather than the fatalistic resignation often imputed to Jewish victims, and it suggested

Figure 198. Livorno, 1958–62, facade nearing completion.

Figure 199. Livorno, 1958–62, interior to ark.

independence instead of willingness to disappear under secular architectural forms.

The building is practical. It was made of concrete for the sake of economy and for structural reasons which serve the purposes of a synagogue. The main supports are the bent vertical "buttresses" which project from the wall surface on the exterior. Concrete and these "buttresses" make it possible for the interior to be a single, undivided room in which everyone can hear and see easily (Fig. 199). The seats, disposed around several sides of the elongated polygonal interior, give a sense of congregational unity, as do the central placement of the bimah and the absence of concealing grilles on the women's gallery.

The form had symbolic uses, too, recalling the tabernacle or Tent in the Wilderness, the central point of religious reference for the Israelites during their exodus from Egypt. Although a synagogue is fundamentally different from the Tent in the Wilderness, the image may have carried poignant meaning for those members of the community who had been dispersed during the war and had been reunited after their own wanderings. The billowing form of the synagogue is even more obvious inside, where the vertical lines and the pale-colored wall spaces between them combine with the light-filled interior space to give the impression of an airy and almost weightless enclosure, comparable to a tent.

Among the other symbolic and commemorative features are the polygonal windows, which refer to those in the destroyed main synagogue of the city. Blood-red stained glass is supposed to recall the blood of the Jewish dead. Parts of the destroyed bimah, reused to make the new one, evoke past tragedy and regeneration, while an early-eighteenth-century ark from the Sephardic synagogue of Pesaro bears witness to the dissolution of other, smaller, Italian Jewish congregations.

If the Livorno synagogue were beautiful, it would be an even more fitting representative of its venerable community and of postwar Jewish ideas. Angelo di Castro, the Jewish architect called from Rome to design it in about 1958, may have been carried away by his desire to erect an active, symbolically meaningful building. It strikes many observers as being awkward, strident, and more in the fashion than in the spirit of its time. But as a bold if somewhat superficial statement, it may have expressed ironically the real situation of a community that wanted earnestly to restore itself to vigorous postwar life but could not do so, owing to the reduced importance of Livorno, and to pressures on young Italian Jews of assimilation, secularization, and Zionist aspirations.

BIBLIOGRAPHY

AJYb, 1962 (1963), p. 323.

U. Fortis, *Jews and Synagogues*, Venice, 1973, pp. 90–95.

Israele XXI, #29–30 (May 7–14, 1936) describes celebration of Ethiopian victory.

Père Labat, *Voyages en Espagne et en Italie*, Amsterdam, 1731, vol. 2, pp. 88ff. recounts visit of 1716.

C. Ligini, "Il tempio di Livorno nell'attività dell'architetto Angelo di Castro," *L'architettura* X, #103 (May 1964), pp. 20–29.

E. H. Lindo, *The History of the Jews of Spain and Portugal*, London, 1848, pp. 334–36.

A. Milano, "La costituzione Livornina del 1593," *Israel. La rassegna mensile* XXXIV, #9/10 (1968), pp. 394–410.

———, *Storia degli ebrei in Italia*, Turin, 1963.

David Mocatta, drawings of interior and an elevation with galleries, Royal Institute of British Architects Drawings Collection, see J. Lever, ed., *Catalogue of the Drawings in the Royal Institute of British Architects Drawings Collection*, London, 1973, vol. L–N, p. 85.

Nahon, *Arks.*.

Pinkerfeld, pp. 36–39.

G. Piombanti, *Guida storica ed artistica della città di Livorno*, 2d ed., Livorno, 1903.

A. Toaff, "Cenni storici sulla comunità ebraica e sulla sinagoga di Livorno," *Israel. La rassegna mensile* XXI, #9–10 (1955), pp. 355–69, 411–26.

———, "On the Jews of Livorno and their Synagogue," *Eretz Israel: Archaeological, Historical and Geographical Studies*, vol. 3, 1954, pp. 249–57 (Hebrew).

G. Vivoli, *Guida di Livorno antico e moderno*, Livorno [1956], citing a manuscript guide of 1835.

Milan

Milanese Jewry was fortunate in that both Christian and Jewish architects devoted great care to its principal synagogue.

Until 1892, the few Jews in Milan worshipped in a room on the second floor of a residential building in Via Stampa, in a synagogue set up in 1840. By 1857, its central bimah, apparently a traditional cage and described as an obstructive "wooden machine thrown between the people and the preacher," had been replaced by a "real reading desk." Among its shortcomings, the synagogue building did not lend itself to embellishment commensurate with the improving position of Jews in the city, and the exits from the room were so narrow that the congregation was in mortal danger in case of fire.

In 1887, a childless community member, Salomone Ottolenghi, bequeathed enough money to pay most of the costs of a new synagogue. Immediately thereafter, the congregation formed a building committee under the direction of Giuseppe Sullum, an engineer. They secured a site in Via Guastalla in central Milan, on land that had belonged to the noble Archinto family. The committee entrusted the design to Luca Beltrami (1854–1933), a prominent Milanese Christian architect who already had designed a new facade for the cathedral, a restoration plan for the Castello Sforzesco, and a number of prestigious buildings.

Beltrami undertook the synagogue commission with a much-appreciated sense of responsibility and with much-appreciated speed. He prepared detailed drawings two months after receiving the commission in the spring of 1890, designed the entire building including its fittings, and watched it go up between February and September of 1892 (Fig. 200). Beltrami also

Figure 200. Milan, 1890–92, facade drawn by Luca Beltrami.

impressed his clients and the architectural community by keeping just about within his budget.

During the preceding several years, new synagogues had been built at Alessandria, Asti, Bologna, Florence, Modena, Parma, Reggio Emilia, Soragna, Turin, and Vercelli. Some of them were inconspicuous externally or designed in commonly used classical styles, while others among them, such as those of Florence, Vercelli, and Turin, had exotic Moorish and Byzantine forms like those of many synagogues erected north of the Alps (see Figs. 193, 194, 216). Beltrami's building belongs to the latter group, but he tried to invent a style specific to Jews in northern Italy, one that combined local and exotic elements.

The two-storey facade is about 30 m. high. Dividing a central gabled section from the lower sides are two piers that rise to the full height of the building. Arched windows open on the second floor—paired on the sides and trebled in the center—and a niche in the gable encloses tablets of the Law. The scheme is not significantly different from that of local churches, and the materials were familiar local stones. The major piers, however, were meant to evoke Jakhin and Boaz; the mosaic decoration in blue and gold which surrounded the door and filled an arch over the three central windows alluded to the Jews' oriental origin; and the windows lit galleries along three sides of the interior, a feature particular to Jewish rather than to local modern Roman Catholic buildings.

Inside the synagogue, a shadowy vestibule flanked by stairs to the galleries prepared visitors for the well-lit prayer hall. The hall had a nave and galleried aisles and a slightly elevated apse where the bimah stood near the ark. Wooden vaults soared to the impressive height of 20 m. in a building 25 m. long and 22 m. wide. The architect was able to combine thinness and height because wooden vaults, as compared to stone vaults, do not need thick walls to buttress their thrusts. The use of wood and of thin walls also made construction cheaper and quicker.

Beltrami's architectural ideas seem to reflect north European precedent. He had made a study trip to Paris as a young man and read widely in professional literature. His *Rundbogenstil* mixed Romanesque and Renaissance elements to express rational theories about their use. He used masonry where it was structurally necessary rather than for effects of mass and ornament, and he applied decorative details principally to junction points, such as the springing points of an arch and cornices. An arch did not have to be of any predetermined shape. If there was enough room, as at gallery level, for piers tall enough to carry a semicircular arch, Beltrami used that form; on the ground floor, where the piers were shorter and thicker, he employed a lower and broader segmental arch. At the top of the interior wall, where there were round clerestory windows, he articulated the wall only by short pilasters which carried a straight cornice. Each part was designed to express its height and its position in the wall composition. Marble paneling and an ark in the form of a little domed temple adorned with blue and gold rays lent a note of festivity.

The transalpine aspects of both exterior and interior found their reflection in the atmosphere of the services. A German visitor compared the tone to that of the Fasanenstrasse synagogue (1912) in Berlin, describing the feeling of both as "aesthetic Judaism."

In August 1943, during the aerial bombardment of Milan, the synagogue was almost entirely destroyed; Fascists had already seized all its metalwork. Only the facade and the community school and apartment building at the rear of the site escaped the bombs. After the war, Jews worshipped in a modest room and sponsored a competition as early as February 1947 for a new synagogue. The prizewinners were Eugenio Gentili and Manfredo d'Urbino, both Jews, who submitted separate but equally admired projects proposing the demolition of the old facade and the construction of an entirely new synagogue. Gentili designed a solid rectilinear building with massive blocks of stone covering the exterior that might evoke stonework in Jerusalem. The building had a central cupola in a sloping ceiling formed of visible beams of reinforced concrete, perhaps recalling arrangements in Polish wooden synagogues of the seventeenth and eighteenth centuries. These traditional features may have been responses to the presence of east European refugees who were generally orthodox and who could not have worshipped in a synagogue with the original disposition of the bimah near the ark. At the same time, the building looked modern in its unadorned planar simplicity, in the frank revelation of its structural elements, and in the use of an exterior stairway to the galleries, an idea familiar in the prewar work of Le Corbusier and Mies van der Rohe. The result of these mixed influences did not look eclectic but, rather, simple and comfortably solid. Manfredo d'Urbino's project was commended for its use of the second floor for the main sanctuary and the ground floor for oratories for Sephardic and Ashkenazic congregations.

Neither scheme was built, because the Ministry of Public Works intervened to require that the synagogue be reerected on the same site. This led to the preservation of the old facade in a new plan proposed by the prizewinning architects aided by Alessandro Rimini, another Jewish architect, and by Ruggiero Rossi, an engineer. Complex financing arrangements and problems in locating a contractor delayed the start of work until September 1951, but the synagogue was completed by 1954 (Fig. 201).

The architects created a sober room made largely of reinforced concrete but relieved by applications of marble at the ark and in the vestibule wall behind a plaque recovered from the former synagogue. The building is oblong, but more centralized in feeling than was Beltrami's building because the galleries are not separated from the nave by several storeys of arches. Instead, with their low parapets, the galleries allow the eye to take in the lateral spaces as well. All the lines are rectilinear, as opposed to the curves and arches that Beltrami used, but by introducing skylighting above the bimah and by softening the harshness of concrete with red marble, yellow window glass, blue window blinds, and the old facade walls, the architects created a room in which the clear and earthbound aspects of Judaism mingle with elements appealing to mood and spirit.

Figure 201. Milan, interior as remodeled in 1951–54.

The synagogue includes small prayer rooms for Sephardic and Ashkenazic groups on the lower floor, and the usual schoolrooms, staff apartments, and offices in an annex. Although it remains the center of the Milanese Jewish community, the Jews of the city are more diverse than a single large synagogue building suggests. In 1971, there were adherents of the German and Polish Ashkenazic, Persian, Spanish-Portuguese, Italian, North African, and Lubavitch Hasidic rites—a variety appropriate to a metropolis like Milan.

BIBLIOGRAPHY

Allgemeine unabhängige jüdische Wochenzeitung, April 16, 1971.

M.M. Armato, O.P., *Luca Beltrami, 1854–1933.*

L'uomo sulla scorta di documenti inediti, Fribourg, 1952, p. 49.
Bachi, pp. 25–46.
P. Chessa, "La sinagoga nell'opera di Gentili," *Metron* X, #51 (1954), pp. 13–19.
Il Vessillo israelitico XXXIX, #1 (1891), pp. 9–10; XL, #10 (1892), pp. 337–38.
Jewish Chronicle, Dec. 25, 1857, p. 12.
C.L.V. Meeks, *Italian Architecture, 1750–1914,* New Haven and London, 1966, p. 272.
G. Romano, "Sally Mayer," *Scritti in memoria di Sally Mayer (1875–1953). Saggi sull'ebraismo italiano,* Jerusalem, 1956, pp. 15–16.
C. Roth, *History of the Jews in Italy,* Philadelphia, 1946, p. 513.
A. Saranno, *Sette anni di vita e di opere della comunità israelitica di Milano (Aprile 1945–Maggio 1952)* [Milan, 1952], esp. pp. 24–28.
L. Tenenti, "Tempio Israelitico di Milano," *Edilizia moderna* I (1892), fasc. VII, pp. 1–4.

I am grateful to JoAnne Gitlin Bernstein for obtaining photographs of the Beltrami drawings of the synagogue in the Castello Sforzesco, Milan.

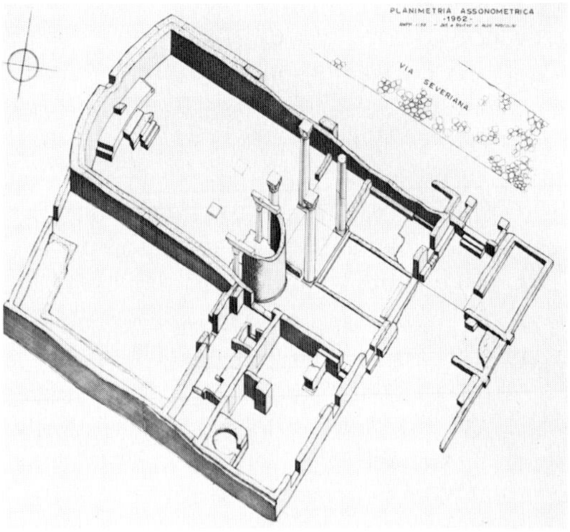

Figure 202. Ostia Antica, as remodeled in 4th century, axonometric plan.

Ostia Antica

The synagogue of Ostia, Rome's ancient port, was discovered in the same accidental way as were many other monuments in and around Rome: It was unearthed during the construction of a highway, in this case the road from Rome via Ostia to the airport at Fiumicino.

The building lay at one end of a major street, beyond the official city limits, and near the river, which supplied the flowing water needed for certain ceremonies and the ritual bath. Excavations carried out in 1961 and 1962 revealed a synagogue in two parts, one comprising the prayer hall, ritual bath, and two rooms of unknown use, and the other part housing the matzah-baking oven and two other spaces, one with benches which may have been the meeting room or school (Fig. 202). In the prayer hall area, four columns arranged in a rectangle reached from a dividing wall toward the entrance side of the building. Archaeologists also found a well near the entrance, and an architrave carved with Jewish ritual objects. The group of spaces formed a community center for a congregation that could have had about five hundred members. The rooms extended over an area of 36.6 m. by 23.5 m., of which 24.9 m. by 12.5 m. were given over to the prayer hall.

Investigators interpreted the remains as showing a fourth-century rebuilding of a first-century synagogue. Remains of *opus sectile* masonry, and the style of the four Corinthian columns, suggest first-century work. There are no traces of a women's gallery, the bimah, or the ark, which a second-century inscription implies was a portable wooden cabinet. From the first-century building, the later one retained the general plan, the four columns, the main entrance, the center door to the prayer hall, and the doorway to the oven room.

The building in its definitive fourth-century form was made of *opus vittatum,* rectangular courses of bricks or small blocks of tufa. It is rectangular on three sides and partly slanted, then gently curved on the northwest side, farthest from the entrance. The prayer hall occupies the eastern part of the site and has its entrance at the east-southeast, toward Jerusalem. An entrance area sunk two steps below grade leads to a room with a wellhead beside the ritual bath room. South of the bath room is an area into which the four columns protrude, with a fourth-century apse inserted between two of them and the wall dividing the westernmost room from the prayer hall. Beyond that is a room with a raised floor paved in white mosaic. Some scholars suggest that women sat there, but there is no evidence to support this idea.

The prayer hall, north of the space with the four columns, had a podium 79 cm. high in the center of the curved wall. Perhaps this was the site of the bimah or of seats for community leaders. The apse at the south corner is certainly a fourth-century addition, because it destroyed the symmetry of the partitions that originally extended from the four columns and because it blocks easy access to a doorway. The apse is exceptional in being freestanding and protruding into a vestibule. Approached by four steps, the apse had an entrance decorated with freestanding marble composite colonnettes, that supported architraves reaching back to join the apse walls. If the architraves were connected by a transverse element that held a pediment, the composition would have recalled the ark aedicula at the Dura-Europos synagogue of ca. 245. The apse at Ostia also had polychromed marble-covered small niches on the low podium walls encasing the colonnettes and bases, and had gilded reliefs of Jewish ritual objects on the corbels of the architraves above the colonnettes.

In the first century, on entering at the southeast, the worshipper would have faced a double portico formed by the four columns and the arches or architraves between them; the architraves extended to projections like antae on the side walls. The area near the entrance could have been a vestibule or meeting room or school, or perhaps the religious court, while the area beyond the columnar portico would have been the prayer hall. Later, in the fourth century, the synagogue received its present form including interior partitions, the apse, the podium, and most of the annexed rooms. The largest room, at the west, had built-in benches and might have been the study room and the courtroom. The apse was probably introduced because by that time other synagogues had given the ark a special permanent architectural setting. The apse was located awkwardly since it had to face southeast toward Jerusalem, preferably without ruining the effect of the imposing columnar portico.

The arrangement at Ostia differs from that of other ancient synagogues, but there was little uniformity of planning or decoration in the earliest centuries of synagogue building. It can be so difficult to identify an ancient synagogue, either in the Diaspora or in the Holy Land, that controversy persists over the identity of "synagogues" on the island of Delos, at Elche in Spain, and at Masada in the Holy Land, to name a few examples from various regions.

Ostia's synagogue merits examination along with the other famous ruins there. We have a plausible explanation of a puzzling plan, thanks to Dr. Maria Floriani Squarciapino, who directed the excavations and wrote the important articles about it. We have physical evidence of a flourishing Jewish community which endured for several hundred years. We have a rare and therefore precious example of an ancient synagogue on European soil. Without other substantial remains of early European synagogues, we can connect the Ostia synagogue to later European ones, mainly because of the ark orientation, which was evidently important enough by the fourth century to engender an ungainly interior arrangement, and because of the community rooms which were intimately connected to the place of worship.

BIBLIOGRAPHY

M. Floriani Squarciapino, "Ebrei a Roma e ad Ostia," *Studi romani* XI (1963), pp. 129ff.

———, "La sinagoga, di Ostia," *Bollettino d'arte,* ser. 4, XLVI, #4 (1961), pp. 326–37.

* ———,"La sinagoga di Ostia: Seconda campagna di scavo," *Atti del VI Congresso internazionale di Archeologia Cristiana, Ravenna, 1962,* Vatican City, 1965, pp. 299–315.

* ———, "La sinagoga recentemente scoperta ad Ostia," *Atti della Pontificia Accademia Romana di Archeologia. Rendiconti,* ser. 3, XXXIV, Vatican City, 1962, pp. 119–32.

———, "The Most Ancient Synagogue Known from Monumental Remains," *Illustrated London News,* Sept. 28, 1963, pp. 468ff.

———, "The Synagogue at Ostia," *Archaeology* XVI, #3 (Sept. 1963), pp. 194–203.
U. Fortis, *Jews and Synagogues,* Venice, 1973, pp. 118–28.
Wischnitzer, *Architecture,* pp. 5–7.
F. Zevi, "La sinagoga di Ostia," *Israel. La rassegna mensile,* 2 ser., XXXVIII, #3 (1972), pp. 131–45.
*Translated into German in *Raggi. Zeitschrift für Kunstgeschichte und Archäologie* IV, #1 (1962), pp. 1ff., and V, #1 (1963), pp. 13ff. respectively.

I am grateful to Raina Fehl for her energetic help in securing photographs.

Rome

Even a brief account of the synagogues in Rome illustrates the extraordinary endurance of the Jewish community from Roman imperial times to the present. As we have seen, there were Jews in Ostia, the port of the capital, in the first to fourth centuries; traces of Roman Jewry reappear after about 1000, when Jews moved near the Ponte Quattro Capi—also known as the Ponte Fabricio and Pons Iudaeorum—and built a prayer house named for a certain Joseph. Then the Jews moved to the *rione* of Regola where they built a synagogue near the church of San Tomasso. This was not the main synagogue of the time, which the *Life of Cola di Rienzo* described as near to Cola's birthplace in what is now the end of via Fiumara near via San Bartolommeo de' Vaccinari. It replaced an earlier synagogue in Trastevere which had been burned in 1268. Other synagogues erected before the mid-sixteenth century were:

1. A small synagogue founded in 1101 by the lexicographer and Talmudist Nathan ben Jechiel (1035–1106) and his brother, Abraham. A building at #13–14 Vicolo dell'Atleta, with a Hebrew inscription on a second storey column that has been read as "Nathan Chai," is sometimes identified with this synagogue. It was shown to Ferdinand Gregorovius, the nineteenth-century historian, as the site of the oldest Roman synagogue then known, but the undated building may have been built after Nathan's death.
2. Bozecchi synagogue, which existed at the end of the thirteenth century.
3. Rabbi Joab synagogue, early fourteenth century.
4. Gallichi synagogue, which existed in 1323.
5. A synagogue that existed in 1337; its main entrance was on the Piazza Giudea, the commercial center of the ghetto.
6. Porta and/or Porta Portese or Portaleone synagogue. Fused with the Quattro Capi or Thores synagogue, their combined possessions were taken later to the Catalan and Levantine synagogues in Rome.
7. A synagogue in Trastevere near the (later) church of San Salvatore in Curte.
8. Catalan-Aragonese, originally perhaps two separate congregations. Permission was given to them by Leo X in 1519 to erect a synagogue on land purchased from the Cenci family in *rione* Sant'Angelo.
9. Scuola Tempio, the synagogue for the oldest Roman families.
10. Tempio Nuovo, probably originally for Italian Jews who came to Rome, but also used by German Jews.
11. Castilian, in which French Jews also worshipped.
12. Sicilian.
13. "Scuola dei Tementi di Dio."

These need not all have been separate buildings. There were other synagogues mentioned in Rome before 1555. A small one was in the Pierleoni residence near S. Nicola in Carceri. A Roman and a Catalan one were neighbors in the *Rione* Sant'Angelo; they may be those numbered 8 and 10 above. A bull issued by Leo X limited the number to eleven.

On July 14, 1555, Paul IV issued the infamous bull, *Cum nimis absurdum,* which instituted the ghetto between the Ponte Quattro Capi, the Portico di Ottavia, the Piazza Giudea, and the Tiber. On the holy day of lamentation for the destruction of the Temple of Jerusalem, July 26, 1555, all Jews were forced to move to the ghetto, where the population was walled in for about three hundred years. The Jews were permitted officially to have only one synagogue, so that several existing ones had to be shut within

Figure 203. Rome, "Cinque Scole," exterior in late 19th century.

two years. The Porta synagogue seems to have been in use outside the ghetto as late as 1558, and its congregation survived as a separate group until 1667; the building itself stood, though unused, until the 1730s. In 1566, under Pius V, all but the Catalan synagogue finally closed and even that one was shut for four months.

Cinque Scole

Later, Pius V agreed to have one building contain five separate synagogues (Fig. 203). The site of the "Cinque Scole" was that of a parish church, S. Maria in Candelabrio, which was demolished under Gregory XIII (1572–85). The five-in-one arrangement satisfied the literal restriction to a single synagogue building and it also satisfied the Jews of several rites and origins who could not agree on common practices. The Castilian, Catalan, Sicilian, "Temple," and "New" synagogues were distributed in various sections of the two-part structure. Some of the synagogues were superimposed. In one wing were the Catalan, Sicilian, and Italian-rite New synagogues, and in the other wing were the Castilian on the ground floor and the Italian-rite Temple one flight up (Fig. 204). The synagogue building also embraced the Talmud Torah school on the top floor, the library, the cloakroom, and, on the side facing the Tiber, a wretched house from which no one wished to evict the poor tenants.

The enforced proximity created problems. The main stairway was preempted by the Temple, which caused inconvenience to the remaining congregations. To settle this dispute and

Figure 204. Rome, "Cinque Scole," Tempio Italiano, late 16th century, interior to ark after restoration in 1868.

others, architects were consulted including Giuseppe Valadier (1762–1839) whose firm may have designed the four-columned, early-nineteenth-century porch built to give access to the New synagogue from an external passageway. Earlier, in 1622–28, Girolamo Rainaldi (1570–1655) designed the twin-columned, pedimented wooden ark and marble seats beside it, as well as the women's gallery balustrade for the Catalan-Aragonese synagogue. The Temple interior had a coffered ceiling decorated with painted ornament and a frieze of stucco relief showing the Temple of Jerusalem and the objects inside it. One synagogue pavement included an image of the Temple of Jerusalem, and it had windows colored in twelve hues, one for each tribe of Israel.

The five synagogues were all rectilinear in plan, lit with windows that were arched in some rooms and straight-headed in others. At least one synagogue—Gregorovius did not say which—had a ceiling "raised by stages into a bizarre kind of dome." All had arks with columns and pediments. Details differed, of course. In the Temple, four columns stood before the ark doors; the other arks had only one column on either side of the doors. The synagogues were of different sizes, too. In 1868, the year of the Temple's restoration, government reports stated that of 5,175 Jews in Rome, almost 1,400 belonged to the Temple, about 1,075 to the New synagogue, about a thousand to the Castilian synagogue, and about 850 to the Sicilian and Catalan synagogues.

Tempio Israelitico

After 1870, when they gained rights equal to those of other Italian citizens and when Rome became the capital of Italy, the Jews were released from papal rule and were free to live elsewhere. Statutes and royal confirmation in 1883 allowed them to form a new community, a corporate entity that could build new places of worship. Beginning in 1885, the unsanitary ghetto was demolished and was replaced by new Tiber embankments and by an open space suitable for a new synagogue. The Jews bought the site from the city in 1888 and sponsored a design competition in early 1889. The sponsors specified the capacity of the building, but did not require that it be oriented.

Twenty-six entries came from Jewish and Christian architects. All of them seem to have taken for granted that a synagogue would not look like any other type of building, especially not a church. Several of the rejected designs had exterior surfaces crowded with ornament, generally Moorish or faintly ancient Near Eastern or Egyptian.

The first-prize winner was Attilio Muggia, a Jewish architect from Bologna who was a professor of architecture at the engineering school in Rome and, later, a judge at the League of Nations competition. He submitted a design for a twin-towered, four-storey building of striped masonry (inspired by the Florence synagogue) with a square drum covered by an elongated cupola (borrowed from the Mole Antonelliana), because Muggia felt that the shape fostered mysticism and gave a special aspect to the

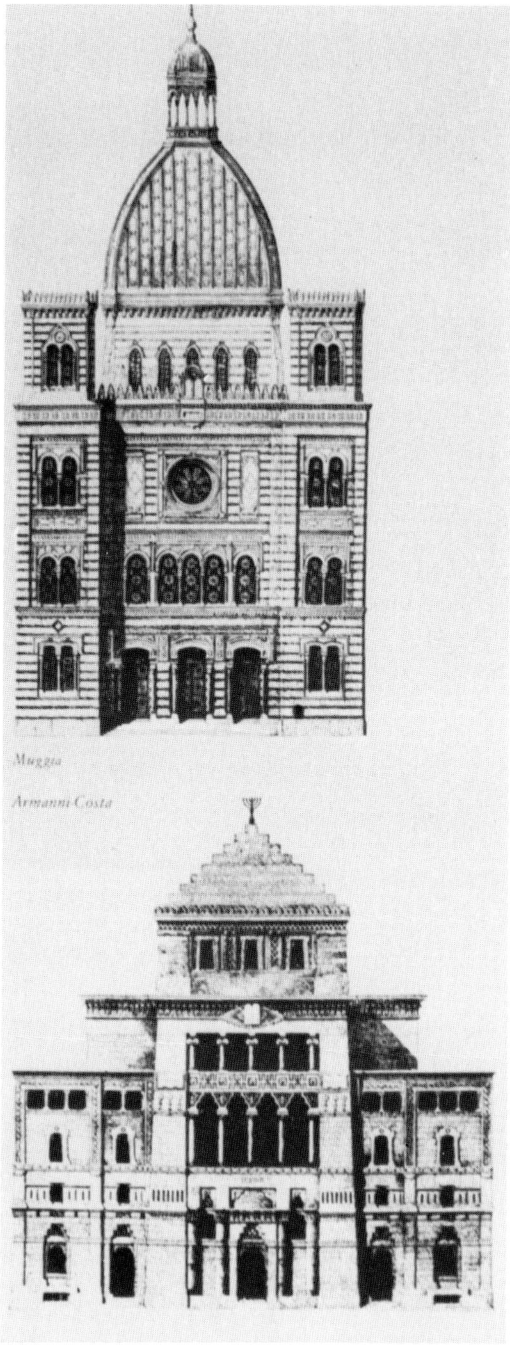

Figure 205. Rome, projects, 1889, by Attilio Muggia and by Costa & Armanni.

building without copying the domed forms found in churches (Fig. 205, see Figs. 193, 214). Muggia took from descriptions of Herod's Temple in Jerusalem the idea of twin towers and a reentrant center section, and he added elements of Phoenician, Assyrian, Byzantine, and Arabic styles. Although Muggia criticized the Florence synagogue for looking like a splendid mosque, his ungainly creation was obviously derived from the Tuscan synagogue. The difference, he felt, was that his design was appropriately eclectic. The mixture of styles would remind Jews that they had been indissolubly associated with where they had lived—the kind of sentiment to be expected more from an assimilated Jew than from a Christian—and it would simultaneously remind them of the Temple of Jerusalem, which learned sources had assured him was also eclectic. Finally, Muggia proposed that his synagogue be light and colorful to give joy and to avoid the shadows of Gothic art.

The Roman architects, Costa & Armanni, designed a synagogue with the exterior silhouette of a five-aisled basilica, stepping down from the high central nave to the lower outer aisles. The building was not actually a basilica, but a Greek cross with a vestibule in front of it. The salient center of the facade had the sloping outline of an Egyptian pylon. Behind it lay the vestibule with adjacent rooms in two bays on each side of the central pylon. The body of the synagogue shared an Egyptian cornice line with the top of the sloping pylon, and behind that rose the square drum under a crowning step pyramid based upon the design of the summit of the Mausoleum of Halicarnassus. The ornament came mainly from Mesopotamian, Egyptian, and Islamic sources. The silhouette was clear, the massing bold. The contrast between the thin columns and foiled arches on the pylon and the large, smooth surfaces elsewhere was energetic and unusual. This design would have looked extraordinary anywhere, especially in Rome, but it was interesting and original, while Muggia's design would have looked equally odd in Rome but it had elements known in other recent synagogues. As it happened, neither design suited the competition terms adequately, and neither one was built.

Figure 206. Rome, 1901–4, exterior.

An important reason for deferring construction was that funds had to be diverted from planning to repair, for in 1893 a fire broke out in the Cinque Scole. The Temple was ruined, the Castilian synagogue ceiling and floor sustained damage, and the New synagogue floor needed restoration.

In 1896, the Jewish community and the city abrogated the 1888 agreement and concluded a new one. They exchanged a strip of land in the ghetto for a new building site, and the community reduced the building fund by a third. The Jewish leaders then asked the prizewinning architects to compete under these new terms by May 1899 for a building that would be visible from the river and offer a harmonious prospect from the Portico di Ottavia. Only Costa & Armanni submitted a design, and they therefore received the commission. The jury included eminent Jews and Camillo Boito, an architect and art historian.

Costa & Armanni, and their supervising architect, Jacobassi, produced a central-plan domed synagogue that covers 1,200 of 3,373 square meters, with the rest of the site left for a garden (Fig. 206). Its forms are compact and massive, emphasizing compressed squares and rectangles.

A two-storey vestibule with an open portico of "Assyrian" columns leads to a prayer hall in the shape of a Greek cross rising 46 m. to the top of a four-sided cupola (Fig. 207). Ungainly columns and pilasters articulate the corners and support the galleries in the north, south, and west cross arms. The ark and the bimah stand on two adjacent platforms as they do in Florence. Painters named Bruschi and Brugnoli executed warm-toned decorations representing tapestries on the walls and a starry firmament on the ceiling. Painted surfaces on the cupola

Figure 207. Rome, 1901–4, interior to ark.

were especially brilliant and transparent, according to the architects, because the cupola was made of aluminum. Inscriptions inside and out and light fixtures, including a tiara of seven-branched candlesticks in the polygonal ark recess, add further richness to the building. The contrast between the compression of the compact plan and the imposing height gives the building a stature which is not supported by the confused detail.

The "style" mixed Roman, Greek, Assyro-Babylonian, and Egyptian elements. The architects believed that ancient Jewish architecture fused Egyptian and Assyrian styles and that later Jewish buildings such as Herod's Temple reflected Greek ideas. (The style could be connected to Rome because Greece was the intermediary.) They did not want to create an archaeological reconstruction, because they knew that ancient buildings would not suit modern needs; Luca Beltrami had said the same thing in relation to his synagogue design for Milan.

The Assyro-Babylonian and Egyptian elements appear only in decorative details, including column capitals and abundant moldings. Perhaps the architects thought that the decorations, combined with awkward and unclassical proportions in a massive building, produced a pre-Greek—that is, Mesopotamian or Egyptian—impression. Nineteenth-century architectural theory associated rational structure, simplicity, and fitness of forms with Greek architecture; the architects may have connected these characteristics to the synagogue's style. Greek and Roman emphasis on symmetry and on clear divisions between building parts, and the Roman emphasis on significant features such as stairs, entrances, and the cupola, also explain the architects' references to the classical tradition. They thought that their building harmonized perfectly with the other monuments of Rome, an opinion with which others may differ. Certainly, the overall impression is more Roman than exotic. The imaginative and exuberant project of 1889 by Costa & Armanni would have been more commanding than the compromising building that stands stolidly on the Tiber's banks.

The synagogue remains as a monument to attitudes common among Italian Jews of the first emancipated generation. They were grateful to their enlightened countrymen, wanted to participate in the new social order, and looked forward to personal growth in the new Italy. The synagogues of Rome, Florence, Turin, and Modena—to name just four from the late nineteenth century—are all too big for their present congregations and may always have been too big, but they were meant for expansive spirits and overflowing hearts.

Today, the Roman synagogue houses a dwindling congregation that follows the Italian rite in a setting with the connected ark and bimah of the Ashkenazic Reform rite. A Spanish-rite oratory occupies a room adjacent to the main prayer hall. There, the ark and bimah stand at opposite ends of the room, following Sephardic tradition. The ark comes from the Castilian synagogue in the Cinque Scole, which was abandoned and demolished when the new Tempio opened.

Other rooms in the building are devoted to a museum of original documents and objects, and casts and copies of materials illuminating Jewish history in Rome. The main prayer hall itself serves as a museum of sorts, for the aisles under the galleries house the ark of 1586 from the Sicilian synagogue in the Cinque Scole, as well as fragments of several old arks. In addition, the main prayer hall completes the story of Jews in Rome by displaying plaques recording the patriotism of those who fell in the First World War and recounting the tragedies experienced by Roman Jews during the Second World War.

BIBLIOGRAPHY

G. Accasto, V. Fraticelli, R. Nicolini, *L'architettura di Roma Capitale, 1870–1970,* Rome, 1972, pp. 178–79.

E. Amadei, "Gli ebrei di Roma," *Capitolium* VIII (1932), pp. 253–60.

Archives israélites XXXV (1874), pp. 213–15.

Bachi, "Appunti," pp. 25–46.

A. Berliner, *Geschichte der Juden in Rom von den ältesten Zeiten bis zur Gegenwart,* Frankfurt am Main, 1893.

U. Bottazzi, "Ghetto," *Capitolium* VIII (1932), pp. 401–11.

V. Campajola, "Il Ghetto di Roma. Studio urbanistico e ambientale," *Quaderni dell'Istituto di Storia dell'Architettura,* #67–70 (1965), pp. 67–84.

S. Collon, "Remarques sur les quartiers juifs de la Rome antique," *Mélanges d'archéologie et d'histoire de l'École française de Rome* LXVII (1940), pp. 72–94.

Encyclopedia Judaica, 1971, s.v. Jewish Quarter.

E. Fano, *Brief Historical Survey of the Jewish Community of Rome,* Rome, 1961.

U. Fortis, *Jews and Synagogues,* Venice, 1973, pp. 98–112.

H. A., and R. Geller, *Roma Ebraica–Jewish Rome,* Rome, 1970.

F. Gregorovius, *The Ghetto and the Jews of Rome,* New York, 1966, or *Figuren-Geschichte, Leben und Szenen aus Italien,* Leipzig, 1856 (excerpted from his *Wanderjahre in Italien,* 1853).

Il Vessillo israelitico XXXVIII, #5 (1890), pp. 179–80; XLI, #2 (1893), pp. 67–69, #4, pp. 112–16.

Jewish Chronicle, Oct. 20, 1893, Aug. 26, 1904.

D. Kaufmann, "Léon X et les juifs de Rome," *Revue des études juives* XXI (1890), pp. 285–89.

S. Krauss, *Synagogale Altertümer,* Berlin and Vienna, 1922, pp. 247–54.

G. LaPiana, "Foreign Groups in Rome in the First Centuries of the Empire," *Harvard Theological Review* XX (1927), pp. 183–403.

H. J. Leon, *The Jews of Ancient Rome,* Philadelphia, 1960, pp. 135–66.

E. Loevinson, *Roma israelitica,* Frankfurt am Main, 1927.

C.L.V. Meeks, *Italian Architecture 1750–1914,* New Haven, 1966.

A. Milano, *Il Ghetto di Roma,* Rome, 1964.

———, "Le sinagoghe del vecchio ghetto di Roma," *Studi romani* VI (1958), pp. 138–59.

———, "The Church and Roman Jewry in the 13th and 14th Centuries," *Eretz Israel* III (1954), pp. 223–29.

——— and R. Bachi, eds., *Università israelitica di Roma. Storia e riordinamento dell'archivio,* Rome, 1929.

E. Natali, *Il ghetto di Roma,* Rome, 1887.

N. Pavoncello, *Il Tempio Maggiore di Roma nel 75 anniversario della fondazione,* Rome, 1979.

———, *Le "Cinque Scole" a Roma,* Rome, 1979 (Scritto Marta Roccas).

[?] Perugini, "L'inquisition romaine et les israélites," *Revue des études juives* III (1881), pp. 94–108.

Dr. Philipp, *The Ghetto in Rome. As It Was and As It Is,* 3d ed., Florence, 1881.

Pinkerfeld, pp. 16–20.

Ricordi di architettura, 2 ser., II (1891), p. 26a.

E. Rodocanachi, *Le Saint-Siège et les juifs. Le ghetto à Rome,* Paris, 1891.

P. Romanelli, "I quartieri giudaici dell'antica Roma," *Bollettino dell'Associazione archaeologica romana* II (1922), pp. 132–39.

C. Roth, "Mordekhai Dato e la 'Scuola dei Quattro Capi,'" *Revue des études juives* LXXXV (1928), pp. 63–65.

F. Sapori, *Architettura in Roma 1901–1950,* Rome, 1953, pp. 25, 34.

Statuti dell'università israelitica di Roma e delle sue

opere di beneficenza, Rome, 1882, pp. 37–39.
H. Vogelstein and P. Rieger, *Geschichte der Juden in Rom,* Leipzig, 1895–96, esp. vol. 2, pp. 309, 379.

I am glad to thank Raina Fehl for sending me materials and photographs.

Trieste

Inaugurated in 1912 to replace four eighteenth-century predecessors, the present synagogue in Trieste was the first imposing one of this cosmopolitan center. It was praised for its novel style, which supposedly started a new era in synagogue design.

Early Synagogues

Jews had had permission since 1696 to worship in their ghetto in the city. The earliest places for prayer were rooms in private houses. One is known—the Scuola Gentili from the family of that name; its ark may later have been used in the Scuola Grande of 1797. A formal community, constituted in 1746, commissioned a community synagogue finished by 1748 and later known as the Scuola Piccola. An architect named Pfister built this Ashkenazic synagogue on an upper floor of a building at a ghetto streetcorner. Fire damaged it in 1821, leading to a rebuilding in 1824 by Matteo Pertsch; in 1864, Giuseppe Moscotto completed restoration and decorative work. The local yeshivah and community offices occupied the floor below the prayer hall. In 1775, the community bought the private Ashkenazic Morpurgo synagogue which had opened in 1740.

To provide more space for worship for the 876 Jews who lived in Trieste in 1793, an architect known as Bolzoni or Balzano the Elder designed the new Ashkenazic Scuola Grande and a smaller Spanish-rite synagogue on the site of the Morpurgo synagogue. He built them both in the same palatial four-storey building in 1797 (Fig. 208); the Ashkenazic prayer hall (Fig. 209) rose two storeys above the Sephardic one on the ground floor. The windows seen in an old photograph indicate a remodeling (1862–64).

Figure 208. Trieste, 1797, exterior.

Another synagogue was the Sephardic Scuola Vivante, which occupied a private house from 1791 to 1805 or 1829; afterward, the congregation moved to a purpose-built synagogue. That building was restored in 1881 by Daniele Jessurun, a Jewish engineer, but the opening of Trieste's new large synagogue in 1912 drew the congregation away from this and from the other existing buildings, except for the Scuola Piccola, which was used by Jews from Greece. All the old synagogues were demolished between 1927 and 1937 under an urban clearance plan; the ark from the Scuola Spagnola went to the synagogue at Opatija in 1928, the Scuola Grande's ark went to the orthodox synagogue in Rijeka in 1934, and in 1956 the Scuola Piccola's ark was sent to Tel Aviv.

Trieste's synagogues were all of characteristic Italian form—long and narrow, with the ark and the bimah at opposite ends and seats arranged along the walls. Galleries for women ran around the room except above the ark; this is a variant of the galleries embracing the prayer halls at the Spanish- and German-rite synagogues in Venice. All of Trieste's synagogues

Figure 209. Trieste, 1797, Ashkenazic synagogue as remodeled in 1862–64.

Figure 210. Trieste project, 1903, by O. and E. Felgel.

had similar decorations, including arched windows and black-and-white marble floor slabs.

Tempio Israelitico

The city's Jewish population increased several times during the nineteenth century, requiring more synagogues. As early as 1870–71, when there were over 4,400 Jews in Trieste, Dr. Eugenio Geiringer designed a "magnificent" neo-Lombard Renaissance synagogue to hold two thousand people. By 1873, 600,000 florins had been subscribed for the construction. Because the Sephardic and Ashkenazic Jews could not agree on the terms of a community merger, this project was never realized. About thirty years later, the two groups decided to collaborate. A bequest from a community member supplied the necessary funds, and a site was obtained on a plaza. Over forty architectural firms entered a design competition held in 1903 for the synagogue and adjacent community building; the program also included a weekday synagogue, apartments for the rabbi and caretaker, and service areas. O. and E. Felgel of Vienna suggested a monumental domed synagogue in a bizarre style which might best be labeled Assyrian rococo (Fig. 210). Its central plan, dome, and elaborate curvilinear ornament made it akin to the contemporary lavish synagogues of Szeged, Sofia (see Figs. 56–59), Subotica, and Hódmezsővásárhely—in other words, to those in other provincial cities in or near the Austro-Hungarian Empire of which Trieste was then a part. The Viennese architects E. Hoppe and O. Schönthal proposed a less monumental facade with a five-lobed gable and a depressed half-dome over the vestibule, a barrel-vaulted nave, galleries on three sides, and a slightly elevated

Figure 211. Trieste project, 1903 by E. Hoppe and O. Schönthal.

apse for the ark (Fig. 211). The delicate, planar, and geometric version of *art nouveau* ornament favored by the followers of Otto Wagner in Vienna disguised the mass of this building. Although the pastel-colored ornament seemed to have been sprinkled on the facade rather than coordinated with it, the decorative details were attractive.

The seven-man jury, composed mainly of Jewish engineers, judged that none of the competitors had submitted an entirely practical building. One entry had the defect of resembling St. Mark's Basilica in Venice, while another looked like a luxurious railway terminal, complete with two clocks on the facade towers. A new four-man building committee asked Franz Matouschek of Budapest to prepare a more commodious and simple design than his and Emil Adler's "railway terminal" but some now obscure difficulty made these architects abandon the synagogue project in 1906.

Finally, the community awarded the commission in mid-1906 to two Christian architects from Trieste, Ruggiero Berlam (1854–1920) and his son, Arduino (1880–1946), who produced a compact and massive design to be constructed in stone (Figs. 212, 213). A vestibule led to the prayer hall, a domed Greek cross with women's galleries in the three cross arms and a wide apse on the fourth side to house both ark and bimah. The form stressed

Figure 212. Trieste, 1908–12, exterior.

Figure 213. Trieste, 1908–12, interior to ark.

compact massing outside and sturdy loftiness inside.

The exterior style was said to be late Roman of a type found in fourth-century Syria, and the architects chose it because it brought them as close as possible to ancient Jewish architecture. Jews in the Holy Land and throughout the Roman Empire had used Roman forms. Syria was near enough to the Holy Land to incorporate design elements used by Jews. A synagogue in this style could suggest the wide geographic distribution of Jews, both in the Roman Empire and in modern times. It could suggest the proximity of Jews to others within the ancient and the modern Roman (that is, Hapsburg) empires. It could suggest the Jews' Middle Eastern origin without making them look too close to Byzantine Christians or to Moslems.

The Berlams' design incorporates the simple shapes and lines, compact massing, and absence of relief that were seen both in the ancient buildings of Syria and in contemporary works of architects throughout Europe. We see these elements in Vienna, among the "Wagner School" architects, and in the Netherlands, in the architecture of H. P. Berlage and his Dutch followers. The latter also similarly emphasized construction materials—brick in Holland as compared to gray stone at Trieste (see Figs. 229, 230). In Germany at this time, as for example in Mainz, Frankfurt, and Görlitz, architects also designed synagogues with central plans, massive and simple forms, and domed roofs, even if the styles varied (see Fig. 16).

If the synagogue at Trieste looks both contemporary and classicizing, and therefore international on the outside, the interior is richer and more separatist in style. On the piers beneath the galleries, long moldings resembling capitals incorporate both vegetable and geometric forms. They are clumsily juxtaposed because the architects tried to imitate the biblical description of the ornament found on the Temple of Solomon. Some mosaics and painted ornaments use forms mentioned in the Bible. The ark, encased in successively smaller enclosures, recalls the Temple's spatial planning. The dominant impression given by the interior is, however, not one of mood-evoking detail but one of grandeur, due to the domed form and the simplicity of the architectural lines, which are seldom interrupted by salient moldings.

As the congregation had embraced Reform, it needed only low gallery parapets, and no large construction in the center was required to accommodate the bimah. The synagogue had an organ and a choir. An observer remarked caustically that the dedication service in 1912 had included choral but not cantorial singing, and that a cantor would have been more desirable than the champagne reception held after the religious ceremony.

The synagogue survived a riot in 1940 when the facade suffered damage and vandals broke windows. It survived an attack in 1942. After that, services continued until 1943 in the weekday synagogue of the adjacent community building. In that year, the main synagogue was turned into a cinema and then into a repository for books and paintings looted from Jewish houses. In May 1945, however, the synagogue opened its doors for worship again, and the building was restored for use by the ever-shrinking Jewish population of Trieste.

BIBLIOGRAPHY

Projects announced and published in: *Der Architekt* XV (1909), p. 48, Taf. 38, 39; *Schweizerische Bauzeitung* XLII (1903), p. 261; XLIII (1904), p. 99; XLIV (1905), pp. 46–47; *Wiener Bauindustrie-Zeitung* XXII (1904–5), pp. 71–75; XXIX (1912), p. 7, pls. 3, 4; *Zentralblatt der Bauverwaltung* XXIII (1903), p. 620; XXIV (1904), p. 368.

Bachi, "Appunti," pp. 25–46.

A. Boralevi, "Il 'Tempio israelitico' di Trieste. Storia di un concorso," *Comunità religiose di Trieste: Contributi di conoscenza,* Udine, 1979, pp. 7–28.

C. Cervani and L. Buda, *La comunità israelitica di Trieste nel secolo XVIII,* Udine, 1973 (Civiltà del risorgimento, 5).

Corriere israelitico, June 30, 1908, pp. 54ff.; July 31, 1912, p. 54; Nov. 30, 1912, pp. 135–36.

R. Curiel, "A cinquant'anni dalla sua inaugurazione, 12 Tamuz 5672–27 giugno, 1912," *Israel. La rassegna mensile,* 2 ser., XXVIII (1962), pp. 296–300.

———, "Gli ebrei di Trieste nel secolo XVIII," *Scritti in onore di Dante Lattes,* special issue of *Israel. La rassegna mensile,* 1938, pp. 239–55.

S. G. Cusin, "Antiche sinagoghe triestine," *Comunità religiose di Trieste. Contributi di conoscenza,* Udine, 1979.

S. Formiggini, "La comunità israelitica di Trieste," *Corriere israelitico VII* (1867), p. 142.

A. Freud, "Die jüdische Gemeinde von Triest," *Ost und West* XIV (1914), cols. 126–32.

Jewish Chronicle, Feb. 3, 1865, supplement, p.1; June 13, 1873, p. 185.

E. Lavagnino, *L'arte moderna dai neoclassici ai contemporanei,* Turin, 1956, pp. 507–9 (Storia dell'arte classica e italiana, 5).

C. L. V. Meeks, *Italian Architecture 1750–1914,* New Haven and London, 1966.

E. Morpurgo, "Bibliografia della storia degli ebrei nel Veneto," *Rivista israelitica* IX (1912), esp. pp. 66–67.

Nahon, *Arks.*

P. Nissim, "Intorno alle vecchie sinagoghe di Trieste e a due cantiche di Izchaq e Samuel David Luzzatto," *Israel. La rassegna mensile* XXVI (1960), pp. 329–44.

Oesterreichische Wochenschrift, July 12, 1912, p. 474.

Pinkerfeld, pp. 50–51.

"Riapertura del Tempio numero 1 della comunità israelitica," *Corriere israelitico* III, Nov. 1, 1864.

G. Romano, review of Cervani and Buda, see above, *Israel. La rassegna mensile* 2 ser. XL, #10 (1973), pp. 467–68.

M. Stock, *Nel segno di Geremia. Storia della comunità israelitica di Trieste dal 1200,* Udine, 1979 (Collana Comunità, 2).

I. Zoller, "La scuola Vivante a Trieste," *Il vessillo israelitico* LIX, #11 (1911), pp. 592–96.

I am very grateful for the gift of his book and for photographs supplied by Mario Stock, and for the publications and information given by Nikolaus Vielmetti.

Turin

If an architect's ambition and ego had not been bigger than his clients' budget, Turin might have had the most extraordinary synagogue in the world. The tallest columnar, masonry-framed building in Europe, now known as the Mole Antonelliana, was designed at first to be a synagogue, but design changes sent the budget sky-high—just where the roof and spire were heading—and the Jewish community was forced to abandon its plans to occupy the building (Fig. 214). They had to content themselves with an adequate but uninspired substitute.

Figure 214. Turin, Mole Antonelliana, 1862–89, exterior.

Mole Antonelliana

In 1848, the Jews were granted civil emancipation in the Kingdom of Savoy, and because legal and economic opportunity often went together, many of them came to Turin, the kingdom's capital, to improve their lot, just as Christians migrated to cities in the nineteenth century. Feeling secure in Turin, the Jews resolved to erect a new synagogue to replace existing overcrowded prayer rooms.

The impetus was provided in 1859 when the Charity Hospital decided to turn to other uses the part of its property that housed the former ghetto, where the Spanish- and Italian-rite prayer rooms were located. In March 1859, the Jewish community decided to set aside a sum of money each year for a new building, and appointed a committee of seven to establish criteria and to sponsor a competition among architects. A community official later declared that the Jews wanted to dedicate a monument of eternal gratitude for emancipation, and hoped to have a synagogue showing grandeur and elegance without pretentious decoration. To be sure, their aims may have heightened when in 1860 Turin became the capital of the new Kingdom of Italy. The competition program of 1862 included space for 1,500 men with seats for a thousand, as well as a gallery for women, a rabbi's residence, a school, a bakery, a ritual bath, and rooms to accommodate offices, archive and furniture storage, meetings, lectures, and ceremonies at weddings and funerals. The site in central Turin, about 37 m. on each side, had been purchased partly from a private citizen and partly from the crown, which had to approve the design.

The four architects who entered the competition of February 1862 either failed to put all the facilities into the available space, or designed buildings that would have cost more than the 250,000 lire in the budget. The Jewish community then called in as a consultant the brilliant local engineer-architect, Alessandro Antonelli (1798–1888). His proposal, prepared by mid-

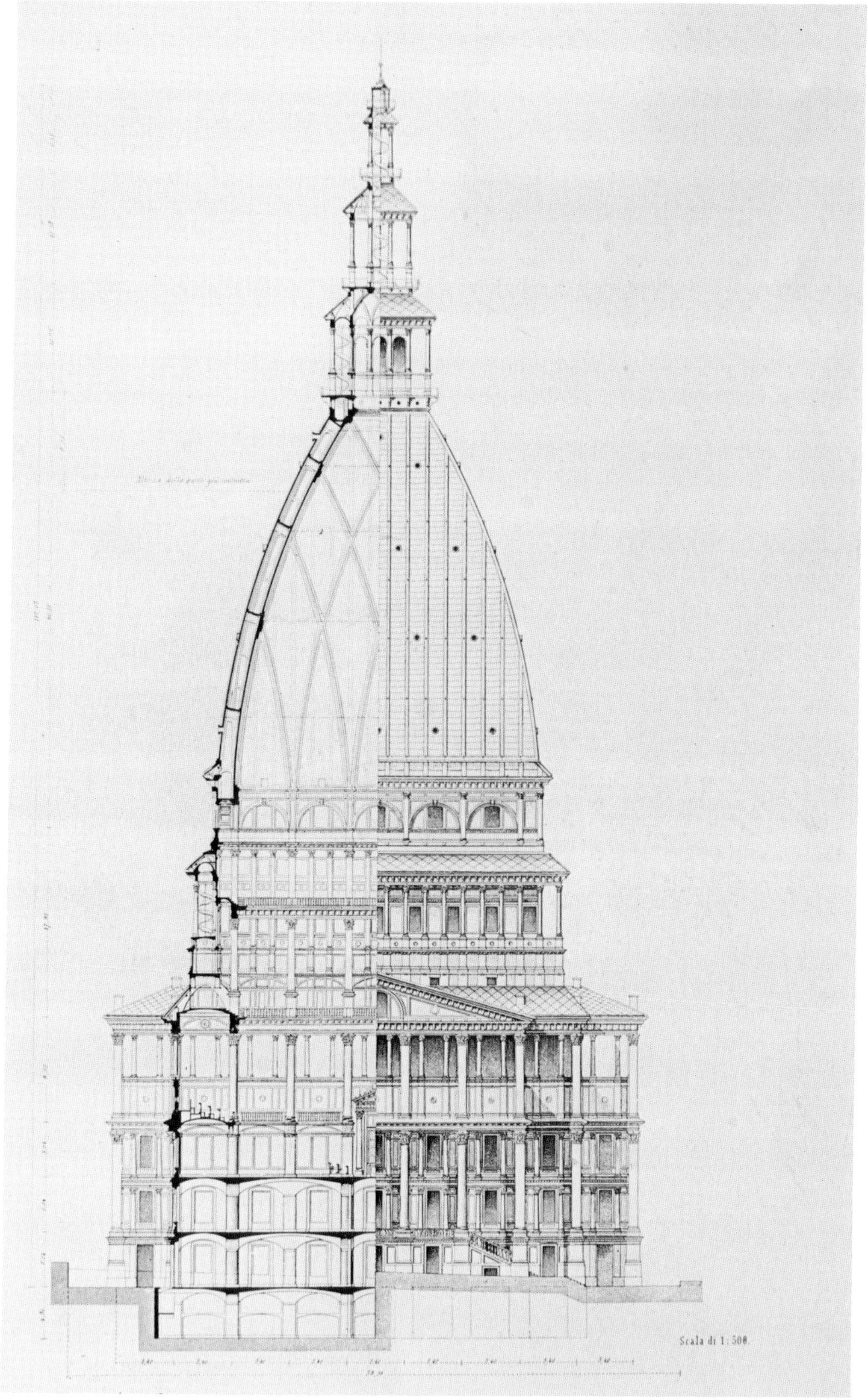

Figure 215. Turin, Mole Antonelliana, 1862–89, section and elevation after 1867.

August of the same year, won the community's approval, since it fitted the necessary auxiliary rooms efficiently under the synagogue and promised to cost only 280,000 lire. Antonelli also proposed a way to provide adequate light to the interior, despite his use of masonry walls, which usually had to be so thick as to make large amounts of window area structurally impossible. He planned a kind of double skeleton frame, but of masonry instead of the iron cages which were increasingly common in technologically advanced cities of Europe and America. (He could not use metal, because at that time Italy lacked the expertise to build what he needed.) He designed a system of columnar piers and lintels, with some relieving arches (Fig. 215). In revised designs of 1863 and 1865, he gave the synagogue a basement, a dome of less than semicircular curve over the prayer hall, and two small side courtyards which were made possible by the purchase of additional land.

But between the second half of 1865, when excavation and construction began, and 1867, the Jews began to notice that, according to the head of the Jewish Community Administrative Council, Antonelli was "consumed by the passion to link his name with a monument of singular mastery and of a form even more singular." He had ordered a "third level raised slowly and almost stealthily . . . with the idea of bringing the upper part to an enormous height." He was, in fact, constructing not a low, curved dome but an immensely tall four-sided cloister vault. It sprang upward toward a three-storey miniature cupola crowned by a seven-branched candlestick. All this soared 47 m. higher than the original project had proposed, with the main prayer hall rising 90 m. under the elongated vault. Antonelli apologized for the changes, which he said he was making for technical reasons, and he offered to take responsibility for them. The offer was meaningless, however, since Antonelli was not rich enough to pay for excess costs himself.

As is the case with many projects, this one, once begun, was hard to stop. As long as they could trust Antonelli's good faith, and as long as their funds held out, the Jews consented to pay for the revised plans. Their hopes of building a suitable monument honoring their emancipation sustained them while Antonelli experimented with such matters of general contemporary technical interest as the covering of large spaces without internal support, or the whittling away of solid mass, or the achievement of great height in a masonry building.

By 1869, however, the Jewish community of about two thousand members ran out of money. The levies for the synagogue had prompted some of its wealthier members to leave town before they could be asked to contribute even more money, and potential new Jewish arrivals avoided a city where they would be assessed immediately for the exorbitant costs of the synagogue. Adding to the troubles of the Turin Jews was the fact that Florence had become the new capital of Italy (1864–71), and the removal of the government diminished the attraction of Turin for Jews who were eager to be in the capital. In February 1870 the congregation had to ask the city council for funds to investigate the building's solidity. When most of the experts agreed that the structure was sound, both laymen and building professionals urged that the synagogue be finished as planned. Despite a municipal subvention in proportion to the city's contribution to Roman Catholic churches, and despite the efforts of the Jews, who had sold various religious objects, melted out the gold from cloth hangings, and taxed themselves faithfully, the community could not afford to complete the building. For a while, it considered demolishing the unfinished vault and constructing a lower cover. A flock of experts offered their own ideas. By 1876, 692,000 lire had been spent and there was still no new synagogue. Amid continuing discussions about demolition and alteration, a group of "Friends of the Monument" was formed from the general public. The pressure of about eight thousand people in favor of having the city retain and complete this extraordinary structure resulted in a municipal decision in 1877 to take over the building, make it into a museum of the Risorgimento, Italy's movement of national unification, and give the Jews in exchange a sum sufficient for a modest synagogue on another site.

The building continued to grow, even after 1887 when an earthquake caused buckling in the drum under the tall cloister vault. Although the drum's form was becoming circular rather than square, the structure remained standing, and finally, in 1889, it was completed with the tall figure of a winged genius of the Savoy dynasty perched upon the spire. The height to the top of the figure was 163.55 m.

It is no wonder that this prodigious building is generally known as the Mole Antonelliana, after its architect, rather than as a synagogue or a shrine honoring a patriotic movement or a king. It is a paradoxical structure—a kind of skyscraper, but one built with preindustrial means; a monument to the end of traditional construction rather than to the future of architecture and engineering; a building designed to represent an ancient religion and then the ancient tradition of kingship, but that in fact evokes modern secular interests and professional expertise. It is somehow fitting that the secular winged genius was blown down by an "act of God" in a great windstorm.

Tempio Israelitico

The synagogue which was built in 1880–84 to replace the Mole was the product of a competition held in the summer of 1879 which specified room for a thousand men, with seven hundred seats, a women's gallery for four hundred worshippers, an organ, a choir area, a pulpit, a bimah, and an ark; offices and annexes also were required. The total cost was to be 300,000 lire and an additional 3,000 lire were to go to the prizewinning architects. Projects came from Enrico Petiti, an engineer in Turin, and from G. Locarni, an architect in Vercelli who had designed the Moorish-style synagogue that opened there in 1878. Their proposals were judged equal in quality, but Petiti won the commission because he adhered more closely

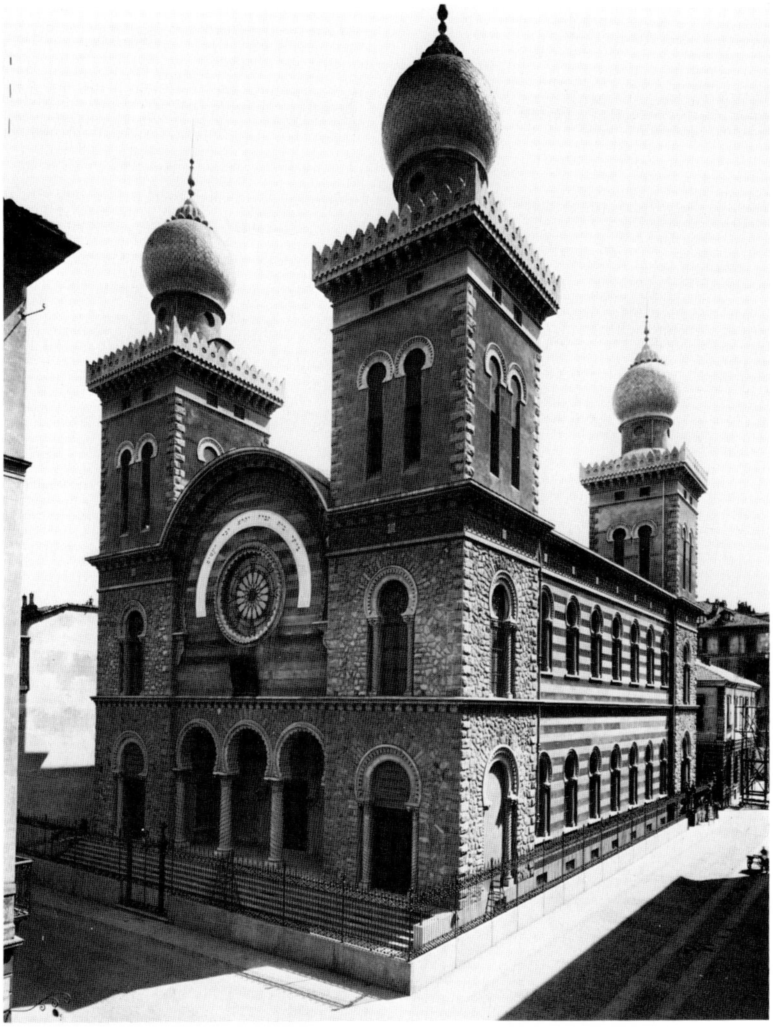

Figure 216. Turin, 1880–84, exterior.

to the program (Fig. 216). The construction at the corners of vie S. Anselmo and Pio Quinto proceeded with little trouble, and the work cost only a bit more than the budgeted amount, thanks to private donations of columns, the pulpit, and other fittings.

The result is a twin-towered oblong building decorated in Moorish style. The congregation abandoned the Renaissance style of the Mole for something more characteristic of northern European interpretations of "Jewish" architecture.

Perhaps this choice reflects the influence of German and Austrian publications describing the many recent "oriental" synagogues, and the influence of the Ashkenazim in Turin's mixed congregation of Italian, Sephardic, and Ashkenazic Jews. Although the number of Moorish synagogues declined in the later 1870s in Germany because Jews there did not want to look strange in a period of rising anti-Semitism, hostility was not virulent in Turin, so that the Moorish style would have carried fewer dangerous messages. The basilican plan and the location of the bimah in the eastern half of the building also reflect central European traditions in this Italian-rite synagogue; Italian traditions kept the bimah farther from the ark, sometimes near the western wall.

The Jews of Turin did not startle the world with this building, which is only 38 m. high to the tops of its bulbous cupolas and only 35 m. long inside the main prayer hall. The exterior is unusual without being beautiful, and the interior is dark because the galleries interfere with the passage of light from the two storeys of windows; gas and electric fixtures were installed later. The coffered ceiling and the ornament were mechanically though carefully executed. Employment of Italian designers and the use of Italian stone and brick satisfied local and patriotic desires. The choice of Moorish forms reflected an affiliation with transalpine Jewry and with those emancipated Jews who were free to express their individuality through artistic style, rather than through height or engineering audacity alone.

BIBLIOGRAPHY

C. C[aselli], "Il tempio israelitico di Vercelli del Comm. G. Locarni," *L'ingegneria civile e le arti industriali* XIV (1889), pp. 8–15.

S. Foà, "Il cinquantenario del Tempio Israelitico in Torino," *Torino* XIV, #3 (March 1934), pp. 34–37.

Pinkerfeld, p. 50.

F. Rosso, *Catalogo critico dell'Archivio Alessandro Antonelli,* I. *I disegni per la Mole di Torino,* Turin, 1975 (with further bibliography).

Venice

In the backwaters of Venice, far from the Piazza San Marco, stand the city's surviving synagogues. With the Jewish quarters of Prague and Cracow, the ghetto of Venice recalls the inward-turning and intense community life of Jews during the Renaissance. Living at the margins of the city, the Jews of Venice nevertheless participated in the commerce for which the city was celebrated, and the synagogues still show both intimate, controlled aspects of Jewish existence and features reflecting the secular brilliance of Venice beyond the ghetto.

Jews established themselves first as money dealers in Venice, and had a *giudecca* (Judaica, or Jewish quarter) by 1090. At some point, they lived on the island still known today as the Giudecca. They were allowed to deal in goods and banking inside the city after 1366, and Venice attracted Jewish migrants from outlying villages. Since they were the bankers, the Ashkenazic and Italian-rite Jews prospered especially. When Venice admitted Jewish refugees from Spain after 1492, Christian commercial competitors tried to control the Jewish population and got city authorities to restrict the Ashkenazic and Italian Jews to a new island district in a marshy area near a monastery of monks who buried executed criminals; it gave the name "ghetto" to all later enclosures of this kind. (The origin of the word *ghetto* is still disputed.) Although this area has recently been "gentrified," it was undesirable at that time, the Venetian equivalent of the flood-prone or pestilential areas given to the Jews in Prague, Rome, and Dresden. About seven hundred Jews were sent there in April 1516. For reasons still unclear, the authorities waited more than seventy years before they confined the Levantine and Iberian Jews; in 1589, these Jews were ordered into a new, adjacent ghetto created because there was no room in the earlier one.

Both ghettoes became so crowded that builders piled new rooms on top of older buildings, until they reached the astounding height of seven or eight storeys (the Jewish districts of Carpentras, Glogów, and Frankfurt am Main also had such "skyscrapers"). Alive with street cries, peddlers, darting children, and the chant of prayers, the area was less elegiac than it seems today. Yet the lanes and narrow canals were dark even then, and something of their old isolation and austerity still pervades the area.

The two main squares, one in each ghetto, were the meeting places, scenes of festivity and of the neighborly ritual of drawing water from a well. The squares burst open to relieve the confinement of the ghetto alleys. The synagogues rose where a lot could be obtained, not in any formal arrangement of theoretical Renaissance urbanism. We reach them today through a chain of darks and lights, from narrow canals and lanes to the open squares, then into modest doorways and dark entrances leading up constricted stairwells into synagogues of unsuspected brilliance. They are rooms densely packed with carved and marbled surfaces, gilded and deep-toned woods, and handsome chandeliers—an appearance little changed since the beginning of the present century. While their walls may be crumbling underneath the interior paneling, the synagogues still record a culture that expressed proud devotion to an isolated faith by endowing the synagogues with the fruits of commerce.

Scuola Grande Tedesca

We do not know where the Jews worshipped during their first dozen years in the ghetto, but a plaque on the west wall of the Scuola Grande Tedesca, the present main Ashkenazic synagogue, records the erection of the building in 1528–29 at the expense of two donors. A second Ashkenazic congregation established the smaller Scuola Canton in 1531–32.

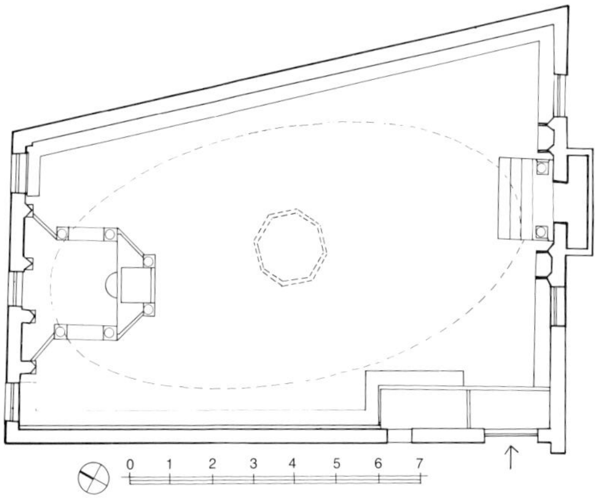

Figure 217. Venice, Scuola Grande Tedesca, 1528–29, ca. 1666(?), 1732–33, plan.

The 1528–29 synagogue was set up in an older, plastered masonry building, with the synagogue added as the fourth and fifth levels of the existing structure. Steep and narrow stairs led to this prayer hall, and possibly to a segregated chamber for women. The prayer hall in its present form is an irregular quadrilateral, surrounded at balcony level by an oval, balustraded and grilled gallery for women (Figs. 217, 218, 219). We know little about the original furnishing and decoration of the main room, but David Cassuto, an architect who studied the Venetian synagogues, noticed that the floor paving, apparently original, contains in the center an octagonal decorative motif under a small central octagonal skylight lantern. According to Ashkenazic tradition, the bimah occupied the center of the synagogue, and the bimah of this synagogue, now on the west wall, probably stood originally in the center of the room under the now-blocked lantern. The carved and gilded ark on the southeastern wall stands between two seats, probably for the rabbi and cantor. The seats project in front of two niches which may once have contained ritual objects and books. The four pink marble steps leading to the ark are dated 1666, the date generally assigned to the ark itself. The two niches beside

Figure 218. Venice, Scuola Grande Tedesca, interior to ark of 1666(?).

Figure 219. Venice, Scuola Grande Tedesca, interior to bimah.

the ark look like slightly cramped abbreviations of the ark, having taller and thinner proportions which are less satisfying. They are surmounted by the same lavish scrolls, pediments, and urns as those above the ark, but the niches do not have enough width to support this superstructure attractively. The design seems to have been popular all the same, for the ark and seats from Sermide, dated 1543, also have densely packed relief carving, paired columns, and elaborate superstructures, and the Scuola Canton at Venice also has an ark and niche arrangement (probably of 1672) like that of the Scuola Tedesca.

The bimah, now at the opposite end of the room, consists of a base on five sides of an octagon, six freestanding balusters which metamorphose into Corinthian columns supporting a cornice, and four half-baluster columns resting against the west wall. Cassuto realized that these half-baluster columns were originally joined so that there were eight full and freestanding supports, forming an octagon. They were later cut apart and redistributed when the bimah was moved from the center of the room to its new position. By blocking the light from some of the windows on the wall behind it, the bimah obstructs the chief sources of natural light.

The date of the bimah in its first form is not known, but its slender balusters and delicate cornice and scrolls are different in style from the more robust and compact forms of the ark. The balusters surrounding the bimah platform are different from those on the women's gallery above them. If urns atop the corners of the bimah remind us of the differently shaped urns of the ark, and look a good deal like the urns over the entrance door, it may be due to minor additions made to the bimah when it was moved—additions made to create more visual cohesion among the wooden furnishings. We do not know when the bimah was moved and remodeled, nor why the Ashkenazic Jews abandoned the traditional central bimah. Perhaps when the changes were made they saw themselves as Venetian Jews rather than Ashkenazic sojourners, and so adopted the practice of other Italian synagogues where the bimah stood opposite the ark.

The most noticeable feature of the room is the oval balcony, which resembles that of the nearby Scuola Spagnola. The late Renaissance development of spaces for women within the main prayer hall is seen in both buildings. The Sephardic synagogue was probably the one for which this solution was invented, but its use in the Scuola Grande Tedesca shows intelligent acceptance of a good new idea. Not only did this provide room for women close to the ceremonies, but it also made the synagogue interior seem more regular in form. The oval gallery links all the oddly shaped parts of the room by making one dramatic sweep which forces the eye to perceive more regularity than there really is. Clearly, however, the interior was not conceived at one time, and there must never have been enough money to redesign it in a single campaign. The ark and bimah are now tucked under the balcony in an awkward way. The gallery, surely added after the ark was constructed in 1666, must therefore be later than the gallery at the Scuola Spagnola, which is supposed to have acquired its gallery in 1655. The gallery parapet balusters in the Scuola Tedesca are lighter and more elongated and graceful in form than those of the Sephardic synagogue. We can no longer examine the original grilles to find dating clues, for they were replaced by late-nineteenth-century metalwork. Could the gallery date from as late as 1732–33, a date inscribed on the same plaque as the date of 1528–29? The later date was that of a major renovation, but perhaps that was only the date of the bimah remodeling and the creation of the present entrance.

The other elements in the room are less important. The principal ceiling decoration is a flat and paneled oval band echoing the gallery. The ceiling surface is painted in vine scrolls and imitation marble. Around the walls runs cherrywood wainscoting with seating attached to the walls. The woodwork is well carved with pilasters, dentil moldings, and angular geometric panels; Cassuto suggests that they date from the mid-seventeenth century. Behind the seats, painted imitation marble covers the walls. Even if sumptuary laws had not forced the congregation to forgo the use of real marble, the cost of this valuable material might have been prohibitive. Moreover, history had taught the Jews how foolish it could be to install valuable materials in a synagogue, lest the whole building be confiscated. The false marble is not attractive to modern eyes but it adds to the rich impression of the room and reveals the community's desire to decorate the premises as well as they could.

On the exterior, the building is a plastered masonry box that resembles many other buildings of the oldest section of the ghetto, but the Scuola Tedesca has five arched windows to indicate its special nature. On the southeastern side, a niche projects outward, identifying the ark recess. There is no porch or Jewish symbol decorating the exterior. The synagogue presses against other buildings on its long sides, so that it cannot even have windows on two sides.

Between 1890 and 1910, the synagogue was embellished and restored. New stairs leading to the men's and women's areas made the ascent less steep and uncomfortable. But few Jews remained active in Ashkenazic synagogue life in Venice, especially after the mid-nineteenth century when they were allowed to live outside the ghetto. The Scuola Tedesca closed for worship in 1917 and has only been reopened as part of the Jewish Museum of Venice, which occupies an adjacent building.

Scuola Spagnola

The second Venetian synagogue with an oval gallery is that of the Spanish-Portuguese Jews, the synagogue known as the Scuola Spagnola or Scuola Ponentina. This plastered masonry building rises on one side of a small open space, called the Campiello delle Scuole, facing the Scuola Levantina erected for Jews from the eastern Mediterranean. As these groups had not been forced into the ghetto in 1516, the Scuola Spagnola must postdate the Iberian Jews' move to their ghetto in 1589.

The building may have been erected in two separate campaigns, as the windows of the ground and mezzanine floors are not coordinated with those of the upper two storeys.

On the north side of the synagogue, a simple round-arched door bordered by Tuscan pilasters and topped by a horizontal cornice leads to an entrance hall and house of study which also served as a small synagogue. The entrance hall was a meeting place for the congregation and was probably also the schoolroom for young boys. It now contains memorial plaques, including some for Venetian Jews who were deported to death camps by the Nazis in 1943–44. The study-synagogue is about 9 m. by 3 m. Its ark and bimah face each other in the center of the long walls so that the ark can stand at the east. The resulting disposition is like that of the Scuola Italiana in Padua. It allows worshippers to see both ark and bimah without having to move if the seats are aligned to face the center short axis. Here, however, the seats run parallel to the long east and west walls as they do in other Venetian synagogues, so that the customary seat arrangement prevailed. The entrance floor also houses the comparatively modern central heating facilities and the stairway to the mezzanine. On the south side of the ground floor is a small courtyard for the Sukkot festival booth.

The mezzanine contains rooms in which the congregation stores ritual appurtenances and other objects; the southern part formerly housed offices. Above the mezzanine is the main prayer hall, reached by stairs terminating at the left and right sides of the bimah (Fig. 220). The room is nearly rectangular (21.5 m. × 12.7 m. × 20.52 m. × 13 m.). A small rectangular ark niche extends outward at the east, and a larger rectangular niche for the choir extends out at the west, lit by a western window. The women's gallery runs above the window level. The gallery seems to be oval, but is actually formed of two semicircles connected by straight walls. As in the Scuola Tedesca, this enclosing gallery unifies the bipolar room and integrates the women's area with the men's.

The details of the room deserve notice both for themselves and for the light they shed on the date and architect of the synagogue (Figs. 221, 222). The windows and the ark framework

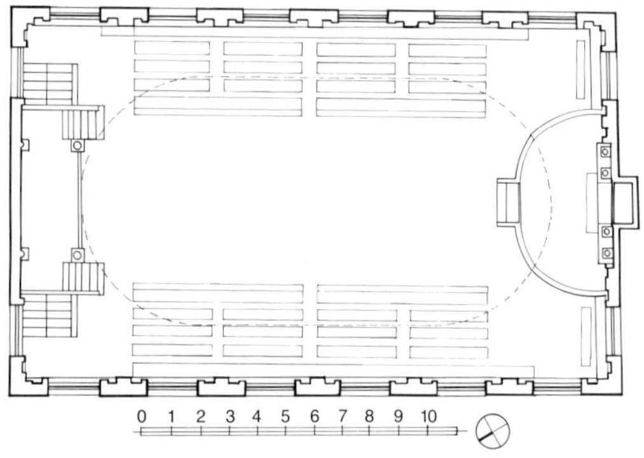

Figure 220. Venice, Scuola Spagnola, after 1589, ca. 1655(?), 1894 plan.

are round-headed, framed by thin pilasters bearing capitals decorated with unclassical brackets. The ark frame has no brackets on its simple molded capitals and may not be coeval with the window frames. Above the window and ark arches and tangent to them is a thin, horizontal terminal strip which turns down at right angles to meet the capitals of the pilasters. In the arch spandrels thus formed are red and purplish decorative inserts, probably made of plaster painted to resemble colored stone which Jews were legally prevented from using. The unpleasantly thin terminal horizontals make the arches and frames seem to stop abruptly and the horizontals intrude into the cornice of the room. Can they be nineteenth-century inventions? (The Scuola Levantina ark, apparently of the Renaissance and identical to the Scuola Spagnola ark, has only a round arch with no terminal horizontal, and the Scuola Levantina windows have cornices over them.) Between the windows rise Ionic pilasters, painted in 1894 to resemble reddish stone; they lack grace in outline and proportion. Their Ionic capitals, however, resemble those in a drawing by the great Venetian architect, Baldassare Longhena, for the Libreria of S. Giorgio Maggiore.

The ark framework consists of a pair of dark, veined columns supporting a cornice and triangular pediment, flanked by another column on each side standing behind the central columns. The side columns also bear cornices. Above the central pediment, dwarf pilasters hold a segmental pediment, forming an attic storey. Tablets of the Law surrounded by gilded rays perch upon the peak of the lower pediment and extend upward to conceal most of the upper one. This design faintly recalls the two-level altarpiece in the Vendramin Chapel in S. Pietro in Castello (1654–65) by Longhena. The altarpiece, however, is more compact and vertical. It lacks a full triangular pediment under the gable and its segmental pediment is ampler in proportion. The altarpiece and ark framework appear to be the products of two different designers. The ark itself may be earlier than its doors, which are dated 1755, but the ark need not be by Longhena.

The balusters of the women's gallery are thicker than those at the Scuola Tedesca and are apparently earlier, close in form to those of Longhena's grand staircase at S. Giorgio Maggiore (1641–45).

Ceiling panels with borders in relief combine semicircles and right angles. Giuseppe Cristinelli, in his book on Longhena, compared the ceiling panel design to that of Longhena's S. Nicolò dei Greci (1658–60), but at that building the ceiling shapes have simpler outlines with fewer curves and angles, and the panels are separated by wider expanses of flat ceiling. In comparison, the Scuola Spagnola looks busy and confused. The flat background of the ceiling was painted in 1894 with a pattern copied from fabric in the synagogue's collection.

We could simply attribute the ark, gallery, and ceiling panels to an anonymous seventeenth-century designer, but F. Zanotto, in his *Nuovissima guida di Venezia* (1856), wrote that Longhena designed the synagogue. He did not document the attribution, however, and it did not appear in earlier guides by J. Lecomte (1844), G. A. Moschini (1847), G. Fontana (1847), or P. Selvatico and V. Lazari (1852). More significantly, it did not appear in A. Lattes's chapter on the Jews of Venice in the Venetian municipal council's *Venezia e le sue lagune* of 1847. Authors of books on Longhena (Semenzato, Cristinelli) copied the attribution from Zanotto or from a later source based on Zanotto's book, and then alluded to vaguely comparable works by Longhena to support the attribution. With more caution, Elena Bassi proposed to associate with the synagogue the name of one of Longhena's assistants, Antonio Gaspari, who was known to have done some work for Jews.

The attribution to Longhena or to his school accords with the date of 1655 given by Lattes for the remodeling of the Scuola Spagnola. The date must be that of the ark, gallery, and ceiling panels, which are of seventeenth-century style. The varied dates of the Longhena monuments that are closest to details in the synagogue suggest that the synagogue designer was a follower rather than a (presumably more consistent) originator of ideas. Cecil Roth's *Venice* confused the dating and attribution by giving the date as 1635, but this was probably a typographical error. The entire population of Venice had just been devastated by plague in 1630–31, and it is unlikely that resources were available to remodel the synagogue. It is true that Longhena designed S. Maria della Salute during the plague years, but that was an *ex voto* for the cessation of the plague, whereas *ex votos* are not part of Judaism and a synagogue would not have been built for such a reason. Besides, the plague had ended as of 1635. The date of 1655 is the preferable one, if either is correct.

By 1655, the Jewish population in Venice is supposed to have increased to 4,800 individuals, twice that of 1630. This came about from natural increase and from the arrival of Jews fleeing Cossack persecution on the Polish-Russian frontier. These Ashkenazic refugees would not have joined the Sephardic synagogue, but the general increase in the Jewish population, added to a natural increase in the Sephardic population, may have led to remodeling of several Jewish institutions, notably the Levantine and Sephardic synagogues. The former, in fact, received the new ark which imitated that of the latter.

The bimah in the Scuola Spagnola is composed of four Corinthian columns, two of them actually half-columns set against the west wall. The columns hold a cornice which supports urns above the two eastern columns and from which scrolls bearing urns rise to a large cen-

Figure 221. Venice, Scuola Spagnola, interior to ark, as redecorated in 1894.

tral urn. The inspiration for a scrolled canopy is likely to have been the baldaquin over the main altar of St. Peter's in Rome; its date in the 1630s gives another reason for preferring 1655 to 1635 for work at the Venetian synagogue. The bimah design is not entirely harmonious, as the lavish baroque scrolls have little to do visually with the sober column and cornice substructure. Curving steps to the left and right of the bimah lead to its reading platform and to the choir space behind it. We do not see that space now, because in 1830 a congregation member named Jacopo Treves de Bonfili donated an organ which was inserted in the bimah. The reading desk was thereupon moved just below the ark. The seats remained aligned along the north and south walls, showing that the synagogue was not entirely influenced by German Reform when the bimah desk moved below the ark.

The Scuola Spagnola has handsome window and gallery grilles and metal chandeliers. The many-armed chandeliers of the main hall add to the sumptuous impression given by the interior. The central lights and those hanging near the long walls appear in a print made before 1830. G. Reinisch Sullam gives 1772 as the date of some of the chandeliers and 1845 as the date on some candlesticks; other fittings may have been installed in a restoration of 1838 which Roth mentioned.

Today, the building is in a state of grave danger. Its physical structure is unsound, the roof leaks, and the interior decoration is in disrepair. Outside plaster has crumbled. The complete restoration of the structure would be costly, but international efforts are being made to save this

Figure 222. Venice, Scuola Spagnola, interior to bimah (now organ framework), after 1830, as redecorated in 1894.

as well as the German, Canton, Italian, and Levantine synagogues—the last three being handsome oblong rooms with bimahs opposite the arks.

All the synagogues, so rich in their interior fittings, give the modern observer a more acute sensation of exoticism than they were meant to convey. The density of these rooms, the firmament of chandeliers in the Scuola Spagnola, and the expanses of carved wood in several synagogues are unfamiliar to Jews raised in modest synagogues or the dignified temples of Reform. Not many churches have survived in their old and crowded state after Christian reformers and restorers "improved" them, but if left alone, churches might have seemed as full, intense, and exotic as these synagogues.

BIBLIOGRAPHY

E. Bassi, *Architettura del sei e settecento a Venezia,* Naples [ca. 1962], pp. 118, 120.

D. Cassuto, *Ricerche sulle cinque sinagoghe (scuole) di Venezia,* Jerusalem, 1978.

———, "The Scuola Grande Tedesca in the Venice Ghetto," *Journal of Jewish Art* III-IV (1977), pp. 40–57.

Consiglio comunale di Venezia, *Venezia e le sue lagune,* Venice, 1847, vol. 1, part 2, appendix 8, pp. 103–7 for A. Lattes, "Gli ebrei a Venezia."

G. Cristinelli, *Baldassare Longhena, architetto del '600 a Venezia,* Padua, 1972, pp. 64–71.

U. Fortis, *Jews and Synagogues,* Venice, 1973, pp. 32–75.

C. D. Lewis, review of Cristinelli, op. cit., *Arte Veneta* XXVII (1973), pp. 328–30.

A. Milano, *Bibliotheca historica Italo-Judaica,* Florence, 1954, and *Supplement,* for articles on the Venetian Jews and on all the synagogues.

———, *Storia degli ebrei in Italia,* Turin, 1963.

E. Morpurgo, "Bibliografia della storia degli ebrei nel Veneto," *La rivista israelitica* VII, #1 (1910), pp. 188ff.; IX, #1–2 (1912), pp. 49ff.

———, "Inchiesta sui monumenti del Veneto interessanti la storia religiosa, civile, e letteraria degli ebrei," *Il corriere israelitico* L, 4 (1911), pp. 41–43.

G. Navarra, "Il restauro del Tempio Spagnolo di Venezia," *Il vessillo israelitico* XLII, #4 (1894), p. 127.

A. Piattelli, "The Merger of the Sephardic and Ashkenazic Congregations of Venice," *American Sephardi* V, #1–2 (Autumn 1971), pp. 29–31.

Pinkerfeld, pp. 5–16.

G. Reinisch Sullam, *Jewish Art Treasures in Venice,* New York, 1973, pp. 31–32.

C. Roth, "Masterpieces of Sephardi Art. IV: The Italian Scuole," *Le judaïsme séphardi,* n.s., #4 (May 1954), pp. 172–76, esp. p. 175.

———, *Venice* (Jewish Communities Series), Philadelphia, 1930 (also published in other languages as *The History of the Jews in Venice*).

C. Semenzato, *L'architettura di Baldassare Longhena,* Padua, 1954 (Università di Padova. Pubblicazioni della Facoltà di Lettere e Filosofia, 29), esp. p. 30.

Wischnitzer, *Architecture,* pp. 59–65.

F. Zanotto, *Nuovissima guida di Venezia,* Venice, 1856, pp. 333–34.

The Netherlands

Amsterdam: Seventeenth-Century Synagogues

"Amsterdam is a large Hamburg, a small Jerusalem." So wrote J. J. Schudt, a German observer around 1700 who noted the prominence of Amsterdam as a trading center and the prominence of Jewish businessmen there. Two synagogues survive from the seventeenth century, when Jews became active inhabitants of the city. The Grote Sjoel, or Great Ashkenazic Synagogue of 1670–71, the Sephardic synagogue of 1671–75, and the latter's destroyed predecessor of 1639 show how the Jews gave architectural expression to their culture. They also illustrate the development of the galleried basilican synagogue.

Sephardic Synagogue of 1639

The Sephardic congregation that built the synagogue of 1639 consisted of descendants of Iberian Jews and Marranos. After the late sixteenth century, the Dutch government was run by relatively tolerant Protestants, so that Marranos who wanted to return to Judaism found the Netherlands a desirable place to live. In the early seventeenth century, Sephardic Jews with Portuguese names set up three synagogues in buildings in the Jewish quarter on the Vloonburg island and merged into a single congregation in 1639 when they remodeled buildings on the Houtgracht (later paved over to become the Waterlooplein). The synagogue was built inside two contiguous houses and may have been an enlargement of one of the earlier three synagogues that amalgamated to form the united congregation (Figs. 223, 224).

A broad staircase led upstairs to the prayer hall, a two-storey room with windows so large that the interior seemed to be framed in glass. This was the earliest known synagogue with lateral galleries integrated with the space of the main prayer hall. Since these converted houses lacked room for the annexes in which women usually were segregated, a galleried basilica became the *ad hoc* but prophetic solution to that problem. This unusual synagogue was based probably on such local galleried buildings as the Remonstrant Church (1629) and the Lutheran Church (1632–33), on structural inventions used in Dutch house churches, and perhaps on the more remote galleried Huguenot churches of France. Galleries allowed many people to occupy a compact space while they sat for a long time, hearing sermons and reading prayers. Recognizing that Jews had similar needs, Christian architects familiar with galleried churches adapted the idea to Jewish use. Some of the gallery space was reserved for women, as can be seen in an engraving by I. Veenhuysen, which showed the grillework that concealed the women from view. Closer to the bimah at the western end of the nave, there was no grillework, revealing that men sat behind the balustrade fronting the gallery. A barrier made of wooden slats separated the men's and women's parts of the galleries.

Stretching upward from the four pairs of Tuscan columns and from the gallery balustrades between them were square posts holding beams spanning the nave; simply cut brackets gave additional support to the beams. Upon the beams rested the central two of four parallel wooden barrel vaults of equal span, emphasizing the east-west axis and the distance between the ark and bimah at opposite ends of the main axis.

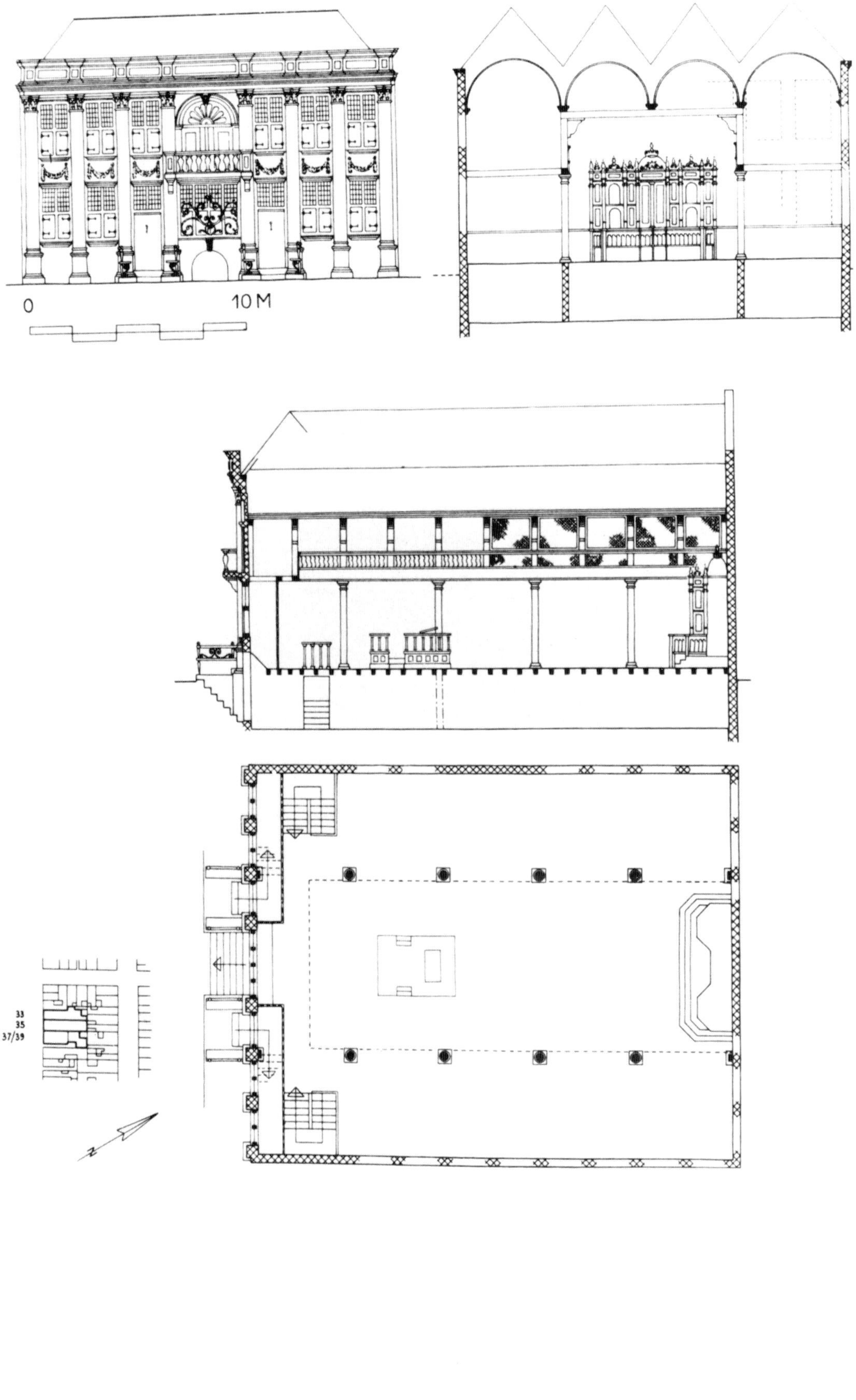

Figure 223. Amsterdam, Sephardic synagogue, 1639, facade, sections, site plan, plan at men's seating level.

Figure 224. Amsterdam, Sephardic synagogue, 1639, interior to ark, engraving designed by I. Veenhuysen.

Grote Sjoel

The synagogue that introduced the galleried basilica as it was seen in later synagogue architecture was the Grote Sjoel, designed by or under the influence of Daniel Stalpaert, municipal architect, and built from March 1670 to March 1671 (Figs. 225, 226). Easily visible along a canal facing the later Sephardic synagogue of 1671–75, the new Ashkenazic synagogue was flanked by two small houses, one for the ritual bath and the other for the residence of the caretaker.

The building presented a picture of stately dignity among the nearby low and narrow gabled houses of the seventeenth century. It is squarish, about 16 m. by 18 m. inside, within brick walls articulated outside by pilasters with molded capitals which indicate the wider nave and narrower aisles. The building lies at an angle to the street, leaving room for a vestibule and staircase annex which has changed in form several times; the present entrance portal dates from about 1823. A triangular pediment on the central section of the principal facade, the pitched roof, vertical pilasters, and high, round-headed windows on the second of three window levels increase the building's apparent height.

Inside, heavy Tuscan columns hold the cornice of the nave under a semicircular barrel vault; slightly lower barrel vaults cover the aisles. The large columns interrupt the gallery parapet and help to support it. This arrange-

Figure 225. Amsterdam, Grote Sjoel, 1670–71 (left) and Nieuwe Sjoel, 1750–52 (right), exterior, engraving designed by J. de Beyer.

ment became standard for many later synagogues, even those built in other styles or materials. As in the synagogue of 1639, some of the gallery space was reserved for men; at least one of the galleries which ran around three sides of the interior held men, as fragments of a balustrade reveal.

The interior design maintains the importance of the east-west axis by means of the long barrel vaults and because the synagogue is longer on that axis. Attention is drawn to the center by the galleries on three sides, and by the presence of only two pairs of freestanding columns creating a central bay. Nevertheless, this building is clearly different from contemporary squarish masonry synagogues in eastern Europe that emphasized the center and the bimah, and separated the women's areas from the main room.

The style of the building and of its furnishings was severe, characteristic of an austere stage of Dutch religious architecture. The ark framework, slightly more delicate than the building itself, had Ionic pilasters and a broken pediment with an ornamental finial in the center and carved leaves in the semicircular tympanum over the doors. The original seats were straight-backed, plain in design, and probably uncomfortable.

The galleried basilica had a long afterlife. The Nieuwe and Uilenburgerstraat synagogues of Amsterdam and the Great Synagogue of London were eighteenth-century examples, followed soon afterward by those of Portsmouth and Vienna-Seitenstettengasse (see Figs. 63, 245). In many of them, the ground floor piers end at gallery level, and supports of another design continue upward to sustain the ceiling, as in Amsterdam's synagogue of 1639. There were examples of this design throughout Europe, some of them especially lofty after architects in the second half of the nineteenth century used slender supports of cast iron rather than the more massive brick and stone of earlier times.

Figure 226. Amsterdam, Grote Sjoel, interior to ark before 1940.

Sephardic Synagogue of 1671–75

The stateliest synagogue in all Europe faces the Grote Sjoel across a filled-in canal. This is the Sephardic synagogue erected in 1671–75 to the design of Elias Bouman, a Christian contractor who had worked on the Grote Sjoel. The red-brown brick structure rises on the eastern portion of a lot which had been the site of the former St. Anthony's Gate (until the city boundaries were expanded), in front of the hospital for contagious diseases. For the imposing edifice they had in mind, the Sephardic Jews needed a lot of this size and may only have been able to obtain it at the edge of town on a site associated with a pesthouse—the dwelling quarter allotted to the Jews earlier in the century. The synagogue, like the smaller Grote Sjoel, rose well above the surrounding buildings, because in their own neighborhood the Jews were allowed to obey the Talmudic prescription to make their house of worship preeminent (Fig. 227). The synagogue's height is all the more impressive in contrast to the low community buildings that cluster around its courtyard (see Fig. 225, far right).

Inside, the effect of a vast and mighty room comes from the large scale of the building's parts, characteristic of contemporary important civic and Christian structures as well (Fig. 228). The building contract specified dimensions of 110 by 175 Amsterdam feet; the synagogue is about 38 m. by 26 m. inside. The entire space can be seen at once, and as the room holds about two thousand seats, the sight is awe-inspiring. Seventy-two windows admit light of exceptional brilliance for a synagogue. Ionic columns, rising more than 13 m. from bases

Figure 227. Amsterdam, Sephardic synagogue, 1671–75, exterior in 18th century, drawn by Jan Spaan.

almost 2 m. square, divide the nave from the aisles. The unfluted columns are thick and massive. They hold three smooth, parallel wooden barrel vaults which cover the nave and the slightly lower aisles; the vaults' smooth surfaces and simple shape add to the impression of forceful directness. The apparent size of these building components is enhanced by the smaller size and scale of the columns that hold the women's galleries. They stand in the aisles, free of other structural elements. The impossibility of relating them to the major design features makes them seem for a fleeting moment equal in size to the large structural columns but seen at a great distance. The huge bimah, a balustraded enclosure raised a few steps above the floor, and the magnificent ark, which resembles a columned and pedimented altarpiece filling the width of the nave, maintain the larger-than-life scale of the interior's principal features. It is the scale, more than the details of carving or design, which makes the building so imposing.

All the same, refinements were carefully considered. The most famous exterior details are the buttresses that curve outward at the base, imitating the reconstruction of Solomon's Temple made in 1642 by Rabbi Jehuda Jacob Leon. The other exterior details, mainly light-colored stone dressings, were executed in the contemporary classical taste and made the building look like many other contemporary Dutch structures.

The interior embellishments included the handsome carved rosewood ark which incorporated the first dated tablets of the Law associated with an ark. There were also gleaming brass chandeliers and wall sconces. A visitor of ca. 1930, Marvin Lowenthal, reported that at that time there were 613 tapers, one for each traditional Jewish law. He also found symbolic content in the seventy-two windows, one for each name of God. This kind of interpretation associated with the Kabbalah is known in eastern Europe from the late sixteenth century onward, but we do not know how widespread it was in western Europe. The chandeliers now in the synagogue did not all come from this building originally, but they give the correct general impression, especially as no electric lights have been introduced. The dignified bearing and handsome clothing of the wealthy merchants of the congregation also lent the synagogue a distinctive character at many periods in the past.

Because few other congregations were rich enough to need a synagogue of this size, and

Figure 228. Amsterdam, Sephardic synagogue, 1671–75, interior to ark on dedication day, engraving by Romeyn de Hooghe.

because Ashkenazic congregations were in the majority in Europe, the 1671–75 Sephardic synagogue had only one direct heir, the Mikve Israel Synagogue of 1730–32 in the Dutch colonial city of Willemstad, Curaçao. It is possible that the aisle-within-an-aisle design of galleries was meant at Amsterdam to imitate the *diplostoon* arrangement which Philo described at the Great Synagogue of Alexandria, for the word *diplostoon* can be interpreted in this way. This meaning might have been lost by other congregations.

The synagogue with columns separated from the galleries recurred occasionally in altered form. At the Nieuwe Ashkenazic Synagogue of Amsterdam (1750–52) beside the Grote Sjoel, the galleries run immediately behind the columns that define the nave. At the concrete-pillared basilican Synagogue de la Paix in Strasbourg (1952–58), the galleries are cantilevered from the side walls. In this case, the difference from the Amsterdam Sephardic type is caused by changes in the structural material and by the architect's desire to introduce as few obstructions as possible. The beauty of the Amsterdam synagogue has, however, been much celebrated in paintings, prints, and literary descriptions, even if the form has seldom inspired followers.

Amsterdam's Sephardic synagogue has undergone remodelings and restorations, none substantial enough to change its basic appearance. The staircase annex (probably 1773–74) on the east replaces the original cantilevered access balcony. The low annexes on the west, north, and south that house the community rooms were formerly colonnaded toward the interior of the synagogue courtyard. Inside, the number of seats was originally larger—about 440 for women and about 1,230 for men—but some of the benches were taken to the winter or weekday synagogue room around 1957. The galleries rest on stone columns which were inserted after 1691 to replace the original wooden ones. The present entrance and vestibule, and the present windows, date from 1852–53, executed under the direction of Isaac Warnsinck, an architect who also replaced the stonework. The women's benches were products of the 1852–53 renovation, and the women's gallery parapets were altered slightly around 1900. The synagogue suffered vandalism during the Second World War, but the sanctuary and community buildings were restored in 1953–59 by Jacob S. Baars and J. W. Kuiper, who made minor modifications and who discovered some forgotten benches from the 1639 synagogue. The government contributed 60 percent of the cost of further repairs initiated in 1966.

The synagogue is seldom used, owing to its imperfect physical condition and to the high cost of heating it. The congregation is dwindling; about a decade ago it included fewer than eight hundred people, even counting Ashkenazic spouses. When the synagogue is used, officiants still wear traditional dark garb with tall hats and white bib collars, and the candles are lit for evening services. At other times, the synagogue is open to visitors.

The Ashkenazic synagogue across the street, and its later neighbors, the Nieuwe (1750–52), Obbene (1685), and Dritt (1700) synagogues, are about to become simply tourist attractions, with no services at all to be held in them. These buildings suffered badly during the war, and after 1945 their surviving members moved to other districts. Eager to find a new use for the empty structures, the government and the Jewish community endorsed the idea of moving the Jewish Historical Museum to them, and an opening in 1986 is being planned. About twenty thousand people come each year to visit the Sephardic synagogue, and surely they will cross the street—a filled-in canal—to see the remains of the Ashkenazic synagogues put to dignified use.

BIBLIOGRAPHY

J.C.E. Belinfante and E. van Voolen, *Museum in wording. Stand van zaken rond de restauratie van het synagogencomplex aan het Jonas Daniël Meijerplein,* Amsterdam, 1982.

M. Lowenthal, *A World Passed By,* New York, 1933, pp. 193–96.

J. J. Schudt, *Jüdische Merckwürdigkeiten,* Frankfurt am Main, 1714, vol. 1, book 4, p. 271 for the quote of ca. 1700. Part of chap. 18, pp. 270–315, is devoted to the Jews and synagogues of Amsterdam.

J. F. van Agt, *Synagogen in Amsterdam,* The Hague, 1974, with extensive bibliography.

I am most indebted to Drs. van Agt and van Voolen for their kindness in sending publications to me.

Amsterdam: 1928–38

Within a single decade between the two world wars, Amsterdam's 65,000 Jews sponsored three synagogue buildings which offered a variety of architectural forms and a level of quality not duplicated anywhere in a comparable period of time. The synagogues rose in the southern and eastern quarters of the city, where extensive building works had been in progress since about 1910, and where many Jews had moved when they left the former Jewish quarter in central Amsterdam.

One synagogue, that of Linnaeusstraat (1927–28), was characteristic of the Amsterdam School of architecture, giving the worshippers a specific local identity. The second, the Dutch-cubist synagogue on Jacob Obrechtplein (1927–28), linked the Jews to modern architectural and cultural currents in the Netherlands. The third, on Lekstraat (1936–37), an example of broader International Style architecture, suggested the universality of Jewish values and bonds between Jews and other progressive people. If the congregations themselves did not have these ideas in mind initially, the architects surely understood the implications of architectural style.

The three synagogues differed markedly in appearance, demonstrating that Jews never agreed on any single form of appropriate architecture, not even in the same city in the course of ten years. Consciously selected architectural forms established ideological or social-cultural distinctions among congregations.

Linnaeusstraat

On the Linnaeusstraat in Amsterdam-East, Jacob S. Baars (1886–1956), a Jewish architect who also built the Talmud Torah school in Amsterdam, designed a synagogue for a congregation with about three hundred heads of family for whom Judaism was not a passionate subject of interest (Figs. 229, 230). They were solid middle- and working-class people, and had the only Dutch-born cantor in the major synagogues of the city. For a group implicitly linked to the here and now, Baars solved problems arising from the restricted and improperly oriented site; he gave the congregation a cost-efficient building about 500 square meters in size; employed Jews as contractors and workmen; and offered an attractive, well-crafted design in a local style but not in the latest or most challenging form of the style.

The site was squarish and thus not irregular, but no side faced due east. In order to orient the ark wall, Baars turned the building at a 45-degree axis to its lot and cut off the projecting angles, creating an octagonal building. By doing so, he obtained space for a raised entrance platform bordered by low pavilions that sheltered covered walkways. The door was emphasized by a parabolic arch at the base of the rectangular facade wall, which rose to a steep triangular gable. Farther east rose a slightly taller wall of the same shape, forming the west end of the prayer hall. Brickwork patterns in abstract designs adorned the gables, and paired tablets of the Law crowned the higher wall.

The principal feature of the facade wall was a large, pointed window of five lights with a triangular field at the top made of geometric brick mullions. A large, pointed facade window had been a feature of many northern European Gothic churches. The ecclesiastical character of the facade of the synagogue was emphasized by a slender, four-sided steeple at the northwest corner which had near its summit some projecting stones recalling gargoyles on Gothic towers. The community building with a ritual bath and staff apartments, on the northwest boundary of the site, could have been a parish

Figure 229. Amsterdam, Linnaeusstraat, 1927–28, exterior.

house as easily as a Jewish congregational building. The character of the synagogue as a Jewish church was balanced only by the presence of Hebrew letters on a vertical brick projection toward the south. Nevertheless, the facade had some links to other synagogues (see Figs. 138, 139, 140, 144). The Frankfurt am Main-Israelitische Religionsgesellschaft and Poznań synagogues had gabled facades, and the latter also had a large facade window, projecting wings, and a centralizing plan. The Essen synagogue had several aspects in common with the Amsterdam building: an adroit adaptation to an imperfect site; low pavilions that hugged the entrance platform; a decorative handling of building materials; and the architect's desire to design everything, including the interior fittings.

Figure 230. Amsterdam, Linnaeusstraat, interior to entrance.

As in many other examples, it was the internal form, arrangements, and decoration that identified the Amsterdam building as a synagogue, providing another example of a building which looked more Jewish on the interior in private than outside, in public. The main room was octagonal, and as a central form it focused on the bimah rather than on the ark. The bimah, made of Slavonic oak and coromandel, was elevated and surrounded by tall, cylindrical candlesticks. The ark drew attention because it, too, was elevated; it was decorated with somewhat discordant black and white marble, framed by a parabolic arch, and crowned on the eastern wall by a triangle-topped window, identical to the one on the facade. Both windows had cubistic stained glass designs by the Jewish artist, Leo Pinkhof, representing symbols of the Ten Commandments in the tall vertical areas, and symbols of major and minor feasts in the triangular zones above. Other decorations were meant to be Jewish in character also. The women's galleries on three sides of the sanctuary had parapets painted with varied symmetrical designs of angular vines, rather than images of living creatures. Entwined plant forms clustered into medallions in each of the plaques of the sloping ceiling. Metal gallery grilles in a net-like design and metal lamps made of diminishing metal polygonal planes added abstract decorations and other textures to a synagogue in which the principal materials were yellow brick on the walls and piers, and the wood of the conspicuous roof arches and furniture.

The architect's evident interest in the texture and variety of materials links his work to the Arts and Crafts Movement at the turn of the century, and to the architecture of H. P. Berlage, whose follower Baars claimed to be. This synagogue was an example of Amsterdam School building—in its use of local brick, its angularity, its unusual curves such as the parabolic arches, and its large sweeps of wall contrasting with details that revealed craftsmanlike attention to both traditional and modern materials. This building was less imaginative than the most inventive work of other Amsterdam School architects—for instance, that of the Jewish architect, Michel de Klerk—but Baars's buildings show that he was a man who walked at a deliberate pace behind the architectural innovators and had no wish to shock his clients with new forms. When asked about his architectural principles, he replied with ideas which had been fresh a generation earlier: Buildings should have simple form and beautiful line, construction determines the result, and style should follow contemporary currents rather than revive ideas of the past. Throughout his life, Baars adapted his style to recent fashion. In 1938, at Carpentierstraat in The Hague, he designed a synagogue in a massive stripped-classical style, widely employed in early-twentieth-century Germany, which had become commonplace by then for public buildings throughout Europe. As a result, when that synagogue was converted to a cinema after the war, it did not appear to be a particularly unusual motion picture theater. Baars eventually adopted the International Style when he and Jan van Duin designed a new synagogue for Rotterdam (1954–56). This building has the thin rectangular planes intersecting and bypassing each other that Mies van der Rohe and Dutch architects of the de Stijl group had developed during the 1920s.

The arts-and-crafts warmth of the Linnaeusstraat synagogue found distant echoes in several English synagogues built during the 1930s, such as that of London-Walm Lane. The Linnaeusstraat synagogue itself, plundered during the Second World War, ceased holding services after 1956. When it was demolished in 1962, the copper grillework and the stained glass windows were rescued and taken to a synagogue in Ramat Gan, Israel.

Jacob Obrechtplein

In the Amsterdam-South area, on Jacob Obrechtplein, another brick synagogue, but one of a very different style, was dedicated in the same year as that of the Linnaeusstraat, and for about the same number of people—about 330 men and 120 women (Figs. 231, 232). This one, by the Jewish architect Harry Elte (1880–1945),

Figure 231. Amsterdam, Jacob Obrechtplein, 1927–28, exterior.

cost 70,000 florins more than Baars's synagogue but included fewer facilities in the community building. As Elte had already remodeled the Utrecht synagogue in 1926 and the Amersfoort synagogue of 1727, he might have been experienced in making the most efficient use of synagogue spaces, but he evidently put design ahead of pure efficiency (an instance was a recess at the street corner intended to preserve a tree which then grew on the site). Having the chance to design something of his own rather than remodel, he produced a complex geometric building in a style derived from Frank Lloyd Wright's early works, especially Unity Temple near Chicago and the Larkin Company Administration Building in Buffalo. In so doing, and by using brick, he followed a style then current in the Netherlands, as in Robert van't Hoff's Villa Henny at Huis ter Heide (1916) and W. M. Dudok's Town Hall at Hilversum (1928–32).

At the east end of the lot, the architect designed a prayer hall longer in its north-south axis, reflecting the conditions of the site. The community building at the southwest is connected to the main structure in one continuous composition of light-colored brick planes and solids. The tall prismatic steeple at the west end of the community house balances the broad mass of the synagogue hall. The combination of community center and sanctuary suggests the close ties between prayer and Jewish community life.

The synagogue interior is about 21.5 m. wide and about 10 m. high. It is a tall rectangular room with smooth white walls, marble floors, fixed oak seats with no decorative moldings, a rectilinear choir gallery, and twelve tall and thin rectangular windows (to symbolize the twelve tribes)—all smooth, simple, and clear. Max Eisler, a contemporary Jewish critic, remarked on

Figure 232. Amsterdam, Jacob Obrechtplein, interior to bimah and entrance.

the building's lack of mysticism or display, and on its modesty and sincerity. A taste for clarity, rectilinearity, and planarity can be found also in the contemporary International Style synagogues of Plauen, Brno, and Hove-Liberal; in Josef Hoffmann's unexecuted designs of the late 1920s for Žilina; and in several other simple buildings of the 1920s and 1930s, including synagogues at Bratislava and Budapest-Lágymányos orthodox (see Figs. 28, 156–161). At Amsterdam, however, the simplicity is tempered by aestheticism and a sense of dramatic effect. This is seen outside in the interplay of rectangles, and in the contrasts between low parts and a steeple or between building cubes and thin white cornices. It is seen inside in the height of the thin windows, in the unusually large tubular clusters of the chandeliers, and in the contrast between a low entrance aisle beneath the low gallery and the leap upward of the remainder of the wall. The tile incrustation on the squat piers under the gallery and under the ark arch, the ornament on the ark doors, and the candelabra near the ark, which looks like skyscraper towers decorated with bulbs, show Elte's interest in applied decoration. His artistry and dramatic sense are most visible in the composition of the ark, where he said that he hoped to emphasize the Torah's eternal guidance. As constraints of the site precluded an ark wall window, Elte substituted a dark reflective-surfaced typanum set in a tall parabolic arch, a form that can be high and impressive without being pointed, so that it avoids introducing Gothic Christian connotations. The ark doors open behind a round arch at the base of the tympanum. The whole composition receives light and emphasis from three colored glass bands set into the soffit of the parabolic arch. They add color and variety without resorting to a Moorish tabernacle or an altarpiece. Elte's parabolic arches and glazed bands were probably inspired by those in the Utrecht Post Office (1918–24 by J. Crouwel), where Elte surely saw them while he worked on the synagogue of that city.

The prewar congregation is remembered for eastern European warmth and for relative prosperity. As entrepreneurs rather than employees, many members could have developed a vision that took them beyond Amsterdam to the country at large, and to ideas of modernity which one could learn from the young industrial cities of America. Indeed, even before approving Elte's new design, synagogue members had worshipped in an older building with modern strip windows and simplified forms taken from domestic architecture.

The synagogue on Jacob Obrechtplein had no imitators, but synagogues in London, including Hendon-United and Whitfield Street-Liberal, employ prisms and broad planes in their geometric designs. The parabolic arch as an ark-area motif reappeared after the Second World War at London-St. John's Wood United and in Germany at the new Essen synagogue (see Fig. 142). The Amsterdam synagogue itself, renamed the Rav Aaron Schuster Synagogue, received an insensitive restoration in 1969 which destroyed some of its ornament and gold leaf decoration, but the exterior is still a handsome Modernist work of its time.

Lekstraat

The Lekstraat synagogue is completely different from the synagogues of the late 1920s, and is allied to the International Style. It looks like a plain stone box pierced only by square windows of two sizes and groupings, and covered by a thin lid (Figs. 233, 234). The architect, A. Elzas (1907–4?), was associated with the advanced artistic group, De 8. Its journal published photographs of the building, which Elzas discussed at its dedication in terms of its architectural simplicity, its use of natural materials, and its consequent emphasis on the essentials—the ark and the bimah. In an interview, he spoke of building for the ages by reducing a design to elementary shapes and smooth surfaces. We now see that his building remains firmly tied to its own age, sharing these characteristics of style with contemporary synagogues in Rotterdam-Botersloot, Brno, and Hove-Liberal.

Elzas won a competition among nine Jewish architects, judged by congregation leaders and three architects. The competition terms had little to do with designing for the ages. They specified that 450 men and 250 women had to be seated, that there be community rooms and staff apartments in an adjacent building, that the sanctuary be so well lit by windows that no electric lights would be needed even on dark winter days, and that no tower was wanted (a clear criticism of the synagogues of Baars and Elte). Elzas's design looked as spare and economical as the competition terms implied, but he faced his reinforced concrete building with stone for the sake of dignity, and used color and textural contrasts inside—dark red floors, white walls, copper lights, oak seats. To emphasize the ark, he faced much of the east wall with pavonazzo marble set in a rectilinear niche with rounded corners. A smaller, dark-faced but identically shaped form constituted the front of the ark. As in the other modern orthodox synagogues of Amsterdam, the bimah was low so as to allow good visibility beyond it.

The building was completed too soon before the onset of war to have had immediate descendants, but the synagogue at Dublin-Terenure (1953) has comparable smooth surfaces, small square windows in a row contrasting with larger windows in other rigid rows, and a lidlike roof.

Different as they are, the Amsterdam synagogues of 1928–38 are comparable in that all of them could have been something other than a synagogue. The first two resemble churches in Amsterdam which are made of brick, have parabolic arches and geometric window-framing that hint at Gothic tracery, or have geometric blocks used in the Dudok-Wright manner. One may, for instance, compare Elte's synagogue to F. B. Jantzen's Jerusalemkerk of 1929 in Amsterdam. The Lekstraat synagogue could be confused with a school or a clinic if it did not have Hebrew letters on the entrance facade. The Jews evidently thought they were suggesting universal values in these buildings, or values held in common with their fellow Amsterdammers, for they deemphasized specific Jewish identification. These Dutch Jews built as if they were Dutch first and Jewish second. At least in comparison with the German and French Jews, they were correct in assessing their place in society. Amsterdam dockworkers later struck in response to Nazi persecution of Jews; they did so, it has been said, not because the dockworkers loved Jews in general but because foreigners were attacking residents of Amsterdam. Dutch Christians who protected Jews during the Second World War confirmed the Jews' faith in their countrymen and in the

Figure 233. Amsterdam, Lekstraat, 1936–37, exterior in 1971.

Figure 234. Amsterdam, Lekstraat, interior to ark.

universal values of brotherhood. The local, national, and universal styles of synagogue architecture prophesied the most heartening aspects of Dutch Jewish experience in the following decade.

BIBLIOGRAPHIES

J. F. van Agt, *Synagogen in Amsterdam,* The Hague, 1974, to be supplemented by: P. Bregstein et al., *Herinnering Joods Amsterdam,* Amsterdam, 1978, and M. Gans, *De oude Amsterdamse Jodenhoek nu,* Baarn, 1975.

LINNAEUSSTRAAT

M. Danvers, "De nieuwe synagoge in Amsterdam-Oost. Een onderhoud met den architect, Den Heer Jac. S. Baars," *Het Vrijdagavond* V (1928), pp. 362–63.

M. Eisler, "Die neue Synagoge Amsterdam-Oost," *Menorah* VIII, #3/4 (1930), pp. 165–73.

OBRECHTPLEIN

M. Eisler, "Eine moderner Tempel in Amsterdam," *Menorah* VII, #11/12 (1929), pp. 559–67.

———, "Vom Geist der Synagoge," *Menorah* VIII, #1 (1930), pp. 77–86, esp. p. 80.

Moderne Bouwkunst in Nederland, XIII, *Kerken,* Rotterdam, 1932, pp. 19–23.

"Synagogue by Harry van [sic] Elte," *Architectural Forum* LIX (Oct. 1933), pp. 297–98.

Synagoge Jacob Obrechtplein.Orde van de plechtige inwijding . . . 8 mei, 1928, Amsterdam, 1928.

LEKSTRAAT

"De Synagoge aan de Lekstraat te Amsterdam," *Bouwkundig Weekblad. Architectura,* LXIX (1938), pp. 429–34.

A. Elzas, "Die nieuwe Synagoge aan de Lekstraat," *Nieuwe Israëlietisch Weekblad,* Nov. 26, 1937.

"Juryrapport betreffende de ingekomen ontwerpen voor den bouw eener Synagoge," *Bouwkundig Weekblad. Architectura* LVI (1935), pp. 297–306, with most or all of the competition entries.

I. Salomons, "Lekstraat Synagoge. Functionalisme als ruimtekunst," *Wonen TA/BK,* June 1978, pp. 7–15 (not consulted).

J. B. van Loghem, "Een synagoge te Amsterdam," *De 8 en Opbouw* IX (1938), pp. 239–48.

Scandinavia

Copenhagen and Stockholm

Synagogues in Scandinavia, although different in style and date of origin, reveal varied responses to the problem of synagogue design in an area with few Jews and a short history of Jewish settlement. The synagogue of Oslo looks like a simple and charming country chapel, while that of Trondheim is a remodeled nineteenth-century *Rundbogenstil* railway building. The Turku synagogue is a brick building in a *Rundbogenstil* of no memorable character except for the central drum and cupola, which can be seen from several vantage points. The Helsinki synagogue has smooth walls broken by a triad of two-storey round-headed windows, with a row of circular windows above and a cupola pitched higher than that of Turku to be more easily seen. Both synagogues have street-corner sites and, like most synagogues in Scandinavia, were allowed general visibility. The Göteborg synagogue stands free on a waterfront site. The prominent location, unusual for so early a date (1855), indicates local toleration of the Jews. It has a tripartite facade articulated by vertically striped side bays, a horizontally striped, three-windowed central bay, and little corner lanterns with cupolas topped by six-pointed stars. Originality in design reflected the modernity of the Reform service inside. Modern, too, was the cast iron which helped to hold the two tiers of galleries. The Norrköping synagogue, erected three years later, has a squarish plan and a drum and small dome, perhaps to suggest the Jews' oriental origins.

The two most distinguished works of synagogue architecture in Scandinavia are those of Copenhagen and Stockholm. The former is exceptionally handsome, in the neoclassical taste that was current in the 1830s, while the latter is a fine example of the stylistic experiments that we have just noted in Scandinavian synagogue architecture generally.

Copenhagen

The Copenhagen synagogue, dedicated in 1833, has a street-front entrance on Krystalgade, enjoying a more open situation than that of most other city synagogues of the time (Fig. 235). Relieving the smooth-walled rectangular exterior is a row of crisp-edged, rectilinear clerestory windows which accelerate the rhythm of three windows on the main seating level.

The prayer hall is a galleried basilica about 22 m. by 24 m. and about 13.5 m. high (Fig. 236), with over 650 seats, and standing room for about a hundred people. Two tiers of polygonal piers support cornices and a coffered ceiling. When G. F. Hetsch (1788–1864), the German-born architect, presented his plans in 1829, he said that he had tried to introduce a slight oriental touch. This accounts for several Egyptian details: trapezoidal windows on the main level and in the clerestory of the east and west facades; sloping pilaster strips and door openings on the east and west sides; and the coved cornice of the ark frame. When Hetsch designed this synagogue, and when David Mocatta designed the contemporary synagogue in Ramsgate (see Fig. 253), architects still suggested orientalism by using Egyptian style. Hetsch, who was born in Stuttgart, may have known Friedrich Weinbrenner's Egyptian design for nearby Karlsruhe (1798), either from having seen the building or a print of it. Prints of synagogues in Munich and Frankfurt am Main showed their Egyptian details. In Copen-

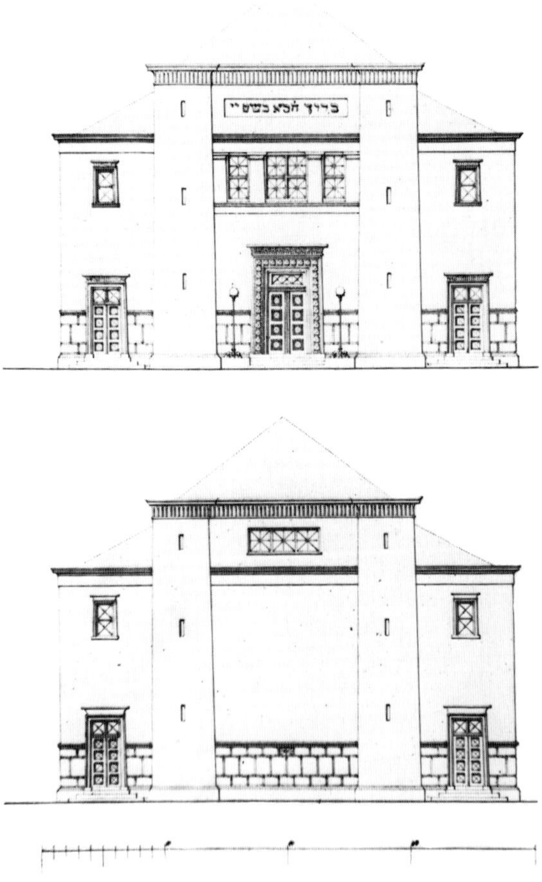

Figure 235. Copenhagen, 1831–33, exterior of facade and east (ark) end, drawn by G. F. Hetsch.

hagen itself, M.G.B. Bindesbøll later designed Egyptian details in the Thorwaldsen Museum; he had been a consultant to the synagogue officials in January 1829, and may then have recommended the style's permanence, dignified strength, and appropriate Near Eastern connections. The synagogue's overall character stresses neoclassical simplicity rather than orientalism, however, and the building has a delicate gravity. Unusual features, such as the Egyptian details and the bracketed stilt blocks above the ground floor capitals, do not disturb this impression. The building suggests that Danish Jews in the 1820s and 1830s wanted to adopt Danish tastes. The choice of consulting architects shows their interest in contemporary society and its finest interpreters.

Stockholm

A generation later, the Jews of Stockholm erected a freestanding synagogue in the center of the city, but only in a byway (Figs. 237, 238). The location reflected the Jews' position on the brink of the full legal equality they obtained in 1870, the year of the building's dedication. Like Copenhagen's Jews, those of the Swedish capital tried to find a good architect. In Fredrik Vilhelm Scholander (1816–81) they found a man who provided a synagogue in harmony with their functional requirements and with their need for self-expression. The legal and social situation here was akin to (but more open than) that of the Berlin Jews a decade earlier, when the imposing but unusual Oranienburgerstrasse synagogue was begun (see Figs. 122, 124). Since the Jewish leaders in Stockholm surely knew about the Berlin synagogue, which opened in 1866, we may imagine them taking some lessons from the larger community in Berlin and applying them with appropriate modifications. Ideas of nationhood had by then become so strong in Germany and Scandinavia that the Jews seem to have accepted the inevitability, if not the desirability, of a special "national" expression of their own within a larger national culture. The Stockholm building lacks the exotic shiny dome of Berlin, but the Swedish synagogue does not look like other architecture of its time or neighborhood any more than did the German synagogue.

The Stockholm synagogue is a massive plastered brick structure. Its rectilinear body is framed by four flat-topped corner towers holding staircases. Between the two western towers, the higher central bay projects slightly. The resulting three-part facade with its heavy cornices is close enough to ancient Near Eastern forms and Temple descriptions to give the synagogue an Eastern identity. When the architect wanted to add a religious aspect by suggesting Gothic windows while avoiding Gothic style, he designed triangular-topped windows rather than pointed arches.

Inside, too, the galleried basilica shows stylistic freedom. Like many buildings which used Gothic revival principles more than forms, this one lays bare its structural elements. As much inert, solid matter as possible has been eliminated. Compound piers support galleries and the ceiling; they are clearly made of iron, and their design as compound piers breaks up their mass and indicates the differences among various elements supported by the individual parts of the piers. Big brackets hold the ceiling. Scholander distinguished the ceiling filling from its framework. He placed skylights in the ceiling bays even though they are insignificant sources of light as compared with the windows and light fixtures; this suggests that he wanted to eliminate or make transparent as many surfaces as he could. Scholander's desire to peel away extra surfaces can also be seen in the opening of his walls by triads of tall windows, in the piercing of brackets and parapets, and in the breaking up of arch and bracket borders by cusps. Within the simple building structure, all elements are lively and sharp. By combining the galleries of a conventional masonry basilica with piers, brackets, and windows of a type seen in wood and iron buildings, and by freely incorporating details from Assyrian, Gothic, and Moorish architecture, the architect made the Stockholm synagogue interior more original and personal than most synagogue designs.

The structure has been maintained and restored. It seats 830 worshippers who follow Reform practice; the bimah stands near the ark, and an organ and women's choir provide music during services. This community has grown, unlike many others on the Continent, because Sweden accepted displaced persons after 1945 as well as Polish Jews who later left their native country during anti-Semitic episodes.

Figure 236. Copenhagen, interior to ark, drawn by G. F. Hetsch.

Figure 237. Stockholm, 1869–70 exterior in 1982

Figure 238. Stockholm, interior to ark in 1982.

BIBLIOGRAPHY

C. V. Jacobowsky, *Goeteborgs Mosaiska Foersamling,* Göteborg, 1955, pp. 69ff.

Jewish Chronicle, July 20, 1866, p. 5 (on the first Oslo synagogue project).

Jewish Community, Stockholm, *A Few Facts about Jewish Life in Sweden,* n.d.

Jødisk Familieblads Festnummer i Anledning af Synagogens 100 Aars Jubilaeum, Copenhagen, 1933, pp. 2–19.

J. Lever, ed., *Catalogue of the Drawings in the Royal Institute of British Architects, Drawings Collection,* London, 1973, vol. G–K, p. 106. Hetsch presented his signed drawings in 1838.

M. H. Narrowe, "The Synagogues of Stockholm," *World Over* XXX (March 14, 1969), pp. 8–9.

C. R. Nyblom, *Fredrik Vilhelm Scholander,* Stockholm, 1899.

Wischnitzer, *Architecture,* pp. 183–85, 216–17, 227–28.

Good photographs of the Oslo synagogue are at YIVO, New York. For photographs and information about Trondheim, I am indebted to Staale Sinding-Larsen, and for photographs of Stockholm, I thank Rabbi Morton H. Narrowe.

United Kingdom*

Belfast

In 1829, Daniel O'Connell, the "Irish Liberator," wrote that Ireland "is the only Christian country that I know of unsullied by any act of persecution of the Jews." This honorable record has been maintained to the present day. The reasons may include the sensitivity of some Irishmen to their own position as subordinate to the English, and a feeling of kinship with others who have experienced discrimination. It may also be due to the absence of Jewish settlement during the Middle Ages and Renaissance, when obscurantist persecution was common elsewhere. From the seventeenth through the nineteenth century, the number of Jews was so small as hardly to warrant notice, much less excite fear or hostility. By the end of the 1880s, when the population was swelled by migrants from eastern Europe, the rights of all religions were enshrined in laws which were no more burdensome to Jews than they were to Catholics.

The earliest reference to a Jew in Belfast dates from 1652, but there is no evidence of other Jews or a synagogue in the city. In 1771, a Jewish butcher is documented, which has led some writers to assume the existence of a Jewish community that required a ritual slaughterer. After the Napoleonic wars, the Jews in Belfast were too few to form a *minyan;* the congregation was organized only in 1861 by German-born merchants who began holding regular synagogue services later in the decade, in a house in the Holywood area.

*There is a discussion of the London-Upper Berkeley Street (Reform) temple in the Hamburg-Poolstrasse section.

Great Victoria Street

By 1871, one of these immigrant merchants, Daniel Joseph Jaffe, was wealthy enough to pay for a synagogue in Great Victoria Street. The congregation then had fifty-five individuals; the building could hold eighty. The foundation stone was laid in 1871, and the synagogue opened in 1872. Nathan Solomon Joseph, an English Jewish architect, designed a colorful yellow and red brick structure with Moorish detail that gave an Eastern identity to the synagogue, making a statement which his clients must have approved. The dedication address, dealing with the Jews' progress in Ireland in the preceding decades, explains the Jews' sense of security in showing their uniqueness.

Annesley Street

By 1903, there were eleven hundred Jews in Belfast, owing to the eastern European migration that had augmented the Jewish population throughout the British Isles. The Russo-Polish Jews left a modest synagogue in Regency Street, having merged with the earlier German congregation in 1903, and erected a new building. Most of its £4,000 cost was obtained from Daniel Joseph Jaffe's son, Sir Otto Jaffe, who had been Lord Mayor of Belfast. Young & Mackenzie, a firm of Christian architects, designed the synagogue, but the advisory architect was B. S. Jacobs of Hull, probably a Jew.

The site lay in Annesley Street, Carlisle Circus, and was about 90 feet by 50 feet, easily able to accommodate a structure of 75 feet by 37 feet. The synagogue held 355 men on the ground floor and 212 women in the gallery. It contained a vestibule with a staircase, a ritual bath, a vestry room, and modern arrangements for heating, lighting, and sanitation. The brick building was trimmed with local Giffnock stone; observers at the time of its dedication in 1904 pointed out the glazed tile dadoes in the vestibule and staircase, and the varnished pitch pine internal woodwork and roof timbers. Its style was described as "a simple treatment of the early round-arched type," which meant a mixture of Romanesque and classical elements. On the building's sides, round-headed windows, filled with leaded lights in geometrical shapes, occupied the center of panels articulated by brick pilasters, forming distinct bays on the exterior. Stone jambs in high relief and a carved tympanum accentuated the main door. In every other way, the synagogue was reticent, reminiscent of modest chapels built throughout Great Britain for Protestant denominations other than the Church of England.

New Synagogue

After the Second World War, the congregation realized that it would eventually need a new synagogue, and it established a building committee which included a local architect. Eugene Rosenberg, of the well-known London architectural firm of Yorke, Rosenberg & Mardall, provided the design; Karl Kapolka was an associate architect. They submitted a model in 1961, began building in 1963, and completed the work in October 1964 (Fig. 239).

The site is located in a pleasant northern residential area where many Jews live. Synagogues built a hundred years earlier tended to be in city centers and were seldom associated with trees and lawns. Synagogues built since about 1920, however, have usually been in outlying areas to which Jews moved once residence restrictions were lifted on the Continent and when public or private transportation made suburban living generally more practical. The perimeter of the site is planted with trees which soften the impact of a specially shaped structure in a neighborhood of sloping-roofed and cozy houses, and the synagogue itself is only about 22 feet high so that it does not impose itself upon the area.

The site's main axis runs approximately north-south, but because of the synagogue's east-west orientation it must lie perpendicular to the main axis, and fills much of the available width. It had to be placed at the northern end of the site because an existing community center occupied some of the land to the south. The sanctuary had to be the easternmost element so that the ark could be directed toward Jerusalem. The synagogue's western portion, which faces the main access street, might have incorporated the facade, as was usual, but the architect made the main access from the parking lot south and west of the community center building. This meant that the street front is only a blank wall forming one side of the windowless cloakroom annex.

The synagogue as a whole was designed in three clearly separated sections: prayer hall, service wing, and connecting entrance. The prayer hall is polygonal, while the other parts are rectilinear and perpendicular to each other. The prayer hall is faced with gray textured concrete and has a few vertical strip windows. The entrance, by contrast, is glazed, while the service wing has solid brick walls and is clearly subordinate to the other parts.

The architects arranged the functional requirements to suit seven hundred worshippers. Because the six supporting piers are relegated to the perimeter of the sanctuary, the interior is unobstructed and everyone enjoys a clear view of the services (Fig. 240). (This modern orthodox congregation does not conceal women behind grilles, but separates them only by a brass railing and by a slight rise in the floor level under their seats.) The sanctuary has excellent acoustics, aided by textured walls and carpeting which also enhance the comfort, quiet, and overall feeling of restrained elegance. The limited fenestration focuses the congregation's attention inside, makes window breakage less likely, and keeps the temperature constant.

The Belfast design is characteristic of its period in having clearly separated elements, chastely simple and planar exterior surfaces, and walls that look like thin shells rather than

Figure 239. Belfast, 1961–64, exterior.

sculptural masses (see Figs. 17, 250). The differentiation of each area formally and spatially puts this building in the mainstream of the rational-functional architectural theory current at the time, and to other work by Yorke, Rosenberg & Mardall, including Gatwick Airport near London. Like other buildings of the 1960s, however, this one has strong contrasts of solid and void with an emphasis on the former, and its windows are vertical strips. Individual elements are akin to those of other well-known buildings that immediately preceded it. The glazed entrance, raised slightly on low and broad steps, recalls Ludwig Mies van der Rohe's Crown Hall, a much-publicized building at the Illinois Institute of Technology in Chicago, where other structures are blank-walled and brick-faced like the cloakroom wing in Belfast.

A few aspects of the form carry emotionally charged or symbolic meaning. The central plan expresses both the unity of the Lord as described in essential Hebrew prayers, and the unity of the congregation. The reinforced-concrete ceiling beams, extending from six

Figure 240. Belfast, interior to ark.

supporting piers of the same material, intersect to form a six-pointed star of David in the center of the ceiling. It is visible only inside the building and is, thus, a private symbol. The symbolic suggestions do not force the whole building to look like a six-pointed star, the tablets of the Law, or the Tent in the Wilderness.

As an example of tasteful contemporary design and undramatic presence, the Belfast synagogue may show the congregation's and the architects' understanding that they had nothing to prove. It is a building free of manifestoes where the congregation could satisfy only itself. It did not have to express Jewish survival or Jewish success. The Jewish communities in Ireland, despite their small number, had provided mayors for both Belfast and Dublin, and had been commended for their contributions to Irish industry and commerce. The Jews were as well accepted as they were anywhere in Europe.

Moreover, by this time, it was commonplace in Europe for synagogues to use contemporary styles free of exotic elements. That a synagogue no longer looks like an oddity among religious buildings is due in part to the fact that churches now rarely use cross-shaped or basilican designs, either. The central plans employed since the Second Vatican Council and the earlier use by Protestants of unified congregational rooms have minimized the differences between places of Christian and Jewish worship. Here at Belfast, we see an International Style, but also an interfaith style.

BIBLIOGRAPHY

Architect and Building News CCXXIX, #8 (Feb. 23, 1966), pp. 342–46.

Architects' Journal CXLIII, #11 (Mar. 16, 1966), pp. 709–19, 721–22.

Architectural Review CXXXI, #1 (Jan. 1962), pp. 28–29.

Architecture d'Aujourd'hui XXXVI (Apr.–May 1966), p. 97.

AZJ XXXV, August 15, 1871.

R. Banham, *The Architecture of Yorke, Rosenberg, and Mardall,* London, [1972], for buildings by the most recent architects.

L. Hyman, *The Jews of Ireland from the Earliest Times to the Year 1910,* Shannon, 1972.

Jewish Chronicle, Sept. 2, 1904; supplement to July 30, 1965.

B. Shillman, *A Short History of the Jews in Ireland,* Dublin and London [1945].

Canterbury

The former synagogue in King Street, Canterbury, is the most charming and purest example of the Egyptian revival in synagogue architecture (Fig. 241). Set back from the small street behind a gate, it is in an inconspicuous location that corresponded to the position of Jews in Canterbury. Never a significant element in the population, the congregation had only fourteen full members in 1842, representing about thirty families.

The modern history of Canterbury's Jews began in the mid-eighteenth century. In 1762 or 1763, resident Jews seem to have built a synagogue in the St. Dunstan's area, probably with funds given by a wealthy Jewish inhabitant. The building had to be outside the city walls, as synagogues were not allowed inside the city, a circumstance common at the time.

In 1846, the South Eastern Railway Company took the synagogue site for a convenient ap-

Figure 241. Canterbury, 1846–48, exterior in 1983.

proach to the city's West Station. In compensation, the Jews received no more than a quarter of the money needed to build elsewhere because, as usual, they held the site only on lease. They had to launch a fund appeal for a new building in a crowded old area in the middle of town. Following a custom initiated by other congregations, they sent letters to all the Jewish congregations of the British Empire, and received donations from as far away as Dublin and Montego Bay, Jamaica. Three zealous congregation members, all related, gave over ten pounds each. Christians in Canterbury contributed one hundred pounds, a fact that signified to the Jews the "liberality of sentiment and religious toleration" fostered by the Jews' own integrity. The cost reached about £1,250, and some of the deficit was made up by Sir Moses Montefiore, the great philanthropist residing not far away at Ramsgate, who had the honor of laying the cornerstone in September 1847, and of opening the door a year later. The congregation saved the ark, bimah, chandeliers, and wainscoting from the old synagogue to use in the new one, a gesture of economy as well as of filial piety; the ark, moreover, was said to have come from the eighteenth-century Hambro Synagogue in London, making it especially precious, although its imitation veined-marble and lotus-leaf columns may have been added in nineteenth-century Canterbury.

The synagogue itself is an oblong building, about 40 feet long, 27 feet wide, and 30 feet high, resembling a small Egyptian temple. Two columns with lotus capitals form its porch. It has a simple entrance door and narrow windows on the three other sides. The openings scarcely detract from the building's severely mural appearance, and the impression of solidity is intensified by the use of Portland cement, imitating granite, on the facade.

The interior had a central bimah, columns with lotus-leaf capitals, a western women's gallery on obelisk-shaped supports, and the often-used inscription, "Know Before Whom Thou Standest."

The designer was a local Christian, Hezekiah Marshall, aided by Thomas French Cousins (or Cozens), a builder in Canterbury. No surviving documents explain their use of Egyptian style. One local Jew wrote about the "medieval" (he meant Gothic) style as evoking memories of (Christian) persecution. Those memories were evidently more vivid to him than thoughts of ancient Egyptian persecution. He also resisted suggestions that only "medieval" styles would harmonize with other architecture in Canterbury. Later in the nineteenth century, a Jewish leader suggested that Marshall wanted to remind the Jews to appreciate living in England rather than in Egyptian bondage. There was also a model of an Egyptian building in the local museum, which might have inspired the designer in his efforts to find something unusual to use in a commission for unusual clients whose origin lay in ancient Mediterranean lands. Perhaps some knowledge had reached him of Egyptian details in earlier synagogues such as those of Munich (1826), Copenhagen (1833), and Hobart, Tasmania (1843). Perhaps he took his cue from the old ark, if its lotus capitals were not his own modifications. Early-nineteenth-century architectural critics had also linked the Jews with Egyptian architecture because both were seen to be enduring but not progressive.

Even though some Jews might have been made uneasy by the unflattering connotations of Egyptian style, they had, at least, an attractive and distinctive synagogue. Enthusiasm for antique style was so marked that even the ritual bath was built in 1851 as a miniature brick-faced temple set in the garden behind the synagogue. The congregation was pleased that the synagogue stood on the site of a Knights Templar hospice, because the Templars had been egregious enemies of the medieval Jews, and that the synagogue site also adjoined the monastic foundation called the Black Prince's Chantry, named for Edward, Prince of Wales (1330–76), who also was hostile to Jews. The synagogue's location was taken as an indication of the security and peace eventually achieved by the Israelites of England.

The synagogue was repainted and renovated in 1861, and repaired in 1889, but in the late nineteenth century the Canterbury congregation declined, as did all old Jewish communities in market towns of the provinces. Services were held in the building during the First World War but by 1931 some furnishings including two Torah scrolls had been given to a synagogue in Oxford. The building was sold in 1937 and used during the 1950s for secular purposes. In the 1960s, St. Alphege's Church undertook to repair it and convert it into a church hall. Further repairs were made in the early 1980s. Although it is hard to imagine a suitable connection between Egyptian design and modern English Protestantism, there is at least historic consistency in the development from Egyptians to Jews to Christians. Despite the fact that the building is now leased to sponsors of band concerts, the Jews of England and all lovers of modest and charming old buildings can be glad that it survives.

BIBLIOGRAPHY

S. Cantacuzino, *Canterbury,* London, 1970 (City Buildings Series).

D. Cohn-Sherbok, "Sir Moses Montefiore and the Canterbury Jewish Community," *Bygone Kent* II, #5 (May 1981), pp. 309–12.

——— and L. Grace, "Jewish Community of Canterbury," *Kent Life,* Nov. 1978, pp. 42–43.

J. Jacobs, *Narrative of the Erection of the New Synagogue at Canterbury,* MS written in 1851, London, United Synagogue Library and Archives; typed copy in Canterbury Public Library.

Jewish Chronicle, Oct. 1, 1847, May 24, 1889, Sept. 27, 1889.

Kentish Observer, Sept. 21, 1848.

C. Roth, *The Rise of Provincial Jewry,* London, 1950, pp. 46–49.

S. Williamson, "The Jewish Community of Canterbury," *Bygone Kent* IV, #3 (March 1983), pp. 174–76.

I am grateful to the local history librarians at the Canterbury Public Library, to officials of the United Synagogue, London, and to Canon C. Tufton, Canterbury.

London

In the medieval City of London, after the Crown relaxed canon law restrictions on synagogue building, synagogues stood in several streets and even near churches. At various periods, synagogues existed in Basinghall, Coleman, Gresham, and Threadneedle streets, and in Ironmonger Lane. The one best known to archaeologists was built in 1280, donated to the Jewish community by one Aaron, son of Vives, who was protected by the king's brother. The floor area was about 27 feet by 36 feet. An adjacent courtyard was larger than the building.

Creechurch Lane

After the Jewish expulsion from England in 1290, no officially acknowledged synagogues existed there until the Jews were readmitted under Oliver Cromwell in the mid-seventeenth century. In 1657, they converted a building in Creechurch Lane into a synagogue, and in 1674 made it a galleried basilica. At first, the women were hidden behind lattices, apparently on the men's level; the 1674 alterations included the cutting away of much of an upper floor of the building and the insertion of two women's galleries, each 40 feet long, raised above the principal floor. There had been a comparable alteration in Amsterdam, producing the synagogue of 1639 there (see Figs. 223, 224). In London, Tuscan columns under the gallery continued upward until they were joined by arches that held the coved nave ceiling. The design was already known in London church architecture, as in St. Sepulchre-without-Newgate (1666–70), but arches were unusual in synagogue galleries until the nineteenth century.

Bevis Marks

London's oldest surviving synagogue, known as Bevis Marks, serves a Sephardic congregation that was established in the seventeenth century. It stands in Heneage Lane in the East End of London, beyond the limits of the City where Jews could not yet own property. The synagogue was built in a lane because Jews were not allowed to erect a synagogue on Bevis Marks, the nearest public street.

The building looks today much as it did in 1699–1701, when it was constructed (Figs. 242, 243). It is a two-storeyed galleried box, 80 by 50 feet, built of red brick with cornices and openings marked with painted stone dressings. The simple facade door is flanked by two small windows; on the upper floor a central elliptical-headed window opens between narrower round-headed ones. A simple exterior was typical of synagogues of that period, but this is handsomer than most because its congregation was wealthy.

The interior has smooth plaster walls and a flat ceiling decorated with rosettes, from some of which hang chandeliers. The galleries run along three sides of the room, as at Livorno's synagogue which had just been remodeled using this plan (1693ff.) (see Fig. 195), though in London the galleries curve outward toward the walls at the eastern end. The galleries rest on twelve Tuscan columns, varied by square piers at the corners; they were originally punctuated over each pier by a finial holding a candelabrum. Rosettes and plaster cornices are the only applied ornament. The furnishings are substantial and elegant. As in the Sephardic synagogue of Amsterdam (1671–75) (see Fig. 228), the ark is a multipart two-storey chest with columns dividing the lower storey and flanking the raised portion of the upper storey, where gilt-lettered Ten Commandments are displayed. The ark at Amsterdam, however, looks more like a cabinet, while that of London looks like a late-Renaissance church facade because its two storeys are connected by scrolls. The bimah, at the west, is much like that of Amsterdam—a raised platform with low parapets—but in London, the balusters are turned rather than carved. Wooden seats run along the east-west axis, facing the center as is usual in Spanish-Portuguese and Italian-rite synagogues.

The building's basic form and its fittings are sober, but the synagogue is saved from being dull by the ample light admitted through its large windows. The interior is animated by reflections and highlights on the turned surfaces of the woodwork, and on the beautiful brass chandeliers and candlesticks which have never been supplanted by electric fixtures.

Figure 242. London, Bevis Marks, 1699–1701, exterior in 1983.

The synagogue was built because increasing Jewish immigration had made the Creechurch Lane synagogue so crowded that women were asked to go home so that men could occupy the galleries. The builder was Joseph Avis, a Quaker carpenter who had worked on the Merchant Taylors' Hall and on St. Bride, Fleet Street, where the synagogue supervisors could have seen his work. It is tempting to think that they hired him also because his religious beliefs were out of the mainstream and he could not have been part of the "Establishment." Moreover, he was a man of moral distinction, if it is true that when he found the building costs to be less than the allotted £2,650, he returned the leftover money. We know that Avis superin-

Figure 243. London, Bevis Marks, interior to ark in 1928.

tended the construction from 1699 to 1701, but we are not sure that he designed it, for documents record payment to Henry Ramsay, a joiner, who made a model of the building in 1694, perhaps to someone else's design. In comparison with the newly rebuilt City of London churches, the Bevis Marks Synagogue is modest both outside and in, but it has features seen in those churches: comparable proportions in smaller size, similar windows, galleries, an ark design like that of altarpieces, and marbleized columns. The synagogue is comparable in style to up-to-date religious buildings of a metropolis, whereas the synagogues of Fürth (1692) (see Fig. 147) and Frankfurt am Main (1711) had Gothic vaults and women's annexes on one side which made them look like old-fashioned buildings for an exceptional group of people. Bevis Marks is comparable to the contemporary synagogue in Berlin-Heidereutergasse (see Figs. 117, 118), in having a logical and well-coordinated design, abundant light, and a nonsectarian style which gave the impression that confident and prosperous people worshipped there. Queen Anne herself is said to have donated a wooden beam for the Bevis Marks Synagogue, revealing the official benevolence accorded to useful and rich Jews, a phenomenon known in Berlin as well. (A ruler's favor also resulted in a fine synagogue at Düsseldorf [1798], where galleries on three sides may have been derived from those of Bevis Marks.)

Few changes have been made since 1701, apart from new shapes of window panes, two steps added to the bimah around 1730, and the rebuilding of the vestry. The original social setting has changed, however, because the Jews' movement away from the East End deprived this synagogue and its former neighbor, the Great Ashkenazic Synagogue, of the population and institutions that once clustered nearby. To accommodate the migrating population, the Sephardic congregation eventually established branches in Wigmore and then Bryanston streets, in Maida Vale-Lauderdale Road (1896), Holland Park, Golders Green, Stamford Hill, and Wembley. Fortunately, their awareness of history led the Sephardic Jews to keep the Bevis Marks Synagogue, which is now officially designated as a national monument worthy of preservation.

BIBLIOGRAPHY

L. D. Barnett, *Bevis Marks Records*, Oxford, 1940–73.

R. Barnett, *The Synagogue of Bevis Marks*, London, 1960.

El Libro de los Acuerdos: Being the Records and Accounts of the Spanish and Portuguese Synagogue of London from 1663 to 1681, trans. L. D. Barnett, Oxford, 1931.

M. Gaster, *History of the Ancient Synagogue of the Spanish and Portuguese Jews*, London, 1901, esp. pp. 50–52, 61–72.

A. M. Hyamson, *The Sephardim of England*, London, 1951.

Royal Commission on Historic Monuments (England), *An Inventory of the Historical Monuments in London IV. The City*, London, 1929, pp. 10–12.

W. A. Samuel, *The First London Synagogue of the Resettlement*, London, 1924, pp. 44–46.

"Sketches of Anglo-Jewish History: V," *Jewish Chronicle*, Sept. 26, 1873, p. 429.

London–Great Synagogue

By the last decade of the seventeenth century, the Jews of London had separated into Sephardic and Ashkenazic congregations. The former commissioned the synagogue near Bevis Marks, while in 1692, the latter opened a synagogue nearby in Duke's Place. This one and its successors of 1722 and 1790 were known as the Great Synagogue. The 1790 synagogue, on the same site, was a handsome brick building donated largely by Judith Hart Levy, who contributed £4,000, a third of the cost. Men usually financed synagogues, and her ancestor, Moses Hart, had borne the expense of the synagogue of 1722, but Mrs. Levy was a widow whose children had died, so that she controlled the family money. The commission went to James Spiller, a Christian who confirmed his good professional reputation by building an unusually handsome galleried basilica (Figs. 244, 245).

The spacious building was large enough to seat about 500 men on the main floor and about 250 women upstairs. It had a broad coved-ceilinged nave separated from the lower aisle by unfluted Ionic columns made of stone. Light entered through clerestory windows and large round-headed windows in the north and south walls. The style was simple. The flat panels in the center of the ceiling, the gallery parapets and grilles, and the fronts of the men's benches were all plain, and the windows had rectangular panes of glass with radial panes only at the tops of the large gallery-level windows. The eastern wall alone had additional decoration: marbleized stone columns, a triumphal arch framing the curved apse for the ark, and plaster swags and garlands under the arch cornice and above the semicircular window in the coving above the ark. Gilt-edged plaques hung on the sides of the eastern wall, no doubt inscribed with prayers for the royal house, as is often seen in synagogues. A poem praising the donors, and the names of donors to the building fund later were painted in gold letters on panels around the walls under the women's gallery (as was also done at Livorno), but these were removed during a restoration in 1930. Seven brass chandeliers lit the room. The bimah was a large platform enclosed in a wooden balustrade with curved ends. Originally, there were no seats between it and the ark, but later in the nineteenth century seats were placed in the open space.

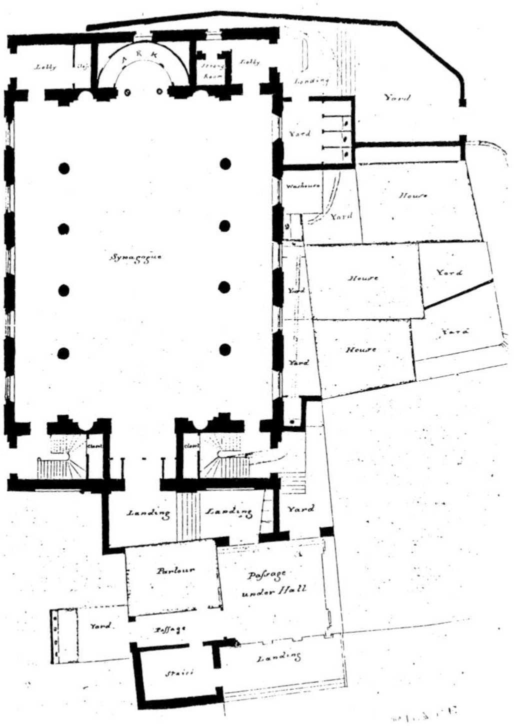

Figure 244. London, Great Synagogue, 1790–91, plan drawn by James Spiller.

The synagogue was redecorated and repaired in 1823, in 1852 by John Wallen, in

Figure 245. London, Great Synagogue, interior to ark, aquatint by A. C. Pugin and Thomas Rowlandson, ca. 1819.

1899–1900, and in 1930. The entrances were altered and the choir gallery was enlarged, changes which improved access and safety in case of fire. Two other alterations had social consequences. The first was the removal of the brass grilles shielding the women's gallery; this was done in 1852 or between 1879 and 1895. The other was the removal before 1895 of a large pew where the poor were kept to prevent their mingling with those who could pay for seats and for building maintenance; this occurred elsewhere in the nineteenth and twentieth centuries, for example, at Casale Monferrato.

The street front was a rectangle divided by a heavy stringcourse and enlivened by the emphatic window archivolts. At each end, a doorway led into the courtyard of Duke's Place itself, and from there one reached the synagogue vestibule with the wedding hall above it; this was not part of the original building.

In its courtyard location, external reticence, architectural contemporaneity, and financing largely by a single donation, the Great Synagogue of London was typical. The interior was exceptionally fine, however, and also exceptionally church-like—a later version of Sir Christopher Wren's St. James Garlickhythe. The building won praise from a number of Christian visitors, a fact which Jewish accounts of the synagogue seldom fail to mention. But not all Christians viewed the occupants of this church-like building as much like themselves, as is evident in the most famous view of the synagogue, one produced by A. C. Pugin and Benjamin Rowlandson for Ackermann's *Microcosm of London*. While Pugin drew the architecture with his usual respect, Rowlandson drew a disagreeable caricature of Jews with hunched postures and ugly faces. At least the print preserves a careful picture of the architecture, an aerial bomb having left the synagogue a ruin in May 1941. After the war, so few congregation members remained in the East End that rebuilding the synagogue seemed unreasonable. A plaque on an office building now marks the site.

BIBLIOGRAPHY

E. Jamilly, "Synagogue Art and Architecture," *A Century of Jewish Life*, London, 1971, p. 77.
C. Roth, *The Great Synagogue, London, 1690–1940*, London, 1950, with further bibliography.
W. Samuel, *The First London Synagogue of the Resettlement*, London, 1924, pp. 44–46.
United Synagogue Archives, London.

London–Spitalfields Great Synagogue

The Spitalfields Great Synagogue illustrates the architectural problems that may arise when a church or chapel or meetinghouse is converted to a synagogue. A congregation's acceptance of apparently awkward adjustments suggests that those who worship in the building are concerned with religious needs and with adequate seating space and light, but are relatively indifferent to harmonious architectural form.

The handsome structure at Fournier Street and Brick Lane was built in 1743 as a Huguenot

Figure 246. London, former Spitalfields Great Synagogue, 1743, exterior between 1897 and ca. 1975.

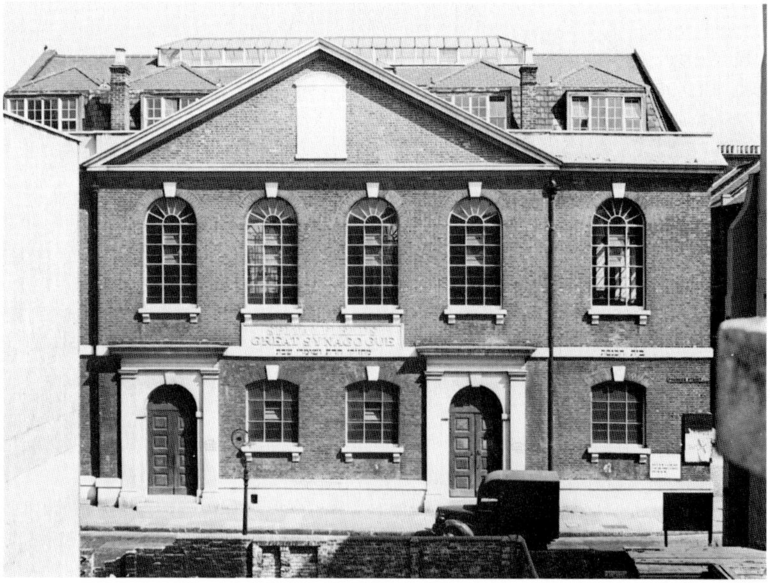

Figure 247. London, former Spitalfields Great Synagogue, interior to ark between 1897 and ca. 1975.

church by Charles Dunn, a mason, and John Jull, a carpenter. It became a Wesleyan chapel in 1819 and, later, a Mission for the Conversion of the Jews, whose residences surrounded this building in the East End.

The facade has been little altered despite these changes in ownership, but the interior originally had galleries on three sides of the ample, large-windowed auditorium, as it no longer does (Figs. 246, 247). Protestant churches commonly use galleries because they increase seating capacity without adding to the floor space, and they allow more people to sit close to the minister. Galleries are equally desirable in synagogues, but those of Spitalfields had to be altered after the ultraorthodox Machzike Hadath congregation acquired the building in 1896. The new occupants had to turn toward Jerusalem during prayer, but they found that the eastern wall was interrupted by one of the three galleries. They therefore ordered the removal of part of the eastern gallery, providing a more appropriate liturgical focus and room for the ark against the eastern wall. While the new arrangement satisfied Jewish religious needs, it left an awkward gallery fragment, destroying the former simple but coherent arrangement of the room with three galleried sides and an open, fourth, side. Had the Jews destroyed all the galleries for the sake of architectural harmony, they would not have had adequate and segregated accommodation for the women. Had they built a gallery on the side originally without one, they would have incurred unnecessary expense.

It was no doubt in order to save money that the congregation incorporated part of the Protestant reredos into the ark, raising the Christians' furniture to a higher degree of sanctity under Talmudic law. The general impression of the room remained that of a sober and dignified eighteenth-century auditorium.

We do not know whether the Methodists altered the building. The changes in the prayer hall which we have already described were designed by A. J. Hopkins and carried out in 1897 by Maple & Co., contractors who received £4,500 for executing Hopkins's plans and for adding twelve classrooms covered by a new roof above the synagogue. The congregation, augmented by members of the Machzike Shomrei Shabbat Synagogue which had been in Booth (now Princelet) Street nearby, moved into the Brick Lane building in a festive inaugural procession in September 1898. The combined congregations bought the synagogue as a freehold in 1922. The building suffered damage from a fire in 1930 and was probably restored shortly thereafter. In 1939, there were 610 male members forming the substantial congregation. The synagogue's seating capacity was about two thousand.

The Great Synagogue survived the bombing of London during the Second World War, but it needed redecoration which was completed in June 1951. It was reconsecrated as one of the largest traditional orthodox houses of worship in London and as an ornament to the orthodox Federation of Synagogues.

The general postwar movement of Jews away from the East End caused membership to decline from 369 men in 1958 to 294 in 1970 and 201 in 1976. By 1972, when a quorum did not assemble even on Saturday, the question arose of closing the synagogue and selling the building for use as a mosque by the Islamic immigrants who now form a significant part of the East End population. In November 1976, the building became the Jamme Masjid of Pakistani Moslems.

BIBLIOGRAPHY

B. Homa, *A Fortress in Anglo-Jewry. The Story of the Machzike Hadath,* London, 1953. I thank Mr. Homa for a long and helpful interview.

Jewish Chronicle, Sept. 16, 1898, pp. 24–25.

V. D. Lipman, *Social History of the Jews in England,* London, 1954, esp. pp. 125–26.

S. Sharot, "Religious Change in Native Orthodoxy in London, 1870–1914," *Jewish Journal of Sociology* XV, #1 (June 1973), pp. 57–78.

F. H. W. Sheppard, ed., *Survey of London XXVII: Spitalfields and Mile End New Town,* London, 1957, pp. 221–25, pls. 40–41.

London–Dollis Hill

The innovative forms of the Dollis Hill synagogue make it one of the most noteworthy of twentieth-century Jewish religious buildings. Progressive architectural magazines of the 1930s were glad to have an example of a functional synagogue that looked entirely different from older ones built in various period styles. They devoted more than usual attention to this one, because synagogues tended to be conservative in form, like most other English architecture of the interwar years. The building was designed by a distinguished British engineer, Sir E(van) Owen Williams, who is celebrated for his work at the Boots Chemical factory in Nottingham, but who was apparently known to his Dollis Hill clients because he had built the Empire Pool and Stadium in 1934 at Wembley, a short distance down the road.

Dollis Hill was one of the areas north of inner London in which the Jewish population increased markedly during the first decades of the century. The congregation first met in 1929 in a private house. They then used houses and rented premises including the Neasden Mission Hall until 1933 when they opened a small synagogue costing about £1400, which is now the community center. By 1936, the congregation had exceeded the capacity of this modest structure, and in February 1937, they laid the cornerstone of the new one, just a few yards away, on a site facing the lawns of a park. The building was meant for about a thousand people, with seats for 524 men and 392 women. The services follow the practices of the United Synagogue

Figure 248. London, Dollis Hill, 1933–34, exterior, south side, in 1983.

organization, separating men and women and emphasizing Hebrew, but removing high grilles from the women's gallery, allowing an organ and male choir, permitting recognizable subject matter in colored glass windows, and sometimes—as is the case here—placing the bimah near the ark. Within a few miles are several other United synagogues built at about the same time for members who lived in semidetached houses on gently curving streets lined with rose bushes.

In this conservative suburban setting rises the concrete synagogue which looks like nothing else in Britain. It has accordion-pleated walls, a bulky, box-like vestibule and office wing facing the street, and hexagonal and arched windows (Figs. 248, 249). The congregation had no fixed ideas about a synagogue's appearance. They just wanted a large but economical building with good sightlines and acoustics. Williams—and Gray's Ferro Concrete Company, Ltd.—satisfied their needs at a cost of only £18,250, and completed construction by the end of 1937.

The prayer hall is an oblong room, but its walls "pleat" outward and inward on the long sides, adding lateral strength to walls that would have been, if straight, too thin to carry the cantilevers of the galleries; the cantilevers are located at the apexes of the pleats. The roof is also "pleated," again in order to strengthen material of a mere 5–inch thickness. The underside of the roof was paneled in cork board for thermal and acoustical reasons.

In his economical use of materials and calculation of their strength, Williams showed his understanding of reinforced-concrete technology and of the congregation's needs. By making internal supports unnecessary, he allowed a generally uninterrupted view of the ritual activities, and he gave to the large room a visual and spatial unity which had been available earlier only in rooms that were too small to need internal supports for roof and galleries.

The designer also made a forceful show of the imposing qualities of functionalist modern architecture. The concrete walls, left in their natural color, revealed in their lightly rubbed surfaces that they were cast against building board shuttering, as though proclaiming the honesty of their construction and the dignity of nontraditional or humble materials.

Inside, Williams avoided the trivial details that diminished the impact of impressive twentieth-century synagogue interiors at Essen, Frankfurt am Main (see Figs. 140, 145), and Sarajevo, leaving a plain interior to be animated primarily by the worshippers. Among nearly contemporary synagogues, only a few were as restrained. This mode of design is far removed in spirit from the grandiose porticoed Liberal Synagogue in London, the late *art nouveau* facade treatment at the London-Walm Lane synagogue, the hesitant modernism at Bratislava (see Figs. 28–30), and the outdated orientalism at Enschede—all buildings erected within the interwar years.

Williams and the congregation did not, however, produce a merely functional box. The unusual pleated walls, the solemn grayish white of the exterior, and the distinctive window shapes make it clear that this is no ordinary building. The convergence of angles where the ceiling folds down to meet the wall pleats provides visual interest, as do changes in the perspective of the windows as they turn outward and inward along the wall. Thirty-four hexagonal windows bring light into the prayer hall. (Konstantin Melnikov's house of 1929 in Moscow also had a smooth-surfaced [plastered] exterior and hexagonal windows, but there is no known connection between that and the synagogue design.) At one time the windows contained six-pointed-star designs, but congregation members later donated colored glass windows embellished with images of Torah scrolls, the Lion of Judah, and other biblical or symbolic subjects. Polygonal spandrels between the walls and ceiling contain polygonal windows, while the vestibule-office wing and other auxiliary spaces are lit by windows which look like inverted tablets of the Law—square at the top and rounded below, designed to enclose menorah designs in metal.

The synagogue has not suffered essential modifications, although the window glass with its conventional images gives an impression of ordinariness which is uncongenial to the remarkable building. In June 1952, a building improvement fund was established to decorate the synagogue and community center. Because economic heating proved difficult, some paneling was added to aid heat retention. The congregation also found the wooden paneling more familiar and beautiful than the original concrete wall surface, and would have extended the woodwork beyond the present wainscoting to cover the ceiling if funds had been available. The exterior was painted a cold, stark white, possibly to conceal repairs or to cover up raw concrete which does not age well in the English climate. These alterations, however, cannot destroy the impact of a bold experiment by a man of imagination and expertise. If the synagogue is not a perfectly beautiful work of art, it is nevertheless a useful one, and a strong, satisfying introduction to the work of a distinguished engineer. It is also a testimonial to clients who were not afraid to take chances.

Figure 249. London, Dollis Hill, interior to ark in 1979.

BIBLIOGRAPHY

"Landmarks in the History of the Dollis Hill Synagogue," typescript in the cantor's archive.

"Synagogue at Dollis Hill, Cricklewood," *Architect and Building News* CLIII (Mar. 25, 1938), pp. 365–67.

"Synagogue at Dollis Hill, Cricklewood," *Architects' Journal* LXXXVII (Mar. 24, 1938), pp. 480, 489–91.

The North West Jewish Monitor, March 5, 1937, p. 10.

Interviews with Harry Cohen, Rev. and Mrs. M. H. Taylor, and Jack Singer were most helpful.

London–Finchley United

The Finchley synagogue is a concrete building of imposing size, built by the firm of Dowton & Hurst in 1965–67 (Figs. 250, 251). It is characteristic of many suburban synagogues in post-war Britain that are affiliated with the United Synagogue, a group of congregations in which orthodox Ashkenazic practices are accompanied by some English prayers. The United Synagogue congregations have more members in the aggregate than any other group of British Jews, such as the orthodox Federation of Synagogues, or the various Reform, or Liberal and Progressive associations. The relative prosperity of the United Synagogue and its members is reflected in its buildings.

During the 1930s and after 1945, the center of London's middle-class Jewish population shifted from the immigrants' first home in the East End to suburban districts, particularly in the north and northwest. Such areas as Golders Green, Hendon, and more recently Edgware, Hampstead, and Finchley, received the immigrants' culturally assimilated children. To accommodate a rapidly growing number of worshippers, and to offer Jewish education to their children, congregation officials commissioned large synagogues and community centers in Hendon (1935), Dollis Hill (1937) (see Figs. 248, 249), St. John's Wood (1956–63), Stanmore (1959–63), and during the last two decades in Finchley, Kingsbury, Pinner (see Fig. 6), and other districts—increasingly, those of outer London. Between 1961 and 1971, sixty-seven new synagogues were acquired or built in the London area.

Many of the largest new synagogues are cold in feeling, at least when empty. It is hard, after all, to design a modest or intimate building for several hundred people. Buildings made of smooth concrete walls rarely look warm or impart a sense of communal piety. In addition, the buildings must follow strict requirements for women's galleries, and must adhere to structural and safety codes. The result is likely to be appreciated more for usefulness than for beauty.

At Finchley, Dowton and Hurst fulfilled their practical obligations well. They avoided the errors made by one United Synagogue architect who left inadequate leg room for about a third of the women, and who designed slippery steps to the ark. The Finchley synagogue has comfortably spaced seating for eight hundred men below and five hundred women in the galleries. Windows provide abundant daylight. The ark platform is broad enough to be both safe and impressive. In the basement, meeting rooms and a kitchen facilitate service at festive events.

In order to moderate the tone of practical efficiency, the congregation installed thick blue carpeting in the main corridor, colored glass windows in the prayer hall, and even a ruffled dressing table in the brides' waiting room. Although some of these additions give the building more the appearance of a hotel than a house of worship, the congregation clearly meant them to soften the effect of hard rectilinear forms.

The facade reveals equally laudable intentions. The architects had to provide a backdrop for the ark on the inside and a suitable main facade on the reverse side of the ark wall. They had to light the ark end, while maintaining the privacy of the ark area and of the congregation in the prayer hall. To do this, they framed the ark in an angular space appropriately different from the area occupied by the worshippers. The angular projection outside also sets the building apart from nearby houses, and may muffle noise from a highway. Alternating vertical strips of concrete and glass set at angles to the street make it difficult for passersby to peer inside or to commit acts of vandalism. The design was perhaps more admirable in theory than in realization, however, for a cartoon in the London *Jewish Chronicle* noted its resemblance to a Rolls-Royce grille.

In general, the recent United synagogues recall those of well-to-do suburban congregations in the United States. They combine synagogue halls of impressive size (filled on High Holy Days) with the facilities of a community center, including youth rooms, women's guild rooms, offices, schoolrooms, lecture halls, and kitch-

Figure 250. London, Finchley United, 1965–67, exterior of ark end.

Figure 251. London, Finchley United, interior to ark.

ens. If the buildings look grandiose at times, they also express a vigorous Jewish community, in which the immigrants' grandchildren share their material prosperity with the central institutions of Jewish life. The conspicuous buildings also assert, as German and Austrian synagogues had done a century earlier, the British Jews' confidence in their country as a secure home in which Jews may assume a public posture.

Comparable facilities, at a comparably imposing scale, are offered in a number of independent synagogues, such as the Golders Green Beth Hamedrash built in the 1960s by Shaw & Lloyd. The chief Liberal synagogue, in St. John's Wood Road, has the largest seating capacity of any British synagogue. A domed, central-plan building in modified neo-Georgian style, it emphasized grandeur and conservative contemporary taste (1925 by Ernest M. Joseph with later additions and postwar restorations). The Reform synagogue at Hove, Sussex, completed in 1966 by Derek Sharp, is another large synagogue and community center in the modern idiom, with arches and decorative details to soften its modern style and box-like shape.

BIBLIOGRAPHY

A Century of Jewish Life, 1870–1970, Catalogue of exhibition at Christie's, London, 1971, including E. Jamilly, "Synagogue Art and Architecture," pp. 75–91.

Jewish Chronicle, map of 1939 synagogue locations, on display in the London Museum exhibition, *London in the 1930s,* London, 1973.

L.E. Kochan, "Anglo-Jewry Since World War II," *American Jewish Year Book* LXXVIII (1978), pp. 339–47.

S.J. Prais, "Synagogue Statistics and the Jewish Population of Great Britain, 1900–1970," *Jewish Journal of Sociology* XIV, #2 (Dec. 1972), pp. 215–28.

C. Roth, *Archives of the United Synagogue. Report and Catalogue,* London, 1930.

S. Sharot, "Religious Change in Native Orthodoxy in London, 1870–1914," *Jewish Journal of Sociology* XV, #1 (June 1973), pp. 57–78.

See also:

"Synagogue. St. John's Wood. T. P. Bennett & Son, Architects," *Architectural Review* CXXIII, #1 (Jan. 1958), p. 27.

"United Synagogue, Great Cumberland Place," *Builder* CCIII (Oct. 12, 1962), pp. 729–31.

I am grateful to the staffs and officers of the synagogues mentioned, especially to Messrs. Cohen and Press at the United Synagogue, John Levinson at the Liberal Synagogue, and Rabbi Dow Marmur of the Reform congregation in Alyth Gardens.

Ramsgate–Sir Moses Montefiore's Synagogue

The small Sephardic synagogue in the coastal resort of Ramsgate on the English Channel is important both for its architecture and for its patron. This was the private synagogue of Sir Moses Montefiore (1784–1885), who devoted a fortune made in finance to the welfare of his fellow Jews and mankind in general. Sir Moses and his wife, Lady Judith, purchased land in Ramsgate, a more fashionable town then than it is today, and built a house and outbuildings on the property. Sir Moses, who was very pious, wished to worship frequently, but there was no synagogue in Ramsgate. In gratitude for his safe completion of a hazardous journey to the Holy Land, he bought property adjacent to his estate in 1831, and began to build. His synagogue remains the Sephardic synagogue of the coastal region, opening to serve holiday visitors to the local resort towns as well as the few Sephardic Jews who live year-round in nearby communities such as Broadstairs and Margate.

The synagogue is perched upon a knoll which rose in Sir Moses' time above a well-tended landscape with lawns, gardens, ornamental trees, and an orchard; its situation made it slightly higher than other buildings on the estate, following the tradition of elevating the synagogue (Fig. 252). An octagon with longer north and south sides and short diagonals, the synagogue has at the west an additional bay containing the vestibule with its (later) marble fountain and basin, and stairs to the women's gallery. The exterior is simply a shell around the plan, with white-painted stucco covering the masonry, smooth walls articulated by pilasters at the angle corners, and a slightly higher wall serving as a modest facade. A horizontal molding divides the facade, and the two storeys thus marked indicate that the women's gallery was provided from the start. In the upper storey, the top window molding is interrupted by a clock, an unusual but not unique fixture on a synagogue. The lower part of the facade must have had symmetrical pilasters flanking a window, but one pilaster is now missing.

While the chaste neoclassical facade retains its original reticence, later interior modifications gave a more colorful and sumptuous aspect than Sir Moses intended (Fig. 253). In 1833, when he and his wife inaugurated the synagogue on their wedding anniversary, they entered a relatively dark octagonal room, lighted only by windows at the gallery level, a central skylight, and one tiny window high on the ark wall. The plastered walls were all painted white, and the few moldings on the pilasters and window frames were kept as simple as possible. This conforms to the restrained neoclassical taste of England's wealthy classes in the years before the synagogue was built, and Sir Moses would surely not have wanted to build anything less conservative than this.

The walls and pillars are now lined with marble in cream and pink tones, the gift of Mrs. Harriett Sebag-Montefiore in 1912. The ark surround, with its pediment supported by smooth, sloping pilasters with lotus capitals, does not appear in a late-nineteenth-century drawing, possibly based on a photograph; this image shows a horizontal lintel above the ark door. Perhaps the ark was also altered in 1912. Several changes were made to celebrate the centenary of the building in 1933. At that time, Mrs. Ida Sebag-Montefiore donated stained-glass windows, perhaps those in strong colors on the northeast and southeast walls; the windows do not appear in the old drawing. A new bimah and new seats also were made for the centenary

Figure 252. Ramsgate, Sir Moses Montefiore's Synagogue, 1831–33, exterior in ca. 1930.

Figure 253. Ramsgate, Sir Moses Montefiore's Synagogue, interior to ark in ca. 1930.

celebration, and the seating was directed toward the east rather than to the central axis as was customary in Sephardic synagogues (and as it appears in the old drawing). The older remaining woodwork was restored at the same time, while iron supports were added to give stability to the women's gallery.

The synagogue meant a great deal to Sir Moses and his wife, standing as it did on the grounds of their house. Its designer was his cousin, David Mocatta, one of the few Jewish architects of his time, and its builder was a local man, Mr. Crosford. The synagogue was also an offering of thanks by Sir Moses for the many blessings God had bestowed upon him. On its inauguration day, he remembered all the poor near his home by giving money to two Church of England parishes for distribution as alms. In his diary he called the inauguration one of the great days of his life, along with those of his marriage and his knighthood. It is also possible that Sir Moses thought of the building as a permanent record of his devotion to Judaism, especially since he and his wife had no children to carry on after them.

In its modesty and clarity of form, the Ramsgate synagogue stands as a suitable memorial to a clear-headed and active individual who knew that he had been elevated above many of his fellow men, but who also knew that this was the Lord's work and meant for a noble purpose. The building is now hidden in the grounds of the Montefiore estate where little activity goes on, now that the Judith, Lady Montefiore theological college makes only intermittent use of the house and grounds. People nevertheless find their way to the site to visit the synagogue and the adjacent tomb, built later in domed Middle Eastern style. There, in a clearing in the overgrown wood and orchard, they see the buildings of a man who behaved like the perfect Englishman in many aspects of his life on earth, and who prayed in an English-style building, but who always identified himself with the ancient heritage of Judaism and wanted to do so for all time, in his tomb.

BIBLIOGRAPHY

E. Jamilly, "Anglo-Jewish Architects and Architecture in the 18th and 19th Centuries," *Jewish Historical Society of England, Transactions,* XVIII (1958), p. 134.

D. A. Jessurun Cardozo and Paul Goodman, *Think and Thank: The Montefiore Synagogue and College, Ramsgate, 1833–1933,* London and Oxford, 1933.

L. Loewe, ed., *The Diaries of Sir Moses and Lady Judith Montefiore,* London and Sydney, 1890.

I am grateful to R. D. Barnett, London, and George DaCosta, Broadstairs, for answering queries and opening the synagogue for me.

Appendix I

List of Selected Architects

Synagogues that the architect(s) designed and built appear first in chronological order. Then follow competition entries and synagogues that the architect(s) altered or rebuilt. Any synagogues without dates are listed at the end of the entry in alphabetical order.

CHRISTIAN

Court and government architects who designed synagogues include:

Antoine d'Allemand: Carpentras (redesign), 1741–42
Friedrich Wilhelm von Erdmannsdorf: Wörlitz, 1788–90
Ludwig von Förster: Vienna-Tempelgasse, 1853–58; Budapest-Dohány Street, 1854–59; Miskolc, 1861–63
M. Hermans: Maastricht, 1839–40
J. A. Joffroy: Avignon, 1846–48
A. Matuszynski: Goersdorf, 1851–ca. 1855; Trimbach, 1865
G. F. Maybaum: Amsterdam-New Ashkenazic, 1750–52
Johann B. Métivier: Munich, 1824–26
J. A. Mulock Houwer: Deventer, 1891–92
Leopold Retti: Ansbach, 1744–46
Daniel Stalpaert: Amsterdam-Great Ashkenazic, 1670
Friedrich Weinbrenner: Karlsruhe, 1798–1806
District architects prepared at least the site plans for synagogues at: Remiremont (1870s), Wissembourg (ca. 1869–70), Sourbourg (ca. 1864).
District architects prepared synagogue plans at: Hochfelden, 1854; Minversheim, 1865; Osthouse, Uttenheim, Westhouse, and Zellwiller, all in the 1860s.
City architects prepared plans for synagogues at: Vesoul, 1873–75; Szczecin, 1871–75; Amersfoort, 1727; Ansbach (remodeling), 1842–43.

The following architects with significant local or international reputations designed synagogues:

Alessandro Antonelli: Turin, 1863ff.
Peter Behrens: Žilina, 1928–30
Luca Beltrami: Milan, 1891
P. J. H. Cuypers: Eindhoven, 1866
Friedrich Eisenlohr: Mannheim, 1853
Ludwig von Förster: see above for Vienna, Budapest, Miskolc.
Hector Guimard: Paris-rue Pavée, 1911–13
G. F. Hetsch: Copenhagen, 1831–33
Josef Hoffmann: projects for Žilina, ca. 1927–28
Peter Jürgensen and Jürgen Bachmann: Frankfurt am Main-Israelitische Religionsgesellschaft, 1904–7
Eduard Knoblauch: Berlin-Heidereutergasse enlargement, 1853–56; Oranienburgerstrasse, 1859–66
Edmund Körner: Essen Steelerstrasse, 1908–13; competition entry for Frankfurt am Main-Westend, 1907
Josef Kornhäusel: Vienna-Seitenstettengasse, 1824–26
Peter Joseph Krahe: Düsseldorf, 1787–90
András Landherr (with Mihály Pollak?): Budapest-Obuda, 1820; perhaps also Hunkovče, 1821, and Abony
Karl F. Langhans: Wrocław-Storch, ca. 1820
Franz Roeckle: Frankfurt am Main-Westend, 1907–10
Fredrik Vilhelm Scholander: Stockholm, 1870
Gottfried Semper: Dresden, 1838–40; project for Paris, 1849
James Spiller: London-Ashkenazic Great, 1788–90
Gustav Stier: Berlin-Johannisstrasse, 1854
Vojtěch Ignac Ullmann: Prague-Dušní Street, 1868
Friedrich von Gärtner: Ingenheim, 1830–32
Otto Wagner: Budapest-Rumbach Street, 1869–72

Friedrich Weinbrenner: see above for Karlsruhe
Sir E. Owen Williams: London-Dollis Hill, 1937
Ernst Zwirner: Cologne-Glockengasse, 1857–61

JEWISH

Architects of synagogues in AUSTRIA-HUNGARY include:

Lipót Baumhorn, designed twenty-four synagogues including: Esztergom, 1888–90; Zrenyanin, 1895; Szeged, 1899–1903; Budapest-Aréna (Dossa György) Street, Páva Street, 1923, Csáky Street, 1927; Gyöngyös, 1929; Budapest-Bethlen Square, 1931 (for the last three, associated with György Somogyi); Rijeka; competed for Žilina
Otto Eisler: Brno-Agudath Achim, 1936
Max Fleischer: Vienna-Schmalzhofgasse, 1883–84; České Budějovice, 1888; Hohenau, Krems, and Pelhřimov, late 1880s and early 1890s; Vienna-Müllnergasse, 1888–89, Neudeggergasse, 1900–1903; General Hospital synagogue, 1903; small ones, mentioned imprecisely; remodeled interiors at Břeclav, Mikulov
Dezsö Freund: Budapest-Nagyfuvaros Street, 1922
Jacob Gartner: Olomouc, 1896–97; Opava, 1896–97; Vienna-Humboldtgasse, 1896; Kluckygasse, 1898; Braunhubergasse, 1898; Debrecen, Hlohovec; Holešov; Plzeň
Alfred Grotte: Tachov, 1912; Pniewy, 1912–13; Poznań-Latz Foundation Old Age/Invalid Hospital synagogue, 1914; Milicz, 1928; remodeled Prague-Meisel, 1893–1905
Karl König: Vienna-Turnergasse, 1871–72; Liberec, 1888
Béla Lajta: Budapest-Pest Hevrah Kaddisha Almshouse prayer hall, 1910, Abony Street Boys' High School synagogue, 1923
Henryk and József Lipovzky: Szeged, 1842
Béla and Sándor Löffler: Budapest-Kazinczy Street Orthodox, 1911–13; one of them competed for Antwerp-van den Nestlei, 1923, and remodeled a warehouse into the Paris-Rashi Synagogue, rue Ambroise Thomas, 1935
Oskar Marmorek: competed for Trieste, 1903
Berthold Marmorstein and Richard Strassmann (Jewish?): Moravská-Ostrava
Matouschek (Jewish?) and Adler: competed for Trieste, 1903
Richard Neutra: competed for Vienna-Hietzing, 1924
Ede Novák and István Hamburger: Budapest-Lágymányos district synagogue, 1926
Károly Hugo Schönteil: Budapest-Kőbánya, 1911
Izidor Sterck: Budapest-Girls' Orphanage Synagogue, 1911
Wilhelm Stiassny: Teplice-Šanov, 1882; Malacky, 1886–87; Vienna-Leopoldgasse, 1893; Prague-Královské Vinohrady, 1896–98, Jerusalémská Street (with L. Richter), 1906; Časlav; Jablonec nad Nisou; remodeled Vienna-Seitenstettengasse and Tempelgasse; projects for Regensburg
Oskar Strnad: competed for Trieste, 1903
László Vago and Ferenc Faragó: Budapest-"Heroes' Temple" war memorial chapel adjacent to Dohány Street synagogue, 1935

Architects of synagogues in FRANCE include:

Alfred Philibert Aldrophe: Paris-rue de la Victoire, 1865–74, Rothschild Orphanage oratory, ca. 1874; Versailles, 1886
Braun and Dayan: Sarcelles, 1965
Abraham Hirsch: Lyon, 1864–68
Edmond Lévy: signed cost estimates for Rouen, ca. 1864
Gustave Lévy: rebuilt and enlarged Bayonne, 1867
Robert Lévy: Niederroedern, Bischwiller, rebuilt Osthoffen, may have enlarged Duttlenheim, all between 1858 and 1865
Claude Meyer-Lévy: Strasbourg, 1958; St. Dié
Nathan Nathan, alias Salomon (probably identical with Salomon Nathan): Fontainebleau, 1857; Marseille, 1860–64 (by Salomon Nathan)
Alexandre Persitz (with A. G. Heaume, religion unknown): Paris-Abrabanel, 1962; competed for Strasbourg
Ionel Schein: Paris-rue Gaston-de-Caillavet, 1980
Jacob Silveyra: Paris-rue Notre Dame de Nazareth, 1819–22 (with J. P. Sandrié, Christian)
Stern and Pietrasanta: Fontainebleau, 1964
Émile Ulmann: Neuilly, 1877–78

Architects of synagogues in GERMANY (1939 boundaries) include:

Friedrich Adler: Cologne-Werkbund Exhibition model synagogue, 1914
Felix Ascher with Robert Friedmann: Hamburg-Oberstrasse, 1929–30;
Alexander Beer: Berlin-Kottbuser (now Fraenkel) Ufer, 1912–16; Prinzregentenstrasse, 1922–30; projects for Klopstockstrasse, 1928; Agricolastrasse, 1930
Oskar Bloch: Schwäbisch-Gmünd (with Ernst Guggenheimer), 1926; competed for Zürich, late 1920s

S. Engel: Hamburg-Bornplatz (with E. Friedheim), 1905–6, Hoheluftchaussee, 1909
Max Fraenkel: Berlin-Münchenerstrasse, 1909–10
E. Friedheim: see above, S. Engel; Hamburg-Oppenheimer Foundation synagogue, 1907–8
Eduard Fürstenau (Jewish?): Dortmund, 1895–1900; Bielefeld, 1900–1905
Carl Gerle: Aachen, Bremen, Hagen, Minden, Mühlheim, Paderborn, Recklinghausen; all 1950s
Helmut Goldschmidt: Bonn, Dortmund; remodeled Cologne-Roonstrasse; all ca. 1956–59
Ernst Guggenheimer: see above, O. Bloch; Stuttgart, 1952
Hermann Guttmann: Offenbach, 1956; Düsseldorf, 1958; Villeurbanne, France (with Raymond Carpe, Christian), 1964; Osnabrück, 1969; Würzburg (with Rudolf Schlick, religion unknown), 1970
Wilhelm Haller: competed for Hamburg-Oberstrasse; projects for cemetery chapel
Emil Hecht: stabilized the Nuremberg synagogue of 1874 in 1902
Johann Höniger (with partner Sedelmeier, religion unknown): Berlin-Rykestrasse, 1902–4, Artilleriestrasse, 1903–4, Levetzowstrasse, 1912–14 (dedicated 1919); competed for Berlin-Lindenstrasse, and Lützowstrasse, Darmstadt, Dortmund, Frankfurt am Main-Israelitische Religionsgesellschaft; Karl-Marx-Stadt; Poznań
Rudolf Joseph: Dieburg, 1927–29; Paris-orthodox synagogue, not named, ca. 1934–35 (Leo Baeck Institute Archives, R. Joseph collection)
Richard Kaufmann: Bad Nauheim, 1929
Siegfried Kusnitzky: Frankfurt am Main-Horovitz, 1881–82; projects for Gdańsk, 1881
Fritz Landauer: Augsburg (with Heinrich Lömpel), 1912–17; Plauen, 1927–29; London-Alyth Gardens, 1935–36; Willesden (with Wills and Kaula), 1937–38; competed for Würzburg, 1922, Vienna-Hietzing, 1924; Hamburg-Oberstrasse, 1929
Ludwig Levy: Kaiserslautern, 1882–86; Pforzheim, 1893; Luxembourg, 1883–94; Baden-Baden, 1899; Bingen, 1905; Barmen, Rastatt, Rostock; projects for Bamberg, 1907; Saarbrücken; consultant at Augsburg, ca. 1907
Emanuel Josef Margold: project for Dieburg, 1926
Erich Mendelsohn: Sovetsk, 1925–26
Leo Nachtlicht: competed for Berlin-Klopstockstrasse, 1929
Fritz Nathan: built or remodeled Frankfurt am Main, Friedberg in Hessen, Konstanz, Mannheim-main, and Klaus; competed for Zürich, ca. 1928
W. Nathanson, master mason: Randers, 1858
Edwin Oels Oppler: Hannover, 1864–70; Wrocław, 1865–72; Świdnica, 1877; Hameln, 1878–79; Bleicherode, 1882; competed for Munich, 1871–72; Karlovy Vary, 1874; Nuremberg; perhaps Norderney, ca. 1877
A. Rosengarten: Kassel, 1836–39; Hamburg-Sephardic, 1852, Kohlhöfen, 1854, Alte und Neue Klaus, 1858
Harry Rosenthal: private house synagogue (for exhibitions at Berlin and Stuttgart, 1929 and 1930); competed for Berlin-Klopstockstrasse (with F. Nathan), 1929
Franz Salomon: Berlin-Siegmundshof, 1924–29
Otto Simonson: Leipzig, 1853–54
Robert Stern: Cologne-Ehrenfeld, 1927
P. L. Wiener (with partner Jaretzki, religion unknown): competed for Berlin-Klopstockstrasse, 1929
Adolf Wolff (Jewish?): Ulm, 1870–73; Nuremberg, 1870–74; Heilbronn, 1871–77; Karlovy Vary, 1876–77; finished Stuttgart, 1861
Richard Wolffenstein (with partner Wilhelm Cremer, Christian): Berlin-Lindenstrasse, 1888–91; Kaliningrad, 1892–96; Berlin-Spandau, 1894, Lützowstrasse, 1896–98; Poznań, 1907–13; Dessau, ca. 1907–9; competed for Dortmund, Essen-Steelerstrasse

Architects of synagogues in ITALY include:

Angelo di Castro: Livorno, 1959–62
Eugenio Gentili (with Manfredo d'Urbino and Alessandro Rimini): remodeled Milan, 1953–54
Marco Treves: Pisa, 1863; Florence (with Christian associates), 1874–82

Architects of synagogues in THE NETHERLANDS and BELGIUM include:

Jacob Baars: Amsterdam-Linnaeusstraat, 1927–28; The Hague-Carpentierstraat, 1938; Rotterdam (with Jan van Duin, religion unknown), 1955–56; remodeled Bussum church into a synagogue, 1931
Joseph DeLange: Ostend, ca. 1900–10; Antwerp-Hovenierstraat, ca. 1910–13, van den Nestlei, 1923–29
Harry Elte: Amsterdam-Jacob Obrechtplein, 1928; Den Helder, ca. 1930; rebuilt Utrecht, 1926; restored Amersfoort, 1927

A. Elzas: Amsterdam-Lekstraat, 1934–38
Jules Hofman: Antwerp-Oostenstraat, 1911–13
Oscar Leeuw (Jewish?): Nijmegen, 1911–12
E. M. Rood: Amsterdam-Gerard Doustraat, 1892; Monnikendam, 1894
Abraham and G. B. Salm (Jewish?): Amsterdam-Rapenburgerstraat, 1881–83, rebuilt Lange Houtstraat, 1894
L. Waterman: Amsterdam-Liberal, 1966
Leon Winkel: Delft, 1861–62

Architects of synagogues in the UNITED KINGDOM include:

Cyril Adler: London-Smith Terrace, 1959
Hyman Henry Collins: London-Bryanston Street Sephardic, 1862–63; Southampton, 1865; Chatham, 1866–70; London-Borough New, 1867; Barnsbury, 1868; Bristol, 1871; competed for London-Upper Berkeley Street, 1867, Liverpool, 1872; repaired London-Western, 1857, and Abbey Road, 1880
Barrow Emanuel (with partner Henry David Davis, Christian): London-Upper Berkeley Street, 1867–70, Stepney Green, 1876, Lauderdale Road, 1896
C. J. Epril (or Eprile, with associate, Hersh): London-Walm Lane; Cambridge, both in 1930s
Alexander Flinder: London-Pinner, 1979–82
Ernest Freud: London-Stepney Green Jewish Hospital Oratory, 1958
Delissa Joseph (nephew of N. S. Joseph): London-Hammersmith, 1890, Hampstead, 1892, South Hackney, 1897, Finsbury Park, 1901, New Cross, 1904; Cardiff, 1897; Manchester-Withington
Nathan Solomon Joseph, sometimes with associates: London-Bayswater, 1862–64; Central, 1866–70; Belfast-Victoria Street, 1870; London-New West End, 1878–79; Dalston, 1885; project for Manchester
B. S. Jacobs: consultant at Belfast, 1904
Karl Kapolka (with Eugene Rosenberg of Yorke, Rosenberg & Mardall): Belfast, 1961–64
Fritz Landauer: see above, Germany
Eric Lyons: London-Belsize Square, 1950s
David Mocatta: Ramsgate, 1831–33; London-Bruton Street, 1842, Margaret Street, 1849; consultant at London-Upper Berkeley Street
Edward Salomons: London-Bayswater (with N. S. Joseph), 1862–63; Manchester-Cheetham Hill Sephardic, 1872–74; competed for Liverpool, 1872
Derek Sharp: London-Amhurst Park; Hove Reform, 1960s
Lewis Solomon: London-Old Castle Street, 1872, Spital Square, 1886, Bethnal Green, 1891, New Hambro, 1899, Stoke Newington, 1903
David Stern and Partners: London-Kingsbury, ca. 1970
Joseph Sunlight: completed Manchester-Withington, 1927
Harald Weinreich: London-Woodford, 1954

The architects' names have been culled primarily from the following sources:
Archives:
Paris-Archives Nationales, file F 19; Consistoire Israélite
London-United Synagogue Archives; R.I.B.A. Drawings Collection
Düsseldorf-Zentralrat der Juden in Deutschland, *Allgemeine unabhängige jüdische Wochenzeitung*
Vienna-Oesterreichische Nationalbibliothek photographic collection
New York-Leo Baeck Institute
Zeist-Rijksdienst voor Monumentenzorg
Jewish encyclopedias cited in Bibliography
General histories of synagogue art and architecture cited in Bibliography, especially those of Roth and Wischnitzer; Hammer-Schenk, Bendt & Bothe, Eschwege, Osborn, and Wolf for Germany; E. Jamilly for England; van Agt for the Netherlands; Heller and Vajda for Hungary
Jewish community histories, cited in Jewish encyclopedias and in bibliographies listed in my own Bibliography, especially those by Kreutzberger and Foerg, L. A. Mayer, and I. Wolff for Germany; Blumenkranz for France; Milano for Italy; Jacobs and Wolf, Roth, and Lehmann for England
Indexes to Jewish periodicals, and the index to the *Jewish Chronicle*

Appendix II

List of Extant Polish Synagogues

Polish prewar synagogues survive in the following towns and perhaps elsewhere:

- Biecz: hotel
- Bobowa: workshop or school
- Bochnia: warehouse
- Chęciny: cinema
- Chełm: technical school
- Chrzanów: warehouse
- Cieszanów: warehouse
- Cracow: now synagogues, museum, factory, house
- Częstochowa: concert hall
- Czortków (now Chertkov, Ukrainian S.S.R.): restaurant
- Dąbrowa: warehouse
- Dębica: warehouse
- Dukla: market
- Gora Kalwaria: warehouse
- Gorlice: bakery
- Jarosław: art school
- Jasło: restaurant
- Józefów: wheat silo
- Katowice: apartment house
- Kazimierz Dolny: Wisła Cinema
- Kielce
- Kolbuszowa: wheat silo and offices
- Konin: abandoned
- Kórnik: 19th-century Moorish synagogue
- Koval: workshop
- Krasnik: abandoned
- Krośniewice: cinema
- Kutno: office (or shop and club)
- Łańcut: Jewish museum
- Łeczna: warehouse
- Lesko: museum
- Lódź, Poludniowa Street #28
- Lubaczów: warehouse
- Międzyrzecz: neoclassical 19th-century synagogue
- Nowy Sącz: abandoned
- Olsztyn: cemetery ceremonial hall
- Orla: warehouse
- Ostrolęka: garage
- Pinczów: museum
- Piotrków Trybunalski: library
- Praszka
- Przemyśl: (Sheinbach) library; (Zassanie) garage
- Przysucha: 18th-century synagogue
- Rabka: house
- Radymno: factory
- Rymanów: library and cultural institution
- Rzeszów: (Old Town) city archives; (New Town) museum
- Sandomierz: archives
- Sanok: commercial building
- Slutsk: bakery (since the 1920s)
- Strzyzów: commercial building
- Szczebrzeszyn: library
- Szczecin
- Szydłów
- Szydłowiec: warehouse
- Tarnów (only the four columns of the bimah canopy remain)
- Turek: cooperative
- Tykocin
- Ustrzyki Dolne: silo
- Warsaw-Nozyk: historic monument
- Wielkie Oczy: silo
- Włodawa: historic monument; garage
- Wrocław-Storch: decrepit
- Zamość: tourist hotel, library, or post office

These may not all be accessible to the visitor. The local tourist office may be consulted for advice.

Glossary

ark (aron ha-kodesh, [h]ekhal): Cabinet in which the Torah scrolls are kept in a synagogue. Originally freestanding against the eastern wall of the synagogue, often placed in a niche or apse. Generally approached by steps and covered with an embroidered curtain.

Ashkenazic (Ashkenaz = Germany, in Hebrew): Referring to Ashkenazim, Jews of Franco-German origin and religious ritual, who later migrated to eastern Europe and to other parts of western and central Europe.

bar mitzvah: An adult male Jew (one over thirteen years of age) who must perform the religious commandments and who takes part in religious services. Also used to mean the ceremony conducted when a boy is thirteen years old, to mark his adulthood for religious purposes.

bet ha-midrash: *See* house of study.

bimah (tevah): Platform or table in a synagogue from which the Torah scrolls are read. The platform supporting a table is often of squarish or polygonal shape, and usually is approached by steps on two sides. A railing used for security and beauty encloses it. The bimah usually is placed on the main (east-west) axis, in the center of the synagogue in Ashkenazic orthodox synagogues, at the east end in Ashkenazic Reform synagogues, and opposite the ark in Sephardic-, Italian-, and Comtadin-rite synagogues.

cantor ([c]hazan): Originally the superintendent of the prayer meeting, eventually the chanter and leader of prayer in a synagogue.

Crystal Night: Nov. 9–10, 1938, when organized vandals broke windows and destroyed synagogues and shops owned by Jews in Germany and Austria.

Diaspora: Dispersion of Jews outside the Holy Land.

Gemara: A commentary on the Mishnah, forming part of the Talmud.

Haggadah: Service read during the Passover meal (Seder).

Hasid ([c]has[s]id): Adherent of a movement that originated in the Ukraine in the mid-eighteenth century. Hasids emphasize faith and mystical religious emotion, rather than scholarship, although modern Hasidism includes both ecstatic activity and scholarship.

High Holy Days: Autumnal days inaugurating the new year (Rosh Hashanah) and providing a day of atonement (Yom Kippur). These days and the time between them constitute ten days of penitence.

house of study: School and religious discussion room for Jewish male adults. It is holier than a synagogue in religious standing. It may be annexed to a synagogue or separately built, either in a purpose-built structure or in a room in a building used for other activities. It may have an ark and a bimah so that people can use it for prayer. It may be called in Yiddish a *kloyz* or *shtibl* (cf. German *Klaus, Stübe*) especially if it is private (rather than owned by a congregation or by an officially designated Jewish community) or if it is used by Hasids.

Karaite: Adherent of a Jewish movement originating in Babylonia. Karaites do not accept the authority of the Talmud, believing in the sole authority of the Bible, especially the Pentateuch. They have their own traditions, liturgy, scholars, and charities.

Marrano: Iberian Jew who converted to Christianity to escape religious persecution.

minyan: Quorum of ten adult male Jews, required for the establishment of a congregation and for recitation of certain prayers.

Mishnah: The core of the Talmud, it is a digest of the Oral Law, i.e., the authoritative interpretations of the Written Law (Pentateuch). Oral Law is so called because its contents had been transmitted orally in successive generations.

mizrah: Marker in the home, indicating the direction

of Jerusalem toward which prayers are addressed.

Neolog: Reform-oriented movement in Hungary, somewhat more conservative than German Reform.

orthodox: Strictly adherent to traditional doctrine as embodied in the Torah, Talmud, and legal codes and commentaries.

rabbi: Term of respect originally used for religious sages and teachers, now used for ordained Jewish ministers of religion. Rabbis historically have been scholars whose learning entitled them to be Jewish community judges, performers of weddings, and religious representatives.

rebbe (tzadik): Hasidic rabbi believed to have special powers to mediate between the divine will and man's desires, and thus considered a wonder-worker. There were hereditary dynasties of these men. Some maintained substantial households or "courts" filled with their adherents.

Reform: Movement in Ashkenazic Judaism, of German origin ca. 1800. It was meant to remove accrued superfluities from Judaism, thus simplifying the liturgy. To make services intelligible to those who knew little Hebrew, Reformers introduced more vernacular elements. Reformers tended originally to be comparatively wealthy Jews who had some secular education. The movement flourished especially in western and central Europe.

responsum (*pl.* responsa): Jewish legal opinion.

ritual bath (mikvah, mikveh): Facility employing fresh-flowing water, used for monthly cleansing ritual for women, and used for analogous rituals by men. Generally not used by Jews who follow Reform tendencies. Ritual baths were usually located near or even below the synagogue or community center.

Rundbogenstil (= round-arched style, in German): Nineteenth-century style based upon elements of ancient, early Christian, Romanesque, and Renaissance architectural styles.

Sephardic (Sefarad = Spain, in Hebrew): Adjective referring to the Sephardim, Jews who trace their origin to the Iberian peninsula, or who use some form of the rite initiated there.

Shavuot: One of three pilgrimage festivals, now a festival celebrating the presentation of the Torah to the Jews, accomplished by Moses at the foot of Mount Sinai.

shtetl (cf. *Stadt* = city, in German): Small-town Jewish community or settlement in eastern Europe.

Sukkot: Seven-day Feast of Booths, originally a harvest festival. The celebration takes place at home, in a booth decorated with branches, fruits, and flowers. A booth of this sort may be erected also in a synagogue courtyard or on a synagogue terrace.

Talmud: Record of legal decisions and discussions of ancient Jewish sages, the fundamental work of the Oral Law that complements the Written Law (Pentateuch). There are two versions of the Talmud—"Babylonian" and "Palestinian" or "Jerusalem." Each is divided into the Mishnah and the Gemara.

Temple: Used in this book with a capital *T* to indicate the central sacrificial sanctuary at Jerusalem, built by King Solomon, rebuilt after the Jews' exile in Babylonia and under King Herod. Used in this book with a lower-case *t* to refer to other religious structures of ancient pagans, French Protestants, and Reform Jews.

Torah: Written Law, the Pentateuch. Handwritten on parchment scrolls, it is kept in the synagogue ark.

yeshivah: *See* house of study. The term *yeshivah* may connote advanced learning in a formally constituted school.

Notes for the Visitor

Several hundred synagogues exist in Europe. Some antedate 1939, and have either been repaired or converted to new uses, while about a hundred were built after 1945, principally in western Europe.

Those who wish to visit the buildings are welcome during religious services, held on Fridays at sundown and on Saturday mornings. Services also are held at other times including the festival days and High Holy Days, which can be determined by using a Jewish calendar or consulting the synagogue office; the dates change each year with the lunar calendar. Synagogues may not be open at other times except by prior appointment.

Men and women probably will be seated separately during religious services, because most European congregations follow the orthodox practice of separating the sexes. Men will be asked to cover their heads; skullcaps are sometimes available for those who have come without hats. Long trousers rather than shorts, and shirts with long sleeves are appropriate. Women in orthodox synagogues may be expected to wear long-sleeved garments, stockings, and a head scarf, even in summer. People should not bring handbags, cameras, or other travel paraphernalia to orthodox services, since those who follow orthodox rules do not carry burdens on the Sabbath. Visitors may telephone the Jewish community office in advance to determine the strictness of traditional observance.

Inquiries may be made in English in many places, and in Yiddish (or German) in much of Europe north of the Alps. In Italy and the Balkans, the Jewish *lingua franca* may be Ladino, a language based on Spanish.

Travelers in eastern Europe should check with the local Jewish community or the national tourist office before attempting to visit present or former synagogue buildings. This recommendation is offered for the visitor's own security, a consideration which should override curiosity or the frustration of being denied entrance to a particular building. One reason why admission to many European synagogues is restricted is the fear of anti-Semitic activity. A prudent person whose credentials are not well known in the city he is visiting will wish to protect himself from accusations of suspicious behavior, and will therefore not take photographs surreptitiously or attempt to persuade guards to let him into a building.

Synagogues that have been converted to new uses may not be open to the public. Those that are now museums, archives, cinemas, or the like normally have hours of opening posted outside or are listed in tourist literature. Photography may be forbidden in these institutions, as well as in former synagogues now in private hands. It is best to inquire at the Jewish community office (rather than of the present occupants) concerning the circumstances of the building's conversion to new uses.

Anyone who is denied admission to present or former synagogue buildings may be able to obtain photographs from government or institutional bureaus. Every European country has an office dedicated to the study and care of architectural monuments; the national tourist office will supply the name and address of the national monuments service, which may have photographs of synagogues, but not of every one. Commercial photographers who supply magazines and television companies with pictures may have synagogue pictures. The Central Archive for the History of the Jewish People, Jerusalem, has a large photographic archive, as does the Holocaust memorial institution, Yad Vashem. In New York City, three institutions have large collections of photographs and illustrated books: New York Public Library (Jewish Division and Picture Collection); Leo Baeck Institute, 129 East 73rd Street, New York, NY 10021, for German-speaking areas; YIVO, 1048 Fifth Avenue, New York, NY 10028, for eastern Europe. Jewish theological seminaries and Jewish museums in the U.S.A. and abroad also may have photographic archives. Not all the photographs are of good quality, nor are there images of all synagogues, but thousands of photographs are available.

There are several guides to Jewish monuments in Europe that contain information about synagogues, war memorials, Jewish community buildings, Jewish museums, and former ghettoes. The information varies in its accuracy, but the prospective visitor will probably find what he or she needs in the following sources:

S. Lightman, ed., *The Jewish Travel Guide,* published annually by the *Jewish Chronicle,* London. Lists synagogues and Jewish institutions by country and usually by city. Gives street addresses and telephone numbers for most of western Europe, and gives basic information for eastern Europe, particularly for capital cities, where the visitor may obtain data concerning communities elsewhere. The guide also contains information on holy days, kasher restaurants, hotels catering to Jewish guests, and suppliers of commercial services, including Jewish bookshops.

B. Postal and S. Abramson, *The Traveler's Guide to Jewish Landmarks in Europe,* New York, 1971. Lists essential addresses; fewer are given than in the *Jewish Travel Guide;* no telephone numbers. In a conversational tone the book recounts legends and traditions, interesting circumstances attending synagogue building, streets named for Jewish martyrs and public figures, etc. Stresses human interest, as compared with the businesslike *Jewish Travel Guide.*

Guides devoted to specific parts of Europe include:

F. Ambrière, ed., *Guide religieux de France,* Bibliothèque des Guides Bleus, Paris, 1967, pp. 75–99 on "Le judaïsme français," by J. Eisenberg.
R. Berg, C. Chemouny, and F. Didi, *Guide juif de France,* Paris, ca. 1968, the most comprehensive French guide with addresses, telephone numbers, historical information, libraries, organizations, bookshops, biographies, etc.
E. Haymann, *Paris Judaica,* Paris, 1979.
V. Issembert-Gannat, *Guide du Judaïsme à Paris,* Paris, ca. 1964.

V. Benda, *The State Jewish Museum in Prague,* Prague, 1967. Describes in detail the synagogues of Prague that have been converted into exhibition rooms for the museum. Discusses their contents.
J. Heřman and M. Vilímkova, *Prague's Synagogues,* Prague, 1970. A good brief guide to the buildings written by serious students of the architecture.

Jewish Historical Monuments in Dubrovnik, Dubrovnik, n.d., pamphlet.

U. Fortis, *Jews and Synagogues: Venice, Florence, Rome, Leghorn. A Practical Guide,* Venice, 1973. Contains addresses, telephone numbers, and opening hours. Good historical and architectural information, though it is awkwardly translated from the Italian. Exceptionally well illustrated, including building plans.
G. Reinisch Sullam, *Jewish Art Treasures in Venice,* New York, 1973.

F. J. Dubiez, *The Sephardi Community of Amsterdam,* Amsterdam, n.d.

The visitor intending to visit German synagogues should consult a list of German synagogues destroyed in 1938ff. in A. Diamant, *Zerstörte Synagogen von November 1938. Eine Bestandsaufnahme,* Frankfurt am Main, 1978. He gives an alphabetical list of towns and notes the later fate of the buildings; some have been rehabilitated and others have new uses.

The visitor to Hungary should consult pictures in I. Heller and Z. Vajda, *The Synagogues of Hungary,* eds. R. Braham and E. Farkas, New York, 1968. Many survive, usually with new uses. The Jewish Museum in Budapest has hundreds of photographs of synagogues in present and former Hungarian territory.

For Polish buildings, see Appendix II.

Bibliography

In this list of selected references, general works are given first, then works dealing with specific subjects and geographical areas. I use current country boundaries and city names, although this leads to problems in nomenclature (for example, using *Leningrad* for *St. Petersburg,* or using Slavic names for Silesian and East Prussian towns that were German before 1945 and where the Jewish culture was German-oriented). Consequently, it seemed best to follow usage in modern atlases. Locations are listed under both their current and former names in the Index.

DICTIONARIES AND ENCYCLOPEDIAS

Encyclopedia Judaica, Berlin, ca. 1928–32. Vols. A–Lyra only were published.

Encyclopedia Judaica, Jerusalem, 1971–72.

Jewish Encyclopedia, New York and London, 1901–6.

Jüdisches Lexikon, Berlin, 1927–30.

Philo-Lexikon. Handbuch des jüdischen Wissens, Berlin, 1935.

Pinkas ha-Kehillot [Encyclopedia of Jewish Communities], Jerusalem, continuing.

Universal Jewish Encyclopedia, New York, 1939–43.

PERIODICALS

Index of Articles on Jewish Studies, Jerusalem, 1966–.

Index of Articles Relative to Jewish History and Literature Published in Periodicals from 1665 to 1900, ed. M. Schwab, Paris, 1923; reprint ed., New York, 1972. Original title: *Répertoire des articles d'histoire et de littérature juives parus dans les périodiques de 1665 à 1900.*

Index to Jewish Periodicals, ed. M. Leikind, Cleveland, 1963.

Among monthly or quarterly periodicals, those with the most articles on synagogues include: *Israel. La rassegna mensile; Monatsschrift für Geschichte und Wissenschaft des Judentums; Menorah; Ost und West; Revue des études juives.*

Among weekly periodicals, the most useful have been: *Allgemeine Zeitung des Judentums* (1837–1922), superseded by *C.-V. Zeitung* (1922–38), then by *Allgemeine unabhängige jüdische Wochenzeitung* (1945–); *Jewish Chronicle; Oesterreichische Wochenschrift; De Vrijdagavond.*

BIBLIOGRAPHIES

Bibliographie der Dissertationen über Judentum und jüdische Persönlichkeiten die 1872–1962 an oesterreichischen Hochschulen (Wien, Graz, Innsbruck) approbiert wurden, ed. W. Bihl, Vienna, 1965.

S. Brisman, *A History and Guide to Judaic Bibliography,* Cincinnati, 1977 (Bibliographica Judaica, 7: Jewish Research Literature, 1).

G. Kisch and K. Roepke, *Schriften zur Geschichte der Juden: eine Bibliographie der in Deutschland und der Schweiz 1922–1955 erschienenen Dissertationen,* Tübingen, 1959 (Schriftenreihe wissenschaftlicher Abhandlungen des Leo Baeck Institute of Jews from Germany, 4).

L. A. Mayer, *Bibliography of Jewish Art,* Jerusalem, 1967.

J. Rothenberg, *Judaica Reference Materials: A Selective Annotated Bibliography,* Waltham, Mass., 1971.

S. Shunami, *Bibliography of Jewish Bibliographies,* 2d ed., Jerusalem, 1965; supplement, 1975.

YIVO. *Doctoral Dissertations and Masters' Theses Accepted by American Institutions of Higher Learning* [on Jewish subjects], New York, 1963, continuing.

GENERAL WORKS

A. Bachi, "Appunti sulla architettura della sinagoga," *Israel. La rassegna mensile* 2 ser., VIII (1933), pp. 25–46.

R. D. Barnett, ed., *The Sephardi Heritage,* New York, 1971.

J. Carlebach, "Architektur der Synagoge," *Jeschurun* XVI, #3–4 (1929), pp. 109–31.

A. Charim, *Die toten Gemeinden,* Vienna, etc., 1976.

M.J.S. Chiat, *A Handbook of Synagogue Architecture,* Chico, Calif., 1982 (Brown Judaic Studies, 29).

B. deBreffny, *The Synagogue,* New York, 1978.

"Die Einweihung zweier neuer grosser Tempel in Nürnberg und Paris," *Allgemeine Zeitung des Judentums* XXXVIII (1874), pp. 669–72.

A. Eisenberg, *The Synagogue through the Ages,* New York, 1974.

D. J. Elazar, ed., *Balkan Jewries Today,* Jerusalem and Philadelphia, 1974.

I. Feuer, "Magyarországi középkori zsinagógák az általános európai fejlődés tükrében," *Magyar Izraelita Országos Kommittee, Evkönyv* 1971/1972, pp. 43–46.

M. Fleischer, "Über Tempelbau," *Die Neuzeit* XIV, #14 (April 4, 1884), pp. 134–37, #16 (April 18, 1884), pp. 154–56.

R. Gordis and M. Davidowitz, eds., *Art in Judaism. Studies in the Jewish Artistic Experience,* New York, 1975.

A. Grotte, *Deutsche, böhmische und polnische Synagogentypen vom XI bis Anfang des XIX Jahrhunderts,* Berlin, 1915 (Mittheilungen der Gesellschaft zur Erforschung jüdischer Kunstdenkmäler, Frankfurt, #7, 8).

———, "Kultbauten der Vergangenheit," *C.-V. Zeitung* X, #27 (July 3, 1931), pp. 343–44.

———, "Ostjüdische Sakralkunst und ihre Ausstrahlung auf deutsches Gebiet," *Monatshefte für Kunstwissenschaft* XI, #5 (1918), pp. 135–38.

M. Grünwald, "Wie baut man Synagogen?" *AZJ,* LXV (1901), pp. 115–17.

C. Gurlitt, *Handbuch der Architektur. Kirchen,* Part 4, VIII, #1, Darmstadt, 1906, pp. 126–65.

J. Gutmann, ed., *Ancient Synagogues: The State of Research,* Chico, Calif., 1981 (Brown Judaic Studies, 22).

———, ed., *The Synagogue. Studies in Origins, Archaeology, and Architecture,* New York, 1975.

E. Hiller, "Betrachtungen über den modernen Synagogenbau," *Ost und West* VI (1906), cols. 28–36.

K. Hruby, *Die Synagoge. Geschichtliche Entwicklung einer Institution,* Zurich, 1971 (Schriften zur Judentumskunde, 3).

U. Kaploun, *The Synagogue,* Philadelphia, 1973.

A. Kohut, *Berühmte israelitische Männer und Frauen in der Kulturgeschichte der Menschheit,* Leipzig, 1900.

A. Kosel and L. Eisenberg, eds., *Deutsch-oesterreichisches Künstler und Schriftsteller Lexikon,* Vienna, 1902–5.

S. Krauss, *Synagogale Altertümer,* Berlin, 1922.

R. Krautheimer, *Mittelalterliche Synagogen,* Berlin, 1927.

J. Kreppel, *Juden und Judentum von Heute,* Zurich, 1925.

H. Künzl, "Die Architektur der mittelalterlichen Synagogen und rituellen Bäder," *Judentum im Mittelalter,* exhibition at Schloss Halbturm, catalogue ed. K. Schubert, Eisenstadt, 1978, pp. 40–59.

———, *Islamische Stilelemente im Synagogenbau des 19. und frühen 20. Jahrhunderts,* Frankfurt am Main, 1984 (Judentum und Umwelt, vol. 9). (Not consulted.)

F. Landsberger, "The Sacred Direction in Synagogue and Church," *Hebrew Union College Annual* XXVIII (1957), pp. 181–203.

I. Levy, *The Synagogue: Its History and Function,* London, 1963.

B. Litvin, *The Sanctity of the Synagogue,* New York, 1959.

L. Löw, *Gesammelte Schriften,* ed. I. Löw, Szeged, 1898; reprinted New York and Hildesheim, 1979.

M. Lowenthal, *A World Passed By,* New York, 1933.

T. and M. Metzger, *Jewish Life in the Middle Ages,* New York, 1982, esp. pp. 59–75.

P. Meyer, B. D. Weinryb, and E. Dushinski, *The Jews in the Soviet Satellites,* Syracuse, 1953.

H. Rosenau, "The Architectural Development of the Synagogue," diss., Courtauld Institute, 1939.

———, "The Synagogue and Protestant Church Architecture," *Journal of the Warburg and Courtauld Institutes* IV (1940–41), pp. 80–84.

C. Roth, ed., *Jewish Art,* New York, 1961; rev. ed., B. Narkiss, ed., 1971.

S. Rubenstein, *The Synagogue. An Illustrated Analy-*

sis of the Synagogue, Bronx, N.Y., 1973.

S. Seeligman, "Assimilatie in architectuur," *De Vrijdagavond* VI, #25 (Sept. 20, 1929), pp. 387–90.

S. Waetzoldt and V. Haas, *Bibliographie zur Architektur im 19 Jahrhundert. Die Aufsätze in den deutschsprachigen Architekturzeitschriften 1789–1918,* Munich, 1977, vol. 3, pp. 1603–20.

R. Wischnitzer, *The Architecture of the European Synagogue,* Philadelphia, 1964.

———, "The Problem of Synagogue Architecture," *Commentary* III, #3 (March 1947), pp. 233–41.

ART

D. Davidowicz (also spelled Davidovitch), *Art and Artists in Polish Synagogues,* Jerusalem, Kibbutz Amuhad, 1982 (Hebrew; not consulted).

———, *Wall Paintings of Synagogues in Poland,* Jerusalem, 1968 (Hebrew; to be translated into German by H. Künzl).

———, *Wandmalereien in alten Synagogen. Das Wirken des Malers Elieser Sussmann in Deutschland,* Hameln and Hannover, 1969.

Encyclopedia Judaica, Jerusalem, 1971, s.v. Art.

F. Feuchtwanger, "Die bildenden Künste im jüdischen Kultus," *Ost und West* III, #5 (1903), cols. 335–47.

H. Frauberger, "Über Bau und Ausschmückung alter Synagogen," *Mitteilungen der Gesellschaft zur Erforschung jüdischer Kunstdenkmäler* II (1901).

R. Gordis and M. Davidowitz, eds., *Art in Judaism,* New York, 1975.

J. Gutmann, ed., *Beauty in Holiness: Studies in Jewish Customs and Ceremonial Art,* New York, 1970.

———, *No Graven Images. Studies in Art and the Hebrew Bible,* New York, 1971.

———, *The Jewish Sanctuary,* Leiden, 1983 (Iconography of Religions, Section XXIII, Judaism, fasc. 2; not consulted).

I. Z. Kahana, "Omanut bet ha-keneset be-halakha," *Bet ha-keneset,* M. Hacohen, ed., Jerusalem, 1955, pp. 255–308.

F. Landauer, "Jüdische Kultbauten von Heute," *C.-V. Zeitung* X, #27 (July 3, 1931), pp. 341–42.

L. A. Mayer, *Bibliography of Jewish Art,* Jerusalem, 1967.

M. Osborn, "Baukünstler und Bauten von Hitzig bis Mendelsohn," *C.-V. Zeitung* X, #27 (July 3, 1931), pp. 337–39.

C. Roth, ed., *Jewish Art,* London, 1961; rev. ed., B. Narkiss, ed., 1971.

K. Schwarz, *Die Juden in der Kunst,* Berlin, 1928.

H. Strauss, "The Horb Synagogue and Polish Synagogue Murals," *Ariel* #24 (Spring, 1969), pp. 75–80.

E. Toeplitz, *Die Malerei in den Synagogen (besonders in Franken),* Frankfurt am Main, 1929 (Beiträge zur jüdischen Kunstgeschichte, 3).

A. Wolf, "Etwas über jüdische Kunst and ältere jüdische Künstler," *Mitteilungen der Gesellschaft für jüdische Volkskunde* V, Heft IX, #1 (1902), pp. 12–74.

POSTWAR SYNAGOGUES

(See also Bibliographies for Belfast, Essen, Hamburg, Livorno.)

Wischnitzer, *Architecture,* pp. 248–77, including illustrations.

AUSTRIA

Salzburgs wiederaufgebaute Synagoge. Festschrift zur Einweihung, Dezember, 1968, Salzburg, 1969.

FRANCE

"Centro comunitario e sinagoga a Parigi," *L'architettura* XXVIII (June 1982), pp. 407–11.

"Concours pour la reconstruction d'une synagogue à Strasbourg," *L'architecture d'aujourd'hui* XXIII, #44 (Sept. 1952), p. xxv.

La Synagogue de la Paix, Strasbourg, 1958.

E. Roditi, "Les centres communautaires. Un nouveau visage du judaïsme français," *L'Arche* #113 (July 1966), pp. 14–19.

"Strasbourg, Synagogue de la Paix," *Techniques et architecture* XXI, #2 (March 1961), pp. 8–11.

"Synagogue à Paris," *L'architecture d'aujourd'hui* XXXVI (Apr.–May 1966), pp. 92–93; also "Projet de synagogue," (Oct.–Nov. 1966), p. 30.

GERMANY

Einweihung der Synagoge Würzburgs, Würzburg, 1970.

H. Eschwege, *Die Synagoge in der deutschen Geschichte,* Dresden, 1980, pp. 171–76.

Festschrift zur Einweihung der neuen Synagoge in Stuttgart, Stuttgart, 1952.

Festschrift zur Weihe der neuen Synagoge in Münster/Westf., Münster, 1961.

R. R. Geis, "Kirchen der letzten Jahre in Deutschland," *Das Münster* XVII (Nov.–Dec. 1964), pp. 365–89.

C. Gerle, "Zur Fertigstellung der neuen Synagoge," *Allgemeine unabhängige jüdische Wochenzeitung* XIV (Nov. 27, 1959), p. 17.

H. Goldschmidt, "Neubau der Synagoge in Bonn," newspaper clipping courtesy of Rachel Wischnitzer.

H. Guttmann, "Das Düsseldorfer Gemeindezentrum," *Die neue Synagoge in Düsseldorf. Zur Einweihung am 7 September, 1958,* Düsseldorf, 1958, pp. 28–31.

———, "Modernes Gemeindezentrum in Osnabrück," *Allgemeine unabhängige jüdische Wochenzeitung* XXIV (May 30, 1969), p. 6.

"Jüdisches Gemeindehaus, Berlin, Fasanenstrasse," and "Neue Synagoge mit Gemeindezentrum in Essen," *Baumeister* LVIII, #2 (Feb. 1961), pp. 96–100 (Essen), pp. 100–105 (Berlin).

K. Kuehling, *Die Juden in Osnabrück,* Osnabrück, 1969.

H. Lamm, "Synagogenbauten Gestern und Heute," *Baumeister* LXIII, #2 (Feb. 1966), pp. 53–59.

Leben und Schicksal. Zur Einweihung der Synagoge in Hannover, Hannover, 1963, esp. pp. 199–206.

O. K., "Eine Dankesschuld abgetragen," *Allgemeine unabhängige jüdische Wochenzeitung* XXVI, July 16, 1971, p. 3.

GREAT BRITAIN

"Jewish Centre. West London." *Architect and Building News* CCXXIX, #12 (Mar. 23, 1966), pp. 523–28.

Jewish Chronicle, July 10, 1964 (Romford), July 31, 1964 (Wallingford, Carmel College Synagogue).

"Synagogue, St. John's Wood. T. P. Bennett & Son, Architects," *Architectural Review* CXXIII (Jan. 1958), p. 27.

"Synagogue, Woodford, Essex," *Architect and Building News* CCVI (Dec. 16, 1954), pp. 759–60.

"United Synagogue. Great Cumberland Place, W. 1," *Builder* CCIII (Oct. 12, 1962), pp. 729–31.

NETHERLANDS

J. Bijnen, "Synagoge te Oss," *Bouwkundig Weekblad* LXXIII (May 27, 1960), pp. 236–39.

"Synagoge van de Nederl. Israel. Gemeente te Rotterdam," *Bouwkundig Weekblad* LXXIV (April 17, 1956), pp. 177–80.

GEOGRAPHIC AREAS

AUSTRIA-HUNGARY AND THE BALKANS

H. Gold, *Gedenkbuch der untergegangenen Judengemeinden des Burgenlandes,* Tel Aviv, 1970.

F. Grünvald and E. Fülöp-Naményi, *Budapesti zsinagógák,* Budapest, 1949.

I. Heller and Z. Vajda, *The Synagogues of Hungary. An Album,* eds. R. Braham and E. Farkas, New York, 1968.

K. Lohrmann, ed., *1000 Jahre österreichisches Judentum. Ausstellungskatalog, Eisenstadt, 1982 (Studia Judaica Austriaca, 9).*

L. Moses, "Synagogenbauten und deren Reste in Niederösterreich," *Unsere Heimat. Monatsblatt des Vereins für Landeskunde von Niederösterreich* n.F. V, #10 (1932), pp. 297–307.

M. Paul, *Technischer Führer durch Wien,* Vienna, 1910, pp. 281–86.

J. Pick, *Jüdisch-geschichtliche Stätten in Wien und den oesterreichischen Bundesländern,* Vienna, 1935.

M. Pollák, "Zsidó templomépités Magyarországon a XIX századtól a mai napig," *Az Izraelita Magyar Irodalmi Társulat Kiadványai,* LVI, *Evkönyv,* 1934.

P. Ujvari, ed., *Magyár Zsidó Lexikon,* Bụdapest, 1929.

BELGIUM

Brussels. La Grande Synagogue de Bruxelles. Contributions à l'histoire juive de Bruxelles, 1878–1978, Brussels, 1978.

J. Gutwirth, "Antwerp Jewry Today," *Jewish Journal of Sociology* X, #1 (June 1968), pp. 121–37.

Z. Szajkowski, "Bibliography of Jewish Periodicals in Belgium," *Studies in Bibliography and Booklore* IV, #3 (1960), pp. 103–22.

CZECHOSLOVAKIA

E. Bachmann, *Eine spätstaufische Baugruppe in mittelböhmischen Raum,* Brno and Leipzig, 1940

(Kunstgeschichte in Sudeten und Carpathienländer, 3).

V. Benda, *The State Jewish Museum in Prague,* Prague, n.d.

L. Ehrmann, "Synagogen," *Die jüdische Denkmäler in der Tschechoslowakei,* ed. S. H. Lieben, Prague, 1933, pp. 6–9.

B. Foges and D. Podiebrad, *Altertümer der Prager Josefstadt,* Prague, 1855.

H. Gold, *Die Juden und judengemeinden Mährens in Vergangenheit und Gegenwart,* Brno, 1929.

A. Grotte, "Historische Baudokumente Jüdischer Wanderung in Böhmen und Mähren," *Jahrbuch der Gesellschaft für die Geschichte der Juden in der Čechoslovakischen Republik* VII (1935), pp. 399–410.

———, "Vergessene Sakralbauten in Westböhmen," *Technische Blätter. Zeitschrift des Deutschen Polytechnischen Vereins in Böhmen* L (1918), pp. 7–14.

J. Heřman and M. Vílímkova, *Die Prager Synagogen,* Prague, 1970.

E. Laor, *Vergangen und ausgelöscht. Erinnerungen an das slowakisch-ungarische Judentum,* Stuttgart, 1972 (Veröffentlichung des Leo Baeck Instituts, I).

O. Muneles, *Bibliographical Survey of Jewish Prague,* Prague, [1952].

H. Volavková, *Zmizelá Praha, 3. Zidovské mésto Pražské,* Prague, 1947.

R. Weltschied, *Das jüdische Prag,* Kronberg, 1978.

EASTERN EUROPE AND THE U.S.S.R.

R. Abramovitch, *The Vanished World,* New York, 1947.

Z. Baker, "Bibliography of Eastern European Memorial Books: Updated and Revised," *Toledot* III, #2/3 (Fall, 1979/Winter, 1980), pp. 7–42.

M. Bałaban, *Bibliografia historii żydów w Polsce . . . 1900–1939,* Warsaw, 1939; reissued in Polish with English title: *Bibliography on the History of the Jews in Poland and in Neighboring Lands,* Introduction by E. Mendelsohn, Jerusalem, 1978.

———, *Bóżnice obronne na wschodnich kresach Rzeczpospolitej. Studia historyczne,* Warsaw, 1927.

———, *Dzielnica żydowska, jej dzieje i zabytki,* L'vov, 1909 (Biblioteka Lwowska, 5, 6).

———, *O warownych bóżnicach w Polsce, 1900–1939,* Warsaw, 1939.

———, *Przewodnik po żydowskich zabytkach Krakowa,* Cracow, 1935.

———, "Wehrhafte Synagogen in den östlichen Randgebieten der polnischen Republik," *Menorah* V, #6/7 (1927), pp. 369–76.

———, *Zabytki historyczne żydów w Polsce,* Warsaw, 1929.

M. Bersohn, *Dyplomataryusz dotyczący żydów w dawnej Polsce . . . 1388–1782,* Warsaw, 1910.

———, *Kilka słów o dawniejszych bóżnicach drewnianych w Polsce,* Cracow, 1895–1903.

Black Book of Localities Whose Jewish Population Was Exterminated by the Nazis, Jerusalem, 1965.

M. Borwicz, *A Thousand Years of Jewish Life in Poland,* Paris, 1956.

R. Braham and M. Hauer, *Jews in the Communist World. A Bibliography, 1945–1962,* New York, 1963.

A. Breier, M. Eisler, and M. Grünwald, *Holzsynagogen in Polen,* Baden bei Wien, 1934.

D. Buxton, *The Wooden Churches of Eastern Europe: An Introductory Survey,* Cambridge, 1981.

D. Davidowicz, *Bate keneset be-Polen ve-Hurbanam,* Jerusalem, 1960. English title: *The Synagogues of Poland and their Destruction.*

L. Dobroszycki and B. Kirshenblatt-Gimblett, *Image before my Eyes: A Photographic History of Jewish Life in Poland, 1884–1939,* New York, 1977.

Entsiklopedia shel Galuyot [Encyclopedia of the Diaspora], Jerusalem, 1953, continuing. Volumes to date deal with eastern Europe.

Z. Gloger, *Budownictwo drzewne i wyroby z drzewa w dawnej Polsce,* vol. 1, Warsaw, 1907.

H. Gold, *Geschichte der Juden in der Bukowina,* 1, Tel Aviv, 1958.

M. Goldstein, *Kultura i sztuka ludy żydowskiego na ziemach polskich,* Warsaw, 1935.

Z. Gostynski, *Les pierres racontent,* Paris, 1973.

A. Grotte, "Die Beeinflüssung jüdischer östlicher Sakralkunst durch Prager Vorbilder," *Jahrbuch der Gesellschaft für Geschichte der Juden in der Čechoslovakischen Republik* VI (1934), pp. 457–69.

———, "Neuere Forschungen über kirchliche Verteidigungsbauten," *Die Denkmalpflege* XXIII, #7/8 (1921), pp. 56–59.

———, *Synagogenspuren in schlesischen Kirchen,* Wrocław, 1931 (Schriften der Gesellschaft zur Förderung der Wissenschaft des Judentums, 41).

M. Grünwald, "Was geschieht für die jüdischen Kunstdenkmäler in Polen?" *Menorah* VIII, #5/6 (1930), pp. 261–63.

A. Heppner and I. Herzberg, *Aus Vergangenheit und Gegenwart der Juden und der jüdischen Gemeinden in den posener Landen,* Koschmin, 1904–28.

P. Juckoff-Skopau, *Architektonischer Atlas von Polen (Kongress-Polen),* Berlin, 1921 (Beiträge zur polnischen Landeskunde, Reihe B, Band 8).

Die Juden in Polen. Sonderheft of *Menorah* V (1927); originally *Menorah* V, #5/6 (1927).

A. Kubiak, "Żydowska architektura zabytkowa w Polsce," *Biuletyn Żydowski Instytut Historyczny,* 1953, #6–7, pp. 122–68, #8, pp. 73–96.

I. Levitats, *The Jewish Community in Russia, 1844–1917,* Jerusalem, 1981.

G. Lukomskii, *Jewish Art in European Synagogues,* London and New York, 1947.

Y. L. Hacohen Maimon (Fishman), ed., *Arim va-imahot be-Yisroel,* Jerusalem, 1969 continuing.

K. Mokłowski, *Sztuka ludowa w Polsce,* L'vov, 1903.

A. Penkalla and J. Szczepański, "Żydowskie Budowle Instytutowe w miastach Guberni Radomskiej w Polowie XIX w.," *Biuletyn Żydowski Instytut Historyczny* 1/101 (1977), pp. 77–83.

K. and M. Piechotka, *Wooden Synagogues,* Warsaw, 1959.

L. Ran, *Jerusalem of Lithuania,* New York, 1974.

J. Rothenberg, *The Jewish Religion in the Soviet Union,* New York, 1972, esp. chap. 2, "Synagogues."

———, *Synagogues in the Soviet Union, Report to the Institute of East European Jewish Affairs, Brandeis University,* March 1966.

I. Schiper, A. Tartakower, and A. Hafftka, eds., *Żydzi w Polsce Odrodzonej,* Warsaw, [ca. 1932].

A. Shulman, *The Old Country. The Lost World of East European Jewry,* New York, 1974.

Sistematicheskii ukazatel literatury o evreikakh na russkom Iazike, Leningrad, 1893.

P. Stoyanov, *Churches and Religions in the People's Republic of Bulgaria,* Sofia, 1975, pp. 72–75.

A. Szyszko-Bohusz, "Materjaly do architektury bóżnic w Polsce," *Prace komisji Historji Sztuki* IV, #1 (1927), pp. 1–25.

E. Vinecour, *Polish Jews. The Final Chapter,* New York, 1977.

P. Wasserman, ed., *Glos gminy żydowskiej,* vol. 3, Warsaw, 1939.

R. Wischnitzer, "Mutual Influences between Eastern and Western Europe in Synagogue Architecture from the 12th to the 18th Centuries," *YIVO Annual of Jewish Social Science* II–III (1947–1948), pp. 25–68.

———, "Synagogen im ehemaligen königreich Polen," *Das Buch von den polnischen Juden,* eds. S. J. Agnon and A. Eliasberg, Berlin, 1916, pp. 89–105.

Yevreiskaia Entsiklopedia, 1912.

A. Y. Yodfat, "The Closure of Synagogues in the Soviet Union," *Soviet Jewish Affairs* III, #1 (1973), pp. 48–56.

S. Zajczyk, "Architektura barokowych bóżnic murowanych w Polsce," *Biuletyn Naukowy* (= *Biuletyn Historii Sztuki*), 1933, #4, pp. 106–95.

———, *Bóżnice drewniane na terenic woj. białostockiego. Woj. białostockie Przeszlość i zabytki,* Białystok, 1928.

FRANCE

F. Ambrière, ed., *Guide religieux de la France,* Paris, 1967.

R. Berg, C. Chemouny, and F. Didi, *Guide juif de France,* Paris, ca. 1967.

B. Blumenkranz, *Art et archéologie des juifs en France médiévale,* Toulouse, 1980 (Collection Franco-Judaica, 9).

———, *Documents modernes sur les juifs XVIe–XXe siècles. I: Dépots parisiens,* Toulouse, 1979.

——— and M. Levy, *Bibliographie des juifs en France,* Toulouse, 1974 (Collection Franco-Judaica).

Centre de documentation juive contemporaine. Bibliothèque, Catalogue I: *La France de l'Affaire Dreyfus à nos jours,* Paris, 1964.

H. Gross, *Gallia Judaica: Dictionnaire géographique d'après les sources rabbiniques,* Paris, 1897 (Société des études juives, Publications); rev. ed., S. Schwarzfuchs, ed., Amsterdam, 1969.

E. Haymann, *Paris Judaica,* Paris, 1979.

V. Issembert-Gannat, *Guide du judaïsme à Paris,* Paris, ca. 1964.

A. Lunel, *Juifs du Languedoc, de la Provence et des états français du pape,* Paris, 1975.

F. Narjoux, *Paris. Monuments élévées par la ville 1850–1880. Édifices religieux,* Paris, 1883.

F. Raphael and R. Weyl, *Les juifs en Alsace. Culture,*

société, histoire, Toulouse, 1977 (Collection Franco-Judaica, 5).

E. Roditi, "Les centres communautaires. Un nouveau visage du judaïsme français," *L'Arche* 113 (July 1966), pp. 14–19.

P. R. Roland-Marcel, *A Guide to Jewish Monuments,* Paris, 1937.

Seine (Département), *Direction des Travaux de Paris. Inventaire général des oeuvres d'art appartenant à la ville de Paris,* vol. 4, 1886.

Z. Szajkowski, *Analytical Franco-Jewish Gazetteer, 1939–1945,* New York, 1966.

———, *Franco-Judaica: An Analytical Bibliography of Books, Pamphlets, Decrees, Briefs, and other Documents Pertaining to the Jews in France, 1500–1788,* New York, 1962.

———, *Jews and the French Revolutions of 1789, 1830, and 1848,* New York, 1970.

GERMANY

Arbeitsinformationen über Studienprojekte auf dem Gebiet der Geschichte des deutschen Judentums und des Antisemitismus, serial publication.

N. B. Bamberger, "Synagogen in Württemberg," *Israelitisches Wochenblatt* (Zurich) LXXXIV (Feb. 3, 1984), pp. 15–19.

V. Bendt and R. Bothe, eds., *Synagogen in Berlin. Zur Geschichte einer zerstörten Architektur,* Berlin, 1983 (Stadtgeschichtliche Publikationen herausgegeben von Rolf Bothe, 1).

A. Diamant, *Zerstörte Synagogen vom November 1938. Eine Bestandsaufnahme,* Frankfurt am Main, 1978.

I. Elbogen, M. Brann, and A. Freimann, eds., *Germania judaica* I, Frankfurt am Main, 1934 (Gesellschaft zur Förderung der Wissenschaft des Judentums. Schriften).

H. Eschwege, *Die Synagoge in der deutschen Geschichte,* Dresden, 1980.

A. Freimann, ed., *Katalog der Judaica und Hebraica, I: Judaica,* Frankfurt am Main (Stadtbibliothek), 1932.

H. Hammer-Schenk, "Aesthetische und politische Funktionen historisierender Baustile im Synagogenbau des ausgehenden 19 Jahrhunderts," *Kritische Berichte. Mitteilungsorgan des Ulmer Vereins für Kunstwissenschaft* III, #2–3 (1975), pp. 12–24.

———, *Synagogen in Deutschland. Geschichte einer Baugattung im 19 und 20 Jahrhundert (1780–1933),* Hamburg, 1981, with extensive bibliography.

———, "Untersuchungen zum Synagogenbau in Deutschland von der ersten Emanzipation bis zur gesetzlichen Gleichberechtigung der Juden (1800–1871)," diss., Tübingen, 1974 (supplanted by *Synagogen in Deutschland*).

F. Hundsnurcher and G. Taddey, *Die jüdische Gemeinde in Baden,* Stuttgart, 1968 (Veröffentlichungen der Archivverwaltung, Baden-Württemberg, 19).

A. Kober, "Jewish Communities in Germany from the Age of Enlightenment to their Destruction by the Nazis," *Jewish Social Studies* IX, #3 (1947), pp. 195–238.

M. Kreutzberger and I. Foerg, eds., *Leo Baeck Institute. New York. Bibliothek und Archiv. Katalog,* vol. 1, Tübingen, 1970.

H. Künzl, "Zur Aufnahme islamischer Architekturstile im Synagogenbau des 19 Jahrhunderts," *Zeitschrift der deutschen Morgenländischen Gesellschaft. Supplement,* vol. 3, part 2, *19 Deutscher Orientalistentag . . . , 1975 in Freiburg im Breisgau, Vorträge,* ed. W. Voigt, 1977, pp. 1626–31.

———, "Synagogen," *Die Kunst des 19 Jahrhunderts im Rheinland, I: Architektur,* eds. E. Trier and W. Weyres, Düsseldorf, 1980, pp. 339–46.

H. Ottenheimer, "The Disappearance of Jewish Communities in Germany, 1900–1938," *Jewish Social Studies* III (1941), pp. 189–206.

P. Rieger, *Jüdische Gotteshäuser und Friedhöfe in Württemberg,* Augsburg, 1932.

H. Rosenau, "German Synagogues in the Early Period of Emancipation," *Publications of the Leo Baeck Institute. Yearbook* VIII (1963), pp. 214–25.

———, "Gottfried Semper and German Synagogue Architecture," *Publications of the Leo Baeck Institute. Yearbook* XXII (1977), pp. 237–44.

H. O. Schembs, ed., *Bibliographie zur Geschichte der Frankfurter Juden, 1781–1945,* Frankfurt am Main, 1978.

K. Schwarz, "Jüdische Kultbauten," *Kunst und Kirche* VII, #2/3 (1930), pp. 89–92.

R. Thalmann and E. Feinermann, *Crystal Night, 9–10 November, 1938,* New York, 1974.

Verband der jüdischen Gemeinden in der DDR, *Gedenke! Vergiss nie! 40 Jahrestag des faschis-*

tischen "Kristallnacht" Pogrom, Berlin, 1979.

Wiener Library Catalog Series: no. 3, *German Jewry: Its History, Life, and Culture,* vol. 1, ed. I. R. Wolff, London, 1958; no. 8 (= vol. 2), ed. H. Kehr, London, 1978.

H. Zopf and G. Heinrich, *Berlin-Bibliographie bis 1960 in der Senatsbibliothek Berlin,* Berlin, 1965 (Veröffentlichungen der Historischen Kommission zu Berlin beim Friedrich Meinecke Institut der Freien Universität 15, Bibliographie, Band 1).

IBERIAN PENINSULA

R. Amador de los Rios y Villalta, *Toledo,* Madrid, 1905, pp. 242–285 (Monumentos arquitectónicos de España, 1).

E. Ashtor, *The Jews of Moslem Spain,* Philadelphia, 1973.

F. Baer, *Die Juden in christlichen Spanien,* Berlin, 1936.

F. Cantera y Burgos, "Identificación de nuevas sinagogas en España," *Sefarad* XXII (1962), pp. 3–16.

———, *Sinagogas de Toledo, Segovia, y Córdoba,* Madrid, 1973.

———, *Sinagogas españolas, con especial estudio de la de Córdoba y la toledana de El Tránsito,* Madrid, 1955.

J. Contreras y Lopez de Ayala, Marques de Lozoya, *Historia del arte hispánico,* Barcelona, 1932–1949, vol. 2, pp. 439–68.

M. Kayserling, *Biblioteca española-portugueza judaica. Dictionnaire, Bibliographie,* Nieuwkoop, 1961.

H. Künzl, "Die Mittelalterliche Synagogen in Spanien," *Emuna* VII (1972), pp. 175–81.

P. Riera Vidal, *The Jews of Toledo and Their Synagogues,* Toledo, 1975 (English edition of a Spanish work of 1958).

R. Singerman, *The Jews in Spain and Portugal. A Bibliography,* New York and London, 1975.

L. Torres Balbas, *Arte almohade, Arte nazarí. Arte mudéjar,* Madrid, 1949 (Ars hispaniae, 4).

ITALY

V. Campajola, "Il ghetto di Roma," *Quaderni dell' Istituto di storia dell'architettura (Università, Roma),* ser. 12, fasc. 67–70 (1965), pp. 67–84.

D. Cassuto, *Ricerche sulle cinque sinagoghe (scuole) de Venezia. Suggerimenti per il loro ripristino,* Jerusalem, 1978.

U. Fortis, *Jews and Synagogues,* Venice, 1973.

S. Kirchstein, "Eine italienische Reise," *Menorah* VII, #1 (1929), pp. 50–62, #2, pp. 76–85.

H. J. Leon, *The Jews of Ancient Rome,* Philadelphia, 1960, esp. pp. 135–66.

E. Loevinson, "Die Juden Italiens," *Ost und West* XII, #9 (1912), cols. 845–54.

A. Milano, *Bibliografia degli studi sulla storia degli ebrei in Italia (1964–66), Israel. La rassegna mensile* XXXII (1966), special supplement.

———, *Bibliotheca historica italo-judaica,* Florence, 1954; supplement, Florence, 1964.

———, *Il ghetto di Roma,* Rome, 1964.

———, "Immagini del passato ebraico," *Israel. La rassegna mensile* XXXIII (1967) and XXXIV (1968), *passim* (articles on many small Italian Jewish communities).

———, "Le sinagoghe del vecchio ghetto di Roma," *Studi romani* VI (1958), pp. 138–59.

E. Morpurgo, "Bibliografia della storia degli ebrei nel Veneto," *Rivista israelitica* VII (1910), pp. 180–90; VIII (1911), pp. 14–29, 68–81, 106–26, 215–29; IX (1912), pp. 49–79, 127–52, 214–33.

J. Pinkerfeld, *Bate ha-keneset be-Italyah,* Jerusalem, 1954 [The Synagogues of Italy].

THE NETHERLANDS

P. Bregstein, *Herinnering Joods Amsterdam,* Amsterdam, 1978.

H. Brugmans and A. Frank, eds., *Geschiedenis der Joden in Nederland,* vol. 1, Amsterdam, 1940.

Encyclopaedia sefardica neerlandica, Amsterdam, 1940–50.

M. H. Gans, *De Amsterdamse Jodenhoek in foto's, 1900–1940,* Baarn, [1974].

———, *De oude Amsterdamse Jodenhoek nu,* Baarn, 1975.

———, *Memorbook. History of Dutch Jewry from the Renaissance to 1940,* Baarn, 1977.

D. Hausdorff, *Jizkor. Platenatlas van drie en een halve eeuw geschiedenis van de Joodse gemeente in Rotterdam van 1610 tot ca. 1960,* Baarn, 1978.

J. J. van Agt *Synagogen in Amsterdam,* The Hague, 1974.

——— et al., *De Tempel van Salomo. Een terugblik in het nabije en verre verleden ter gelegenheid van de feestelijke opening van de Synagoge bij de Prinsessegracht in Den Haag,* The Hague, 1976, esp. pp. 14–40.

J. Verheul, *De nederlandsch-israelitische gemeente en hare oude synagoge te Rotterdam,* Rotterdam, 1938.

———, "Synagogues in the Netherlands," *Studies on the History of Dutch Jewry* III (1981), pp. 89–123 (Hebrew, with English title).

UNITED KINGDOM

Catalogue of the Exhibition of Anglo-Jewish Art and History in Commemoration of the Tercentenary of the Resettlement of the Jews in the British Isles, London, 1956.

J. Jacobs and L. Wolf, eds., *Anglo-Jewish Historical Exhibition 1887,* London, 1888.

———, *Bibliotheca Anglo-Judaica,* London, 1888.

E. Jamilly, "Anglo-Jewish Architects and Architecture in the 18th and 19th Centuries," *Jewish Historical Society of England. Transactions* XVIII (1958), pp. 127–41.

———, "Synagogue Art and Architecture," *A Century of Jewish Life, 1870–1970,* London, 1971, pp. 75–91.

R. P. Lehmann, *Anglo-Jewish Bibliography, 1937–1970,* London, 1971, esp. pp. 160–80, 291–321.

———, *Nova Bibliotheca Anglo-Judaica, 1937–1960,* London, 1961, esp pp. 65–84, 175–93.

S. S. Levin, ed., *A Century of Anglo-Jewish Life, 1870–1970,* London, 1970.

V. D. Lipman, "The Rise of Jewish Suburbia," *Jewish Historical Society of England. Transactions* XXI (1968), pp. 78–103.

———, *Social History of the Jews in England,* London, 1954.

S. J. Prais, "Synagogue Statistics and the Jewish Population of Great Britain, 1900–1970," *Jewish Journal of Sociology* XIV, #2 (Dec. ,1972), pp. 215–28.

C. Roth, *The Federation of Synagogues, 1912–1937,* London, 1937.

———, *The Rise of Provincial Jewry: The Early History of the Jewish Communities in the English Countryside, 1740–1840,* London, 1950.

A. Rubens, *A Jewish Iconography,* London, 1954. (Rev. ed. ca. 1980 not consulted).

S. Sharot, "Reform and Liberal Judaism in London, 1840–1940," *Jewish Social Studies* XLI, #3–4 (1979), pp. 211–28.

———, "A Religious Change in Native Orthodoxy in London, 1870–1914: The Synagogue Service," *Jewish Journal of Sociology* XV, #1 (June 1973), pp. 57–78.

Index

Variations of place names appear in parentheses. Figure numbers are given in italics following page numbers.

Illustration Credits

All numbers refer to figures.

Drawn by Madelaine Fava: 1, 6, 31, 40, 44, 50, 60, 127, 167, 195, 217, 220.
Menorah 1923/24: 2, 3; 1929: 161; 1931: 158.
Kupferstichkabinett SMPK, Berlin: 4.
Trustees of the British Library (MS Or. 2884): 5.
Author: 7, 16, 17, 21–23, 36, 42, 51, 70–73, 80, 81, 102, 111, 113, 233, 241, 242, 248, 249.
Courtesy Helmut Eschwege: 8, 9.
Polska Akademia Nauk. Instytut Sztuki, Warsaw: 10, 78, 79, 92, 95–97.
Jagiellonian University, Cracow, Photographic Archive: 11, 77, 84, 86.
From the Archives of the YIVO Institute for Jewish Research: 12, 35, 52, 53, 94, 188–190.
Courtesy of the Leo Baeck Institute, New York: 13, 125, 126, 144, 165, 179.
Rudolf Mosse Buchverlag Berlin, *Erich Mendelsohn, Das Gesamtschaffen des Architekten*: 14, 15.
Bundesdenkmalamt, Vienna: 18, 19.
Courtesy Nikolaus Vielmetti: 20.
Courtesy Sándor Scheiber: 24, 55, 57.
H. Gold, *Die Judengemeinde Bratislava in Vergangenheit und Gegenwart*: 25–27.
Lúdovit Dojč: 28.
Deutsche Bauzeitung 1907: 143; 1929: 29, 30; 1931: 156.
Der Architekt 1906: 210, 211; 1916/19: 32, 33; 1919: 66.
Courtesy Ellen C. Schwartz: 34.
Courtesy Rachel Wischnitzer: 37, 93, 118, 164, 172, 173.
Courtesy National Monuments Service, Budapest: 38, 39, 41, 54.
Der Bautechniker 1891: 43, 45.
Savez Jevreijskih opština Jugoslavije, Belgrade: 46.
Courtesy Antun Tasovac: 47.
Bildarchiv und Porträtsammlung, Oesterreichische Nationalbibliothek, Vienna: 48, 56, 58, 63–65, 69.
National Museum, Prague: 49.
Courtesy Mark Epstein: 59.
Graphische Sammlung Albertina, Vienna: 61, 62.
Royal Institute of British Architects Drawing Collection: 67, 155, 235, 236.
Courtesy Dione Neutra: 68.
Grotte, *Deutsche*: 74, 75, 82, 83, 85, 87, 169.
Drawn by Anne Lacy: 76, 166, 186.
Courtesy Jonathan Porath: 88.
Central Archives for the History of the Jewish People, Jerusalem, photo no. 2662: 89.
Jesse Zel Lurie: 90, 91.
Courtesy Leon Joelson: 98–100.
Courtesy Andrzej Stasiak: 101.
Courtesy Norman Golb: 103.
Photo Daniel Franck, Paris: 104, 105, 107.
Photo Roger-Viollet, Paris: 106, 114.
Archives Nationales, Paris: 108, 109.
Oscar Israelowitz: 110, 119, 231.
Photo Couturier: 112.
Courtesy Alfred E. Willis: 115, 116.
Courtesy Jochen Littkemann: 117.
Bayerisches Landesamt für Denkmalpflege, Munich: 120, 121.
Märkisches Museum, Berlin-East: 122.
Zeitschrift für Bauwesen 1886: 123.
Illustrated London News 1866: 124.
Innen-Dekoration 1917: 128.
Bildarchiv Foto Marburg: 129, 130, 139, 140.
Aargauische Kantonsbibliothek, Aarau (MS BNQ 50:1): 131–133.
Aargauische Denkmalpflege, Aarau/Schweiz: 134–137.
R. Klapheck, *Die neue Synagoge in Essen*: 138.
Courtesy Bernhard Schaub: 141.
Courtesy Oberstadtdirektor, Amt für Wirtschafts- und Verkehrsförderung (Verkehrsamt) der Stadt Essen, Photo Guenter Schleder: 142.
Der Baumeister 1907: 145.

Krautheimer, *Mitt. Syn.*: 146, 147.
Germanisches Nationalmuseum, Nuremberg: 148.
Oskar Wolfsberg-Aviad, *Judische Gemeinde in Hamburg*: 149.
Courtesy Gert Von Bassewitz: 150, 153.
Courtesy Page Ayres Cowley: 151, 152.
B. Italiener, *Festschrift zum 120–jährigen Bestehen des israelitischen Tempels in Hamburg*: 154.
Baugilde 1932: 157.
Forum 1931: 158–160.
Historisches Museum am Hohen Ufer, Hannover: 162, 163.
Foto Stadtarchiv Worms: 168, 170, 171.
Muzeum Architektury we Wrocławiu, Wrocław: 174–177.
F. Schorbach, ed., *Edwin Oppler, Architektonische Entwürfe*: 178.
Arquitectura 1931: 180, 183.
The New York Public Library. Astor, Lenox, and Tilden Foundations. Art, Prints, and Photograph Division (P. de la Escosura, *España artístico y monumental*): 181.
Fotografías y ampliacciones MAS, Barcelona: 182, 184, 185.
Foto Nabão, Tomar. Courtesy Manuel de Oliveira: 187.
Foto Francesco Colonelli. Courtesy Comunità Israelitica, Ancona: 191.
Foto Giulio Borbon: 192.
Alinari: 193, 194, 206, 214, 216.
Courtesy Foto Arte, Livorno: 197–199.
Courtesy Museo d'arte antica, Milan: 200.
Metron 1954: 201.
Courtesy Maria Floriani Squarciapino: 202.
Gabinetto Comunale Stampe. Archivio Fotografico Comunale (Roma): 203, 204.
G. Accasto et al., *L'architettura di Roma capitale*: 205.
Courtesy Robert Kupferman: 207.
Courtesy Mario Stock: 208, 209, 212, 213.
L'ingegneria civile e le arti industriali 1875: 215.
Museo Correr, Venice: 218, 219, 222.
Osvaldo Böhm, Venice: 221.
Rijksmuseum-Stichting, Amsterdam: 224, 225, 228.
Gemeente Archief Amsterdam: 227, 229, 230, 232.
Rijksdienst voor de Monumentenzorg, Zeist, The Netherlands: 223.
Algemeen Nederlands Persbureau (ANP), Amsterdam: 226, 234.
Photo PAT–Per Anders Thunqvist, Stockholm: 237, 238.
Photograph by Henk Snoek. Courtesy Yorke, Rosenberg and Mardall, Architects: 239, 240.
Courtesy Royal Commission on Historical Monuments (England): 243.
United Synagogue, London. Archives: 244.
The New York Public Library. Astor, Lenox, and Tilden Foundations. Art, Prints, and Photograph Division (R. Ackermann, *Microcosm of London* III): 245.
Courtesy Greater London Council Photograph Library: 246, 247.
Paul Press: 250, 251.
D. A. Jessurun Cardozo and P. Goodman, eds., *Think and Thank*: 252, 253.